FOURTH EDITION

INTRODUCTION TO
GLOBAL POLITICS

Steven L. Lamy
University of Southern California

John S. Masker
Temple University

John Baylis
Swansea University

Steve Smith
University of Exeter

Patricia Owens
University of Sussex

New York   Oxford
OXFORD UNIVERSITY PRESS

To our students and our mentors.

Published in the United States of America by Oxford University Press USA
198 Madison Avenue, New York, NY 10016, United States of America.

Library of Congress Cataloging-in-Publication Data

Names: Lamy, Steven L., author.
Title: Introduction to global politics / Steven L. Lamy, University of
    Southern California; John S. Masker, Temple University; John Baylis,
    Swansea University; Steve Smith, University of Exeter; Patricia Owens,
    University of Sussex.
Description: Fourth edition. I Oxford University Press : New York, [2017]
Identifiers: LCCN 2016015013 I ISBN 9780190299798 (pbk.)
Subjects: LCSH: Geopolitics. I World politics. I International relations.
Classification: LCC JC319 .I66 2017 I DDC 327—dc23 LC record available at https://lccn.loc.gov/2016015013

9 8 7 6 5 4 3 2

Printed by R. R. Donnelley, United States of America

BRIEF CONTENTS

CONTENTS

PART I: FOUNDATIONS OF GLOBAL POLITICS

PART II: GLOBAL ACTORS

CHAPTER 4 Making Foreign Policy 114

Steven L. Lamy and John Masker

CHAPTER 5 Global and Regional Governance 156

Devon Curtis, Christian Reus-Smit, Paul Taylor, Steven L. Lamy, and John Masker

PART III: GLOBAL ISSUES

CHAPTER 6 Global Security, Military
Power, and Terrorism 206

John Baylis, Darryl Howlett, James D. Kiras, Steven L. Lamy,
and John Masker

W̶e have written this edition of *Introduction to Global Politics* with an increasingly interdependent world in mind. Perhaps the word *globalization* has become so overplayed that it has not retained much of its original force. Yet there is no unifying topic more important than globalization, no political trend of the same magnitude. Even our everyday decisions—those as seemingly trivial and isolated as what food to eat, what clothes to wear, what books to read, or what movies to see—affect the quality of life of everyone around us and of billions of people in distant countries. Meanwhile, decisions made around the world affect our daily life.

Not only is the world changing, becoming more complex and interconnected than ever before, but the nature of this course is also evolving. No matter what it is called—international relations, world politics, or global politics—the course has transformed in recent years, asking us to examine not only relations among countries but also a broader context of global events and issues. In this book, we therefore take a global approach that fosters an awareness of and appreciation for a variety of worldviews. To quote the French writer Marcel Proust, we believe that "the real voyage of discovery consists not in seeking new landscapes but in having new eyes."

A Global Approach

So what does it mean to take a "global" view of world politics? By this, we mean two things: First, this textbook brings together **academics from around the world**, drawing from a diversity of thought unmatched by other textbooks. Despite the range of views represented here, all of the contributors teach international relations courses, and we agree on emphasizing the challenges we all face as members of a global community. This book thus introduces students not only to the diversity of thinking in our field but also to its common elements.

Second, we discuss in some detail the various **critical actors in global politics**. We explore the role of individual nation-states as well as international institutions such as the United Nations, the European Union, and critically important economic institutions, including the World Bank Group and the World Trade Organization. We carefully assess how different groups and individuals have shaped these global institutions, holding different views on how best to govern this world of nearly two hundred independent nation-states. We also explore the growing number and significance of **nongovernmental actors**, both multinational corporations, such as Nike and McDonald's, and nongovernmental organizations, such as Oxfam and Doctors Without Borders. The entire world saw how important these actors are as we experienced several significant events early in the twenty-first century: the 2008 global economic crisis; the 2011 earthquake, tsunami, and nuclear crisis in Japan, estimated to be the most expensive disaster in history; the 2015 terror attacks in Paris, which demonstrated that the Islamic State is more than just a regional threat; the 2015 Paris Climate Change Conference; and the current migrant and refugee crisis. The field is changing as the world changes. With this new edition of *Introduction to Global Politics*, we hope to improve on the standard conversation; to bring the introductory course more in line with today's research; to ask (and try to answer) the kind of questions most relevant for students of world politics today.

This textbook will introduce students to the mainstream theoretical traditions of realism and liberalism and to critical approaches that are often left out of other texts, including constructivism, Marxism, feminism, and utopianism (Chapter 3). Our goal is to introduce students to all relevant voices so they can make an informed choice about how best to both explain and understand our world. We clearly lay out important theories so that they illuminate the actors and issues we discuss, rather than cloud them in further mystery. In short, we hope these pages will help each student develop a more informed worldview.

Learning Goals

An important assumption of this text is that *theory matters*. Every individual sees the world through theories and uses them to organize, evaluate, and critically review contending positions in controversial policy areas. Unfortunately, many people take positions that lack supporting evidence; they accept a statement or position as true or valid because it fits with their beliefs or reinforces what they believe to be true.

After completing a course using this text, students will know more about the global system, the most important global actors, and the issues that shape the priorities and behavior of states and other actors in that system. This text encourages students to approach global politics in an informed, well-reasoned, and theoretically grounded manner. Overall, the chapters in this edition focus on four core learning objectives:

1. To develop a comprehensive understanding of the various theoretical traditions in global politics and the roles they play.
2. To understand the relationship between theory and policymaking or problem-solving in global politics.
3. To appreciate the diversity of worldviews and theoretical assumptions that may inform political situations.
4. To develop an understanding of the global system and thereby increase the capacity to act or participate at various levels within it.

At the beginning of each chapter, we identify specific learning objectives that stem from these overarching goals. The review questions at the end of the chapter check that students have met the learning objectives.

REVIEW QUESTIONS

1. Is globalization a new phenomenon in world politics?
2. In what ways are you linked to globalization?
3. How do ideas about globalization shape our understanding of the trend?
4. How can different levels of analysis lead to different explanations of the impact of globalization on global politics?
5. Why do theories matter?
6. International relations began as a problem-solving discipline in response to World War I. What are the global problems that now define our field of study?

LEARNING OBJECTIVES

After reading and discussing this chapter, you should be able to:

Describe key global actors and their role in addressing global issues.

Begin to define theories of international relations.

Explain the concept of levels of analysis.

Define the term *globalization*.

Explain academic disagreements about the character of globalization.

Organization

This edition of *Introduction to Global Politics* includes ten chapters and is divided into three parts:

Foundations of Global Politics

Covers the basic concepts, history, and theories of global politics.

Global Actors

Introduces the main actors on the world stage—from states, to intergovernmental organizations, to transnational actors and nongovernmental agencies.

Global Issues

Focuses on issues of crucial importance to the security and prosperity of the people in the world.

In the last section of the book, we discuss war, terrorism, human rights, and human security. We also focus on global trade and finance and the environment, with an emphasis on development and environmental sustainability. Each chapter provides essential information about the issue area and presents case studies and worldview questions that encourage students to think about these issues from contending perspectives.

Pedagogical Features

To aid students in the development of their own, more well-informed worldview, we supply several **active-learning** features, outside the main text, within every chapter. These boxed essays and other elements provide **discussion questions** and bring into sharp relief some of the unique themes of this book:

- **Global Perspectives**—Each one of these feature essays opens a window onto another part of the

GLOBAL PERSPECTIVE

The Trans-Pacific Partnership

Once the Trans-Pacific Partnership (TPP) is ratified, it will be the world's largest trade agreement linking twelve countries that account for 40 percent of the world's gross domestic product. What does this mean for the states involved, and those not involved? Any trade agreement creates sharp divisions between members and nonmembers. Obviously, it becomes more attractive to trade within the community created by the agreement. However, these agreements often create divisions at home as well. Many domestic interests such as labor unions and environmental groups complain about the loss of jobs, lowering of wages, decreases in benefits, and the failure to enact stricter environmental regulations. Within each of the member countries, there will be changes in policies that will shape future debates.

For example, Japanese agricultural workers oppose the TPP because it would eliminate the current tariffs on agricultural imports from other countries that make the prices of Japanese agricultural products much lower. According to Japanese Prime Minister Shinzō Abe, the TPP is critical for both the economy and security of Japan. The government hopes that the TPP will jump-start a moribund economy that has not grown much in the last twenty years. Japan and some of the other Asian member countries, namely Vietnam and Malaysia, are concerned that China's dominance in the region will soon extend to setting the economic rules of engagement in Asia. These states see the TPP as a way of countering Chinese influence in both economic and political sectors. In recent disputes with Japan over the control of the Senkaku Islands and navigation and fishing rights, China cut off Japan's access to rare earth minerals that are essential for the production of many of Japan's high-tech instruments. The TPP will reduce the effectiveness of this form of coercive diplomacy and reduce the vulnerability of member states.

The United States has been trying to create a free trade pact in this region since the early 1990s. The TPP is a critical element of President Obama's pivot to Asia with the primary goal being the establishment of a set of trading rules that will work in the United States' favor and counter China's effort to create trading rules for the region. U.S. leaders are not opposed to China joining the pact but they expect China to play by the rules that were negotiated by the United States and the other eleven partner countries. Opposition in the United States is mainly from labor unions and some Democratic members of Congress who are concerned about the loss of jobs and the lack of environmental protections in the agreement.

Participants at a 2015 rally held by the Central Union of Agricultural Co-operatives in Japan hold signs to protest the Trans-Pacific Partnership trade agreement. Why do you think domestic workers in Japan and the other eleven states feel that this trade agreement will work against them?

In Australia, industries that rely on exports strongly support the deal because it will create new trading partners and help to grow existing trade deals. Outside the business sector, there are some real concerns about several of the treaty's clauses that suggest that large corporations can prevent governments from passing legislation that protects consumers, workers, and the environment. Labor union representatives have focused on the danger of trading away Australia's sovereign rights, as well as trading away Australian jobs.

All parties to the agreement must figure out ways to manage the processes of globalization to serve their interests and meet their obligations to their citizens. This often requires giving up some sovereignty and opening up their national economies to the forces of globalization that promote competition between economic and political actors.

For Discussion

1. Clearly, domestic interest groups shape global trade policy. Which groups favor more open global treaties and which groups work against them? Why?
2. The TPP is a trading pact but it is also designed to prevent Chinese economic control in the Asia Pacific region. Will great-power rivalry like this extend into other regions?
3. Why is this trade agreement so controversial in the United States?

world, showing how other countries and world organizations perceive and manage global politics.

- **Theory in Practice**—These features examine real-world scenarios through a variety of theoretical lenses, demonstrating the explanatory power of theories in global politics.
- **Case Studies**—For a more in-depth analysis of a subject, students can turn to these essays that delve into world events.
- **What's Your Worldview?**—These short, critical-thinking questions in every chapter challenge students to develop their own, more well-informed ideas about global actors and issues.
- **Thinking About Global Politics**—This feature at the end of each chapter presents in-class activities dealing with real-world political issues. These activities give students the opportunity to develop their critical-thinking skills and apply what they have learned. Each activity includes follow-up questions or writing prompts.
- **Engaging with the World**—These short boxes highlight opportunities to get involved with organizations working for positive change in the world.

CASE STUDY

A Failed Intervention

The Darfur Genocide refers to the current mass slaughter of civilians in Western Sudan, which has claimed the lives of more than 300,000 people and displaced nearly 2.5 million others. The killings began in the early 2000s and continue today. The genocide is being carried out by a group of government-armed and -funded Arab militias known as the Janjaweed, which translated Arab militias to "devils on horseback." The Janjaweed are destroying Darfurians by burning villages, raping, and torturing civilians.

U.S. Secretary of State Colin Powell declared the ongoing conflict in Darfur genocide on September 4, 2004, and on February 18, 2006, President George W. Bush called for the number of international troops in Darfur to be doubled. On September 17, 2006, British Prime Minister Tony Blair wrote an open letter to the members of the European Union calling for a unified response to the crisis. In supporting the United Nations Security Council Resolution in 2007 to authorize the deployment of up to 26,000 peacekeepers to try to stop the violence in Darfur, British Prime Minister Gordon Brown said in a speech before the UN General Assembly that the Darfur crisis was "the greatest humanitarian disaster the world faces today." The British government also endorsed the International Criminal Court's (ICC) indictment

against Sudanese President Omar al-Bashir for committing crimes against humanity, war crimes, and genocide and urged the Sudanese government to cooperate with the ICC.

Unfortunately, the world seems to have forgotten about Darfur but the killing and human rights violations have continued. The government of Sudan has been able to contain the flow of information by closing the UN Human Rights Office in the capital of Khartoum and convincing peacekeepers to leave regions they deem stable. Once the peacekeepers leave, the atrocities begin again. In 2014, the Satellite Sentinel Project, an organization dedicated to ending genocide and crimes against humanity, was able to confirm evidence that the Sudanese government had burned and bombed some six villages in Darfur's eastern Jebel Marra region.

The government of Sudan has used aid money from Qatar to build model villages for those displaced by the continuing violence. However, Human Rights Watch recently uncovered an incident of mass rape in one of these model villages. In October 2014 in the village of Tabit, soldiers from the Sudanese army raped over 200 women in a thirty-six-hour period. Human rights courts have ruled that rape by police or soldiers is an act of torture because it is used as an instrument of terror and is a tactic of social control and ethnic domination.

The crimes against humanity continue today with only NGOs demanding action. The international community has imposed some sanctions but enforcement is uneven. The United States and its European allies have no stomach for another intervention after Afghanistan, Iraq, Libya, and Syria. A major constraint is the fact that both China and Russia have worked to block many UN resolutions in attempts to appease the Sudanese government. From its seat on the UN Security Council, China has been Sudan's chief diplomatic ally. China invests heavily in Sudanese oil (Sudan is China's largest overseas oil provider) and China supplies Sudan's military with helicopters, tanks, and fighter planes. For decades, Russia and China have maintained a strong economic and politically strategic partnership and have opposed the presence of UN peacekeeping troops in Sudan. Russia strongly supports Sudan's territorial integrity and opposes the creation of an independent Darfur state. Russia is also Sudan's strongest investment partner and considers Sudan an important global ally in Africa.

Women and children living in the ZamZam camp for displaced people in northern Darfur. The Sudanese government is trying to convince the United Nations that things are stable, citizens are protected, and the peacekeeping forces should leave, yet several NGOs claim that atrocities continue and the world must return its attention to this region. Why do you think the world seems to have moved on and forgotten these victims of violence?

Every part of this textbook has been developed with today's college student in mind. The book includes a number of integrated study aids—such as chapter opening learning objectives, a running glossary, lists of key terms, and review questions—all of which help students read and retain important information while extending their learning experience. Two opposing quotations open every chapter, setting up two sides of one possible debate for students to consider while reading. At the end of every chapter, rather than simply summarizing the contents for students, we provide a conclusion that requires students to analyze the various topics and themes of the chapter a bit more critically, placing everything they have learned into a broader context across chapters. Students need to acquire strong critical-thinking skills; they need to learn how to make connections among real-world events they hear about in the news and the ideas they learn about in class—and so it is with these goals in mind that the authors and editors have developed this edition.

One last point with regard to pedagogical features: the art program has been carefully selected to support critical thinking as well; not only do we present a number of maps that offer unique global perspectives on historic events and modern world trends, but we have also incorporated data graphics and compelling photographs to engage students visually. The captions of many of these images include questions for further thought—once again connecting the reader back to the core content of the course, with an interesting prompt or relevant point.

New to This Edition

We have thoroughly updated this edition of *Introduction to Global Politics* in light of recent trends and events that are shaping our world, such as the rise of the Islamic State and the continuing effects of the global economic crisis. In addition, we have streamlined each chapter, revised for more balanced coverage, and strengthened our focus on active learning. In making these revisions, we have taken into account the helpful comments from reviewers as well as our own experience using the first, second, and third editions in our classes.

Revision Highlights

The first three editions of *Introduction to Global Politics* were published in two formats, a fourteen-chapter edition and a brief ten-chapter edition. The fourth edition is a ten-chapter hybrid edition, which contains balanced coverage of the major theoretical perspectives of international relations, a thorough examination of global actors, and an engaging introduction to global issues such as global trade and finance and the environment. This briefer text encourages students to examine the world by applying foundational concepts to historical and contemporary events, issues, and headlines. We have combined essential concepts with classic and current research, learning aids, and contemporary examples. The following tables illustrate how chapters from the third editions were streamlined to create the fourth edition:

Adopters of *Introduction to Global Politics* will find the same content previously covered in fourteen chapters now covered in ten chapters:

Fourth Edition Chapters	Third Edition Chapters
Chapter 1: Introduction to Global Politics	Chapter 1: Introduction to Global Politics
Chapter 2: The Evolution of Global Politics	Chapter 2: The Evolution of Global Politics
Chapter 3: Realism, Liberalism, and Critical Theories	Chapter 3: Realism and Liberalism Chapter 4: Critical Theories
Chapter 4: Making Foreign Policy	Chapter 5: Making Foreign Policy
Chapter 5: Global and Regional Governance	Chapter 6: Global and Regional Governance Chapter 7: Nongovernmental Actors
Chapter 6: Global Security, Military Power, and Terrorism	Chapter 8: Security and Military Power Chapter 9: Terrorism
Chapter 7: Human Rights and Human Security	Chapter 10: Human Rights and Human Security
Chapter 8: Global Trade and Finance	Chapter 11: International Political Economy Chapter 12: Global Trade and Finance
Chapter 9: Poverty, Development, and Hunger	Chapter 13: Poverty, Development, and Hunger
Chapter 10: Environmental Issues	Chapter 14: Environmental Issues

Adopters of *Introduction to Global Politics Brief Edition* will find the same number of chapters and chapter organization as previous editions, although the chapter titles have been revised slightly:

Fourth Edition Chapters	Brief Third Edition Chapters
Chapter 1: Introduction to Global Politics	Chapter 1: Introduction to Global Politics
Chapter 2: The Evolution of Global Politics	Chapter 2: The Evolution of Global Politics
Chapter 3: Realism, Liberalism, and Critical Theories	Chapter 3: Theories of Global Politics
Chapter 4: Making Foreign Policy	Chapter 4: Making Foreign Policy
Chapter 5: Global and Regional Governance	Chapter 5: International Law and Nonstate Actors
Chapter 6: Global Security, Military Power, and Terrorism	Chapter 6: Global Security, Military Power, and Terrorism
Chapter 7: Human Rights and Human Security	Chapter 7: Human Rights and Human Security
Chapter 8: Global Trade and Finance	Chapter 8: Global Economics and Trade
Chapter 9: Poverty, Development, and Hunger	Chapter 9: Poverty, Development, and Hunger
Chapter 10: Environmental Issues	Chapter 10: Environmental Issues

Additionally, adopters of *Introduction to Global Politics* will find:

- We have threaded critical international relations theories throughout the text more evenly.
- Revised Case Studies offer updated and further analysis on topics such as global production and the failed intervention to stop genocide in Darfur.
- Throughout the textbook, figures, tables, maps, and graphs have been added, replaced, or updated with the latest and most accurate statistics and information.
- We have significantly updated our photo program, replacing more than half of the photos in the text to coincide with textual updates and keep pace with current events.

Chapter-by-Chapter Improvements

Chapter 1: Introduction to Global Politics
- Expanded theoretical coverage introduces students to the three theoretical traditions in international relations theory: Machiavellian, Grotian, and Kantian.
- New Case Study: "Global Production and the iPhone."

Chapter 2: The Evolution of Global Politics
- Revised chapter-opening vignette addresses the goals of nation-states for survival and influence in the global system and how critical trends, such as the diffusion of power and increasing demands for vital resources, influence such goals.
- Expanded coverage of U.S.-Cuba relations addresses the restoration of diplomatic ties.
- Further examination of the war on terrorism, including the completion of NATO's International Security Assistance Force mission in Afghanistan and its subsequent transition to the ongoing Resolute Support Mission.
- Global Perspective "Perception, Continuity, and Change After January 20, 2009" has been updated to address the course of the Arab Spring.
- Updated statistics and graphics include Estimated Global Nuclear Warheads, as of 2015, and Number of Wars in Progress Since 1950.

Chapter 3: Realism, Liberalism, and Critical Theories
- Elimination of overlapping content between Chapter 3 and the first two introductory chapters, effectively streamlining the chapter and bringing its objectives of defining and describing the origins of international relations theories, as well as explaining the relation among the levels of analysis and the different variations of the five schools of thought, into clearer focus.
- The latest on the most pertinent international relations matters including how world leaders should deal with extremist networks like the Islamic State.

Chapter 4: Making Foreign Policy
- Further coverage and analysis of the UN Framework Convention on Climate Change, including the goals of the 2015 Paris Climate Change Conference.
- Expanded discussion of fragile states, including updates to the Fragile State Index.
- Discussion of foreign policy evaluation has been expanded to include criticism of the CIA's detention and treatment of prisoners taken in the wars in Iraq and Afghanistan.
- Additional examples of NGO influence on human rights—e.g., Human Rights Watch pressuring the Chinese government to abolish its re-education through labor detention system.
- Updated statistics and graphics include Top Ten Foreign Aid Donors and the addition of a new figure, "Share of World Military Expenditures of the Fifteen States with the Highest Expenditure."

Chapter 5: Global and Regional Governance
- Revised chapter-opening vignette addresses the impact of the Tunisian National Dialogue as a civil society organization and winner of the Nobel Peace Prize.
- Updated examples of venture philanthropy include Facebook cofounder and CEO Mark Zuckerberg's pledge to donate 99 percent of his wealth.

- Case Study "A Global Campaign: The Baby Milk Advocacy Network" has been updated to include recent statistics from the World Health Organization.
- Updated statistics and graphics include "INGO Growth Continues" and "Distribution of Think Tanks in the World."

Chapter 6: Global Security, Military Power, and Terrorism

- Updated information on conflicts including the Syrian civil war, the rise of the Islamic State and their goal to establish an Islamic Caliphate, and the UN peacekeeping mission in the Central African Republic to prevent civil wars and sectarian conflicts.
- Condensed coverage of mainstream and critical approaches to security in order to eliminate overlapping content found in Chapter 3.
- Added examples of the importance of collective action and reliance on international/regional organization—e.g., in the case of the 2015 Iran nuclear deal.
- Expanded discussion of the effects of nuclear weapons and the idea that the international community is experiencing a new nuclear age in which weapons of mass destruction are used to secure strategic advantage.
- Case Study "U.S. Drone Warfare: A Robotic Revolution in Modern Combat" has been updated to include recent statistics on drone strikes.
- Updated information on the spread of jihadists, Al-Qaeda, and ISIS and the geographical extent to which the Obama administration (and future administrations) will have to go to find them.
- Updated statistics and graphics include "Arms Deliveries Worldwide" and "Arms Transfer Agreements Worldwide"; the addition of two new figures: "Top Locations of Islamic State Twitter Users" and "Thirteen Years of Terror in Western Europe"; the addition of a new map: "Where ISIS Has Directed and Inspired Attacks"; and the addition of a table detailing the inter-actor relationship of those involved in the Syrian civil war.

Chapter 7: Human Rights and Human Security

- Added information on the latest human rights crises—e.g., the refugee crisis, the Syrian civil war, and South Sudan.
- New Case Study "A Failed Intervention" on the genocide occurring in Darfur.
- Updated statistics on current UN peacekeeping operations.

Chapter 8: Global Trade and Finance

- Updated analysis on the current status of global economic interconnection—e.g., the role that governmental intervention has on the economy of their nation-states (free markets included), the impact of the slowdown of China's economy, and the effects of increasing global foreign direct investment.
- New discussion of the Trans-Pacific Partnership and its subsequent implications as the largest regional trade agreement in history.

- Theory in Practice "Contending Views of Capitalism" updated to reflect recent changes in the Chinese economy and the cyberwarfare tactics it uses against the United States.
- Updated statistics and graphics include "Main Trading Nations," "Real GDP Growth," and the addition of a new graph, "Holdings of U.S. Treasury Securities."

Chapter 9: Poverty, Development, and Hunger
- Added discussion on the results of the Millennium Development Goals process (including an updated "Progress Chart for UN Millennium Development Goals") and the United Nations' subsequent adoption of the new 2030 Agenda for Sustainable Development (illustrated by "Sustainable Development Goals").
- Updated discussions of world population statistics and estimated population growth projections, including new graphics "Projected World Population" and "Fastest-Growing Populations."

Chapter 10: Environmental Issues
- Discussion of the latest environmental issues including the rising number of carbon emissions emitted on the planet, the effect climate change and environmental degradation are having as causes of major violence in regards to specific ethnic communities that compete for scarce resources, and how 2015 was the hottest year in recorded history.
- Added discussion of how climate change is the greatest challenge to economic and political stability across the world.
- Revised discussion of the latest Intergovernmental Panel on Climate Change report addresses the rise of global surface temperatures, the continued shrinking of sea ice, and how human influence correlates to climate change and increasing levels of greenhouse gas emissions in the atmosphere.
- Added information and analysis of the 2015 Paris Climate Change Conference, its outcomes, and the importance of adhering to pledges to curb emissions and keeping global temperature rises under 2 degrees Celsius; new concluding thoughts and analysis added as well.
- Table detailing "Recent Global Environmental Actions" was revised to focus on events and actions of the past thirty years.
- Updated statistics and graphics include Global Greenhouse Gas Emissions by Type of Gas, and two new graphics: "Number of Oil Spills Between 1970–2015" and "Largest Producers of CO_2 Emissions Worldwide."

Supplements

Oxford University Press offers instructors and students a comprehensive ancillary package for qualified adopters of *Introduction to Global Politics*.

Companion Website at www.oup.com/us/lamy

This open access companion website includes a number of learning tools to help students study and review key concepts presented in the text including learning objectives, key-concept summaries, quizzes, essay questions, web activities, and web links.

Ancillary Resource Center (ARC)

This convenient, instructor-focused website provides access to all the up-to-date teaching resources for this text—at any time—while guaranteeing the security of grade-significant resources. In addition, it allows OUP to keep instructors informed when new content becomes available. Register for access and create your individual user account by clicking on the Instructor's Resources link at www.oup.com/us/lamy. Available on the ARC:

- **Instructor's Manual:** The Instructor's Resource Manual includes chapter objectives, a detailed chapter outline, lecture suggestions and activities, discussion questions, video resources, and web resources.
- **Test Item File:** This resource includes nearly 1,000 test items, including multiple-choice, short answer, and essay questions. Questions are identified as factual, conceptual, or applied, and correct answers are keyed to the text pages where the concepts are presented.
- **Computerized Test Bank:** Using the test authoring and management tool Diploma, the computerized test bank that accompanies this text is designed for both novice and advanced users. Diploma enables instructors to create and edit questions, create randomized quizzes and tests with an easy-to-use drag-and-drop tool, publish quizzes and tests to online courses, and print quizzes and tests for paper-based assessments.
- **PowerPoint Presentations:** Each chapter's slide deck includes a succinct chapter outline and incorporates relevant chapter graphics.

Course Cartridges

For qualified adopters, OUP will supply the teaching resources in a course cartridge designed to work with your preferred Online Learning Platform. Please contact your Oxford University Press sales representative at (800) 280-0280.

E-Book

The E-Book ISBN is 9780190299811. A discounted E-Book version of this text is available for 180-day rental at www.redshelf.com, www.chegg.com, or www.vitalsource.com.

CNN Videos

Offering recent clips on timely topics, this DVD provides up to fifteen films tied to the chapter topics in the text. Each clip is approximately 5–10 minutes in length, offering a great way to launch your lectures. Contact your local OUP sales representative for details.

Interactive Media Activities

Invite students to "learn by doing," reinforcing key concepts presented in the book across chapters and demonstrating their practical application. The five interactive media activities include *Negotiating a Climate Change Treaty, Keeping the Peace in Guinea-Bissau, Negotiating with China, Stopping an Epidemic,* and *Preventing World War.*

Packaging Options

Adopters of *Introduction to Global Politics* can package **ANY** Oxford University Press book with the text for a 20 percent savings off the total package price. See our many trade and scholarly offerings at www.oup.com, then contact your local Oxford University Press sales representative to request a package ISBN.

- *Introduction to Global Politics: A Reader*, edited by John Masker, offers the best variety of readings, the best coverage of alternative theories, and the best price. Package it with this text and save your students 20 percent!
- *Current Debates in International Relations*, edited by Eric B. Shiraev and Vladislav M. Zubok, presents forty-nine readings drawn from major scholarly journals, magazines, and newspapers including *Foreign Affairs, Foreign Policy, International Relations,* and *The Wall Street Journal.* It provides a broad selection of articles—both classical/theoretical and practical/applied—and steers students through major international issues, offering contending yet complementary approaches.

In addition, the following items can be packaged with the text for FREE:

- *Oxford Pocket World Atlas,* **Sixth Edition:** This full-color atlas is a handy reference for international relations and global politics students.
- **Very Short Introductions:** These very brief texts offer succinct introductions to a variety of topics. Titles include *Terrorism,* Second Edition, by Charles Townshend; *Globalization,* Third Edition, by Manfred Steger; and *Climate Change,* Third Edition, by Mark Maslin, among others.
- *Now Playing* **Video Guide:** Through documentaries, feature films, and YouTube videos, *Now Playing: Learning Global Politics Through Film* provides video examples of course concepts to demonstrate real-world relevance. Each video is accompanied by a brief summary and three to five discussion questions. Qualified adopters will also receive a Netflix subscription that enables them to show students the films discussed in the book.

- ***Research and Writing Guide for Political Science:*** This brief guide provides students with the information and tools necessary to conduct research and write a research paper. The guide explains how to get started writing a research paper, describes the parts of a research paper, and presents the citation formats found in academic writing.

Please contact your Oxford University Press Sales Representative at (800) 280-0280 for more information on supplements or packaging options.

Acknowledgments

The authors wish to thank all members of Oxford University Press, in particular Jennifer Carpenter, executive editor, for her tireless sponsorship of this complex project, for her guidance, enthusiasm, and insights; Maegan Sherlock, development editor, for guiding the revision process; Matt Rohal, assistant editor, who worked efficiently to research art and secure permissions; Roxanne Klaas, senior project manager, who managed the project with skill and grace; Timothy J. DeWerff, copy editor, who provided the right amount of polish; and last but not least, art director Michele Laseau, who updated the book's inviting design for this edition. Beyond the individual authors and editors of this edition, Steve Lamy would like to thank his research assistants Sara Watar, Dersim Heimervall, and Barron Omega and his students in the School of International Relations at USC.

Likewise, there are many others who are unaffiliated with the authors and editors, who contributed to this new edition's shape and success as well.

We owe a debt of gratitude to the following people, who reviewed the previous three editions and have provided invaluable insight into putting together the past and future editions of this book:

Supplements Author

John Masker, Temple University

First Edition Reviewers

Ali R. Abootalebi
*University of Wisconsin,
Eau Claire*

Linda S. Adams
Baylor University

Klint Alexander
Vanderbilt University

Youngshik D. Bong
American University

Marijke Breuning
University of North Texas

Alison Brysk
*University of California,
Irvine*

Jeanie Bukowski
Bradley University

Manochehr Dorraj
*Texas Christian
University*

John S. Duffield
Georgia State University

Michelle Frasher-Rae
Ohio University

Brian Frederking
McKendree University

Matthew Fuhrmann
*University of South
Carolina*

David M. Goldberg
College of DuPage

Jeannie Grussendorf
Georgia State University

James R. Hedtke
Cabrini College

Jeanne Hey
Miami University

Jeneen Hobby
Cleveland State University

Arend A. Holtslag
*University of Massachusetts,
Lowell*

Christopher Housenick
American University

Aida A. Hozic
University of Florida

Maorong Jiang
Creighton University

Michael D. Kanner
*University of Colorado
at Boulder*

Aaron Karp
Old Dominion University

Joyce P. Kaufman
Whittier College

Bernd Kaussler
James Madison University

Howard Lehman
University of Utah

Steven Lobell
University of Utah

Domenic Maffei
Caldwell College

Mary K. Meyer McAleese
Eckerd College

Mark J. Mullenbach
*University of Central
Arkansas*

William W. Newmann
*Virginia Commonwealth
University*

Miroslav Nincic
*University of California,
Davis*

Michael Nojeim
Prairie View A&M University

Richard Nolan
University of Florida

Asli Peker
New York University

Meg Rincker
Purdue University Calumet

Brigitte H. Schulz
Trinity College

Shalendra D. Sharma
University of San Francisco

David Skidmore
Drake University

Michael Struett
*North Carolina State
University*

James Larry Taulbee
Emory University

Faedah Totah
*Virginia Commonwealth
University*

John Tuman
*University of Nevada,
Las Vegas*

Brian R. Urlacher
University of North Dakota

Thomas J. Vogly
University of Arizona

Kimberly Weir
*Northern Kentucky
University*

Yi Yang
*James Madison
University*

Brief First Edition Reviewers

Ali R. Abootalebi
*University of Wisconsin,
Eau Claire*

Nicole Burtchett
Washington State University

Donovan C. Chau
*California State University,
San Bernardino*

Daniel Chong
Rollins College

Michaelene Cox
*Illinois State
University*

Roberto Dominguez
Suffolk University

Joseph J. Foy
University of Wisconsin, Waukesha

Daniel K. Gibran
Tennessee State University

James Michael Greig
University of North Texas

Steven W. Hook
Kent State University

Jeffrey Lewis
Cleveland State University

Fredline M'Cormack-Hale
Seton Hall University

Jessica Peet
University of Florida

Amanda M. Rosen
Webster University

James C. Ross
University of Northern Colorado

Donald H. Roy
Ferris State University

Barbara Salera
Washington State University

Noha Shawki
Illinois State University

M. Scott Solomon
University of South Florida

Jelena Subotic
Georgia State University

Milind Thakar
University of Indianapolis

Glenn Dale Thomas III
University of Memphis

Kimberly Weir
Northern Kentucky University

Min Ye
Coastal Carolina University

Second Edition Reviewers

Michael R. Baysdell
Saginaw Valley State University

Pamela Blackmon
Pennsylvania State University

Richard P. Farkas
DePaul University

Stefan Fritsch
Bowling Green State University

Robert F. Gorman
Texas State University, San Marcos

Jeannie Grussendorf
Georgia State University

Clinton G. Hewan
Northern Kentucky University

Carrie Humphreys
The University of Utah

Michael G. Jackson
Stonehill College

Michael D. Kanner
University of Colorado at Boulder

Lisa Kissopoulos
Northern Kentucky University

Greg Knehans
University of North Carolina at Greensboro

Cecelia Lynch
University of California, Irvine

Domenic Maffei
Caldwell College

Eduardo Magalhães III
Simpson College

Lawrence P. Markowitz
Rowan University

Emily Rodio
Saint Joseph's University

Anna M. Rulska
North Georgia College & State University

Maria Sampanis
California State University, Sacramento

Edwin A. Taylor III
Missouri Western State University

Alana Tiemessen
University of Massachusetts Amherst

Robert E. Williams
Pepperdine University

Brief Second Edition Reviewers

Leah Michelle Graham
University of North Alabama

Eric A. Heinze
University of Oklahoma

Courtney Hillebrecht
University of Nebraska, Lincoln

Paul E. Lenze, Jr.
Northern Arizona University

Andrea Malji
University of Kentucky

Timothy Schorn
University of South Dakota

Jacob Shively
Indiana University

Jelena Subotic
Georgia State University

Richard Tanksley
North Idaho College

Scott Wallace
Indiana University Purdue University Indianapolis

Third Edition Reviewers

Jennifer Bloxom
Colorado State University

Kevin J.S. Duska, Jr.
The Ohio State University

John J. Jablowski, Jr.
Penn State University

Paul A. Mego
University of Memphis, Lambuth

Alexei Shevchenko
California State University Fullerton

Veronica Ward
University State University

Winn W. Wasson
University of Wisconsin, Washington County

Fourth Edition Reviewers

We also owe a debt of gratitude to the following people who reviewed, and gave special attention to, this edition of the book.

Richard W. Coughlin
Florida Gulf Coast University

Mariam Dekanozishvili
Coastal Carolina University

Ryan Gibb
Baker University

Michael Huelshoff
University of New Orleans

Michael D. Kanner
University of Colorado, Boulder

Paul A. Mego
University of Memphis, Lambuth

Sara Moats
Florida International University

Jason J. Morrissette
Marshall University

Amit Ron
Arizona State University

Elton Skendaj
University of Miami

Stacy B. Taninchev
Gonzaga University

Daniel Tirone
Louisiana State University

Krista Tuomi
American University

Robert E. Williams, Jr.
Pepperdine University

The book would not have been the same without the assistance and insight from these outstanding scholars and teachers. Meanwhile, any errors you may find in the book remain our own. We welcome your feedback and thank you for your support.

Steven L. Lamy
John S. Masker
John Baylis
Steve Smith
Patricia Owens

ABOUT THE AUTHORS

Amitav Acharya is the UNESCO Chair in Transnational Challenges and Governance and Professor of International Relations at American University, Washington D.C. His recent books include *The End of American World Order* (Polity 2013), *Rethinking Power, Institutions, and Ideas in World Politics: Whose IR?* (Routledge 2013); *Why Govern? Rethinking Demand and Progress in Global Governance*, editor (Cambridge 2017) and *Human Security: From Concept to Practice*, co-editor (World Scientific 2011). His articles on international relations theory, norm diffusion, comparative regionalism, and Asian security have appeared in *International Organization, World Politics, International Security, Journal of Peace Research*, and *International Studies Quarterly*.

David Armstrong is Emeritus Professor of International Relations at the University of Exeter. His books include *Revolutionary Diplomacy* (California University Press 1977), *The Rise of the International Organization* (Macmillan 1981), *Revolution and World Order* (Clarendon Press 1993), *International Law and International Relations* (co-authored with Theo Farrell and Hélène Lambert; Cambridge University Press 2007), and *Routledge Handbook of International Law* (editor; Routledge 2009).

John Baylis is Emeritus Professor at Swansea University. Until his retirement in 2008 he was Professor of Politics and International Relations and Pro-Vice-Chancellor at the university. His Ph.D. and D.Litt. are from the University of Wales. He is the author of more than twenty books, the most recent of which are *The Globalization of World Politics: An Introduction to International Relations* (7th ed. with Steve Smith and Patricia Owens; OUP 2017), *Strategy in the Contemporary World: An Introduction to Strategic Studies* (5th ed.

with James Wirtz and Colin S. Gray; OUP 2016), *The British Nuclear Experience: The Role of Beliefs, Culture and Identity* (with Kristan Stoddart; OUP 2015), and *The United States and Europe: Beyond the Neo-Conservative Divide?* (edited with John Roper; Routledge 2006).

Alex J. Bellamy is Professor of Peace and Conflict Studies and Director of the Asia-Pacific Centre for the Responsibility to Protect at The University of Queensland, Australia. He is also Senior Advisor at the International Peace Institute (New York) and Fellow of the Academy of Social Sciences in Australia. His books include *The Responsibility to Protect: A Defense* (Oxford 2015) and *Massacres and Morality: Mass Atrocities in an Age of Non-Combatant Immunity* (Oxford 2012). He is currently writing a book on the decline of mass atrocities in East Asia (Oxford).

Chris Brown is Emeritus Professor of International Relations at the London School of Economics and Political Science and the author of *International Relations Theory: New Normative Approaches* (Columbia 1992), *Understanding International Relations* (Palgrave Macmillan 1997; 4th ed. 2009), *Sovereignty, Rights and Justice* (Polity 2002), *Practical Judgement in International Political Theory* (Routledge 2010), and *International Society, Global Polity* (Sage 2015) as well as numerous book chapters and journal articles in the field of international political theory. He edited *Political Restructuring in Europe: Ethical Perspectives* (Routledge 1994) and co-edited (with Terry Nardin and N. J. Rengger) *International Relations in Political Thought: Texts from the Greeks to the First World War* (Cambridge 2002). A former Chair of the British International Studies Association (1998/99), he was Head of the Department of International Relations at LSE from 2004 to 2007.

Professor **Michael Cox** holds a Chair in International Relations at the London School of Economics and Political Science. He is the author, editor, and co-editor of over twenty books, including *Soft Power and U.S. Foreign Policy* (Routledge 2010), *The Global 1989* (Cambridge University Press 2010), *U.S. Foreign Policy* (Oxford University Press 2008), *Twentieth Century International Relations* (eight volumes; Sage 2006), *E. H. Carr: A Critical Appraisal* (Palgrave 2000), *A Farewell to Arms: Beyond the Good Friday Agreement* (2nd ed., Manchester University Press 2006), *American Democracy Promotion* (Oxford University Press 2000), *U.S. Foreign Policy After the Cold War: Superpower Without a Mission?* (Pinter 1995), and *The Interregnum: Controversies in World Politics, 1989–1999* (Cambridge University Press 1999). His work has been translated into several languages, including Japanese, Chinese, Russian, Ukrainian, German, Italian, French, and Spanish. Formerly Chair of the European Consortium for Political Research (2006–2009) and Research Fellow at the Norwegian Nobel Institute in 2002 and 2007, he is currently Chair of the United States Discussion Group at Chatham House, London, and Co-Director of IDEAS, a Centre for the Study of Strategy and Diplomacy at the LSE.

Devon E. A. Curtis is Senior Lecturer in the Department of Politics and International Studies at the University of Cambridge and a Fellow of Emmanuel College. Her main research interests and publications deal with power-sharing and governance arrangements following conflict, UN peacekeeping, non-state armed movements in the Great Lakes region of Africa, and critical perspectives on conflict, peacebuilding, and development. She is the co-editor of *Peacebuilding, Power and Politics in Africa* (Ohio University Press 2012).

Tim Dunne is Executive Dean of the Faculty of Humanities and Social Sciences at the University of Queensland where he is also Professor of International Relations in the School of Political Science and International Studies. Previously he was Director of the Asia-Pacific Centre for the Responsibility to Protect, where he continues to be a Senior Researcher. He has written and edited twelve books, including *Inventing International Society: A History of the English School* (Palgrave 1998), *Liberal World Orders* (co-edited with Trine Flockhart, Oxford University Press, in association with the British Academy 2013), and *The Handbook of the Responsibility to Protect* (co-edited with Alex J. Bellamy, Oxford University Press 2016).

Stephen Hobden is Senior Lecturer in International Politics at the University of East London, where he teaches courses on international relations theory and China's changing international role. He is currently working on a research project, together with his colleague Erika Cudworth, on complexity theory and international relations. This has resulted in the publication of a number of articles, together with the book *Posthuman International Relations: Complexity, Ecology and Global Politics* (Zed 2011).

Darryl Howlett is Senior Lecturer in the Division of Politics and International Relations at the University of Southampton. His most recent publications include *NPT Briefing Book* (2015 edition with John Simpson, Hassan Elbahtimy and Isabelle Anstey; Centre for Science and Security Studies, King's College London, UK in association with the James Martin Center for Nonproliferation Studies (CNS) at the Middlebury Institute of International Studies at Monterey (MIIS), US), (with Jeffrey S. Lantis) "Strategic Culture," in *Strategy in the Contemporary World* (John Baylis, James Wirtz, Colin S. Gray, editors; 5th ed., Oxford University Press 2016) and "Cyber Security and the Critical National Infrastructure," in *Homeland Security in the UK* (Paul Wilkinson, editor; Routledge 2007).

Richard Wyn Jones is Professor of Welsh Politics and Director of the Wales Governance Centre at Cardiff University. He has written extensively on Welsh politics, devolution, nationalism, and security studies. His book *Security, Strategy and Critical Theory* (Rienner 1999) is regarded as an important work in the area of critical theory. His most recent books are *Wales Says*

Yes: The 2011 Referendum and Welsh Devolution (University of Wales Press 2012—with Roger Scully); (in Welsh) *"Y Blaid Ffasgaidd yng Nghymru": Plaid Cymru a'r Cyhuddiad o Ffasgaeth* (University of Wales Press 2013), and *The Fascist Party in Wales? Plaid Cymru, Welsh Nationalism and the Accusation of Fascism* (University of Wales Press 2014).

James D. Kiras is Associate Professor at the School of Advanced Air and Space Studies, Maxwell Air Force Base, Alabama, where he has directed the School's course of instruction on irregular warfare for almost a decade. He is also an Associate Fellow of the Joint Special Operations University, Tampa, Florida, and worked for a number of years in the defense policy, counterterrorism, special operations, and consulting world. Dr. Kiras publishes and lectures on subjects including special operations, counterterrorism, and irregular warfare. His most recent book, co-authored with other contributors, is the revised second edition of *Understanding Modern Warfare* (Cambridge University Press 2016). Dr. Kiras's first book was entitled *Special Operations and Strategy: From World War II to the War on Terrorism* (Routledge 2006).

Steven L. Lamy is Professor of International Relations in the School of International Relations at the University of Southern California. He is also the Vice Dean for Academic Programs in the College of Letters, Arts and Sciences. His latest research focuses on religion and international relations and is funded by a grant from the Luce Foundation.

John S. Masker is Associate Professor of Political Science at Temple University, where he teaches international relations and political theory. He has had visiting appointments at Williams College, Mount Holyoke College, and Clark University. Masker has written about nuclear nonproliferation, Russian foreign policy, and U.S. foreign policy.

Anthony McGrew is Professor and Pro-Vice Chancellor at La Trobe University, Melbourne and Director of the Confucius Institute. He is also currently a special Visiting Professor at the Shanghai Academy of Social Sciences. He has written extensively on globalization and global governance and is currently researching China's role in global institutions.

Patricia Owens is Professor of International Relations at the University of Sussex. She is author of *Economy of Force* (Cambridge 2015), *Between War and Politics* (Oxford 2007/9) and co-editor of the *European Journal of International Relations*. She is a former fellow of the Radcliffe Institute for Advanced Study at Harvard University; past Procter Fellow at Princeton University; and Seton-Watson Fellow at Oriel College, Oxford University.

Christian Reus-Smit is a Fellow of the Academy of the Social Sciences in Australia, and Professor of International Relations at the University of Queensland. He is author of *Individual Rights and the Making of the International System* (Cambridge 2013), *American Power and World Order* (Polity Press 2004) and *The Moral Purpose of the State* (Princeton University Press 1999), co-author of *Special Responsibilities: Global Problems and American Power* (Cambridge University Press 2012), editor of *The Politics of International Law* (Cambridge University Press 2004), and co-editor of *The Oxford Handbook of International Relations* (Oxford University Press 2008), *Resolving International Crises of Legitimacy* (special issue, *International Politics* 2007), and *Between Sovereignty and Global Governance* (Macmillan 1998).

Brian C. Schmidt is Associate Professor of Political Science at Carleton University, Ottawa, Canada. He is the author of *The Political Discourse of Anarchy: A Disciplinary History of International Relations* (SUNY 1998), *Imperialism and Internationalism in the Discipline of International Relations*, co-edited with David Long (SUNY 2005), and *International Relations and the First Great Debate* (Routledge 2012).

Len Scott is Emeritus Professor of International History and Intelligence Studies at Aberystwyth University. His recent publications include *The Cuban Missile Crisis: A Critical Reappraisal* (London: Routledge, 2015), co-edited with R. Gerald Hughes; *An International History of the Cuban Missile Crisis: A 50-year Retrospective* (London: Routledge, 2014), co-edited with David Gioe and Christopher Andrew; *The Cuban Missile Crisis and the Threat of Nuclear War: Lessons from History* (London: Continuum Books, 2007).

Sir Steve Smith is Vice Chancellor, and Professor of International Relations, at the University of Exeter. He has held Professorships of International Relations at the University of Wales, Aberystwyth, and the University of East Anglia and has also taught at the State University of New York (Albany) and Huddersfield Polytechnic. He was President of the International Studies Association for 2003–2004 and was elected to be an Academician of the Social Sciences (AcSS) in 2000. He was the editor of the prestigious Cambridge University Press/British International Studies Association series from 1986 to 2005. In 1999 he received the Susan Strange Award of the International Studies Association for the person who has most challenged the received wisdom in the profession. He is the author or editor of fifteen books, including (with the late Professor Martin Hollis) *Explaining and Understanding International Relations* (Oxford University Press 1989) and (co-edited with Ken Booth and Marysia Zalewski) *International Theory: Positivism and Beyond* (Cambridge University Press 1995), and some one hundred academic papers and chapters in major journals and edited collections. From 2009 to 2011 he was President of Universities UK.

Paul Taylor is Emeritus Professor of International Relations and, until July 2004, was the Director of the European Institute at the London School of Economics, where he specialized in international organization within the European Union and the United Nations system. Most recently he has published *The End of European Integration: Anti-Europeanism Examined* (Routledge 2008), *International Organization in the Age of Globalization* (Continuum 2003; paperback version June 2005), and *The Careless State* (Bloomsbury 2010). He is a graduate of the University College of Wales, Aberystwyth, and the London School of Economics.

The late **Caroline Thomas** was Deputy Vice-Chancellor and Professor of Global Politics at the University of Southampton. She specialized in North–South relations and published widely on the global politics of security, development, environment, and health.

John Vogler is Professor of International Relations in the School of Politics, International Relations and Environment (SPIRE) at Keele University, UK. He is a member of the ESRC Centre for Climate Change Economics and Policy. His books include *Climate Change in World Politics* (Palgrave 2016), *The Global Commons: Environmental and Technological Governance* (John Wiley 2000) and, with Charlotte Bretherton, *The European Union as a Global Actor* (Routledge 2006). He has also edited, with Mark Imber, *The Environment and International Relations* (Routledge 1996) and, with Alan Russell, *The International Politics of Biotechnology* (Manchester University Press 2000).

Nicholas J. Wheeler is Professor of International Relations and Director of the Institute for Conflict, Cooperation, and Security at the University of Birmingham. His publications include (with Ken Booth) *The Security Dilemma: Fear, Cooperation, and Trust in World Politics* (Basingstoke: Palgrave Macmillan 2008); (edited with Jean-Marc Coicaud) *National Interest Versus Solidarity: Particular and Universal Ethics in International Life* (Tokyo: United Nations University Press 2008); and (with Ian Clark) *The British Origins of Nuclear Strategy 1945–55* (Oxford: Oxford University Press). He has also written widely on humanitarian intervention and is the author of *Saving Strangers: Humanitarian Intervention in International Society* (Oxford: Oxford University Press, 2000). His new book, *Trusting Enemies* is under contract with Oxford University Press. He was the academic lead on the Sixth Birmingham Policy Commission on "The Security Impact of Drones: Challenges and Opportunities for the UK" and is the PI on an

ESRC funded project under RCUK's "Science and Security" programme on "The Political Effects of Unmanned Aerial Vehicles on Conflict and Cooperation Within and Between States." He is co-editor with

Professor Christian Reus-Smit and Professor Evelyn Goh of the prestigious Cambridge Series in International Relations.

MAPS OF THE WORLD

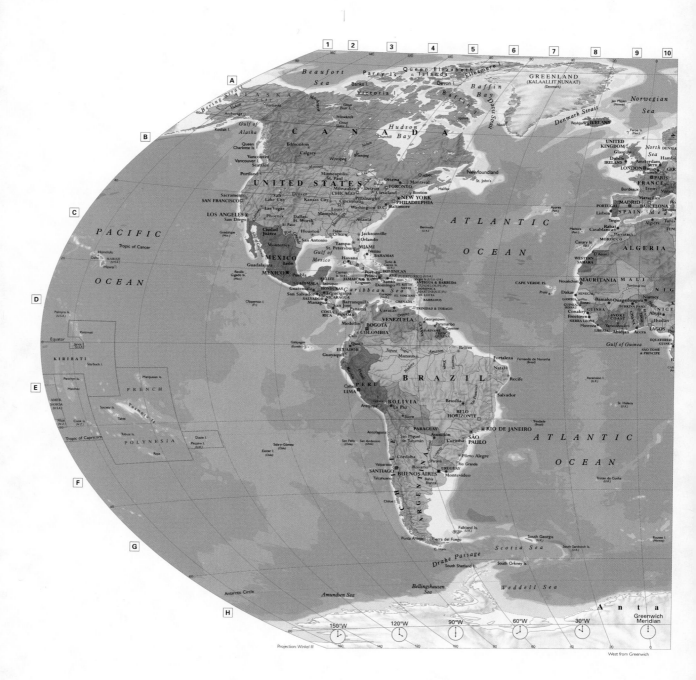

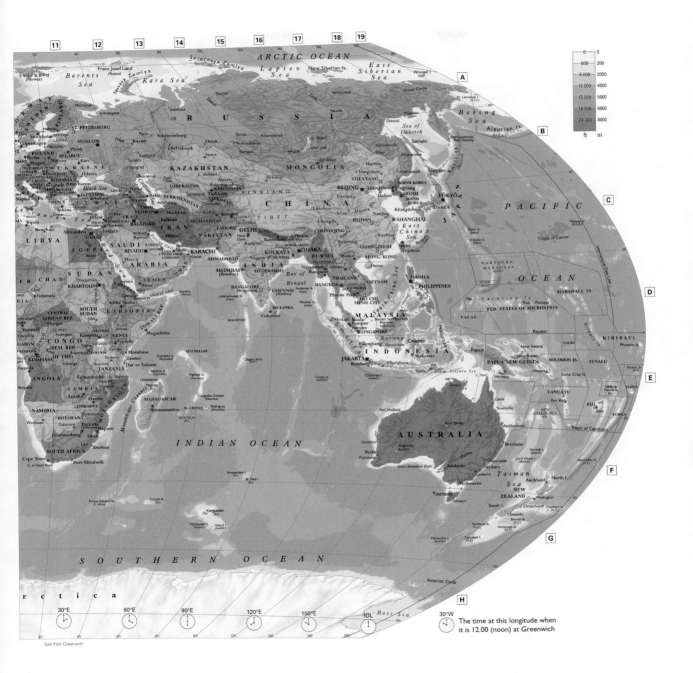

The time at this longitude when it is 12.00 (noon) at Greenwich

East from Greenwich

1:47 000 000

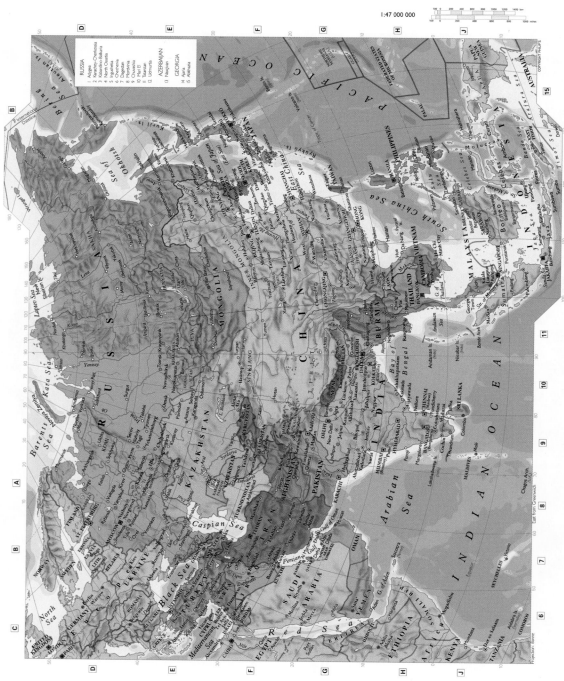

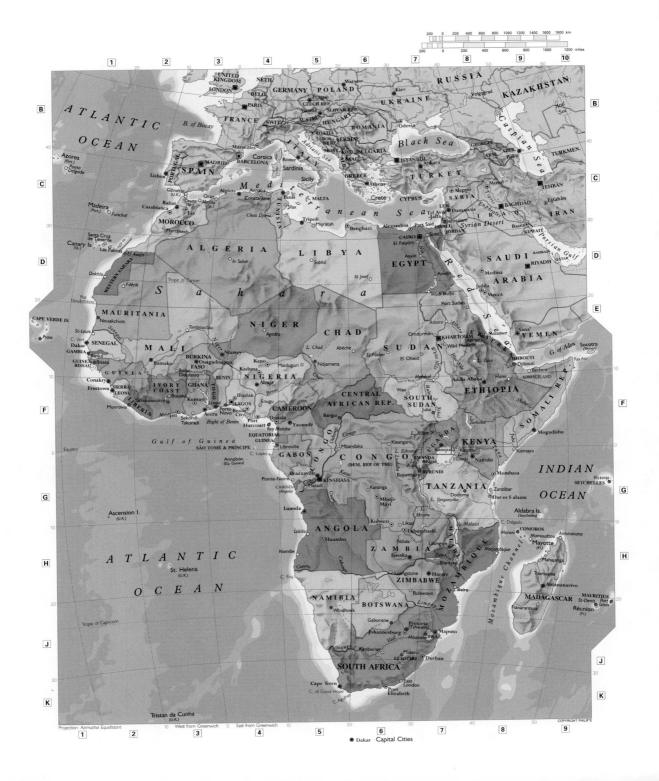

Africa map. Scale: 200 0 200 400 600 800 1000 1200 1400 1600 1800 km; 200 0 200 400 600 800 1000 1200 miles.

Projection: Azimuthal Equidistant. West from Greenwich. East from Greenwich. COPYRIGHT PHILIP'S

● Dakar Capital Cities

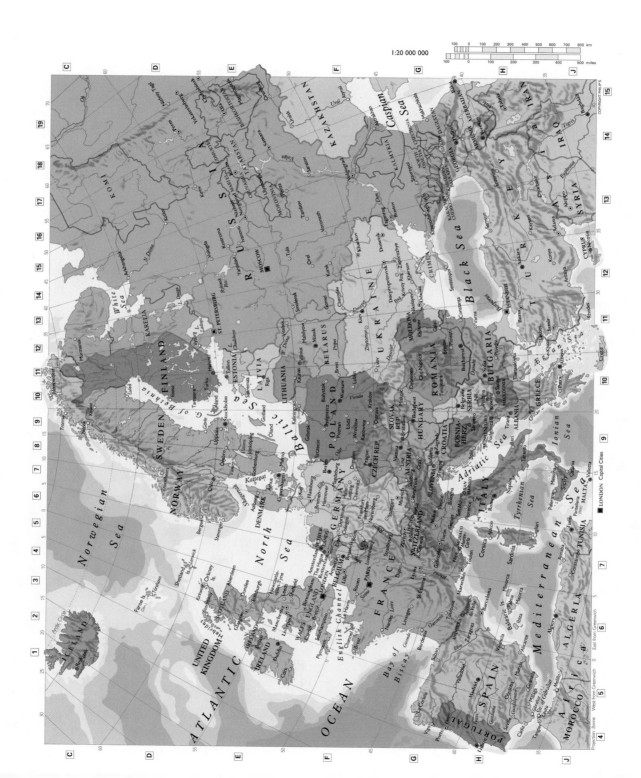

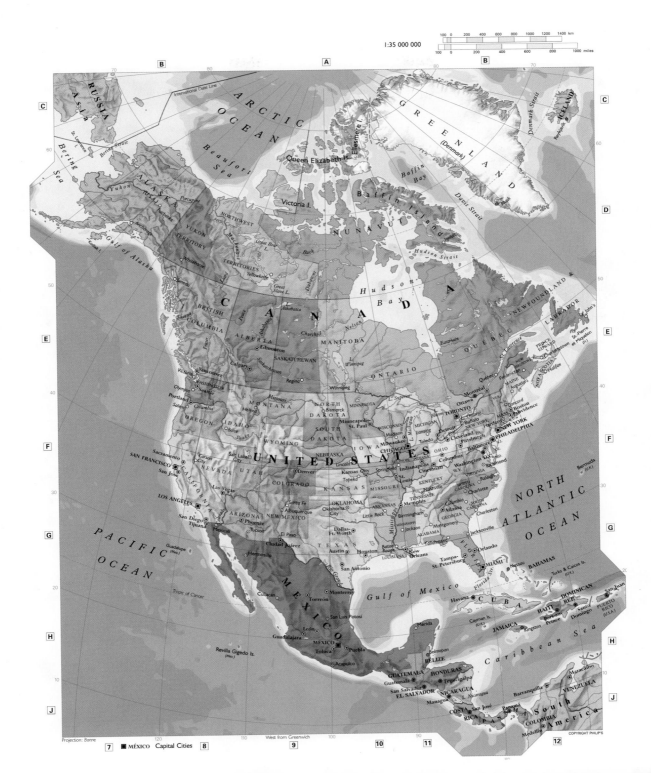

1:35 000 000

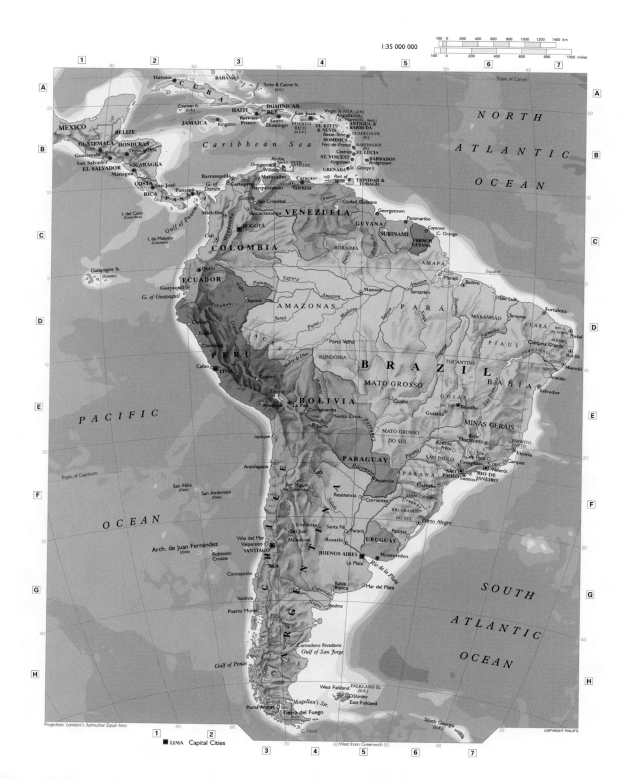

1:35 000 000

100 0 200 400 600 800 1000 1200 1400 km

100 0 200 400 600 800 1000 miles

Projection: Lambert's Azimuthal Equal Area

■ LIMA Capital Cities

West from Greenwich

COPYRIGHT PHILIP'S

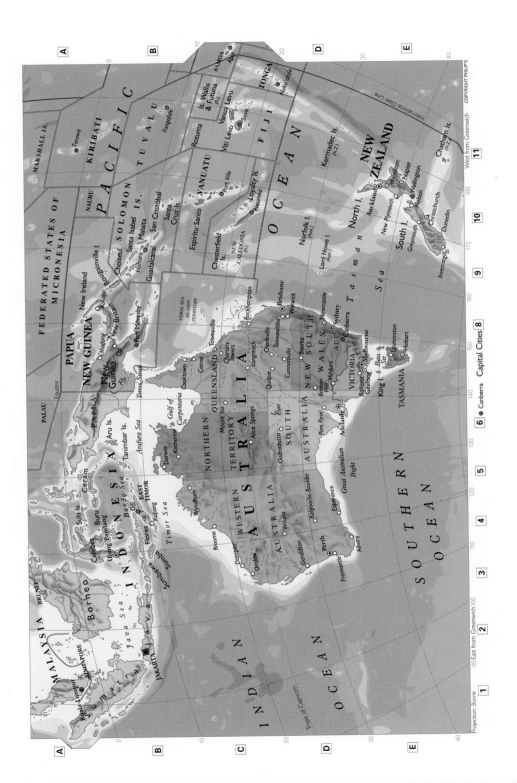

Projection: Bonne

INTRODUCTION TO
GLOBAL POLITICS

1

Introduction to Global Politics

Indian Prime Minister Narendra Modi traveled to China for negotiations with President Xi Jinping of the People's Republic of China. Both countries hope to overcome territorial disputes and forge economic and political partnerships.

I am a citizen of the world.

—DIOGENES

I am not a citizen of the world. . . . I am not even aware that there is a world such that one could be a citizen of it. No one has ever offered me citizenship, or described the naturalization process, or enlisted me in the world's institutional structures, or given me an account of its decision procedures . . . or provided me with a list of the benefits and obligations of citizenship, or shown me the world's calendar and the common celebrations and commemorations of its citizens.

—MICHAEL WALZER

Who will lead the world in this century, in this era of globalization? Will the American empire come to an end because of its internal economic problems and a dysfunctional polarized political system? Will China or India assume the mantle of leadership, and will this new global leader be willing to set aside national interests for the good of the global system? Although both India and China are emerging as major economic players, both have millions of citizens mired in poverty, and each country has significant domestic challenges that may preclude an activist role in global politics. We need to remember that the United States and its allies have created a global system that has provided opportunities for most countries to prosper. This is not to say, however, that the current system does not struggle with significant global challenges, such as how to help the "bottom billion," the poorest billion people in the world. But will the new superpowers take responsibility for providing the material and resources needed to manage global problems?

The world is changing, and that change is not only about terrorist networks or about the end of the Cold War. Globalization—especially economic globalization—has dramatically reshuffled global power arrangements and created new alliances and coalitions with the power to shape our future security and well-being. By **globalization**, we mean *the process of increasing interconnectedness among societies such that events in one part of the world more and more have effects on peoples and societies far away.* This is still a world without a central government or common power, but we all depend on the willingness of some states to provide order, enforce the rule of law, and lead and manage

3

the institutions essential to controlling the processes of globalization. At the same time, we expect our governments to provide security and opportunities for economic growth, and that is not easily done in this era. Who will lead is one question, and who can afford to lead is maybe an even more important question. Still, the global war on terrorism, with tremendous costs in terms of blood and treasure, continues to shape foreign policies of many states. And we know that all nation-states are being dramatically affected by the global economic crisis—now manifested in the crisis in Greece—which is pinching the wealthy and crushing those without the natural and human resources necessary to compete.

Like societies in the past, citizens across this world face more challenges than just economic ones. The world is facing a major refugee cricsis caused by wars in Africa, the Middle East, and other failed or fragile states, such as Syria. The U.S. interventions in both Afghanistan and Iraq did not result in the creation of stable multiethnic democratic states. Communal violence is now destabilizing both nation-states, which has caused many Afghan and Iraqi citizens to flee.

Recently, Europe battled its own debt crisis, which threatened the entire global financial system. This crisis started in 2009 with Greece's inability to stabilize its finances. The euro area continues to face economic issues, which are heightened by the influx of refugees from conflict regions around the world. Germany is taking the lead to stabilize the euro, prevent the collapse of Greece, and contain the crisis. Germany has also taken the lead in accepting refugees. Many of the world's leading economies, like the United States and China, have been asked to help, but they are not willing to commit resources or to assume risks if changes are not made in the fiscal policies of the struggling countries.

How we react to momentous events like the current refugee crisis in Europe and global climate change is linked to how we identify ourselves. Are you a citizen of the world, like Diogenes, or a citizen of a specific place, like Michael Walzer? You might be surprised to know how connected you are to the world. Look at the labels in your clothing. The tag says, "Made in someplace," but have you ever wondered how the pieces of your sneakers, for example, got to the factory where they were assembled? Or how the shoes traveled from that factory in Asia to the store in California, Kansas, Texas, or Vermont where you purchased them? Have you ever asked yourself who made your sneakers? How does that person live? How do others in the world view the United States or other wealthy and powerful states? How you are connected goes beyond looking at the goods and services you purchase in a given day. Do you have a passport and have you traveled internationally? Do you have a web-capable cell phone and are you constantly plugged into Internet applications like Facebook? Are you on Skype talking to friends you met while on a study abroad program? Have you signed up for news alerts from news agencies? Do you also read the international news from foreign sources such as the BBC or Al Jazeera? Do you belong to a global nongovernmental organization (NGO) like Human Rights Watch, Oxfam, or Greenpeace?

All of us have connections to the world that we are not aware of. Other connections we make, like joining a political group or student club on campus, are more personal and immediate. Yet both types of connections—known and unknown—help shape our identities as individuals in the wider world. The purpose of this book is to help you understand the world of politics that provides those connections. Along the way, you will see how interdependent we all are and how our way of life is shaped by forces of globalization.

We need to remember that globalization is a multidimensional process. Economic or market globalization involves processes of trade, production, and finance that are pushed by communications, technology, and the networking of national markets into a global economy (Hebron and Stack 2011). Political globalization is the spread of political ideas, values, norms, practices, and policies. Those who study globalization also look at its impact on the state and the ability of the state to do what is expected by its citizens. There are two positions here: (1) *hyperglobalists*, who see the state losing authority and sharing power with other actors, and (2) *skeptics*, who believe that states can use globalization to enhance their power and authority.

Perhaps as important as economic globalization is cultural globalization. This involves the spread of popular culture, in areas such as music, film, literature, and consumerism, and the global diffusion of more traditional cultural ideas found in religious and ethnic communities. Globalization is a powerful force that may challenge or at times enhance the authority of both state and nonstate actors in a variety of policy sectors.

This chapter presents an overview of the textbook—the main actors and topics that we will examine. It also introduces the theories that will guide us in our study of global politics. You will learn more about globalization, and you will begin that important journey of discovery by developing new eyes. You will begin to see how different theories construct our world.

Introduction

Probably more than any other series of events, the ongoing global economic crisis and the terrorist attacks of September 11, 2001, in the United States (referred to as

Many Americans celebrated the killing of Osama bin Laden in May 2011. Unfortunately, other terrorist networks have joined with Al-Qaeda and are spreading their extremist message across the world. Is there any region of the world safe from this extremist violence?

9/11), as well as those of March 11, 2004, in Madrid and July 7 and 21, 2005, in London, brought home just how globalized the contemporary world is. The subsequent war in Afghanistan and the controversial invasion of Iraq in 2003, followed by insurgency and civil war, and the rise of the Salafi jihadist extremist group Islamic State of Iraq and Syria, or ISIS, further demonstrate how the current era is globalized. These matters involved international coalitions of nation-states and transnational violent non-state networks in conflicts that linked events in seemingly unrelated parts of the world. Let us look at how aspects of these terrorist attacks illustrate the impact of globalization.

Although 9/11 was an event that took place in the United States, it was immediately observed throughout the world; the television pictures of the second plane crashing into the World Trade Center are probably the most widely seen images in television history. Thus, 9/11 was a world event, which had far more of an effect than represented by the number of deaths involved (about 3,000 died in the four attacks that day). The Madrid and London attacks seemed to underscore the seriousness of those who wanted a war against Western culture and its political and economic dominance.

The attacks in the United States were carried out by nineteen individuals in the name of an organization known as Al-Qaeda. This organization was not a state or formal international body but a loose coalition of committed men based, it was claimed, in more than fifty countries. This was a truly globalized network and not a traditional organization. The London and Madrid attacks were also directed or inspired by Al-Qaeda. Currently, the ISIS network, an affiliate of Al-Qaeda, controls territory in Iraq and Syria and smaller territories in Libya, Nigeria, and Afghanistan. ISIS attacks such as those in Brussels, Belgium which killed more than 30 people in March 2016; Paris, France, which in November 2015 killed more than 100 people; as well as the March 2015 downing of a Russian passenger jet killing 224, illustrate the expanding threat posed by ISIS.

The attacks were coordinated by using some of the most powerful technologies of the globalized world—namely, mobile phones, international bank accounts, and the Internet. Moreover, the key personnel traveled regularly among continents, using yet another symbol of globalization, mass air travel.

The reactions to these events throughout the world were intense, instantaneous, and very mixed: in some Arab and Muslim countries, there was jubilation that the West generally, and the United States specifically, had been hit; in many other countries, there was profound shock and an immediate empathy with the attacked countries.

With respect to the 9/11 attacks, they were not on ordinary buildings; the Pentagon is the symbol of U.S. military power and hegemony, and the World

Trade Center was (as the name implies) an icon of the world financial network and the triumph of capitalism led by the United States and other Western countries.

It is worth noting that although the 9/11 attacks targeted the United States, many individuals of other nationalities were killed; it is estimated that citizens from about ninety countries were killed in the attacks on the World Trade Center.

Finally, though there is a lot of disagreement over why Osama bin Laden ordered the attacks, the main reasons seem to have concerned events in yet other parts of the world. Bin Laden himself cited the plight of the Palestinians, as well as the continued support of the United States and its allies for the current Saudi regime and the presence of U.S. advisers on that country's "holy" soil. Therefore, although there are many indicators that the world has become increasingly globalized over the last thirty-five years, in many ways, 9/11, the European attacks, and the ongoing conflicts in the Middle East are the clearest symbols of how distant events reverberate around the world. Other "wicked global problems," such as climate change and global poverty, demand a global response and the 2015 Paris agreement on climate change and the recently announced UN Sustainable Development Goals suggest that nation-states are willing to cooperate to respond to these global challenges.

Still, globalization can also be seen as one of the causes of these attacks. In many parts of the world dominated by traditional cultures and religious communities, fundamentalists see globalization as a Western process bringing popular culture and Western ideas that undermine their core values and beliefs. This "Westoxification" pushed and promoted by globalization is the enemy, and the United States is the leader of this noxious process. Many fundamentalist communities are trying to control, manage, and, if possible, stop the process of globalization. This is possible in totalitarian societies, but it is becoming more difficult as the Internet and global communications spread around the world. The upheavals in North Africa and the Middle East—the so-called Arab Spring—were organized using social networks like Facebook and messaging services like Twitter. Change agents across the globe are certainly aided by new communication technologies, and these are transboundary tools that states cannot effectively contain.

Generally, people care most about what is going on at home or in their local communities. We usually elect people to office who promise to provide jobs, fix roads, offer loans for housing, build good schools, and provide quality health care. These promises may get candidates votes, but people in office soon learn that many of the promises cannot be fulfilled without considering the dynamics of the global economy and the impact of major global events. Leaders are now realizing that to provide for their citizens they must manage the processes of globalization, and this is not a task one country can do alone. We all became aware of the breadth and depth of globalization with the economic crisis that began in 2008 and has continuing effects in 2016. The costs of this global financial crisis are unemployment, home foreclosures, bank failures, a collapse in the stock markets around the world, and a general anger and dissatisfaction with political leaders for failing to anticipate these problems and respond before the near collapse.

Group of Twenty (G20) An assembly of governments and leaders from twenty of the world's largest economies: Argentina, Australia, Brazil, Canada, China, France, Germany, India, Indonesia, Italy, Japan, Mexico, Republic of Korea, Russian Federation, Saudi Arabia, South Africa, Turkey, United Kingdom, United States, and the European Union.

Presently, fears of a European recession could grow worse if a rescue plan for Greece does not work. The potential failure of the plan threatens to derail any stock market rally in the United States and to hinder global economic growth and recovery. Governments and regional organizations like the European Union must prove they can regulate global finance and manage the processes of globalization. World leaders and corporate executives are concerned about China's economic slowdown. Although China's 8 percent growth is the envy of most countries, any slowdown might have a major negative impact on trade in areas of global commodities like iron ore and other minerals. At the 2014 **G20**, or **Group of Twenty**, meetings in Brisbane, Australia, the assembled leaders made a commitment to raise gross domestic product (GDP) by 2 percent by 2018. European and U.S. leaders also supported the controversial transatlantic trade deal in an effort to add jobs and increase trade. With both of these efforts, leaders are now hoping that government spending might stimulate demand and that they can work together to regulate global finance. Further, they hope to direct more funds to countries in the developing world and reform the global institutions that must monitor and manage the forces of globalization. Slowly, people throughout the world are realizing that their own well-being or quality of life is directly tied to the well-being of others in distant lands.

Again, the aim of this book is to provide an overview of global politics in this globalized world. Let us start, though, with a few words about the title. It is not accidental. First, we want to introduce you to global politics as distinct from international politics or international relations (a distinction we will explain shortly). Second, many think the contemporary, post–Cold War world is markedly different from previous periods because of the effects of globalization. We think it is especially difficult to explain global politics in such an era because globalization is a particularly controversial term. There is considerable dispute over just what it means to talk of this being an era of globalization and whether it means the main features of global politics are any different from those of previous eras. In this introduction, we explain how we propose to deal with the concept of globalization, and we offer you some arguments for and against seeing it as an important new development in global politics.

Before turning to globalization, we want to set the scene for the chapters that follow. We will first discuss the various terms used to describe international relations, world politics, and global politics, and then we will spend some time looking at the main ways global politics has been explained.

Representatives from global and regional institutions participate in talks about the Greek economy. German Chancellor Angela Merkel, Managing Director of the International Monetary Fund Christine Lagarde, European Commission President Jean-Claude Juncker, and European Central Bank Governor Mario Draghi are essential partners in managing economic challenges. What does this tell us about the power of globalization?

International Relations and Global Politics

Why does the title of this book refer to **global politics** rather than to international politics or **international relations**? These are the traditional names used to describe the kinds of interactions and processes that are the concern of this text. Our reason for choosing the phrase *global politics* is that it is more inclusive than either of the alternative terms. With this phrase, we mean to highlight our interest in the politics and political patterns in the world, and not only those among nation-states (as the term *international politics* implies). We are interested in relations among organizations that may or may not be states—for example, multinational companies, terrorist groups, or **nongovernmental organizations (NGOs)**; these are all known as **transnational actors**. Although the term *international relations* does represent a widening of concern from simply the political relations among nation-states, it still restricts focus to *inter-national* relations. We think relations among cities or provinces and other **governments** or international organizations can be equally important. Therefore, we prefer to characterize the relations we are interested in as those of world politics—or more specifically, given the powerful influences of globalization, global politics.

However, we do not want such fine distinctions regarding word choice to force you to define politics too narrowly. You will see this issue arising repeatedly in the chapters that follow because many academics want to define politics very widely. One obvious example concerns the relationship between politics and economics; there is clearly an overlap, and a lot of bargaining power goes to the person who can persuade others that the existing distribution of resources is simply economic rather than political. So we want you to think about politics very broadly for the time being. Several features of the contemporary world that you may not have previously thought of as political will be described as such in the chapters that follow. Our focus is on the patterns of political relations, defined broadly, that characterize the contemporary world.

Global Actors

After reviewing the foundational and theoretical aspects of global politics in Chapters 2 and 3, we will take a close look at a number of important actors on the world stage. Nation-states (countries) are the most important actors in global politics because they are the actors that engage in diplomatic relations, sign the treaties that create the legal foundation for world politics, and go to war.

Increasingly, however, **nonstate actors** are playing important roles in global politics. These can be international or regional organizations that are composed of states. The United Nations (discussed further in Chapter 5) is the most famous actor in this category; others include the European Union, the Organization of American States (OAS), the Shanghai Cooperation Organization, and the African Union. **Multinational corporations (MNCs)** have also become important players in world politics. These large business organizations can have their headquarters

Global politics The politics of global social relations in which the pursuit of power, interests, order, and justice transcends regions and continents.

International relations The study of the interactions of states (countries) and other actors in the international system.

Nongovernmental organization (NGO) An organization, usually a grassroots one, with policy goals but not governmental in makeup. An NGO is any group of people relating to each other regularly in some formal manner and engaging in collective action, provided the activities are noncommercial and nonviolent and are not on behalf of a government.

Transnational actor Any nongovernmental actor, such as a multinational corporation or a global religious humanitarian organization, that has dealings with any actor from another country or with an international organization.

Government The people and agencies that have the power and legitimate authority to determine who gets what, when, where, and how within a given territory.

Nonstate actor Any participant in global politics that is neither acting in the name of government nor created and served by government. Nongovernmental organizations, terrorist networks, global crime syndicates, and multinational corporations are examples.

Multinational corporation or enterprise (MNC/MNE) A business or firm with administration, production, distribution, and marketing located in countries around the world. Such a business moves money, goods, services, and technology around the world depending on where the firm can make the most profit.

Nation A community of people who share a common sense of identity, which may be derived from language, culture, or ethnicity; this community may be a minority within a single country or live in more than one country.

State A legal territorial entity composed of a stable population and a government; it possesses a monopoly over the legitimate use of force; its sovereignty is recognized by other states in the international system.

in one country, their design staff in another, and their production facilities in several other countries. Multinational corporations are important in many ways but perhaps most significantly because a factory can provide vital jobs in a developing country.

In Chapter 5, we will provide an in-depth look at these and other nonstate actors, including a discussion of nongovernmental organizations, which have increased in numbers and influence in global politics. Nongovernmental organizations like Oxfam or World Vision provide expertise for policymakers and provide programs and resources to address global problems like poverty and global health issues. To clarify the difference, some authors call MNCs for-profit nonstate actors and NGOs not-for-profit nonstate actors. We will also look at foundations and research think tanks that are playing more important roles in global politics. Finally, we will explore the role played by individuals, including celebrities, who become involved in diplomacy. To lay the groundwork for that future discussion, let's take a moment now to look more closely at the definitions—and debates—involving states and nation-states, as well as to consider the problems of the traditional state-centered approach to studying global politics.

Like many of the terms used in the study of global politics, the terms *state* and *nation-state* can be somewhat confusing. The two parts of the term nation-state derive from different sources. **Nation** derives from the idea that a group of people sharing the same geographic space, the same language, the same culture, and the same history also share a common identity. As most political scientists use the term, nation conveys a group identity that is bigger than a family group or tribal unit. **State** has its origins in Latin and in the legal system of the Roman Empire. In political science, state is a particularly divisive term because, as we will see in Chapter 3, academics disagree about what the term means. At a minimum, political scientists agree that the state is the highest-level political structure that makes authoritative decisions within a territorially based political unit. What makes the term confusing for many students in the United States is that the country comprises subunits called "states." When nation and state are combined in the pair nation-state, we have a term that describes a political unit within which people share an identity. It is important to note that *the state is not always coincidental with a nation*. While the state for many political scientists is a set of governing institutions, *nation* refers to the people who share a history, language, religion, or other cultural attributes. The Flemish in Belgium, the Welsh in the United Kingdom, and the Iroquois of the United States and Canada are examples of nations found within states. Most states, even when

The Swedish home furnishing store IKEA has 42 stores in the United States, only 8 fewer than in Germany, with 50 IKEA locations. But did you know that China, with only 18 IKEA stores, produces more than a fifth of all IKEA's products?

called nation-states, actually comprise several nations. As we will see in this book, many problems in the modern international system result from nations with historical rivalry that are forced to live within the borders of one state.

The concepts of state and sovereignty are critical to understand if you are a student of international relations, a diplomat, or a political leader. The **nation-state**—sometimes called "country" or simply "state"—is the primary unit of analysis in the study of international relations. As we will discuss in Chapter 2, the Peace of Westphalia (which ended the Thirty Years' War in 1648) recognized the state as supreme and the sovereign power within its boundaries. The Westphalian ideal of sovereignty emphasizes the principle of the inviolability of the borders of a state. Furthermore, all states agreed with the idea that it was not acceptable to intervene in the internal affairs of other states. **Sovereignty** is a complex and contested concept in international relations; essentially, it suggests that within a given territory the leaders of a state have absolute and final political authority. However, international relations scholar Manuel Castells (2005) has suggested that the modern nation-state might be adversely affected by globalization in four ways; indeed, all our political institutions are facing the same four crises:

> **Nation-state** A political community in which the state claims legitimacy on the grounds that it represents all citizens, including those who may identify as a separate community or nation.

> **Sovereignty** The condition of a state having control and authority over its own territory and being free from any higher legal authority. It is related to, but distinct from, the condition of a government being free from any external political constraints.

1. States cannot effectively manage global problems unilaterally and thus suffer a *crisis of efficiency.*
2. Policymakers are not always representative of their citizens' interests, and as policymaking becomes more global, decisions are made further away from citizens. This is a *crisis of legitimacy.*
3. Citizens are being pulled toward their cultural identity and toward identity and affiliation with NGOs and other civil-society actors. A variety of forces pull them away from citizen identity and have created a *crisis of identity.*
4. Globalization has increased inequality in many states and created a *crisis of equity.*

Castells argues that nation-states must create collaborative networks with NGOs and other nonstate actors to respond effectively to these crises. The nation-state will survive, but states might be forced to share sovereignty with other global actors to provide for their citizens, meet their obligations, and combat world issues.

Global Issues

In Chapters 6 through 10, we will turn to global issues, demonstrating the connections among state and nonstate actors in the international system and consider how these global issues are

Celebrity activism is common in global politics. Akon is famous mostly for his music, but he is also a human rights activist. His current Akon Lighting Project seeks to bring electricity to millions of households in Africa using solar energy and other sources.

WHAT'S YOUR WORLDVIEW?

Are you a member of a nation? Do you identify with a particular ethnic community? Are you a member of an NGO, like Amnesty International or Greenpeace International? How do these identities affect your responsibilities as a citizen of a nation-state?

inextricably linked. First, we consider global security and military power—that is, the traditional responsibility of countries to provide for the physical security of the state's territory. We also examine terrorism, including the various groups that use this method and the ways that countries have responded to both global and domestic threats. Chapter 7 discusses an emerging issue area of global politics: human rights and human security. The last three chapters examine the intersections of trade, finance, poverty, development, and environmental issues. Each of these topics overlaps with the others, and it's important not to read these chapters merely in a straightforward fashion but also to review the information from previous chapters as you progress through your coursework.

ENGAGING WITH THE WORLD

Kiva

Do you want to know more about those who are struggling in our global community and find ways to help them? Do you want to work with 300 field partners and 450 volunteers in 83 different countries? Get involved with Kiva by becoming a fellow or starting a campus club.

Kiva is a nonprofit organization that lends money to help people around the world start a business and work their way out of poverty. Kiva has more than 1.3 million lenders with close to $806 million in loans, and Kiva has a 98.42 percent repayment rate. Check out www.kiva.org.

Theories of Global Politics

Theory A proposed explanation of an event or behavior of an actor in the real world. Definitions range from "an unproven assumption" to "a working hypothesis that proposes an explanation for an action or behavior." In international relations, we have intuitive theories, empirical theories, and normative theories.

The basic problem facing anyone who tries to understand contemporary global politics is that there is so much material to look at; it is difficult to know which things matter and which do not. Where would you start if you wanted to explain the most important political processes? How, for example, would you explain the U.S. decision to use military force to support rebels in Syria? Why did Russia counter with its own military force to support the current Syrian government? How will the world respond to the challenges created by climate change? Where in the world did the current economic crisis originate? Where will it end—and when? What policies will global leaders develop to respond to this economic crisis? Why are the number of extremist groups and the use of violence on the rise? Is this violence the result of failed states or a failure of leadership? Questions such as these seem impossible to answer definitively. Whether we are aware of it or not, whenever we are faced with such questions, we have to resort to **theories** to understand them and to develop effective responses.

What Are Theories?

A theory is not simply some grand formal model with hypotheses and assumptions. Rather, *a theory is a kind of simplifying device that allows you to decide which facts matter and which do not.* A good analogy is sunglasses with different colored lenses. Put on a red pair and the world looks red; put on a yellow pair and it looks yellow. The world is not any different; it just looks different. So it is with theories. Below we will briefly mention the main theoretical views that have dominated the study of global politics to give you an idea of the colors they paint the world. But before we do, please note that we do not think of theory as merely an option. It is not as if you can avoid theory and instead look directly at the facts. This is impossible because the only way you can decide which of the millions of possible facts to look at is by adhering to some theory that tells you which ones matter the most.

Demonstrators in South Africa are protesting attacks on immigrants and economic refugees who have come to South Africa for work. Poverty, violence, and repression may be the drivers for those who leave their homes. The number of refugees in 2015 is 60 million. What can be done?

You may not even be aware of your theory. It may just be the view of the world you have inherited from family, a group of friends, or the media. It may just seem to be common sense to you and not anything complicated like a theory. But your theoretical assumptions are implicit (implied though not plainly expressed) rather than explicit (stated clearly and in detail), and we prefer to be as explicit as possible when it comes to thinking about global politics.

Theoretical Traditions in International Relations

Martin Wight (1913–1972), one of the founding scholars in the English School of international relations, introduced his students to three **traditions** in international relations theory: **Machiavellian** (named for the Italian Renaissance politician, philosopher, and writer Niccolò Machiavelli), **Grotian** (after Dutch jurist Hugo Grotius), and **Kantian** (named for German philosopher Immanuel Kant). Each tradition describes the "nature of international politics," according to its adherents, which informs policy **prescriptions** for state survival in the international system. For Machiavellians, the international system is anarchic and states are constantly in conflict: states pursue their own interests as they see fit and systems of law and diplomacy cannot prevent future wars. The Machiavellian tradition describes the most pessimistic shade of realism, which is discussed in the following section. It is important to note that not all realists embrace such a negative view of human relations or accept the best description of international politics as a "war of all against all."

The Grotian tradition focuses on law and order. For Grotians, the international system is not anarchic. Instead, political and economic exchanges result in

Tradition In international relations, a way of thinking that describes the nature of international politics. Such traditions include Machiavellian, Grotian, and Kantian.

Machiavellian tradition A tradition in international relations theory named for Niccolò Machiavelli that characterizes the international system as anarchic; states are constantly in conflict and pursue their own interests as they see fit.

Grotian tradition A liberal tradition in international relations theory named for Hugo Grotius that emphasizes the rule of law and multilateral cooperation. Grotians believe the international system is not anarchic, but interdependent: a society of states is created in part by international law, treaties, alliances, and diplomacy, which states are bound by and ought to uphold.

Kantian tradition A revolutionary tradition in international relations theory named for Immanuel Kant that emphasizes human interests over state interests.

Prescription Recommendations for state survival in the international system based on international relations traditions.

an interdependent society of states, created in part by international law, treaties, alliances, and diplomacy. Grotians recognize that no central authority governs international society, and that conflict and cooperation can both occur. Nevertheless, states are bound by legal and moral constraints they themselves intentionally embed in the international institutions they create. Since all states benefit from the order provided by this rule-based society, they are morally obligated to uphold it.

Kantians, on the other hand, argue that human, not state, interactions properly define international relations; therefore, the latter should promote individual well-being and protect the community of humankind. For many modern day Kantians, the state system preferred by Machiavellians and Grotians actually causes most global problems, conflict, and violence.

Wight recognized that his traditions were ideal types and that there were many "subdivisions" in each. As students of international relations, we must recognize that most leaders borrow from several traditions.

The Rise of Realism

Idealism Referred to by realists as *utopianism* since it underestimates the logic of power politics and the constraints this imposes on political action. Idealism as a substantive theory of international relations is generally associated with the claim that it is possible to create a world of peace based on the rule of law.

Normative theory The systematic analyses of the ethical, moral, and political principles that either govern or ought to govern the organization or conduct of global politics. The belief that theories should be concerned with what ought to be rather than merely diagnosing what is.

Realism A theoretical approach that analyzes all international relations as the relation of states engaged in the pursuit of power. Realists see the international system as anarchic, or without a common power, and they believe conflict is endemic in the international system.

People have tried to make sense of world politics for centuries, especially since the separate academic discipline of international politics was formed in 1919, when the Department of International Politics was set up at the University of Wales, Aberystwyth. The man who established that department, a Welsh industrialist named David Davies, saw its purpose as to help prevent war. By studying international politics scientifically, many scholars believed they could find the causes of the world's main political problems and put forward solutions to help politicians solve them. After the end of World War I, the discipline was marked by this commitment to changing the world, and a number of antiwar organizations embraced this **idealism**. We call such a position **normative**, as its proponents concerned themselves with what *ought to be*.

Opponents of this normative position characterized it as overly idealistic in that it focused on means of preventing war and even making war and violence obsolete. They adopted a theory they called **realism**, which emphasized seeing the world as it really is rather than how we would like it to be. The world as seen by realists is not a very pleasant place; human beings are at best self-interest-oriented and probably much worse. To them, notions such as the perfectibility of human beings and the possibility of an improvement of world politics seem far-fetched. This debate between idealism and realism has continued to the present day, but it is fair to say that realism has tended to have the upper hand. It appears to accord more with common sense than does idealism, especially when the media bombard us daily with images of how awful humans can be to one another.

Having said this, we would like you to think about whether such a realist view is as neutral as it may seem commonsensical. After all, if we teach global politics to generations of students and tell them that people are selfish, then doesn't that become common sense? And don't they simply repeat what they have been taught when they go off into the media, or to work for the government, or the military, or when they talk to their children at the dinner table, and, if in positions

Members of the North Korean military salute the statues of North Korea's founder Kim Il-sung and his son Kim Jong-il in Pyongyang on April 25, 2015, the 83rd anniversary of the founding of the Korean People's Army. North Korea's intransigent foreign policy is based on the use and threat of force. How does this strategy shape the foreign policies of neighboring states?

of power, act accordingly? We will leave you to think about this. For now, we would like to keep the issue open and point out that we are not convinced that realism is as objective or nonnormative as it is often portrayed.

Rival Theories

Although realism has been the dominant way of explaining global politics in the last nearly 100 years, it is not the only way. In Chapter 3, we will examine not only realism but its main rival, **liberalism** (which essentially holds that states and non-state actors want peace and prosperity), and critical approaches such as **Marxism**, **constructivism**, **feminist theory**, and utopian views. Both realism and liberalism are considered mainstream or traditional theories. We use the word *critical* to identify theories or approaches that critique traditional theories—that advocate transforming the present global system and creating an alternative system.

In the 1980s, it became common to talk of an **interparadigm debate** among realism, liberalism, and Marxism; that is, these three major theories (designated **paradigms** by influential philosopher of natural science Thomas Kuhn) were in competition, and the truth about global politics lay in the debate among them. At first glance, each seems to be particularly good at explaining certain aspects of global politics, and an obvious temptation is to try to combine them into some overall account. But this is not the easy option it may seem. These three theories, along with the more recently influential constructivism, are not so much different views of the same world as *four views of different worlds*.

Let us examine this claim more closely. It is clear that each of these four broad theoretical traditions focuses on different aspects of global politics (realism on the power relations among states, liberalism on a much wider set of interactions among states and nonstate actors, Marxist theory on the patterns of the

Liberalism A theoretical approach that argues for human rights, parliamentary democracy, and free trade—while also maintaining that all such goals must begin *within a state*.

Marxism A theory critical of the status quo, or dominant capitalist paradigm. It is a critique of the capitalist political economy from the view of the revolutionary proletariat, or workers. Marxists' ideal is a stateless and classless society.

Constructivism An approach to international politics that concerns itself with the centrality of ideas and human consciousness. As constructivists have examined global politics, they have been broadly interested in how the structure constructs the actors' identities and interests, how their interactions are organized and constrained by that structure, and how their very interaction serves to either reproduce or transform that structure.

Feminism A political project to understand so as to end women's inequality and oppression. Feminist theories tend to be critical of the biases of the discipline. Many feminists focus their research on the areas where women are excluded from the analysis of major international issues and concerns.

Interparadigm debate The debate between the main theoretical approaches in the field of global politics.

Paradigm A model or example. In the case of international relations theory, the term is a rough synonym for "academic perspective." A paradigm provides the basis for a theory, describing what is real and significant in a given area so that we can select appropriate research questions.

world economy, and constructivism on the ways ideas and values shape our image of the world). However, each is saying more than this. Each view claims that it is picking out the most important features of global politics and that it offers a better account than the rival theories. Thus, the four approaches are really in competition with one another, and while you can certainly choose among them, it is not so easy to add bits from one to the others. For example, if you are a Marxist theorist, you think state behavior is ultimately determined by class forces—forces that the realist does not think affect state behavior. Similarly, constructivism suggests that actors do not face a world that is fixed but rather one that they can in principle change—in direct contrast to the core beliefs of realists and Marxists alike. That is, these four theories are really versions of what global politics is like rather than partial pictures of it. They do not agree on what global politics is fundamentally all about.

We should note that most scholars view constructivism, which has become increasingly influential since the 1990s, as a critical *approach* to studying international relations rather than a *theory*. Nick Onuf, a key constructivist scholar, has stated that constructivism is not a theory but a way of studying social relations. We like the way Michael Barnett (2011) compares constructivism with rational choice theory. Rational choice theory is a social theory suggesting that all actors act with fixed preferences, which are to always maximize benefits and minimize costs (see Table 1.1). Constructivism is also a social theory that is concerned with the relationship between agents and structures and the importance of ideas. From Barnett's view, constructivism is not a substantive theory; that is, it does not have common views about states, the international system, and human behavior, as realism and liberalism do.

We do not think any one of these theoretical perspectives has all the answers when it comes to explaining world politics in an era of globalization. In fact, each

---

TABLE 1.1 Decision Makers: Rationality and Politics

Rational choice: An economic principle that assumes that individuals always make prudent and logical decisions that provide them with the greatest benefit or satisfaction and that are in their highest self-interest.

Bounded rationality: Decision-makers do not always have the ability and information to make a rational decision or one that is optimal. Instead, they first simplify the list of choices available and then apply rationality. Thus, instead of value maximizing, the decision-maker is value satisficing. Herbert Simon, who proposed this model, suggested that people are only partly rational and emotions, values, and previous experiences may help shape the decision.

Prospect theory: Involves risk aversion and risk acceptance. Decision-makers in an environment of gain will avoid risky options and those in an environment of losses will accept risky options.

Poliheuristic theory: A two-stage analysis in which decision-makers first eliminate choices based on cognitive shortcuts and then subject the remaining choices to rational processing.

sees globalization differently. We do not want to tell you which theory seems best, since the purpose of this book is to give you a variety of conceptual lenses. By the end of the book, we hope you will work out which of these theories (if any) best explains globalization and other elements of global politics. However, we want to reinforce here our earlier comment that theories do not portray "the" truth. The theories see globalization differently because they presume what is most important in global politics. There is no answer as to which theory has the "truest" or "most correct" view of globalization.

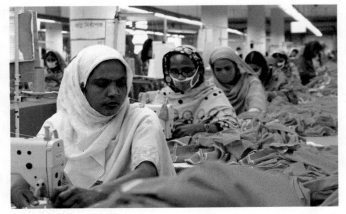

Women work in the textile factory One Composite Mills in Gazipur, a suburb of Dhaka, Bangladesh, where they make products for German mail-order company Klingel, sports articles producer Uhlsport (Kempa), Toys"R"Us, Desigual, and Paul R. Smith. Have you thought about the work conditions for people making the items that you consume on a regular basis?

Research Approaches and Levels of Analysis

As curious individuals, we are all interested in understanding the nature of global politics and the behavior of different actors in this global society. Two of the more traditional ways of doing research are the historical and social scientific approaches. A less traditional method of understanding the world is the constructivist approach. These three research approaches, in combination with theories, help us explain and understand decisions and events in global politics.

The Historical Approach

Historians arrive at an understanding of why states take certain actions, or why events happen, after careful review of public documents, memoirs, and interviews with key actors. Their goal is to understand a particular decision or event and create a thorough description or narrative that helps us understand decisions that key actors made. The goal is not to understand all wars or all actions by states but to create a history of a particular war or a very thorough description of a country's decision to take a certain policy position.

The Social Scientific Approach: Levels of Analysis

The intellectual interests of social scientists are slightly different. Social scientists want to bring the precision and certainty of the natural sciences to the social world. Uncomfortable with the subjectivity and ambiguity of many historical accounts, social scientists develop hypotheses based on dependent (Y) and independent (X) variables (e.g., "if X, then Y"); they then test and confirm these hypotheses or revise and refine them until they are accurate. They seek to explain international relations behavior, predict what others may do in similar situations, and develop a list of policy options or prescriptions for relevant policymakers. Research, then, is the search for the independent variable. For example, how do we explain a nation-state's allocation of development assistance or foreign aid? We know the amount of development assistance (dependent variable), but we now must find the independent variable that might explain this allocation.

Independent variables reside in one of four **levels of analysis** (which we will discuss in greater depth in Chapter 4):

Levels of analysis Analysts of global politics may examine factors at various levels—such as individual, domestic, systemic, and global—to explain actions and events. Each level provides possible explanations on a different scale.

- *Individual/Human Dimension:* This level explores the range of variables that can affect leaders' policy choices and implementation strategies. Current research reveals that individuals matter, particularly in the midst of crises, when decisions require secrecy and/or involve only a few actors, or when time is of the essence. The influence of individuals increases when they have a great deal of latitude to make decisions and when they have expertise and a keen interest in foreign policy.

- *Domestic Sources or National Attributes:* Factors at this level include a state's history, traditions, and political, economic, cultural, and social structures, as well as military power, economic wealth, and demographics, and more permanent elements like geographic location and resource base.

- *Systemic Factors:* To most realists, the anarchic nature of international relations may be the most important factor at this level. However, the individual and collective actions states have taken to cope with anarchy via treaties, alliances, and trade conventions—formal contracts created by states in an attempt to provide order—also constitute significant systemic factors. More informal constraints based on traditions, common goals, and shared norms shape state behavior as well. For example, most states respect the sovereignty of all states and follow the rule of international law because they expect others to do the same. This notion of reciprocity is the primary incentive for states to support a rule-based international system. Finally, distribution of power in the system (e.g., bipolar, multipolar) and the nature of order (e.g., balance of power, collective security) are also important systemic factors. Remember, the international system is created by the interaction of states and other powerful actors like international and regional organizations.

- *Global Factors:* Often confused with system-level factors, global-level variables challenge notions of boundaries and sovereignty. The processes that define globalization are multidimensional and originate from multiple levels. Globalization and its economic, political, cultural, and social dimensions derive from decisions made or actions taken by individuals, states, and international and regional organizations or other nonstate actors, but they are seldom traceable to the actions of any one state or even a group of states. A technological innovation (e.g., the Internet and the information revolution) that diffuses through the system affecting all but does not belong to any single actor is an obvious example. The movement of capital by multinational banks, the broadcasts of CNN, and the revolutionary ideas of religious fundamentalists all represent global factors that shape policy behavior. Natural conditions such as environmental degradation, pandemics (AIDS, SARS, and the flu), and weather patterns also affect foreign policy. Consider, for example, how global climate change and resulting changes in weather patterns might result in excessive rain or the opposite, a drought. Might these conditions influence a country's trade policies? Will a country now need to import food and establish trade relations with other food-producing states? Climate is a global factor that may have an impact on the globalization process.

What is exciting about research in our field is that there is always disagreement about which variables explain the most. The strength of any one argument is based on the quality of the empirical evidence collected to support the hypothesis being tested. Since we are not lab scientists, we cannot conduct experiments with control groups to test our propositions. Instead, we look to the work of historians, public-policy records, government documents, interviews, budgets, and journalist accounts to gather evidence to confirm or reject hypotheses.

The level chosen as a source for an independent variable depends on the situation you wish to examine, the availability of data or evidence, your research skills and interests, and, finally, your creativity and imagination. Each level is like a drawer in a toolbox; the analytic approaches or variables at each level are the tools that the researcher uses to develop and explore the explanatory power of three kinds of hypotheses: (1) causal hypotheses: if it rains, it will flood; (2) relational hypotheses: if it rains, flooding in certain geologic and geographic areas will worsen; and (3) impact hypotheses: if it rains more than *n* amount, the flooding will be particularly severe.

None of this is new. Both the ancient Greek historian Thucydides and the Enlightenment philosopher Immanuel Kant indirectly discussed levels of analysis in their efforts to explain state behavior. Thucydides focused on the explanatory potential of power capabilities and even suggested that the distribution of power in the international system influenced a state's behavior. Kant referred to the first three levels of analysis when he suggested that nation-states could avoid war by eliminating standing armies, managing the self-interests of rival leaders, and finding ways to provide order in the international system.

The Constructivist Approach

Constructivists question the underlying assumptions supporting historical and social scientific approaches to understanding international relations. Instead, these scholars postulate that there is no single historical narrative. Rather, the interests of specific actors shape the story, and it is their control of that story that gives them power. No perspective offers the truth because words, meanings, symbols, and identities are subjective and are used by individuals, groups, and society to gain and maintain power.

Further, constructivists argue that all of us interpret events and global conditions according to our beliefs, interests, values, and goals. We are not free to do anything we want in any given situation; instead, we are handed a menu reflective of the dominant interests and goals of powerful groups within a state or in the international system.

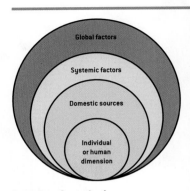

Levels of analysis.

In the study of global politics, there are four levels of analysis. Some scholars would say there are only three levels, but the authors of this book make a distinction between *systemic* (or international) factors and *global* factors. What is the argument for this distinction?

Dimensions of Globalization

As we have said, our goal in this book is to offer an overview of world politics in a globalized era. A globalized world is one in which political, economic, cultural, and social events become more and more interconnected and also one in which they have more impact. That is, societies are affected more extensively and more deeply by events of other societies. These events can conveniently be divided into three types: social, economic, and political. In each case, the world seems to be shrinking, and people are increasingly aware of this. The World Wide Web is the most graphic example, since it allows you to sit at home and have instant communication with websites around the world. Electronic mail has also transformed communications in a way that the authors of this book would not have envisaged fifteen years ago.

But these are only the most obvious examples. Others include worldwide television communications, global newspapers, global production of goods (see the Case Study: Global Production and the iPhone in this chapter), global franchises such as McDonald's and IKEA, and risks such as global warming. It is this pattern of events that seems to have changed the nature of world politics from what it was just a few years ago. The important point is not only that the world has changed but that the changes are qualitative and not merely quantitative; a strong case can be made that a new world political system has emerged as a result of globalization.

Having noted this, we want to point out that globalization is not some entirely new phenomenon in world history. Indeed, as we will examine later on, many argue that it is merely a new name for a long-term feature. We leave it to you to judge whether in its current manifestation it represents a new phase in world history or merely a continuation of processes that have been around for a long time, but we do want to note that there have been several precursors to globalization. Hence, looking beyond this quick history of globalization that follows, in Chapter 2 we will also present more detailed examples of previous international orders.

Our final task in this introductory chapter is to offer a summary of the main arguments for and against globalization as a distinct new phase in world politics. We do not expect you to decide where you stand on the issue at this stage, but keep this information in mind as you read the rest of this book. The main arguments in favor of globalization comprising a new era of world politics are the following:

1. *The pace of economic transformation is so great that it has created a new world politics.* States are no longer closed units; they cannot fully control their own economies. The world economy is more interdependent than ever, with trade and finances ever expanding.

2. *Communications have fundamentally revolutionized the way we deal with the rest of the world.* Now events on one side of the world can be immediately observed

on the other side. Electronic communications are also converging and thus altering our notions of the social groups we work with and live in. For example, consider how the Arab Spring events from 2010–2012 in Tunisia and Egypt and the revolution in Libya were influenced by social networking tools.

    3. *There is now, more than ever before, a global culture* such that most urban areas resemble one another. The urban world shares a common culture, much of it emanating from Hollywood and shaped by a global consumer culture.

    4. *The world is becoming more homogeneous in some material and ideational areas.* Differences in political and economic thinking among peoples are diminishing. The desire for democracy is universal, and many want a car, a house, and a television.

    5. *Time and space seem to be collapsing.* Our old ideas of geography and chronology are undermined by the speed of modern communications and media.

    6. *A **global polity** is emerging*, with transnational social and political movements and the beginnings of a transfer of allegiance from the state to substate, transnational, and international bodies. Global governance has become an important part of managing globalization.

    7. *A **cosmopolitan culture** is developing.* People are beginning to "think globally and act locally."

    8. *A **risk culture** is emerging.* People realize both that the main risks that face them are global (e.g., climate change and pandemics) and that states are unable to deal with the problems without some form of cooperation.

However, just as there are powerful reasons for seeing globalization as a new stage in world politics, often allied to the view that globalization is

Global polity The collective structures and processes by which "interests are articulated and aggregated, decisions are made, values allocated and policies conducted through international or transnational political processes" (Ougaard 2004, 5).

Cosmopolitan culture A pattern of relations within which people share the same goals and aspirations, generally to improve that culture for all members.

Risk culture A pattern of relations within which people share the same perils.

A positive element of globalization is the emphasis on human rights, including the right to secure an education. Here, Afghan girls walk toward the Mollia Girls School in the Ghorband District of Parwan Province. Why do extremists often use violence to stop the spread of education?

Global Production and the iPhone

Apple uses several different global manufacturers to build the iPhone. Take a closer look at any of its components and you will see just how global the iPhone manufacturing process truly is. In the iPhone 6s and 6s Plus, the central A series microchip, which makes the smartphone run, is made by two suppliers: the Taiwan Semiconductor Manufacturing Company and Samsung, a South Korean multinational company. InvenSense, a San Jose, California–based company, designed the iPhone's gyroscope, which makes the screen rotate between portrait and landscape mode. Japanese multinational corporation Sony supplies the image sensor for the front and back cameras, and another Japanese company, Toshiba, supplies storage, as does SK Hynix of South Korea. These components and more come together in factories in mainland China where the iPhone is assembled.

Relative to Western standards, working conditions and wages in China are low: workers typically live in dormitories and work up to 12 hours a day. Nevertheless, such factories help to reduce rural poverty by employing large numbers of workers. Apple executives argue that outsourcing to countries such as China and Taiwan is crucial to the development of the company and its innovation. Not only is labor cheaper but "the vast scale of overseas factories as well as the flexibility, diligence and industrial skills of foreign workers have so outpaced their American counterparts that 'Made in the U.S.A.' is no longer a viable option for most Apple products."

Since the first iPhone launched in 2007, it has become a major revenue driver for Apple, which made more than $234 billion in 2015. In its last sales quarter of 2015, Apple sold 48 million iPhones worth $33.2 billion. Those who own shares in Apple have benefited immensely from the globalization of the iPhone.

For Discussion

1. Many people are what we call economic nationalists—they support policies and practices that help keep jobs in their home country. How much more would you be willing to pay for your iPhone if it were made in your country? Is where it's manufactured at all important to you? Why or why not?

2. Some critics of globalization suggest that it allows companies to search for the lowest common denominator, meaning low wages, no labor or safety laws, and no environmental standards. Without these constraints, profits can be quite high. Should consumers consider these factors before buying products? Should there be global standards for wages, worker safety, and protection of the environment? Why or why not?

3. Most global production takes advantage of each country's comparative strengths or assets, and the result is a great product at a good price. Is this not how capitalism should work? Explain.

SOURCES

Compare Camp, "How & Where iPhone Is Made: Comparison of Apple's Manufacturing Process," September 17, 2014, http://comparecamp.com/how-where-iphone-is-made-comparison-of-apples-manufacturing-process/.

Charles Duhigg and Keith Bradsher, "How the U.S. Lost Out on iPhone Work," *New York Times*, January 21, 2012, http://www.nytimes.com/2012/01/22/business/apple-america-and-a-squeezed-middle-class.html?hp.

Jordan Golson, "Apple's iPhone Chips Aren't as Different as Some Have Reported," October 13, 2015, http://www.techrepublic.com/article/apples-iphone-chips-arent-as-different-as-some-have-reported/.

Grace Huang, "Sony to Spend 45 Billion Yen to Boost Sensor Capacity," *Bloomberg Business*, April 7, 2015, http://www.bloomberg.com/news/articles/2015-04-07/sony-to-spend-45-billion-yen-to-boost-sensor-capacity.

Rupert Neate, "Apple Calls 2015 'Most Successful Year Ever' after Making Reported $234bn," *The Guardian*, October 27, 2015, http://www.theguardian.com/technology/2015/oct/27/apple-2015-revenue-iphone-sales.

World Bank (2006), *Global Economic Prospects 2007: Managing the Next Wave of Globalization* (Washington, D.C.: World Bank), p. 118.

progressive—that is, it improves the lives of people—there are also arguments that suggest the opposite. Some of the main ones are as follows:

1. One obvious objection to the globalization thesis is that it is *merely a buzzword to denote the latest phase of capitalism*. In a very powerful critique of globalization theory, Hirst and Thompson (1999) argue that one effect of the globalization thesis is that it makes it appear as if national governments are powerless in the face of global trends. This ends up paralyzing governmental attempts to subject global economic forces to control and regulation. Believing that most globalization theory lacks historical depth, they point out that it paints the current situation as *more special than it is* and also as more firmly entrenched than it might in fact be. Current trends may be reversible. They conclude that the more extreme versions of globalization are "a myth," and they support this claim with five main conclusions from their study of the contemporary world economy (1999, 2–3): First, the present internationalized economy is not unique in history. In some respects, they say, it is less open than the international economy was between 1870 and 1914. Second, they find that genuinely transnational companies are relatively rare; most are national companies trading internationally. There is no trend toward the development of international companies. Third, there is no shift of finance and capital from the developed to the underdeveloped worlds. Direct investment is highly concentrated among the countries of the developed world. Fourth, the world economy is not global; rather, trade, investment, and financial flows are concentrated in and among three blocs—Europe, North America, and Asia. Finally, they argue that this group of three blocs could, if they coordinated policies, regulate global economic markets and forces. Note that Hirst and Thompson are looking only at economic theories of globalization, and many of the main accounts deal with factors such as communications and culture more than economics. Nonetheless, theirs is a very powerful critique of one of the main planks of the more extreme globalization thesis, with their central criticism that seeing the global economy as something beyond our control both misleads us and prevents us from developing policies to control the national economy.

2. Another obvious objection is that globalization is very *uneven in its effects*. At times, it sounds very much like a Western theory applicable only to a small part of humankind. To pretend that even a small minority of the world's population can connect to the World Wide Web is clearly an exaggeration, when in reality most people on the planet have probably never made a telephone call in their lives. Thus, globalization applies only to the developed world. We are in danger of overestimating globalization's extent and depth.

3. A related objection is that globalization may be *the latest stage of Western imperialism*. It is the old modernization theory (a controversial theory that suggests nation-states move naturally from traditional societies that are rural and agricultural to modern societies that are complex, urban, and industrial) in a new guise. The forces that are being globalized are conveniently those found in the

Western world. What about non-Western values? Where do they fit into this emerging global world? The worry is that they do not fit in at all, and what is celebrated in globalization is the triumph of a Western worldview at the expense of the worldviews of other cultures.

4. Critics have also noted that there are *people who have much to lose* as the world becomes more globalized. This is because it represents the success of liberal capitalism in an economically divided world. Perhaps one outcome is that globalization allows the more efficient exploitation of less well-off states, and all in the name of openness. The technologies accompanying globalization are technologies that automatically benefit the richest economies in the world and allow their interests to override local economies. So not only is globalization imperialist, but it is also exploitative.

5. We also need to make the straightforward point that *not all globalized forces are necessarily good ones.* Globalization makes it easier for drug cartels and terrorists to operate, and the World Wide Web's anarchy raises crucial questions of censorship and preventing access to certain kinds of material.

6. Turning to the so-called **global governance** aspects of globalization, the main worry here is about *responsibility*. To whom are the transnational social movements responsible and democratically accountable? If Microsoft or Shell becomes more and more powerful in the world, does this not raise the issue of how accountable it is to democratic control? David Held has made a strong case for the development of what he calls **cosmopolitan democracy** (1995), but this cosmopolitan democracy has clearly defined legal and democratic features. The concern is precisely that most of the emerging powerful actors in a globalized world are not accountable. This argument also applies to seemingly good global actors such as Oxfam and the World Wildlife Fund.

7. Finally, *there seems to be a* **paradox** *at the heart of the globalization thesis.* On the one hand, globalization is usually portrayed as the triumph of Western, market-led values. But how do we then explain the tremendous economic success that some national economies have had in the globalized world? Consider the economic success of China and India and the so-called Tigers of Asia, countries such as Singapore, Taiwan, Malaysia, and South Korea. These countries have enjoyed some of the highest growth rates in the international economy but subscribe to very different views of the role of the state in managing the economy and to the place of individual rights, privileges, political rights, and freedoms. The paradox, then, will be if these countries can continue to modernize so successfully without adopting many Western values. If they can, what does this do to one of the main themes of globalization—namely, the argument that globalization represents the spreading across the globe of a set of values? If these countries do continue to follow their own roads toward economic and social modernization, then we must anticipate future disputes between Western and non-Western values over issues like human rights, gender, and religion.

We hope these arguments for and against the dominant way of representing globalization will cause you to think deeply about the utility of the concept

Global governance The regulation and coordination of transnational issue areas by nation-states, international and regional organizations, and private agencies through the establishment of international regimes. These regimes may focus on problem-solving or the simple enforcement of rules and regulations.

Cosmopolitan democracy A condition in which international organizations, transnational corporations, and global markets are accountable to the peoples of the world.

Paradox A seemingly absurd or self-contradictory statement that, when investigated or explained, may prove to be well founded or true.

in explaining contemporary world politics. The chapters that follow do not take a common stance *for* or *against* globalization. We will end by posing some questions that we would like you to keep in mind as you read the remaining chapters:

- Is globalization a *new* phenomenon in world politics?
- Which theory best explains the effects of globalization?
- Is globalization a positive or a negative development?
- Does globalization make the state obsolete?
- Does globalization make the world more or less democratic?
- Is globalization merely Western imperialism in a new guise?
- Does globalization make armed conflicts more or less likely?
- Last but not least, what will *your* role be in world politics? How will you choose to identify yourself and participate locally, nationally, and globally? Has globalization increased your opportunities to engage with the world?

A homeless man tries to sleep during the monsoon rains in India. Globalization has not improved quality of life for all. Do wealthy states benefiting from globalization have an obligation to the poor?

Conclusion

We hope this introduction and the chapters that follow help you answer these questions. We also hope this book as a whole provides you with a good overview of the politics of the contemporary world.

Returning to 9/11 and the global reach of terrorism and extremist politics, we think it important to conclude this chapter by stressing that globalization clearly is a very complex phenomenon that is contradictory and difficult to comprehend. Just as the Internet is a liberating force, it is also how the terrorists who planned the attacks communicated. Similarly, television can bring live stories right into our living rooms so that we understand more about the world. But on 9/11, television was also a means of communicating a very specific message about the vulnerability of the United States and ultimately a way of constructing the categories within which we

Migrants on a dinghy arrive at the southeastern island of Kos, Greece, after crossing from Turkey. Greece has become the main gateway to Europe for tens of thousands of refugees and economic migrants, mainly Syrians fleeing war, as fighting in Libya has made the alternative route from North Africa to Italy increasingly dangerous. Consider how globalization shapes this crisis.

reacted. Finally, maybe the most fundamental lesson of 9/11 is that not all people in the world share a view of globalization as a progressive force in world politics. Those who undertook the attacks were rejecting, in part, the globalization-as-Westernization project. *Globalization is therefore not one thing.*

How we think about it will reflect not merely the theories we accept but also our own positions in this globalized world. In this sense, the ultimate paradox of 9/11 is that the answers to questions such as what it was, what it meant, and how to respond to it may themselves ultimately depend on the social, cultural, economic, and political spaces we occupy in a globalized world. That is, world politics suddenly becomes very personal: How does your economic position, your ethnicity, your gender, your culture, or your religion determine what globalization means to you?

CONTRIBUTORS TO CHAPTER 1: *John Baylis, Anthony McGrew, Steve Smith, Steven L. Lamy, and John Masker.*

KEY TERMS

Constructivism, p. 15
Cosmopolitan culture, p. 21
Cosmopolitan democracy, p. 24
Feminist theory, p. 15
Global governance, p. 24
Global politics, p. 9
Global polity, p. 21
Globalization, p. 3

Government, p. 9
Grotian tradition, p. 13
Group of Twenty (G20), p. 8
Idealism, p. 14
International relations, p. 9
Interparadigm debate, p. 15
Kantian tradition, p. 13
Levels of analysis, p. 18
Liberalism, p. 15
Machiavellian tradition, p. 13

Marxism, p. 15
Multinational corporation (MNC), p. 9
Nation, p. 10
Nation-state, p. 11
Nongovernmental organization (NGO), p. 9
Nonstate actor, p. 9
Normative, p. 14
Paradigm, p. 15

Paradox, p. 24
Prescription, p. 13
Realism, p. 14
Risk culture, p. 21
Sovereignty, p. 11
State, p. 10
Theory, p. 12
Tradition, p. 13
Transnational actor, p. 9

REVIEW QUESTIONS

1. Is globalization a new phenomenon in world politics?
2. In what ways are you linked to globalization?
3. How do ideas about globalization shape our understanding of the trend?
4. How can different levels of analysis lead to different explanations of the impact of globalization on global politics?

5. Why do theories matter?
6. International relations began as a problem-solving discipline in response to World War I. What are the global problems that now define our field of study?

For more information, quizzes, case studies, and other study tools, please visit us at **www.oup.com/us/lamy**.

Why Should I Care?

In this chapter, we have discussed how forces of globalization shape all of our lives. We know that these forces of globalization influence nation-states, but how do they shape your life and the activities of your family and friends? How is your quality of life shaped by global factors that have created a global economy and a global consumer culture? How are your personal choices influenced by the actions of distant actors and economic, political, and cultural conditions pushed by globalization?

PART ONE: YOU AS A GLOBAL CONSUMER

Consider the following questions in small groups, with a focus on how you are linked in a web of interdependence that may shape the choices you make. Also understand that you are making choices in different sectors of global society. It is like playing chess on three or four different chessboards. You are making choices in the economic sector, political sector, and cultural sector. In turn, these choices affect social relations and have profound implications for the natural world, or the environmental sector.

1. With the iPhone case in mind, consider how many items in your daily commodity basket (the sum total of goods and services purchased in a given time frame) are not local and are imported from a foreign country.
2. Do you think dependency on foreign goods and services matters? How might your choices influence people in your community and people in distant lands?
3. Individuals, like countries, need to avoid situations where their choices create an unhealthy dependency on foreign goods and services. For example, a country's dependency on oil makes it vulnerable to corporations and countries that supply it. It is okay to depend on products, but you hope this dependency has low political and economic costs. For example, our dependency on oil makes us vulnerable because it is too hard to find a substitute. This is called *vulnerability interdependency*. But our dependency on good French wine can be replaced by a dependency on good Chilean or Australian wine. The cost of finding an alternative is low; thus, this is called *sensitivity interdependency*. These sensitivity situations are unavoidable in a global economy. Again, considering your lifestyle, are you in the vulnerability or sensitivity category? Is it easy to stay in the sensitivity category?

PART TWO: ASSESSING YOUR POLITICAL CONNECTIONS

1. The entire world changed with the terrorist attacks against the United States, Spain, the United Kingdom, and recently, Paris and Beirut. How have global politics changed and how have these changes affected you and your family?
2. Identify four international events that have occurred in the last six months that have had a direct impact on political life in your country. Be specific about how these events have changed the game of domestic politics.
3. What about leadership in this world of global politics? When you consider the impact of globalization and the complex issues we all face as citizens in rich and poor states, what skills and competencies do you think leaders need to be successful in securing the interests of their citizens and providing for world order?

WRITING ASSIGNMENT: MORAL INTERDEPENDENCY

We have become so interdependent economically and politically, but do we recognize our moral responsibility to people who are not our citizens? Do we have any responsibility for the impact of our foreign policy decisions on other countries? For example, in the pursuit of wealth and prosperity, we may trade for oil with authoritarian regimes that oppress their citizens. Are we also culpable? By providing that regime with financial resources, are we contributing to its reign of terror?

2

The Evolution of Global Politics

Heads of State and royals from twenty European countries, including, front row from right German President Roman Herzog, Austrian President Thomas Klestil, and Italian President Oscar Luigi Scalfaro, walking through the streets of Münster, Germany, to celebrate the 350th anniversary of the Peace of Westphalia on Saturday, October 24, 1998. This agreement ended the Thirty Years' War but also provided the foundation for secular nation-states and emphasized the equality and independence of states. As globalization becomes more intensive and extensive, is the Westphalian system at risk?

Those who cannot learn from history are doomed to repeat it.

—GEORGE SANTAYANA

We learn from history that we learn nothing from history.

—G. B. SHAW

All nation-states have goals that may be unstated but are essential for survival and influence in the global system. These goals include the following:

1. Maintain and protect the state's sovereignty.
2. Protect autonomy, which allows for both independence and flexibility.
3. Maintain existing levels of power and influence and work to increase both relative to other policy actors.
4. Secure representation in global and regional institutions and gain a voice in global policy formulation.

Most nation-states have think tanks or special task forces that explore possible future world scenarios. This is how states prepare for the uncertainty of global politics. In the United States, the National Intelligence Council publishes reports that provide a framework for thinking about the future by focusing on "critical trends and possible discontinuities," such as those in the areas of globalization, demography, and the environment. In their most recent publication, *Global Trends 2030: Alternative Worlds* (2012), the authors discuss megatrends, game changers, and potential future worlds.

Among the megatrends is the *diffusion of power*, meaning that there will be no dominant world power and that power will shift to networks and coalitions of public and private actors. Another critical megatrend will be *increasing demands for food, water, and energy*. With climate change, scarcity may increase the competition for these resources.

Some of the *game changers* or events and conditions discussed in the study entail:

• Crisis and disputes among players in the *global economy* that threaten economic stability. The challenge is to encourage cooperation and multilateralism and discourage economic nationalism and trade disputes. These are problems that have plagued the international system for centuries.

- The *governance gap* or the inability of governments to manage the processes of globalization, which stimulate a variety of changes in the international system.
- The potential for more conflict as power shifts within and between nation-states.
- Regional instability in critical regions, such as the Middle East and South Asia. It is very possible that these conflicts will spill over and recent moves by Russia in Syria, for example, might result in a new Cold War and thus another great power conflict.

Sometimes, it's difficult to imagine how things might ever improve; other times, it's easy to get caught up in the moment, when something significant or strange occurs on the world stage. Yet each of the events and enduring conditions listed here stems from a deeper world history, and knowing about these histories takes us a step closer to understanding global politics—past, present, and future.

Perhaps, despite our cautious list of future scenarios, the international system has actually moved in a positive direction. After all, countries that were enemies in 1944—including France, Germany, and Great Britain—are today working together to bring economic prosperity to the world as members of the European Union. The accumulation of human history—political change, economic progress, medical breakthroughs, the lives of ordinary people—is part of the fabric of struggle and cooperation, strife and comity.

Our goal in this chapter is to demonstrate, briefly, how the international system, and in some ways the global society, has evolved during the last 400 years. It is, of course, not possible to cover all of international political history in one chapter. Therefore, our attention here will be primarily on significant political events; in other chapters, we will discuss social and economic trends.

Introduction

The history of international relations did not begin in 1648, but as we'll explain, it's a good place to begin our story. Kingdoms, empires, city-states, and nation-states have for centuries interacted in the same kinds of patterns that emerged after the end of the Thirty Years' War (1618–1648).

In China, Africa, India, and ancient Greece, political units of various sizes had engaged in economic relations, exchanged ambassadors, and fought wars for centuries prior. And globalization is not a new phenomenon; it dates back to the premodern era, when the Silk Road constituted one of the first overland and transcontinental trade routes, connecting eastern, southern, and western Asia with the Mediterranean and European world. Similarly, early maritime trade routes, particularly the Indian Ocean trade route, played an important part in east-to-west exchanges of culture, language, and goods, all the way from the Roman period to the seventeenth century.

But we choose to begin with 1648 because an event during that year represents a major dividing line in history: the Peace of Westphalia, which ended the

Thirty Years' War, established the principle of sovereignty. Crucial in delimiting the political rights and authority of monarchs, it added significantly to the developing template for the international system, now referred to as the "globalized system," that is a theme of this book: arrangements for governance, human rights, and economics that form the basis of the contemporary world.

In this chapter, we will discuss wars and political upheavals. It is a sweeping tale, covering the American and French Revolutions, two world wars, the end of European colonization of Africa and Asia, the Cold War and the changes in the international political system that followed its end, and the terrorist attacks of the early and mid-2000s. Our goal is to provide some background, or context, for you to understand the topics that we will examine in depth in Chapters 6 through 10.

After reading and discussing this chapter, you should have a better understanding of the origins of the modern international system. This is primarily a Western, Eurocentric system—one that spread even as former empires tried to contain European expansion. You will also have a better understanding of the Cold War and its effects on the world. Some have called the Cold War "World War III," as it was a global ideological battle for the hearts and minds of all peoples. If it was a war about two contending rulebooks—one being the U.S. or Western view of capitalism and democratic governance and the other being the Soviet brand of socialism and authoritarian government—is the post–Cold War crisis about how to apply the Western rules? Some authorities have suggested that the current global war on terrorism is actually World War IV. This chapter encourages you to explore various dimensions of the U.S.-led war on terrorism that is now centered on Afghanistan, Pakistan, Syria, Iraq, and Somalia.

Most important, you'll gain a sense that history matters because it shapes political institutions and influences how leaders make decisions. Leaders in situations of uncertainty often refer to lessons from historical events. Analogical reasoning, or learning from history, is an important element of decision-making in our complex international environment.

The Significance of the Peace of Westphalia

When Martin Luther nailed his Ninety-Five Theses to the door of the cathedral in Wittenberg, Germany, in 1517, he launched more than the **Protestant Reformation**. For the next century, monarchs across Europe found in religion a justification to begin wars that were actually about politics and economics. The **Thirty Years' War** (1618–1648) was the last of these religious conflicts in Europe and ostensibly began over a disagreement about the right of political leaders to choose a state religion. The opponents—including at various times Denmark, France, Austria, Sweden, Spain, and the principalities of the Holy Roman Empire—conducted most of their operations in Germany, killing tens of thousands of soldiers and civilians and devastating cities and farmland.

Protestant Reformation
A social and political movement begun in 1517 in reaction to the widespread perception that the Catholic Church had become corrupt and had lost its moral compass.

Thirty Years' War
(1618–1648) The last of the great wars in Europe fought nominally for religion.

Peace of Westphalia (1648) Ended the Thirty Years' War and was crucial in delimiting the political rights and authority of European monarchs.

Sovereign equality The idea that all countries have the same rights, including the right of noninterference in their internal affairs.

Society of states An association of sovereign states based on their common interests, values, and norms.

Balance of power In the international system, a state of affairs in which there is parity and stability among competing forces, and no one state is sufficiently strong to dominate all the others.

Peace of Utrecht (1713) The agreement that ended the War of the Spanish Succession and helped to consolidate the link between sovereign authority and territorial boundaries in Europe. This treaty refined the territorial scope of sovereign rights of states.

The **Peace of Westphalia** in 1648 not only ended this catastrophic conflict but also ushered in the contemporary international system by establishing the principle of sovereignty (a state's control and authority over its own territory). Political leaders, aware that the fighting had solved nothing and brought only widespread destruction, codified in the accord the right of the more than 300 German states that constituted the Holy Roman Empire to conduct their own diplomatic relations—a very clear acknowledgment of their sovereignty. They were also to enjoy "an exact and reciprocal Equality": the first formal acceptance of **sovereign equality** (the idea that countries have the same right to sovereignty) for a significant number of states.

More generally, the peace may be seen as encapsulating the very idea of a **society of states**, an association of sovereign states based on their common interests, values, and norms. The participants of the conference, including ambassadors from the Netherlands, Spain, Sweden, France, Austria, and several of the larger German principalities, very clearly and explicitly took over from the papacy the right to confer international legitimacy on individual rulers and states and to insist that states observe religious toleration in their internal policies (Armstrong 1993, 30–38). The **balance of power**—parity and stability among competing powers—was formally incorporated in the **Peace of Utrecht**, which ended the War of the Spanish Succession (1701–1714), when a "just equilibrium of power" was formally declared to be the "best and most solid basis of mutual friendship and durable harmony."

The period from 1648 to 1776 saw the international system that had been taking shape over the previous 200 years come to fruition. Wars were frequent, if lacking the ideological intensity that religion brought to the Thirty Years' War. Some states, notably the Ottoman Empire, slowly declined; others, such as Britain and Russia, rose. Hundreds of ministates still existed, but it was the interaction among no more than ten key players that determined the course of events.

Yet despite constant change and many wars, Europe in its entirety constituted a kind of republic, as eighteenth- and nineteenth-century European writers argued. Some pointed to religious and cultural similarities in seeking to explain this phenomenon, but the central elements that all agreed on were a determination by all states to preserve their freedom, a mutual recognition of one another's right to an independent existence, and, above all, a reliance on the balance of power. Diplomacy and international law were seen as the other two key institutions of international society, as long as the latter was based clearly on state consent. As Torbjørn Knutsen (1997) points out, the Peace of Westphalia supported a new view of international law among states: they moved from seeing it as divinely inspired to seeing it as a set of customs, conventions, and rules of conduct created and enforced by states and their leaders.

Revolutionary Wars

Against this background of a polite, nominally rule-based European international society, the American and French Revolutions (1776 and 1789, respectively) had profound consequences. In the case of the United States, one consequence was its eventual emergence as a global superpower in the twentieth century; the consequences of the French Revolution were more immediate. First, the revolutionary insistence that sovereignty was vested in the nation rather than in the rulers gave a crucial impetus to the idea of **national self-determination**. This principle would increasingly dominate international politics in the nineteenth and twentieth centuries and endanger imperial systems that were seen as denying the rights of nations (people connected by linguistic, ethnic, and cultural bonds) to become sovereign states themselves.

The second consequence of the French Revolution stemmed from the response of the main European powers. After the defeat of the French Emperor Napoleon in 1815, the leading states increasingly set themselves apart from the smaller ones as a kind of great powers' club. This system, known as the **Concert of Europe**, lasted until World War I. Its aims were to maintain the European balance of power drawn up at the end of the Napoleonic Wars and reach decisions on potentially divisive issues. The leading dynastic powers, Austria and Russia, wanted the concert to give itself the formal right to intervene against any revolution. Britain, which was the least threatened by revolution, strongly resisted this proposition on the grounds that such a move would violate the key principle of nonintervention. However, the concert unquestionably marked a shift away from the free-for-all and highly decentralized system of eighteenth-century international society toward a more managed, hierarchical system. This shift affected all three of the key institutional underpinnings of the Westphalian international society: the balance of power, diplomacy, and international law.

In 1814, the powers had already formally declared their intention to create a "system of real and permanent balance of power in Europe," and in 1815, during

National self-determination
The right or desire of distinct national groups to become states and to rule themselves.

Concert of Europe An informal institution created in 1815 by the five great powers of Europe (Austria, Britain, France, Prussia, and Russia), whereby they agreed on controlling revolutionary forces, managing the balance of power, and accepting interventions to keep current leaders in power. This system kept the peace in Europe from 1815 until World War I.

British troops charge unmounted Indian civilians during the Sepoy Rebellion in 1857.

Congress of Vienna A meeting of major European leaders (1814–1815) that redrew the political map of Europe after the Napoleonic Wars. The congress was an attempt to restore a conservative political order in the continent.

the **Congress of Vienna**, they carefully redrew the map of Europe to implement this system. The main diplomatic development was the greatly increased use of conferences to consider and sometimes settle matters of general interest. In a few technical areas, such as international postal services, telegraphy, and sanitation, permanent international organizations were set up. In international law, the powers sought to draft "a procedure of international legitimation of change" (Clark 1980, 91), especially in the area of territorial change.

Developments external and internal to the European concert system brought about its demise. Externally, after the American Civil War, the United States began to become a world power. Two events indicate this changing status. First, President Theodore or Teddy Roosevelt brokered the Treaty of Portsmouth, New Hampshire, that ended the Russo-Japanese War in 1905. Second, Roosevelt sent the new American battle fleet, called the Great White Fleet for its paint scheme, around the world in a cruise that lasted from December 1907 to February 1909.

Meanwhile, a critical internal change to the European concert system was the hardening of the Great Powers, as they were called, into two rival blocs after the Franco-Prussian War of 1870–1871. Previously, the balance-of-power mentality had meant that the major countries would realign themselves as necessary to keep any one power from becoming dominant. Prussian statesman and first chancellor of Germany Otto von Bismarck's creation of the German Empire in 1871 caused a major imbalance in the concert system. His alliance system was flexible and complex, and it maintained order among European states, but with Bismarck out of power since 1890, less skilled leaders let the alliance rules and protocols lapse. France focused more on Europe and less on Africa, and the German kaiser let the Russians ally with Great Britain. One result of these developments was the carnage of World War I.

World Wars: Modern and Total

Wars on a global scale shocked international society. Although separated by twenty years, World Wars I and II have some similarities beyond mere geography (see Map 2.1). Changes in military technology shaped the ways combatants fought: machine guns, airplanes, and submarines all influenced operations. Both wars also featured controversies over the treatment of civilians. Indiscriminate bombing of cities occurred during both wars and reached its lowest point with the British and American firebomb air raids on Germany and Japan. Yet one major distinction between the two world wars is this: the Nazi death camps were at the time without parallel in human history. Unfortunately, genocide and ethnic cleansing have since continued to plague the world.

For the victorious Allies, the question of how World War I began became a question of how far the Germans and their allies should be held responsible. In 1919, at the Versailles Palace outside Paris, the victors imposed a statement of German war guilt in Article 231 of the final settlement, primarily to justify the reparations they demanded. Debates among historians about the war's origins

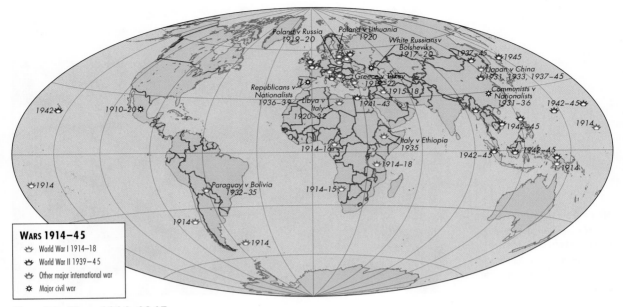

Map 2.1 Wars 1914–1945.
The two world wars were responsible for perhaps more than 80 million deaths. World War I was essentially a European territorial dispute, which, because of extensive European empires, spread as far afield as Africa and Southeast Asia. World War II also started as a European conflict but spread to the Pacific when Japan seized territory. In the interwar period, disputes broke out over territory in South America and East Asia, but elsewhere, the reluctance of the colonial powers to become embroiled in territorial disputes maintained an uneasy peace.

have focused on political, military, and systemic factors. Some have suggested that responsibility for the war was diffuse, as its origins lay in complex dynamics of the respective alliances and their military imperatives. One of the more influential postwar interpretations, however, came from West German historian Fritz Fischer, who, in his 1967 book *Germany's Aims in the First World War*, argued that German aggression, motivated by the internal political needs of an autocratic elite, was responsible for the war.

However complex or contested the origins of the war are in retrospect, the motivations of those who fought are more explicable. The masses of the belligerent states shared nationalist beliefs and patriotic values. As they marched off to fight, most thought the war would be short, victorious, and, in many cases, glorious. The reality of the European battlefield and the advent of **trench warfare** determined otherwise. Defensive military technologies, symbolized by the machine gun, triumphed over the tactics and strategy of attrition, though by November 1918 the Allied offensive finally achieved the rapid advances that helped bring an end to the fighting. It was total war in the sense that whole societies and economies were mobilized: men were conscripted into armies, and women went to

> **WHAT'S YOUR WORLDVIEW?**
>
> *Who or what factors were to blame for the start of World War I? In general, what causes wars?*

Trench warfare Warfare in which armies dug elaborate defensive fortifications in the ground, as both sides did in World War I. Because of the power of weapons like machine guns and rapid-fire cannons, trenches often gave the advantage in battle to the defenders.

After a rapid German advance into France in August 1914, troops on both sides created extensive networks of defensive trenches. Millions of combatants died.

Fourteen Points President Woodrow Wilson's vision of international society, first articulated in January 1918, included the principle of self-determination, the conduct of diplomacy on an open (not secret) basis, and the establishment of an association of nation-states to provide guarantees of independence and territorial integrity (League of Nations).

Armistice A ceasefire agreement between enemies in wartime. In the case of World War I, the armistice began at 11 A.M. on November 11, 1918.

Treaty of Versailles, 1919 Formally ended World War I (1914–1918).

work in factories. The western and eastern fronts remained the crucibles of the fighting, although conflict spread to various parts of the globe. Japan, for example, went to war in 1914 as an ally of Britain.

In response to German aggression on the high seas and domestic public opinion that supported the Allies, the United States entered the war in 1917 under President Woodrow Wilson. His vision of international society and world order, articulated in his **Fourteen Points**, would drive the agenda of the Paris Peace Conference in 1919. The overthrow of the Russian tsar in February 1917 by what became known as the Provisional Government, and the seizure of power by the Bolsheviks in November 1917, soon led Russia's new leaders to negotiate withdrawal from the war. Germany no longer fought on two fronts but faced a new threat as the United States mobilized resources. With the failure of Germany's last great military offensive in the west in 1918 and with an increasingly effective British naval blockade, Germany agreed to an **armistice** (ceasefire).

The **Treaty of Versailles**, which formally ended the war, established the **League of Nations**, and specified the rights and obligations of the victorious and defeated powers (including the notorious regime of reparations on Germany). It failed, however, to tackle what was for some the central problem of European security after 1870: a united and frustrated Germany. The treaty precipitated German revenge by creating new states out of former German and Austrian territories and devising contested borders. The League of Nations failed because the major powers—namely, France, Great Britain, and the United States—were not able to set aside their national interests for the good of a collective global interest. France sought to punish Germany, Great Britain was focused on its empire, and the United States failed to join the League, wanting nothing to do with settling European conflicts.

For some scholars, 1914–1945 represents two acts in a single play, or a thirty-year war. The British international relations theorist E. H. Carr, for example, saw the period from 1919 to 1939 as a twenty-year crisis, which he believed resulted from an unrealistic and utopian peace treaty that did not address the real causes of the war. Economic factors were also crucial contributors to the outbreak of World War II. World War I boosted production levels for Japan and the United States, but it devastated production facilities in Europe. Britain and France demanded reparations from Germany to pay for their reconstruction.

The Great Depression of the 1930s, though not caused by World War I, also contributed to the outbreak of World War II. It crippled not only the U.S. economy but the global economy. The damage it caused lowered the prestige of **liberal democracy** (a representative form of democracy), thereby strengthening extremist forces. Long-term consequences of the Great Depression included widespread unemployment and economic stagnation. Global trade and financial transactions increased, but this growing interdependence of national economies did not result in free trade; instead, protectionist policies (e.g., tariffs to protect domestic interests) increased. The resulting change in the international political system helped bring about the collapse of the trade, finance, and economic management systems.

The effect on German society was particularly significant. All modernized states suffered mass unemployment, but in Germany, inflation was acute. Economic and political instability provided the ground in which support for the Nazis took root. By 1933, Adolf Hitler had achieved power, and the transformation of the German state began. There remain debates about how far Hitler's ambitions were carefully thought through and how much he seized opportunities. A. J. P. Taylor provided a controversial analysis in his 1961 book *Origins of the Second World War,* in which he argued that Hitler was no different from other German political leaders. What was different about Germany this time was the particular philosophy of Nazism and ideas of racial supremacy and imperial expansion.

British and French attempts to negotiate with Hitler culminated in the **Munich Agreement of 1938**. In an effort to appease Germany, Britain and France acquiesced to Hitler's territorial claims over the Sudetenland in Czechoslovakia, but within months, Germany had seized the rest of Czechoslovakia and was preparing for war on Poland. Since then, **appeasement** has generally been seen as synonymous with a craven collapse

League of Nations The first permanent collective international security organization aimed at preventing future wars and resolving global problems. The League failed due to the unwillingness of the United States to join and the inability of its members to commit to a real international community.

Liberal democracy A state with democratic or representative government and a capitalist economy that promotes multilateralism and free trade. Domestic interests, values, and institutions shape foreign policy. Liberal democracies champion freedom of the individual, constitutional civil and political rights, and laissez-faire economic arrangements.

In 1923, the German Weimar Republic created after World War I suffered from hyperinflation. The currency was so worthless that children used it as building blocks. This economic collapse led to political unrest and helped the Nazis come to power.

Munich Agreement of 1938 An agreement negotiated after a conference held in Munich between Germany and the United Kingdom and other major powers of Europe along with Czechoslovakia. It permitted Nazi Germany's annexation of Czechoslovakia's Sudetenland, an area along the Czech border that was inhabited primarily by ethnic Germans.

Appeasement A policy of making concessions to a territorially acquisitive state in the hope that settlement of more modest claims will assuage that state's expansionist appetites.

Blitzkrieg The German term for "lightning war." This was an offensive strategy that used the combination of mechanized forces—especially tanks—and aircraft as mobile artillery to exploit breaches in an enemy's front line.

before the demands of dictators—encouraging, not disarming, their aggressive designs. Recent debates about appeasement have focused on whether there were realistic alternatives to negotiation, given the lack of military preparedness to confront Hitler.

By 1939, the defensive military technologies of World War I gave way to armored warfare and air power, as the German **blitzkrieg** brought speedy victories over Poland and in the west. Hitler was also drawn into the Balkans and North Africa in support of his Italian ally, Mussolini. The invasion of the Soviet Union in June 1941 plainly demonstrated the scale of fighting and scope of Hitler's aims. Although Germany had massive early victories on the eastern front, winter saw a stalemate and the mobilization of Soviet peoples and armies. German treatment of civilian populations and Soviet prisoners of war reflected Nazi ideas of racial supremacy and resulted in the deaths of millions. German anti-Semitism and the development of concentration camps gained new momentum after a decision on the "Final Solution of the Jewish Question" in 1942. The term **Holocaust** entered the political lexicon of the twentieth century, as the Nazis attempted the **genocide** of the Jewish people and other minorities, such as the Roma, in Europe.

By 1941, German submarines and American warships were in an undeclared war. The imposition of American economic sanctions on Japan precipitated Japanese military preparations for a surprise attack on the U.S. fleet at Pearl Harbor on December 7, 1941. When Germany and Italy declared war on America in support of their Japanese ally, President Franklin Roosevelt decided to assign priority to the European over the Pacific theater of war. After a combined strategic bombing offensive with the British against German cities, the Allies launched a second front in France, which the Soviets had pressed for.

Defeat of Germany in May 1945 came before the atomic bomb was ready. In an effort to shorten the war, avoid an invasion of Japan, and push the Japanese government to surrender, the United States dropped the first atomic bomb on Hiroshima on August 6, 1945, and the second on Nagasaki on August 9, 1945. The United States was the first and is still the only state to use these weapons of mass destruction in war. The destruction of the two Japanese cities remains enormously controversial. Aside from voicing moral objections to bombing civilian populations, historians have engaged in fierce debate about why the bombs were dropped.

When World War II ended, the United States and the Soviet Union remained as the two dominant countries in world politics. For some people in the United States, their homeland largely untouched by the destruction of the war,

On August 6, 1945, the United States dropped an atom bomb on Hiroshima, killing 140,000 and unleashing a weapon system that the world is still trying to control. Now, with the number of nuclear weapons in the world, we can destroy the world as we know it. How can we control these weapons?

the country seemed poised to take its proper position as world leader. For the leaders of the Soviet Union, the world looked ready for the expansion of the Soviet style of rule. In the next section, we examine the process of decolonization of Western European holdings. This process provided both countries, soon to be called **superpowers**, with many opportunities to expand their influence. The United States was willing to commit resources to stabilize the world economy and build global political structures to manage trade, development, and financial affairs.

Legacies and Consequences of European Colonialism

The effects of World War II helped cause the demise of European imperialism in the twentieth century (see Maps 2.2 and 2.3). More than marking an end of Western European dominance in world politics, the end of imperialism seemed to be the death knell for the European style of managing international relations. This change took place against the background of the Cold War, which we will discuss in the next section. But it's important first to appreciate the context of decolonization because it reflected and contributed to the decreasing importance of Europe as the arbiter of world affairs.

Holocaust The attempts by the Nazis to murder the Jewish population of Europe. Some 6 million Jewish people were killed in concentration camps, along with a further million that included Soviet prisoners, Roma, Poles, communists, homosexuals, and the physically or mentally disabled.

Genocide The deliberate and systematic extermination of an ethnic, national, tribal, or religious group.

Superpower A state with a dominant position in the international system. It has the will and the means to influence the actions of other states in favor of its own interests, and it projects its power on a global scale to secure its national interests.

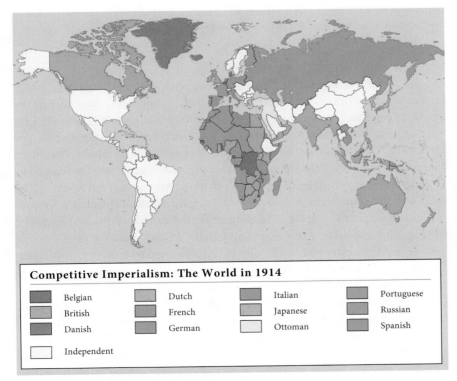

Competitive Imperialism: The World in 1914

Belgian	Dutch	Italian	Portuguese
British	French	Japanese	Russian
Danish	German	Ottoman	Spanish
Independent			

Map 2.2 **Former Colonial Territories.**

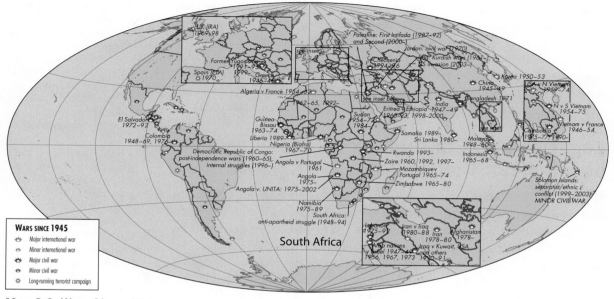

Map 2.3 Wars Since 1945.

As European colonial control was largely destroyed between 1945 and 1970, new nation-states were created. One result was an increase in localized wars, mainly arising from boundary disputes, and in civil wars caused by conflicts between different ethnic groups or between those with conflicting religious or political beliefs. Note that many of these wars directly or indirectly involved the United States and Soviet Union. An estimated 25–30 million people died in these wars, two-thirds of whom were civilians.

The belief that national self-determination should be a guiding principle in international politics marked a transformation of attitudes and values; during the age of imperialism, political status accrued to imperial powers. However, after 1945, imperialism became a term of disgrace. Colonialism of the past and the new UN Charter (which established the United Nations) were increasingly recognized as incompatible, though independence was often slow and sometimes marked by prolonged and armed struggle, especially in many African and Asian states. The Cold War also complicated and hindered the transition to independence. Various factors influenced the process of decolonization: the attitude of the colonial power, the ideology and strategy of the anti-imperialist forces, and the role of external powers. Political, economic, and military factors played various roles in shaping the transfer of power. Different imperial powers and newly emerging independent states had different experiences of withdrawal from empire.

There was no one pattern of decolonization in Africa and Asia, and the paths to independence reflected attitudes of colonial powers, the nature of local nationalist or revolutionary movements, ethnic and racial factors, and, in some cases, the involvement of external states, including the Cold War protagonists. How far these divisions were created or exacerbated by the imperial powers is an important question in examining the political stability of the newly independent states.

Equally important is how capable the new political leaderships in these societies were in tackling their political and economic problems.

The decolonization process in Africa was complicated by the number of European states involved in formal empire and the different national interests of these colonizing states. The economic crises created by the war forced the British, French, and Belgians to exploit the riches of their colonies. Portugal saw its colonies Angola, Mozambique, and Portuguese Guinea as essential elements in Portugal's economic and political survival. Belgium held on to its colonies in Central Africa until 1960, and France worked to assimilate its colonies into a French imperial order. The British strategy was to devolve more authority to local elites and create a more informal empire.

With the end of the Belgian Congo, the new Democratic Republic of the Congo was embroiled in a civil war, with the Russians and Americans supporting opposing forces. Here the leader of the pro-Western province of Katanga, Moise Tshombe, greets mercenaries fighting to support his secession from the Congo.

The 1960s was a period of accelerated decolonization and the beginning of many internal conflicts in Africa. Many of these new states failed because they did not have adequate political or economic structures, lacked experienced and educated leaders, and they were culturally diverse, with little or no loyalty toward any newly created nation-state. Each was still dependent on its former colonial masters. This dependency still shapes the domestic and foreign policies of these states today.

In Asia, the relationship between nationalism and revolutionary Marxism was a potent force. In Malaya (now part of Malaysia), the British defeated a communist insurgent movement (1948–1960). In Indochina, a peninsula in Southeast Asia consisting of Burma (Myanmar), Thailand, Malaya, Laos, Cambodia, and Vietnam, the French failed to do likewise (1946–1954). For the Vietnamese, resentment toward centuries of foreign oppression—Chinese, Japanese, and French—soon focused on a new imperialist adversary, the United States. Early American reluctance to support European imperialism gave way to incremental and covert commitments, and then, from 1965, to open military and political support of the newly created state of South Vietnam.

American leaders and a very influential anticommunist interest community spoke of a domino theory, in which if one state fell to communism, the next would be at risk. Chinese and Soviet support provided additional Cold War contexts. Washington failed, however, to coordinate limited war objectives with an effective political strategy and, once victory was no longer possible, sought to disengage from Vietnam through "peace with honor." The Tet (Vietnamese New Year) offensive of the Vietcong guerrillas in 1968 marked a decisive moment, convincing many Americans that the war would not be won, though it was not until 1973 that American forces finally withdrew, two years before South Vietnam was defeated.

Many wars in Asia and Africa started as colonial wars and quickly became proxy wars in the Cold War struggle between the superpowers.

The global trend toward decolonization was a key development in the twentieth century, though one frequently offset by local circumstances. Yet while imperialism withered, other forms of domination, or **hegemony**, took shape. Simply stated, hegemony means a state has the capacity and the will to shape and govern the international system. Both the United States and the Soviet Union were vying for global hegemony during the Cold War. The notion of hegemony has been used to criticize the behavior of the superpowers, most notably with Soviet hegemony in Eastern Europe and American hegemony in Central America. For both countries, this struggle for dominance, regardless of the term used, was the central element of the period we discuss in the next section, the Cold War.

Hegemony A system regulated by a dominant leader, or political (and/or economic) domination of a region. It also means power and control exercised by a leading state over other states.

Cold War

The rise of the United States as a global power after 1945 was of paramount importance in international politics. Its conflict with the Soviet Union provided one of the crucial dynamics in world affairs—one that affected, directly or indirectly, every part of the world. In the West, historians have debated with vigor and acrimony which country was responsible for the collapse of the wartime alliance between Moscow and Washington. The rise of the USSR as a global power after 1945 is equally crucial in this period. Relations between Moscow and its Eastern European "allies," with the People's Republic of China (PRC), and with revolutionary forces in the third world have been vital issues in world politics as well as key factors in Soviet-American affairs. If one feature of the **Cold War** was its **bipolar** structure, another was its highly divided character, born out of profoundly opposing views about the best way of organizing society: the Western system of market **capitalism** or the Eastern bloc's centrally planned economies.

Yet for all its intensity, the Cold War was very much a managed conflict in which both sides recognized the limits of what they could do. Certainly, policymakers in the East and the West appeared to accept in private—if not in public—that their rival had legitimate security concerns. The Cold War was thus fought within a framework of informal rules. This framework helps explain why the conflict remained "cold"—at least in terms of general war between the United States and the Soviet Union, since millions of people died during the period of 1945 to 1990 in what have been called "brushfire" or "proxy" wars in Africa and Asia.

Indeed, how and why the Cold War remained cold have been subjects of much academic debate. Few, however, would dispute the fact that whatever else may have divided the two superpowers—ideology, economics, and the struggle for global influence—they were in full agreement about one thing: the overriding need to prevent a nuclear war that neither could win without destroying the world and themselves. In the end, this is why the superpowers acted with such caution for the greater part of the Cold War era. In fact, given the very real fear of outright nuclear war, the shared aim of the two superpowers was not to destroy the

Cold War The period from 1946 to 1991 defined by ideological conflict and rivalry between the United States and the Soviet Union. This was a global struggle for the hearts and minds of citizens around the world that was characterized by political conflict, military competition, proxy wars, and economic competition.

Bipolar An international political order in which two states dominate all others. It is often used to describe the nature of the international system when the two superpowers, the Soviet Union and the United States, were dominant powers during the Cold War.

Capitalism A system of production in which human labor and its products are commodities that are bought and sold in the marketplace.

other—though a few on both sides occasionally talked in such terms—but rather to contain the other's ambitions while avoiding anything that might lead to dangerous escalation (only once, in 1962, with the Cuban Missile Crisis, did the two superpowers come close to a nuclear exchange). This situation in turn helps explain another important feature of the Cold War: its stalemated and hence seemingly permanent character.

Some historians date the origins of the Cold War to the Russian Revolution of 1917, but most focus on events between 1945 and 1950. Whether the Cold War was inevitable, whether it was the consequence of mistakes and misperceptions, and whether it reflected the response of Western leaders to aggressive Soviet intent are central questions in debates about the origins and dynamics of the Cold War. Until 1989, these debates drew only from Western archives and sources and reflected Western assumptions and perceptions. With the end of the Cold War, greater evidence has emerged of Soviet and U.S. motivations and understanding.

> **WHAT'S YOUR WORLDVIEW?**
>
> *The United States and the USSR fought many proxy wars across the globe. One writer lists some fifty-eight wars from 1945 to 1989 (Holsti 1991). Roughly 52 percent of the current armed conflicts began during the Cold War. Given these statistics, is it correct to call the period 1945 to 1989 a "Cold War"?*

Onset of the Cold War

The start of the Cold War in Europe reflected failure to implement the principles agreed on at the 1945 wartime conferences of Yalta and Potsdam. The futures of Germany and various Central and Eastern European countries, notably Poland, were issues of growing tension between the former wartime allies. Reconciling principles of national self-determination with national security was a formidable task. In the West, there was growing feeling that Soviet policy toward Eastern Europe was guided not by historic concern with security but by ideological expansion. In March 1947, the Truman administration sought to justify limited aid to Turkey and Greece with rhetoric designed to arouse awareness of Soviet ambitions and a declaration that America would support those threatened by Soviet subversion or expansion. The **Truman Doctrine** and the associated policy of **containment** expressed the self-image of the United States as inherently defensive. These were underpinned by the **Marshall Plan** for European economic recovery, proclaimed in June 1947, which was essential to the economic rebuilding of Western Europe. In Eastern Europe, democratic socialist and other anticommunist forces were undermined and eliminated as Marxist-Leninist regimes, loyal to Moscow, were installed. The only exception was in Yugoslavia, where the Marxist leader, Marshal Tito, consolidated his position while maintaining independence from Moscow.

The first major confrontation of the Cold War took place over Berlin beginning in 1948 (see Table 2.1). During the Yalta and Potsdam Conferences, Germany was divided among the four victorious powers: the United States, the Soviet Union, Great Britain, and France. Its former capital, Berlin, although positioned deep in the heart of the Soviet zone of occupation, was also divided into four sectors, with the result that the Western zones of the city were surrounded

Truman Doctrine A statement made by U.S. President Harry Truman in March 1947 that it "must be the policy of the United States to support free people who are resisting attempted subjugation by armed minorities or by outside pressures."

Containment An American political strategy for resisting perceived Soviet expansion.

Marshall Plan Officially known as the European Recovery Program, it was a program of financial and other economic aid for Europe after World War II. Proposed by Secretary of State George Marshall in 1948, it was offered to all European states, including the Soviet Union.

The U.S. Air Force brings milk to citizens of Berlin during the Soviet road blockade of the city in 1948. This may have been the first time the world saw the true intentions of the Soviet Union and its totalitarian regime.

by Soviet-controlled territory. In June 1948, Stalin sought to resolve Berlin's status by severing road and rail communications to the three Western-controlled sectors of the city. West Berlin's population and political autonomy were kept alive by a massive U.S. airlift, and Stalin ended the blockade in May 1949. The crisis saw the deployment of American long-range bombers in Britain, officially described as "atomic capable," though none was armed with nuclear weapons. U.S. military deployment was followed by political commitment enshrined in the **North Atlantic Treaty Organization (NATO)** treaty signed in April 1949. The key article of the treaty—that an attack on one member would be treated as an attack on all—accorded with the principle of collective self-defense enshrined in Article 51 of the UN Charter. In practice, the cornerstone of the alliance was the commitment of the United States to defend Western Europe. In reality, this soon meant the willingness of the United States to use nuclear weapons to deter Soviet aggression. For the Soviet Union, political encirclement soon entailed a growing military, and specifically nuclear, threat.

Although the origins of the Cold War were in Europe, events and conflicts in Asia and elsewhere were also crucial. In 1949, the thirty-year Chinese civil war ended in victory for the communists under Mao Zedong. This had a major impact on

North Atlantic Treaty Organization (NATO)
Organization established by treaty in April 1949 including twelve (later sixteen) countries from Western Europe and North America. The most important aspect of the NATO alliance was the U.S. commitment to the defense of Western Europe. Today NATO has twenty-eight member states.

TABLE 2.1	**Cold War Crises**	
Years	**Crisis**	**Key Actors**
1948–1949	Berlin	USSR/US/UK
1950–1953	Korean Conflict	North Korea/South Korea/US/People's Republic of China
1954–1955	Taiwan Strait	US/People's Republic of China
1961	Berlin	USSR/US/NATO
1962	Cuba	USSR/US/Cuba
1973	Arab-Israeli War	Egypt/Israel/Syria/Jordan/US/USSR
1975	Angola	US/USSR/Cuba/China/South Africa
1979–1992	Afghanistan	USSR/US/Saudi Arabia/Pakistan
1979–1990	Nicaragua–El Salvador	US/USSR/Cuba

Asian affairs and on perceptions in both Moscow and Washington. In June 1950, the North Korean attack on South Korea was interpreted as part of a general communist strategy and as a test case for American resolve and the will of the United Nations to withstand aggression. The resulting American and UN commitment, followed in October 1950 by Chinese involvement, led to a war lasting three years in which more than 3 million people died before prewar borders were restored. North and South Korea themselves remained locked in seemingly perpetual hostility, even after the Cold War.

Conflict, Confrontation, and Compromise

One consequence of the Korean War was the buildup of American forces in Western Europe, lest communist aggression in Asia distract from the American-perceived real intent in Europe. The idea that communism was a monolithic political entity controlled from Moscow became an enduring American fixation not shared in London and elsewhere. Western Europeans nevertheless depended on the United States for military security, and this dependency deepened as the Cold War confrontation in Europe was consolidated. The rearmament of the Federal Republic of Germany (West Germany) in 1954 precipitated the creation of the **Warsaw Pact** in 1955, an agreement of mutual defense and military aid signed by communist European states of Eastern Europe under Soviet influence. The military buildup continued apace, with unprecedented concentrations of conventional and, moreover, nuclear forces. By the 1960s, there were some 7,000 nuclear weapons in Western Europe alone. NATO deployed nuclear weapons to offset Soviet conventional superiority, and Soviet short-range, or "theater nuclear," forces in Europe compensated for overall American nuclear superiority.

The death of Stalin in March 1953 portended significant consequences for the USSR at home and abroad. Stalin's eventual successor, Nikita Khrushchev, strove to modernize Soviet society, and in the process he helped unleash reformist forces in Eastern Europe. While Poland was controlled, the situation in Hungary threatened Soviet hegemony, and in 1956, the intervention of the Red Army brought bloodshed to the streets of Budapest and international condemnation on Moscow. Soviet intervention coincided with an attack on Egypt by Britain, France, and Israel, precipitated by Colonel Nasser's nationalization of the Suez Canal in a manner that displeased Britain, the former colonial occupier. The French took part in the attack because Nasser's government was providing support to anti-French rebels in Algeria. The British government's actions provoked fierce domestic and international criticism and the most serious rift in the "special relationship" between Britain and the United States. President Dwight Eisenhower was strongly opposed to the actions of the U.S. allies, and in the face of what were effectively U.S. economic sanctions (a threat to cut off American oil exports to Britain), the British abandoned the operation as well as their support for the French and Israelis.

Khrushchev's policy toward the West mixed a search for political coexistence with the pursuit of ideological confrontation. Soviet support for movements of

Warsaw Pact An agreement of mutual defense and military aid signed in May 1955 in response to West Germany's rearmament and entry into NATO. It comprised the USSR and seven communist states (though Albania withdrew support in 1961). The pact was officially dissolved in July 1991.

national liberation aroused fears in the West of a global communist challenge. American commitment to liberal democracy and national self-determination was often subordinated to Cold War perspectives as well as to U.S. economic and political interests. The Cold War saw the growth of large permanent intelligence organizations, whose roles ranged from estimating intentions and capabilities of adversaries to covert intervention in the affairs of other states. Crises over Berlin in 1961 and Cuba in 1962 marked the most dangerous moments of the Cold War. In both, there was a risk of direct military confrontation and, certainly in October 1962, the possibility of nuclear war. How close the world came to Armageddon during the Cuban Missile Crisis and exactly why peace was preserved remain matters of debate among historians and surviving officials.

The events of 1962 were followed by a more stable period of coexistence and competition. Nuclear arsenals, nevertheless, continued to grow. Whether this is best characterized as an **arms race** or whether internal political and bureaucratic pressures drove the growth of nuclear arsenals is open to interpretation. For Washington, commitments to NATO allies also provided pressures and opportunities to develop and deploy their own shorter-range (tactical and theater) nuclear weapons. The global nuclear dimension increased with the emergence of other nuclear-weapon states: Britain in 1952, France in 1960, and China in 1964. Growing concern at the spread, or proliferation, of nuclear weapons led to the negotiation of the Nuclear Nonproliferation Treaty (NPT) in 1968, wherein states that had nuclear weapons committed themselves to halt the arms race, and those that did not possess them promised not to develop them. Despite successes of the NPT, by 1990, several states had developed or were developing nuclear weapons, notably Israel, India, Pakistan, and apartheid South Africa. (Libya and South Africa later gave up their nuclear weapons programs and remain the only states to have done so.)

The Rise and Fall of Détente

At the same time that America's commitment in Vietnam was deepening, Soviet-Chinese relations were deteriorating. Indeed, by 1969, the People's Republic of China and the Soviet Union had fought a minor border war over a territorial dispute. Despite (or because of) these tensions, the foundations for what became known as **détente** were laid between the Soviet Union and the United States and for what became known as **rapprochement** between China and the United States. Both terms, long a part of the language of diplomacy, refer to the processes by which countries seek to improve their relations. Détente in Europe had its origins in the **Ostpolitik** of German Chancellor Willy Brandt and resulted in agreements that recognized the peculiar status of Berlin and the sovereignty of East Germany. For his efforts, which finally bore fruit with the end of the Cold War in 1989, Brandt won the Nobel Peace Prize. Soviet-American détente had its roots in mutual recognition of the need to avoid nuclear crises and in the economic and military incentives in avoiding an unconstrained arms race. Both Washington and Moscow also looked toward Beijing when making their bilateral calculations.

Arms race A central concept in realist thought. As states build up their military to address real or perceived threats to their national security, they may create insecurity in other states. These states in turn develop their military capacities and thus begin an arms race. This never-ending pursuit of security creates the condition we know as a security dilemma.

Détente The relaxation of tension between East and West; Soviet-American détente lasted from the late 1960s to the late 1970s and was characterized by negotiations and nuclear arms control agreements.

Rapprochement The reestablishment of more friendly relations between the People's Republic of China and the United States in the early 1970s.

Ostpolitik The West German government's "Eastern Policy" of the mid-to-late 1960s, designed to develop relations between West Germany and members of the Warsaw Pact.

In the West, détente was associated with the political leadership of President Richard Nixon and his adviser Henry Kissinger, who were also instrumental in Sino-American rapprochement. This new phase in Soviet-American relations did not mark an end to political conflict, as each side pursued political goals, some of which were increasingly incompatible with the aspirations of the other superpower. Both sides supported friendly regimes and movements and subverted adversaries. All this came as various political upheavals were taking place in the third world. The question of how far the superpowers could control their friends, and how far they were entangled by their commitments, was underlined in 1973 when the Arab-Israeli War embroiled both the United States and the Soviet Union in what became a potentially dangerous

Did Mao Zedong and Richard Nixon change the balance of Cold War politics when they shook hands in Beijing in 1972?

confrontation. Getting the superpowers involved in the war—whether by design or serendipity—helped create the political conditions for Egyptian-Israeli rapprochement. Diplomatic and strategic relations were transformed as Egypt switched its allegiance from Moscow to Washington. In the short term, Egypt was isolated in the Arab world. For Israel, fear of a war of annihilation fought on two fronts was lifted. Yet continuing political violence, terrorism, and the enduring enmity between Israel and other Arab states proved insurmountable obstacles to a more permanent regional settlement.

In Washington, Soviet support for revolutionary movements in the third world was seen as evidence of duplicity. Some American politicians and academics claim that Moscow's support for revolutionary forces in Ethiopia in 1975 killed détente. Others cite the Soviet role in Angola in 1978. Furthermore, the perception that the USSR was using arms control agreements to gain military advantage was linked to Soviet behavior in the third world. Growing Soviet military superiority was reflected in growing Soviet influence, it was argued. Critics claimed the Strategic Arms Limitation Talks (SALT) process enabled the Soviets to deploy multiple independently targetable warheads on their large **intercontinental ballistic missiles (ICBMs)**, threatening key American forces. America faced a "window of vulnerability," critics of détente claimed. The view from Moscow was different, reflecting different assumptions about the scope and purpose of détente and the nature of nuclear deterrence. Other events were also seen to weaken American influence. The overthrow of the shah of Iran in 1979 resulted in the loss of an important Western ally in the region, though the ensuing militant Islamic government was hostile to both superpowers.

December 1979 marked a point of transition in East-West affairs. NATO agreed to deploy land-based Cruise and Pershing II missiles in Europe if

Intercontinental ballistic missiles (ICBMs) Weapons system the United States and Soviet Union developed to threaten each other with destruction. The thirty- to forty-minute flight times of the missiles created a situation that is sometimes called "mutually assured destruction" (MAD) or "the balance of terror."

negotiations with the Soviets did not reduce what NATO saw as a serious imbalance. Later in the month, Soviet armed forces intervened in Afghanistan to support their revolutionary allies. The USSR was bitterly condemned in the West and in the third world for its actions and soon became committed to a protracted and bloody struggle that many compared to the American war in Vietnam. In Washington, President Jimmy Carter, who had sought to control arms and reduce tensions with the USSR, hardened his view of the Soviet Union. The first reaction was the Carter Doctrine, which clearly stated that any Soviet attack on countries in the Persian Gulf would be seen as a direct attack on U.S. vital interests. Another result was the Carter administration's decision to boycott the 1980 Summer Olympics in Moscow. Nevertheless, Republicans increasingly used foreign and defense policy to attack the Carter presidency. Perceptions of American weakness abroad permeated domestic politics, and in 1980 Ronald Reagan was elected president. He was committed to a more confrontational approach with the Soviets on arms control, third world conflicts, and East-West relations in general.

From Détente to a Second Cold War

In the West, critics of détente and arms control, some of whom would later advise the George W. Bush presidential administration, argued in the 1970s and 1980s that the Soviets were acquiring nuclear superiority. Some suggested that the United States should pursue policies and strategies based on the idea that victory in nuclear war was possible. The election of Ronald Reagan in 1980 was a watershed in Soviet-American relations. Reagan had made it clear during the election campaign that the United States would take a tough stance in its relations with the Soviet Union. In two monumental speeches delivered in March 1983, Reagan stated that the Soviet Union was the "focus of evil in the modern world," and he coined the phrase "evil empire" to describe the USSR. In the second speech, he outlined his idea for a strategic defense against Soviet missiles. One issue that Reagan inherited, and which loomed large in the breakdown of relations between East and West, was nuclear missiles in Europe. NATO's decision to deploy land-based missiles capable of striking Soviet territory precipitated a period of great tension in relations between NATO and the USSR and political friction within NATO.

Strategic Defense Initiative (SDI) A controversial strategic policy advocated by the Reagan administration and nuclear physicists such as Edward Teller, who helped create the hydrogen bomb. The plan, which is often derisively nicknamed "Star Wars," called for a defensive missile shield that would make Soviet offensive missiles ineffective by destroying them in flight.

Reagan's own incautious public remarks reinforced perceptions that he was as ill informed as he was dangerous in matters nuclear, though key arms policies were consistent with those of his predecessor, Jimmy Carter. On arms control, Reagan was disinterested in agreements that would freeze the status quo for the sake of getting agreement, and Soviet and American negotiators proved unable to make progress in talks on long-range and intermediate-range weapons. One particular idea had significant consequences for arms control and for Washington's relations with its allies and its adversaries. The **Strategic Defense Initiative (SDI)**, quickly dubbed "Star Wars" after the movie, was a research program designed to explore the feasibility of space-based defenses against ballistic missiles. The

Soviets appeared to take SDI very seriously and claimed that Reagan's real purpose was to regain the nuclear monopoly of the 1950s. The technological advances claimed by SDI proponents did not materialize, however, and the program was eventually reduced and marginalized, although never fully eliminated from the U.S. defense budget.

The resulting period of tension and confrontation between the superpowers has been described as the second cold war or the end of détente and compared to the early period of confrontation and tension from 1946 to 1953. In Western Europe and the Soviet Union, there was real fear of nuclear war. Much of this fear was a reaction to the rhetoric and policies of the Reagan administration. The world viewed American statements on nuclear weapons, military intervention in Grenada in 1983, and an air raid against Libya in 1986 as evidence of a new belligerence. Reagan's policy toward Central America and his support for the rebel Contras in Nicaragua were sources of controversy within the United States and internationally. The International Court of Justice (ICJ), a judicial court of the United Nations (which we'll discuss in Chapter 5), found the United States guilty of violating international law in 1986 for sowing sea mines in Nicaraguan harbors. The Reagan administration ignored this ruling, claiming the ICJ lacked jurisdiction in this situation.

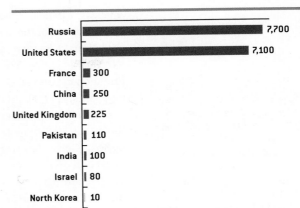

Estimated Global Nuclear Warheads, as of 2015.
The world's nuclear-armed states possess a combined total of approximately 16,000 nuclear warheads.

The Reagan administration's use of military power was nonetheless limited: rhetoric and perception were at variance with reality. Nevertheless, there is evidence that the Soviet leadership took very seriously the words (and deeds) of the Reagan administration and there were some who believed that Washington was planning a nuclear first strike. In 1983, Soviet air defenses shot down a South Korean civilian airliner in Soviet airspace. The American reaction and the imminent deployment of U.S. nuclear missiles in Europe created a climate of great tension in East-West relations.

Throughout the early 1980s, the ill health of a series of Soviet leaders (Brezhnev, Andropov, and Chernenko) inhibited Soviet responses to the American challenge and the American threat. In 1985, however, Mikhail Gorbachev became general secretary of the Soviet Communist Party. Gorbachev's "new thinking" in foreign policy and his domestic reforms created a revolution both in the USSR's foreign relations and within Soviet society. At home, **glasnost** (or openness) and **perestroika** (or restructuring) unleashed nationalist and other forces that, to Gorbachev's dismay, were to destroy the Union of Soviet Socialist Republics.

Gorbachev paved the way for agreements on nuclear and conventional forces that helped ease the tensions of the early 1980s. In 1987, he traveled to Washington to sign the Intermediate Nuclear Forces (INF) Treaty, banning intermediate-range

Glasnost A policy of greater openness pursued by Soviet leader Mikhail Gorbachev from 1985, involving more toleration of internal dissent and criticism.

Perestroika Gorbachev's policy of restructuring, pursued in tandem with glasnost and intended to modernize the Soviet political and economic system.

nuclear missiles, including Cruise and Pershing II. This agreement was heralded as a triumph for the Soviet leader, but NATO leaders, including Margaret Thatcher and Ronald Reagan, argued that it was vindication of the policies pursued by NATO since 1979. The INF Treaty was concluded more quickly than a new agreement on cutting strategic nuclear weapons, in part because of continuing Soviet opposition to SDI. And it was Reagan's successor, George H. W. Bush, who concluded a **Strategic Arms Reductions Treaty (START)** agreement that reduced long-range nuclear weapons (though only back to the level they had been in the early 1980s). Gorbachev used agreements on nuclear weapons as a means of building trust and demonstrated the serious and radical nature of his purpose. However, despite similar radical agreements on conventional forces in Europe (culminating in the Paris agreement of 1990), the end of the Cold War marked success in nuclear arms control rather than nuclear disarmament. The histories of the Cold War and of the atomic bomb are very closely connected, but although the Cold War is now over, nuclear weapons are still very much in existence. We will discuss the issues surrounding nuclear weapons in Chapter 6.

Strategic Arms Reductions Treaty (START) Negotiations between the United States and Soviet Union over limiting nuclear arsenals began in 1982 and progressed at a very slow pace over eight years. The eventual treaty in 1991 broke new ground because it called for a reduction of nuclear arms rather than just a limit on the growth of these weapons.

From the End of the Cold War to the War on Terrorism

The first major global conflict after the Cold War ended was the 1990 Iraqi invasion of neighboring Kuwait. The United States led a comprehensive multilateral diplomatic and military effort to punish former President of Iraq Saddam Hussein for his actions and to signal to the world that this kind of violation of international law would not stand. The war to liberate Kuwait lasted only forty-two days, and an international coalition of diplomats and military forces helped define the "New World Order" espoused by President George H. W. Bush. The United States wisely included the Soviet Union in its plans and effectively used the UN Security Council to pass more than twelve resolutions condemning the actions of Iraq. What the first President Bush created was a U.S.-led global coalition that was supported by all five permanent members of the Security Council (China, France, the Russian Federation, the United Kingdom, and the United States)—a first since the establishment of the United Nations. The invasion of Kuwait was illegal under international law, and the major powers were willing to work together to protect and promote a "rule-based system."

The world in 1990 was full of promise (especially for the victors of the Cold War) but full of potential risk as well. It was also replete with the sources of further conflict. This New World Order, as U.S. President George H. W. Bush called it, existed briefly between two eras: one defined by an ongoing struggle between two competing secular ideologies and another shaped by an emerging clash between two conceptions of civilization itself.

The Cold War divided the world for more than forty years, threatened humanity with near destruction, and led to the death of at least 25 million people, mostly in the highly contested zone that came to be referred to as the "third world" during the Cold War. Yet in spite of these dangers and costs, the Cold War in its core areas still managed to create a degree of stability that the world had not experienced since the early part of the twentieth century. For this reason, many came to view the bipolar order after 1947 as something that was not merely the expression of a given international reality but also desirable and defensible. As we will see in Chapter 3, some realists seemed to celebrate the superpower relationship on the grounds that a world with two balancing powers, each limiting the actions of the other, was likely to be a far more stable world than one with several competing states.

What happened in Eastern Europe in 1989, of course, produced enormous shock waves. Many people hoped that Gorbachev's reforms would make the world a safer and more humane place. Hardly anybody, though, seriously anticipated the collapse of communism and the destruction of the Berlin Wall. Moreover, few believed that this revolutionary process could be achieved peacefully. It was all rather surprising for those who had thought this superpower rivalry would never end without some type of nuclear confrontation. Now world leaders had to remake the world and find ways to integrate former enemies back into the West.

The tasks they confronted certainly seemed very great, ranging from the institutional one of devising new tasks for bodies such as NATO, the United Nations, and the European Union (created in 1992) to the more economic challenge of facilitating the transition in countries that had little experience running **market democracies**. Many questioned the need for high military spending, arguing that if the world was now becoming a safer and more integrated place, what then was the purpose of spending billions on weapons?

> ### WHAT'S YOUR WORLDVIEW?
>
> *With the end of the Cold War, many analysts talked optimistically about a "peace dividend"—that is, a chance to shift spending from military to social programs like education, health, and job training. Many European states and NATO partners cut their spending, but the United States did not cut military spending and shift funding to domestic priorities. Why do you think this happened? Do you think U.S. leaders feared a new rival like China, or did they anticipate the need for a strong military to support their hegemonic position?*

Market democracies See *liberal democracy.*

Globalization: Challenging the International Order?

If the Cold War period was marked by a clear and sharp divide between opposing socioeconomic systems operating by radically different standards, then the post–Cold War order could readily be characterized as one in which many states were compelled to play by a single set of rules within an increasingly competitive world economy. The term most frequently used to describe this new system of international relations was *globalization*.

Globalization, however, meant different things to different theorists. For one school, the hyperglobalists, it was assumed to be undermining borders and states—quite literally abolishing the Westphalian system. Journalist and author Thomas Friedman (2005) argued that globalization has changed world politics forever, giving individuals more tools to influence markets and governments and create networks that challenge the power of states. Skeptics agreed that

Anarchy A system operating in the absence of any central government. It does not imply chaos but, in realist theory, the absence of political authority.

globalization provided a different context within which international relations was now being played out, but rejected the notion that it was doing away with the state or destroying the underlying logic of **anarchy**. As we discussed in Chapter 1, some writers were even skeptical of whether there was anything especially novel about globalization. Such skepticism, however, did not prevent globalization's critics and defenders from engaging in an extended debate about the impact of globalization on global inequality, climate change, and the more general distribution of power in the international system. Globalization was a fact of economic life and there was no escaping its logic. The only thing one could do (using the oft-repeated words of President Clinton) was to "compete not retreat." Moreover, if one did not do so, the future for one's own people, and by implication one's state, was bleak.

If there was little meeting of minds among politicians and academics, there was little doubt about the impact globalization was having on the world economy, in particular in North America, Europe, and East Asia. Here, at least, the theoretical debate about the novelty, existence, and meaning of the phenomenon was being resolved, as this triad of economic power (over 80 percent of the world's total) experienced reasonable growth, increased economic interdependence, and massive wealth creation.

There was also something distinctly unethical about an apparently unregulated economic process that made billions for the few (especially those in the financial sector) while generating insecurity for the many. Globalization's defenders inferred this was a price worth paying if there was to be any semblance of economic progress. In a world where extreme competition ruled and money moved at the flick of a switch, there was only one thing worse than being part of this runaway system—and that was not being part of it.

From Superpower to Hyperpower: U.S. Primacy

If a one-world economy operating under the same set of highly competitive rules was at least one consequence of the end of the Cold War, another was a major resurgence of American self-confidence in a new international system where it seemed to have no serious rival. This was not only a development that few had foretold (in the 1970s and 1980s, many analysts believed that the United States was in decline); it was one that many had thought impossible (most realists in fact believed that after the Cold War the world would become genuinely multipolar). It was also a situation many feared on the grounds that an America with no obvious peer competitor would act more assertively and with less restraint. That aside, all of the most obvious indicators by the late 1990s—military, economic, and cultural—seemed to point to only one conclusion: as a result of the Soviet collapse, followed in short order by an economic crisis in Japan and Europe's failure to manage two ethnic wars in the former Yugoslavia, the United States had been transformed from a mere superpower to what the French Foreign Minister Hubert Vedrine in 1998 termed a **hyperpower**. Former Secretary of State Madeleine Albright may have also agreed, in her own way, with this assessment,

Hyperpower The situation of the United States after the Cold War ended. With the Soviet Union's military might greatly diminished and China having primarily only regional power-projecting capability, the United States was unchallenged in the world.

although she used more diplomatic language; she called the United States "the indispensable power" in global politics.

This claim to unilateral privilege was linked to a particularly bleak view of the world shared by many, though not all, U.S. policymakers. The Cold War may have been over, they agreed: America may have emerged triumphant. But this was no reason to be complacent. To repeat a phrase often used at the time, although the "dragon" in the form of the USSR had been slain, there were still many "vipers and snakes" lurking in the tall grass. Among the five most dangerous and pernicious of these were various rogue states (Iran, Iraq, North Korea, Libya, and Cuba), the constant threat of nuclear proliferation (made all the more likely by the disintegration of the USSR and the unfolding nuclear arms race between Pakistan and India), and the

People stand amid bodies covered with blankets in a mosque after a suicide attack during the noon prayer in Sanaa, Yemen, in March 2015. The attack was aimed at Shiite rebels controlling the capital city. This civil war has entangled the United States, Saudi Arabia, and Iran in a dangerous battle with a number of terrorist groups including Al-Qaeda in the Arabian Peninsula (AQAP), a Sunni extremist group based in Yemen.

threat of religious fundamentalists and ideological extremists (all the more virulent now because of the fallout from the last great battlefield of the Cold War in Afghanistan). Indeed, long before 9/11, the dangers posed by radical Islamism were very well known to U.S. intelligence, beginning with the bombing of the U.S. Marine barracks in Beirut, Lebanon, in October 1983, that caused the deaths of almost 300 American personnel. The devastating bombing of the World Trade Center in 1993 and of the U.S. embassies in Tanzania and Kenya five years later, as well as the audacious attack on the USS *Cole* in 2000, all pointed to a new form of **terrorism** that could be neither deterred nor easily defeated by conventional means.

Yet in spite of these threats, there was no clear indication that the United States was eager during the 1990s to project its power with any serious purpose. The United States may have possessed vast capabilities, but there appeared to be no real desire in a post–Cold War environment to expend American blood and treasure in foreign adventures. The desire sank even further following the debacle in Somalia in 1993: the death of eighteen U.S. soldiers there created its own kind of syndrome that made any more U.S. forays abroad extremely unlikely. The United States after the Cold War was thus a most curious hegemon. On the one hand, its power seemed to be unrivaled (and was); on the other, it seemed to have very little idea about how to use this power other than to bomb the occasional rogue state when deemed necessary, while supporting diplomatic solutions to most problems when need be (as in the cases of the Middle East and North Korea). The end of the Cold War and the disappearance of the Soviet threat may have rendered the international system securer and the United States more powerful, but it also made the United States a very reluctant warrior. In a very important sense, the United States during the 1990s remained a superpower without a mission.

Terrorism The use of violence by nonstate groups or, in some cases, states to inspire fear by attacking civilians and/or symbolic targets and eliminating opposition groups. This is done for purposes such as drawing widespread attention to a grievance, provoking a severe response, or wearing down an opponent's moral resolve to effect political change.

Perception, Continuity, and Change after January 20, 2009

The study of global politics depends to a great extent on perception. How we think about the world often determines what we think is important. This habit of mind helps explain how political leaders and opinion makers in the United States were unprepared for two key events of the late twentieth century: the collapse of the Soviet Union and the rise of militant Islamic fundamentalism. The signs of the two events were in plain sight if you knew what to look for.

ISIS extremists slaughter non-believers in Iraq. As the new face of terrorism, ISIS is seen as more dangerous and more intolerant. A global coalition is fighting ISIS in Iraq and Syria and the Russians have joined the fight supporting the Syrian government. Instability in the region is increasing and the chance to control the process of change is disappearing quickly.

In the case of Islamic fundamentalism, certainly if you lived in a country with a large Muslim population, you would have been aware of the growing appeal of fundamentalist strains of Islam. The Wahabi sect in Saudi Arabia, for instance, forms the basis for society there. Egypt has had problems with violence linked to the Muslim Brotherhood since the time of British colonization. Indeed, the Brotherhood is often blamed for the assassination of President Anwar Sadat. In Afghanistan, the United States itself helped arm Islamic fundamentalists in their war against the Soviet invasion during the 1980s. The trend was visible every day in public as people rejected European styles of dress: more men grew beards, and more women adopted the clothing styles the fundamentalists preferred.

If North American and European leaders were not ready for the impact of Islamic fundamentalism, how unprepared are people in the rest of the world for trends resulting from the Arab Spring, the killing of Osama bin Laden, the end of the war in Iraq and Afghanistan, and the rise of the Islamic State or ISIS? Politics and society remain the same in most of the other Arab states, but the civil wars in Syria and Yemen have increased instability in these areas. The Obama administration abandoned the unilateral strategies of the Bush years in favor of the multilateralism that framed the intervention in Libya and shaped the decision to lift sanctions on Iran after it agreed to halt its production of nuclear weapons. If we start with the global war on terrorism, we can see that some things now are the same, and some are not. For example, in the early months of 2009, the newly elected Obama administration continued to use Predator drone aircraft to attack suspected Islamic militants in tribal areas in Pakistan along the Afghanistan border. Operation Geronimo, which resulted in the death of Osama bin Laden, was launched without the permission of Pakistani leaders. Pakistani officials objected to drone attacks during the Bush years, but President Obama decided that the raids must continue, and it is likely these kinds of attacks will continue with or without the support of Pakistan, and with the election of a new U.S. president in 2016. A major change in U.S. policy from the Bush administration could be seen, however, in the fundraising efforts to rebuild Palestinian homes in Gaza. Moreover, as the United States increased the number of its troops in Afghanistan to fight the resurgent Taliban, officials in Washington also quietly expressed their dissatisfaction with the actions of the Karzai government there.

Change does not always occur in a direction that can be controlled. One result of the Arab Spring is the move away from autocratic regimes toward democratic systems. Unfortunately, only one nation-state involved in the Arab Spring movement has remained democratic. A moderate Islamic party won more than 40 percent of the vote in the 2011 elections in Tunisia. The Muslim Brotherhood's Freedom and Justice Party and the ultraconservative Salafis together won more than 70 percent of the seats in the new

Egyptian parliament in early 2012. However, in 2013, the Egyptian military overthrew the legally elected government led by President Mohammed Morsi. The United States and its allies in the West and in the Middle East are in a political bind. Should they support religious parties that represent extremist views, or nondemocratic forces like the Egyptian military that overthrew an elected government?

For people outside the United States, it is difficult to assess the meaning of apparent continuity or change in U.S. foreign policy. One source of this difficulty is the perception popular in the developing world that the United States is the global hegemonic oppressor. People have been socialized by family members, schools, and religious and political leaders to blame the United States for their sufferings. This perception may not be based on fact, and it could be as incorrect as the perception that all Muslims are terrorists or that Islamic fundamentalism poses a threat to Europe and the United States. However, perceptions and images are often more powerful than reality.

For Discussion

1. Images die a slow death. Many people in the West still distrust Russians because of the Cold War, which has been over since the late 1980s. How do we overcome the misperceptions that shape our views of other cultures?

2. Do you think countries like the United States and other major powers need an enemy? Does having foes serve political or economic interests? Explain.

3. Do you think the United States and the West will be able to work with the Islamist parties in Egypt, Tunisia, Iraq, and Afghanistan? Why or why not?

Europe in the New World System

If the most pressing post–Cold War problem for the United States was how to develop a coherent global policy in a world where there was no single major threat to its interests, then for Europe, the main issue was how to manage the new enlarged space that had been created as a result of the events in 1989. Indeed, while more triumphant Americans would continue to proclaim that it was they who had won the Cold War in Europe, it was Europeans who were the real beneficiaries. A continent that had once been divided was now whole again. Germany had been peacefully united. The states of Eastern Europe had achieved the right of self-determination. The threat of war with potentially devastating consequences for Europe had been eliminated. Naturally, the transition from one order to another was not going to happen without certain costs, borne most notably by those who would now have to face up to life under competitive capitalism. And the collapse of communism in some countries was not an entirely bloodless affair, as ethnic conflict in former Yugoslavia (1990–1999) revealed only too tragically. With that said, a post–Cold War Europe still had much to look forward to.

Although many in Europe debated the region's future, policymakers were confronted with the more concrete issue of how to bring the East back into the West, a process that went under the general heading of enlargement. In terms of policy outcome, the strategy scored some notable successes. By 2007, the European Union had grown to twenty-seven members, and NATO was one fewer at twenty-six, with most of the new members coming from the former Soviet bloc. The two bodies also changed their club-like character in the process, much to the consternation of some people in the original member states, who found the entrants from the former Soviet bloc to be as much trouble as asset. According to critics, enlargement had proceeded so rapidly that the essential core meaning of both organizations had been lost. The European Union, some argued, had been so keen to enlarge that it had lost the will to integrate. NATO meanwhile could no longer be regarded as a serious military organization with an integrated command structure. One significant aspect of this was the "out of area" problem that limited NATO activities to Europe itself. This would change after September 11, 2001. Still, it was difficult not to be impressed by the capacity of NATO and the European Union in their new roles. These institutions had helped shape part of Europe during the Cold War and were now being employed to help manage the relatively successful (though never easy) transition from one kind of European order to another. For those who had earlier disparaged the part institutions might play in preventing anarchy in Europe, the important roles played by the European Union and NATO seemed to prove that institutions were essential.

Europe, it was generally recognized, remained what it had effectively been since the end of World War II: a work in progress. The problem was that nobody could quite agree when, if ever, this work would be completed and where, if anywhere, the European Union would end. Some analysts remained remarkably upbeat. The European Union's capacity for dealing with the consequences of the end of the Cold War, its successful introduction of a single currency (the euro, in January 2002), and its ability to bring in new members all pointed to one obvious conclusion: the European Union's future was assured. Many, however, were more skeptical. After a decade-long period of expansion and experimentation, Europe, they believed, had reached a dead end. It was more divided than united over basic constitutional ends, and it faced several challenges—economic, cultural, and political—to which there seemed to be no easy answers. Indeed, according to some commentators, European leaders not only confronted older issues that remained unsolved, but they also faced a host of new ones (e.g., the euro crisis with a debt-ridden Greece and refugees arriving from conflict regions in the Middle East and Africa) to which they had no ready-made solutions. Europe, today, may have been well aware of where it was coming from, but it had no blueprint for where it wanted to go.

Russia: From Yeltsin to Putin

One of the many problems facing the new Europe after the Cold War was how to define its relationship with post-communist Russia, a country confronting several degrees of stress after 1991 as it began to transform itself from a Marxist superpower with a planned economy to a democratic country that was liberal and market

The European refugee crisis has brought millions of displaced people to the continent in what the United Nations has called the worst refugee crisis since World War II. After landing in Piraeus, Greece, these refugees continue their journey north through Europe.

oriented. As even the most confident of Europeans accepted, none of this was going to be easy for a state that had experienced the same system for nearly three-quarters of a century. And so it proved during the 1990s, an especially painful decade during which Russia lost its ability to effectively challenge the United States and was instead a declining power with diminishing economic and ideological assets. Furthermore, there was not much in the way of economic compensation. On the contrary, as a result of its speedy adoption of Western-style privatization, Russia underwent something close to a 1930s-style economic depression, with industrial production plummeting, living standards sinking, and whole regions once devoted to Cold War military production experiencing free fall.

President Boris Yeltsin's foreign policy, meanwhile, did little to reassure many Russians. Indeed, his decision to get close to Russia's old capitalist enemies gave the distinct impression that he was selling out to the West. This made him a hero to many outside Russia. However, to many ordinary Russians, it seemed as if he (like his predecessor Gorbachev) was conceding everything and getting very little in return. Nationalists and old communists, still present in significant numbers, were especially scathing. Yeltsin and his team, they argued, had not only given away Russia's assets at "discount prices" to a new class of **oligarchs**, but he was also trying to turn Russia into a Western dependency. In short, he was not standing up for Russia's national interest.

Oligarchs A term from ancient Greece to describe members of a small group that controls a state.

Whether his successor Vladimir Putin, a former official in the KGB, had a clear vision for Russia when he took over the presidency matters less than the fact that, having assumed office, he began to stake out very different positions. These included greater authoritarianism and nationalism at home, a much clearer recognition that the interests of Russia and those of the West would not always be one and the same, and what turned into a persistent drive to bring the Russian economy—and Russia's huge natural resources—back under state control. This did not lead to turning back the clock to Soviet times. What it did mean, though, was that the West's leaders could no longer regard the country as a potential strategic partner. Certainly, Western governments could not assume that Russia would forever be in a state of decline. The West must instead confront a state with almost unlimited supplies of oil and gas and with a leadership determined to defend Russia's interests and to restore Russia to a position of global leadership.

Still, the West had less to fear now than during the Cold War. Economic reform had made Russia dependent on the West (though some Western countries, like Germany, depended on Russia for their energy requirements). Furthermore, the official political ideology did not in any way challenge Western institutions or values. Nor was Russia the military power it had once been during Soviet times. Indeed, not only was it unable to prevent some of its former republics from either signing up to former enemy institutions like NATO or moving more openly

WHAT'S YOUR WORLDVIEW?

President Putin supported the invasion of Ukraine and the takeover of Crimea in 2014. He also has been silent on the downing of Malaysian Airlines Flight 17, which according to American and German intelligence was shot down by pro-Russian insurgents, also in 2014. Recently, he has sent Russian military forces into Syria to support the Assad regime. Is Russia trying to reestablish its role as a major superpower by challenging Western views of liberal democracy and presenting an illiberal authoritarian governing option?

The "stare-down" at the G8 summit in Northern Ireland between the leaders of two powerful states may reveal the deep divisions between President Obama and President Putin over the conflict in Syria and the negotiations over Iran's nuclear weapons. Now one might add the serious disagreement over the Russian takeover of Crimea and the support of rebels in Ukraine, as well as the recent support for the Assad government in Syria.

into the Western camp, but by 2007, it was effectively encircled by the three Baltic republics to the northwest, an increasingly pro-Western Ukraine to the south, and Georgia in the Caucasus. Adding to its potential woes was the fact that many of its more loyal, regional allies ran highly repressive and potentially unstable governments: Belarus, Turkmenistan, and Azerbaijan, for example.

Meanwhile, in Chechnya, Russia faced an insurgency beginning in 1994 that not only revealed deep weaknesses in the Russian military but also brought down Western outrage on its head—perhaps not to the point of causing a rupture but certainly enough to sour relations. Many in the United States and a few in Europe were compelled to conclude that while Russia may have changed in several positive ways since the collapse of the USSR, it still maintained an authoritarian outlook, a disregard for human rights, a willingness to use military force, and an inclination toward empire.

East Asia: Primed for Rivalry?

If perceived lessons from history continue to play a crucial role in shaping modern Western images of post-Soviet Russia, then the past also plays a part in defining the international relations of East Asia—and a most bloody past it has been. The time following World War II was punctuated by several devastating wars (in China, Korea, and Vietnam), revolutionary insurgencies (in the Philippines, Malaya, and Indonesia), authoritarian rule (nearly everywhere), and revolutionary extremism (most tragically in Cambodia). The contrast with the postwar European experience could not have been more pronounced. Scholars of international relations point out that whereas Europe managed to form a new liberal security community during the Cold War, East Asia did not. In part, this was the result of the formation of the European Union and the creation of NATO (organizations that had no equivalents in Asia). But it was also because Germany managed to effect a serious reconciliation with its immediate neighbors while Japan (for largely internal reasons) did not. The end of the Cold War in Europe transformed the continent dramatically, but this was much less true in East Asia, where powerful communist parties continued to rule in China, North Korea, and Vietnam. Additionally, several territorial disputes, one between Japan and Russia and another between China and its neighbors over islands and navigation rights in the South China Sea, threatened the security of the region.

ENGAGING WITH THE WORLD

Give Peace a Chance

Interested in working for peace? Many groups are committed to this initiative and offer ways to get involved. One is the Quaker religious community, whose peace testimony states that their "opposition to all forms of violence imposes on them responsibility to seek alternative responses to conflict and injustice." Visit www.quaker.org.uk and www.friendspeaceteams.org.

Another is the Ecumenical Accompaniment Program in Palestine and Israel (EAPPI), a peace project of the World Council of Churches. Volunteers monitor and report violations of human rights and international law and work with Palestinian and Israeli peace activists to promote nonviolent responses to the problems in this region. Check out www.eappi.org.

For all these reasons, East Asia, far from being primed for peace, was still ripe for new rivalries. Europe's very bloody past between 1914 and 1945, went the argument, could easily turn into Asia's future. This was not a view shared by every commentator, however. In fact, as events unfolded, this uncompromisingly tough-minded realist perspective came under sustained criticism. Critics did not deny the possibility of future disturbances: how could they, given Korean division, North Korea's nuclear weapons program, and China's claim to Taiwan? But several factors did suggest that the region was not quite the powder keg some thought it to be.

The first and most important factor was the great economic success experienced by the region itself. The sources of this have been much debated, with some people suggesting that the underlying reasons were cultural and others that they were directly economic (cheap labor plus plentiful capital); a few believed they were the byproduct of the application of a nonliberal model of development employing the strong state to drive through rapid economic development from above. Some have also argued that the United States played a crucial role by opening its market to East Asian goods while providing the region with critical security on the cheap. Whatever the cause or combination of causes, the fact remains that by

Gross domestic product (GDP) The sum of all economic activity that takes place within a country.

Association of Southeast Asian Nations (ASEAN) A geopolitical and economic organization of several countries located in Southeast Asia. Initially formed as a display of solidarity against communism, it has since redefined its aims and broadened to include the acceleration of economic growth and the promotion of regional peace.

Soft power The influence and authority deriving from the attraction that a country's political, social, and economic ideas, beliefs, and practices have for people living in other countries.

the end of the twentieth century East Asia had become the third-largest powerhouse in the global economy, accounting for nearly 25 percent of world **gross domestic product (GDP)**.

Second, although many states in East Asia may have had powerful memories of past conflicts, these were beginning to be overridden in the 1990s by a growth in regional trade and investment. Economic pressures and material self-interest appeared to be driving countries in the region together rather than apart. The process of East Asian economic integration was not quick—the **Association of Southeast Asian Nations (ASEAN)** was only formed in 1967. Nor was integration accompanied by the formation of anything like the European Union. However, once regionalism began to take off during the 1990s, it showed no signs of slowing down.

A third reason for optimism lay with Japan. Here, in spite of an apparent inability to unambiguously apologize for past misdeeds and atrocities—a failure that cost it dearly in terms of **soft power** (see Chapter 4) influence in the region—its policies could hardly be characterized as disturbing. On the contrary, having adopted its famous peace constitution in the 1950s and renounced the possibility of ever acquiring nuclear weapons (Japan was one of the strongest upholders of the original 1968 Nonproliferation Treaty), Japan demonstrated no interest in upsetting its neighbors by acting in anything other than a benign manner. Furthermore, by spreading its considerable largesse in the form of aid and large-scale investment, it went some of the way in fostering better international relations in the region. Even its old rival China was a significant beneficiary, and by 2003, more than 5,000 Japanese companies were operating on the Chinese mainland. However, in a move that perhaps reflects concern for aggressive behavior by China and North Korea, the Japanese parliament approved legislation that allows for the Japanese self-defense forces to engage in foreign conflicts.

This leads us to China. Much has been written about "rising China," especially by analysts who argue—in classical realist fashion—that when new powerful states emerge onto the international stage, they are bound to disturb the existing balance of power. China looks benign now, they agree. It will look different in a few years' time—once it has risen. However, there may be more cause for guarded optimism than pessimism, largely because China has adopted policies (both economic and military) whose purpose clearly is to reassure its neighbors that it can rise peacefully and thus effectively prove the realists wrong. It has also translated policy into action by supporting regional integration, exporting its considerable capital to other countries in East Asia, and working as a responsible party rather than a spoiler inside regional multilateral institutions. Such policies are beginning to bear fruit, with greater numbers of once-skeptical neighbors viewing China as a benevolent instrument of development rather than a threat. However, recent Chinese moves to build artificial islands in

WHAT'S YOUR WORLDVIEW?

Both China and India are gaining power and influence in global affairs. Both countries are members of the G20, and both have strong economies that were not devastated by the recent economic crisis. These two states are also increasing their military spending, including the expansion of their naval power. Some experts argue that this is only the beginning of a shift of global power toward Asia. What do you think? Is this a real challenge to other major powers or just a rebalancing of the world?

An Indian soldier cleans missiles in preparation of a visit to India by President Obama. India increased its military spending by 11 percent in 2015. Is this a new arms race in Asia with China, India, and Pakistan seeking military supremacy?

order to extend their territorial waters and, thus, their control of strategic waterways, seem to have adversely affected some of the more positive feelings about this rising power.

In the end, however, all strategic roads in China (and in East Asia as a whole) lead to the one state whose presence in the region remains critical: the United States. Though theoretically opposed to a unipolar world in which there is only one significant global player, the new Chinese leadership has pursued a most cautious policy toward the United States. No doubt some Americans will continue to be wary of a state run by the Communist Party, whose human rights record can hardly be described as exemplary. However, as long as China continues to act in a cooperative fashion, there is a good chance that relations will continue to prosper. There is no guaranteeing the long-term outcome. With growth rates around 10 percent per year, with its apparently insatiable demand for overseas raw materials, and with enormous dollar reserves at its disposal, China has already changed the terms of the debate about the future of international politics. Of course, it remains to be seen what effects the global economic collapse that began in 2008 will have on China; in 2015, China devalued its currency, which caused world financial markets to suspect a potential weakening of its economy. China may be overly dependent on foreign investment and militarily light years behind the United States, but even so, it presents a set of challenges that did not exist in the much simpler days of the Cold War. Indeed, one of the great ironies of international history may be that China as a rising capitalist power playing by the rules of the market may turn out to be more of a problem for the West than China the communist power of the past.

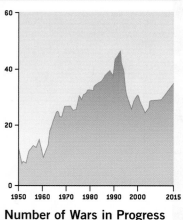

Number of Wars in Progress Since 1950.

Based on what you have read in this chapter, what accounts for these trends—for the increases, spikes, and decreases?

Latin America: Becoming Global Players

Early in the nineteenth century, a patron-client relationship developed between the United States and Latin America. The Monroe Doctrine (1823) stated that any European country attempting to intervene in the Americas would be seen as an aggressor, and the United States would respond in kind. President Theodore Roosevelt added his corollary in 1904 that proclaimed the U.S. right to intervene in cases of "flagrant wrongdoing" by a Latin American government, which usually meant a country was acting against U.S. interests.

In the great ideological struggle between the United States and the Soviet Union, Latin American countries were expected to be client states of the United States and to take pro-U.S. positions in disputes with the Soviet Union. Cuba was the pariah state because of its alliance with the USSR and its communist government. Any government that strayed from the U.S. orbit was usually replaced in a covert coup or overthrown by local forces loyal to the United States for the sake of its own economic and strategic interests. The United States tried to overthrow the regimes in Cuba and Nicaragua, and it was successful in removing pro-communist leaders in Guatemala, Chile, and Grenada. Unfortunately for the United States, its image in Latin America today has been tarnished due to the fact that many of the authoritarian military leaders in Latin America were supported by the United States.

Since 9/11, the United States has not prioritized relations with Latin America, and other countries, such as China, have become more influential in the region. Meanwhile, Brazil, Venezuela, and Chile have become important global and regional players. Brazil, owing in part to its energy and manufacturing industries, has become an important member of the newly emerging Brazil, Russia, India, China, and South Africa (BRICS) powers, and its soft power diplomacy campaigns have landed it the 2014 World Cup and the 2016 Summer Olympics. Chile has become a major player in global trade and in regional and global institutions such as the Organization of American States and the United Nations. As a very stable social democratic state, Chile is emerging as an active middle power in global politics. Venezuela under the late President Hugo Chávez presented a challenge to U.S. leadership, if not hegemonic practices in Latin America. He increased trade and investment with China, conducted military exercises with Russia, and created an alternative economic development program that allocates five times more aid than the United States in Latin America.

Recent history, including the war on terrorism and the Bush administration's emphasis on unilateralism and preemptive war, has hurt the image of the United States in the region. The European Union is now the largest investor in Latin America, and trade with China is increasing. For decades, the U.S. policy of not recognizing and boycotting Cuba was considered obsolete, but in December 2014 President Obama announced the restoration of full diplomatic relations with the island nation. Although the U.S. trade embargo remains in effect, the

United States plans to ease restrictions on remittances, travel, and banking, marking a dramatic turning point in U.S.-Cuba relations and, more broadly, U.S.-Latin American relations.

The War on Terrorism: From 9/11 to Iraq, Afghanistan, and Syria

The end of the Cold War marked one of the great turning points of the late twentieth century, but 9/11 was a reminder that the international order that had come into being as a result was not one that found ready acceptance everywhere. Osama bin Laden was no doubt motivated by far more than a dislike of globalization and American primacy. As many analysts have pointed out, bin Laden's vision was one that pointed back to a golden age of Islam rather than forward to something modern. That said, his chosen method of attacking the United States using four planes, his use of video to communicate with followers, his employment of the global financial system to fund operations, and his primary goal of driving the United States out of the Middle East could hardly be described as medieval. He represented a very modern threat, one that could not be dealt with by traditional means. Old strategies, such as containment and deterrence, were no longer relevant. If this was the beginning of a "new global war on terrorism," as some argued at the time, then it was unlikely to be fought using policies and methods learned between 1947 and 1989.

This new nonstate network threat, led by a man whose various pronouncements owed more to holy texts than anything else, made it difficult for some in the West to understand the true character of radical Islamic movements and their use of terrorist tactics. As the controversial war on terrorism unfolded—first in Afghanistan and then in Iraq, Iran, and Pakistan, some began to view the United States as the imperial source of most of the world's growing problems.

The new threat environment provided the United States with a fixed point of reference around which to organize its international affairs. It built close relations with many states—Russia, India, Pakistan, and China perhaps being the more important—that were now prepared to join it in waging a global war against terror. After the 9/11 attacks, the Bush administration officials felt compelled to act in a far more assertive fashion abroad. Indeed, some of Bush's more conservative supporters believed that one of the reasons for the attack on the United States in the first place was that it had not been assertive enough in the 1990s. Finally, policymakers in the Bush administration seemed to abandon the defense of the status quo in the Middle East. The events of 9/11, they argued, had changed the original formula whereby the United States turned a blind eye to autocratic regimes that existed in the region in exchange for cheap oil and stability. U.S. dependency on these two commodities was no longer enough to justify making deals with states like Saudi Arabia that produced the dangerous ideologies that inspired terrorism.

A German soldier puts his hand on the shoulder of a Kurdish peshmerga fighter, left, during training at the Infantry School of the German Federal Armed Forces Bundeswehr. Germany is part of the alliance training the Kurdish peshmerga in their fight against the Islamic State in Syria.

This sort of thinking paved the way for the war against Iraq in 2003. However, Iraq had not been involved in 9/11; the regime itself was secular and it shared the same goal as the United States in seeking to contain the geopolitical ambitions of Islamic Iran. For these reasons, different analysts have identified different factors to explain the war, including the ideological influence exercised by the neoconservatives on President Bush, America's close relationship with Israel, and America's desire to control Iraq's oil (see the Case Study in this chapter). This leaves us with more questions than answers, with possibly the most credible answer being the less conspiratorial one: the United States went to war partly because it thought it would win fairly easily, partly because it got its intelligence wrong, and partly because some political leaders thought—rather unwisely—that building a new regime in Iraq would be just as easy as getting rid of the old one.

Regardless of the motive, it was clear by 2009 that the Iraq War was a strategic blunder that neither delivered stable democracy to Iraq nor inspired others in the region to undertake serious political reform. It also had the doubly dangerous consequence of disturbing the whole of the Middle East, while making it possible for Iran to gain even greater influence in the region than it had before. In fact, by undermining the old regime in Iraq, the United States effectively created a vacuum into which an increasingly self-confident Iranian regime has marched. Finally, as a result of their action in Iraq, the United States and its allies provided radical Islamists around the world with a rallying point that they appear to have exploited with some skill, as is illustrated by the rise of the Islamic State.

After the 9/11 attacks, Al-Qaeda was given sanctuary by the Taliban government in Afghanistan. The United States immediately demanded that the leaders of this terrorist network be turned over to the United States for trial. The Taliban refused, and on October 7, 2001, the U.S. military invaded Afghanistan, destroyed Al-Qaeda's terrorist training camps, and overthrew the Taliban-controlled government. NATO members invoked Article 5 and came to the aid of the United States.

NATO took command of the International Security Assistance Force (ISAF) in 2003. Since 2009, the United States has moved away from a counterinsurgency policy that put an emphasis on protecting civilians, providing services, and nation building toward more direct military action: increasing airstrikes in both Afghanistan and Pakistan, the use of drones for surveillance and attacks on suspected terrorist leaders, a dramatic increase in covert operations, and the use of

The Iraq War and Its Origins

International relations, as a field, has always been concerned with the origins of wars. Long-term changes in the balance of power, fear of encirclement, imperial ambition—not to mention misperception and ideology—have all been employed at one time or another to explain why states engage in military action. The Iraq War presents a useful, and possibly difficult, test case for various theories of war origins. Several competing explanations have been advanced so far to explain the U.S. decision to go to war against Iraq in 2003. These include, among others, the official argument that Iraq represented a serious and potentially rising threat to a critically important region; the more materialist thesis that the United States was determined to secure direct control of Iraq's massive reserves of oil; and the popular claim that the war was the product of pressures arising from within the United States itself—here identified as the Israel lobby, the ideologically inclined neoconservatives, and their various supporters on the Christian Right. This coalition was joined by a few liberals who wanted a regime change and Saddam Hussein punished as a brutal dictator.

The student of world politics, however, is still left with a number of unanswered questions. First, would the war have happened without the quite unexpected election of George W. Bush in late 2000? That is, did the president make a huge difference to the decision taken? Second, could Bush have then led the United States into war without the profound shock created by the equally unexpected attack of 9/11? Considered this way, wasn't the war largely the byproduct of fear and insecurity? Third, what role did British Prime Minister Tony Blair play? Indeed, was this a war made possible by an alliance with a middle power? Fourth, would it have been feasible at all if various American writers and policymakers had not thought the United States so powerful that it could more or less do anything in the world? That is, to what extent did the notion of the "unipolar moment" contribute to the final decision to go to war? Furthermore, were the intellectual grounds for the war not also laid by those during the post–Cold War period who thought it wise to promote democracy and encouraged others to intervene in the internal affairs of sovereign states for humanitarian purposes? Finally, to what extent could one

2013 was the tenth anniversary of British participation in the invasion of Iraq. Here George Bush and Tony Blair meet to finalize the British role in this war of choice. How did British citizens react to this decision to support the United States?

argue that the Iraq War was in the U.S. national interest; and if it was, then why did so many realists oppose the war?

For Discussion

1. The debates about the role of think tanks like the Project for a New American Century and individuals like William Kristol, Richard Perle, and Paul Wolfowitz in shaping the decisions of the Bush administration will continue for years. How important are policy advisers like these, and when do they have the most influence?

2. Did the ideas of George W. Bush, Dick Cheney, and Colin Powell matter in shaping U.S. policy? Were their advisers just as important? Explain.

3. Some experts have suggested that the Bush administration was very Wilsonian in that it aimed to rebuild the Middle East based on American values of liberal democracy. Is there anything new about a country wanting to project its values? Could this have been done without the preemptive use of force? Explain.

4. Although American troops remain in Iraq, the Iraq War is now officially over. Was it worth the human and financial costs? Why or why not?

special forces surprise attacks on terrorist camps in the tribal regions that extend into Pakistan.

With the successful covert operation that resulted in the killing of Osama bin Laden in 2011, many citizens in NATO countries were wondering why their men and women continued to fight and die for a corrupt and ineffective government in Afghanistan. Suicide bombers continued to kill civilians who cooperated with the United States and the Afghan government, and the Taliban resurged, taking refuge in Pakistan. One of the most dangerous terrorist groups, the Haqqani network, is based in Pakistan and funded by the Pakistani intelligence agency, the Inter-Services Intelligence directorate (ISI). The Afghanistan government claims that the ISI has supported a fivefold increase in insurgent attacks since 2006.

Meanwhile, the NATO ISAF mission was completed in 2014 and in January 2015, NATO began to train, advise, and assist Afghanistan's security forces in non-combat roles under the Resolute Support Mission. However, renewed Taliban military activities, including the taking of Kunduz, a major northern Afghan city, suggest that the Afghan government might have trouble containing insurgent forces.

The United States and Pakistan are allies, but they have different interests in Afghanistan. The United States hopes that when it withdraws, Afghanistan will be a relatively stable, prosperous, and democratic state that is no longer an incubator for terrorists. Pakistan does not want a strong Afghanistan that might be governed by ethnic Tajiks, who are traditionally allies of India. We must remember that India and Pakistan are rivals in this region and both have nuclear weapons. When the United States and NATO withdraw completely, peace and stability in this region may not yet be achieved.

With or without the war in Afghanistan, however, the West would still likely be confronted by the challenge of violent radical Islam. This is a movement that not only feeds off Western blunders and policies (especially American ones in the Middle East and South Asia) but is also based on a set of cultural values, state practices, and historical grievances that make it almost impossible to deal with effectively—without compromising what it means to be part of the West. Herein, though, lays another problem: how precisely to define this conflict.

It was fashionable to characterize it as one between two different "civilizations" (a term originally made popular by American writer Samuel Huntington in 1993). Nevertheless, there was something distinctly uncompromising about a conflict between those on the one side who supported democracy, **pluralism**, individualism, and a separation between state and church and those on the other who preached intolerance and supported **theocracy** while calling for armed struggle and **jihad** against the unbeliever. Not that these views were shared by all Muslims. Indeed, these radical views were roundly condemned by the overwhelming majority of Muslim clerics and followers of Islam. Still, as the antagonism unfolded, there seemed to be enough disaffected people in enough societies—including Western ones—to make this aggressive ideology

Pluralism A political theory holding that political power and influence in society do not belong just to the citizens nor only to elite groups in various sectors of society but are distributed among a wide number of groups in the society. It can also mean a recognition of ethnic, racial, and cultural diversity.

Theocracy A state based on religion.

Jihad In Arabic, *jihad* means "struggle." Jihad can refer to a purely internal struggle to be a better Muslim or a struggle to make society more closely align with the teachings of the Koran.

an occasional but potent threat. The way the world in general and the West in particular deal with it will likely determine the shape of international relations for many years to come.

Conclusion

In this chapter, we have seen some of the trends and events that created the contemporary globalized system. War (both "hot" and "cold"), revolutions, and colonization and its collapse each had a role in the evolution of international society. The irony might be found in this fact: religion played a role in both 1648 and 2001. The signatories of the Peace of Westphalia wanted to remove religion from European international politics. Members of Al-Qaeda and now the Islamic State and its allies want to bring religion back into global politics.

The Peace of Westphalia in the seventeenth century created an international system in Europe that many people at the time believed would make for more orderly politics on the continent. In the same way, the end of the Cold War in the twentieth century seemed to promise a more peaceful world. But as we have seen in this chapter, these hopes went unfulfilled. The effects of revolutions, wars, and European imperialism have revealed the hollow nature of the European international system. Moreover, during the Cold War—while much of the attention of politicians and academics in the developed world was focused on the U.S.-USSR confrontation—other wars, economic trends, and social movements around the world were too often ignored. As a result, the euphoria in Western Europe and the United States that followed the end of the Soviet Union soon gave way to a new set of challenges and threats.

CONTRIBUTORS TO CHAPTER 2: *David Armstrong, Michael Cox, Len Scott, Steven L. Lamy, and John Masker.*

KEY TERMS

Anarchy, p. 52
Appeasement, p. 37
Armistice, p. 36
Arms race, p. 46
Association of Southeast
 Asian Nations
 (ASEAN), p. 60
Balance of power, p. 32
Bipolar, p. 42
Blitzkrieg, p. 38
Capitalism, p. 42
Cold War, p. 42
Concert of Europe, p. 33

Congress of Vienna, p. 34
Containment, p. 43
Détente, p. 46
Fourteen Points, p. 36
Genocide, p. 38
Glasnost, p. 49
Gross domestic product
 (GDP), p. 60
Hegemony, p. 42
Holocaust, p. 38
Hyperpower, p. 52
Intercontinental ballistic
 missiles (ICBMs), p. 47

Jihad, p. 66
League of Nations, p. 36
Liberal democracy, p. 37
Market democracies, p. 51
Marshall Plan, p. 43
Munich Agreement of
 1938, p. 37
National self-determination,
 p. 33
North Atlantic Treaty
 Organization (NATO),
 p. 44
Oligarchs, p. 57

Ostpolitik, p. 46
Peace of Utrecht (1713),
 p. 32
Peace of Westphalia (1648),
 p. 32
Perestroika, p. 49
Pluralism, p. 66
Protestant Reformation,
 p. 31
Rapprochement, p. 46
Society of states, p. 32
Soft power, p. 60
Sovereign equality, p. 32

REVIEW QUESTIONS

1. Was the international system of nineteenth-century Europe merely a means of legitimizing imperialism? Explain.
2. How did the method by which European colonies in Africa and Asia gained their independence determine their post-independence internal politics?
3. Why did the United States become involved in wars in Asia after 1950? Illustrate your answer by reference to either the Korean War or the Vietnam War.
4. How have scholars of international relations attempted to explain the end of the Cold War?
5. Why did liberal theorists predict that the world would become a more stable place after the end of the Cold War, and why did realists disagree with them?
6. If the United States won the Cold War, why did it have such problems defining a grand strategy for itself after 1989 and before 9/11?
7. How has globalization since the Cold War changed the basic character of world politics?
8. How successfully has Europe adapted to the challenges facing it since the end of the Cold War?
9. How has the war on terrorism changed global politics?

For more information, quizzes, case studies and other study tools, please visit us at **www.oup.com/us/lamy.**

THINKING ABOUT GLOBAL POLITICS

Understanding and Resolving International Conflicts

INTRODUCTION

In this exercise, you will be asked to analyze several conflict situations from the perspective of different state and non-state actors or players directly or indirectly involved in a given conflict. First, we ask you to explore the causes of this conflict, and second, we ask you to consider possible ways of managing or resolving the conflict. You might have to do some research to find answers to our questions. This is a great opportunity to explore the wide variety of sources on the web and in your university or college library.

PROCEDURE

This is a cooperative learning exercise. In groups of three or four, begin by reviewing the Cold War conflicts in this chapter and the conflicts in Chapter 6.

1. Review the Cold War conflicts and identify those that might still be going on. For those that have ended, how did they end? What were the reasons these conflicts were resolved?

THINKING ABOUT GLOBAL POLITICS *continued*

2. Now look at the conflicts from 1946 to 2009. Pay particular attention to conflicts that began after the Cold War and respond to the following questions:
   a. Who is involved in this conflict? Primary actors? Secondary actors?
   b. What do these actors claim are the causes of the conflict?
   c. What other factors serve to accentuate the conflict and increase its lethality?

3. In Chapters 1 and 4, we introduce you to levels of analysis: tools for explaining decision-making and the behavior of states in the international system. Since war and conflict are a constant in the international system, we can use levels to explain why wars begin and how they might end. With your cooperative learning team, come up with plausible explanations for the start of each conflict. Was it caused by the leader's desire for power (level 1) or the state's need for oil (level 2) or the fear of a neighbor's military buildup or the security dilemma (level 3)? Now share your list of plausible explanations with the rest of the class. See if you can reach agreement on the most frequent reasons that countries go to war. Are there any patterns that develop? You might also check your ideas with the work of historians or official records on the war. If we know why countries go to war, can we anticipate and even prevent future wars?

4. Now, with some understanding of why wars begin, let's review several examples of peacemaking efforts. There are many examples of conflicts that have ended peacefully. Select at least two of these conflicts and identify the factors that helped all the parties reach an acceptable peace. For example, was one party defeated and forced to accept a peace agreement, like Japan and Germany in World War II, or was peace achieved because a third party offered mediation and assistance, as Norway did to help reach a peace agreement in Sri Lanka?

WRITING ASSIGNMENT

What has this exercise taught you about the difficulties of preventing future wars and the problems associated with peacemaking? Do you think peace, defined as an absence of war, is a utopian dream? Must we live in a world where all we can hope to do is manage conflict and prevent systemic war?

3

Realism, Liberalism, and Critical Theories

Liberalism emphasizes the role of international institutions and the importance of diplomacy—both bilateral and multilateral. Prime Minister of India Narendra Modi and U.S. President Barack Obama talked trade, the environment, and security issues in Asia at the heads of state lunch in honor of the visiting dignitaries for the General Debate of the 70th UN General Assembly.

Though it be true that democratic government will make wars less likely, it will not eliminate all causes of conflict between nations, and if the enormous sacrifices of this war are not to be made in vain, not merely must democracy triumph in individual states, but in the society of states as well.

—WOODROW WILSON

Theory is always *for* some one, and *for* some purpose.

—ROBERT W. COX

There are several "states of concern" for the leading world powers, and the Islamic State in the Levant (otherwise known as ISIL) or Daesh, or the Islamic State of Iraq and Syria, or ISIS may present one of the most difficult problems for those concerned with national security, terrorism, extremism, and violence. The terror attacks in Beirut, Paris, Brussels and the destruction of a Russian airliner in Egypt in 2015 suggest to the world that the Islamic State and other extremists are going global with their messages of violence and extremism. The security forces in most countries are organized to fight other states. Fighting terrorist networks began in earnest after the September 11, 2001, terrorist attacks; however, these groups are difficult to defeat, and the wars that began then are still going on. Now we face new challenges and new extremist networks. These extremist networks act like Machiavellian states in the sense that they use military force to secure their interests, thus forcing other states to react with equal force.

ISIS originated as an Al-Qaeda splinter group in Iraq in 2003. The CIA estimates that ISIS fields more than 30,000 fighters, of whom about half are foreign, including at least 2,000 who hold Western passports. The goal of ISIS is to create a new Caliphate that is similar to a nation-state with Sharia law, public services, and an economy based on natural resources. Since the attacks in Paris, Western intelligence services consider ISIS to be a bigger threat than Al-Qaeda. ISIS has demonstrated that it is focused on taking their message to the world and being the primary challenger to the non-believers and the decadent West. How do world leaders deal with this extremist network willing to use force to serve its interests?

From the realist perspective, negotiations and diplomacy have costs as well as benefits. Realists believe one must always negotiate from strength and be prepared to act with force or the threat of force when

LEARNING OBJECTIVES

After reading and discussing this chapter, you should be able to:

Define the term *theory* and give examples.

Describe the historical origins of the realist, liberal, Marxist, constructivist, and feminist schools of thought.

Name the key theorists of the five schools of thought.

Explain the relation among the levels of analysis and the different variants of the five schools of thought.

Explain the benefits and shortcomings of the different variants of the five schools of thought for the study of international relations.

dealing with rogue states or terrorist networks that have no intention of following international rules. On the other hand, liberal internationalists believe that international institutions and diplomatic efforts can reduce the power and influence of radical networks and rogue states. For example, in the area of nuclear weapons, the power, prestige, and influence of the United States and liberal institutions like the International Atomic Energy Agency (IAEA) are being undermined by North Korea and Iran. Realists argue that the basic flaw of liberal thinking is that a rogue state can be talked out of developing nuclear weapons. Instead, realists believe the major powers must put pressure on North Korea by choking off its ability to export and import weapons and military equipment, cut off all access to financial resources, and pressure China to rein in its North Korean ally. Similarly, realists argue that all states must respond collectively to defeat ISIS. Liberal thinkers still hold out hope for arms control talks and successful coercive diplomacy efforts aimed at convincing North Korean leaders to end their intransigence and join the international community of nation-states and containing or ending the extremist strategies of ISIL and other radical networks.

As we will discuss in this chapter, both realism and liberalism are effective theories by which we can more closely examine interactions among states. Both have become important in the study of international relations at universities around the world. Yet both have their limitations as well. You will see that the basis for both theories is a very different understanding about human nature, the goal of a state's policy, and the nature of the international system.

The narratives on international relations that we call "critical" ask us to reconsider our assumptions about politics. You will learn that many people in this world do not accept the dominant theories that define the international system; they therefore seek change or transformation. It is important to understand all theoretical views. If we decided to discard or marginalize these critical approaches, we would abandon the intellectual goal of being careful and comprehensive critical thinkers. We would also abandon the people behind these ideas, theories, and ways of knowing. The narratives of those on the margins are as important as those in the center of power. In addition, these critical theories offer alternatives to state-centric and power-politics theories.

Introduction

In Chapter 1, we asked you to consider your personal worldview, or perspective on global events and conditions, which can result from your experiences, education, personal identity, citizenship, and other factors. In this chapter, we begin to present the concept of **theory**. By theory, we mean a set of propositions that help us understand events or behaviors. You are subconsciously using theories all the time. Like pairs of sunglasses that can block different amounts of sunlight, a theory can limit what we see yet also help us see certain characteristics better.

As we will see in this chapter, the theories called realism and liberalism have an impact on the ways political leaders view and understand the world. We do not mean that a leader one day announces, "I am a realist" or "I am a liberal" and then follows a recipe for foreign policy. Instead, we believe that theories can help us look at actions and be able to describe and explain events. Theories can also help us predict future actions based on what has occurred in the past. However, we must keep in mind that the theories we use—like sunglasses—might also restrict what we think.

Although realism and liberalism are the dominant traditional theories of international relations, they are not always effective in helping us understand some of the transformative actors and issues in today's globalized world, such as NGOs, transnational networks, the importance of economic structures, and minority voices that have been marginalized over the years. These limitations have led to the development of alternative theories, which will be explored in the second part of this chapter, including Marxism, constructivism, and feminist theory, each of which can provide important ideas to understand trends and events in global politics and globalization in ways that realism and liberalism cannot.

Theories are essential in your development as an informed critical thinker and an effective decision maker. One of the basic skills of citizenship in this era of globalization is to be able to *describe, explain, predict, and prescribe* (DEPP) from these different theoretical positions. The DEPP skills are essential for you as a scholar in this field. They also will help determine your level and form of *participation* in the global system. Thus, after you finish reading and discussing this chapter, you should know how realists and liberals *describe, explain, predict, prescribe, and participate in* (DEPPP) global politics.

> **Theory** A proposed explanation of an event or behavior of an actor in the real world. Definitions range from "an unproven assumption" to "a working hypothesis that proposes an explanation for an action or behavior." In international relations, we have intuitive theories, empirical theories, and normative theories.

What Is Realism?

Over the centuries, various world leaders have sought to create international rules to make life more stable and predictable by decreasing outbreaks of violent aggression. As you will recall from Chapter 2, the Peace of Westphalia (1648) established a principle that still governs international relations: sovereignty. The key European nations who signed the peace treaties agreed that only a legitimate government could exercise

Ukrainian servicemen put their dogs under their jackets to keep them warm while fighting with Russian-backed separatists in eastern Ukraine. This is a power move by Russia and part of its realist strategy to increase Russia's influence and control in the region and its image as a great power.

control over its citizens and territory, could act independently and flexibly in its relations with other states, and could craft its own strategies and policies aimed at securing perceived national interests. By inference, no state could interfere in the domestic affairs of any other state. Of course, the principle of sovereignty applied more to the continent of Europe and less to societies anywhere else on Earth; nevertheless, sovereignty was—and still is today—a critically important concept.

By declaring some regions of the world sovereign and agreeing that sovereign states could not legally interfere with the internal business of other sovereign states, political leaders *thought* they had solved the problem of foreign wars. However, this attempt to eliminate war failed early and often: within a year of the Peace of Westphalia, England invaded Ireland; within four years, the English and the Dutch were at war; within six years, Russia and Poland were at war; and so it went.

With this reality in mind, it is relatively easy to understand why the earliest perspective on international relations, referred to as **realism**, is based on the following three assumptions:

Realism A theoretical approach that analyzes all international relations as the relation of states engaged in the pursuit of power. Realists see the international system as anarchic, or without a common power, and they believe conflict is endemic in the international system.

1. States are the only actors in international relations that matter.
2. A policymaker's primary responsibility is to create, maintain, and increase national **power**—the means available to a state to secure its national interests—at all costs.
3. No central authority stands above the state. The anarchic nature of the international system is an essential assumption for realist thinkers and, in fact, for most liberal thinkers and even some critical-approach thinkers.

Power This is a contested concept. Many political scientists believe that power is the capacity to do things and, in social and political situations, to affect others to get the outcome one wants. Sources of power include material or tangible resources and control over meaning or ideas.

The world perceived by realists is lawless, competitive, and uncertain. In fact, one influential philosopher who helped define realism, Thomas Hobbes, published this pessimistic observation about life in his political treatise *Leviathan*: "The life of man is solitary, poor, nasty, brutish and short." The only way to avoid misery and anarchy, according to Hobbes (1651), was to have a strong ruler of a strong state impose order and provide protection from external attack.

The Essential Realism

In later sections, we will see how realism can be regarded as a broad theoretical umbrella covering a variety of perspectives, each with its own leading authors and texts. Despite the numerous denominations, keep in mind that, essentially, all realists subscribe to the following three S's: *statism*, *survival*, and *self-help*. Let's discuss these three essential elements in more detail and also examine some of realism's shortcomings.

Statism

For realists, the state is the main actor, and sovereignty is its distinguishing trait. The meaning of the sovereign state is inextricably bound up with the use of force. In terms of its internal dimension, to illustrate this relationship between violence and the state, we need to look no further than Max Weber's famous definition of the state as "the monopoly of the legitimate use of physical force within a given territory" (M. J. Smith 1986, 23). Within this territorial space, **sovereignty** means that the state has supreme authority to make and enforce laws. This is the basis of the unwritten contract between individuals and the state. According to Hobbes, for example, we trade our liberty in return for a guarantee of security (safety and protection of a way of life). Once security has been established, **civil society** can begin—a society of individuals and groups not acting as participants in any government institutions or in the interests of commercial companies. But in the absence of security, people are in the state of nature where there can be no business, no art, no culture, no society. The first move for the realist, then, is to organize power domestically. Only after power has been organized can community begin.

Realist international theory assumes that, domestically, the problem of order and security is solved. However, in the real world—in the relations among independent sovereign states—insecurities, dangers, and threats to the very existence of the state loom large. Realists primarily explain this on the basis that the very condition for order and security—namely, the existence of a sovereign world government—is missing from the international realm. Realists claim that in this condition of anarchy, states compete with other states for power and security.

The nature of the competition is viewed in zero-sum terms; more for one state means less for another. This competitive logic of power politics makes agreement on universal principles difficult, apart from the principle of nonintervention in the internal affairs of other sovereign states. But realists suspend even this principle—as we saw in the previous chapter, designed in seventeenth-century Europe to facilitate coexistence—and argue that in practice, nonintervention does not apply in relations between great powers and their regional neighbors. As evidenced by the most recent behavior of the United States in Afghanistan and Iraq, modern hegemonic (dominant) states are able to influence events far beyond their borders, overturning the nonintervention principle on the grounds of national security and international order.

Given that the first move of the state is to organize power domestically and maintain law and order, and the second is to accumulate power internationally, it is important to consider in more depth what realists mean by power. The classical realist Hans Morgenthau offers the following definition of power: "Man's control over the minds and actions of other men" (1948/1955, 26). There are two important points that realists make about the elusive concept of power. First, power is a relational concept; one does not exercise power in a vacuum but in relation to another entity. Second, power is a relative concept; calculations need to be made not only about one's own power capabilities but also about the power that other states possess. Yet the task of accurately assessing the power of states is infinitely complex. Too often, power calculations are reduced to counting the number of troops, tanks, aircraft, and naval ships a country possesses in the mistaken belief that

Sovereignty The condition of a state having control and authority over its own territory and being free from any higher legal authority. It is related to, but distinct from, the condition of a government being free from any external political constraints.

Civil society The totality of all individuals and groups in a society who are not acting as participants in any government institutions or acting in the interests of commercial companies.

this translates into the ability to get other actors to do something they would not otherwise do.

Survival

The second principle that unites realists is the assertion that in international politics the preeminent goal is survival. Although realists disagree as to whether the accumulation of power is an end in itself, one would think there is no dissenting from the argument that security is states' ultimate concern. Survival is held to be a precondition for attaining all other goals, whether these involve conquest or merely independence. According to Kenneth Waltz, "beyond the survival motive, the aims of states may be endlessly varied" (1979, 91).

Niccolò Machiavelli tried to make a science out of his reflections on state survival. His book *The Prince* codifies a set of maxims that would enable leaders to maintain their hold on power. In important respects, we find two related Machiavellian themes recurring in the writings of modern realists; both derive from the idea that international politics requires different moral and political rules from those of domestic politics. The first is the task of understanding what realists believe to be the true nature of international politics; the second is the need to protect the state at all costs (even if this means the sacrifice of one's own citizens). These concerns place a heavy burden on the shoulders of state leaders. In the words of Henry Kissinger, the academic realist who became secretary of state during the Nixon presidency, "a nation's survival is its first and ultimate responsibility; it cannot be compromised or put to risk" (1977, 204). Their guide must be an **ethic of responsibility**: the careful weighing of consequences and the realization that individual immoral acts might need to be carried out for the greater good.

Ethic of responsibility For realists, it represents the limits of ethics in international politics; it involves the weighing up of consequences and the realization that positive outcomes may result from amoral actions.

An ethic of responsibility is frequently used as a justification for breaking the laws of war, as in the case of the British nighttime firebombing raids on Nazi Germany, or the Bush administration's decision to alter its obligations on the issue of torture as it concerned suspected terrorists held at Guantánamo Bay. The principal difficulty with the realist formulation of an ethic of responsibility is that, while instructing leaders to consider the consequences of their actions, it does not provide a guide for how state leaders should weigh the consequences (M. J. Smith 1986, 51).

Not only does realism provide an alternative moral code for state leaders, proponents claim, it also suggests a wider objection to the whole enterprise of bringing **ethics** into international politics. (Morality is what is good, right, and proper, and ethics is the examination, justification, and analysis of morality as custom or practice.) Starting from the assumption that each state has its own particular values and beliefs, realists argue that the state is the supreme good and there can be no community beyond borders. This moral relativism has generated a substantial body of criticism, particularly from some liberal theorists who endorse the notion of universal human rights.

Ethics Ethical studies in international relations and foreign policy include the identification, illumination, and application of relevant moral norms to the conduct of foreign policy and assessing the moral architecture of the international system.

Self-Help

Kenneth Waltz's *Theory of International Politics* (1979) brought to the realist tradition a deeper understanding of the international system itself. Unlike many other realists, Waltz argued that international politics is not unique due to the regularity of war and conflict because this is also familiar in domestic politics. The key difference between domestic and international orders lies in their structure. In the domestic polity, citizens usually do not need to defend themselves. In the international system, there is no higher authority, no global police officer, to prevent and counter the use of force. Security can therefore be realized only through **self-help**. In an anarchic structure, "self-help is necessarily the principle of action" (Waltz 1979, 111). But in the course of providing for one's own security, the state in question will automatically be fueling the insecurity of other states.

The term given to this spiral of insecurity is the **security dilemma**. According to Nick Wheeler and Ken Booth, security dilemmas exist "when the military preparations of one state create an irresolvable uncertainty in the mind of another as to whether those preparations are for 'defensive' purposes only (to enhance its security in an uncertain world) or whether they are for offensive purposes (to change the status quo to its advantage)" (1992, 30). This scenario suggests that one state's quest for security is often another state's source of insecurity. States find it very difficult to trust one another and often view the intentions of others in a negative light. Thus, the military preparations of one state are likely to be matched by neighboring states. The irony is that at the end of the day, states often feel no more secure than before they undertook measures to enhance their own security.

In a self-help system, structural realists argue that the balance of power, or parity and stability among competing powers, will emerge even in the absence of a conscious policy to maintain it (i.e., prudent statecraft). Waltz argues that balances of power result irrespective of the intentions of any particular state. In an **anarchic system** populated by states with leaders who seek to perpetuate themselves, alliances will be formed that seek to check and balance the power against threatening states. Classical realists, however, are likelier to emphasize the crucial role state leaders and diplomats play in maintaining the balance of power. That is, the balance of power is not natural or inevitable; the leaders of states construct it.

However, various kinds of realists debate the stability of a balance-of-power system. Many argue that the balance of power has been replaced by an unbalanced unipolar order. It is questionable whether other countries will actively attempt to balance against the United States as structural realism might predict. But whether it is the contrived balance of the Concert of Europe in the early nineteenth century or the more fortuitous balance of the Cold War, balances of power are broken—through either war or peaceful change—and new balances emerge. What the perennial collapsing of the balance of power demonstrates is that states

A fleet of Chinese warships, including a missile destroyer, a missile frigate, and a replenishment ship, visited Europe's Nordic states in a show of goodwill and as an attempt to learn more about the Arctic region in anticipation of gaining more access to the region's resources and new transportation routes. Chinese national interests guide this naval exercise.

Self-help In realist theory, in an anarchical environment, states cannot assume other states will come to their defense even if they are allies. Each state must take care of itself.

Security dilemma In an anarchic international system, one with no common central power, when one state seeks to improve its security it creates insecurity in other states.

Anarchic system A realist description of the international system that suggests there is no common power or central governing structure.

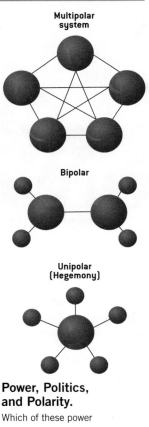

Multipolar system

Bipolar

Unipolar (Hegemony)

Power, Politics, and Polarity.

Which of these power arrangements best represents the world today? What about the world of the early twentieth century? Nineteenth century? How does theory help us understand these global power dynamics?

Comparative advantage A theory developed by David Ricardo stating that two countries will both gain from trade if, in the absence of trade, they have different relative costs for producing the same goods. Even if one country is more efficient in the production of all goods than the other (absolute advantage), both countries will still gain by trading with each other as long as they have different relative efficiencies.

are at best able to mitigate the worst consequences of the security dilemma but are not able to escape it due to the absence of trust in international relations.

Historically, realists have illustrated the lack of trust among states by reference to Enlightenment thinker Jean-Jacques Rousseau's parable of the stag hunt. In *Man, the State and War*, Kenneth Waltz revisits the parable:

> *Assume that five men who have acquired a rudimentary ability to speak and to understand each other happen to come together at a time when all of them suffer from hunger. The hunger of each will be satisfied by the fifth part of a stag, so they "agree" to cooperate in a project to trap one. But also the hunger of any one of them will be satisfied by a hare, so, as a hare comes within reach, one of them grabs it. The defector obtains the means of satisfying his hunger but in doing so permits the stag to escape. His immediate interest prevails over consideration for his fellows. (1959, 167–168)*

Waltz argues that the metaphor of the stag hunt provides a basis for understanding the problem of coordinating the interests of the individual versus the interests of the common good and the payoff between short-term interests and long-term interests. In the self-help system of international politics, the logic of self-interest mitigates against the provision of collective goods, such as "security" or "free trade." In the case of the latter, according to the theory of **comparative advantage**, all states would be wealthier in a world that allowed freedom of goods and services across borders. But individual states, or groups of states like the European Union, can increase their wealth by pursuing **protectionist** policies, such as tariffs on foreign goods, as long as other states do not respond in kind. Of course, the logical outcome is for the remaining states to become protectionist, international trade to collapse, and a subsequent world recession to reduce the wealth of each state. Thus, the question is not whether all will be better off through cooperation but rather who will likely gain more than another. It is because of this concern with relative-gains issues that realists argue that cooperation is difficult to achieve in a self-help system.

One Realism or Many?

So far in this chapter, we have treated the realist lens as if it were a unified set of beliefs and propositions; it is, however, not at all that way, as both the model's supporters and critics have pointed out. The belief that there is not one realism but many leads logically to a delineation of different types of realism. Next, we will outline key differences between classical realism and structural realism, or neorealism. A summary of the varieties of realism outlined appears in Table 3.1.

Classical Realism

The lineage of **classical realism** begins with Thucydides' representation of power politics as a law of human behavior. The classical realists argued that the drive for power and the will to dominate are the fundamental aspects of human nature. The behavior of the state as a self-seeking egoist is understood to be merely a reflection of the characteristics of the people that comprise the state.

Therefore, it is human nature that explains why international politics is necessarily power politics. This reduction of realism to a condition of human nature is one that frequently reappears in the leading works of the doctrine, most famously in the work of Hans Morgenthau. The important point for Morgenthau is, first, to recognize that these laws exist and, second, to devise the most appropriate policies that are consistent with the basic fact that human beings are flawed creatures.

Another distinguishing characteristic of classical realism is its adherents' belief in the primordial character of power and ethics. Classical realism is fundamentally about the struggle for belonging, a struggle that is often violent. Patriotic virtue is required for communities to survive in this historic battle between good and evil, a virtue that long predates the emergence of sovereignty-based

Protectionist An economic policy of restraining trade between states through methods such as tariffs on imported goods, restrictive quotas, and a variety of other government regulations designed to allow "fair competition" among imports and goods and services produced domestically.

| TABLE 3.1 | A Taxonomy of Realisms | | |

Type of Realism	Key Thinkers	Key Texts	Big Idea
Classical Realism (Human Nature)	Thucydides (ca. 430–406 BCE)	*The Peloponnesian War*	International politics is driven by an endless struggle for power that has its roots in human nature. Justice, law, and society either have no place or are circumscribed.
	Machiavelli (1532)	*The Prince*	Political realism recognizes that principles are subordinated to policies; the ultimate skill of the state leader is to accept, and adapt to, the changing power-political configurations in global politics.
	Morgenthau (1948)	*Politics Among Nations*	Politics is governed by laws that are created by human nature. The mechanism we use to understand international politics is the concept of interests defined in terms of power.
Structural Realism (International System)	Rousseau (c. 1750)	*The State of War*	It is not human nature but the anarchical system that fosters fear, jealousy, suspicion, and insecurity.
	Waltz (1979)	*Theory of International Politics*	Anarchy causes logic of self-help, in which states seek to maximize their security. The most stable distribution of power in the system is bipolarity.
	Mearsheimer (2001)	*Tragedy of Great Power Politics*	The anarchical, self-help system compels states to maximize their relative power position.
Neoclassical Realism	Zakaria (1998)	*From Wealth to Power*	The systemic account of world politics provided by structural realism is incomplete. It needs to be supplemented with better accounts of unit-level variables such as how power is perceived and how leadership is exercised.

Classical realism The belief that it is fundamentally the nature of people and the state to act in a way that places interests over ideologies. The drive for power and the will to dominate are held to be fundamental aspects of human nature.

Structural realism (neorealism) A theory of realism that maintains the international system and the condition of anarchy or no common power push states and individuals to act in a way that places interests over ideologies. This condition creates a self-help system. The international system is seen as a structure acting on the state with individuals below the level of the state acting as agency on the state as a whole.

notions of community in the mid-seventeenth century. Classical realists therefore differ from contemporary realists in the sense that they engaged with moral philosophy and sought to reconstruct an understanding of virtue in light of practice and historical circumstance.

Thucydides was the historian of the Peloponnesian War, a conflict between two great powers in the ancient Greek world, Athens and Sparta. Though he was a disgraced general on the losing side, Thucydides' work has been admired by subsequent generations of realists for its insights into many of the perennial issues of international politics. One of the significant episodes of the war between Athens and Sparta is known as the "Melian dialogue" and provides a fascinating illustration of a number of key realist principles. At the end of this chapter, the "Thinking About Global Politics" feature reconstructs Thucydides' version of the dialogue between the Melians and the Athenian leaders who arrived on the island of Melos to assert their right of conquest over the islanders. In short, what the Athenians are asserting over the Melians is the logic of power politics and the duty of a hegemon to maintain order. Because of their vastly superior military force, they are able to present a fait accompli to the Melians: either submit peacefully or be exterminated. Citing their neutrality in the war, the Melians for their part try to buck the logic of power politics, appealing in turn with arguments grounded in justice, God, and their lack of support for the Spartans. As the dialogue makes clear, although at a military disadvantage and bound to lose, the Melians chose to fight. Their defeat became the basis for a maxim of realism: "The strong do what they have the power to do and the weak accept what they have to accept."

How is a leader supposed to act in a world animated by such malevolent forces? The answer given by Machiavelli is that all obligations and treaties with other states must be disregarded if the security of the community is under threat. Moreover, imperial expansion is legitimate, as it is a means of gaining greater security. Other classical realists, however, advocate a more temperate understanding of moral conduct. Mid-twentieth-century realists such as Butterfield, Carr, Morgenthau, and Wolfers believed that wise leadership and the pursuit of the national interest in ways that are compatible with international order could mitigate anarchy. Taking their lead from Thucydides, they recognized that acting purely on the basis of power and self-interest without any consideration of moral and ethical principles frequently results in self-defeating policies.

Structural Realism, or Neorealism

Structural realists, sometimes called **neorealists**, concur that international politics is essentially a struggle for power, but they do not endorse the classical-realist assumption that this is a result of human nature. Instead, structural realists attribute security competition and interstate conflict to the lack of an overarching authority above states and the relative distribution of power in the international system.

Kenneth Waltz, the best-known structural realist, defines the structure of the international system in terms of three elements—organizing principle, differentiation of units, and distribution of capabilities, or power. He identifies two different organizing principles: anarchy, the decentralized realm of international politics, and hierarchy, the basis of domestic order. He argues that the units of the international system are functionally similar sovereign states; hence, unit-level variation is irrelevant in explaining international outcomes. It is the third tier, the distribution of capabilities across units, that is, according to Waltz, the key independent variable to understanding important international outcomes such as war and peace, alliance politics, and the balance of power. Many structural realists are interested in providing a rank ordering of states so as to differentiate and count the number of great powers that exist at any particular point in time. The number of great powers in turn determines the structure of the international system.

How does the international distribution of power impact the behavior of states, particularly their power-seeking behavior? In the most general sense, Waltz argues that states, especially the great powers, must be sensitive to the capabilities of other states. The possibility that any state may use force to advance its interests results in all states being worried about their survival. According to Waltz, power is a means to the end of security: "Because power is a possibly useful means, sensible statesmen try to have an appropriate amount of it." He adds, "In crucial situations, however, the ultimate concern of states is not for power but for security" (1989, 40). In other words, rather than being power maximizers, states, according to Waltz, are *security* maximizers. He argues that power maximization often proves to be dysfunctional because it triggers a counterbalancing coalition of states.

A different account of the power dynamics that operate in the anarchic system is provided by John Mearsheimer's theory of **offensive realism**, another variant of structural realism. While sharing many of the basic assumptions of Waltz's structural-realist theory, frequently termed **defensive realism**, Mearsheimer differs from Waltz when it comes to describing the behavior of states. Most fundamentally, "offensive realism parts company with defensive realism over the question of how much power states want" (Mearsheimer 2001, 21). According to Mearsheimer, the structure of the international system compels states to maximize their relative power position. Under anarchy, he agrees that self-help is the basic principle of action. Yet he also argues that while all states possess some offensive military capability, there is a great deal of uncertainty about the intentions of other states. Consequently, Mearsheimer concludes that there are no satisfied or status quo states; rather, all states are continuously searching for opportunities to gain power at the expense of other states. Contrary to Waltz, Mearsheimer argues that states recognize that the best path to peace is to accumulate more power than anyone else. The ideal position is to be the global

Offensive realism A structural theory of realism that views states as power maximizers.

Defensive realism A structural theory of realism that views states as security maximizers—more concerned with absolute power as opposed to relative power. According to this view, it is unwise for states to try to maximize their share of power and seek hegemony.

hegemon of the international system; however, Mearsheimer believes that global hegemony is impossible and therefore he concludes that the world is condemned to perpetual great-power competition.

Contemporary Realist Challenges to Structural Realism

Neoclassical realism A version of realism that combines both structural factors such as the distribution of power and unit-level factors such as the interests of states.

Although offensive realism makes an important contribution to realism, some contemporary realists are skeptical of the notion that the international distribution of power alone can explain the behavior of states. **Neoclassical-realist** scholars have attempted to build a bridge between international structural factors and unit-level factors, such as the perceptions of state leaders, state-society relationships, and the motivations of states (we will learn more about the various levels of analysis—*individual, national, systemic,* and *global*—in Chapter 4). According to Stephen Walt, the causal logic of neoclassical realism "places domestic politics as an intervening variable between the distribution of power and foreign policy behavior" (2002, 211).

One important intervening variable is leaders themselves—namely, how they perceive the international distribution of power, given that there is no objective, independent reading of the distribution of power. Structural realists assume that all states have a similar set of interests, but neoclassical realists such as Randall Schweller (1996) argue that historically this is not the case. He argues, with respect to Waltz, that the assumption that all states have an interest in security results in neorealism exhibiting a profoundly status quo bias. Not only do states differ in terms of their interests, but they also differ in terms of state strength, or the ability to extract and direct resources at their disposal in the pursuit of particular interests. Neoclassical realists argue that different types of states possess different capacities to translate the various elements of national power into state power. Thus, contrary to Waltz, all states cannot be treated as "like units" with similar goals, interests, and values.

Given the varieties of realism that exist, it is perhaps a mistake to understand traditions as a single stream of thought, handed down in a neatly wrapped package from one generation of realists to another. Instead, it is preferable to think of living traditions like realism as the embodiment of both continuities and conflicts. Despite the different strands running through the tradition, there is a sense in which all realists share a common set of propositions.

In the next section, we will examine liberalism, another tradition within the field of international relations theory. We will see that realism and liberalism share certain assumptions about the international systems but disagree strongly about others.

As Brazil grows as an economic leader in global politics, it has increased its military strength and its involvement in many UN peacekeeping efforts around the world, including in Haiti, Timor-Leste, and the Ivory Coast.

What Is Liberalism?

After World War I, the leaders of the victorious states—the United States, the United Kingdom, and France—adapted the underlying principles of political and economic **liberalism** they had been practicing domestically since the seventeenth and eighteenth centuries to international relations in an attempt to avoid a second devastating war. Liberal thought is grounded in the notion that human nature is good, not evil; that states can thrive best in a world governed by morality and law; and that reason and rationality will compel states to cooperate to achieve mutually held goals in peace (see Table 3.2 for a list of noteworthy liberal thinkers). Envisioning a world where compliance with the principles of liberalism would facilitate more harmonious relationships among global actors, the United States, the United Kingdom, and France sought to recast the rules of international relations as they drafted the 1919 Treaty of Versailles and the charter for the League of Nations.

Just as realism derives from the observations and interpretations of political situations, so does liberalism. The seeds of a liberal perspective had been sown in

> **Liberalism** A theoretical approach that argues for human rights, parliamentary democracy, and free trade—while also maintaining that all such goals must begin *within a state*.

TABLE 3.2	**Taxonomy of Liberalism**		
Classical Liberals			
Hugo Grotius	*On the Law of War and Peace* (1625)	Natural law gives way to international law where contracts, oaths, and a system of just war exist and must be abided.
John Locke	*Two Treatises of Government* (1689)	The State of Nature provides for the equality and freedom of every man before the law as well as the right to own property.
Immanuel Kant	*Perpetual Peace* (1795)	Peace is to be secured by the abolishment of standing armies, the proliferation of democratic states, and the respect for state sovereignty.
Richard Cobden	*England, Ireland and America, by a Manchester Manufacturer* (1835)	Free trade would create a more peaceful world order and lead to increased individual liberty, prosperity, and interdependency.
Contemporary Liberals			
Woodrow Wilson	*Fourteen Points* (1918)	Transparency among states, the proliferation of free trade, the reduction of arms, and the creation of a multinational institution to ensure the implementation of mutual agreements—idealism.
David Mitrany	*The Functional Theory of Politics* (1975)	Inter-state trade and cooperation in common sectors are mutually beneficial and will spill over to include other sectors—functionalism.
Hedley Bull	*The Anarchical Society* (1977)	Defines the state as having control over its people and a certain territory and advocates a "society of states" bound by common rules and interests—pluralism.

the wake of the fifteenth century's so-called Age of Discovery, which fostered the rampant expansion of global commerce as states, explorer entrepreneurs, and trading companies became involved in the business of exchanging goods and services. Commerce across political and cultural boundaries was never just a simple matter of private individuals swapping one commodity for another (otherwise known as *barter*) or for money. To engage in commerce, these pioneer global traders had to negotiate the terms of trade—that is, how much of one commodity was worth how much of another, or how much money; they had to abide by new and different cultural norms and legal systems; and they had to bargain with political leaders to gain and maintain market access. Trade formed linkages that transcended political, social, cultural, and economic boundaries.

As trade expanded to include the exchange of a wider variety of commodities from all over the world, so did the linkages. Over time, a complex web of connections evolved along with the multitude of formal and informal agreements needed to facilitate commerce. As economic and social interactions crossed political boundaries with increasing frequency, trade and immigration patterns rendered realist guidelines decreasingly useful to policymakers. It was no longer so easy to engage in unilateral actions without experiencing economic repercussions, as World War I had emphatically demonstrated.

Realism, however, prevailed. Its logic, combined with the realities of the world, led to its continued domination of global and foreign policymaking. The major world powers of the twentieth century were not willing to abandon unilateralism. The United States never ratified the treaty creating the League of Nations (due to concerns about future entanglements in European wars), France sought revenge over Germany, and the United Kingdom sought to limit the power of the League. Then, one by one, Germany, Japan, and Italy violated Versailles Treaty covenants and sought to regain lost power by acquiring resources and invading other states.

The world was soon consumed by World War II, which, like its predecessor, committed combatant and noncombatant alike to the national cause of winning. In a desperate effort to end the war and to signal to others evidence of its military might, the United States dropped atomic bombs on Hiroshima and Nagasaki, Japan, triggering a profound and fundamental change in international and human relations.

As World War II came to an end, key decision makers in the United States recognized that the United States needed to be an active player on the world scene; they also saw that the United States had the financial and military power to enforce a new world order based on its political and economic visions. Moreover, they realized that, in a world where sovereignty remained the reigning principle, decisions affecting two or more states required the participation of all affected stakeholders and the backing of the rule of law. Embedded in this **multilateralist** approach to global governance is a principle of political liberalism—namely, that the "governed" (in this case, states) should have a say in the development of those rules, norms, and principles by which they will be governed. The political leaders

Multilateralism The process by which states work together to solve a common problem.

of the United States and its allies created a host of international governmental organizations (IGOs), such as the United Nations and the Bretton Woods economic institutions, to manage global relations in key political and economic arenas. The mandates of these IGOs were informed by **liberal internationalism**, a combination of

- Democratic values (political liberalism);
- Free trade markets (economic liberalism);
- Multilateral cooperation (multilateralism); and
- A rule-based international society that respects sovereignty and human rights.

We will discuss these principles further as we define the boundaries of liberal thinking and begin to understand how neoliberalism and radical liberalism have since evolved their own set of arguments from the liberal tradition.

> **Liberal internationalism** A perspective that seeks to transform international relations to emphasize peace, individual freedom, and prosperity and to replicate domestic models of liberal democracy at the international level.

ENGAGING WITH THE WORLD

Global Zero: A World Without Nuclear Weapons

This global citizens' movement is committed to the total elimination of nuclear weapons. As its website suggests, governments spend over $1 trillion on nuclear weapons, which in the wrong hands could lead to the end of life as we know it. This organization has opportunities for interns and volunteers. Many college and university campuses have Global Zero organizations. Check out www.globalzero.org.

Defining Liberalism

In essence, liberalism argues for human rights, parliamentary democracy, and free trade—while also maintaining that all such goals must begin *within a state*. The early European liberals thought that reforms within one's own country would be the first step in a long process that could eventually extend to world affairs. Although the belief in the possibility of progress is one identifier of a liberal approach to politics (Clark 1989, 49–66), there are other general propositions that define the broad tradition of liberalism.

Perhaps the appropriate way to begin this discussion is with a four-dimensional definition (Doyle 1997, 207). First, all citizens are equal before the law and possess certain basic rights to education, access to a free press, and religious toleration. Second, the legislative assembly of the state possesses only the authority invested in it by the people, whose basic rights it may not abuse. Third, a key dimension of the liberty of the individual is the right to own property, including productive forces. Fourth, liberalism contends that the most effective system of economic exchange is one that is largely market-driven and not one that is subordinate to bureaucratic regulation and control, either domestically or internationally. When these propositions are taken together, we see a stark contrast between liberal values of individualism, tolerance, freedom, and constitutionalism and realism's conservatism, which places a higher value on order and authority and is willing to sacrifice the liberty of the individual for the stability of the community.

Although in the past many writers have tended to view liberalism as a theory of domestic government, what is becoming more apparent is the explicit connection between liberalism as a *domestic* political and economic theory and liberalism as an *international* theory. Properly conceived, liberal thought on a global scale embodies a domestic political and economic system *operating at the international level*. Like individuals, states have different characteristics; some are bellicose and war prone, whereas others are tolerant and peaceful. In short, the identity of the state determines its outward orientation. Liberals see a further parallel between individuals and sovereign states. Although the character of states may differ, all states in a global society are accorded certain "natural" rights, such as the generalized right to nonintervention in their domestic affairs. We see this in the "one state, one vote" principle in the UN General Assembly (see Chapter 6 for more on the United Nations).

On another level, the domestic analogy refers to the extension of ideas that originated inside liberal states to the international realm, such as the coordinating role played by institutions and the centrality of the rule of law to the idea of a just order. Historically, liberals have agreed with realists that war is a recurring feature of the anarchic states system. But unlike realists, they do not identify **anarchy** as the cause of war. Certain strands of liberalism see the causes of war located in **imperialism**, others in the failure of the balance of power, and still others in the problem of undemocratic regimes. And can we prevent war through collective security, commerce, or world government? While it can be productive to think about the various strands of liberal thought and their differing prescriptions (Doyle 1997, 205–300), given the limited space permitted to deal with a broad and complex tradition, the emphasis here is on the core concepts of international liberalism and the way these relate to the goals of order and justice on a global scale.

Unlike what we learned about realism, liberalism is at its heart a doctrine of change and belief in progress. Liberalism pulls in two directions: its commitment to freedom in the economic and social spheres leans in the direction of a minimalist role for governing institutions, while the democratic political culture required for basic freedoms to be safeguarded requires robust and interventionist institutions. This has variously been interpreted as a tension between different liberal goals and more broadly as a sign of rival and incompatible conceptions of liberalism. Should a liberal polity—no matter what the size or scale—preserve the right of individuals to retain property and privilege, or should liberalism elevate equality over liberty so that resources are redistributed from the strong to the

Anarchy A system operating in the absence of any central government. It does not imply chaos but, in realist theory, the absence of political authority.

Imperialism The practice of foreign conquest and rule in the context of global relations of hierarchy and subordination. It can lead to the establishment of an empire.

weak? When we look at politics on a global scale, it is clear that inequalities are far greater while at the same time our institutional capacity to do something about them is that much less. As writers on globalization remind us, the intensification of global flows in trade, resources, and people has weakened the state's capacity to govern.

The Essential Liberalism

Immanuel Kant and Jeremy Bentham were two of the leading liberals of the **Enlightenment**. Both were reacting to the barbarity of international relations, what Kant described as "the lawless state of savagery," at a time when domestic politics was at the cusp of a new age of rights, citizenship, and constitutionalism. Their abhorrence of the lawless savagery led them individually to elaborate plans for "perpetual peace." Although written more than two centuries ago, these manifestos contain the seeds of core liberal ideas, in particular the belief that reason could deliver freedom and justice in international relations. For Kant, the imperative to achieve perpetual peace required the transformation of individual consciousness, republican constitutionalism, and a federal contract between states to abolish war (rather than to regulate it, as earlier international lawyers had argued). This federation was likened to a permanent peace treaty rather than a "superstate" actor or world government.

Kant's claim that liberal states are peaceful in their international relations with other liberal states was revived in the 1980s. In a much-cited article, Michael Doyle argued that liberal states have created a "separate peace" (1986, 1151). According to Doyle, there are two elements to the Kantian legacy: restraint among liberal states and "international imprudence" in relations with nonliberal states.

Although empirical evidence seems to support the **democratic peace thesis**, it is important to bear in mind the limitations of the argument. For the theory to be compelling, believers in the thesis need to provide an explanation of why war has become unthinkable between liberal states. Kant argued that if the decision to use force was taken by the people rather than by the prince, then the frequency of conflicts would be drastically reduced. Democratic or liberal states tend not to go to war with other liberal or democratic states, but they *will* go to war with nonliberal or undemocratic states. Historical evidence supports this point. Thus, Kant's idea that democratic states will not go to war cannot be supported.

An alternative explanation for the democratic peace thesis might be that liberal states tend to be wealthy and therefore have less to gain—and more to lose—by engaging in conflicts than poorer, authoritarian states. Perhaps the most convincing explanation of all is the simple fact that liberal states tend to be in relations of amity with other liberal states. War between Canada and the United States is unthinkable, perhaps not because of their liberal democratic constitutions but because they are friends with a high degree of convergence in economic and political matters (Wendt 1999, 298–299). Indeed, war between states with

WHAT'S YOUR WORLDVIEW?

Liberal internationalism emerged as a dominant perspective after the two world wars. After these conflicts, most states wanted to return to a rule-based system that promotes democracy and free trade. Yet, historically, this view does not last. What are some possible reasons that liberal-internationalist thinking does not prevail?

Enlightenment A movement associated with rationalist thinkers of the eighteenth century. Key ideas (which some would argue remain mottoes for our age) include secularism, progress, reason, science, knowledge, and freedom. The motto of the Enlightenment is *"Sapere aude!"* (Have courage to know!) (Kant 1991, 54).

Democratic peace thesis A central plank of liberal-internationalist thought, the democratic peace thesis makes two claims: first, liberal polities exhibit restraint in their relations with other liberal polities (the so-called separate peace), but second, they are imprudent in relations with authoritarian states. The validity of the democratic peace thesis has been fiercely debated in the international relations literature.

German Chancellor Angela Merkel listens to European Commission President Jean-Claude Juncker at an emergency EU heads of state summit on the immigrant crisis at the EU Commission headquarters in Brussels. Kantian liberals believe that refugees have universal rights and should be accepted by all states. What do you think?

contrasting political and economic systems may also be unthinkable because they have a history of friendly relations. An example here is Mexico and Cuba, which maintain close bilateral relations despite their history of divergent economic ideologies.

Two centuries after Kant first called for a "pacific federation," the validity of the idea that democracies are more pacific continues to attract a great deal of scholarly interest. The claim has also found its way into the public discourse of Western states' foreign policy, appearing in speeches made by U.S. presidents as diverse as Ronald Reagan, Bill Clinton, George W. Bush, and Barack Obama. Less crusading voices within the liberal tradition believe that a legal and institutional framework must be established that includes states with different cultures and traditions. At the end of the eighteenth century, Jeremy Bentham advocated such a belief in the power of law to solve the problem of war. "Establish a common tribunal" and "the necessity for war no longer follows from a difference of opinion" (Luard 1992, 416). Like many liberal thinkers after him, Bentham showed that federal states such as the German Diet, the American Confederation, and the Swiss League were able to transform their identity from one based on conflicting interests to a more peaceful federation.

Because liberal politics and capitalism are intimately linked, many writers believe, with Adam Smith, that the elimination of tariffs, duties, and other restrictions on imports would be a vital step in dissemination of liberalism's program. For example, the belief of Richard Cobden, a British politician and public intellectual, that **free trade** would create a more peaceful world order is a core idea of nineteenth-century liberalism. Trade brings mutual gains to all the players irrespective of their size or the nature of their economies. It is perhaps not surprising that this argument found its most vocal supporters in Britain; the supposed universal value of free trade brought disproportionate gains to the hegemonic power. There was never an admission that free trade among countries at different stages of development would lead to relations of dominance and subservience.

Like free trade, the idea of a "natural harmony of interests" in international political and economic relations came under challenge in the early part of the twentieth century. The fact that Britain and Germany had highly interdependent economies before World War I seemed to confirm the fatal flaw in the association of economic interdependence with peace. From the turn of the century, the contradictions within European civilization, of progress and exemplarism on the one hand and the harnessing of industrial power for military purposes on the other, could no longer be contained. Europe stumbled into a horrific war, resulting in

Free trade An essential element of capitalism that argues for no barriers or minimal barriers to the exchange of goods, services, and investments among states.

the deaths of 15 million people. Not only did the war end three **empires**, but it was also a contributing factor to the Russian Revolution of 1917.

World War I shifted liberal thinking toward a recognition that peace is not a natural condition but one that must be constructed. Perhaps the most famous advocate of an international authority for the management of international relations was Woodrow Wilson. According to this U.S. president, peace could only be secured with the creation of an international organization to regulate the international anarchy. Security could not be left to secret bilateral diplomatic deals and a blind faith in the balance of power. Just as peace had to be enforced in domestic society, the international domain needed a system of regulation for coping with disputes and an international force that could be mobilized if nonviolent conflict resolution failed. In this sense, more than any other strand of liberalism, idealism rests on the idea that we can replicate the liberalism we know domestically at the international level (Suganami 1989, 94–113).

Along with calls for free trade and self-determination, in his famous "Fourteen Points" speech to Congress in January 1918, Wilson argued that "a general association of nations must be formed" to preserve the coming peace; the League of Nations was to be that general association. For the League to be effective, it needed to have the military power to deter aggression and, when necessary, to use a preponderance of power to enforce its will. This was the idea behind the **collective security** system that was central to the League of Nations. Collective security refers to an arrangement where "each state in the system accepts that the security of one is the concern of all, and agrees to join in a collective response to aggression" (Roberts and Kingsbury 1993, 30). It can be contrasted with an alliance system of security, where a number of states join together, usually as a response to a specific external threat (sometimes known as "collective defense"). In the case of the League of Nations, its charter noted the obligation that, in the event of war, all member states must cease normal relations with the offending state, impose sanctions, and, if necessary, commit their armed forces to the disposal of the League Council should the use of force be required to restore the status quo. The League's constitution also called for the self-determination of all nation-states, another founding characteristic of liberal-idealist thinking on international relations.

Unfortunately, the overall experience of the League of Nations as a peacekeeper was a failure. While the moral rhetoric at the creation of the League was decidedly liberal and idealist, in practice states remained imprisoned by self-interest in the style of realism. There is no better example of this than the U.S. decision not to

Empire A distinct type of political entity, which may or may not be a state, possessing both a home territory and foreign territories. This may include conquered nations and colonies.

Collective security An arrangement where "each state in the system accepts that the security of one is the concern of all, and agrees to join in a collective response to aggression" (Roberts and Kingsbury 1993, 30).

U.S. President Woodrow Wilson, a liberal internationalist, thought the key to international security was an international organization, the League of Nations. Why did the League fail?

join the institution it had created. With the Soviet Union initially outside the system for ideological reasons, the League of Nations quickly became a debating society for the member states. Hitler's decision in March 1936 to reoccupy the Rhineland, a designated demilitarized zone according to the terms of the Treaty of Versailles, effectively ended the League.

According to the realist's version of the history of the discipline of international relations, the collapse of the League of Nations dealt a near-fatal blow to liberal idealism. There is no doubt that the language of liberalism after 1945 was more pragmatic; how could anyone living in the shadow of the Holocaust be optimistic? Yet familiar core ideas of liberalism—belief in the benefits of progress, free trade, and respect for human rights—remained. Key political leaders in Europe and North America recognized the need to replace the League with another international institution with responsibility for international peace and security. Only this time, in the case of the United Nations, there was an awareness of the need for a consensus between the great powers for enforcement action to be taken. The framers of the UN Charter therefore included a provision (Article 27) allowing any of the five permanent members of the Security Council the power of veto. This revision constituted an important modification to the classical model of collective security (A. Roberts 1996, 315). The framers of the UN Charter also acknowledged that security was more than guns and thus created the Economic and Social Council (see Chapter 5) to build what became known as *human security,* which we will examine in Chapter 7. With the ideological polarity of the Cold War, the UN procedures for collective security were ineffectual (as either of the superpowers and their allies would veto any action proposed by the other). It was not until the end of the Cold War that a collective security system was put into operation, following the invasion of Kuwait by Iraq on August 2, 1990.

An important argument advanced by liberals in the early postwar period concerned the state's inability to cope with modernization. David Mitrany (1943), a pioneer **integration** theorist, argued that transnational cooperation was required to resolve common problems. His core concept was **functionalism**, meaning the likelihood that cooperation in one sector would lead governments to extend the range of collaboration across other sectors, known as *spillover.* As states become more embedded in an integration process, the benefits of cooperation and the costs of withdrawing from cooperative ventures increase. The history of the European Union supports Mitrany's assertion.

Academic interest in the positive benefits from transnational cooperation informed a new generation of scholars whose argument was not simply about the mutual gains from trade but that other **transnational nonstate actors** were beginning to challenge the dominance of sovereign states. Global politics, according to pluralists, was no longer an exclusive arena for states. The inability of the United States to win the Vietnam War provided the impetus to this research because that conflict seemed to challenge realism's central claims about power determining outcomes in international politics. In one of the central texts of this genre, Robert Keohane and Joseph Nye (1972) argued that the centrality of other actors,

Integration A process of ever-closer union between states in a regional or international context. The process often begins with cooperation to solve technical problems.

Functionalism An idea formulated by early proponents of European integration that suggests cooperation should begin with efforts aimed at resolving specific regional or transnational problems. It is assumed that resolution of these problems will lead to cooperation, or spillover, in other policy areas.

Transnational nonstate actor Any nonstate or nongovernmental actor from one country that has relations with any actor from another country or with an international organization.

such as interest groups, transnational corporations (e.g., Shell Oil or AIG), and nongovernmental organizations (NGOs), like Oxfam or Human Rights Watch, had to be taken into consideration. They also asserted that military power had a declining utility in international politics. The overriding image of international relations is one of a cobweb of diverse actors linked through multiple channels of interaction.

Although the phenomenon of transnationalism was an important addition to the international relations theorists' vocabulary, it remained underdeveloped as a theoretical concept. Perhaps the most important contribution of **pluralism** was its elaboration of **interdependence**. Due to the expansion of capitalism and the emergence of a global culture, pluralists recognized a growing interconnectedness in which "changes in one part of the system have direct and indirect consequences for the rest of the system" (Little 1996, 77). Absolute state autonomy, so keenly entrenched in the minds of state leaders, was being circumscribed by interdependence. Such a development brought with it enhanced potential for cooperation as well as increased levels of vulnerability.

In the course of their engagement with other neorealists, early pluralists modified their position. Neoliberals, as they came to be known, conceded that the core assumptions of neorealism were indeed correct: the anarchic international structure, the centrality of states, and a rationalist approach to social scientific inquiry. Where they differed was in the argument that anarchy does not mean durable patterns of cooperation are impossible; the creation of international regimes matters here, as they facilitate cooperation by sharing information, reinforcing reciprocity, and making defection from norms easier to punish. Moreover, neoliberals argued that actors would enter into cooperative agreements if the gains were evenly shared. Neorealists disputed this hypothesis, saying that what matters is a question not so much of mutual gains as of **relative gains**: a neorealist (or structural-realist) state needs to be sure that it has more to gain than its rivals from a particular bargain or regime.

Neoliberalism

There are two important arguments that set **neoliberalism** apart from democratic peace liberalism and the liberal idealism of the interwar period. First, academic inquiry should be guided by a commitment to a scientific approach to theory building. Whatever deeply held personal values scholars maintain, their task must be to observe regularities, formulate hypotheses as to why that relationship holds, and subject these to critical scrutiny. This separation of fact and value puts neoliberals on the positivist or social scientific research side of the methodological divide. Second, writers such as Keohane are critical of the naive assumption of nineteenth-century liberals that commerce breeds peace. A free trade system, according to Keohane, provides incentives for cooperation but does not guarantee it.

Neoliberal institutionalism (or institutional theory) shares many of the assumptions of neorealism; however, its adherents claim that neorealists focus excessively on conflict and competition and minimize the chances for cooperation

Pluralism A political theory holding that political power and influence in society do not belong just to the citizens nor only to elite groups in various sectors of society but are distributed among a wide number of groups in the society. It can also mean a recognition of ethnic, racial, and cultural diversity.

Interdependence A condition where states (or peoples) are affected by decisions taken by others. Interdependence can be symmetric (i.e., both sets of actors are affected equally), or it can be asymmetric (i.e., the impact varies between actors).

Relative gains One of the factors that realists argue constrain the willingness of states to cooperate. States are less concerned about whether everyone benefits (absolute gains) and more concerned about whether someone may benefit more than someone else.

Neoliberalism Theory shaped by the ideas of commercial, republican, sociological, and institutional liberalism. Neoliberals see the international system as anarchic but believe relations can be managed by the establishment of international regimes and institutions. Neoliberals think actors with common interests will try to maximize absolute gains.

even in an anarchic international system. Neoliberal-institutional organizations such as the Bank for International Settlements, the International Monetary Fund (IMF), and the World Bank are both the mediators and the means to achieve cooperation among actors in the system. Currently, neoliberal institutionalists are focusing their research on issues of global governance and the creation and maintenance of institutions associated with managing the processes of globalization.

For neoliberal institutionalists, the focus on mutual interests extends beyond trade and development issues. With the end of the Cold War, states were forced to address new security concerns like the threat of terrorism, the proliferation of nuclear weapons, and an increasing number of internal conflicts that threatened regional and global security. Graham Allison (2000) states that one of the consequences of the globalization of security concerns like terrorism, drug trafficking, and pandemics like HIV/AIDS is the realization that threats to any country's security cannot be addressed unilaterally. Successful responses to security threats require the creation of regional and global regimes that promote cooperation among states and the coordination of policy responses to these new security threats.

Robert Keohane (2002a) suggests that one result of the 9/11 terrorist attacks on the United States was the creation of a very broad coalition against terrorism involving a large number of states and key global and regional institutions. Neoliberals support cooperative multilateralism and are generally critical of the preemptive and unilateral use of force as is condoned in the 2002 Bush Doctrine. Most neoliberals would believe that the U.S.-led war with Iraq undermined the legitimacy and influence of global and regional security institutions that operated so successfully in the first Gulf War (1990–1991) and continue to work effectively in Afghanistan.

The neoliberal-institutional perspective is more relevant in issue areas where states have mutual interests. For example, most world leaders believe that we will all benefit from an open trade system, and many support trade rules that protect the environment. Institutions have been created to manage international behavior in both areas. The neoliberal view may have less relevance in areas in which states have no mutual interests. Thus, cooperation in military or national security areas, where someone's gain is perceived as someone else's loss (a zero-sum perspective), may be more difficult to achieve.

Pictured here are leaders of the EU and China during a summit to discuss future trade and political relations. China has become the EU's second biggest trading partner, with both parties looking to increase trade and investments between the entities, thus emphasizing interdependence and mutual gains. This is the goal of most liberal states. Was Jeremy Bentham correct when he said that capitalism may lead to peace?

Liberalism in Practice

When applying liberal ideas to international relations today, we find two clusters of responses to the problems and possibilities posed by globalization. Before outlining these responses, let

The Power of Ideas: Politics and Neoliberalism

BACKGROUND

A very good example of the hegemonic power of the United States, many Marxists would argue, is the success that it has had in getting neoliberal policies accepted as the norm throughout the world.

THE CASE

The set of policies most closely associated with the neoliberal project (in particular, reduction of state spending, currency devaluation, privatization, and the promotion of free markets) are known as the Washington Consensus. Many would argue that these are commonsense policies and that third world countries that have adopted them have merely realized that such economic policies best reflect their interests. However, Marxists would argue that an analysis of the self-interest of the hegemon and the use of coercive power provide a more convincing explanation of why such policies have been adopted.

The adoption of neoliberal policies by third world countries has had a number of implications. Spending on health and education has been reduced, they have been forced to rely more on the export of raw materials, and their markets have been saturated with manufactured goods from the industrialized world. It does not take a conspiracy theorist to suggest that these neoliberal policies are in the interests of capitalists in the developed world. There are three main areas where the adoption of neoliberal policies in the third world is in the direct interest of the developed world. First, there is the area of free trade. We need not enter into arguments about the benefits of free trade, but it is clear that it will always be in the interest of the hegemon to promote free trade; this is because, assuming it is the most efficient producer, its goods will be the cheapest anywhere in the world. It is only if countries put up barriers to trade to protect their own production that the hegemon's products will be more expensive than theirs. Second, there is the area of raw materials. If third world countries are going to compete in a free trade situation, the usual result is that they become more reliant on the export of raw materials (because their industrial products cannot compete in a free trade situation with those of the developed world). Again, this is in the interest of the hegemon, as increases in the supply of raw material exports mean that the price falls. Additionally, where third world countries have devalued their currency as part of a neoliberal package, the price of their exported raw materials goes down. Finally, when third world governments have privatized industries, investors from North America and Europe have frequently been able to snap up airlines, telecommunications companies, and oil industries at bargain prices.

If neoliberal policies appear to have such negative results for third world countries, why have they been so widely adopted? This is where the coercive element comes in. Through the 1970s, 1980s, and continuing to today, there has been a major debt crisis between the third world and the West. This debt crisis came about primarily as a result of excessive and unwise lending by Western banks. Third world countries were unable to pay off the interest on these debts, let alone the debts themselves. As a result, they turned to the major global financial institutions, such as the IMF, for assistance. Although the IMF is a part of the UN system, it is heavily controlled by Western countries, in particular the United States. For example, the United States has 22.64 percent of the votes, while Mozambique has only 0.06 percent. In total, the ten most industrialized countries have more than 50 percent of the votes.

OUTCOME

For third world countries, the price of getting assistance was that they would implement neoliberal policies. Only once these were implemented, and only on the condition that the policies were maintained, would the IMF agree to provide aid to continue with debt repayment.

Hence, Marxists would argue that a deeper analysis of the adoption of neoliberal policies is required. Such an analysis would suggest that the global acceptance of neoliberalism is very much in the interests of the developed world and has involved a large degree of coercion. That such policies seem "natural" and "commonsense" is an indication of the hegemonic power of the United States.

For Discussion

1. China's economic policies are based on state control of the economy. All capitalist activities serve the interests of the nation-state. This system, called the Beijing Consensus, is seen as a challenge to the dominance of the neoliberal Washington Consensus. Will China's economic success encourage other nation-states to take more control over their economies?

us quickly recall the definition of liberalism, the four components being *juridical equality, democracy, liberty*, and the *free market*. As we will see, these same values can be pursued by very different political strategies.

Liberalism of privilege The perspective that developed democratic states have a responsibility to spread liberal values for the benefit of all peoples of the earth.

The first response we will address is that of the **liberalism of privilege** (Richardson 1997, 18). According to this perspective, the problems of globalization need to be addressed by a combination of strong democratic states in the core of the international system, robust regimes, and open markets and institutions. For an example of the strategy in practice, we need look no further than the success of the liberal hegemony of the post-1945 era. In the aftermath of World War II, the United States took the opportunity to embed certain fundamental liberal principles into the rules and institutions of international society. Contrary to realist thinking, U.S. leaders chose to forfeit short-run gains in return for a durable settlement that benefited all the world's states.

According to U.S. writer G. John Ikenberry, a defender of the liberal order, the United States signaled the cooperative basis of its power in a number of ways. First, the United States was an example to other members of international society insofar as its political system is open and allows different voices to be heard. Second, the United States advocated a global free trade regime in accordance with the idea that free trade brings benefits to all participants. Third, the United States appeared, to its allies at least, as a reluctant hegemon that would not seek to exploit its significant power-political advantage. Fourth, the United States created and participated in a range of important international institutions that constrained the country's actions (see Chapters 2 and 8 for discussions of such institutions as the Bretton Woods system, the World Trade Organization, and NATO).

Let us accept for a moment that the neoliberal argument is basically correct: the post-1945 international order has been successful and durable because U.S. hegemony has been liberal. The logic of this position is one of institutional conservatism, meaning that to respond effectively to global economic and security problems, there is no alternative to working within the existing institutional structure. At the other end of the spectrum, critics see the current liberal international order as highly unresponsive to the needs of weaker states and peoples. According to the International Monetary Fund, income inequality has increased in both advanced and developing economies in recent decades. The UN Development Programme's 2015 Human Development Report states that nearly 830 million people around the world are classified as working poor and live on less than $2.00 a day;

Liberal internationalists believe in diplomacy as a way to prevent war and promote peaceful cooperation. Representatives from the negotiating countries meet in Vienna, Austria, to discuss the parameters of the Iranian nuclear program including the permission of International Atomic Energy Agency inspectors at military sites in exchange for the lifting of sanctions. Nuclear arms control depends on global cooperation and an effective treaty regime.

according to the Multidimensional Poverty Index (MPI), the ten poorest countries are in sub-Saharan Africa.

Given that liberalism has produced such unequal gains for the West and the rest, it is not surprising that the United States as a hegemonic power has become obsessed with the question of preserving and extending its control of institutions, markets, and resources, just as realists predicted it would. When this hegemonic liberal order comes under challenge, as it did on 9/11, the response is uncompromising. It is notable, in this respect, that President George W. Bush mobilized the language of liberalism against Al-Qaeda, the Taliban, and Iraq. He referred to the 2003 war against Iraq as "freedom's war," and defenders of Operation Iraqi Freedom frequently use the term "liberation."

This strategy of preserving and extending liberal institutions is open to a number of criticisms. For the sake of simplicity, we will gather these under the umbrella of **radical liberalism**, which sees liberalism as benefiting only a few states and individuals. Table 3.3 summarizes the core assumptions of realism, liberalism, and radical liberalism/utopianism. Proponents of radical liberalism object to the understanding of liberalism embodied in the neoliberal defense of contemporary international institutions. The liberal character of those institutions is assumed rather than subjected to critical scrutiny. As a result, the incoherence of the purposes underpinning these institutions is often overlooked. The kind of economic liberalization advocated by Western financial institutions, particularly in economically impoverished countries, frequently comes into conflict with the norms of democracy and human rights. Three examples illustrate this dilemma.

First, the more the West becomes involved in the organization of developing states' political and economic infrastructure, the less those states can be accountable to their domestic constituencies. The critical democratic link between the government and the people, which is central to modern liberal forms of representative democracy, is therefore broken (Hurrell and Woods 1995, 463). Second, to qualify for Western aid and loans, states are often required to meet harsh economic criteria requiring cuts in many welfare programs. The example of the poorest children in parts of Africa having to pay for primary school education (Booth and Dunne 1999, 310)—which is their right according to the Universal Declaration of Human Rights—is a stark reminder that economic liberty and

WHAT'S YOUR WORLDVIEW?

The new liberal economic order has left many countries and their people in poverty. Are there ways to create programs that give capitalism a more human face? What do you think could be done to address global poverty?

Radical liberalism The utopian side of liberalism best exemplified by the academic community called the World Order Models Project (WOMP). These scholars advocate a world in which states promote values like social justice, economic well-being, peace, and ecological balance. The scholars see the liberal order as predatory and clearly in need of transformation.

New security challenges involve protecting vulnerable populations and providing basic human needs. These Kenyan children lost their parents to HIV, and 70 percent of global HIV victims are in sub-Saharan Africa. Radical liberals would support more funding for these types of programs and less funding for neoliberal infrastructure projects—people, not buildings, should be the priority.

TABLE 3.3	Realism, Liberalism, and Radical Liberalism/Utopianism: A Review of Core Assumptions		
	Realism	**Liberalism**	**Radical Liberalism/ Utopianism**
Main Actors	States	States, nonstates, and groups	States, nonstates, groups, and individuals
Central Concern	Relative power	Welfare and security	Peace, social justice, and human security
Typical Behavior	Self-help	Cooperation	Promotion of ideas
Basis for Power	Tangible resources (military/economic)	Issue specific, both hard and soft power	Political legitimacy and value of ideas
Nature of Interstate Relations	Unregulated competition and limited alliances	Interest-based regimes, coordination and collaboration among states	Norm-based regimes
Ideal State of the World	Stability through balance of power	Equitable system managed by regional organizations/ international organizations	World community

political equality are frequently opposed. Third, the inflexible response of the IMF, World Bank, and other international financial institutions to various crises in the world economy has contributed to a backlash against liberalism. Richard Falk puts this dilemma starkly: there is, he argues, a tension between "the ethical imperatives of the global neighborhood and the dynamics of economic globalization" (1995a, 573). Radical liberals argue that the hegemonic institutional order has fallen prey to the neoliberal consensus, which minimizes the role of the public sector in providing for welfare and elevates the market as the appropriate mechanism for allocating resources, investment, and employment opportunities.

If we take the area of political economy, the power exerted by the West and its international financial institutions perpetuates structural inequality. A good example here is the issue of free trade, which the West has pushed in areas where it gains from an open policy (e.g., in manufactured goods and financial services) but resisted in areas where it stands to lose (e.g., agriculture and textiles). At a deeper level, radical liberals worry that *all* statist models of governance are undemocratic, as elites are notoriously self-serving.

A second critique that radical liberals pursue focuses on the illiberal nature of the regimes and institutions. There is a massive **democratic deficit** at the global level; policy decisions are not subject to review by citizens. Only the fifteen members of the UN Security Council can determine issues of international peace and security, and only the five permanent members (the United States, the United

Democratic deficit Leaders have created many policymaking institutions at the global, regional, and national levels with policymaking power led by individuals who are appointed and not elected. Thus, policy decisions are not subject to review by citizens.

Kingdom, France, China, and Russia) can exercise veto power. Thus, it is hypothetically possible for up to two hundred states in the world to believe that military action ought to be taken, but such an action would contravene the UN Charter if one of the permanent members cast a veto.

In place of the Westphalian and UN models, David Held outlines a **cosmopolitan democracy**. This requires, in the first instance, the creation of regional parliaments and the extension of the authority of such regional bodies (e.g., the European Union) that already exist. Second, human rights conventions must be entrenched in national parliaments and monitored by a new International Court of Human Rights. Third, reform of the United Nations, or its replacement, with a genuinely democratic and accountable global parliament "is necessary." Held espouses that if democracy is to thrive, it must penetrate the institutions and regimes that manage global politics.

Radical liberals place great importance on the civilizing capacity of global society. While the rule of law and the democratization of international institutions are core components of the liberal project, it is also vital that citizens' networks are broadened and deepened to monitor and cajole these institutions. These groups form a linkage among individuals, states, and global institutions. It is easy to portray radical-liberal thinking as utopian, but we should not forget the many achievements of global civil society so far. The evolution of international humanitarian law and the extent to which these laws find compliance are largely due to the millions of individuals who are active supporters of human rights groups like Amnesty International and Human Rights Watch (Falk 1995b, 164). Similarly, global protest movements have been responsible for the heightened sensitivity to environmental degradation everywhere.

Cosmopolitan democracy A condition in which international organizations, transnational corporations, and global markets are accountable to the peoples of the world.

Critical Theories

As we have seen, realism and liberalism offer valuable insights into the interplay of states; however, they have certain shortcomings. With the exception of Marxism, the critical theories or perspectives we examine in this latter part of the chapter have recently become part of the international relations discourse, in part as a response to these shortcomings but also in reaction to a different set of stimuli. Indeed, Marxism, feminist theory, and constructivism can each provide important tools to understand trends and events in global politics and globalization in ways that realism and liberalism cannot. Many might ask, why spend time on Marxism since the Soviet Union collapsed? Most socialists or Marxists have two very convincing answers. First, the Soviet Union never provided a model of the ideal socialist or Marxist society. Michael Harrington (1989, 79), an American socialist, describes Soviet socialism as follows:

> [Soviet] Socialism was a bureaucratically controlled and planned economy that carried out the function of primitive accumulation and thus achieved rapid modernization. The state owned the means of production, which made some people

think it must be socialist; but the party and the bureaucracy owned the state by virtue of a dictatorial monopoly of political power.

Harrington called the Soviet system a moral disaster for socialism. It was a totalitarian state and not an ideal expression of Marxism.

A second reason is globalization. Karl Marx and Friedrich Engels, the founders of Marxist theory (1848), described how increasing interdependence will inevitably create a single global market and a global consumer culture.

The need for a constantly expanding market for its products chases the bourgeoisie over the surface of the globe. In place of wants, satisfied by the production of country, we find new wants, requiring for their satisfaction the products of distant lands and climes.

A global economy shifts the key elements of Marxist thought from the domestic level to the global level.

We have emphasized the point that theory matters because we all embrace theories that help us understand the world and explain how and why things happen. After reading and discussing this chapter, you will have a better understanding of critical voices—those that question the assumptions of the dominant theories and paradigms (see Table 3.4 for an overview of these alternative theories). Marxists ask us to look at the world from the perspective of workers and not the owners; feminists ask us to look at the lives of women; and constructivists ask us to consider how ideas, images, and values shape our worldview and our construction of reality.

TABLE 3.4 **Alternative International Relations Theories at the Beginning of the Twenty-First Century**

	Central Idea	View of International System	Key Authors
Marxism	Global capitalist system eliminates harmony of interests of workers.	Core-periphery relationship. Unfair terms of international trade. Underdevelopment in periphery.	Prebisch, Frank, Cardoso, O'Donnell
Constructivism	Seeks to understand change. Ideas are social creations. Relationships result from historical processes. Ideas can evolve, replace older ways of thinking.	A process. Result of hegemonic ideas. Can change as a result of evolving ideas.	Onuf, Walker, Wendt
Liberal Feminism	Change women's subordinate position in existing political systems.	Improve women's representation in INGOs. End gender bias in INGOs and NGOs.	Caprioli, Enloe, Elshtain, Tickner, Tobias

The Essential Marxism

We turn our attention first to **Marxism**, the oldest of the challengers. Marxist ideas inspired many political movements in the developing world in the period of decolonization through the 1970s and 1980s. Although the Communist Party state of the Soviet Union is gone and never reached the goal of a pure expression of Marxism, and the authoritarian Chinese Communist Party permits a form of capitalism in China, the central ideas of Marxism can still help us understand the inequality that characterizes the globalized economy.

A Marxist interpretation of world politics has been influential since the mid-1800s. In his inaugural address to the Working Men's International Association in London in 1864, Karl Marx told his audience that history had "taught the working classes the duty to master [for] themselves the mysteries of international politics." However, despite the fact that Marx himself wrote copiously about international affairs, most of this writing was journalistic in character. He did not incorporate the international dimension into his theoretical description of capitalism. This omission should perhaps not surprise us. The sheer scale of the theoretical enterprise in which he was engaged, as well as the nature of his own methodology, inevitably meant that Marx's work would remain contingent and unfinished.

Marx was an enormously prolific writer whose ideas developed and changed over time. The *Collected Works* produced by Progress Publishers in Moscow, for instance, contains fifty volumes of very thick books. Hence, it is not surprising that his legacy has been open to numerous interpretations. In addition, real-world developments have led to the revision of his ideas in light of experience. A variety of schools of thought have emerged that claim Marx as a direct inspiration or whose work can be linked to Marx's legacy.

Four strands of contemporary Marxist thought have made major contributions to thinking about global politics. Before we discuss what is distinctive about these approaches, it is important that we examine their essential commonalities.

First, all the theorists discussed in this section share with Marx the view that the social, political, and economic world should be analyzed as a totality. The academic division of the social world into different areas of inquiry—history, philosophy, economics, political science, sociology, international relations, and so on—is both arbitrary and unhelpful. None can be understood without knowledge of the others: the social world has to be studied as a whole. Regardless of the scale and complexity of the social world, for Marxist theorists, the disciplinary boundaries that characterize the contemporary social sciences need to be transcended if we are to generate a proper understanding of the dynamics of global politics.

Another key element of Marxist thought, which underlines this concern with interconnection and context, is the materialist conception of history. The central contention here is that economic development is effectively the motor of history. The central dynamic that Marx identifies is tension between the means of production (e.g., labor, tools, technology) and relations of production (technical and

Marxism A theory critical of the status quo, or dominant capitalist paradigm. It is a critique of the capitalist political economy from the view of the revolutionary proletariat, or workers. Marxists' ideal is a stateless and classless society.

Economic base For Marxists, the substructure of the society is the relationship between owners and workers. Capitalists own the means of production and control technology and resources. The workers are employed by the capitalists, and they are alienated, exploited, and estranged from their work and their society.

Superstructure The government or political structure that is controlled by those who own the means of production.

Class A social group that in Marxism is identified by its relationship with the means of production and the distribution of societal resources. Thus, we have the bourgeoisie, or the owners or upper classes, and the proletariat, or the workers.

institutional relationships) that together form the **economic base** of a given society. As the means of production develop—for example, through technological advancement—previous relations of production become outmoded, limiting effective utilization of the new productive capacity. This limitation in turn leads to a process of social change that transforms relations of production to better accommodate the new configuration of means. For example, computer-driven machines for manufacturing might replace auto-factory workers, or the workers' jobs might be moved to a country where labor and production costs are lower. Workers are still needed, but fewer, and most of those must be retrained to repair computers or develop software and no longer make car doors. The recent crisis in the U.S. auto industry is still having profound negative effects in industrial cities like Detroit and Cleveland, forever changing the political, economic, and social landscape. In other words, developments in the economic base act as a catalyst for the broader transformation of society as a whole. This is because, as Marx argues in the preface to his *Contribution to the Critique of Political Economy*, "the mode of production of material life conditions the social, political and intellectual life process in general." Thus, the legal, political, and cultural institutions and practices of a given society reflect and reinforce—in a more or less mediated form—the pattern of power and control in the economy. It follows logically, therefore, that change in the economic base ultimately leads to change in the "legal and political **superstructure.**"

Class plays a key role in Marxist analysis. Marx defines class as "social relations between the producers, and the conditions under which they exchange their activities and share in the total act of production" (Marx 1867). For most Americans, class is simply a way of designating an individual's position within the income distribution of a society. Upper, middle, and lower income classes represent income groups in our society. For Marxists, your income does not determine your class. Instead, your class is defined by your position within the hierarchy of production. In contrast to liberals, who believe that there is an essential harmony of interest between various social groups, Marxists hold that society is systemically prone to class conflict. *The Communist Manifesto*, which Marx coauthored with Friedrich Engels, argues that "the history of all hitherto existing societies is the history of class struggle" (Marx and Engels 1848). In capitalist society, says Marx, the main axis of conflict is between the bourgeoisie (the capitalists) and the proletariat (the workers).

The founders of "scientific socialism," Karl Marx and Friedrich Engels, together in a park that was once in communist-controlled East Berlin. Can you think of ways in which socialist ideas still influence politics in your country?

The Marxist perspective on globalization seeks to describe the ways inequality affects the lives of millions of people. Marx and his coauthor Engels predicted that capitalism would spread around the world and then, and only then, would the proletariat become aware of their exploitation as workers, alienation from their government, and estrangement from society ruled by the bourgeoisie. In this situation, globalization might be the catalyst for awareness and eventual transformation.

Despite his commitment to rigorous scholarship, Marx did not think it either possible or desirable for the analyst to remain a detached or neutral observer of this great clash between capital and labor. He argued that "philosophers have only interpreted the world in various ways; the point, however, is to change it" (Marx 1888). Marx was committed to the cause of emancipation. He was not interested in developing an understanding of the dynamics of capitalist society simply for the sake of it. Rather, he expected such an understanding to make it easier to overthrow the prevailing order and replace it with a communist society—a society in which wage labor and private property are abolished and social relations transformed.

It is important to emphasize that the essential elements of Marxist thought are also contested. There is disagreement as to how these ideas and concepts should be interpreted and how they should be put into operation. Analysts also differ over which elements of Marxist thought are most relevant, which have been proven to be mistaken, and which should now be considered as outmoded or in need of radical overhaul. Moreover, there are substantial differences between them in terms of their attitudes toward the legacy of Marx's ideas. The work of the more contemporary Marxists, for example, draws far more directly on Marx's original ideas than does the work of the critical theorists. Indeed, the critical theorists would probably be more comfortable being viewed as post-Marxists than as straightforward Marxists. But even for them, as the very term *post-Marxism* suggests, the ideas of Marx remain a basic point of departure.

International relations theorist Robert W. Cox provides a transition from contemporary Marxism to more recent theoretical developments. In his 1981 article "Social Forces, States, and World Orders: Beyond International Relations Theory," Cox analyzes the state of international relations theory as a whole and one of its major subfields, international political economy. This article became an important wedge in the process of toppling realism's dominance in international relations. The sentence that has become one of the most often-quoted lines in all of contemporary international relations theory reads as follows: "Theory is always *for* some one, and *for* some purpose" (1981, 128). This quote expresses a worldview that follows logically from a broad Marxist position that has been explored in this section. If ideas and values are (ultimately) a reflection of a particular set of social relations and are transformed as those relations are themselves transformed, then this suggests that all knowledge of political relations must reflect a certain context, a certain time, a certain space. Thus, politics cannot be objective and timeless in the way some traditional realists and contemporary structural realists, for example, would like to claim.

What Makes a Theory "Alternative" or Critical?

If you grew up in the United States, you have probably internalized a combination of the liberal and realist perspectives. To keep with our simile that theories are like eyeglasses, you are in essence wearing bifocals, combining both liberal and realist visions of different worlds. You probably think that you live in a mostly peaceful and law-abiding society with a free market economic system in which anyone can become rich. This is the rough outline of the liberal model. While you have this view of the domestic situation, you most likely look at international events quite differently. Here, the realist model describes what you see: if countries are not at war, then they are constantly seeking some kind of an advantage, such as in trade negotiations, for example. Individuals and states are self-interest oriented, and international politics is a constant struggle for power and material resources.

However, for someone who grew up in the former Eastern bloc of communist countries, the view of your society could be quite different, especially if that person were a child of a member of the ruling Communist Party. For that person, Marxism, not capitalism, is the dominant political-economic model. In fact, in some ways, the theory of Marxism in the USSR was like a religion: it had an explanation for history, it described how to live properly, and it offered a utopian workers' paradise as a reward for living correctly.

A Marxist could look at life in the United States and see exploitation everywhere. Workers in factories are alienated from the products they make. Without an employee discount, for instance, an assembly line worker at a General Motors factory could never afford to own the car that went by on the conveyor belt. Schools are designed to create good future workers by teaching the benefits of arriving on time, being polite to the teacher, and submitting perfect homework. The income gap between rich and poor is wide and getting wider.

For this imagined child of the Communist Party in the USSR, life is good and not based on exploitation. There are special shops for party members, where shortages of meat are rare and you can purchase white bread, not the rough rye loaves found in other stores. You would probably also attend school with other children like yourself and have science labs with the latest equipment. When you catch the flu in the winter, you do not have to wait in long lines to see a doctor.

The Marxist perspective on international affairs would sound a bit like realism but with a socialist spin. Where realism sees constant struggles for power, the Marxist

doctrine of the USSR saw capitalist encirclement of the Soviet Union and the exploitation of the developing world. The doctrine preached class warfare on a global scale, and the USSR extended foreign aid in "fraternal cooperation" with its socialist friends.

Imagine still that you were a student born into the USSR: in your classes on foreign relations, you would learn that the "correlation of forces" was beginning to turn in the direction of the socialist world. You would also learn that your country was peace-loving and had pledged that it would never use nuclear weapons first in a war with the capitalist NATO countries.

Although this is a stylized reality we have asked you to imagine, it does prove a point: what is "alternative" depends on your perspective. An alternative perspective can also be critical of the status quo. In all likelihood, you, this hypothetical student in the USSR, would know that you had a privileged status in society. You might be uncomfortable with it because you could see the exploitation of people in the "workers' paradise": tiny apartments with a shared bathroom down the hall; food shortages; drab clothing selections; a yearlong wait to purchase a car, and then no choice of color. In the workplace, people seem like the assembly line workers in the capitalist West: bored and underpaid. A popular joke in the 1970s Soviet Union was "we pretend to work, and the state pretends to pay us."

However, for all its shortcomings, it would be *your* Marxist perspective, and you might feel good about it. Meanwhile, you would consider the liberal capitalist model perilous until perhaps 1989, when you would learn what it meant to see things from the other perspective.

For Discussion

1. We suggest in the text that the Soviet Union was an authoritarian/totalitarian state capitalist system and not truly a communist or Marxist society. Its authoritarianism made it an alternative to democracy. What examples are there, if any, of Marxist societies? Is Marxism at all relevant today?

2. Does realism help us understand Russian society better than Marxism? Why or why not? What about utopian societies?

3. What examples do we have, if any, of experiments in utopian societies? Would you say a real Marxist society was utopian?

One key implication is that there can be no simple separation between facts and values. Whether consciously or not, all theorists inevitably bring their values to bear on their analysis. Cox suggests that we need to look closely at each theory, each idea, and each analysis that claims to be objective or value-free and ask who or what it is for and what purpose it serves. He subjects realism, and in particular its contemporary variant structural realism, to an extended criticism on these grounds.

According to Cox, these theories serve the interests of those who prosper under the prevailing order—that is, the inhabitants of the developed states and, in particular, the ruling elites. Their purpose, again whether consciously or not, is to reinforce and legitimate the status quo. They do this by making the current configuration of international relations appear natural and immutable. When realists (falsely, according to Cox and many other analysts) claim to be describing the world as it is, as it has been, and as it always will be, what they are in fact doing is reinforcing the ruling hegemony in the current world order. In the same way, according to a contemporary neoliberal argument, blindly accepting globalization as a beneficial process reinforces the hegemony of the countries, corporations, and their stockholders. Cox extends his argument by contrasting **problem-solving theory** with **critical theory**. Problem-solving theory accepts the parameters of the present order while attempting to fix its problems and thus helps legitimate an unjust and deeply iniquitous system.

Third World Socialists

Following World War II, many former European colonies declared independence. To build sovereign states, they rejected prevailing economic theories of the day—especially Soviet-style socialism and Western capitalism—in favor of political-economic development strategies based on autarchy (economic self-sufficiency), which were sensitive to the history, values, experience, resources, and specific attributes of each region. They recognized that, for most developing states, the major resources are people and land, so states must intervene to replace exploitation with citizen access to economic resources and opportunities. Finally, they stressed the importance of producing for local consumption, presciently fearing that development strategies requiring rapid industrialization or reliance on export-driven industries would increase dependency levels.

Although defined by different experiences and context, Julius Nyerere, the first president of Tanzania, Kwame Nkrumah, the first prime minister and president of Ghana, Mohandas Gandhi, leader of the Indian independence movement, and Mao Zedong, former Chairman of the Chinese Communist Party, led socialist and populist revolutions against former colonial powers. Subsequently, they battled new "colonizing" economic forces that increased their countries' dependency on the North, thereby reducing their power and independence in the international system. Each of these third world socialist movements shared five critical elements:

1. Intensely nationalistic, they targeted all forms of colonialism and foreign economic domination.

Problem-solving theory Realism and liberalism are problem-solving theories that address issues and questions within the dominant paradigm or the present system. How can we fix capitalism? How can we make a society more democratic? These are problem-solving questions that assume nothing is wrong with the core elements of the system.

Critical theory Theories that are critical of the status quo and reject the idea that things can be fixed under the present system. These theories challenge core assumptions of the dominant paradigm and argue for transformation and not just reform.

2. As radical movements, they rejected exploitation and injustice and were willing to use force to initiate change.
3. Capitalism was identified with imperialism, an immoral system, wherein wealth accumulation came at the expense of others.
4. Their inspiration was the masses—city workers and rural peasants—whose needs should have been served by the political and economic systems that govern them.
5. They were socialist, meaning the state owned much of the core industries.

Feminist Theory

Feminism A political project to understand so as to end women's inequality and oppression. Feminist theories tend to be critical of the biases of the discipline. Many feminists focus their research on the areas where women are excluded from the analysis of major international issues and concerns.

Often misunderstood as an attack on men, **feminist theory** provides useful tools with which to analyze a range of political events and policy decisions. The title of this section, "Feminist Theory," is both deliberate and misleading. It is deliberate in that it focuses on the socially constructed roles that women occupy in world politics. It is misleading because this question must be understood in the context of the construction of differences between women and men and contingent understandings of masculinity and femininity. In other words, the focus could more accurately be on gender than on women because the very categories of women and men, and the concepts of masculinity and femininity, are highly contested in much feminist research. Similarly, distinctions such as liberal and socialist are slightly misleading because these categories do not exactly correspond to the diverse thinking of feminist scholars, especially in contemporary work, in which elements from each type are often integrated.

The term *gender* usually refers to the social construction of the difference between men and women. Although it is a complex concept, here is one way to think of it: biology determines your sex; a mix of social and cultural norms, as well as your own sense of identity, determines your gender. Some theories assume natural and biological (e.g., sex) differences between men and women; some do not. What all of the most interesting work in this field does, however, is analyze how gender both *affects* global politics and *is an effect of* global politics. That is, feminist theorists examine how different concepts (e.g., the state or sovereignty) are "gendered" and in turn how this gendering of concepts can have differential consequences for men and women (Steans 1998). Feminists have always been interested in how understandings of gender affect the lives of men and women (Brittan 1989; Seidler 1989; Connell 1995; Carver 1996; Zalewski and Parpart 1998). As with all theoretical traditions, there are different shades of feminism that combine with some of the more traditional theoretical ideas in global politics.

Liberal feminism A position that advocates equal rights for women but also supports a more progressive policy agenda, including social justice, peace, economic well-being, and ecological balance.

Feminist theory in international relations originally grew from work on the politics of development and peace research. By the late 1980s, a first wave of feminism, **liberal feminism**, was more forcefully posing the question of "where are the women in global politics?" The meaning of liberal in this context is decidedly *not* the same as the meaning we discussed earlier in the chapter. This definition is more in line with traditional views of liberalism that put equal and nondiscriminatory liberty at the center of the international debate.

In the context of feminism, the term *liberal* starts from the notion that the key units of society are individuals, that these individuals are biologically determined as either men or women, and that these individuals possess specific rights and are equal. One strong argument of liberal feminism is that all rights should be granted to women equally with men. Here we can see how the state is gendered insofar as rights, such as voting rights and the right to possess property, have been predicated solely on the experiences and expectations of men—and typically, a certain ethnic or racial class of men. Thus, taking women seriously made a difference to the standard view of global politics. Liberal feminists look at the ways women are excluded from power and prevented from playing a full part in political activity. They examine how women have been restricted to roles critically important for the functioning of things but not usually deemed important for theories of global politics. To give you an example of political discrepancies by gender, Table 3.5 shows the percentage of women in national parliaments by region in 2015.

To ask, "where are the women?" was at the time quite a radical political act, precisely because women were absent from the standard texts of international

TABLE 3.5 Percentage of Women in National Parliaments by Region (as of November 2015)

	Regional Averages		
	Single House or Lower House	Upper House or Senate	Both Houses Combined
Nordic countries	41.0%	—	—
Americas	27.0%	25.7%	26.8%
Europe—OSCE member countries (including Nordic countries)	25.7%	24.2%	25.4%
Europe—OSCE member countries (excluding Nordic countries)	24.2%	24.2%	24.2%
Sub-Saharan Africa	23.3%	22.0%	23.1%
Arab States	19.1%	11.9%	17.9%
Asia	19.3%	16.2%	19.0%
Pacific	13.4%	36.0%	15.9%

Source: Inter-Parliamentary Union (percentages as of December 1, 2015)
http://ipu.org/wmn-e/world.htm

Lebanese women hold posters to mark International Women's Day during a rally of thousands demanding that parliament approve a law that protects women from domestic violence. Lebanon appears very progressive on women's rights compared to other countries in the Middle East, but domestic violence remains an unspoken problem. What about other states in the Middle East? How do they protect the rights of women?

relations, and thus they appeared invisible. Writers such as Cynthia Enloe (1989, 1993, 2000) began from the premise that if we simply started to ask "where are the women?" we would be able to see their presence in and importance to global politics, as well as the ways their exclusion from global politics was presumed a "natural" consequence of their biological or natural roles. After all, it was not that women were actually absent from global politics. Indeed, they played central roles either as cheap factory labor, as prostitutes around military bases, or as hotel maids.

The point is that traditional international theory either ignored these contributions or, if it recognized them at all, designated them as less important than the actions of states*men*. Enloe demonstrated just how critically important were the activities of women—for example, as wives of diplomats and soldiers or as models of correct European behavior—to the functioning of the international economic and political systems both during the era of European colonialism and afterward. She illustrated exactly how crucial women and the conventional arrangements of "women's and men's work" were to the continued functioning of international politics.

Most specifically, Enloe documented how the concept and practice of militarization influenced the lives and choices of men and women around the world. "Militarization," she writes, "is a step-by-step process by which a person or a thing gradually comes to be controlled by the military or comes to depend for its well-being on militaristic ideas" (2000, 3; also see Elshtain 1987; Elshtain and Tobias 1990). Enloe is an example of a scholar who begins from a liberal premise—that women and men should have equal rights and responsibilities in global politics—but draws on socialist feminism to analyze the role of economic structures and on standpoint feminism to highlight the unique and particular contributions of women.

Constructivism

Constructivism An approach to international politics that concerns itself with the centrality of ideas and human consciousness. As constructivists have examined global politics, they have been broadly interested in how the structure constructs the actors' identities and interests, how their interactions are organized and constrained by that structure, and how their very interaction serves to either reproduce or transform that structure.

Most writers who call themselves **constructivists** argue that our actions and words make society, and society in turn shapes our actions and words. Ideas, beliefs, and values are important because they influence the identities and interests of states and the eventual selection of policies and strategies that transform our world. As part of this process, we construct rules that first identify for us the key players (i.e., who has agency) in a given situation, recognizing that no one actor in the international system is an agent in all policy situations; then those rules

Jane Addams and the Women's International League for Peace and Freedom

The Women's Peace Party (WPP), led by activist Jane Addams (1860–1935), was one of the first groups to protest against World War I. On January 10, 1915, more than 3,000 people met in Washington, D.C., and endorsed a platform that inspired President Wilson's Fourteen Points for peace; their planks included the following (Addams and Joslin 1922/2002, 6–7):

1. Convene a meeting of neutral nations to promote peace.
2. Limit arms production and nationalize the arms industries.
3. Oppose militarism in the United States.
4. Promote peace through education.
5. Insist on democratic control over foreign policy.
6. Extend suffrage to women, thereby humanizing governments.
7. Replace the "balance of power system" with a "concert of nations" system.
8. Develop a global governance system based on the rule of law, not coercion.
9. Deploy non-force options to control rivals.
10. Work to eliminate the causes of war, like poverty.
11. Appoint a commission of experts to promote international peace.

Addams and her colleagues strongly believed that, if an international organization had been in place when dialogue among European powers failed, it could have mediated the dispute before it exploded into a major war.

The WPP became the American section of the pacifist Women's International League for Peace and Freedom (WILPF), which was established in the Netherlands in spring 1915 as a federation of women organized in twenty-one countries. Participants argued that the choice "between violence and passive acceptance of unjust conditions" was a false one. As true Kantians, they believed that "courage, determination, moral power, generous indignation, active good-will, and education can be used to secure goals rather than violence" (Addams and Joslin 1922/2002, 145–146). Delegates of WILPF visited fourteen countries, both belligerent and neutral, and urged leaders to end the war and to address the causes of violence in the international system. Repeatedly, they confronted the dominance of realist thinking:

We heard the same opinion expressed by these men of the governments responsible for the promotion of the war; each one said that his country would be ready to stop the war immediately if some honorable method of securing peace were provided; each

one disclaimed responsibility for the continuance of war; each one predicted European bankruptcy if the war were prolonged, and each one grew pale and distressed as he spoke of the loss of his gallant young countrymen . . . (Addams and Joslin 1922/2002, 11).

Considered by many to be the "most dangerous woman in America" for her opposition to the U.S. entry into World War I and her challenges of the world's leaders and their vested interests, Addams was awarded the Nobel Peace Prize in 1935 for her efforts aimed at ending the war and providing relief for the victims of war.

For Discussion
1. What organizations are promoting both a pacifist and feminist agenda in today's global politics debates?
2. How important were pacifist groups in the period between World War I and World War II?
3. Women like Jane Addams played an important role in both American and international politics. Why do students of international relations never hear about her?
4. Why does the study of global politics often neglect the contributions of individual people? How do their contributions matter?

instruct, direct, and commit actors to take certain actions. For example, realist rules during the Cold War dictated that all states were subservient to and would follow the lead of the United States or Soviet Union. However, actual practice does not always comply with the rules: frequently, states found areas where these superpowers had little interest—such as development or peacekeeping—and established a niche to serve their interests. The George W. Bush administration tried to assert a similar pattern of hegemonic rules after the attacks of September 11, 2001, with phrases like "coalition of the willing" and "you are either with us or you are with the terrorists."

Over time, rules and practices can form a stable pattern that serves the interests of key agents. These patterns become "institutions." The Cold War was a twentieth-century institution, and the global economy is a good example of a twenty-first-century institution. Its rules and practices are based on neoliberal free market capitalism that best serves the interests of corporations, global economic institutions, and the wealthy states. The wealthy states' power in the system is based on both material factors (e.g., control of resources) and discursive power (based on knowledge and the control of language and ideas within a society).

A leading constructivist, Alexander Wendt, seeks to understand "how global politics is socially constructed" (1995, 71). Wendt claimed that "anarchy is what states make of it" (1992, 391), arguing that anarchy in the international system does not have to result in competition, security dilemmas, arms races, or conflict. States have plenty of options; they are only limited by rules, practices, and institutions that they themselves have created. How a country reacts to anarchy reflects its particular understanding of that condition.

Constructivists argue that the international system is defined by socially constructed realities, and therefore, to understand the system, one must focus on shared rules, practices, meanings, identities, and norms. These factors define the interests, identities, preferences, and actions of each state in the system. By emphasizing the social construction of reality, we also are questioning what is frequently taken for granted. This raises several issues. One is a concern with the origins of social constructs that now appear to us as natural and are part of our social vocabulary. After all, the notion of sovereignty did not always exist; it was a product of historical forces and human interactions, which generated new distinctions regarding where political authority resided. Although individuals have been forced to flee their homes throughout the course of human history, the political and legal category of refugees is only a century old. To understand the origins of these concepts requires attention to the interplay between existing ideas and institutions, the political calculations by leaders who had ulterior motives, and morally minded actors who were attempting to improve humanity.

Also of concern to constructivists are alternative pathways. Although world history can be seen as patterned and somewhat predictable, there are contingencies— historical accidents and human intervention can force history to change course. The events of 9/11 and the response by the Bush administration arguably transformed the direction of global politics. Would the world be different today if Al Gore had been elected president instead? This interest in possible and counterfactual worlds works against historical determinism. Wendt's (1992) claim that "anarchy is what states make of it" calls attention to how different beliefs and practices will generate divergent patterns and organization of global politics. A world of nonviolent activists like Mahatma Gandhi would be very different from a world of violent extremists like Osama bin Laden.

Constructivists also examine how actors make their activities meaningful. Following Max Weber's insight that "we are cultural beings with the capacity and the will to take a deliberate attitude toward the world and to lend it *significance*" (1949, 81), constructivists attempt to recover the meanings that actors give to their practices and to the objects they create. Constructivists argue that culture, rather than private belief, informs the meanings people give to their action. Sometimes, constructivists have presumed that such meanings derive from a hardened culture. However, because culture is fractured and society comprises different interpretations of what is meaningful activity, scholars must consider these cultural fault lines. To pinpoint or fix any precise meaning is largely a political and temporary accomplishment; it is not to discover some transcendent truth.

Some of the most important debates in global politics are about how to define particular activities. Development, human rights, security, humanitarian intervention, sovereignty—topics that we discuss in later chapters—are important orienting concepts that can have any number of meanings. States and nonstate actors have rival interpretations of the meanings of these concepts and will fight to try to have their preferred meaning collectively accepted.

The fact that these meanings are fixed through politics, and that once these meanings are fixed they have consequences for the ability of people to determine their fates, suggests an alternative way of thinking about power. Most international relations theorists treat power as the ability of one state to compel another state to do what it otherwise would not and tend to focus on the material technologies, such as military firepower and economic statecraft, that have this persuasive effect. Constructivists have offered two important additions to this view of power. The forces of power go beyond **material**: they also can be **ideational** or discursive. Ideational power is more than control over meaning; it is also the acceptance of ideas or a way of life. The notion that *your* way of thinking is the norm is but one example of ideational power.

Consider the issue of **legitimacy**. States, including great powers, crave legitimacy—the belief that they are acting according to and pursuing the values of the broader international community. There is a direct relationship

Material Things we can see, measure, consume, and use, such as military forces, oil, and currency.

Ideational/ideal interest The psychological, moral, and ethical goals of a state as it sets foreign and domestic policy.

Legitimacy An authority that is respected and recognized by those it rules and by other rulers or leaders of other states. The source of legitimacy can be laws or a constitution and the support of the society.

Bernard Kouchner, former French Foreign Minister and one of the founders of Doctors Without Borders, meets with representatives seeking peace and stability in Lebanon. Kouchner is a medical doctor and someone who believes in universal rights and human security. Kouchner was also a Kantian utopian providing cosmopolitan rights for many.

between state legitimacy and the costs associated with a course of action: the greater the legitimacy, the easier time state leaders will have convincing others to cooperate with their policies. The lesser the legitimacy, the more costly the action. This means that even great powers will frequently feel the need to alter their policies to be viewed as legitimate—or bear the consequences. Further evidence of the constraining power of legitimacy is offered by the tactic of "naming and shaming" by human rights activists. For example, human rights advocates led by Mia Farrow used the threat of a boycott of the 2008 Olympics to persuade China to stop jailing dissidents and persecuting religious and ethnic minorities. China did allow for some changes, but because of its economic and political power, it was able to ignore calls for major reforms. If states did not care about their legitimacy—about their reputation and the perception that they were acting in a manner consistent with prevailing international standards—then such a tactic would have little visible impact.

Conclusion

In this chapter, we learned that for realists, global politics is an endless struggle for dominance and power. Power can be control over something tangible, like resources and territory, or it can be a struggle for something intangible, like prestige. However, because of its pessimistic opinion about human nature, realist doctrine tends to see enemies or competitors everywhere and assumes that all states are constantly on the verge of war. Although it shares some of realism's ideas about international systemic anarchy, liberalism offers a less violent explanation for global politics. Many proponents of the liberal perspective believe that long-term international cooperation is possible and will lead to human material and spiritual progress. Both realism and liberalism are valuable theories because they can help us understand some of the various interactions, events, and behaviors of global politics.

However, in recent history, the dominance of the theories of realism and liberalism have been challenged within mainstream scholarly thinking, which has led to growing intellectual appeal of a range of new approaches developed to understand world politics in ways that realism and liberalism cannot. The theories that we call "critical" suggest other ways of interpreting global events.

Although proponents of the critical theories presented in this chapter seek to challenge the conventionally dominant theories of international relations, their work does more than that. In addition to offering new critical ways to view the field, these critical theories, if combined with aspects of realism and liberalism, give us a richer understanding of international processes. We can see, for example, that war might not result only from countries' struggle for material power but also from the power of ideas or constructed notions of a proper masculine role in society. A student of international relations who aims to become a critical thinker must consider all theoretical perspectives in attempting to understand our world.

As you continue reading, think of the various theories as eyeglasses to help you see the central problem of each issue. You should be open to multiple interpretations of events and remember that no one theory can explain everything because, by accepting a single theory as your basis for understanding and explaining global politics, you are excluding other perspectives that might also be valid.

CONTRIBUTORS TO CHAPTER 3: *Tim Dunne, Brian C. Schmidt, Stephen Hobden, Richard Wyn Jones, Steve Smith, Steven L. Lamy, and John Masker.*

KEY TERMS

Anarchic system, p. 77
Anarchy, p. 86
Civil society, p. 75
Class, p. 100
Classical realism, p. 78
Collective security, p. 89
Comparative advantage, p. 78
Constructivism, p. 106
Cosmopolitan democracy, p. 97
Critical theory, p. 103
Defensive realism, p. 81
Democratic deficit, p. 96

Democratic peace thesis, p. 87
Economic base, p. 100
Empire, p. 89
Enlightenment, p. 87
Ethic of responsibility, p. 76
Ethics, p. 76
Feminism, p. 104
Free trade, p. 88
Functionalism, p. 90
Ideational/ideal interest, p. 109
Imperialism, p. 86
Integration, p. 90
Interdependence, p. 91

Legitimacy, p. 109
Liberal feminism, p. 104
Liberal internationalism, p. 85
Liberalism, p. 83
Liberalism of privilege, p. 94
Marxism, p. 99
Material, p. 109
Multilateralism, p. 84
Neoclassical realism, p. 82
Neoliberalism, p. 91
Offensive realism, p. 81
Pluralism, p. 91
Power, p. 74

Problem-solving theory, p. 103
Protectionist, p. 78
Radical liberalism, p. 95
Realism, p. 74
Relative gains, p. 91
Security dilemma, p. 77
Self-help, p. 77
Sovereignty, p. 75
Structural realism (neorealism), p. 80
Superstructure, p. 100
Theory, p. 73
Transnational nonstate actor, p. 90

REVIEW QUESTIONS

1. Is realism anything more than the ideology of powerful, satisfied states?
2. How would a realist explain the origins of the war on terrorism?
3. How might realists explain the impact globalization has on world politics?
4. Should liberal states promote their values abroad? Is force a legitimate instrument in securing this goal?
5. Whose strategy of dealing with globalization do you find more convincing: those who believe that states and institutions should maintain the current order or those who believe in reform driven by international or regional organizations or global civil society?
6. Why have critical theoretical approaches become more popular in recent years?
7. How would you explain the continuing vitality of Marxist thought in a post–Cold War world?
8. Feminists define gender as a social construction. What does this mean? What kinds of questions does international relations feminism try to answer using gender as a category of analysis?

9. Women's participation at the highest levels of international and national policymaking has been extremely limited. Do you think this is important for understanding global politics?

10. What is the core concept of constructivism?

11. What do you think are the core issues for the study of global change, and how does constructivism help you

address those issues? Alternatively, how does a constructivist framework help you identify new issues that you had not previously considered?

12. Which of the three critical approaches discussed in this chapter do you think offers the best account of global politics? Why?

➤ For more information, quizzes, case studies, and other study tools, please visit us at **www.oup.com/us/lamy.**

The Melian Dialogue: Realism and the Preparation for War

BACKGROUND

Thucydides, the former Athenian general and historian, wrote that the history of the Peloponnesian War was "not an essay which is to win applause of the moment, but a possession of all time." Most realists find references to all of their core beliefs in this important document. The Melians were citizens of the Isle of Melos, which was a colony of Sparta. The Melians would not submit to the Athenians as many of the other islands had. Athens was a dominant sea power, and Sparta was more of a land power. At first, Melos tried neutrality, but Athens attacked and plundered the territory and then sent envoys to negotiate. A short excerpt from the dialogue appears below (Thucydides 1954/1972, 401–407). Note that the symbol [. . .] indicates one or more line breaks from the original text.

THE DIALOGUE

ATHENIANS: Then we on our side will use no fine phrases saying, for example, that we have a right to our empire because we defeated the Persians. [. . .] You know as well as we do that, when these matters are discussed by practical people, the standard of justice depends on the equality of power to compel and that in fact the strong do what they have the power to do and the weak accept what they have to accept.

MELIANS: . . . You should not destroy a principle that is to the general good of all men—namely, that in the case of all who fall into danger there should be such a thing as fair play and just dealing. . . .

ATHENIANS: This is no fair fight, with honor on one side and shame on the other. It is rather a question of saving your lives and not resisting those who are far too strong for you.

MELIANS: It is difficult . . . for us to oppose your power and fortune. . . . Nevertheless we trust that the gods will give us fortune as good as yours. . . .

ATHENIANS: Our opinion of the gods and our knowledge of men lead us to conclude that it is a general and necessary law of nature to rule whatever one can. This is not a law that we made ourselves, nor were we the first to act upon it when it was made. We found it already in existence, and we shall leave it to exist forever among those who come after us. We are merely acting in accordance with it, and we know that you or anybody else with the same power as ours would be acting in precisely the same way. [. . .] You seem to forget that if one follows one's self-interest one wants to be safe, whereas the path of justice and honor involves one in danger. [. . .] This is the safe rule—to stand up to one's equals, to behave with deference to one's superiors, and to treat one's inferiors with moderation.

MELIANS: Our decision, Athenians, is just the same as it was at first. We are not prepared to give up in a short moment the liberty which our city has enjoyed from its foundation for 700 years.

ATHENIANS: . . . You seem to us . . . to see uncertainties as realities, simply because you would like them to be so.

For Discussion

1. As you think of all the assumptions of realism discussed in this chapter, how many of these do you see articulated in this brief dialogue?

2. Later in this dialogue, the Athenians tell the Melians "the strong do what they will and the weak do what they must." Do you think this phrase is still relevant today?

3. Melos was an ally of the great military power, Sparta. What should Sparta do once it finds out what Athens has done? What theory informed your strategy?

4

Making Foreign Policy

Japanese Prime Minister Shinzō Abe at a meeting with leaders from eleven Pacific island states in New York on September 28, 2015. Abe spoke of Japan's further interest in contributing to countermeasures for climate change and increased efforts for disaster prevention in the Pacific region. Should this become a global effort to save these states?

Statecraft is the strategy of power. Power is the capacity to direct the decisions and actions of others. Power derives from strength and will.

—CHARLES FREEMAN

However conceived in an image of the world, foreign policy is a phase of domestic politics—an inescapable phase.

—CHARLES BEARD

Middle powers like Japan see themselves as global problem-solvers and they often work with other states and international organizations to find solutions to major global problems. Middle powers often lead major global policy debates; examples include Canada and Norway as leaders in the area of human security and the establishment of the International Criminal Court. Global factors affect all states, however, and therefore play a role in shaping the foreign policy of all states. In the opening photo, Japanese Prime Minister Shinzō Abe is reaching out to the leaders of small island states that could be overwhelmed by rising ocean levels caused by climate change. Japan must also act to make certain it survives the expected changes. In December 2015, world leaders met in Paris to create and implement policies to address the dangers presented by global climate change at the UN Conference on Climate Change. The goal of the conference was to achieve a new international agreement on climate change aimed at keeping global warming below 2 degrees centigrade. It is a new foreign policy challenge that goes beyond protecting economic interests. For many states, this is an *existential* issue—their very survival depends on the Paris agreement. Climate change cannot be blamed for a specific weather event, but the melting of Arctic ice, increases in CO_2 levels, and warming of the oceans have contributed to unusual and severe weather events. Sea level is projected to rise three feet by the end of the century—and that would be the end of several sovereign states with their own culture, language, and history. Citizens in Papua New Guinea and the Solomon Islands have already been forced to flee their homes due to rising tides, and Tuvalu, Kiribati, and the Marshall Islands may vanish entirely within the next fifty years.

Climate change, a global phenomenon, is shaping the foreign policy priorities of many small developing states like the Philippines and

LEARNING OBJECTIVES

After reading and discussing this chapter, you should be able to:

Describe differences among state, country, government, nation, and nation-state.

Explain three kinds of foreign policy tools.

Define the terms *soft power* and *hard power* and cite examples of each.

Explain causes of foreign policy behavior at each level of analysis.

Describe the four phases of the foreign policy–making process.

Explain how size (e.g., in terms of resources, geography) affects foreign policy behavior.

Discuss the concept of foreign policy tradition as it applies to U.S. foreign policy.

Vietnam as well as Asian middle powers like Japan and South Korea, and even European middle powers like Sweden, Norway, and Denmark. In 2007, the Pacific Small Island Developing States was established as an informal group of eleven island countries. They list their first challenge as climate change and they use the forums of the United Nations to promote their national and regional interests. Ambassador Marlene Moses of Nauru suggested that these eleven states share vulnerabilities such as their size and remoteness, and that their "low-lying nature exposes them to adverse effects of climate change," which has a major impact on national security. Since 2009, the UN General Assembly has recognized the link between climate change and global security. Recently in his encyclical, *Laudato Si: On Care for Our Common Home*, Pope Francis made a convincing argument that climate change is linked to poverty and social justice. To Pope Francis and many others, this is the critical issue of today and the future. Most states put military and economic security over environmental policies that might address the causes of climate change. The small states of the Pacific and Japan, the European members of the Arctic Council, and the participants of the 2013 African Climate Conference are working to convince the rest of the world that global consumerism is altering Earth's climate and threatening human survival, especially in vulnerable states.

As we will see in this chapter, there may be both concrete and abstract limits to what one person can accomplish in foreign policy. We will discuss the methods that political leaders around the world use in pursuit of their foreign policy goals, including promoting and securing what they see as the national interests of their countries. All countries in the post–Cold War world—rich and poor, large and small, democratic and authoritarian—operate within the same set of limits and possibilities in the domestic and international arenas.

Introduction

Each of the theories we examined in Chapter 3 describes the behavior of an actor called the state. As you will recall from Chapter 1, there is a lot of disagreement in international relations theory about what we mean by "the state." But for this chapter, we need to begin by accepting that the state *exists* and that it is the most important actor in the contemporary globalized international system so that we can better understand the relationship among nations and states, nationalism and national interests, and globalization and global politics. (As a review, we define *state* as a legal territorial entity, *nation* as a community of people who share a common sense of identity, and *nation-state* as a political community in which the state claims legitimacy on the grounds that it represents the nation.) Only by accepting that the state exists will we be able to discuss the process by which the system of states interacts. We call this process **foreign policy**.

Foreign policy The articulation of national interests and the means chosen to secure those interests, both material and ideational, in the international arena.

We begin this chapter with a definition of foreign policy and explore the questions of who makes foreign policy and what we expect from it. We then present a brief overview of levels of analysis and the study of foreign policy behavior. Here we show you how to explain *why* states make certain choices over others. In the next section of the chapter, we offer an analytic framework of the foreign policy process, providing an overview of how most states make foreign policy. We go on to explore **statecraft**, the methods and tools that governmental leaders use to secure and promote their national interests. We also consider the growing importance of *soft power* in the post–Cold War era, which is defined more by globalization and global challenges. We will see how, in global politics, foreign policy actors often pursue different goals simultaneously because foreign policy connects domestic politics and international relations. For example, a leader might advocate human rights policy to satisfy domestic interest groups but maintain trade relations with an authoritarian state to satisfy a need for natural resources. In the final section of the chapter, we look at foreign policy styles and traditions across great, middle, and small states around the world.

After reading and discussing this chapter, you will have a sense of how most states make foreign policy and the factors that shape it—how citizens and their leaders articulate, promote, and eventually secure their national interests. You will have a deeper understanding of levels of analysis, categories of analytic tools that students and scholars in our field use to explain the foreign policy of all states. You will also be introduced to some of the strategies, tools, and approaches that nation-states use to secure their interests and promote their ideas and values in our global system.

Statecraft The methods and tools that national leaders use to achieve the national interests of a state.

What Is Foreign Policy?

Foreign policy is the articulation of **national interests** (the goals of a nation-state) and the means chosen to secure those interests, both material and ideational, in the international arena. **Material interests** may be trade agreements, energy resources, and even control over strategic territory. **Ideational interests** include the promotion of values, norms, and policy ideas that enhance the security and prosperity of a nation-state. Individuals (especially political leaders or elites), interest groups, geographic position, traditions, norms, and values all shape the national interests of any state. International events, global factors such as the Internet and climate change, and the actions of both friends and enemies can also influence a country's national interests.

National interest The material and ideational goals of a nation-state.

Material interest The physical goals of state officials as they set foreign and domestic policy.

Ideational/ideal interest The psychological, moral, and ethical goals of a state as it sets foreign and domestic policy.

States, Nationalism, and National Interests

Since foreign policy aims to secure a country's national interests and promote its values, it is critically important to understand the relationship among states, nationalism, and national interests. To do so, we must keep in mind the following points:

1. From about the mid-seventeenth century, an order of sovereign, territorial states known as the Westphalian system (discussed in Chapter 2) developed in Europe.

2. The rise of nationalism from the late eighteenth century rationalized this state order, later extending beyond Europe until the whole world was organized as a series of nation-states. International relations were, and to many still are, primarily relations among nation-states.
3. Globalization may undermine this political order by eroding sovereign territorial power and by creating competing identities and multiple loyalties.

With these points in mind, we will first outline key concepts and debates concerning nationalism and nation-states, which will inform our discussion of foreign policy.

Nationalism is the idea that the world is divided into nations, and these nations provide the overriding focus of political identity and loyalty that in turn demands **national self-determination**. Nationalism can be considered as ideology, as politics, and as sentiments. Definitions of nationalism usually frame it as ideology, a political worldview. **Civic nationalism** is defined by a common citizenship regardless of ethnicity, race, religion, gender, or language. All citizens are united in their loyalty toward and identity with a nation-state. They also embrace a set of political practices, traditions, and values that we call a political culture. Civic nationalism and **ethnonationalism** differ in the fact that civic nationalism maintains loyalty to the state and lacks a racial or ethnic element, whereas ethnonationalism is defined by loyalty toward a specific ethnic community such as a language or religious community. Ethnic nationalists generally seek to create their own sovereign nation-state separate from the state in which they reside.

However, we might ignore nationalist ideology unless it becomes significant. This can happen if nationalism shapes people's sense of identity: nationalism as sentiments. It can also happen if nationalism is taken up by movements able to form nation-states: nationalism as politics empowered via self-determination. Nationalism is an important element of any country's foreign policy and the formation of national interests.

As defined by Goldstein and Keohane (1993), ideas as beliefs held by individuals matter (1) when they provide road maps for decision makers who are formulating and implementing policy and (2) when they become embedded in institutions that are part of the foreign policy process. Ideas and interests help us explain the actions of all states. In the case of the United States, many Americans believe it is a nation unlike any other, and that other states should emulate its values and traditions; this is often called "American exceptionalism." Many of the original settlers to the United States, especially in the New England colonies, brought with them an idea that they had a covenant with God to create a new nation that would lead humanity to greatness. This notion of exceptionalism has often translated into a foreign policy that promotes U.S. values and traditions across the world and frames all U.S. actions as blessed by a higher power. Presidents from Washington to Obama have sought to promote U.S. democracy and free market values around the world.

Of course, this idea of exceptionalism and national purpose is not unique to the United States. In Russia, after the fall of the Soviet Union, some argued for

Nationalism The idea that the world is divided into nations that provide the overriding focus of political identity and loyalty, which in turn should be the basis for defining the population of states. Nationalism also can refer to this idea in the form of a strong sense of identity (*sentiment*) or organizations and movements seeking to realize this idea (*politics*).

National self-determination The right or desire of distinct national groups to become states and to rule themselves.

Civic nationalism The idea that an association of people can identify themselves as belonging to the nation and have equal and shared political rights and allegiance to similar political procedures.

Ethnonationalism A strain of nationalism marked by the desire of an ethnic community to have absolute authority over its own political, economic, and social affairs. Loyalty and identity shift from the state to an ethnic community that seeks to create its own state.

Do governments matter? Belgium, a state made up of three nations—Flemish, French, and German regions—was without a national government from June 2010 until December 2011. Here citizens march in Brussels in January 2011 in support of national unity, drawing attention to Belgium's record-breaking length of time without a government.

Russian exceptionalism based on a more humanitarian, postcapitalist, Russian spiritualism. Certainly, Putin's policy toward Ukraine and Syria and his efforts to create a coalition of authoritarian states suggest that he wants to restore Russia's exceptional "Great Power" status. Every state has a vision about how the world should be ordered, but only a few have the means to follow through with their beliefs about order, security, and justice. In short, this is how nationalism can shape foreign policy as a sentiment and political ideology.

Robert Cooper (2000) provides an interesting view of the evolution of the nation-state and the role of nationalism in a global age. Cooper suggests that the world can be divided into three types of states: premodern, modern, and postmodern states. In **premodern states**, individuals are more loyal to subnational, religious, and ethnic communities. People do not always identify as citizens of these very weak states, which are essentially what we call **failed (collapsed)** or **fragile states**. Afghanistan, Zimbabwe, Somalia, North Korea, and Iraq are examples (see Table 4.1). These states lack complete control over their own territory and their key governing institutions are unstable and ineffective. They are also incapable of executing meaningful agreements with other countries and do not have the capacity to provide even basic services for their citizens. These are states that have minimal or nonexistent foreign policies except for the relationships they have with states that provide them with aid and essential services.

Modern states are traditional nation-states with control over their territory and the ability to protect their citizens and provide services that allow for the

Premodern state A state within which the primary identity of citizens or subjects is to national, religious, or ethnic communities.

Failed or **collapsed state** A state that fails to provide basic services and provide for their citizens. Such a state cannot protect its boundaries, provide a system of law and order, or maintain a functioning marketplace and means of exchange.

Fragile state A state that has not yet failed but whose leaders lack the will or capacity to perform core state functions.

Modern state A political unit within which citizens identify with the state and see the state as legitimate. This state has a monopoly over the use of force and is able to provide citizens with key services.

TABLE 4.1	The Fragile State Index Top Twelve	

Rank	State	Factors Contributing to the State's Fragility
1	South Sudan	poverty, corruption, food shortages, armed conflict, human rights abuses
2	Somalia	jihadist terrorism, piracy, poverty, food insecurity
3	Central African Republic	natural disasters, inadequate infrastructure, terrorism, violent protests, governmental coups
4	Sudan	civil war, authoritarian government, terrorism, poverty, overdependence on oil
5	Congo, Democratic Republic of the	civil war, massive human rights abuses, disease, mass rape and torture
6	Chad	poverty, influx of refugees, radicalized youth population, tribal/religious conflicts
7	Yemen	jihadist terrorism, human rights abuses, external interference, poverty, disease, lack of food and clean water
8	Afghanistan	violent protests, assassinations by Taliban, external interference, drug trade
9	Syria	civil war, religious conflicts, economic issues, political instability, human flight, authoritarian rule
10	Guinea	economic issues, humans rights abuses, political instability and corruption
11	Haiti	corruption, forced evictions, poverty, crime, continued inability to cope with effects of natural disasters
12	Iraq	destroyed infrastructure, terrorism, ethnic conflict, external interference

Source: Fund for Peace, Fragile States Index 2015
http://fsi.fundforpeace.org/rankings-2015

accumulation of wealth. China, India, and Brazil are examples of modern states. Their foreign policies tend to focus on economic interests and a desire to become a major power in their region. In these states, citizens identify with the state, and nationalism tends to be very high. For example, the 2008 Summer Olympics in China gave world viewers an indication of the strength of Chinese nationalism. We all saw the same form of nationalism during the 2014 World Cup in Brazil and again during the 2016 Summer Olympics. India's acquisition of nuclear weapons, its rise as a leader of the G20 economic group, and the favorable nationalist reaction within India serve as another example of the relationship between nationalism and foreign policy in a modern state.

Postmodern states include the states that make up the liberal Western world, such as the United States and the European states. Postmodern states are linked with other states in both formal and informal arrangements at the regional and global levels. Citizens are less nationalistic and more cosmopolitan in their outlook on both domestic and foreign policy. Indeed, in most postmodern states, the

Postmodern state A political unit within which citizens are less nationalistic and more cosmopolitan in their outlook on both domestic and foreign policy.

distinction between domestic and foreign policies is virtually nonexistent. Policy-making authority is shared among a variety of actors at the local, national, regional, and international levels. For example, the European Union now develops common foreign policy positions, and most postmodern states depend on NATO for their external security. Postmodern states share, trade, and borrow sovereignty with other public and private actors.

While modern states are consumed with economic growth and building up their power and authority at home and abroad, postmodern states are multilateralists, busy building regional and global regimes to deal with the security challenges presented by modern and premodern states. Premodern states can become incubators for terrorism, drug sales, human trafficking, arms trading, and even piracy. Many are also kleptocracies, or states ruled by corrupt leaders who steal the state's resources and use its police and security forces to repress dissidents. In a kleptocracy, corrupt leaders often benefit if the state is failed or fragile, as there are no institutions of government to punish them for their crimes. A revolution is often the only way to get rid of these corrupt leaders. The Arab Spring that began in late 2010 led to the end of three kleptocracies: Egypt, Tunisia, and Libya. Unfortunately, only Tunisia survives as a democratic state.

> ## WHAT'S YOUR WORLDVIEW?
>
> *Is nationalism essential for a state to be strong and to take on global leadership or is it simply confidence and political stability at home? Does excessive nationalism diminish efforts toward multilateralism and cooperative problem-solving?*

Foreign policy decisions result from premodern, modern, and postmodern political circumstances. It should be noted that even in undemocratic or authoritarian states, domestic interests such as those favored by military leaders, government bureaucrats, and business leaders shape both domestic and foreign policy. Citizens might not have as much to say about what their leaders decide to do in the international system, but bureaucratic agencies and elites do have a voice. Consider how the Chinese business community has worked to open up the communist regime in that country. As we will see later in this chapter, the foreign policy process is essentially a balancing act between domestic and international factors.

Foreign Policy from Different Perspectives

So which interests are *national*? Why these interests over others? Who determines these interests? In broad terms, a state's national interests fall into the following categories:

1. Security: the survival of the society, maintaining independence, and protecting territory.

Leona Aglukkaq, Canadian Minister for the Arctic Council, greets U.S. Secretary of State John Kerry as he arrives in Iqaluit, Nunavut. Ministers from the eight Arctic nations and the leaders of northern indigenous groups attended the Arctic Council Ministerial meeting in April 2015. The Arctic is both a domestic and an international policy arena, as well as an arena for resource competition.

Refugees

BACKGROUND

Who is a refugee? As refugees, can they be called citizens of any country? Why does this category matter and how has it changed? How do refugee issues challenge those making foreign policy? Do we have a responsibility to protect and provide food and shelter to refugees who are not our citizens? There are many ways to categorize people who leave their homes, including migrants, temporary workers, displaced peoples, and refugees.

THE CASE

Prior to the twentieth century, "refugee" as a legal category did not exist, and it was not until World War I that states recognized people as refugees and gave them rights. Who was a refugee? Although World War I displaced many people, Western states limited their compassion to Russians who were fleeing the Bolsheviks (it was easier to accuse a rival state of persecuting its people); only they were entitled to assistance from states. However, High Commissioner Fridtjof Nansen took his mandate and the category and began to apply it to others in Europe who also had fled their country and needed assistance. Although states frequently permitted him to expand into other regions and provide more assistance, states also pushed back and refused to give international recognition or assistance to many in need—most notably, when Jews were fleeing Nazi Germany. After World War II, and because of mass displacement, states reexamined who could be called a refugee and what assistance they could receive. Because Western states were worried about having obligations to millions of people around the world, they defined a refugee as an individual "outside the country of his origin owing to a well-founded fear of persecution" as a consequence of events that occurred in Europe before 1951. This definition excluded those outside Europe who were displaced because of war or natural disasters arising from events after 1951. Objecting to this arbitrary definition that excluded so many, the UN High Commissioner for Refugees, working with aid agencies and permissive states, seized on events outside Europe and argued that there was no principled reason to deny to others what was given to Europeans. Over time, the political meaning of *refugee* came to include anyone who was forced to flee his or her home and crossed an international border. Eventually, states changed the international legal meaning to reflect the new political realities.

In the contemporary era of Rwanda, Darfur, Bosnia after the Cold War, and now Syria, Afghanistan, and Iraq, we are likely to call someone a refugee if he or she is forced to flee their home because of circumstances caused by others, without having to cross an international border. To capture the idea of those who flee but are still in their homeland, we use the term "internally displaced persons." Indeed, the concept of refugees has expanded impressively over the last 100 years, resulting in millions of people who are now entitled to forms of assistance that are a matter of life and death. Watching this world tragedy unfold has led many states to support the human security movement and the UN resolution on the Responsibility to Protect (see Chapters 5 and 7).

A young girl in a refugee camp in Mogadishu, Somalia. United Nations experts predict that more than 850,000 people are experiencing food insecurity in Somalia's current drought-induced crisis. Refugees present a moral and practical dilemma for the international community. Do states have a responsibility to feed and protect refugees?

OUTCOME

One reason states wanted to differentiate "statutory" refugees from internally displaced persons is that they have little interest in

CASE STUDY *continued*

extending their international legal obligations to millions of people and do not want to become too involved in the domestic affairs of states. For example, in the early 1990s, refugees fleeing the civil war in the former Yugoslavia flooded into Germany. However, the German government was already paying for the reunification with East Germany and could not afford to support more refugees at the time. Therefore, because of domestic political reasons, the German government had to look to other states for a solution to a foreign policy problem. The German government chose to lobby for intervention by the European Union, NATO, and the United Nations.

For Discussion

1. Do states have a responsibility to accept political refugees?
2. Should states intervene in other states to alleviate refugee crises?
3. Should domestic political considerations—such as electoral politics—shape the foreign refugee policy of a state?

2. Economic welfare: economic well-being and market stability.
3. Prestige: status, image, and level of respect and trust.
4. Promoting values and political ideology: making the world like you.
5. Expanding territory or control over vital resources: increasing power or resources.
6. Seeking peace and stability: playing a role in maintaining world order and being a rule-maker.

As we have seen so far in this book, however, different theoretical views provide different perspectives on both issues and policies. Neoclassical realists, for example, believe that domestic political interests play a role in shaping foreign policy, and thus, a state's priorities may change. For classical realists, however, national interests are relatively unchangeable over time. Hans Morgenthau argued that a state's national interest is the pursuit of power and that power, once acquired, is used to secure material aims, protect social and physical quality of life, and promote specific ideological or normative goals. As we saw in Chapter 3, classical realists like Morgenthau believe in a state-centric international system in which states act as a single coherent actor that pursues national interests in a rational manner. Here, "rational" means selecting a policy path that maximizes benefits for the state and minimizes risks. Morgenthau and his disciples considered "national interest as the pursuit of power" the essence of politics.

For realists, the principal national interest is national security, or maintaining the integrity of a country's territory and its economic, political, and cultural institutions. Power is essential for national security, and most realists define power in military terms. Morgenthau argued that to understand foreign policy one needs to understand the "political and cultural context within which foreign policy is formulated" and that interests and ideas shape foreign policy actions and priorities. He quotes the noted scholar Max Weber to make his point: "Interests (material and ideal), not ideas, dominate directly the actions of men. Yet the 'images of the world' created by these ideas have very often served as switches determining the tracks on which the dynamism of interests kept actions moving" (1960, 9).

Robert Pastor (1999) argues that a state's leaders rank their foreign policy goals from *vital* or *essential* to *desirable*. From his realist view, Pastor ranks national interests as follows:

1. National security that includes the defense of borders and the prevention of external influence over domestic affairs.
2. The pursuit of economic interests and securing vital resources.
3. The defense of a country's traditions and values, and the promotion of its ideals in the international system.
4. The implicit and explicit effort to make the world more like itself.

The objectives of foreign policy, according to many realists, must be defined in terms of material national interests and must be supported by adequate power. Military power is dominant in the realm of realism; however, in this era of globalization, the tools of statecraft have changed in both their utility and efficacy. All major states today, for instance, have substantial armed forces, yet all states face the potential of attacks by terrorist groups, and a strong military is not always an effective deterrent.

As we discussed in Chapter 3, proponents of the liberal perspective on international relations believe that a state's power is not measured by force alone. Liberals seek power not only in terms of military power; power and influence in the international system may also depend on diplomacy and skills of persuasion. For Grotian liberals, a state may be able to secure its national interests by (1) maintaining rule of law in the international system and (2) empowering international institutions and regimes that promote global governance in policy areas such as economic development and global finance. Liberal internationalists like former Canadian Foreign Minister Lloyd Axworthy (2003, 5) have taken bold steps to reform the international system and shift foreign policy priorities from narrow national interests to a much more universal focus on human security and human interests. Axworthy described a goal that many liberal middle powers have embraced:

> *We propose a way of seeing the world and tackling global issues that derives from serving individual human needs, not just those of the nation-state or powerful economic interests.*

Liberal internationalism in this case has evolved to embrace a more Kantian or normative view of national priorities and interests.

Constructivists, meanwhile, believe that state interests and foreign policy goals are "defined in the context of internationally held norms and understandings about what is good and appropriate" (Finnemore 1996b, 2). Awareness that this normative context changes over time helps us understand shifts in foreign policy behavior. For example, the more internationalist context that came with the end of the Cold War supported a shift from ideological conflict to engagement and cooperation, and as a result, many states returned to their own traditions and values as guideposts for foreign policy.

Marxists, on the other hand, believe that foreign policy is generally controlled by economic and political elites who also control power at home. National interests are determined by the wealthy and powerful, not the average citizen. This belief leads to the conclusions that wars are fought primarily for economic reasons and the goals of a country's development-assistance programs are to make poor countries dependent on the donor state, thus keeping them in the position of providing cheap labor, cheap resources, and a welcome place for foreign investors. Utopians such as the academics who comprised the World Order Models Project (WOMP) advocate a foreign policy that shifts national interests to more global interests such as peace, social justice, economic well-being, and ecological balance.

Who Makes Foreign Policy?

We need to remind ourselves that human beings have agency in foreign policy. It is not the state that decides; it is individuals representing the state. Leaders, bureaucrats, members of parliament, and ministers make decisions, and these decisions are shaped by a variety of factors, such as past events, national attributes, dominant values or the narrative that defines a country's political culture, policy decisions made by both internal and external actors, and the nature of global politics. The values and beliefs of the individual clearly shape the final decisions. We discuss the various factors that shape foreign policy decision-making later in this chapter when we discuss levels of analysis.

When exploring the question of who makes foreign policy, we are interested in those who make decisions on behalf of states or organizations within a state. Both public and private actors may shape foreign policy. At each phase of the foreign policy process, different actors will become involved and attempt to shape policy.

It is important to start with individuals in formal government positions: foreign ministers, a secretary of state in the United States, or a key minister of trade or defense. Generally, members of the executive branch or the prime minister's cabinet are the ones who *initiate* foreign policy, and they work through the legislature and parliament to *formulate* the policy. Government agencies generally work with the private sector or other governments to *implement* policy decisions. Private actors such as banks, transnational enterprises, nongovernmental organizations (NGOs), universities, and think tanks may play a role in any part of the foreign policy process. Other governments and regional and international organizations may also be involved in helping formulate and implement foreign policy. NGOs and corporations do not directly make policy, but they can have a profound influence on public officials who do make the final policy decisions.

WHAT'S YOUR WORLDVIEW?

Who do you think determines a country's foreign policy priorities? What are your country's top foreign policy interests, and are they what you would expect them to be?

What Do We Expect from Foreign Policy?

National interests are usually related to what we, as citizens, expect from our governments. At the basic level, we want the state to protect our borders, provide internal security and a system of law and order, and support and maintain a means of exchange or a marketplace. This is the point at which domestic and international policy distinctions begin to blur. Foreign policy and domestic policies are clearly interdependent in this global age. Most foreign policy experts believe that citizens expect their state's foreign policy to deliver in seven areas (Hill 2003, 44–45):

1. Protecting citizens living or traveling in a foreign country.
2. Projecting an image or identity in the international system that enhances a state's prestige and makes that state's values, beliefs, and traditions attractive to other states in the international system.
3. Maintaining the "status quo" in terms of providing stability and protecting citizens against external threats.
4. Advancing prosperity and providing the ways and means for accumulating wealth.
5. Assisting leaders in making decisions about whether to intervene in a global crisis or get involved in an alliance or international institution.
6. Providing support for international negotiations aimed at creating and maintaining a stable world order.
7. Working toward protecting the global commons (e.g., oceans) and for providing global public goods (e.g., clean air).

A variety of internal and external actors and structures influence and shape these foreign policy goals. Globalization has pushed domestic and foreign policy processes into a complex and interconnected relationship. Domestic societies are more exposed to external or international developments, and foreign policies both shape and are shaped by domestic developments. In capitals across the world, foreign policy leaders talk about policy issues that are transnational in nature, like migration, poverty, environmental challenges, and trade. In crafting government policies to slow climate change, for example, political leaders must contend with the demands of business and industry groups and those of concerned citizens at home—not to mention demands that leaders, corporations, and citizens of other states bring to negotiations. These leaders also understand how domestic interests often prevent the realization of foreign policy goals. One of the most difficult issues for foreign policy leaders is how to make bold foreign policy decisions without alienating a powerful domestic group that might influence the next election. For example, the leaders of the world knew that genocide was taking place in Darfur, and yet few states were willing to intervene in the area to stop the killing. Humanitarian intervention presents a difficult policy choice for most leaders because it is hard to convince domestic groups to sacrifice blood and treasure for people from distant lands.

Now that we have covered some foundational aspects of what foreign policy is, who makes it, and what we expect from it, we revisit levels of analysis (introduced in Chapter 1) to look at *why* states make the foreign policy decisions they do.

Levels of Analysis in Foreign Policy

As a student of foreign policy, you might be interested in finding answers to puzzles or unexpected actions by a state. For example, why did North Korea's leaders decide to develop nuclear weapons? Why do Nordic governments give so much development assistance? These are complex issues, but some explanations are better than others. Foreign policy analysis is the search for factors or variables that explain the most about a state's behavior. Scholars doing research in this area are interested in questions like the following: Why do states behave in a certain way? What factors explain a state's behavior? Why do leaders pick one option over another? If a state spends a significant amount of money on its military, what factors explain that choice? Although there are always questions about "agency," or which actors actually make foreign policy, foreign policy analysis offers plausible explanations for foreign policy behavior. We say plausible explanations because this is not an exact science: the social scientist trying to explain foreign policy puzzles can never replicate the certainty of the natural scientist working in the lab and controlling all the variables. Yet if the social scientist can identify factors that shape foreign policy, it might help us better understand the foreign policy process and even predict how states might behave in similar situations. In this section, we will discuss one such approach to the agency question: levels of analysis.

In Chapter 1, we discussed how some research in international relations attempts to replicate the research methods and assumptions of the natural sciences. The idea here is that one can develop theories, test them by gathering evidence, and find useful explanations for the decisions made by leaders. Foreign policy analysis, a subfield of international relations, puts the individual at the center of decision-making. Most studies of decision-making begin with the assumption that all decision makers act rationally or always act to maximize benefits and minimize costs. In his classic study of decision-making in a crisis situation, *Essence of Decision*, Graham Allison (1971) introduces three models, or analytic tools, for explaining decision-making. The first, the rational-actor model, or RAM, provides a useful example of using rationality. The other two models, organizational behavior and bureaucratic politics, are second-level or domestic-level tools. Unfortunately, some foreign policy decision makers cannot meet the requirements of rationality. For example, it may not be possible for policymakers to know all of their options and assign values to those options. They may lack access to information essential to selecting policies that result in value maximization. Thus, other factors, like a decision maker's belief system, the political structure of a state, or the distribution of power in the international system, may influence the range of choices and the eventual policy choice.

Levels of Analysis in Foreign Policy.

Many factors influence foreign policy. As a scholar, one must consider each level when trying to explain the behavior of nation-states.

Most texts suggest that there are three levels of analysis: *individual*, or the human dimension; *national* attributes, or the domestic factors; and *systemic* conditions, or the nature of the international system. A number of scholars have added a fourth level that focuses on *global* conditions or factors (see Table 4.2). Discussions about the importance of globalization and technological innovations, like the Internet, suggest that these factors potentially influence decisions made by national leaders.

Individual Factors, or the Human Dimension

We assume that all leaders are rational actors (i.e., always selecting a policy path that maximizes benefits and minimizes costs), but other factors like beliefs, personality images, and perceptions also shape decision-making. Foreign policy research suggests that these other factors are most important in a crisis situation, a decision requiring secrecy and thus involving few actors, or a decision demanding a quick response. This level is also important when a leader is given a great deal of latitude to make a decision and when the decision maker has an interest or expertise in foreign policy.

To act rationally, leaders must be able to know all of their options, be capable of assigning values to these options, and have enough information to select the higher-valued options. Those who use these other idiosyncratic factors like *belief systems* or *personality types* to explain behavior do not believe any decision maker can be rational all of the time. Most decision makers operate in an environment of uncertainty with imperfect information. Many leaders talk about "going with their gut" when they are making decisions in crises, but they are usually relying on previous experience (e.g., analogical reasoning) or their worldview (e.g., realism, liberalism, Marxism, feminism, constructivism). Leaders filter information through their worldviews, which include both principled and causal beliefs, and generally seek programs that fit with these beliefs. For example, former British Prime Minister Margaret Thatcher, with a strong realist belief system, convinced George H. W. Bush to take the 1990 Iraqi invasion of Kuwait seriously and respond militarily. She also decided to use force rather than diplomacy to take back the Falkland Islands after the Argentine invasion in 1982.

National Factors, or Domestic Attributes

At the domestic or national level, researchers look at a country's history and traditions and at its political, economic, cultural, and social structures. Regime type—such as whether a state is a parliamentary democracy or authoritarian with unelected leaders and a strong single-party bureaucracy—shapes the choice of foreign policy strategies. The role of political parties and interest groups or NGOs within a society is also an important variable at the domestic level.

An area of study that crosses over to some of the constructivist research in foreign policy is the focus on cultural values and national traditions and ruling narratives. Valerie Hudson (2007) suggests that national identity and cultural variables may be more important today than systemic factors like balance of

TABLE 4.2	**Levels of Analysis: Explaining the Behavior of Global Actors**
Level of Analysis	**Explanation**
Individual	• Bounded rationality/cybernetics • Biological explanations • Motivation/personality • Perception/images • Belief systems/information processing
National	• Power capabilities • Domestic politics: finding coalitions for policy and support for retaining power • Decision-making styles and structures: bureaucratic politics and organizational behavior • Size and resource base • Geographic factors • Political structure • Economic system • Political culture
Systematic	• Level of anarchy or order • Distribution of power • Obligations, treaties, alliances • Regimes or governing arrangements
Global	• Global social movements • Environmental conditions and challenges • Media and popular cultural forces • Decisions by transnational nonstate actors such as transnational enterprises and international NGOs • Ideas, values, and norms that transcend culture and time

power in shaping foreign policy. Citizens in social democratic states with political cultures that promote social justice and economic well-being expect their foreign policy programs to advance these same values. Foreign policy makers have belief systems about how the world works, and this combines with national traditions and dominant or ruling narratives that create a menu from which leaders make their choices.

Changing elements that shape policy include military power, economic wealth, and demographic factors. More permanent elements like geographic location and resource base also matter. A powerful variable in many democratic societies is domestic politics, or electoral calculations. Politicians often find that they are unable to achieve their desired goals because of demands of the election cycle. A further complication is the role of bureaucracies in the policy process. Unelected civil servants can influence outcomes that politicians want. Academic work includes many such examples, notably Graham Allison's study of the Cuban missile crisis, *Essence of Decision*. In his exploration of crisis decision-making

Standard operating procedures (SOPs) The prepared-response patterns that organizations create to react to general categories of events, crises, and actions.

within the Kennedy administration, Allison found that **standard operating procedures (SOPs)**, or the way things are usually done in an organization, are major determinants of foreign policy behavior. Large organizations employ SOPs to respond to a range of events. For instance, when a natural disaster like a hurricane or earthquake happens, agencies have plans ready to provide the correct kind of assistance. Normally, a state's agencies of all kinds—military, intelligence, foreign affairs—have SOPs ready for every foreseeable eventuality. Bureaucratic politics, Allison's third model, suggests that within every government, bureaucratic agencies compete with one another for control over resources and policy. The eventual result of this competition is the policy.

Systemic Factors, or the Nature of the International System

The anarchic nature of the international system—its lack of a central authority—may be the most important factor at the systemic level. However, countries take individual and collective actions to cope with this lack of a global central authority. Thus, treaties, alliances, and trade conventions, which states agree to abide by, are seen as systemic constraints.

Reciprocity A form of statecraft that employs a retaliatory strategy, cooperating only if others do likewise.

A country's behavior is also shaped by more informal systemic constraints based on traditions, common goals, and shared norms. For example, most states respect the sovereignty of all states, and most follow the rule of international law. These laws cannot be enforced, but states abide by them because they expect others to do the same. This notion of **reciprocity** is the primary incentive for states to support a rule-based international system. The distribution of power in the system (e.g., unipolar, bipolar, multipolar, nonpolar) and the nature of order (e.g., balance of power, collective security) are also important system-level factors. Neorealists believe that the lack of a common power or a central government at the global level is the defining element of international relations, and a state's foreign policy is aimed primarily at survival in this anarchic system. Kenneth Waltz describes this anarchic condition of the system (1959, 238):

> Each state pursues its own interests, however defined, in ways it judges best. Force is a means of achieving the external ends of states because there exists no consistent, reliable process of reconciling the conflicts of interest that inevitably arise among similar units in a condition of anarchy.

Liberals, on the other hand, believe that anarchy forces states to create rules and develop regimes or governing arrangements aimed at encouraging cooperation and multilateralism. Today, many liberals focus on more effective global governance across policy areas. As the world has learned with the very recent global economic crisis, rules and regulations that govern all markets are indeed essential.

Global Factors

Global factors are often confused with system-level factors. Simply stated, the difference is that global factors are not necessarily created by states, whereas systemic factors are. Global-level variables can be the outcome of decisions or technology made by individuals, interest groups, states, or nonstate actors. For example, the Internet and social media, created and used by private actors, have played a major role in organizing opposition forces in the Arab Spring countries of Egypt, Tunisia, Libya, and most recently in Syria. Both radical and humanitarian groups use these resources to rally support for their causes and to challenge the power of key states. For example, ISIS has mastered the use of social media for recruiting young Muslims to join their extremist movement and this has prompted the United States, United Kingdom, and other countries to develop social media programs to counter jihadist messaging. No one state owns the Internet or the various social media outlets, and yet these can be valuable tools aimed at shaping foreign policy.

Global factors may also be the results of natural conditions. These factors cannot be traced to the actions of any one state or even group of states. In fact, they usually challenge the ideas of boundaries and sovereignty. The Internet and resulting information revolution, the movement of capital by multinational banks, CNN or BBC broadcasts, and the revolutionary ideas of religious fundamentalists all represent global factors that might shape policy behavior. The process of globalization promotes such factors. Environmental conditions such as pollution, pandemics, climate change, and resulting drought or severe storms can also have a global impact on foreign policy; for example, they may lead to new alliances for resolving the crisis at hand or to conflicts over the control of critical resources, such as clean water.

Social scientists may combine variables to reach an explanation of a particular foreign policy decision. But social science researchers want to isolate key variables or factors that explain the decision made. They are guided by the goals of precision and parsimony. Advocates of the scientific approach, or **positivists**, want to be able to say that U.S. policy toward Iraq, for example, can best be explained by looking at the personality of George W. Bush or the power of the Defense Department and the office of the vice president in shaping policy. Each of these bureaucratic organizations made the case for war. What is exciting about research in our field is that there is always disagreement about which variables explain the most. Thus, someone could say with equal certainty that U.S. economic interests—namely, our dependency on oil—offer a better explanation for the decisions to launch a "war of choice," something we will discuss more in Chapter 6. The strength of anyone's argument is based on the quality of the empirical evidence that one collects to support the hypothesis being tested. We use the work of historians, public policy records, government documents, interviews, budgets, and journalists' accounts to gather evidence to confirm or reject our hypotheses.

By utilizing the different levels of analysis to explain foreign policy, we might be able to predict what states would do in a given situation. Likewise, we can use previous decisions as analogs and make suggestions or prescriptions for future foreign policy. Next, we will discuss how foreign policy is accomplished by examining the strategies and tools that states might use to secure their goals and meet their priorities in the international system.

Positivists Analysts who use the scientific method to structure their research.

The Foreign Policy Process

So far we have examined the explanations and influences of foreign policy, answering questions of why and what for; in this section, we get down to the nuts and bolts and look at the process of how foreign policy comes about. You may be surprised to learn that the foreign policy–making apparatus of most democratic countries is basically the same. Political systems tend to divide the responsibility for decision-making between members of the executive branch, which carries out the policies, and the deliberative or legislative branch, which sets spending priorities and guidelines for the executive to follow. Deliberative bodies often have a responsibility to oversee the actions of the executive branch. Both branches of government might subdivide responsibility further into geographic regions, economic sectors, or military affairs. In addition to the governmental actors with legal authority, there are also any number of individuals and groups outside the government structure that might seek to influence the policy process. The actors that comprise this informal sector vary by issue area, but they can include business groups, religious groups, news media, and private citizens.

As we suggested earlier in the chapter, even authoritarian or totalitarian states have decision-making processes in which government ministries debate issues and work with private interests to promote specific policy positions. Leaders rarely act alone and create a foreign policy that adheres specifically to their own interests. For example, military leaders and various bureaucrats within North Korea support the intransigence of the state in its defiance of the United States and the international community to build nuclear weapons.

Four Phases of Foreign Policy Making

The study of foreign policy making assumes that governmental officials with the legal authority to act do so in a logical manner. Political scientists call this the "rational-actor model" of foreign policy making. Proponents of this model assert that a government's foreign policy officials are able to (1) define a problem, (2) develop responses to the problem, (3) act upon one or more of the responses, and then (4) evaluate the effectiveness of the policy. In the following sections, we discuss these four phases in more depth.

Phase One: Initiation or Articulation

Issues are often first articulated or otherwise promoted by media and interest groups who are attempting to influence the policymaking process. Information about a foreign policy issue is disseminated, and as public awareness of an issue increases, the informed public may pressure elected officials to either act on the issue or, in some cases, stay clear of the problem.

Both internal (formal) and external (informal) actors may push a certain position and pressure leaders to take action. For example, in the case of the conflict and genocide in Darfur, NGOs using the Internet provided the public with information about the atrocities. These same NGOs initiated further global-awareness campaigns with celebrities and notable public leaders that attracted the attention of major media outlets and many elected officials who recognized the importance of the issue for either moral reasons or pragmatic electoral calculations.

Individuals and research institutes (often called "think tanks"; see Table 4.3) can initiate a debate about a foreign policy issue. A natural disaster, unexpected tragedy, or crisis might also inspire some official reaction from governments. For example, in general, the American public is not supportive of increasing foreign aid, but if a flood or earthquake devastates an area, U.S. citizens generally want the government to supply emergency aid.

TABLE 4.3　Some U.S. Foreign Policy Think Tanks

Brookings Institution is a highly authoritative nonprofit public-policy organization whose mission is to conduct high-quality independent research and provide innovative, practical recommendations that strengthen American democracy; foster the economic and social welfare, security, and opportunity of all Americans; and secure a more open, safe, prosperous, and cooperative international system.

Council on Foreign Relations is an independent, nonpartisan membership organization, think tank, and publisher dedicated to being a resource for its members, government officials, business executives, journalists, educators and students, civic and religious leaders, and other interested citizens to help them better understand the world and the foreign policy choices facing the United States and other countries. The council publishes *Foreign Policy*, a leading journal of international affairs and U.S. foreign policy.

Heritage Foundation is a conservative-leaning think tank committed to building an America where freedom, opportunity, prosperity, and civil society flourish.

Carnegie Endowment for International Peace (CEIP) is one of America's leading institutions for researching and analyzing international affairs and making recommendations for U.S. foreign policy. The CEIP, with over 100 employees, is headquartered in Washington, D.C., with offices in four other countries.

RAND Corporation is a nonprofit think tank formed to offer research and analysis to the U.S. armed forces. The organization has since expanded to work with other governments, private foundations, international organizations, and commercial organizations on a host of nondefense issues.

American Enterprise Institute (AEI) is a conservative think tank, founded in 1943. Its mission is "to defend the principles and improve the institutions of American freedom and democratic capitalism—limited government, private enterprise, individual liberty and responsibility, vigilant and effective defense and foreign policies, political accountability, and open debate."

Center for American Progress is a liberal political-policy research and advocacy organization. Its website describes it as "a nonpartisan research and educational institute dedicated to promoting a strong, just and free America that ensures opportunity for all."

New America is dedicated to the renewal of American politics, prosperity, and purpose in the digital age through big ideas, technological innovation, next-generation politics, and creative engagement with broad audiences.

Hudson Institute is an independent research organization promoting new ideas for the advancement of global security, prosperity, and freedom. Founded in 1961 by strategist Herman Kahn, Hudson Institute challenges conventional thinking and helps manage strategic transitions to the future through interdisciplinary studies in defense, international relations, economics, health care, technology, culture, and law.

Technologies like the Internet and cell phones may contribute to the democratization of foreign policy. Today, citizens in industrialized states have an opportunity to be better informed than ever before, and they are presented with a variety of options to become actively involved in a particular issue area. Citizen involvement also now transcends borders: global or transnational social movements have mobilized citizens to work to end hunger, forgive debt, and end the use of certain weapons. These campaigns have been successful in their efforts to persuade governments to use official foreign policy tools to address their concerns. For example, Bono, the lead singer from the musical group U2, spent time with the late Senator Jesse Helms and other members of Congress as a representative of the Jubilee 2000 movement that urged wealthy states to forgive the debts of poor states. Other celebrities have joined members of the domestic Christian Coalition to increase awareness of the issues surrounding poverty and third world debt and to lobby both the executive branch of government and members of Congress.

Global and domestic actors also have an impact on policymakers in authoritarian or nondemocratic states. China continues to be a favorite target for human rights groups, and they have had some impact on Chinese domestic policies. For example, with the help of pressure from groups like Human Rights Watch, in 2013, the Chinese government announced that it would abolish the detention system known as re-education through labor whereby people who had committed crimes, as well as political and religious dissidents, were detained. Tragically, many of these NGOs have had no impact on policymakers in fragile states like Zimbabwe or Syria. In many authoritarian states like Russia and China, they have become targets of government agencies seeking to control their activities.

Phase Two: The Formulation of Foreign Policy

The formulation phase of policymaking involves the creation of an official government policy. Internal and external actors—individuals, interest groups, corporations, and foreign governments—initiate policy debates and put pressure on policymakers to act. Parliaments, executive offices, ministries, and bureaucratic agencies must then work to develop an effective foreign policy. In reference to the aforementioned Jubilee 2000 movement, the idea to forgive the debt of third world countries was discussed by relevant government agencies. The legislative branches debated the cost and benefits of forgiving debt, and specialists in various financial departments provided essential information for the final policy position.

Specialists who work inside and outside government typically provide essential information for policymakers. Often, in the policymaking process, the original intention of the policy is loaded with other priorities that might help the politician get reelected or that might help a bureaucracy gain more power and resources. In noncrisis situations, foreign policy is formulated much like domestic policy. It is a complex process involving legislatures, executive agencies, ministries and departments, and a wide variety of internal and external interest communities.

In crisis situations, foreign policy is made by a smaller group of individuals and agencies. Since the end of World War I, in the United States and many other Western democracies, the executive branch or cabinet has taken over the foreign policy process. Foreign ministries, defense departments, and special advisers to the prime minister or president are usually charged with responding to a crisis. In the administration of George W. Bush, decisions about the war in Iraq were made by a group of advisers comprising members of the National Security Council, the vice president's office, and the Defense Department; the State Department was often left out or its ideas dismissed by the president's inner circle.

Although in most democracies elected members of legislatures serve on committees with foreign policy oversight, most of these committees react to policy plans formulated by the head of government and that person's advisers. Most legislative bodies do have budget responsibilities and can use this power to support or change foreign policy priorities. However, shrewd leaders who appeal to the public for support of their foreign policy actions can neutralize the legislature's power of the purse. For example, few members of the U.S. Congress challenge funding for military actions or aid programs for an important ally, for fear of being called antimilitary or unpatriotic. Generally, when dealing in areas of foreign policy, the old adage applies: "Partisanship ends at the water's edge." After 9/11, it was very easy for the Bush administration to get congressional support for any program that could be framed as part of the global war on terrorism. More recently, in 2014, the U.S. Congress displayed bipartisan support and approved the Obama administration's plan to train and arm Syrian rebels in the fight against Islamic State militants.

Phase Three: Foreign Policy Implementation

Once a policy is decided in a legislature, department, or ministry, it is usually assigned to policy actors in a ministry or department and other affiliated actors in the field, who are expected to implement the policy. For example, if Congress passes a bill allocating funds for development assistance or foreign aid, the money is sent to the most appropriate agency: in this case, the U.S. Agency for International Development (USAID), which receives the funds and distributes them to its various field offices. The money is then given to development projects that may have been organized by local governments, NGOs, and development agencies from other countries. It is not unusual for countries to form coalitions with local communities, NGOs, and other aid agencies. However, funds are not always spent on intended projects, and they are often not spent at all. Corruption, project delays, new priorities, and leadership changes often get in the way of intended consequences. U.S. agencies intending to reduce poverty in developing countries must deal with a variety of factors that might delay a program or prevent it from reaching its goals.

Phase Four: Foreign Policy Evaluation

Policy evaluation is the final step in the policymaking process, and it is often neglected or overlooked. Although a review provision might be built into a given

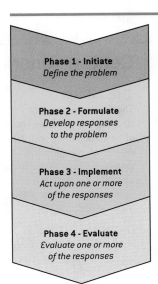

Phase 1 - Initiate
Define the problem

Phase 2 - Formulate
Develop responses to the problem

Phase 3 - Implement
Act upon one or more of the responses

Phase 4 - Evaluate
Evaluate one or more of the responses

A Typical Decision-Making Process.

What do we mean by *rational actor*? What about this model suggests rationality? Of course, this graphic is a simplification. Can you draw a more complex process model, or flow chart, based on what you have read so far? What other steps or loops would your model depict?

Central America: A Perpetual Pursuit of Union?

THE ISSUE

The foreign policies of Central American states can seem to present a paradox. The outside observer sees a number of small countries with a common history, a relatively high degree of common identity, and apparently everything to gain from integration. So why have these states not integrated? This is a case of particularistic domestic goals undermining what seems to some outside observers a logical regional option.

BACKGROUND

Following independence, the Captaincy-General of Guatemala became the Federal Republic of Central America (1823–1839) before splitting into Guatemala, El Salvador, Honduras, Nicaragua, and Costa Rica. Restoration of this union has been a constant theme in integrationist discourse. Yet Central America was more a collection of communities than a clearly defined overarching entity. Non-Guatemalan elites resisted leadership by Guatemala, and Costa Rica early on showed a tendency toward isolationism. Nationalism grew, conflict undermined unionism, and outside involvement was often unhelpful. Various sources of division thus coexisted with a powerful mythology of union.

In 1907, a Central American Peace Conference convened in Washington to help end local conflicts, and led to a short-lived Central American Court of Justice (1908–1918). The Organization of Central American States (ODECA) was created in 1951 with the goal of re-creating regional unity. The first organizations of functional cooperation emerged around this time. Some twenty-five such bodies now exist, covering everything from water to electrical energy and creating a complex web of regional interactions. Formal economic integration began in 1960 with the Central American Common Market (CACM). Intraregional trade grew, but the system entered crisis at the end of the 1960s. Efforts at reform in the 1970s were overtaken by political crises and conflicts. In the 1980s, integration became associated with the Central American peace process. In this context of confidence building, a Central American Parliament was created as a forum for regional dialogue. In

1991, with conflicts in El Salvador and Nicaragua ended, the Cold War over, and a new wave of regional integration across the world, a new period began with the creation of the Central American Integration System (SICA). This system aimed to provide a global approach to integration, with four subsystems—political, economic, social, and cultural.

RECENT HISTORY

Although the Central American Parliament is directly elected, it has no powers and it does not include Costa Rica. As of 2015, only Guatemala, El Salvador, Honduras, and Nicaragua participated in the Central American Court of Justice. There have been repeated discussions of institutional reform, however. In 2005, intraregional trade represented around 27 percent of exports and 12 percent of imports. Most goods originating in Central American countries enjoy free circulation. The same levels of external tariff were applied for 95 percent of goods; thus, general negotiations for a Central American customs union began in 2004. International agreements are also shaping the future of Central America. The Central American countries

Refugees from Central America make their way through Mexico to the United States. Migration is a problem that regional cooperation might be able to solve. With a growing divide between rich and poor and a very competitive global economy, the leaders of this region must address quality-of-life issues such as crime and violence, education, health, housing, and employment.

GLOBAL PERSPECTIVE *continued*

signed a free trade agreement with the United States in 2004 modeled on the North American Free Trade Agreement (NAFTA). In 2006, they also began to negotiate an association agreement with the European Union, including a free trade agreement.

SICA has advanced efforts aimed at encouraging more integration by providing a legal framework for dispute resolution and helping member states avoid war. SICA membership includes the seven nation-states of Central America (Belize, Costa Rica, El Salvador, Guatemala, Honduras, Nicaragua, and Panama) plus the Dominican Republic. In 2008, SICA announced an agreement to begin pursuit of a common currency and common passport for citizens of the member states. However, as of February 2016, none of these goals has been realized. While the pursuit of union continues at the international level, it is hindered by goals and motivations found at the individual and domestic levels.

For Discussion

1. Does it make sense for Central America to have its own political and economic union, or should it be part of a larger Latin American union?
2. Globalization may force countries into creating larger common markets. In what other policy areas would a union make sense?
3. What would the United States and Mexico think about such a union?
4. What are the internal and external factors working either for a union or against more cooperation?

program, the administrators of the policy might have a personal interest in keeping the program active. The media may focus their attention on the policy outcomes if the policy program was a success or a failure. All interested parties will have a position and will try to influence future decisions in this policy area. Often, the very public and private actors involved in the previous phases of the policy process will be involved in the evaluation of policy outcomes.

Most legislatures conduct public hearings related to major foreign policy expenditures. These hearings can become particularly important if a policy program has failed or had a major impact on a society. Consider, for instance, the Iraq Study Group's hearings on the Iraq War or congressional committee hearings on the future of NATO or U.S. trade policy toward China. Congress tends to use every opportunity to evaluate the foreign policy activities of a particular administration. In some political systems, like that of the United Kingdom and Canada, the prime minister must face the parliamentary opposition during a legislative session called "question time." This form of evaluation generally attracts a great deal of public attention and comments from opposition politicians.

Another form of evaluation that usually triggers policy actions is comprehensive studies done by universities, think tanks, research institutions, and NGOs. Human Rights Watch, Greenpeace, the International Crisis Group, the International Committee of the Red Cross, and hundreds of other interest groups provide policymakers with comprehensive studies on nearly every foreign policy issue area. To illustrate, in 2014, the U.S. Senate Select Committee on Intelligence, chaired by Senator Dianne Feinstein, released a 6,700-page report criticizing the CIA's detention and treatment of prisoners taken in the wars in Iraq and Afghanistan. This report may have a major impact on future decisions about how to treat individuals taken prisoner in the war on terrorism; it may also damage the image of the United States among friends and foes alike. This is one reason why some states avoid public hearings and comprehensive reviews of policy programs.

Foreign Policy Strategies and Tools

The organized statements of goals and beliefs that political leaders formulate and the methods they intend to employ to achieve those goals are called foreign policy strategies or **doctrine**. For the political leaders of a state, a foreign policy doctrine acts as a kind of GPS for charting policy strategies and determining national priorities. The doctrine guides decisions such as where to invest critical resources to secure long- and short-term goals.

Doctrine A stated principle of government policy, mainly in foreign or military affairs, or the set of beliefs held and taught by an individual or political group.

Most states have coherent foreign policy strategies to attain both material and ideational goals. For example, after emerging from apartheid and exclusive white rule in the late 1980s, South Africa developed a foreign policy that promotes human rights across the world and supports an African Renaissance. Similarly, after years of rule by military dictators, Chile decided on an activist foreign policy based on the theme of "diplomacy for development." The hope is that this policy will help Chile overcome its structural constraints of size and geographic location and allow it to develop a niche as a regional leader and an honest broker in international affairs.

All countries have three kinds of foreign policy tools to choose from: sticks, carrots, and sermons. "Sticks" refer to threats, "carrots" to inducements, and "sermons" to what diplomats might call moral suasion. We could also add the power that comes with having a positive image or reputation in the international system. Being an honest broker, or a moral leader seeking to help resolve regional conflicts, can also become a source of power in the international world. Leaders from Norway, for example, took the lead to resolve the Middle East conflict with the Oslo Accords in 1993 and mediate the ethnic conflict in Sri Lanka in 2002. Norwegian leaders are supported in these endeavors because Norwegian citizens see it as their responsibility to the global community. Norwegian nationalism includes a strong sense of internationalism. It is important to remember that, because of differences in resources, population, and level of economic development, some countries might not be able to use some or any of the options we discuss in the following sections.

Sticks: Military and Economic Tools

In the international system of the realist perspective that influences many political leaders, states must secure their interests by military power. Since there is no common power or central government and no agreement on rules governing the system, some countries use force or the threat of force to secure their interests and gain more power and influence in the international system. Other military tools include military aid or assistance, sharing intelligence, alliances, military research, and technological innovations.

Sometimes, the decision to deploy a weapon system can be a stick for diplomats to use. The George W. Bush administration supported the development and deployment of a ballistic missile defense system in Eastern Europe to defend Europe against missiles from Iran or terrorist groups in the Middle East. Perhaps fearing growing U.S. power and influence in the region, the Russian government saw the installation of such a defense system as a menace to Russia's security needs. In response, the Obama administration offered the Russians a carrot by declining to build the missile defense system. Now Russian support of rebels in Ukraine and the annexation of Crimea has caused some concerns among Baltic nation-states and the United States has responded with guarantees of military support from NATO.

Unfortunately, spending scarce national resources on military equipment does not guarantee safety. For instance, the United States enjoys military hegemony in the world today and spends more on its military than any other nation-state (see Figure 4.1). Yet the sale of weapons by private actors and even many states has created real security challenges for the entire world. New security challenges presented by global terrorism networks have resulted in a number of new security arrangements and the sharing of both technical resources and military personnel. NATO, for example, has expanded its mandate to address the wars in Afghanistan, Iraq, and Syria.

The use of foreign policy sticks is not limited to leaders who have adopted the realist perspective on global politics. Liberals also recognize the importance of military tools of statecraft. Woodrow Wilson did not shy away from using America's military resources to help end World War I. However, he called for a collective security arrangement with the League of Nations. Today, progressive-liberal states such as Canada, the Netherlands, and Denmark are active members of NATO who have willingly deployed their armed forces in Iraq and Afghanistan. Many middle and small powers are active participants in peacekeeping forces in conflict regions around the world. Collective humanitarian interventions and peacekeeping are military tools that are becoming more important in areas where states have failed to provide basic security or are disintegrating (see Chapter 7 for more information on peacekeeping operations).

A new form of warfare may present major challenges for both liberals and realists. Cyberwarfare, or an attack on a country's computer and information systems, could cause an economic collapse. Russia used cyberattacks in Estonia and Georgia to weaken confidence in these governments and make their citizens and leaders feel vulnerable to outside forces. With our ever-increasing dependency on

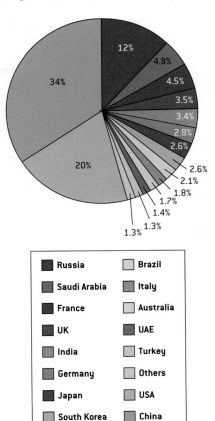

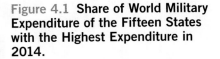

Russia	Brazil
Saudi Arabia	Italy
France	Australia
UK	UAE
India	Turkey
Germany	Others
Japan	USA
South Korea	China

Figure 4.1 Share of World Military Expenditure of the Fifteen States with the Highest Expenditure in 2014.

technology, this form of warfare is likely to increase. China has used cyberwarfare to attack computer systems in the United States, and Israel used a computer worm, Stuxnet, to disrupt Iran's nuclear program. Military resources are not much help here. Most states are not well prepared for such an attack, and the perpetrators could be states, terrorist networks, or a single computer expert.

In addition to military inducements, states can employ economic sticks. This type of influence can include **economic sanctions**, boycotts, **arms embargoes**, and punitive tariffs. Sanctions are used to both alter domestic politics and influence the foreign policy behavior of a target state. In the war on terrorism, the United States froze bank and investment assets from Afghanistan and Iraq as well as several Islamic charity organizations. Blocking access to multilateral lending institutions such as the World Bank and investment restrictions have become major tools in attempts to influence state behavior at home and abroad. Economic sanctions can also involve the buying and selling of large quantities of a target state's currency to manipulate its exchange rate and create an economic crisis. Additionally, restrictions on travel and business are often used to force change in a society.

The best example of an effective sanction effort was the global cultural, political, and economic boycott of South Africa during its apartheid regime. Currently, members of the UN Security Council are using sanctions to punish North Korea for its production and testing of nuclear weapons. Prior to the 2015 Iran nuclear deal, sanctions were imposed on Iran for pursuing nuclear weapons as well. The United States and the European Union have also imposed sanctions on the Syrian government for its use of chemical weapons and its behavior in the ongoing civil war. Economic tools need not be all negative, however. States often use the promise of material assistance to reach a desired goal.

Economic sanctions A tool of statecraft that seeks to get a state to behave by coercion of a monetary kind—for example, freezing banking assets, cutting aid programs, or banning trade.

Arms embargo Similar to economic sanctions, an arms embargo stops the flow of arms from one country to another.

EU High Representative for Foreign Affairs and Security Policy Federica Mogherini, Iranian Foreign Minister Mohammad Javad Zarif, British Foreign Secretary Philip Hammond, and U.S. Secretary of State John Kerry, meet in Switzerland in April 2015 after a round of Iran nuclear talks. The goal of the resulting Iran nuclear deal is to ensure that Iran's nuclear program is and remains peaceful.

Carrots: Foreign Assistance

Most of the wealthy states in the international system are donor states, or states that give a significant amount of development assistance or aid to less wealthy or poor states. For donor states, development assistance is a means of pursuing foreign policy objectives. There are at least five forms of foreign assistance:

1. *Project aid* provides a grant or loan to a country or an NGO for a specific project.
2. *Program aid* is given to a government to create certain policy conditions in the recipient country, such as opening a market or supporting balance of payments.

3. *Technical assistance* provides a country with equipment or technicians in a given policy area.
4. *Humanitarian* or *disaster assistance* provides states funds for food, materials, medicine, and other basic supplies.
5. *Military* or *security aid* is often given to allies or partners in programs like the war on terrorism or to those participating in UN peacekeeping activities.

As we will discuss more fully in Chapter 9, states give aid for a variety of purposes, but most states tie their aid to national interests such as security, economic growth, or prestige. Food aid helps the hungry, but it also helps farmers in the donor state who sell their crops and cattle to the government. Even the most generous states use this economic tool to serve some of their own domestic interests. Assistance programs include the sharing of expertise and technology. Giving humanitarian assistance may also enhance a state's prestige and its image in the international system. Christine Ingebritsen (2006, 283) argues that the small countries of Scandinavia, consistently major donors, have played a pivotal role in promoting global social justice and strengthening norms of ethical behavior (see Chapter 7). These small and middle powers have used carrots such as development assistance, trade agreements, and other nonforce resources to encourage peaceful resolution of conflict, promote multilateralism, and work toward a more equitable distribution of global wealth. A typical Nordic aid program might include funding for public health and education, environmental protection, promotion of human rights and democracy, and family planning. The Nordic countries also give a high percentage of their aid to multilateral organizations and NGOs working in developing regions of the world (see Figure 4.2). About 40 percent of UNICEF's budget comes from Nordic countries, and organizations like Oxfam and Save the Children receive funds from Nordic governments.

Development assistance and aid programs in the United States are administered by the U.S. Agency for International Development (USAID). Under the Clinton administration, the number of USAID goals were trimmed from thirty to five. These reflected the neoliberal goals of the administration for the enlargement of democratic and capitalist states:

1. Provision of human relief.
2. Stabilization of population growth.
3. Promotion of democracy.

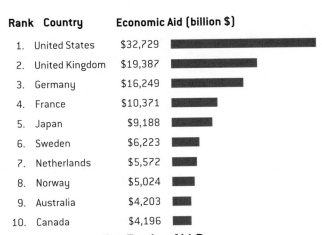

Rank	Country	Economic Aid (billion $)	
1.	United States	$32,729	
2.	United Kingdom	$19,387	
3.	Germany	$16,249	
4.	France	$10,371	
5.	Japan	$9,188	
6.	Sweden	$6,223	
7.	Netherlands	$5,572	
8.	Norway	$5,024	
9.	Australia	$4,203	
10.	Canada	$4,196	

Figure 4.2 Top Ten Foreign Aid Donors.
Do you see a pattern among the countries on this list? What motivates these states to give such large amounts of aid?

An Afghan National Army soldier stands guard at the gate of a Doctors Without Borders hospital in Kunduz, Afghanistan. In October 2015, Taliban fighters took control of the key northern city of Kunduz. During the fighting to retake the city, a U.S. air attack hit the hospital, killing at least twelve Doctors Without Borders staff and ten patients. With the nature of war and fighting changing dramatically, will it become more difficult to protect the lives of innocent civilians?

4. Environmental protection.

5. Economic growth.

These goals changed slightly with the George W. Bush administration. Namely, a focus was placed on preventing HIV/AIDS, and family planning programs were no longer supported.

Other economic tools include trade agreements, the provision of loans, and the sharing of development or trade experts. Countries give economic resources in two main methods: directly to another country, in what are called "bilateral agreements," or indirectly through global institutions like the World Bank, the International Monetary Fund (IMF), and a variety of regional development banks like the Asian Development Bank. World Bank aid in the developing world can finance a range of projects, such as rural electrification or creating an export-driven agricultural market.

ENGAGING WITH THE WORLD

World for World Organization

This Italian NGO was established in 2002 with a mandate to increase public awareness about global development issues and promote policies to help implement the Sustainable Development Goals set by the United Nations. You can volunteer for a solidarity and development program or for many other programs in areas including the environment, education, health, emergency relief, poverty alleviation, food security, and water. You can also apply for internships with the organization in various locations. Check out www.worldforworld.org.

Sermons: Diplomatic Messaging and the Use of the Media

Military and economic sticks address material interests. "Sermons" address ideal interests. These might include *demarches*, or simple warnings, directives, or position statements sent to governments as a form of moral suasion. A charismatic leader giving a speech to the world can be a powerful diplomatic tool. President Obama's speech on June 4, 2009, given in Cairo, Egypt, addressed a global audience and was a clear attempt to convince the Muslim world that the

U.S. policy toward Islam was going to change. Minutes after its completion, the U.S. government had it on the Internet in several languages. Although we have yet to see the full impact of this particular speech, as a kind of public diplomacy, it is an effective use of modern media and global communications to serve political purposes.

Diplomacy plays a critical role in the preservation of peace and world order. Many experts consider it a lost art undermined by advanced communications, summit meetings, the increasing importance of international and regional organizations, and the demands of a global media industry that is persistently looking for information and often exposing secret agreements. Traditional diplomatic historians assert that diplomacy performs four important functions:

1. Communication among actors.
2. Negotiation.
3. Participation in regional and international organizations.
4. Promotion of trade and other economic interests.

Diplomats today must deal with a host of new global challenges that require cooperation among state and nonstate actors. Diplomatic meetings aimed at addressing global challenges like climate change, terrorism, organized crime, human rights, and international investments are becoming major sources of power for countries with basic knowledge, scientific expertise, and the means to implement the policies. The role states play in the development of global regimes is an important source of power in this era of globalization. Small and middle powers tend to value the role of diplomacy and use some of their most qualified foreign policy experts in diplomatic roles.

Public diplomacy is fast becoming an important foreign policy tool. In the past, this form of diplomacy might have been called propaganda, but today, it involves telling the world about the positive characteristics of your society. These educational, cultural, and informational programs are also an important source of power. Countries can provide funds for educational exchanges of students, faculty, and diplomats. The U.S. Fulbright Program, for example, sends students and scholars from the United States around the world and brings foreign scholars to the United States. International foundations can also provide this type of funding. One example is the Aga Khan International Scholarship Foundation, which provides scholarships each

Diplomacy The process by which international actors communicate as they seek to resolve conflicts without going to war and find solutions to complex global problems.

Public diplomacy The use of media, the Internet, and other cultural outlets to communicate the message of a state.

Public diplomacy is a valuable tool for encouraging countries to see the value in the arts and humanities. South African writer and the late Nobel laureate Nadine Gordimer speaks in Calcutta, India, in 2008 having been invited by the public diplomacy division of the Indian Ministry of External Affairs. Talks like these promote our common values and force us to think about our common humanity.

year for postgraduate studies to outstanding students from developing countries. Concerts, book tours, movies, and art exhibits are all part of a country's efforts to promote its values and cultural attributes. During the Cold War, the U.S. Information Agency sponsored tours of jazz bands to the Soviet Union and other communist countries. Media sources are also ways to promote a state's interests and make a state attractive to others. For example, the BBC and the Voice of America provide global radio programs that attract listeners and learners across the world.

Finally, in a world of nuclear weapons and internal wars that kill both civilians and soldiers, **coercive diplomacy** has become a valuable foreign policy tool because "it seeks to persuade an opponent to cease his aggression" rather than go to war (George 1991, 5). In 1990, the George H. W. Bush administration used a strategy of coercive diplomacy in an attempt to get Saddam Hussein to leave Kuwait. The Bush administration made a clear demand, or *ultimatum*, that the Iraqi government ignored. The administration then took a variety of steps that involved the buildup of forces, economic sanctions, and diplomatic maneuvers in the United Nations. This strategy of gradually turning the screw was aimed at getting Iraq to see how costly a war with the United States and a coalition of forces representing some thirty-six countries would be. In this case, coercive diplomacy failed because Iraq did not back down, and the U.S.-led coalition destroyed the Iraqi military with the blessings of the United Nations and most of the world community.

Coercive diplomacy The use of diplomatic and military methods that force a state to concede to another state. These methods may include the threat of force and the mobilization of the military to gradually "turn the screw" but exclude the actual use of force. The implication is that war is the next step if diplomacy fails.

Soft and Hard Power in Foreign Policy

One way to understand the methods of foreign policy making is to think of both carrots and sticks as **hard power** tools. However, these inducements and threats are only part of the diplomatic process in the international system. Harvard professor and former Clinton administration official Joseph Nye introduced the concept of **soft power**, or the ability to "shape the preferences of others" (2004, 5–15). Soft power, as Nye presented the concept, tries to co-opt people and countries rather than threaten or coerce them. Political leaders can use soft power to encourage cooperation and to shape what other states want in the international system. A country's culture and ideology are important sources of soft power.

Hard power The material threats and inducements leaders employ to achieve the goals of their state.

Soft power The influence and authority deriving from the attraction that a country's political, social, and economic ideas, beliefs, and practices have for people living in other countries.

Nye asserts that the soft power of any country is based on three sources: (1) its culture, (2) its political values, and (3) its foreign policy. If a country's culture is attractive to others, it can be a source of power. Similarly, if a country's political values—like democracy and respect for human rights—are attractive to other citizens and other states, then that country can gain power and influence in the international system. Finally, a country with a moral foreign policy can also have power and influence in the international system. From this view, we see that the United States may have lost its international standing because of its use of torture and prisoner abuse in Iraq and secret prisons around the world; when the United States lost moral credibility, its foreign policy activities were more likely to be seen

"Never forget Srebrenica" is the message on this poster as a Dutch activist participates in a 2007 memorial in The Hague to the victims of Europe's worst massacre since World War II. The failure of Dutch troops in 1995 to protect Bosnian Muslims in the designated safe area of Srebrenica still haunts the people of the Netherlands, and this event shapes the foreign policy of the country today.

as unethical by most of the global community. Nye suggests that if a country promotes values that other states want, leadership will cost less.

Soft power is not merely the same as influence. After all, influence can also rest on the hard power of threats or payments. Soft power is more than just persuasion, or the ability to move people by arguments, though that is an important part of it. It is also the ability to attract, and attraction often leads to acquiescence. Simply put, in behavioral terms, soft power is *attractive power*.

Both hard- and soft-power tools are an important part of any leader's foreign policy doctrine and policy agenda. In this **nonpolar** world (Haass 2008), where no one state or group of states controls all power and authority, and where power and influence are distributed among a variety of state and nonstate actors, it will be harder to control these actors and even harder to build multilateral alliances to respond to global challenges. With no clear concentration of power in many policy areas, the number of threats and vulnerabilities is likely to increase, and states will need to work harder to maintain order and stability. Most experts predict that all states and transnational actors will need to combine resources to address the most significant global problems the world faces. The entire global effort aimed at addressing climate change, for example, will require major collective action. Globalization may not have changed enduring national interests such as security and prosperity, but it has certainly changed how states pursue these interests.

Nonpolar An international system in which power is not concentrated in a few states but is diffused among a variety of state and nonstate actors.

Foreign Policy Styles and Traditions

Foreign policy style Often shaped by a state's political culture, history, and traditions, this describes how a country deals with other states and how it approaches any decision-making situation. For example, does it act unilaterally or multilaterally? Does it seek consensus on an agreement or does it go with majority rule?

Foreign policy tradition A tradition that includes national beliefs about how the world works and a list of national interests and priorities based on these beliefs. It also refers to past actions or significant historical events that act as analogs and give guidance to leaders about what strategy would best secure their national interests.

No examination of how foreign policy works would be complete without a discussion of various styles and traditions, as well as the various ways great powers, middle powers, and weak states may differ in their approaches. Analysts of foreign policy behavior often assert that factors such as the geographic size of a country, its resource base, and its population can determine the kind of foreign policy—or style—a country will undertake. A **foreign policy style** is often the result of how a country deals with other members of the international community. When this style continues over a long period of time, we call it a **foreign policy tradition**. The foreign policy style and tradition include a common set of public assumptions about the role of the state in the international system. A tradition includes national beliefs about how the world works and what leaders must do to secure their national interests. Styles and traditions promote different foreign policy strategies, and each suggests different sets of policy priorities. In this section, we discuss some aspects of foreign policy style and foreign policy tradition.

Great Powers, Middle Powers, and Small States

The foreign policy of all states is aimed at securing national interests and responding to the needs, values, and interests of their citizens. All states seek a role, or *niche*, in the international system. James Rosenau (1981) suggested that all states develop a strategy for adapting to the conditions created by the international system. Smaller states with limited resources and little capacity to influence other powers by unilateral actions are likely to select an **acquiescent strategy**. This strategy suggests they will adapt their interests to fit with the interests of larger and more powerful regional or global leaders. Consider, for example, the

Acquiescent strategy A foreign policy strategy in which a state defers to the interests of a major power.

role of "client states" and alliances during the Cold War. These states followed the lead of the United States or Soviet Union and were rewarded with the promise of security and prosperity in the form of aid, military assistance, and trade agreements.

States that were once global leaders and even hegemonic powers at times seek policies aimed at preserving their power and status in the international system. This **preservative strategy** has been employed by countries like the United Kingdom and France. Preservative policies include taking a leadership role in international and regional organizations, identifying issues that need attention, and taking the lead in responding to these challenges. The United Kingdom's efforts to lead the debt-relief campaign and France's role in the recent Paris climate talks (or COP21) are examples of this behavior.

The most powerful states seek to retain and possibly increase their power and authority by adapting a **promotive foreign policy**. The United States and the Soviet Union promoted their views, values, and interests after World War II as they competed for the hearts and minds of citizens around the globe. Each

WHAT'S YOUR WORLDVIEW?

Do you think power gives rise to responsibility? Should powerful states be expected to right the world's wrongs and solve the world's problems?

Preservative strategy A foreign policy aimed at preserving power and status in the international system.

Promotive foreign policy A foreign policy that promotes the values and interests of a state and seeks to create an international system based on these values.

The Impact of Globalization on Different Kinds of States

The Asian economic crisis of 1997, which was triggered by the weakness of Asian financial systems, highlighted states' different capacities for responding to globalization. Even though all states in the region were affected by the crisis, their responses suggested that some enjoyed more choice or sovereignty than others. Indonesia, Thailand, and the Republic of Korea turned to the International Monetary Fund for assistance, which was conditional on several policies mostly defined by the IMF, itself in Washington, D.C. Malaysia, meanwhile, formulated its own strategy for adjustment and imposed policies such as capital controls, which Washington greatly disapproved of. Although globalists and skeptics alike treat all states as equal in their arguments about globalization, we should

question whether this equality is true. (Globalists think that globalization is changing the world and undermining the authority of states, whereas skeptics still see the state as the primary actor in global politics and believe the state can and will manage the processes of globalization.)

One way to think about the impact of globalization is to distinguish between strong states and weak states. At the extreme end, strong states shape the rules and institutions that have made a global economy possible. We have already seen the way U.S. policies shaped the creation, implementation, and breakdown of the Bretton Woods system. A more general description of strong states is that they can control—to some degree— the nature and speed of their integration into the world economy. Into this

category, we might place not only relatively strong industrialized countries but also developing countries such as Brazil, Malaysia, China, and India. In all of these cases, globalization is having a powerful effect, as evidenced by the restructuring of national and private industries in industrialized countries and the past decade of economic liberalization in Brazil and China. Yet, at the same time, in each of these countries, there are high protective barriers in important sectors of the economy and serious debates about capital controls and the regulation of international capital. The capacity of these countries to control their integration into the world economy is doubtless related to their size, resources, geostrategic advantages, and economic strength. However, interestingly, it also seems related to their national ideology and the domestic power of the state. One characteristic that all strong states have in common is that they guard with equal ferocity their independence in economic policy, foreign policy, human rights, and security issues.

Weak states, by contrast, suffer from a lack of choice in their international economic relations. They have little or no influence in the creation and enforcement of rules in the system, and they have exercised little control over their own integration into the world economy. For example, in the aftermath of the debt crisis of the 1980s, many weak states opened up their economies, liberalized, and deregulated, more as a result of coercive liberalization than of a democratic policy choice. In the 1990s, this continued with what an international economist

India's economic growth and rise as both a regional and global power has been fueled by resources like coal and on the backs of a large population living below the poverty line. How will the global climate change movement that seeks to ban the use of coal affect India's economic growth?

Continued

The Impact of Globalization on Different Kinds of States *continued*

called "forced harmonization," whereby, for instance, in the case of trade negotiations on intellectual property, developing countries were coerced into an agreement that transferred "billions of dollars' worth of monopoly profits from poor countries to rich countries under the guise of protecting the property rights of inventors" (Rodrik 1999).

Distinguishing among states according to their capacity to shape and respond to globalization is vital in analyzing the impact on the global economy. The example of the collapse of the international financial system in late 2008 demonstrates that some states, in particular the United States, are rule-makers in the world economy, whereas less powerful states are rule *takers*.

For Discussion

1. Based on this situation, do you think globalization is uneven or predatory, or are the benefits shared equally? Why?

2. In the recent economic crisis, have regional organizations like the European Union or global organizations like the International Monetary Fund been able to respond effectively? Explain.

3. Our international system is based on nation-states, but to our global economy, borders and sovereignty are almost meaningless. Do we need more effective global regimes? Why or why not?

---

superpower created an alliance structure that divided the world into two armed camps with the capacity to destroy the world as we know it. After the Cold War, U.S. leaders talked about establishing a new world order that served the interests of the United States and its allies. Some experts talked about the unipolar moment, a time when the United States could promote its values, traditions, and interests to create a peaceful and prosperous world.

There are always states that believe the existing international system is unfair, oppressive, violent, and alienating. These states seek to transform the international system by promoting an **intransigent foreign policy**. They do not accept the rules of the game and mobilize their resources to challenge the great powers in the international system. During the 1960s and 1970s, leaders of the Nonaligned Movement (NAM)—namely, Cuba, Pakistan, India, and Indonesia—pushed intransigent policy programs that challenged the dominant rules of the international system. Today, North Korea and Iran are challenging great-power rules—namely, the rules that restrict the number of states with nuclear weapons.

To a certain extent, these four **adaptation strategies** describe the foreign policies of states today. States adapt to circumstances and events and the structure of the system. Some international relations theorists propose that the choice from among these strategies is linked to a given country's size or influence in the international system. This assertion has been, at times, the center of a significant debate among academics. Although it is clear that countries choose a foreign policy strategy because of their resources and needs, it is not always the case that size determines a particular policy option. A brief overview of what we might expect from great, middle, and small powers follows. States are constantly adapting to changes in the international system and to the domestic factors that might

Intransigent foreign policy A foreign policy that challenges the rules established by the great powers or rule-making states.

Adaptation strategies Changes in foreign policy behavior in reaction to changes in the international system or international events and adjusting national goals to conform to the effects of events external to that state.

limit a state's ability to act in the system or, conversely, provide opportunities for more active participation.

Great-Power Foreign Policy

Most of the research about **great-power** politics and foreign policy is shaped by traditional realist assumptions about world politics and as a result tends to ignore cases that contradict the academic goal of a parsimonious theory. It is also, as we learned in Chapter 3, an arguably bleak perspective because it sees enemies everywhere. For example, John Mearsheimer (2001, 29–32), an influential realist scholar, contends that great powers always seek to maximize their share of world power, and all great powers seek hegemony in the international system.

For all great powers, survival is the primary goal. These states all think strategically about how to survive in a system where all states are potential threats. More specifically, the goals of great powers include advancing the economic and political interests of their people and maintaining the rules and institutions in the international system that serve their interests. The United States and its allies created the primary institutions of global governance after World War II. The only significant challenge to that system was advanced by the Soviet Union. Some have called the Cold War a war about whose rulebook would be followed. With the end of the Cold War, there is now only one rulebook, and the battle is over which rules to apply and how to apply them. Countries invited to the G8 and G20 meetings are all great global and regional powers. They meet once a year to debate best ways to respond to economic crises, humanitarian challenges, and security issues, and what they decide in these areas affects the entire world.

Mistrust and uncertainty force states to act always in accordance with their own self-interest. Mearsheimer (2001, 33) suggests that great powers act "selfishly in a self-help world." This means the foreign policies of great powers are focused on gaining power and authority in the military world and beyond. Great powers seek to lead in all policy sectors, but the dominant currency is military power, and all great powers must respond to the **security dilemma**. Without any form of central authority in the international system, states must seek security through military power and security alliances.

Middle-Power Foreign Policy

Relying again on realist assumptions and definitions, a scholar might focus on national attributes such as land area, resource base, population, and military capabilities to distinguish **middle powers** from small or weak states and great powers. However, in a world where power and influence are no longer solely defined in terms of physical attributes and military strength, a state's behavior or experience in various policy situations may provide better insights into how that state sees itself and how others see its role in the international system. Most middle powers are liberal states with social democratic political systems and economies based on trade. This means their survival and prosperity depend on global stability and order. These states seek incremental reform by extending a

Great power A state that has the political, economic, and military resources to shape the world beyond its borders. In most cases, such a state has the will and capacity to define the rules of the international system.

Security dilemma In an anarchic international system, one with no common central power, when one state seeks to improve its security, it creates insecurity in other states.

Middle powers These states, because of their position and past roles in international affairs, have very distinctive interests in world order. Middle powers are activists in international and regional forums, and they are confirmed multilateralists in most issue areas.

A Palestinian man takes a selfie with Dutch Foreign Minister Bert Koenders in front of Roots Hotel in Gaza City. Koenders visited the Kerem Shalom Crossing in southern Israel, which borders Gaza, to inaugurate a new security scanning system that aims to increase the number of trucks crossing into Gaza from Israel, an example of middle-power problem-solving.

liberal world order, which they see as the most effective way to achieve both human and national security. Canada, Australia, and the Nordic countries are great examples of active middle powers.

In describing the importance of a "behavioral" measure of middle powers, Cooper, Higgott, and Nossal (1993) describe their attributes as follows:

A. *Catalysts*: States that provide resources and expertise to take leadership roles in global initiatives.
B. *Facilitators*: States that play active roles in setting agendas in global policy discussions and building coalitions for collaborative responses.
C. *Managers*: Middle powers that support institution building at the international level and encourage support for existing international organizations and multinational activities.

Niche diplomacy Every state has its national interests and its areas of comparative advantage over other international actors. This is its area of expertise and where it has the greatest interest. Hence, this is where the state concentrates its foreign policy resources.

The same authors quote Gareth Evans, a former Australian minister for foreign affairs and trade, in describing a concept called **niche diplomacy**. This form of middle-power activism "involves concentrating resources in specific areas best able to generate returns worth having, rather than trying to cover the field" (Cooper et al. 1993, 25–26).

The middle powers, because of their position and past roles in international affairs, have very distinctive interests in the future order. Middle powers are activists in international and regional forums, and they are confirmed multilateralists in most issue areas. They actively support an equitable and pluralistic rule-based system. They are, for the most part, trading states and thus favor a relatively open and stable world market. Since stability is so important to them, most middle powers see themselves as global problem-solvers, mediators, and moderators in international disputes (Holbraad 1984; Wood 1998). Middle powers usually play a leadership role in regional organizations (e.g., the European Union) and in functionally specific institutions such as the World Health Organization (WHO) and the Development Assistance Committee (DAC) of the Organisation of Economic Co-operation and Development (OECD).

Normative orientation In foreign policy, promoting certain norms and values and being prescriptive in one's foreign policy goals.

A third view of middle powers places an emphasis on the **normative orientation** of this group of states. Although subject to much criticism, the image of middle powers as potentially wiser and more virtuous than other states is usually promoted by national leaders and progressive interest groups to gain domestic support for international activism and to enhance the reputation of their states in the international community. This image of global moral leaders, bridging the gap between rich and poor communities, fits well with the egalitarian social democratic values of most Western middle powers. Robert Cox (1989, 834–835) argues that the traditional normative aims of middle powers—namely, greater social equity and a call for more diffusion of power in the system—might give them more leverage as principled problem-solvers in continuing economic and political challenges faced by all states in the system today.

The middle powers may play a critical role as the catalysts of problem-solving initiatives or the managers of regimes initiated by greater powers with less interest for internationalism and little domestic support for egalitarian goals and values.

Small-State Foreign Policy

Researchers agree that small states are defined by a small land mass, gross national product (or GNP), and population. In addition, they usually do not have large military forces or the resources to have a significant impact on global politics. However, if they act in concert with other states, it is possible for small states to have an impact on the international system. For example, the like-minded states that played a pivotal role in the formation of the International Criminal Court (ICC) included a coalition of small and middle powers.

Small states can also identify a niche and develop expertise in a given policy area. Most wealthy small states, like Belgium or New Zealand, often focus their foreign policy on trade and economic issues. They will also participate in regional organizations and at times take leadership roles in crisis situations. New Zealand, along with Australia and the island state of Vanuatu, took the lead to create a nuclear-free zone in the Pacific in 1985. The Reagan administration's response to this action demonstrates the limits to small-state actions: when the New Zealand Labour government banned nuclear-capable U.S. Navy ships from its harbors, the United States terminated security cooperation with the country. Belgium is one of the most active members of the European Union, NATO, and every other regional and international organization. Because of its colonial past, it has worked with many African states in development and peacekeeping activities.

It should be stated that with the end of the Cold War and the intensity of forces of globalization, there has been a change in the valuation of states' capacities and their potential influence in the international system. After all, military power may not be as important as policy expertise or technology in this new world where new security challenges include climate change, pandemics, poverty, and cyberwarfare. Foreign policy in a **nonpolar world** (i.e., power is diffused and held by a variety of state and nonstate actors) is less constrained by the structure of the system and allows for more flexibility and independence. Globalization has also increased the number of opportunities for citizen participation, and technology like the Internet makes it much easier to organize for a specific cause or policy position and to promote a small state's national interest in the global community.

Nonpolar world A world in which there are many power centers, and many of them are not nation-states. Power is diffused and in many hands in many policy areas.

Some small states have taken on the role of norm entrepreneurs in the international system. Christine Ingebritsen et al. (2006, 275) describes this role:

> *Thus, Scandinavia, a group of militarily weak, economically dependent small states, pursues "social power" by acting as a norm entrepreneur in the international community. In three policy areas (the environment, international security, and global welfare), Scandinavia has acted to promote a particular view of the good society.*

Other attributes of small-state foreign policy include the following (Henderson et al. 1980, 3–5):

- Most small states have limited financial and human resources and thus have to decide carefully when and where to participate. Generally, this means a limited global role and a focus on their geographic region and the interests of their own citizens.
- With limited resources (their citizens), most small states focus on economic and trade issues.
- Small states generally take an active role in regional and international organizations. Multilateralism is a preferred strategy, and small states consider it the best way to secure their interests.
- Small states can play critical roles in alliances and in global policy regimes. Many of these states have resources and expertise, and they seek roles as global problem-solvers in policy areas of importance to their domestic population.

As the space between domestic and foreign policy sectors blurs or even disappears, domestic politics and the interests of citizens play a greater role in shaping foreign policy. In both small and middle powers, what citizens expect from states at home has a significant influence on how these states behave internationally.

Conclusion

In this chapter, we provided an overview of the primary issues and actors in the foreign policy process. We saw that many variables shape the world of diplomacy in the contemporary international system: material needs, ideas, and people themselves. The rational-actor model offers one way to understand the policymaking process. We also considered different styles and traditions in foreign policy. In the following chapters,

The United States has increased its training of the military in several small African states. Most recently, the United States deployed troops to Cameroon to help their forces defeat Boko Haram. Here a U.S. naval officer trains Senegalese sailors for future security activities. Great-power engagement in African states has increased with the rise of extremist attacks.

we will turn to specific topics that comprise the critical challenges in the international system; for example, we will see how globalization is undermining the autonomy of the nation-state. International and regional organizations like the United Nations and the European Union, nongovernmental organizations (NGOs), and multinational corporations are each eroding the nation-state's power; they influence some of the core policy areas that were once the sole responsibility of nation-states. This trend is an important factor shaping relations in the contemporary world.

CONTRIBUTORS TO CHAPTER 4: *Steven L. Lamy and John Masker.*

KEY TERMS

Acquiescent strategy, p. 146
Adaptation strategies, p. 148
Arms embargo, p. 140
Civic nationalism, p. 118
Coercive diplomacy, p. 144
Diplomacy, p. 143
Doctrine, p. 138
Economic sanctions, p. 140
Ethnonationalism, p. 118
Failed or collapsed state,
    p. 119
Foreign policy, p. 116

Foreign policy style, p. 146
Foreign policy tradition,
    p. 146
Fragile state, p. 119
Great power, p. 149
Hard power, p. 144
Ideational/ideal interest,
    p. 117
Intransigent foreign policy,
    p. 148
Material interest, p. 117
Middle powers, p. 149

Modern state, p. 119
National interest, p. 117
National self-determination,
    p. 118
Nationalism, p. 118
Niche diplomacy, p. 150
Nonpolar, p. 145
Nonpolar world, p. 151
Normative orientation,
    p. 150
Positivists, p. 131
Postmodern state, p. 120

Premodern state, p. 119
Preservative strategy,
    p. 146
Promotive foreign policy,
    p. 146
Public diplomacy, p. 143
Reciprocity, p. 130
Security dilemma, p. 149
Soft power, p. 144
Standard operating
    procedures (SOPs), p. 130
Statecraft, p. 117

REVIEW QUESTIONS

1. Why has nationalism spread across the world in the last two centuries?
2. How has the rise of the modern state shaped the development of nationalism?
3. In what ways do personal characteristics affect outcomes in the rational-actor model?
4. What are the four levels of analysis? How are they used to explain the behavior of states?
5. How do bureaucracies influence the foreign policy process?

6. Do small states have any power and influence in the international system?
7. "Contemporary globalization erodes nation-state sovereignty but does *not* undermine nationalism." Discuss.
8. Who are the actors in creating foreign policy? What are the phases?
9. What is a foreign policy doctrine?
10. Do you think the foreign policy process is shifting away from the state?

For more information, quizzes, case studies, and other study tools, please visit us at **www.oup.com/us/lamy**.

Designing a New World Order

BACKGROUND

The significant changes in the political and economic landscape in Europe and the former Soviet Union, the unprecedented collective response to Iraqi aggression in Kuwait, and the puzzling failure of the major powers to respond effectively to aggression in Somalia, Rwanda, and the former Yugoslavia suggest that it may be time for the rule-making actors in the international system to establish a new set of standards and rules of behavior for the new world order. This new system of explicit and implicit rules and structures will replace the East-West Cold War "bipolarity," or the "balance of nuclear terror." Many leaders, including former presidents George H. W. Bush and Bill Clinton, have frequently invoked the concept of "new world order" as a justification for foreign policy decisions. However, there does not seem to be any consensus in the United States or in other nation-states about the structure of this new world order. Some world leaders have called for a series of discussions about the future of world politics in an effort to prevent U.S. hegemony and avoid drifting toward a new era of competition and anarchy. They want to know their role in this new system. Who will be the new rule-makers? How will order be maintained? What are the rules? What are the new security challenges? These are some of the questions leaders are asking.

EXPECTATIONS

In this small-group discussion exercise, you will explore various world-order models, review how changes in the structure of the system might influence or shape foreign policies of states, and then make a case for a new U.S. global strategy and a new world order.

PROCEDURE

1. Review the options presented in the "World-Order Models" section below. You may want to review historical periods when these systems were in operation (not all systems of order presented on this sheet have been implemented).
2. With reference to a traditional realist's three system-level challenges and constraints—order, anarchy, and the security dilemma—which world-order system would you find most effective for U.S. interests? What about the interests of other major powers (e.g., Japan, Germany, Russia, and Great Britain)? What about the concerns of developing states or the South?
3. Discuss the nature of foreign policy under each system structure. For example, how would the foreign policy of major, middle, and small powers be influenced if the system moved from bipolarity to hegemony? Review each possible system structure and its influence on foreign policy.

WORLD-ORDER MODELS

One-Country Rule: One country governs the rest of the world, controlling all resources, industry, and trade. The superpower determines the national interest of all other nations and the interest of the world; all are defined in terms of the superpower's interests.

Bipolar: Two superpowers have divided the world. Each controls a large group of countries and controls the resources, industry, and trade within its bloc. Relations between the two blocs are determined by the superpowers to serve their own interests.

Polycentrism: Each country has its own government and controls its own resources, industry, and trade. There are no international organizations or alliances; every country operates in its own interest.

Regionalism: Countries located in the same part of the world have formed regional governments that control resources, industry, and trade within each region. Relations between regions are governed by regional interests.

World Law: All nations of the world have established a world authority that makes laws against international violence and has agencies to enforce these laws, keep the peace, and resolve conflicts. Individual nations control their own resources, industry,

internal security, and trade. The world authority acts only to prevent the use of violence in relations between nations.

Some Other Order: Draw your own model of an international system. Specify how international relations, trade, and security are handled in your model. Why is your model better than any of the other models?

DISCUSSION AND FOLLOW-UP

If time permits, in small groups, discuss what you think will be the major issues facing the world's leaders in the next ten years. Then try to reach consensus on a system structure (i.e., world-order model) that you feel will create an international environment that will enable states to constructively and effectively respond to these issues.

5 | Global and Regional Governance

A Tunisian democracy group won the 2015 Nobel Peace Prize for its contributions to the first and most successful Arab Spring movement. The Norwegian Nobel Committee cited the Tunisian National Dialogue Quartet "for its decisive contribution to the building of a pluralistic democracy" in the North African country following its 2011 revolution. Will regional stability and peace depend upon building pluralistic democracies across the Middle East and North Africa?

The mystery to be overcome is one all peoples share—how divergent historic experiences and values can be shaped into a common order.

—HENRY KISSINGER

This is an ungoverned world. The UN has no autonomous power; it is what its members want it to be, and usually its members don't want it to be anything much. . . . When it is said that it is better if things are done multilaterally, too often this means accepting the lowest common denominator.

—STANLEY HOFFMANN

Peace was the final prize Alfred Nobel mentioned in his will, which established five Nobel Prizes. The first peace prize went to two people: Henry Dunant, who founded the International Committee of the Red Cross, and Frederic Passy, a leading pacifist, in 1901. Clearly, the Nobel committee was signaling to the world that transnational organizations like the Red Cross might provide the way forward in meeting humanitarian challenges, whether natural disasters or human-made crises.

In 2015, the Norwegian Nobel committee awarded the peace prize to the Tunisian National Dialogue, a civil society organization that emerged as a leading advocate for democracy after the 2011 Jasmine Revolution that started the Arab Spring. The National Dialogue Quartet is made up of four key organizations: Tunisian General Labor Union; Tunisian Confederation of Industry, Trade, and Handicrafts; Tunisian Human Rights League; and Tunisian Order of Lawyers. The members of these organizations worked collectively to mediate conflicts and promote peaceful democratic development. They succeeded in overcoming the divisions that brought the country close to a civil war.

The committee that awards the peace prize uses it as a signaling device, to reward behavior that they believe will lead to peace and stability. The prize recognizes the constitutional process that resulted in peace and stability in Tunisia. It also recognizes the importance of civil society actors in the process of democratization. Unfortunately, in many of the countries where the Arab Spring failed to produce a

LEARNING OBJECTIVES

After reading and discussing this chapter, you should be able to:

Identify the principal organs of the United Nations.

Explain key differences between the League of Nations and the United Nations.

Discuss the evolution of UN peacekeeping operations since 1950.

Explain the arguments for reforming the UN organs and operations.

Describe the development of the European Union and its integration process.

Give examples of how various types of nongovernmental actors influence global politics.

Multilateralism The process by which states work together to solve a common problem.

Global governance The regulation and coordination of transnational issue areas by nation-states, international and regional organizations, and private agencies through the establishment of international regimes. These regimes may focus on problem-solving or the simple enforcement of rules and regulations.

viable democratic process there were no civil society actors. Authoritarian regimes in Libya, Syria, and Egypt suppressed secular and religious organizations, eliminating the very important "space between" government, or the public sector, and the business world, or the private sector.

One way to peace is to support more regional cooperation and the building of regional institutions such as the European Union. As far back as 1971, Professor Joseph Nye called this process *peace in parts* as he imagined a world of European Unions linked together to promote the rule of law and encourage **multilateralism** and cooperation. Imagine Tunisia taking the lead to create a regional organization that would bring peace and stability to Northern Africa and the Middle East.

Introduction

Leaders in all countries face the challenge of managing the processes of globalization. States seek to create international institutions and laws that enable them to secure their national interests in a more globalized society. **Global governance** describes the formal and informal processes and institutions that guide and control the activities of both state and nonstate actors in the international system; global governance does not mean the creation of a world government. After all, this governance is not always led by states, nor is it always led by international organizations that are created by states.

Indeed, multinational corporations and even NGOs create rules and regulations to govern behavior in some policy areas. For example, banks will set up informal rules for exchanging currencies, and NGOs have set up ethical rules for fundraising and intervention in crisis regions. As demonstrated by the work of Elinor Ostrom, 2009 Nobel Prize winner in economics, sometimes private, nongovernmental groups can do a better job of creating rules for governing a shared resource. In this case, the state is the primary actor but not the only one in global governance.

In this complex and increasingly global system, states are working with international and regional organizations like the United Nations and the European Union and **nonstate actors** like Oxfam, Save the Children, and Amnesty International through diplomacy, international law, and regimes or international governing arrangements to solve common regional and global problems. Cary Coglianese (2000, 299–301) suggests that international organizations and international law are critical in responding to three types of problems:

1. Coordinating global linkages: In this area, rules and laws are critical for managing the exchanges of information, products, services, money, and finance and even for managing collective responses to criminal activity.
2. Responding to common problems: The global community faces common problems like climate change, poverty, human rights abuses, refugees,

and pandemics, all of which require some form of coordination and collective policy response.

3. Protecting core values: Institutions and laws are essential for protecting and promoting core values like equality, liberty, democracy, and justice across the world.

The problems listed here and others increase with globalization. States will undoubtedly become more dependent on international and regional institutions like the United Nations or the African Union to promote international and regional cooperation in these critical areas. The global system has institutions capable of coordinating responses to global crises, but successful responses depend on voluntary compliance by both state and nonstate actors. If global actors consider the laws, regimes, and institutions to be fair and legitimate, they will be more likely to comply. Here we mean international laws, or the body of legal standards, procedures, and institutions that govern the interactions of sovereign states. A **regime** is a governing arrangement that guides states as well as transnational actors and institutions (described in detail in the next section); it is a set of rules, norms, and practices that shape behavior of all actors in a given issue area. **International law** is an international institution.

Regionalism has become a pervasive feature of international affairs. According to the World Trade Organization (WTO), all of its members are party to one or more regional trade agreements (RTAs), and as of February 2016, nearly 625 notifications of RTAs were received, 419 of which are in force. Regional peacekeeping forces have become active in some parts of the world. In past decades, regionalism has become one of the forces challenging the traditional centrality of states in international relations.

That challenge comes from two directions. The word *region* and its derivatives denote one distinguishable part of some larger geographical area. Yet they are used in different ways. On the one hand, regions are territories within a state, occasionally crossing state borders. On the other hand, regions are particular areas of the world, covering a number of different sovereign states. We focus on this latter description of regionalism in our discussion.

In this chapter, we discuss four linked topics:

- First, we introduce the basics of international law that provide a framework for the interactions of states, international and regional actors, and nonstate actors in global politics.
- Next, we turn to the United Nations, the largest international organization with a mandate to prevent future world wars and protect human rights.
- We then discuss the concept of regional integration, with a focus on the European Union, the most successful and comprehensive regional organization.
- In the final section, we explore the wide variety of nonstate actors and the increasingly important role these actors are playing in global politics.

Nonstate actor Any participant in global politics that is neither acting in the name of government nor created and served by government. Nongovernmental organizations, terrorist networks, global crime syndicates, and multinational corporations are examples.

Regime A set of implicit or explicit principles, norms, rules, and decision-making procedures around which actors' expectations converge in a given area of international relations. Often simply defined as a governing arrangement in a regional or global policy area.

International law The formal rules of conduct that states acknowledge or contract between themselves.

International Law

In this section, we consider the practice of modern international law and the debates surrounding its nature and efficacy. For our purposes, there is one central question: What is the relationship between international law and international politics? If the power and interests of states are what matters, as we discussed in Chapter 4, then international law is either a servant of the powerful or an irrelevant curiosity. And yet, if international law does *not* matter, then why do states and other actors devote so much effort to negotiating new legal regimes and augmenting existing ones? Why does so much international debate revolve around the legality of state behavior, the applicability of legal rules, and the legal obligations incumbent on states? Moreover, why is compliance with international law so high, even by domestic standards?

International institutions
Complexes of norms, rules, and practices that prescribe behavioral roles, constrain activity, and shape expectations.

International law is best understood as a core international institution—a set of norms, rules, and practices created by states and other actors to facilitate diverse social goals, from order and coexistence to justice and human development. It is an institution with distinctive historical roots, and understanding these roots is essential to grasping its unique institutional features.

International Order and Institutions

International organization
Any institution with formal procedures and formal membership from three or more countries. The minimum number of countries is set at three, rather than two, because multilateral relationships have significantly greater complexity than bilateral relationships.

Realists portray international relations as a struggle for power, a realm in which states are "continuously preparing for, actively involved in, or recovering from organized violence in the form of war" (Morgenthau 1985, 52). Although war has certainly been a recurrent feature of international life, it is a crude and deeply dysfunctional way for states to ensure their security or realize their interests. Because of this, states have devoted as much, if not more, effort to liberating themselves from the condition of war than to embroiling themselves in violent conflict. Creating some modicum of international order has been an abiding common interest of most states most of the time (Bull 1977, 8).

To achieve international order, states have created international institutions. People often confuse institutions and organizations, incorrectly using the two terms interchangeably. **International institutions** are commonly defined as complexes of norms, rules, and practices that "prescribe behavioral roles, constrain activity, and shape expectations" (Keohane 1989a, 3; see Table 5.1). **International organizations**, like the United Nations, are physical entities that have staffs, head offices, and letterheads. International institutions can exist without any organizational structure—the 1997 Ottawa Convention banning land mines is an institution, but there

Japanese whaling vessels leave for a trip to the Antarctic, despite the fact that the International Court of Justice (ICJ) ruled Japan's whaling expeditions illegal. Historically, many countries have disregarded international law in order to promote their national interests. What can be done to make international laws more effective? How can international organizations enforce their rulings?

| TABLE 5.1 | **Levels of International Institutions** |

Institution	Description
Constitutional	Constitutional institutions comprise the primary rules and norms of international society without which society among sovereign states could not exist. The most commonly recognized of these is the norm of sovereignty, which holds that within the state, power and authority are centralized and hierarchical, and outside the state no higher authority exists. The norm of sovereignty is supported by a range of auxiliary norms, such as the right to self-determination and the norm of nonintervention.
Fundamental	Fundamental institutions rest on the foundation provided by constitutional institutions. They represent the basic norms and practices that sovereign states employ to facilitate coexistence and cooperation under conditions of international anarchy. They are the rudimentary practices states reach for when seeking to collaborate or coordinate their behavior. Fundamental institutions have varied from one historical system of states to another, but in the modern international system, contractual international law and multilateralism have been the most important.
Issue-specific, or *regimes*	Issue-specific institutions, or *regimes*, are the most visible or palpable of all international institutions. They are the sets of rules, norms, and decision-making procedures that states formulate to define legitimate actors and action in a given domain of international life. Examples of regimes are the Framework Convention on Climate Change and the International Covenant on Civil and Political Rights. Importantly, issue-specific institutions or regimes are concrete enactments of fundamental institutional practices such as international law and multilateralism.

is no head office. Many institutions have organizational dimensions, however. The WTO (formerly the General Agreement on Tariffs and Trade) is an institution with a very strong organizational structure. Whereas institutions can exist without an organizational dimension, international organizations cannot exist without an institutional framework. Their very existence presupposes a set of norms, rules, and principles that empower them to act and that they are charged to uphold. If states had never negotiated the Charter of the United Nations, the organization could not exist, let alone function.

In modern international society, states have created three levels of institutions:

- There are deep constitutional institutions, such as the principle of sovereignty, which define the terms of legitimate statehood.
- States have also created fundamental institutions, like international law and multilateralism, which provide the basic rules and practices that shape how states solve cooperation and coordination problems. These are the institutional norms, techniques, and structures that states and other actors invoke and employ when they have common ends they want to achieve or clashing interests they want to contain.
- Last, states have developed issue-specific institutions or regimes, such as the Treaty on the Nonproliferation of Nuclear Weapons, which enact fundamental

In 2009, the International Criminal Court (ICC) indicted Sudanese President Omar al-Bashir for committing genocide in the Darfur region. However, to this day he remains in power in Sudan. The ICC is a rather new institution and it is criticized for only indicting African leaders. The United States and other major powers have not supported the ICC and that limits its jurisdiction and authority. What are the chances of the ICC becoming an effective institution with global jurisdiction?

Multilateral diplomacy
Cooperation among three or more states based on, or with a view to formulating, reciprocally binding rules of conduct.

institutional practices in particular realms of interstate relations. The treaty is a concrete expression of the practices of international law and multilateralism in the field of arms control.

We are concerned here with the middle-level, fundamental institutions. These are "the elementary rules of practice that states formulate to solve the coordination and collaboration problems associated with coexistence under anarchy" (Reus-Smit 1999, 14). In modern international society, a range of such institutions exist, including international law, multilateralism, bilateralism, diplomacy, and management by the great powers. Since the middle of the nineteenth century, however, the first two (international law and multilateralism) have provided the basic framework for international cooperation and the pursuit of order.

How do states develop international law? Why do states follow international law if there is no international government to enforce these laws? Why is international law not given a higher priority in the study of international relations? These are important questions that might help us understand the development of international law as an international institution.

The principal mechanism modern states employ to legislate international law is **multilateral diplomacy**, commonly defined as cooperation among three or more states based on, or with a view to formulating, reciprocally binding rules of conduct. It is a norm of the modern international legal system that states are obliged to observe legal rules because they have consented to those rules. A state that has not consented to the rules of a particular legal treaty is not bound by those rules. The only exception to this concerns rules of customary international law, and even then, implied or tacit consent plays an important role in the determination of which rules have customary status.

In many historical periods, and in many social and cultural settings, the political and legal realms are entwined. For instance, the absolutist conception of sovereignty bound the two realms together in the figure of the sovereign. In the modern era, by contrast, the political and legal realms are thought to be radically different, with their own logics and institutional settings. Domestically, this view informs ideas about the constitutional separation of powers; internationally, it has encouraged the view that international politics and law are separate spheres of social action. This has not only affected how the academic disciplines of international relations and law have evolved, but also how state practice has evolved.

Realists generally believe that international law should serve the interests of the powerful states. This perspective has led to criticisms of international law and of international organizations like the United Nations, which protects the interests of major powers by focusing decision-making power in the Security Council. As we will discuss, some non-Western states argue that many of these laws do not account for their interests, traditions, and values.

Criticisms of International Law

From one perspective, international law is easily cast as a Western, even imperial, institution. As we have seen, its roots lie in the European intellectual movements of the sixteenth and seventeenth centuries. Ideas propagated at that time drew a clear distinction between international laws that were appropriate among Christian peoples and those that should govern how Christians related to peoples in the Muslim world, the Americas, and, later, Asia. The former were based on assumptions of the inherent equality of Christian peoples and the latter on the inherent superiority of Christians over non-Christians.

Further evidence of this Western bias can be found in the "standard of civilization" that European powers codified in international law during the nineteenth century (Gong 1984). According to this standard, non-Western polities were granted sovereign recognition only if they exhibited certain domestic political characteristics and only if they were willing and able to participate in the prevailing diplomatic practices. The standard was heavily biased toward Western political and legal institutions as the accepted model. Based on this standard, European powers divided the world's peoples into "civilized," "barbarian," and "savage" societies, divisions they used to justify various degrees of Western authority.

Many claim that Western bias still characterizes the international legal order. Critics point to the Anglo-European dominance of major legal institutions, most notably the UN Security Council, and international human rights law, which they argue imposes a set of Western values about the rights of the individual on non-Western societies where such ideas are alien. According to this argument, Western powers use their privileged position on the Security Council to intervene in the domestic politics of weak, developing countries.

There is truth in these criticisms. However, the nature and role of international law in contemporary world politics are more complex than they appear. At the heart of the modern international legal system lies a set of customary norms that uphold the legal equality of all sovereign states, as well as their rights to self-determination and nonintervention. Non-Western states have been the most vigorous proponents and defenders of these cardinal legal norms. In addition, non-Western peoples were more centrally involved in the development of the international human rights regime than is commonly acknowledged. The Universal Declaration of Human Rights (1948) was the product of a deliberate and systematic process of intercultural dialogue, involving representatives of all of the world's major cultures (Glendon 2002). The International Covenant on Civil and Political Rights (1966), often portrayed as a reflection of Western values, was shaped in critical ways by newly independent postcolonial states (Reus-Smit 2001). What's more, international human rights law has been an important resource in the struggles of many subject peoples against repressive governments and against institutions such as colonialism.

From International to Supranational Law?

So long as international law was designed primarily to facilitate international order—to protect the negative liberties (i.e., freedom from outside interference) of sovereign states—it remained a limited, if essential, institution. In recent decades, however, states have sought to move beyond the simple pursuit of international order, toward the objective of global governance, and international law has begun to change in fascinating ways.

First, although states are "still at the heart of the international legal system" (Higgins 1994, 39), individuals, groups, and organizations are increasingly recognized as subjects of international law. An expansive body of international human rights law has developed, supported by evolving mechanisms of enforcement. Examples of enforcement include the war crimes tribunals (discussed later in this chapter) for Rwanda and the former Yugoslavia, the creation of the International Criminal Court (ICC), and the twenty-three cases the ICC is pursuing against war criminals.

Second, nonstate actors are becoming important *agents* in the international legal process. Although such actors cannot formally enact international law, and their practices do not contribute to the development of customary international law, they often play a crucial role in the following:

- Shaping the normative environment in which states codify specific legal rules.
- Providing information to national governments that encourages the redefinition of state interests and the convergence of policies across states.
- Drafting international treaties and conventions (the first of which was the 1864 Geneva Convention, drafted by the International Committee of the Red Cross; Finnemore 1996).

Third, the rules, norms, and principles of international law are no longer confined to maintaining international order, narrowly defined. Recent decisions by the UN Security Council have treated gross violations of human rights by sovereign states as threats to global peace and security, thus legitimating action under Chapter VII of the UN Charter. (Examples include the international intervention in East Timor in 1999 and, more recently, the authorization of measures to protect civilians in Libya in 2011.) In doing so, the Security Council implies that international order is dependent on the maintenance of at least minimum standards of global justice.

Because of these changes, international law might be gradually transforming into a system of supranational law. States are no longer the only subjects and agents of international law, and it has expanded into global regulation, with a scope encompassing issues of justice as well as order.

This desire to promote a rule-based global society that would protect human rights and prevent war led world leaders to create the United Nations in 1945. We now take a step back in time and turn to a discussion of this important international institution.

The United Nations

The **United Nations** has the unique status of being the largest international organization, what some call a **supranational global organization**, and the only one that has a universal focus. Other supranational organizations with more specific responsibilities include the World Bank, the IMF, and the WTO. The states that make up the United Nations created a group of international institutions, which include the central system located in

San Francisco was the scene of the signing of the UN Charter in 1945. Has the time come to revise the document and reform the United Nations?

New York; the Specialized Agencies, such as the World Health Organization (WHO) and the International Labor Organization; and the Programmes and Funds, such as the United Nations Children's Fund (UNICEF) and the United Nations Development Programme (UNDP). When it was created in the aftermath of World War II, the United Nations reflected the hope for a just and peaceful global community.

The United Nations is the only global institution with legitimacy that derives from universal membership and a mandate that encompasses security, economic and social development, and the protection of human rights and the environment. Yet the United Nations was created by states for states, and questions about the meaning of **state sovereignty** and the limits of UN action remain key issues.

Since its founding, UN activities have expanded to address political, economic, and social conditions within states. Threats to global security addressed by the United Nations now include interstate conflict and threats by nonstate actors. In 2005, the United Nations established the **Responsibility to Protect Resolution (R2P)**, asserting the moral obligation for states to intervene in other states that violate human rights.

Despite the expanding scope of UN activities, there are some questions about the relevance and effectiveness of the United Nations. The failure of the United States and the United Kingdom to get clear UN Security Council authorization for the war in Iraq in 2003 led to well-publicized criticism of the United Nations and a crisis in international relations. Yet the troubled aftermath of the invasion and persistent questions about the legitimacy of a war that was not sanctioned by the United Nations show that it has acquired important moral status in international society.

After describing the history and main organs of the United Nations, this section looks at its changing role in addressing matters of peace and security and economic and social development. We also focus on how the United Nations' role

United Nations Founded in 1945 following World War II, it is an international organization composed of 193 member states dedicated to addressing issues related to peace and security, development, human rights, humanitarian affairs, and international law.

Supranational global organization An authoritative international organization that operates above the nation-state.

State sovereignty The concept that all countries are equal under international law and that they are protected from outside interference; this is the basis on which the United Nations and other international and regional organizations operate.

Responsibility to Protect Resolution (R2P) Resolution supported by the United Nations in 2005 to determine the international community's responsibility in preventing mass atrocities, reacting to crises, protecting citizens, rebuilding, and preventing future problems.

Collective security An arrangement where "each state in the system accepts that the security of one is the concern of all, and agrees to join in a collective response to aggression" (Roberts and Kingsbury 1993, 30).

United Nations Charter (1945) The legal regime that created the United Nations. The charter defines the structure of the United Nations, the powers of its constitutive agencies, and the rights and obligations of sovereign states party to the charter.

League of Nations The first permanent collective international security organization aimed at preventing future wars and resolving global problems. The League failed due to the unwillingness of the United States to join and the inability of its members to commit to a real international community.

has evolved in response to changes in the global political context and on some of the problems that it still faces.

A Brief History of the United Nations and Its Principal Organs

The United Nations was established on October 24, 1945, by fifty-one countries as a result of initiatives taken by the governments of the states that had led the war against Italy, Germany, and Japan. As early as 1939, American and British diplomats were discussing the need for a more effective international organization like the United Nations. It was intended to be a **collective security** organization, an arrangement where "each state in the system accepts that the security of one is the concern of all, and agrees to join in a collective response to aggression" (A. Roberts and Kingsbury 1993, 30). Unfortunately, as we will see later in this chapter, the Cold War bipolar international system undermined the effectiveness of the United Nations in security affairs.

There are 193 member states of the United Nations—nearly every state in the world. Notable exceptions include Western Sahara and Kosovo (neither of which is recognized as a self-governing territory), Taiwan (which is not recognized as a separate territory from China), and Palestine and Vatican City (both of which enjoy non-member observer status). Member states agree to accept the obligations of the **United Nations Charter**, an international treaty that sets out basic principles of international relations. According to the Charter, the United Nations has four purposes: to maintain international peace and security, to develop friendly relations among nations, to cooperate in solving international problems and in promoting respect for human rights, and to be a center for harmonizing the actions of nations. At the United Nations, all the member states—large and small, rich and poor, with differing political views and social systems—have a voice and a vote in this process. Interestingly, although the United Nations was clearly created as a grouping of states, the Charter refers to the needs and interests of peoples as well as those of states (see Table 5.2).

In many ways, the United Nations was set up to correct the problems of its predecessor, the **League of Nations**. The League of Nations was established after World War I and was intended to make future wars impossible, but it lacked effective power. There was no clear division of responsibility between the main executive committee (the League Council) and the League Assembly, which included all member states. Both the League Assembly and the League Council could only make recommendations, not binding resolutions, and these recommendations had to be unanimous. Any government was free to reject any recommendation. Furthermore, there was no mechanism for coordinating military or economic actions against miscreant states. Key states, such as the United States, were not members of the League. By World War II, the League had failed to address a number of acts of aggression.

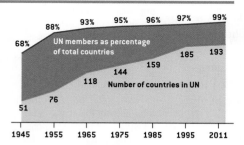

Growth in UN Membership.

There are 196 countries in the world and 193 are members of the United Nations (the most recent member to join was South Sudan in 2011). If the UN Security Council continues to block effective action like preventing mass atrocities in Darfur and punishing the Syrian government for using chemical weapons, do you think countries will quit the United Nations?

TABLE 5.2	**The UN Charter Contains References to Both the Rights of States and the Rights of People**
Type of Right	**Supporting Excerpt from the Charter**
People	**The Preamble** of the UN Charter asserts that "We the peoples of the United Nations [are] determined [. . .] to reaffirm faith in fundamental human rights, in the dignity and worth of the human person, in the equal rights of men and women and of nations large and small."
People	**Article 1(2)** states that the purpose of the United Nations is to develop "friendly relations among nations based on respect for the principle of equal rights and self-determination of peoples and to take other appropriate measures to strengthen universal peace."
State	**Article 2(7)** states that "Nothing contained in the present Charter shall authorize the United Nations to intervene in matters which are essentially within the domestic jurisdiction of any state."
State	**Chapter VI** deals with the "Pacific Settlement of Disputes."
State	**Article 33** states that "The parties to any dispute, the continuance of which is likely to endanger the maintenance of international peace and security, shall, first of all, seek a solution by negotiation, enquiry, mediation, conciliation, arbitration, judicial settlement, resort to regional agencies or arrangements, or other peaceful means of their own choice."
State	**Chapter VII** deals with "Action with Respect to Threats to the Peace, Breaches of the Peace, and Acts of Aggression."
State	**Article 42** states that the Security Council "may take such action by air, sea, or land forces as may be necessary to maintain or restore international peace and security." The Security Council has sometimes authorized member states to use "all necessary means," and this has been accepted as a legitimate application of Chapter VII powers.
State	**Article 99** authorizes the secretary-general to "bring to the attention of the Security Council any matter which in his opinion may threaten the maintenance of international peace and security."

The structure of the United Nations was intended to avoid some of the problems faced by the League of Nations. The United Nations has six main organs: the Security Council, the General Assembly, the Secretariat, the Economic and Social Council, the Trusteeship Council, and the International Court of Justice (see Figure 5.1).

The Security Council

The **United Nations Security Council** was given the main responsibility for maintaining international peace and security. It is made up of fifteen member states, ten nonpermanent members and five permanent members (sometimes called the P5): the United States, Britain, France, Russia (previously the Soviet Union)—the victors in World War II—and China. In contrast to the League of Nations, the United Nations recognized great-power prerogatives in the Security Council, offering each of the P5 a **veto power** over all Security Council decisions. The convention emerged

United Nations Security Council The council made up of five permanent member states (sometimes called the P-5)—namely, Great Britain, China, France, Russia, and the United States—and ten nonpermanent members. The P-5 all have a veto power over all Security Council decisions.

Veto power The right of the five permanent members of the Security Council (United States, Russia, China, France, and Great Britain) to forbid any action by the United Nations.

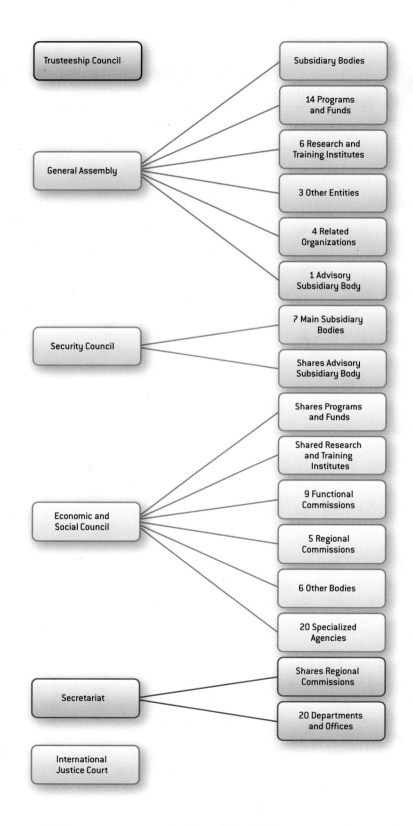

Figure 5.1 **The Structure of the United Nations.**

that abstention by a permanent member is not regarded as a veto. Unlike with the League, the decisions of the Security Council are binding and must be passed by only a majority of nine of the fifteen members. However, if one permanent member dissents, the resolution does not pass.

The five permanent members of the Security Council were seen as the major powers when the United Nations was founded. They were granted a veto on the view that if the great powers were not given a privileged position, the United Nations would not work. This recognition of a state's influence being proportional to its size and political and military power stems from the realist notion that power determines who rules in the international system. Indeed, this tension between the recognition of power politics through the Security Council veto and the universal ideals underlying the United Nations is a defining feature of the organization. There have been widespread and frequent calls for the reform of the Security Council, but this is very difficult. In both theoretical and policy terms, the inability to reform the Security Council shows the limits of a collective security system and liberal thinking that suggests all states are equal.

When the Security Council considers a threat to international peace, it first explores ways to settle the dispute peacefully. It might suggest principles for a settlement or mediation. In the event of fighting, the Security Council tries to secure a ceasefire. It might send a peacekeeping mission to help the parties maintain the truce and to keep opposing forces apart. The Council can also take measures to enforce its decisions under Chapter VII of the Charter, for instance, by imposing **economic sanctions** or ordering an arms embargo. (See Chapter 4 for a discussion of these foreign policy tools.) On rare occasions, the Security Council has authorized member states to use all necessary means, including collective military action, to see that its decisions are carried out. The Council also makes recommendations to the General Assembly on the appointment of a new secretary-general and on the admission of new members to the United Nations.

Economic sanctions A tool of statecraft that seeks to get a state to behave by coercion of a monetary kind—for example, freezing banking assets, cutting aid programs, or banning trade.

> **WHAT'S YOUR WORLDVIEW?**
>
> *The leaders of many states demand respect for their national sovereignty. How might that hurt the chance of success for any international or regional organization? How might that influence the future of the United Nations and other international and regional organizations?*

The General Assembly

The recognition of power politics through veto power in the Security Council can be contrasted with the universal principles underlying the other organs of the United Nations. All UN member states are represented in the **United Nations General Assembly**—a "parliament of nations"—which meets to consider the world's most pressing problems. Each member state has one vote. A two-thirds majority in the General Assembly is required for decisions on key issues such as international peace and security, the admission of new members, and the UN budget. A simple majority is required for other matters. However, the decisions reached by the General Assembly only have the status of recommendations, rather than binding decisions. One of the few exceptions is the General Assembly's Fifth Committee, which makes decisions on the budget that are binding on members.

United Nations General Assembly Often referred to as a "parliament of nations," it is composed of all member states, which meet to consider the world's most pressing problems. Each state has one vote, and a two-thirds majority in the General Assembly is required for decisions on key issues. Decisions reached by the General Assembly only have the status of recommendations and are not binding.

The General Assembly can consider any matter within the scope of the UN Charter. Recent topics discussed by the General Assembly include the impact of globalization on societies, the role of diamonds in fueling conflict, international cooperation in the peaceful uses of outer space, peacekeeping operations, sustainable development, and international migration. Because General Assembly resolutions are nonbinding, they cannot force action by any state, but the Assembly's recommendations are important indications of world opinion and represent the moral authority of the community of nation-states.

The Secretariat

United Nations Secretariat
The Secretariat carries out the administrative work of the United Nations as directed by the General Assembly, Security Council, and other organs. The Secretariat is led by the secretary-general, who provides overall administrative guidance.

The **United Nations Secretariat** carries out the substantive and administrative work of the United Nations as directed by the General Assembly, the Security Council, and the other organs. It is led by the secretary-general, who provides overall administrative guidance. In December 2006, Ban Ki-moon from South Korea was sworn in as the eighth secretary-general.

On the recommendation of the other bodies, the Secretariat also carries out a number of research functions and some quasi-management functions. Yet the role of the Secretariat remains primarily bureaucratic, and it lacks the political power of, for instance, the Commission of the EU. The one exception to this is the power of the secretary-general, under Article 99 of the Charter, to bring situations that are likely to lead to a breakdown of international peace and security to the attention of the Security Council. This article was the legal basis for the remarkable expansion of the diplomatic role of the secretary-general. The secretary-general is empowered to become involved in a large range of areas that can be loosely interpreted as threats to peace, including economic and social problems and humanitarian crises.

The Economic and Social Council

United Nations Economic and Social Council (ECOSOC)
This council is intended to coordinate the economic and social work of the United Nations and the UN family organizations. The ECOSOC has a direct link to civil society through communications with nongovernmental organizations (NGOs).

The **United Nations Economic and Social Council (ECOSOC)**, under the overall authority of the General Assembly, is intended to coordinate the economic and social work of the United Nations and the UN family of organizations. It also consults with NGOs, thereby maintaining a vital link between the United Nations and civil society. ECOSOC's subsidiary bodies include functional commissions, such as the Commission on the Status of Women and regional commissions, such as the Economic Commission for Africa.

The UN Charter established ECOSOC to oversee economic and social institutions. ECOSOC does not have necessary management powers, however; it can only issue recommendations and receive reports. In consequence, the United Nations' economic and social organizations have continually searched for better ways of achieving effective management.

WHAT'S YOUR WORLDVIEW?

Given the global economic troubles we now face, should the United Nations create an Economic Security Council that would replace or work with the G20? Who should belong? What could it do, and could it be effective?

The Organisation of Economic Co-operation and Development

The OECD, which was founded in 1961 and currently has thirty-four member countries, promotes policies to improve the economic and social well-being of people around the world. Through the OECD's Student Ambassador Program, an on-campus, yearlong ambassadorship, you can engage with the OECD and plan activities to raise awareness. The OECD works with governments to understand what drives economic, social, and environmental change; measures productivity and global flows of trade and investment; and analyzes and compares data to predict future trends. To learn more about getting involved, check out www.oecd.org.

The Trusteeship Council

When the United Nations was created, the **United Nations Trusteeship Council** was established to provide international supervision for eleven Trust Territories administered by seven member states and to ensure that adequate steps were taken to prepare the territories for self-government or independence. By 1994, all Trust Territories had attained self-government or independence, either as separate states or by joining neighboring independent countries. The last to do so was the Trust Territory of the Pacific Islands, Palau, which had been previously administered by the United States under special rules with the United Nations called a strategic trust. With its work completed, the Trusteeship Council now consists of the five permanent members of the Security Council. It has amended its rules of procedure to allow it to meet when necessary.

United Nations Trusteeship Council Upon creation of the United Nations, this council was established to provide international supervision for eleven trust territories administered by seven member states in an effort to prepare them for self-government or independence. By 1994, all trust territories had attained self-government or independence, and the council now meets on an ad hoc basis.

The International Court of Justice

The **International Court of Justice (ICJ)** is the main judicial organ of the United Nations. Consisting of fifteen judges elected jointly by the General Assembly and the Security Council, the Court decides disputes between countries. Participation by states in a proceeding is voluntary, but if a state agrees to participate, it is obligated to comply with the Court's decision. The Court also provides advisory opinions to other UN organs and specialized agencies on request. Only states may bring cases before the ICJ. If people who live in one state want to bring a suit against another state, they must get their home state to file the suit.

Three factors reduce the effectiveness of the ICJ:

- First, the competence, or jurisdiction, of the Court is limited, as already noted, to cases that states bring against states. The Court's statutory jurisdiction extends to anything related to a state's undertakings by signing the UN

International Court of Justice (ICJ) The main judicial organ of the United Nations consisting of fifteen judges elected jointly by the General Assembly and Security Council. The ICJ handles disputes between states, not individuals and states, and although a state does not have to participate in a case, if it elects to do so it must obey the decision.

Women in Jakarta, Indonesia, commemorate International Human Rights Day by demanding a more transparent legal system. Although international law and global institutions have prompted countries to protect human rights, there is still a need for improvement in many regions of the world. Beyond promoting international laws, what can the international community do to protect human rights?

Charter and any matter related to a ratified treaty. If a state is not a signatory, there can be no recourse to the ICJ. In addition, if the United Nations itself is a party to the case, at least one state party of the ICJ must be an applicant as well.

- Second is the question of compulsory jurisdiction. States that are party to the ICJ statute are not bound by compulsory jurisdiction unless they agree to it; this is the "option clause" problem. For example, in the *Aerial Incident of July 27, 1955 (Israel v. Bulgaria)* the court found that Bulgaria was not liable for damages because its compulsory jurisdiction option had expired.

- A third factor—the state reservations—follows from the option-clause problems: not only may a state let its compulsory jurisdiction lapse, but also it can refuse to accept the ICJ jurisdiction if the state claims that its own existing national law covers the issue before the courts. This occurred in a 1957 case in which Norway sued France over a debt owed to Norwegian investors. France claimed that its domestic legal system had jurisdiction in the matter, and Norway lost.

In Chapter 7, we discuss the International Criminal Court, an independent international organization that is not part of the United Nations.

Maintenance of International Peace and Security

Political context has shaped the performance of the United Nations in questions of peace and security. Clearly, changes in international society since the United Nations was founded in 1945 have had an impact on the UN system. The Cold War hampered the functioning of the UN Security Council, because the veto could be used whenever the major interests of the United States or Soviet Union were threatened. From 1945 to 1990, 193 substantive vetoes were invoked in the Security Council, compared with only 31 substantive vetoes from 1990 to 2015. Furthermore, although the UN Charter provided for a standing army to be set up by agreement between the Security Council and consenting states, the East–West Cold War rivalry made this impossible to implement. The result was that the UN Security Council could not function in the way the UN founders had expected.

Because member states could not agree on the arrangements laid out in Chapter VII of the Charter, a series of improvisations followed to address matters of peace and security:

- First, the United Nations established a procedure under which the Security Council agreed to a mandate for an agent to act on its behalf. This occurred in the Korean conflict in 1950 and the Gulf War in 1990, when the United States and its allies took principal action.
- Second, the United Nations has engaged in classical peacekeeping, which involves establishing a UN force under UN command to be placed between disputing parties after a ceasefire. Such a force uses its weapons only in self-defense, is established with the consent of the host state, and does not include forces from the major powers. The first instance of this was in 1956, when a UN force was sent to Egypt to facilitate the exodus of the British and French forces from the Suez Canal area and then to stand between Egyptian and Israeli forces. Since the Suez crisis, there have been a number of classical peacekeeping missions, for instance, at the Green Line in Cyprus, in the Golan Heights, and after the decade-long Iraq-Iran War. The primary drawback to this kind of peacekeeping operation is that it is not effective if the warring parties do not want peace. Such operations can also be difficult to conclude.
- Third, a new kind of peacekeeping, sometimes called multidimensional peacekeeping or **peace enforcement**, emerged after the Cold War. These missions are more likely to use force for humanitarian ends when order has collapsed within states (see Chapter 7 for more information). A key problem has been that peacekeepers have found it increasingly difficult to maintain a neutral position and have been targeted by belligerents. Examples include the intervention in Somalia in the early 1990s and intervention in the former Yugoslavia in the mid-1990s. In both cases, until the EU, NATO, or the United States was directly involved in the operations, peace was elusive.

Peace enforcement Designed to bring hostile parties to agreement and may occur without the consent of the parties.

After the end of the Cold War, the UN agenda for peace and security expanded quickly. Then Secretary-General Boutros Boutros-Ghali outlined a more ambitious role for the United Nations in his seminal report, *An Agenda for Peace* (1992). The report described interconnected roles for the United Nations to maintain peace and security in the post–Cold War context. These included four main kinds of activities:

Preventive diplomacy Measures that states take to keep a disagreement from escalating.

Peacemaking Active diplomatic efforts to seek a resolution to an international dispute that has already escalated.

1) **preventive diplomacy**, which involves confidence-building measures, fact finding, and preventive deployment of UN authorized forces;
2) **peacemaking**, designed to bring hostile parties to agreement, essentially through peaceful means;
3) **peacekeeping**, the deployment of a UN presence in the field with the consent of all parties (classical peacekeeping); and
4) **post-conflict peace building**, which ideally will develop the social, political, and economic infrastructure to prevent further violence and to consolidate peace.

Peacekeeping The interposition of third-party military personnel to keep warring parties apart.

Post-conflict peace building Activities launched after a conflict has ended that seek to end the condition that caused the conflict.

WHAT'S YOUR WORLDVIEW?

Why would a country decide to participate in a UN peacekeeping operation? What factors would motivate it to participate in such a collective action? Is this part of a country's domestic political culture? What kind of worldview would they most likely hold?

However, when all peaceful means have failed, peace enforcement authorized under Chapter VII of the Charter might be necessary, and it may occur without the consent of the parties in conflict.

In 2015, the total number of peacekeeping personnel (troops, military observers, police, civilian personnel, and UN volunteers) in the United Nations' sixteen ongoing peacekeeping operations was just over 124,000 (UN 2015). Since 1948, 3,395 UN peacekeeping forces have died; in current operations, 1,620 UN personnel have been killed (see Table 5.3).

Increased Attention to Conditions Within States

The new peacekeeping was the product of a greater preparedness to intervene within states. An increasing number of people believed that the international community, working through the United Nations, should address individual political and civil rights, as well as the right to basic provisions like food, water, health care, and accommodation. Under this view, violations of individuals' rights were a major cause of disturbances in relations between states: A lack of internal justice risked international disorder. The United Nations reinforced this new perception that pursuing justice for individuals, or ensuring **human security**, was an aspect of national interest. (We discuss human security in Chapter 7.)

In some states, contributions to activities such as peacekeeping were defended in terms of national interest. States such as Canada and Norway could justify their contributions to peacekeeping as a "moral" course of action, but these

Human security The security of people, including their physical safety, their economic and social well-being, respect for their dignity, and the protection of their human rights.

| TABLE 5.3 | UN Peacekeeping Operations (as of August 31, 2015) |

Location	Origin of Operation	Location	Origin of Operation
Middle East (UNTSO)	1948	Haiti	2004
India and Pakistan	1949	Côte d'Ivoire	2004
Cyprus	1964	Darfur	2007
Syria	1974	Congo, Democratic Republic of the	2010
Lebanon	1978	South Sudan	2011
Western Sahara	1991	Sudan	2011
Kosovo	1999	Mali	2013
Liberia	2003	Central African Republic	2014

Source: Copyright © United Nations 2015. United Nations Peacekeeping Fact Sheet: http://www.un.org/en/peacekeeping/resources/statistics/factsheet.shtml

contributions also served their national interests by enhancing their status in the international community. The Japanese also responded to moral pressure founded in national interest when they contributed substantially to defraying the cost of British involvement in the 1990–1991 Gulf War. This act can be explained in terms of the synthesis of morality and interest. For some states, a good reputation in the United Nations had become an important national goal.

In the past, the United Nations had helped to promote the traditional view of the primacy of international order between states over justice for individuals, so the new focus on individual rights was a significant change. What accounts for this change? We offer two reasons:

- First, the international environment had changed. The Cold War standoff between the East and the West had meant that member states did not want to question the conditions of the sovereignty of states.
- Second, some analysts made strong arguments that challenged the privileging of statehood over justice during the process of decolonization. Charles Beitz was one of the first, concluding that statehood should not be unconditional and that the situation of individuals after independence demanded attention (Beitz 1979). Michael Walzer (1977) and Terry Nardin (1983) came to similar conclusions: states were conditional entities in that their right to exist should be dependent on a criterion of performance. Such writings helped alter the moral content of diplomacy.

The new relationship between order and justice was, therefore, a product of particular circumstances. After the Cold War, the international community began to sense that threats to international peace and security did not emanate only from aggression between states. Rather, global peace was also threatened by civil conflict (including refugee flows and regional instability), humanitarian emergencies, violations of global standards of human rights, and other conditions such as poverty and inequality.

More recently, other types of non-state-based threats, such as terrorism and the proliferation of small arms and weapons of mass destruction, have had an increasingly prominent place on the UN security agenda. Partly in response to the terrorist attacks in the United States in 2001, as well as the impasse reached in the UN Security Council over Iraq in 2003, then Secretary-General Kofi Annan named a high-level panel to examine the major threats and challenges to global peace. The final report, *A More Secure World: Our Shared Responsibility* (UN 2004) emphasized the interconnected nature of security threats and presented development, security, and human rights as mutually reinforcing. Although many of the report's recommendations were not implemented, it led to the establishment of a new UN Peacebuilding Commission.

The UN Peacebuilding Commission was established in December 2005 as an advisory subsidiary body of the General Assembly and the Security Council. The secretary-general's High-Level Panel on Threats, Challenges, and Change

Neoconservatives and the United Nations

THE CHALLENGE

For analysts from the realist school of thought, states exist in an anarchic, self-help world, looking to their own power resources for national security. This was the perspective of the neoconservatives who dominated the administration of U.S. President George W. Bush. They subscribed to a strain of realist thinking that is best called hegemonist; that is, they believed the United States should use its power solely to secure its interests in the world. They were realists with idealistic tendencies, seeking to remake the world through promoting, by force, if necessary, freedom, democracy, and free enterprise.

Paul Wolfowitz, an important voice in the neoconservative camp, wrote that global leadership was all about "demonstrating that your friends will be protected and taken care of, that your enemies will be punished, and those who refuse to support you will live to regret having done so."* Although it would be wrong to assume that all realist thinkers and policymakers are opposed to international organizations such as the United Nations, most are wary of any organizations that prevent them from securing their national interests. The belief is that alliances should be only short-term events because allies might desert you in a crisis.

For some realists, such as the Bush neoconservatives, committing security to a collective security organization is even worse than an alliance because, in a worst-case situation, the alliance might gang up on your country. Even in the best-case situation, it would be a bad idea to submit your military forces to foreign leadership.

OPTIONS

In its early years, before the wave of decolonization in Africa and Asia, the United Nations' U.S.-based realist critics did not have the ear of the country's political leadership. Presidents Truman and Eisenhower both found a way around the USSR's Security Council veto by working through the General Assembly, a body that at the time was very friendly to the United States and its goals. However, with the end of European control of Africa and Asia, the General Assembly changed. The body frequently passed resolutions condemning the United States and its allies. One result was a growing movement to end U.S. involvement in the United Nations, especially among the key foreign policy advisers to President Reagan.

APPLICATION

In the 1980s, political realists saw no tangible benefit for the United States to remain active in the United Nations once the leaders in Washington could no longer count on a UN rubber stamp for U.S. policies. For a number of years, the United States did not pay its dues to the United Nations.

This rejection of UN-style multilateralism revived with the George W. Bush presidency, beginning in 2001. In a controversial recess appointment, Bush chose John Bolton to be the U.S. ambassador to the United Nations in 2005. This appointment came as a surprise because Bolton was a staunch opponent of multilateral organizations such as the United Nations. The Bush foreign policy advisers were against the peacekeeping operation in the former Yugoslavia. In her criticism of Clinton administration foreign policy, then National Security Adviser Condoleezza Rice said the United States would not send its troops to countries for nation building. More important, the Bush administration did not want to have its hands tied when dealing with Iraq and its alleged store of nuclear, chemical, and biological weapons. President Bush and his top advisers believed that sanctions—an important weapon in the United Nations' moral-suasion arsenal—would never force Iraq to disarm and that only force could do so. The irony is that, after the 2003 invasion, the United States' own weapons inspectors could find no evidence that Iraq had any of the banned weapons.

*Paul Wolfowitz, "Remembering the Future," *National Interest* 59 (Spring 2000), p. 41.

For Discussion

1. What might be a Marxist criticism of the United Nations and its operations?

2. Is there any way to overcome realists' belief of international anarchy and the impossibility of global governance?

3. Some utopians believe that a world government would end war and provide answers to other global challenges. Do you agree or disagree? Why or why not?

4. Do the five permanent members of the Security Council have too much power over the operations of the organization? Why or why not?

argued that existing UN mechanisms were insufficient in responding to the particular needs of states emerging from conflict. Many countries, such as Liberia, Haiti, and Somalia in the 1990s, had signed peace agreements and hosted UN peacekeeping missions but reverted to violent conflict. The Peacebuilding Commission aims to provide targeted support to countries in the volatile post-conflict phase to prevent the recurrence of conflict. It proposes integrated strategies and priorities for post-conflict recovery to improve coordination among the myriad of actors involved in post-conflict activities. The establishment of the Peacebuilding Commission is indicative of a growing trend at the United Nations to coordinate security and development programming.

Intervention Within States

As the international community more clearly understood issues of peace and security to include human security and justice, it expected the United Nations to take on a stronger role in maintaining standards for individuals within states. One difficulty in carrying out this new task was that it seemed to run against the doctrine of nonintervention. **Intervention** was traditionally defined as a deliberate incursion into a state, without its consent, by some outside agency to change the functioning, policies, and goals of its government and achieve effects that favor the intervening agency (Vincent 1974).

Intervention The direct involvement within a state by an outside actor to achieve an outcome preferred by the intervening agency without the consent of the host state.

The founders of the United Nations viewed sovereignty as central to the system of states. States were equal members of international society and were equal with regard to international law. Sovereignty also implied that states recognized no higher authority than themselves and no superior jurisdiction. Intervention in the traditional sense was in opposition to the principles of international society, and it could be tolerated only as an exception to the rule.

By the 1990s, some believed that there should be a return to an earlier period when intervention was justified, but that a wider range of instruments should be used. Supporters of this idea insisted on a key role for the United Nations in granting a license to intervene. They pointed out that the UN Charter did not assert merely the rights of states, but also the rights of peoples: statehood could be interpreted as being conditional on respect for such rights. There was ample evidence in the UN Charter to justify the view that extreme transgressions of human rights could be a justification for intervention by the international community.

Yet there have been only a few occasions where a UN resolution justified intervention because of gross infringements of human rights. The justification of NATO's intervention in Kosovo in 1999 represented a break from the past in that it included a clear humanitarian element. Kosovo was arguably the first occasion in which international forces were used in defiance of a sovereign state to protect humanitarian standards. NATO launched an air campaign in March 1999 in Kosovo against the Republic of Yugoslavia without a mandate from the Security Council because Russia had declared that it would veto such action. Nonetheless, NATO states noted that by intervening to stop ethnic cleansing and crimes against humanity in Kosovo they were acting in accordance with the principles of the UN Charter. The U.S. action against Afghanistan in 2001 is an exceptional case in which the UN Security Council acknowledged the right of a state that had been attacked—referring to the events of 9/11—to respond in its own defense.

The difficulty in relaxing the principle of nonintervention should not be underestimated. For instance, the United Nations was reluctant to send troops to Rwanda, Bosnia, Kosovo, and Sudan to respond to acts of ethnic cleansing and genocide. More recently, the United Nations took several weeks to decide to intervene to protect civilians in Libya in 2011, and they have yet to decide how best to protect civilians in Syria's civil war. Some fear a slippery slope whereby a relaxation of the nonintervention principle by the United Nations will lead to military action by individual states without UN approval. There are significant numbers of non-UN actors, including regional organizations, involved in peace operations, and several states are suspicious of what appears to be the granting of a license to intervene in their affairs.

An increasing readiness by the United Nations to intervene within states to promote internal justice for individuals would indicate a movement toward global governance and away from unconditional sovereignty. There have been some signs of movement in this direction, but principles of state sovereignty and nonintervention remain important. There is no clear consensus on these points. There is still some support for the view that Article 2(7) of the UN Charter should be interpreted strictly: there can be no intervention within a state without the express consent of the government of that state. Others believe that intervention within a country to promote human rights is justifiable only on the basis of a threat to international peace and security. Evidence of a threat to international peace and security could be the appearance of significant numbers of refugees or the judgment that other states might intervene militarily. Some liberal internationalists argue that this condition is flexible enough to justify intervention to defend human rights whenever possible.

Overall, the United Nations' record on the maintenance of international peace and security has been mixed. There has been a stronger assertion of the responsibility of international society, represented by the United Nations, for gross offenses against populations. However, the practice has been patchy.

WHAT'S YOUR WORLDVIEW?

Much was written about the need to invoke the Responsibility to Protect (R2P) doctrine to help the citizens of Libya. NATO members cited R2P to justify intervention. Meanwhile, more than 250,000 people have died in the Syrian civil war. Why has the world done so little about this civil war and the death of innocents?

Economic and Social Questions

As we have discussed, conditions within states, including human rights, justice, development, and equality, have a bearing on global peace. The more integrated global context has meant that economic and social problems in one part of the world might affect other areas. Furthermore, promoting social and economic development is an important UN goal.

The number of institutions within the UN system that address economic and social issues has increased significantly since the founding of the United Nations.

Nonetheless, the main contributor states have been giving less and less to economic and social institutions. In 2000, the United Nations convened a Millennium Summit, where heads of state committed themselves to a series of measurable goals and targets, known as the Millennium Development Goals (MDGs), discussed in detail in Chapter 9. Although these eight goals were not completely achieved by 2015, UN efforts lifted more than one billion people out of extreme poverty and provided access to education and health care to a significant number of people on the margins of their societies. There is still much more to do, which is why the member states of the United Nations agreed to the 2030 Sustainable Development Agenda that includes 17 sustainable development goals and 169 targets. These build on the MDGs and seek to "free the human race from the tyranny of poverty" and focus development on sustainable economic, social, and environmental goals.

The Reform Process of the United Nations

In his important book *The Parliament of Man* (2006), Paul Kennedy suggests that any reform of the United Nations will need to be partial, gradual, and carefully executed. He argues that the need to make the United Nations more effective, representative, and accountable to its members is greater today than it was in the past because of a number of global developments, including the following:

1. The emergence of new great powers like India and Brazil and older powers like Japan and Germany who have been left out of the Security Council. Are the current members of the Security Council willing to add new members or even change the decision-making structure?
2. The presence of truly global issues that threaten the world as we know it. These include environmental degradation, terrorism, the proliferation of weapons of all kinds, and the persistence of global poverty. Is the United Nations interested in or capable of responding to these issues?

In the mid to late 1990s, alongside growing UN involvement in development issues, the UN economic and social arrangements underwent reform at two levels: first, reforms concerned with operations at the country (field) level; and second, reforms at the general, or headquarters, level.

Country Level

The continuing complaints of NGOs about poor UN performance in the field served as a powerful stimulus for reform. A key feature of the reforms at the country level was the adoption of Country Strategy Notes. These were statements about the overall development process tailored to the specific needs of individual countries. They were written on the basis of discussions among the Specialized Agencies, Programmes and Funds, donors, and the host country. The merit of the Country Strategy Notes is that they clearly set out targets, roles, and priorities.

Other reforms at the country level included the strengthening of the resident coordinator's role and enhanced authority for field-level officers. There was also an effort to introduce improved communication facilities and information sharing. The activities of the various UN organizations were brought together in single locations, or "UN houses," which facilitated inter-agency communication and collegiality. The adoption of the MDG framework and subsequent Sustainable Development Goals has also helped country field staff achieve a more coherent approach to development.

Headquarters Level

If the UN role in economic and social affairs at the country level was to be effective, reform was also required at the headquarters level. Because the Security Council is the main executive body within the United Nations, it is not surprising that many discussions of UN reform have focused on it.

The founders of the United Nations deliberately established a universal General Assembly and a restricted Security Council that required unanimity among the great powers. Granting permanent seats and the right to a veto to the great powers of the time was an essential feature of the deal.

The composition and decision-making procedures of the Security Council were increasingly challenged as membership in the United Nations grew, particularly after decolonization. Yet the only significant reform of the Security Council occurred in 1965, when the Council was enlarged from eleven to fifteen members and the required majority grew from seven to nine votes. The veto power of the permanent five members was left intact.

The Security Council does not reflect today's distribution of military or economic power, and it does not reflect a geographic balance. Germany and Japan have made strong cases for permanent membership. Developing countries have demanded more representation on the Security Council, particularly South Africa, India, Egypt, Brazil, and Nigeria. Should the European Union be represented instead of Great Britain, France, and Germany individually? How would Pakistan feel about India's candidacy? How would South Africa feel about a Nigerian seat? What about representation by an Islamic country? These issues are not easy to resolve. Likewise, it is very unlikely that the P5 states will relinquish their veto. Although large-scale reform has proved impossible thus far, changes in Security Council working procedures have made it more transparent and accountable to the member states.

Reform efforts in the 1990s focused on the reorganization and rationalization of the ECOSOC, the UN family of economic and social organizations. These efforts allowed ECOSOC to become more assertive and to take a leading role in the coordination of the UN system. They also aimed to eliminate duplication and overlap in the work of the functional commissions.

Overall, economic and social reorganization meant that the two poles of the system were better coordinated: the pole where intentions are defined through global conferences and agendas and the pole where programs are implemented.

Programs at the field level were better integrated, and field officers were given enhanced discretion. The reform of ECOSOC sharpened its capacity to shape broad agreements into cross-sectoral programs with well-defined objectives. At the same time, ECOSOC acquired greater capacity to act as a conduit through which the results of field-level monitoring could be conveyed upward to the functional commissions. These new processes had the effect of strengthening the norms, values, and goals of a multilateral system.

The European Union and Other Regional Organizations

Regionalism can be seen as one of the few instruments available to states to try to manage the effects of globalization. We define it as the use of regional rather than central systems of administration or economic, cultural, or political affiliation. If individual states no longer have the effective capacity to regulate, regionalism might be a means to regain some control over global market forces—and to counter the more negative social consequences of globalization.

Libyan Prime Minister Fayez al-Sarraj, left, and European Union Foreign Policy Chief Federica Mogherini participate in a media conference in Tunis, Tunisia, in early 2016. Mogherini has announced a major aid package for Libya's UN-supported unity government. The European Union is attempting to develop a foreign policy agenda and strategy that is more independent and reflects the interests of the member states.

The Process of European Integration

In Europe, regionalism after 1945 took the form of a gradual process of integration leading to the emergence of the **European Union (EU)**. It was initially a purely West European creation among the "original six" member states, born out of the desire for reconciliation between France and Germany in a context of ambitious federalist plans for a united Europe. Yet the process has taken the form of a progressive construction of an institutional architecture, a legal framework, and a wide range of policies, which in 2016 encompasses twenty-eight European states.

The European Coal and Steel Community was created in 1951 (in force in 1952), followed by the European Economic Community and the European Atomic Energy Community in 1957 (in force in 1958). These treaties involved a conferral of Community competence, or standards, in various areas—the supranational management of coal and steel, the creation and regulation of an internal market, and common policies in trade, competition, agriculture, and transport. Since then, powers have been extended to include new legislative competences in some fields such as the environment. Since the 1992 Treaty on European Union (the Maastricht Treaty, in force in 1993), the integration process has also involved the adoption of stronger forms of unification, notably monetary union, as well as

European Union (EU) The union formally created in 1992 following the signing of the Maastricht Treaty. The origins of the European Union can be traced back to 1951 and the creation of the European Coal and Steel Community, followed in 1957 with a broader customs union (the Treaty of Rome, 1958). Originally a grouping of six countries in 1957, "Europe" grew by adding new members in 1973, 1981, and 1986. Since the fall of the planned economies in Eastern Europe in 1989, Europe has grown and now includes twenty-eight member states.

cooperation in economic and employment policy, and more intergovernmental cooperation in foreign and security policy.

From very limited beginnings, in terms of both membership and scope, the European Union has gradually developed to become an important political and economic actor whose presence has a significant impact internationally and domestically. This gradual process of European integration has taken place at various levels. The first is the signature and reform of the basic treaties. These are the result of intergovernmental conferences, where representatives of national governments negotiate the legal framework within which the EU institutions operate. Such treaty changes require ratification in each country.

Within this framework, the institutions have considerable powers to adopt decisions and manage policies (Table 5.4), although the dynamics of decision-making differ significantly across arenas. There are important differences between the more integrated areas of economic regulation and the more intergovernmental pillars of foreign policy and police or judicial cooperation in criminal matters. In some areas, a country might have to accept decisions imposed on it by the (qualified) majority of member states. In other areas, it might be able to block decisions.

To understand the integration process, one needs to take account of the role played by both member states *and* supranational institutions. Member states are

TABLE 5.4   Institutions of the European Union

EU Institution	Responsibilities	Location
European Commission	Initiating, administering, and overseeing the implementation of EU policies and legislation	Brussels and Luxembourg
European Parliament (EP)	Acting as directly elected representatives of EU citizens, scrutinizing the operation of the other institutions, and, in certain areas, sharing the power to legislate	Strasbourg, Brussels, and Luxembourg
Council of Ministers	Representing the views of national governments and determining, in many areas jointly with the EP, the ultimate shape of EU legislation	Brussels (some meetings in Luxembourg)
European Council	Holding regular summits of the heads of state or government and the president of the commission, setting the European Union's broad agenda, and acting as a forum of last resort to find agreement on divisive issues (Note: different from the Council of Europe)	Brussels
European Court of Justice	Acting as the European Union's highest court (supported by a Court of First Instance)	Luxembourg
European Central Bank	Setting interest rates and controlling the money supply of the single European currency, the euro	Frankfurt
Court of Auditors	Auditing the revenues and the expenditure under the EU budget	Luxembourg

not just represented by national governments, as a host of state, nonstate, and transnational actors participate in the processes of domestic preference formation and direct representation of interests in the key EU institutions. The relative openness of the European policy process means that political groups and economic interests will try to influence EU decision-making if they feel that their position is not sufficiently represented by national governments. That is one reason the European Union is increasingly seen as a system of multilevel governance, involving a plurality of actors on different territorial levels: supranational, national, and local.

The complexity of the EU institutional machinery, together with continuous change over time, has spawned a lively debate among integration theorists (Rosamond 2000; Wiener and Diez 2004). Some scholars regard the European Union as sui generis—in a category of its own—and therefore in need of the development of dedicated theories of integration. The most prominent among these has been neofunctionalism, which sought to explain the evolution of integration in terms of "spillover" from one policy sector to another as resources and loyalties of elites were transferred to the European level. As aspects of EU politics have come to resemble the domestic politics of states, scholars have turned to approaches drawn from comparative politics or the study of governance in different states.

However, the exchange between "supranational" and "intergovernmental" approaches has had the greatest impact on the study of European integration. Supranational approaches regard the emergence of supranational institutions in Europe as a distinct feature and turn these into the main object of analysis. Here, the politics above the level of states is regarded as the most significant, and consequently the political actors and institutions at the European level receive the most attention.

Intergovernmental approaches, on the other hand, continue to regard states as the most important aspect of the integration process. Consequently, they concentrate on the study of politics *between* and *within* states. But most scholars would agree that no analysis of the European Union is complete without studying both the operation and evolution of the central institutions and the input from political actors in the member states.

The prospect of an ever *wider* European Union has raised serious questions about the nature and direction of the integration process. The 2004 enlargement, when ten additional states joined the European Union, was seen as a qualitative leap. Concerns that the enlarged Union, if not reformed substantially, would find it difficult to make decisions and maintain a reliable legal framework led to several attempts to reform the treaties. The most wide-ranging proposals, and the most significant change in the language of integration, came with the treaty establishing a constitution for Europe that EU governments signed in 2004. The very fact that the European Union should discuss something referred to in the media as a European Constitution is a sign of how far it has developed from its modest beginnings. However, the Constitutional Treaty was rejected in referendums in France and the Netherlands, raising serious doubts not only about this

The summer of 2015 saw thousands of refugees migrating to Europe from conflict-affected areas in the Middle East, Central Asia, and Africa. Here, European Commission President Jean-Claude Juncker, center, and European Commissioner for Economic and Financial Affairs Pierre Moscovici, right, discuss how to deal with the onslaught of refugees. This crisis challenges the future of the European Union. Some member states have closed their borders and refused to take in refugees as prescribed by the European Union.

attempt at institutional reform but also about ambitions for a formal constitutional process more generally.

After years of debate, the European Union's reform treaty came into force on December 1, 2009. EU leaders believe the now-ratified Lisbon Treaty will rejuvenate the decision-making apparatus of all of the EU institutions, making the functioning of the twenty-eight-member Union more efficient and democratic.

During the recent global economic crisis, Germany emerged as the clear leader of the eurozone and the European Union. Some in Germany are talking about a remaking of the European Union that would include more financial union, including some control over the members' budgets and spending; creating a eurobonds program; renegotiating many of the treaties that bind the EU members together; and even going so far as to create a federal Europe. Once again, a major crisis might serve as a catalyst for greater European integration.

Other Regional Actors: The African Union and the Organization of American States

African Union (AU) Created in 2002 and consisting of fifty-four member states, this union was formed as a successor to the Organization of African Unity. It maintains fourteen goals primarily centered on African unity and security, human rights, peace security and stability, economy, sustainable development, and equality.

Organization of African Unity (OAU) A regional organization founded in 1963 as a way to foster solidarity among African countries, promote African independence, and throw off the vestiges of colonial rule. The Organization of African Unity had a policy of noninterference in member states, and it had no means for intervening in conflicts; as a result, this organization could be only a passive bystander in many violent conflicts.

The **African Union (AU)** is the most important intergovernmental organization in Africa. It replaced the **Organization of African Unity (OAU)** in July 2002. The AU is made up of fifty-four African states, all but Morocco, which remains a nonmember at the time of this writing. The OAU was established in 1963 to provide a collective voice for Africa and to work to end all forms of colonization. It also sought to promote economic development and human rights and to improve the quality of life for all Africans. However, the OAU's record was not good, especially considering that nineteen of the twenty-three poorest countries in the world are in Africa. A number of major conflicts are creating almost insurmountable human security problems across the continent. Despite its general ineffectiveness, the OAU did succeed in encouraging its members to cooperate as a voting bloc in international organizations like the United Nations.

The AU still must deal with many of the same challenges as it attempts to fulfill its vision of creating "an integrated, prosperous and peaceful Africa, driven by its own citizens and representing a dynamic force in the global arena." The AU has a long way to go to be considered a successful regional organization. Achieving this success might be even more difficult as major powers like China, India, the United States, and European states all compete for access to African resources and turn a blind eye to abuses of governance in many states.

Turning to the Americas, the **Organization of American States (OAS)** is the world's oldest regional organization, founded in 1890. Known at the time as the International Union of American Republics, it changed its name to the Organization of American States in 1948. Its charter states that the goals of the organization are to create "an order of peace and justice, to promote their solidarity, to strengthen their collaboration, and to defend their sovereignty, their territorial integrity, and their independence." During the Cold War, the U.S. obsession with communism drove the OAS to intervene in the affairs of states and at times use extralegal activities to make certain that friendly governments stayed in power. The main pillars of the OAS are democracy, human rights, regional security, and economic development. In the thirty-five-member organization, the United States remains the dominant power, but with rising powers like Brazil, Chile, and Argentina and the intransigent Venezuela, the OAS could become a very effective regional organization and major player in global politics.

Global and regional state organizations are but one piece of the emerging pattern of global governance. We turn now to nongovernmental actors and examine their role in international life.

The Growth of Global Civil Society

The world of global activism is led by a number of nonstate actors: **international nongovernmental organizations** or **INGOs** (NGOs with members from at least three countries), philanthropic foundations that give money to global social movements, and powerful, wealthy, or famous individuals (e.g., Bill Gates, Bono, and the Dalai Lama) who use their expertise and resources to influence the formulation and implementation of public policy. All of these actors together make up what is known as a global or transnational **civil society**. Anheier, Glasius, and Kaldor (2004) define global civil society as

> *a supranational sphere of social and political participation in which citizen groups, social movements and individuals engage in dialogue, debate, confrontation and negotiation with each other, with governments, international and regional governmental organizations and with multinational corporations.*

Global civil society occupies the space between the state and the market; it is not constrained by national boundaries. Religious organizations, schools and other educational institutions, trade unions, and service organizations like Rotary International make up a traditional list of civil-society actors. Scholars in this area (e.g., Keck and Sikkink 1998) have added to this list INGOs, research groups or epistemic communities, foundations, and media organizations. Global civil society also includes social movements and advocacy networks. A **social movement** is defined as a mode of collective action that challenges ways of life, thinking, dominant norms, and moral codes; seeks answers to global problems; and promotes reform or transformation in political and economic institutions. Transnational social movements (TSMOs), often made up of NGOs and like-minded

Organization of American States (OAS) A regional international organization composed of thirty-five member states. It is the world's oldest regional organization, founded in 1890 as the International Union of American Republics and changing its name to Organization of American States in 1948. The goals of this organization are to create "an order of peace and justice, to promote their solidarity, to strengthen their collaboration, and to defend their sovereignty, their territorial integrity, and their independence."

International nongovernmental organization (INGO) A formal nongovernmental organization with members from at least three countries.

Civil society The totality of all individuals and groups in a society who are not acting as participants in any government institutions or acting in the interests of commercial companies.

Social movement A mode of collective action that challenges ways of life, thinking, dominant norms, and moral codes; seeks answers to global problems; and promotes reform or transformation in political and economic institutions.

governments and international organizations, have led many successful global campaigns to address issues such as famine in Africa, land mines, and corporate social responsibility in developing countries.

Transnational advocacy networks (TANs) are "networks of activists, distinguishable largely by the centrality of principled ideas or values in motivating their formation" (Keck and Sikkink 1998, 1). The advocates or activists in these networks "promote normative positions, lobby for policy reforms, and play an important role in policy debates over a wide variety of social issues" (Keck and Sikkink, 8–9). Both INGOs and governments can play a central role in these networks. TANs and TSMOs have taken advantage of the forces of globalization to increase the political effectiveness of their various campaigns, and the ease of communicating online has contributed to their rise. These movements and networks, which target governments at all levels, in some cases provide critical resources for political change and innovation. Making connections with other actors across the world is much easier with social media, global media outlets, greater financial resources, and INGO links to governments, academic institutions, and even global corporations.

Although not, strictly speaking, part of the global civil society, multinational corporations (MNCs) have formed their own INGOs and pro-business networks to lobby for their own interests and to counter the increasingly effective efforts of more progressive INGOs and TANs. Most global corporations support trade-and-aid policies, which encourage open markets and provide stability and protection for their investments. These corporations and their INGOs are up against numerous public campaigns to make corporations more accountable to the public and to force them to address environmental concerns, human rights, and social justice issues.

Some scholars have suggested that power and authority have shifted from states and public authorities toward actors in the global civil society. Although it is true that INGOs do provide services and resources in areas where states have failed to provide for their citizens, filling those gaps is only part of what these actors do for the world. In many situations, INGOs, think tanks, foundations, and even MNCs act as innovators and catalysts for change. Understanding the complexities of the global economy requires understanding more than states and IGOs. This is the world of global politics, not simply international relations, and we need to understand the specific roles played by the many types of nonstate actors.

> **Transnational advocacy network (TAN)** A network of activists—often, a coalition of NGOs—distinguishable largely by the centrality of principled ideas or values in motivating its formation.

Médecins Sans Frontières, or Doctors Without Borders, is a French secular humanitarian-aid nongovernmental organization. The organization won the Nobel Peace Prize, and it is best known for its projects in war-torn regions and developing countries facing endemic diseases. Here a nurse assists an Iraqi patient in Amman, Jordan. This NGO respects no boundaries that prevent it from taking care of people in need. Immanuel Kant would approve.

In the next sections of this chapter, we will introduce you to the major non-state actors that play important roles in the development of policy at the local, national, and global levels. In some cases, actors such as think tanks and research institutes provide expertise in the *formulation* of policy options. In other cases, actors such as NGOs may partner with states to *implement* policy decisions. We will explore who these actors are and what kind of power and influence they have.

Multinational Corporations

Multinational corporations (MNCs) are firms with subsidiaries that extend the production and marketing of the firm beyond the boundaries of any one country. The foreign subsidiaries of an MNC are directly owned by the parent corporation. Multinational corporations are not included under the umbrella of civil society because they are for profit. Some experts use the terms *MNC* and *transnational corporation* interchangeably; however, Andrew Hines, an expert for BNET (now CBS Money Watch), makes a clear distinction between four types of international businesses:

> **Multinational corporation or enterprise (MNC/MNE)**
> A business or firm with administration, production, distribution, and marketing located in countries around the world. Such a business moves money, goods, services, and technology around the world depending on where the firm can make the most profit.

1. *international companies* are simply importers and exporters with no investments or operations outside the home countries;
2. *multinational companies* have investments around the world, but they adjust their products and services to local markets;
3. *global companies* have investments and a presence in many countries, and they use the same brand and image in all markets; and
4. *transnational companies* are complex organizations that invest in foreign operations, and although they have a central corporate office, they allow foreign markets to make decisions about marketing and research and development.

To simplify our analysis, we will focus on MNCs and assume that transnational corporations are similar in the role they play as global actors. Most MNCs have their origins in developed countries, and they invest throughout the world. The number of MNCs increased exponentially after World War II. Most MNCs at the time were from the United States, United Kingdom, Japan, Germany, and France. Recently, China, India, Russia, Brazil, and Korea have added MNCs to the market. Indeed, because of their interests in global markets and their interests in selling to the world, the nationality of MNCs may be irrelevant. As consumers, we look for the best products at the best price, and we usually make little noise about purchasing a product made by a foreign corporation. National leaders do not seem to be concerned when multinationals build factories in their country or when they purchase critically important industries. MNCs are global because they seek markets for investments, cheap but skilled labor, and access to resources essential for making their products. Multinational corporations have power because they control scarce and critically important economic resources, they have the ability to move resources around the world, and they have advantages in areas of marketing and consumer loyalty.

Generally, MNCs get a bad review as representatives of Western capitalist culture, guilty of exploiting labor and crowding out local businesses. Many MNCs are seen as enemies of the people, supporting oppressive governments and contributing to pollution, poverty, and corruption. This view may be both outdated in some cases and limited, however, and views of MNCs vary according to one's theoretical perspective. Liberals see MNCs as a positive force, spreading technology, efficiency, and wealth. Economic nationalists, or neomercantilists, argue that MNCs threaten national sovereignty and dilute national wealth. Finally, Marxists see MNCs as representatives of the core-capitalist states, creating dependencies in countries where they invest and helping create and maintain a core-periphery global economic structure. According to this view, MNCs participate in predatory globalization, or the search for investment opportunities in countries where labor is cheap and where laws aimed at protecting the welfare of workers and the environment are either not enforced or nonexistent. Essentially, Marxists argue that MNCs put profits above all else.

However, many NGOs work with MNCs to create opportunities for work in developing countries and to respond to human needs such as clean water, basic education, and health care. Multinational corporations also give many small local businesses access to markets, financial credits, and technological infrastructure. The view of MNCs is changing because these corporations realize that they must provide a positive image if they are to attract customers. Their ability to attract customers and make profits depends in part on providing resources, expertise, and training to local populations, thus becoming partners in development. Many governments now compete for investments from MNCs. Not only do they provide jobs and help build infrastructure, MNCs are often engines of change and reform in corrupt and mismanaged governments.

Why do companies invest abroad? The decision to become a multinational firm is not only about access to markets; it is also about finding competitive advantages for the firm. These might be technological innovations and efficient production costs, for example, which make manufacturing more profitable at a foreign location.

We have made the claim that MNCs are playing a more positive role in many developing countries. To address the argument that MNCs are only interested in profits, we will consider the case of India's economy, which is predicted to be as big as China's in ten to fifteen years. The 1.2 billion people living in India are becoming more affluent, more educated, and more politically active, and they are demanding more from both the public and private sectors. At the same time, MNCs are more concerned about attracting customers, and that means providing a good product and being good citizens in this market.

However, India has had its share of problems with MNCs more interested in profit and less interested in the well-being of its workers and neighbors. A prime example is the 1984 Bhopal gas tragedy at a Union Carbide factory, which killed 3,800 people and left several thousand with permanent disabilities. Union Carbide, a U.S.-based MNC, was one of the first U.S. companies to invest in India, and it produced pesticides for India's agricultural sector. In the final settlement, Union Carbide paid out close to $500 million for victims and for building clinics and other facilities in the region.

The 1984 gas leak in Bhopal, India, was a terrible tragedy that continues to impact the quality of life for the people in the region. These children live in a region with polluted water because of the former Union Carbide industrial complex. Transnational or global social movements often form around the injustices revealed by industrial disasters such as Bhopal.

Another MNC with a more than 100-year history in India is Nestlé. This corporation has had to deal with charges of malpractice, corruption, and generally putting profits ahead of the needs and interests of its consumers. (See the Case Study in this chapter.) Nestlé India has eight factories that produce milk, which Indians drink in great quantities. One small factory in the Punjab region depends on about 180 farmers for its supply of milk, and those farmers were having problems with their animals. Nestlé brought in agronomists, veterinarians, and agricultural education experts to work with the local farmers to help maintain healthier herds that produced more milk. Nestlé clearly benefited, but so did the local farmers.

Multinational corporations are also involved in a number of partnership projects with governments and INGOs. Since 2002, the U.S. Agency for International Development (USAID) has been working with Albanian farmers and Land O'Lakes, a food-producing MNC, to increase the quality of dairy products and to provide jobs for 12,000 farmers and dairy processors. In several Latin American countries, the Nature Conservancy, a U.S.-based NGO, has been working with an MNC, FEMSA (along with the Inter-American Development Bank and the Global Environment Facility), to establish a social investment foundation that supports education, science, and technology. FEMSA is the world's largest Coca-Cola bottling company and a major beer distributor in Latin America. More than 50 million people will benefit from this partnership, which will work to restore forests and grasslands where clean water originates. In Colombia, the conservation trust fund is aimed at protecting rivers and watersheds that provide clean drinking water for people in Bogotá.

Several factors make these public and private partnerships more likely in the future. Governments have fewer financial resources for global projects. Citizens are becoming more aware of vital global challenges and more critical of bad

A Global Campaign: The Baby Milk Advocacy Network

BACKGROUND

The prototype for global campaigning by NGOs has been the International Baby Food Action Network (IBFAN), which challenges the marketing of dried milk powder by the major food and pharmaceutical transnational corporations (TNCs). In the early 1970s, medical staff in developing countries gradually became aware that the death rate for babies was rising because of decreased breastfeeding. If the family was poor and used insufficient milk powder, the baby was undernourished. If the water or the bottle was not sterile, the baby developed gastric diseases. Bottle feeding today causes around 1.5 million deaths a year.

THE CASE

The question was first taken up by the *New Internationalist* magazine and War on Want (WoW) in Britain in 1973–1974. A Swiss NGO, the Third World Action Group (AgDW), then published a revised translation of WoW's report, under the title "Nestlé Kills Babies." When Nestlé sued for libel, AgDW mobilized groups from around the world to supply evidence for their defense. The Swiss Court found AgDW guilty in December 1976 on one of Nestlé's four original counts, on the technical basis that Nestlé was only indirectly responsible for the deaths.

The question moved to the United States when religious groups involved in Latin America fought another court case against pharmaceutical company Bristol-Myers Squibb. Increased awareness led to organization by a new group, the Infant Formula Action Coalition, of a boycott of Nestlé's products, which spread to many countries. In the hope of diffusing the increasing pressure, the International Council of Infant Food Industries accepted a proposal by the late Senator Edward Kennedy for the WHO and UNICEF to hold a meeting on infant feeding in October 1979. Rather than seeing the issue depoliticized, the companies found they were facing demands to limit their marketing. The meeting also taught a group of NGOs how much they could benefit from working together with a common political strategy. They decided to continue to cooperate by forming IBFAN, as a global advocacy network.

The new network was able to mobilize a diverse coalition of medical professionals, religious groups, development activists, women's groups, community organizations, consumer lobbies, and the boycott campaigners. Against intense opposition from the TNCs and the U.S. administration, IBFAN succeeded in achieving the adoption of an International Code of Marketing of Breast-Milk Substitutes, by WHO's assembly, in

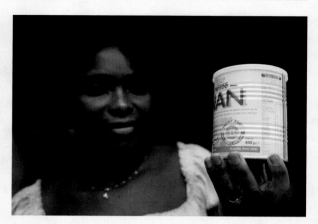

A mother in Cameroon holds a can of milk powder that she feeds her baby. IBFAN challenges the marketing of milk powder by MNCs, citing research linking decreased breast-feeding to an increased death rate for babies.

May 1981. The key provisions of the code were that "there should be no advertising or other form of promotion to the general public" nor any provision of free samples to mothers.

OUTCOME

According to the World Health Organization, as of 2011, 37 out of 199 countries reporting had passed laws reflecting all of the recommendations of the code; another 69 countries fully prohibit advertising of breast-milk substitutes. Many countries however still have weak legal provisions or voluntary policies. IBFAN's work continues along two tracks: It monitors and reports violations of the code by companies, including in countries where marketing is now illegal, and seeks to upgrade the law in countries that are only partially implementing the code.

Sources: This account is based on A. Chetley (1986), The Politics of Baby Foods *(London: Pinter), information at www.ibfan.org, the IBFAN website, and WHO.* Country Implementation of the International Code of Marketing of Breast-milk Substitutes: Status Report 2011. *Geneva, World Health Organization, 2013 (revised).*

For Discussion

1. The global campaign against Nestlé led to this action network. Is this an effective way to shape national policy?
2. When and where do global campaigns work?
3. What is the "boomerang pattern," and what role did it play in the Nestlé campaign?

behavior by both public and private actors, and IGOS and INGOS are providing expertise and other resources to facilitate global responses to address these challenges.

INGOs as Global Political Actors

Nongovernmental organizations (NGOs) are autonomous organizations that are not instruments of any government, are not for profit, and are formal legal entities. These exist within societies as domestic NGOs, like the Sierra Club in the United States, or as international nongovernmental organizations (INGOs). They campaign for certain causes (e.g., Amnesty International for human rights), represent the interests of specific professionals (e.g., international trade unions), and include charitable organizations (e.g., CARE and Oxfam).

As long as nation-states have fought wars or famine has plagued societies, civil-society organizations have played a role in trying to find solutions to these problems. In 1874, there were thirty-two registered INGOs; in 1914, there were more than a thousand. One of the most well-known INGOs is the International Red Cross, which was founded by Jean Henri Dunant in 1859 after the Battle of Solferino, and was awarded the Nobel Peace Prize in 1917, 1944, and 1963. The Red Cross directed the implementation of the first Geneva Convention on the humane treatment of wounded soldiers and prisoners of war. Another INGO, Save the Children, formed after World War I, and Médecins Sans Frontières (Doctors Without Borders) started after the Biafran Civil War in Nigeria in the late 1960s. International nongovernmental organizations have been willing to work in crisis situations when governments are reluctant to become involved. In the 1990s, INGOs began to work more closely with each other and with governments and IGOs like the World Bank and the United Nations.

Nongovernmental organizations often act collectively in pursuit of their interests or values, and some scholars believe that they are shifting political power away from the state. Nongovernmental organizations work with states and regional and international organizations, but most global politics scholars believe that the state no longer monopolizes the political world. Most of the NGOs working in what some have called the most idealist and "imagined" global communities are progressive organizations working to reform or transform the current global system. They aim to do so by making decision-making

Private foundations are important supporters of science and science research. Here Nayanjot Lahiri receives an award at the Infosys Science Foundation award ceremony in Bangalore, flanked by former United Nations Secretary-General Kofi Annan, second left, Infosys Ltd. Executive Chairman N. R. Narayana Murthy, right, and Nobel laureate Amartya Sen. The foundation honors annually outstanding achievements of researchers and scientists across seven categories. The Infosys Foundation is a nonprofit organization based in Karnataka, India, established in 1996 by Infosys to support the underprivileged sections of society. How might foundations like this shape the future of our global society?

Nongovernmental organization (NGO) An organization, usually a grassroots one, with policy goals but not governmental in makeup. An NGO is any group of people relating to each other regularly in some formal manner and engaging in collective action, provided the activities are noncommercial and nonviolent and are not on behalf of a government.

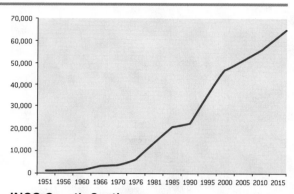

70,000
60,000
50,000
40,000
30,000
20,000
10,000
0

1951 1956 1960 1966 1970 1976 1981 1985 1990 1995 2000 2005 2010 2015

INGO Growth Continues.

What impact does the growth of INGOs have on states?

arenas more democratic, transparent, equitable, and environmentally friendly. As Rischard (2002) argues in his book on global problems, NGOs tend to work in three broad areas:

- *Sharing our planet*—issues such as climate change, ocean pollution, and biodiversity.
- *Sharing our humanity*—issues that focus on global health, education, human rights, war, violence, and repression.
- Governance, or *sharing our rulebook*—issues that involve international laws and institutions.

Thus, trade and investment rules promoted by neoliberal institutions like the WTO and the World Bank have become the target of concern for many global activists.

International nongovernmental organizations are generally seen as independent, altruistic, idealistic, and progressive; however, not all INGOs support progressive changes. Some represent the status quo, and some support authoritarian or racist preferred futures (for example, there are many neo-Nazi INGOs). Transnational or multinational corporations sponsor NGOs and advocacy networks that are also a part of this global civil society.

There are a variety of INGOs, differentiated by their purpose, organization, and sponsorship. These include:

- *BINGOs*: business and industry INGOs like the World Economic Forum, the World Business Council for Sustainable Development, and the Global Business Council on HIV and AIDS;
- *GRINGOs*: government regulated and initiated INGOs; many authoritarian states sponsor these to keep watch on dissidents and the activities of foreign interests;
- *QUANGOs*: sometimes called quasi-INGOs because they receive most of their funds from public sources although they are still independent; and
- *RINGOs*: INGOs that are sponsored by religious groups and often promote religious norms and values; World Vision, Caritas, and Norwegian Church Fund are examples.

What kind of power do these INGOs have? How can they counter the economic and political power of global corporations? Do they have any influence over nation-states?

Sources of INGO Power

A critical question is how much power INGOs and other transnational actors have to implement their own strategic plans and affect the policy of governments and intergovernmental organizations. We know that MNCs can use their money and the promise of jobs, investment, and access to new technologies to influence governments, but what about religious organizations like World Vision or think tanks like the Brookings Institution? Let us look at INGOs to assess their sources of influence.

In many societies, especially the pluralist social-democratic states (e.g., Sweden, Denmark, the Netherlands), domestic NGOs and INGOs play an important role as partners in the policy process. Some NGOs are not as independent from public agencies as they claim to be. These so-called QUANGOs are often supported by governments to carry out policy programs that governments cannot or will not implement.

To illustrate, INGOs have played a critical role in implementing development-assistance programs throughout the world. The International Red Cross claims the INGOs working in the development and human security areas give out more money than the World Bank. Most of this money comes from governments and public agencies. Organizations like Oxfam in the United Kingdom, World Vision (the largest privately funded Christian relief-and-development NGO), and Doctors Without Borders receive anywhere from 25 percent to 50 percent of their funding from various government sources.

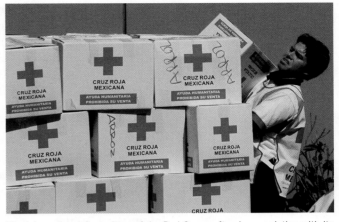

The International Committee of the Red Cross, often in association with its national counterparts, offers disaster-relief services in what is meant to be a nonpolitical manner. Here we see a member of the Red Cross stacking crates of food for victims of the devastating earthquake in Haiti in January 2010. How do states benefit by permitting NGOs to provide these essential services?

International nongovernmental organizations are also supported by private sources like corporations and philanthropic foundations. In December 2011, Google announced that it would provide $11.5 million in grants to ten organizations working to end the practice of slavery. This is about 25 percent of what Google was giving away to charitable organizations during the holiday season. The grant was to be used by a coalition on international antitrafficking organizations. The International Justice Mission (IJM) was the lead organization in this effort. More specifically, IJM in India, one of the fourteen field offices, led intervention and rescue missions. International Justice Mission is a human rights agency that rescues victims of slavery, sexual exploitation, and other forms of violent oppression. Prior to this gift, most of IJM funding came from private sources, and less than 1 percent of its funding had come from major corporations or corporate foundations. Another important member of this coalition is CNN and its CNN Freedom project that started in March 2011. CNN, a global media superpower, has broadcast more than 200 stories about human trafficking and modern-day slavery. This kind of exposure educates citizens and their leaders and pressures them to act.

Obviously, government funding increases the ability of INGOs to assist people in need and to help governments carry out some of their foreign policy goals. As governments are forced to cut back their workforce, many duties are being picked up by INGOs. Not only do INGO employees deliver services to the poor and protect citizens in conflict areas, but INGOs like Amnesty International and Human Rights Watch provide policymakers and interested citizens with valuable information and research reports that can be used to develop new laws and policy programs. Their research expertise gives them access to policymakers, and often, their ideas and interests become part of public policy.

Forms of INGO Power

Forms of INGO power discussed by Keck and Sikkink (1998) include information politics, symbolic politics, leverage politics, accountability politics, and global campaign politics. We will briefly discuss each of these.

Information Politics

International nongovernmental organizations and other civil-society actors use e-mail, fax machines, newsletters, and web pages to keep their followers informed, solicit donations, and mobilize citizens to take positions supporting their causes. During antiglobalization demonstrations at WTO or G8 talks, many activists use digital cameras and audio streams to share the day-to-day events with other activists in distant lands. This builds support and a stronger sense of community among INGOs and other activist groups.

Another part of information politics is the research and studies that many INGOs provide media reporters and government officials. Because of their expertise and their access to critical players in crisis situations, NGOs can also provide important technical and strategic information, which can be used to influence policymakers and inform other activists.

Symbolic Politics

Activist leaders of INGOs identify a critical issue or event and provide explanations that frame the issue so it becomes a catalyst for growth of the movement. The shelling of a café in Sarajevo by Bosnian Serb forces during the civil war in Yugoslavia was used as a symbolic event by human rights INGOs who were demanding U.S. intervention to stop the ethnic cleansing in Bosnia.

International nongovernmental organizations use their position in society and their role in crises as a way of increasing awareness and expanding support for their cause. When the Red Cross, Doctors Without Borders, and the International Campaign to Ban Landmines were awarded the Nobel Peace Prize, it called attention to their cause and gave the groups more legitimacy throughout the world. International nongovernmental organizations and the transnational social movements they participate in often use big stories to gain public attention, more members, financial contributions, and the attention of those with political power. In the 1980s, Irish rock star Bob Geldof (who played Wall in the Pink Floyd–inspired movie) turned the world's attention to famine in western Africa. His activism led musicians in the United Kingdom, the United States, and Canada to each produce their own "We Are the World" records and sponsor a series of globally televised concerts to raise public awareness and collect funds for famine relief.

Some of these big stories that are picked up by the media are based on false or incomplete information. A good example is the 1995 Brent Spar incident. Greenpeace launched an attack on an obsolete oil rig, called the Brent Spar, in the North Sea to protest the decision by Shell to sink it. Greenpeace claimed that the environmental damage would be worse by sinking the rig than by towing it to shore and dismantling it there. Yet independent environmental studies clearly showed that the environmental damage would be greater if the rig were towed to shore and dismantled. Still, Greenpeace continued with its campaign and forced the government of Germany and Shell Oil to dismantle the rig on land. Both traditional and social media sources can be used to turn the facts about natural disasters and the aftermath of war and violence into human stories.

Leverage Politics

International nongovernmental organizations often use material leverage (e.g., money or goods) or moral leverage to persuade governments to act in certain ways or to encourage other INGOs to support their position on an issue. They often shame governments into acting in a certain way. They are adept at using the media to expose hypocritical behaviors and to make certain the public is aware of unpopular practices by governments, transnational corporations, and other actors. With greater access to media and information technology, INGOs have access to larger audiences. These INGOs demand more accountability and have increasing power and influence, which helps them to shape the domestic and foreign policy process.

Accountability Politics

International nongovernmental organizations are able to use a number of information and media sources to act as watchdogs and force governments and political leaders to follow up on their public promises. Unfortunately, this pressure does not always work. Both George H. W. Bush and Bill Clinton promised to push China to improve its human rights record before they would support new trade relations. Once elected, both presidents caved in to trade interests and failed to address human rights concerns. Although INGOs are not always successful, they continue to use their resources to pressure governments to close the gap between promises and performances.

Global Campaign Politics

A relatively new tool for NGOs, civil-society actors, and like-minded governments is a global campaign that uses the media, local activist networks, and, if necessary, product boycotts like the one described in the Nestlé Case Study. The use of social networking sites and the proliferation of NGOs across the world have made it easier to establish and maintain such campaigns. The One Campaign aimed at

Nongovernmental Organizations and Protecting the Rights of Children

Do nongovernmental organizations matter? People on one side of this academic dispute believe that NGOs are important actors that influence a range of behaviors in international relations. On the other side are many realists who believe that governments are the most important—and some believe the only—actor that matters in the study of the discipline. Somewhere in the middle are analysts who think that, by combining the study of states and NGOs, we can begin to understand the complexities of international relations. This dispute is primarily a disagreement of the kind you learned about in Chapter 3: What is the proper unit of analysis in the study of globalization and international relations?

A young Sudan People's Liberation Army child soldier holds a gun during the demobilization of soldiers in South Sudan.

For children around the world, these academic exercises miss the point: NGOs matter. Without the work of NGOs to supply food, provide education, and promote awareness, the lives of children would be much worse. In countries around the world each day, children are forced to be soldiers in civil wars, they starve, lack basic health services, are forced to work in factories for less pay than adults, and are physically abused and forced into sex slavery.

Each day, hundreds of local and transnational NGOs strive to improve living conditions for millions of people under the age of eighteen by attempting to implement the UN Millennium Development Goals and subsequent Sustainable Development Goals. Nongovernmental organizations also hold each country accountable for its ratification of the 1989 Convention on the Rights of the Child. Because the United Nations is an organization of sovereign and nominally equal countries, it is sometimes unable to do as much as some governments would like. Nongovernmental organizations, because they are not responsible to national governments, can apply moral suasion through public-awareness campaigns to help people in need.

Two of the more famous NGOs working to help children are Oxfam and Human Rights Watch, which focus on three main areas of children's rights: basic needs such as food, clothing, shelter, and health care; education; and security, including juvenile justice and ending war. Although these are also problems in industrialized countries, they represent greater challenges in the developing world where governments lack the resources to provide for these needs. For example, Oxfam International's seventeen member groups work in more than 100 countries helping people to help themselves by providing the tools and seeds for them to grow their own food. Oxfam also works in the area of arms control, seeking to encourage governments to stop expensive weapons sales and to redirect the money to basic human needs in developing countries.

Human Rights Watch has programs aimed at ending abuses of people regardless of age; however, the organization believes that children are at risk because of their vulnerable status in many societies. The group raises awareness about the horrible conditions that children face around the world: detention in "social protection

GLOBAL PERSPECTIVE   *continued*

centers" in Vietnam, where they are forced to work long hours for much less than the prevailing local wage scale; being forced to fight in civil wars in Africa and Asia; or used as sex workers in some countries, where they are then denied access to medical care, including HIV/AIDS medicines. The Children's Rights Division of Human Rights Watch has worked with the International Criminal Court to try to end the use of child soldiers and sexual trafficking in children.

Academic analysts of international politics might disagree about the worth of NGOs in the study of international society, but NGOs clearly have a positive effect daily on the lives of millions of people who are most at risk. Nongovernmental organizations are able to assume tasks that governments are unable or unwilling to do themselves.

For Discussion

1. If states fail to protect children, is there not a place for NGO intervention?
2. Children and their rights are hardly the focus of most international relations discussions. How do NGOs bring these concerns to our attention?
3. As the agenda of international relations shifts to human security issues, or freedom from fear and freedom from want, how important will nonstate actors be in the future?

addressing global poverty and campaigns seeking to provide assistance to victims of natural disasters have also benefited from what we know as celebrity diplomacy (discussed in the next section). We are all familiar with the roles played by Bono, Radiohead, and Wyclef Jean in mobilizing public support for their humanitarian causes. Many of these global campaigns play on our love for music, film, and other forms of entertainment. With the Internet and social media, it is relatively easy to identify a global issue, build an organization, promote a particular set of values and actions, and raise both financial and volunteer support for your cause. It is even easier if you can link your cause to a major event or to the popularity of a certain artist or sports hero.

Celebrity Diplomacy

In 2005, *Time* magazine named Bono and Bill and Melinda Gates persons of the year for their contributions to the global community. Bono, lead singer in the Irish rock group U2, has been described by James Traub of the *New York Times* as a "one-man state who fills his treasury with the global currency of fame." He has used this fame to lead major global campaigns to end global poverty. Andrew Cooper suggests that well-known celebrities as global activists are part of a more open and robust process of diplomacy that is the opposite of the insulated and secretive world of traditional diplomacy (2008). Cooper suggests this new form of diplomacy may be eroding the authority and legitimacy of more traditional forms of diplomatic activity. Many celebrities have used their status and resources to achieve goals that reflect their own values. The International Campaign to Ban Landmines was headline news when the late Princess Diana became its international spokesperson. Angelina Jolie and Brad Pitt have become spokespersons for a variety of causes related to children and refugees and created a charitable foundation to aid humanitarian causes around the world. The Jolie/Pitt Foundation gave away $2 million—$1 million to Global Action for Children (now defunct) and $1 million to Doctors Without Borders—to help families affected by HIV/AIDS and extreme poverty.

Not all celebrities promote progressive or cosmopolitan causes like global governance, social justice, human security, and protecting the environment. There are celebrities who represent more conservative political causes and movements, like the late Charlton Heston, president of the National Rifle Association. This is not a new phenomenon; countries have always used movie stars and entertainers to sell war bonds and promote public campaigns.

Celebrities, like any of us, use social media to communicate their messages, but they can also use their celebrity status to sell more than just movies and music. They sell ideas and normative values and positions to their adoring fans and use technology and global media to convince political leaders to embrace their positions. Traditional diplomats are very critical of these celebrity actions and suggest that they lack the expertise and dedication to the real goals of traditional diplomacy. Critics say it is okay for celebrities to raise funds for humanitarian issues, but they are not representatives of states and they need to be careful not to interfere with any official diplomatic agenda.

A new group of celebrities are entrepreneurs who have made billions and have created foundations and philanthropic organizations to promote and fund their special causes. Mark Zuckerberg, the co-founder and chief executive of Facebook, is at the top of the list of the new rich doing something for the world. In 2015, he announced that he and his wife would give 99 percent of their Facebook shares, holdings currently worth more than $45 billion, to charitable purposes over the course of their lives. Their organization, the Chan Zuckerberg Initiative, will focus on education, curing disease, connecting people, and building strong communities. This is a very effective practice called **venture philanthropy**, and it is having an especially large impact in the developing world. British aviation magnate Richard Branson has focused his wealth on global social and environmental problems. He has established a green-energy carbon war room and a fund to reward scientists for finding new ways to control climate change and remove carbon from the environment.

As governments cut social programs at home and development assistance programs, and failed or fragile states are unable or unwilling to provide basic services for their citizens, foundations and individual philanthropists are willing to step up and support innovative programs that encourage local business development and efforts to solve persistent societal challenges.

Venture philanthropy The practice of supporting philanthropists or social entrepreneurs by providing them with networking and leveraging opportunities.

Foundations and Think Tanks

A foundation is a nonstate actor that is established as a charitable trust or a nonprofit INGO with the purpose of making grants to other institutions or to individuals for a variety of purposes. Many world leaders establish foundations when they leave office to continue to make a difference in global affairs. For example, the Nelson Mandela Foundation was established in 1999 to continue the work of this great leader, especially in the areas of reconciliation in divided societies and social justice. Another example is the William J. Clinton Foundation, which sponsors global initiatives that allow governments to respond to major global challenges such as the need for education, safe drinking water, and clean air.

Foundations do not simply step in and provide funding where the state has left a vacuum. Rather, foundations want to be change agents and encourage reform and innovation in societies across the globe. Some of the more successful and enduring foundations are in the United States, but many wealthy individuals in Europe and Asia have established foundations to help their countries and their neighbors. For example, the Bharti Foundation, founded by telecom billionaire Sunil Mittal, has opened more than 200 schools to address the problem of illiteracy and has funded teacher training programs and libraries. Foundations play a major role in funding research institutes and communities of scholars and experts who are essential sources of information for those who formulate, implement, and eventually evaluate policy decisions and processes.

Other notable philanthropic foundations that have had a major impact on global politics include the Bill and Melinda Gates Foundation, the Rockefeller Foundation, the Open Society Foundations, the MacArthur Foundation, the Ford Foundation, and the Aga Khan Foundation. Many of these foundations fund research institutes, universities, and think tanks.

Think tanks (also known as research institutes) vary in size, resource base, policy orientation, and political influence in either national or global politics. Some are scholarly and focus on nonpartisan research, whereas others represent a particular political position or ideology. Many focus on ideas like free market capitalism, socialism, or civic engagement.

Think tanks have increased in number and influence as critical players in global politics, and their increasing importance is the result of a variety of factors. One obvious reason has to do with the complexity of issues now facing policymakers. Most of the officials we elect or appoint to handle these issues are not experts. They depend on the communities of experts often found within think tanks and research institutes. Another reason for the growth of these actors is that although we are flooded with information, it is very hard to decide what information is reliable. Think tanks and research institutes with a long history of producing reliable information based on sound research offer public officials information they can use with confidence. These think tanks play a critical role by providing the following services:

- Disseminating research reports and other briefing documents.
- Promoting specific policy strategies and ideas.

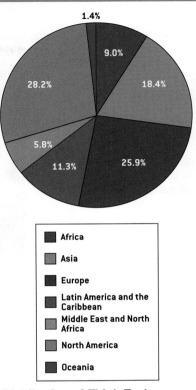

Legend:
- Africa
- Asia
- Europe
- Latin America and the Caribbean
- Middle East and North Africa
- North America
- Oceania

Distribution of Think Tanks in the World, 2015.

Who shapes the policy agenda when European and North American research institutes dominate policy research?

Julian Assange, founder of the WikiLeaks website, noted for publishing confidential documents, news leaks, and classified information. In what ways do nonstate actors influence foreign policy?

- Providing essential information to political parties, public officials, policy bureaucracies, the media, and the general public.
- Evaluating policy programs and decision-making processes.

Criminal and Terrorist Networks as Global Actors

Globalization has provided a number of opportunities for the spread of positive ideas and opportunities as well as trade, travel, and communications. There is, of course, a dark side to globalization, and that is the opportunities it provides for criminal networks to expand their activities, increase their profits, and increase their number of victims. A variety of informal organizations and criminal gangs engage in violent or criminal behavior across the globe. We can make a distinction between activity that is considered criminal around the world—such as theft, fraud, personal violence, piracy, or drug trafficking—and activity that is claimed by those undertaking it to have legitimate political motives. In reality, the distinction becomes blurred when criminals claim political motives or political groups are responsible for acts such as terrorism, torture, or involving children in violence. For all governments, neither criminal activity nor political violence can be legitimate within their own jurisdiction and generally not in other countries.

Politically, the most important criminal industries are illicit trading in arms, drugs, and people. In a 2003 article in *Foreign Policy*, Moises Naim argues that the war on terrorism has obscured the importance of five other global wars that we are losing, on:

- drug interdiction;
- the illegal arms trade;
- the protection of intellectual property and the prevention of piracy and counterfeiting of products;
- human trafficking; and
- money laundering and the smuggling of money, gold coins, and other valuables.

Even when governments are strong and reasonably effective, a range of factors can hinder their ability to respond to the threats presented by global criminal networks. These include inadequate laws, bureaucratic jurisdictional disputes, and enforcement strategies that work well at home but not in a more complex global environment.

While it is possible to win these wars against powerful criminal networks, governments will not win without some serious thinking about how we organize states and how we think about the international system. World leaders must begin to share or even trade sovereignty. They must open their systems to global institutions sponsoring multilateral enforcement activities. States must find ways to regulate transboundary activities and to reach some agreement on a set of regulations that will be enforced in every market across the globe. Successful efforts to end these wars might also depend on a change in our attitudes about community and the individual. If we continue to promote the goal of individual advancement over peace and stability in our communities, these wars could continue for a long time.

WHAT'S YOUR WORLDVIEW?

Is the idea of national sovereignty now obsolete? With globalization becoming a more important factor in shaping our quality of life, should we be more open to collective multilateralism, global governance, and even intervention from external actors?

The number of extremist groups willing to use terrorism and targeting innocents has increased. These are also nonstate actors. Here people place flowers at the entrance to the French consulate in Madrid, Spain, to remember victims of the Paris attacks in November 2015. Do we have any way to stop these global terrorist attacks?

We discuss terrorism and terrorist networks in depth in Chapter 6, so for now we merely want to emphasize that terrorist organizations are nonstate actors that have an impact on all actors in the international system. Terrorism is very difficult to eliminate because groups using terrorism are usually parts of larger, decentralized global networks. President George W. Bush described the battle against it as "fourth-generation warfare," which involves nation-states in wars with nonstate global networks.

Terrorist networks are global networks composed of many different groups who might or might not share a common ideological position. These groups are usually united only in their desire to overthrow a government or a regional or global system of governance or replace a way of life or a hegemonic ideology. This *new terrorism* is characterized by its global reach, decentralized structure, a seemingly wide-open targeting strategy with no regard for civilians, and more obscure and extreme goals and objectives. Radical groups who are likely to use terrorism are often linked to NGOs and foundations that are supported by sympathetic states or by states seeking to keep extremists out of their lands.

We should not forget that some states also support terrorist activities, and in some cases, their military or police forces are the terrorists. In the pursuit of national interests, states might not always follow the rules.

Conclusion

International law, international and regional organizations, and INGOs collectively play an important role in the governance of our global society. These institutions provide the infrastructure of a truly global system in which it is possible to think about a global common good and a world where human interests trump national interests. There are three pillars of global governance (Muldoon 2004):

1. A political pillar that includes diplomacy, international law, and global and regional organizations like the United Nations, the WTO, and the European Union.
2. An economic pillar that includes MNCs, international banking and industry associations, global labor movements, and global economic movements.
3. A social pillar that includes actors within the global civil society, such as INGOs, and global social movements.

International and regional organizations play a critical role in governing the policy areas that transcend the nation-state. The effectiveness and perhaps the fairness of global policy will often depend on the efficacy of international law. Thus, all these institutions play a role in the governance of this global society.

The capacity of the United Nations in its economic and social work, its development work, and its management of peacekeeping and post-conflict reconstruction has expanded since the 1990s. Nonetheless, further changes and adaptations within the UN system are necessary.

With regard to regional organizations, the European Union is the best example of how far the integration process can go and how much sovereignty states are willing to share or surrender. However, the prospect of an ever-wider European Union has raised serious questions about the nature and direction of the integration process.

Nongovernmental actors can also play an important role in making international society work. NGOs can hold governments accountable for their international commitments in a number of ways. Using modern communications methods, transnational social movements can call attention to a problem, recruit members to help, and bring needed relief, often faster than states are able to mobilize. However, nongovernmental actors do not have the stability that most states do, and their effectiveness can vary dramatically from year to year, from region to region, because their support and structure are entirely member-dependent.

For all the reasons we have outlined in this chapter, international law, international organizations, and INGOs remain important elements in our discussions about the future of international politics. Nation-states are not the only actors and NGOs, multinationals, and criminal networks play an increasingly important role in shaping the foreign policy of nation-states. These nonstate actors are shaping the international agenda and forcing states to pay attention to their actions.

CONTRIBUTORS TO CHAPTER 5: *Devon Curtis, Christian Reus-Smit, Paul Taylor, Steven L. Lamy, and John Masker.*

KEY TERMS

African Union (AU), p. 184
Civil society, p. 185
Collective security, p. 166
Economic sanctions, p. 169
European Union (EU), p. 181
Global governance, p. 158
Human security, p. 174
International Court of Justice (ICJ), p. 171
International institution, p. 160

International law, p. 159
International nongovernmental organization (INGO), p. 185
International organization, p. 160
Intervention, p. 177
League of Nations, p. 166
Multilateral diplomacy, p. 162
Multilateralism, p. 158
Multinational corporation or enterprise (MNC/MNE), p. 187

Nongovernmental organization (NGO), p. 191
Nonstate actor, p. 158
Organization of African Unity (OAU), p. 184
Organization of American States (OAS), p. 185
Peace enforcement, p. 173
Peacekeeping, p. 173
Peacemaking, p. 173
Post-conflict peace building, p. 173

Preventive diplomacy, p. 173
Regime, p. 159
Responsibility to Protect Resolution (R2P), p. 165
Social movement, p. 185
State sovereignty, p. 165
Supranational global organization, p. 165
Transnational advocacy network (TAN), p. 186
United Nations, p. 165
United Nations Charter, p. 166

United Nations Economic and Social Council (ECOSOC), p. 170

United Nations General Assembly, p. 169

United Nations Secretariat, p. 170

United Nations Security Council, p. 167

United Nations Trusteeship Council, p. 171

Venture philanthropy, p. 198

Veto power, p. 167

REVIEW QUESTIONS

1. Can you think of other factors, in addition to the ones listed in the chapter, that contributed to the rise of modern international law in the past two centuries?

2. Do you find the argument that states create institutions to sustain international order persuasive?

3. What do you think are the strengths and weaknesses of the international legal system?

4. What have been the driving forces behind processes of regional integration and cooperation?

5. What impact have processes of regional integration had on the state?

6. Compare and contrast European integration with regional cooperation in other areas of the world.

7. How does the United Nations try to maintain world order?

8. How has UN peacekeeping evolved?

For more information, quizzes, case studies, and other study tools, please visit us at **www.oup.com/us/lamy.**

THINKING ABOUT GLOBAL POLITICS

Who Could Help Tomorrow? Twenty Global Problems and Global Issues Networks

This is a *problem-based* exercise that simply asks you to consider which public, private, and civil-society actors should pool their resources and effectively respond to global problems. The idea for this comes from a book by J. F. Rischard, *High Noon: Twenty Global Problems, Twenty Years to Solve Them* (2002). He is a former vice president of the World Bank, and his book has been at the center of discussion at several major global conferences. Now, it is your turn to think about these issues and possible solutions. Rischard believes that two major stresses present unprecedented problems and opportunities. These two are demographic changes, including population growth and income distribution, and the new global economy that includes a technological revolution and the globalization of production, trade, and investment. These stress factors contribute to a number of global issues or challenges that

require the attention of all citizens of the world. Here are the three issue areas and some specific challenges in each category:

- Sharing our planet: Issues involving the global commons, **global warming, biodiversity and ecosystem losses, fisheries depletion, deforestation, water deficits, and maritime safety and pollution.**

- Sharing our humanity: Issues requiring a global commitment, **poverty, peacekeeping, conflict prevention, counterterrorism, education for all, global infectious diseases, the digital divide, and natural-disaster prevention and mitigation.**

- Sharing our rulebook: Issues needing a global regulatory approach; **reinventing taxation for the twenty-first century; biotechnology rules; global financial architecture;**

illegal drugs; trade, investment, and competition rules; intellectual property rights; e-commerce rules; and international labor laws and migration rules.

Who can help to solve or manage these problems? How about a coalition of public, private, and civil-society actors? According to Rischard, partnerships like these are the only way forward. Global coalitions or global information networks (GINs) are similar in purpose to TANs and TSMOs. Each GIN enlists members from governments, international civil society organizations, and businesses to address the issues that challenge global stability and often create real human-security problems.

In small groups of three or four, identify one of the problems or challenges in the three preceding categories. In your group, discuss the nature of the problem and identify actors who you think could help respond to it. You need at least two actors in each of the three categories (six total actors): two governments, two NGOs, and two businesses. This is your problem-solving coalition, or GIN. Why did you select these actors? What resources or expertise do they bring to the problem-solving activities? How will each actor participate in the situation? How will each solve or manage the problem?

For example, if water pollution is the issue, maybe you should involve Canada and Saudi Arabia. Canada has large supplies of clean water, and Saudi Arabia has money to pay for the program and a need for water. NGOs might include the Global Water Campaign and Oxfam; businesses that sell water, like Nestlé and Coca-Cola, might also have skills, interests, and resources.

Your assignment is to put together the most effective coalition to respond to the potential crisis and tell us how it will work.

6

Global Security, Military Power, and Terrorism

Free Syria fighters are one of the many groups now fighting in the Syrian civil war. The United States, Turkey, several Arab states, and other NATO allies are fighting on the part of the rebel forces, and Russia is actively supporting the current Syrian government. If peace talks fail could this conflict lead to a major war?

Only the dead have seen the end of war.

—PLATO

With respect to terrorism, the locus of global concern is mainly restricted to Islamic countries with no *willingness* to address the terrorism of "covert operations" in the North, or to address the social causes of terrorism to the extent that recourse to such forms of political violence rests on injustices.

—RICHARD FALK

W ars in the twenty-first century have been and continue to be conflicts within failed or fragile states. About 39 percent of these conflicts are in Africa, another 39 percent are in Asia, and most of the rest are in the Middle East. The current civil war in Syria is both an ideological and ethnic conflict that has global implications. The November 2015 attacks in Paris were blamed on the Islamic State, who attacked in retaliation for French participation in the Syrian civil war. A recent study by the Institute for Economics and Peace states that conflicts killed 180,000 in 2014 and the total costs of these conflicts equaled 13.4 percent of the world's gross domestic product (GDP); the deadliest wars were in Syria and Iraq. The Islamic State seized territory in both countries and slaughtered their rivals and civilians they labeled as nonbelievers. Radical or extremist Islamist groups like the Taliban in Afghanistan and Pakistan, Boko Haram in Nigeria, and Al-Shabaab in other African states are engaged in violent attacks undermining the power and authority of very weak states.

Consider the war in the Democratic Republic of Congo, which is the world's most lethal conflict since World War II. It has lasted more than fifteen years—although several rebel groups agreed to a ceasefire in late 2013—and taken the lives of over 5.4 million people, including an estimated 2.7 million children. Some twenty rebel groups and armies from nine nation-states are fighting in a territory as large as all of Western Europe, often committing acts of sexual violence in their assaults. Ethnic or tribal disputes, poverty, and the lust for power and treasure all contribute to this war. Fundamentally,

After reading and discussing this chapter, you should be able to:

Define and explain different theoretical views of security.

Explain the changes in warfare in recent years, sometimes called the "revolution in military affairs."

Discuss the threat that nuclear weapon proliferation poses to international peace.

Define terrorism, including the role of perception in defining which groups are "terrorists" and which are legitimate groups that use unconventional methods.

Define the law-enforcement and war-on-terrorism approaches to fighting terrorists.

there is no government to respond, and even 20,000 UN peacekeepers have been unable to contain the conflict. In December 2013, the eighth UN peacekeeping mission in Africa began operations in the Central African Republic. The primary goal of the mission was to stop the sectarian violence where Muslim and Christian groups preyed on each other, creating what UN officials called "pregenocidal" conditions. Human Rights Watch reports that since September 2015 at least 100 people have died in this ongoing ethnic violence and efforts aimed at creating peace and stability are undermined by violence between Muslim Seleka rebels and the "anti-balaka" Christian militia. Civil wars and sectarian conflicts like those in the Democratic Republic of Congo and the Central African Republic present the biggest security challenges to those who seek global order.

We have entered a period where the shape of war is changing. Nation-states are now unlikely to engage in wars of choice. The era of deploying large armies to fight large land wars might be over, replaced by precision strikes and drone raids. The new type of warfare lasts for years, is financially draining, costs thousands or even millions of lives, and poses extraordinary defensive challenges.

Although we seem to have become complacent over nuclear proliferation and the chances of a nuclear confrontation, the chances of a nuclear confrontation are still very real. Authoritarian states like North Korea are seeking to defend their interests in what they perceive as hostile environments, and nuclear powers like India and Pakistan are at each other's throats because of longstanding disputes over Kashmir. We must not forget that there are radicals always in the market for weapons of mass destruction.

Our material interests and lifestyle choices, if not our moral responsibilities, draw us all into these conflicts. For whatever reason, war has been a feature of life for most of recorded history. In this chapter, we examine national security, international or global security, terrorism, and conflict from a number of academic perspectives. We will try to determine whether the arena of human conflict has changed in an age of globalization.

Introduction

Is global security, meaning a world without war and extremist violence, possible to achieve? For much of the intellectual history of the world, a debate has raged about the causes of war. For some writers, especially historians, the causes of war are unique to each case. Other writers believe that it is possible to provide a wider, more generalized explanation. Some analysts, for example, see the causes lying in human nature, others in the outcome of the internal organization of states, and yet others in international anarchy.

The end of the Cold War reshaped the debate. Some liberal and many alternative theorists, like constructivists and radical liberals (discussed in Chapter 3), claimed to see the dawn of a new world order. For other analysts, however, realism or neorealism remained the best approach to thinking about international security. In their view, very little of substance had changed as a result of the events of 1989. The end of the Cold War initially brought into existence a new, more cooperative era between the superpowers. However, this more harmonious phase was only temporary, because countries still interacted in an anarchic international system. For the thousands of people who have died, events seemed to support the realist and neorealist worldviews. With the first Gulf War (1990–1991), the ongoing civil wars in Africa and Asia, the 9/11 attacks, and the wars in Afghanistan, Iraq, and now Syria, it became increasingly clear that states and nonstate actors (including international terrorist groups) continued to view the use of force and violence as an effective way to achieve their objectives.

We begin with a look at the basic definitions and disagreements central to the field, including what is meant by *security*, and we explore the relationship between national and global security. Then we examine the traditional ways of thinking about national security, and the influence these ideas about national security have had on contemporary thinking. We follow this examination with a survey of alternative ideas and approaches that have emerged in the literature in recent years. Next we turn to the pressing question of nuclear weapons proliferation, including a brief overview of these weapons and a discussion of attempts to prevent their spread in the years after the Cold War. Finally, we discuss a transnational trend—terrorism—that has changed the nature of global conflict and security.

Security The measures taken by states to ensure the safety of their citizens, the protection of their way of life, and the survival of their nation-state. Security can also mean the ownership of property that gives an individual the ability to secure the enjoyment or enforcement of a right or a basic human need.

National security A fundamental value in the foreign policy of states secured by a variety of tools of statecraft, including military actions, diplomacy, economic resources, and international agreements and alliances. It also depends on a stable and productive domestic society.

What Is "Security"?

Most writers agree that **security** is a contested concept. There is a consensus that it implies freedom from threats to core values (for both individuals and groups), but there is a major disagreement about whether the main focus of inquiry should be on *individual*, *national*, or *international* security. During the Cold War period, most writing on the subject was dominated by the idea of **national security** and the realist model that asserts states should develop military capabilities to deal with the threats they confront. More recently, however, a number of contemporary writers have argued for an expanded conception of security outward from the limits of parochial national security to include a range of other considerations and avoid ethnocentrism. This conception is

Syrian refugees break through a border fence and enter into Turkey. The conflict in Syria has displaced over 4 million people, creating instability and economic stress in countries hosting large numbers of refugees. The countries bordering Syria—Turkey, Lebanon, and Jordan—have taken in the majority of the refugees. This regional crisis has quickly become a global crisis.

Widening school of international security
Sometimes called the Copenhagen school, these are authors who extend the definition of security to include economic, political, societal, and environmental policy areas.

known as the **widening school of international security** because of proponents' desire to widen the definition to include economic, political, social, and even environmental issues as part of a global security agenda.

Further, not all who study security issues focus on the tension between national and international security (see Table 6.1). Some argue that such an emphasis ignores the fundamental changes that have been taking place in world politics. Others argue that much more attention should be given to "societal security," the idea that growing regional integration is undermining the classical political order based on nation-states, leaving states exposed within larger political frameworks. We see this development in the European Union, and plans for an expanded North American Free Trade Agreement (NAFTA) might indicate a similar trend in the Western Hemisphere. At the same time, the fragmentation of various states, like the Soviet Union and Yugoslavia, has created new problems of boundaries, minorities, and organizing ideologies that are causing increasing regional instability (Weaver et al. 1993, 196). These dual processes of integration and fragmentation have led to the argument that ethnonationalist groups, rather than states, should become the center of attention for security analysts.

TABLE 6.1	Comparing Worldviews

View of National Security as a Policy Issue

Realist	Liberal	Global Humanist	Marxist
• Military power is essential in supporting the primary objective of a state's national interest: survival. • In an anarchic, state-centric system, war is inevitable. • Self-help: no other state or institution can be relied on to guarantee your survival.	• Nations should practice collective security as a means of cooperation and assured protection of national interest, sharing the use of resources. • Nations have shared responsibility for foreign policy successes as well as failures. • Wars undertaken for purposes of expediency are unjust. Defense of life and defense of property are just causes, but if the cause of war is unjust, all acts arising from it are immoral.* • Anticipatory self-defense is forbidden. • Complete security is impossible.	• Arms reduction is a desirable step toward disarmament. • The international norm against the use of nuclear weapons should be strengthened. • Security policy should be guided by a sense of human solidarity that transcends the nation rather than by a desire to maximize national military power. • Human interest should take priority over national interest.	• National security is the protection of those who own the means of production. • There is no need for a large, oppressive military force if people are not oppressed and exploited by a small and powerful group of capitalist elites. • Inequality is the main security threat in the global system.

*Murphy, Cornelius F., Jr. "The Grotian Vision of World Order." American Journal of International Law Jul. 76.3 (1982): 477–498. JSTOR. Web. Sept. 31, 2011. 481. http://www.jstor.org/stable/2200783.

Disagreements about definitions of security matter, because these academic arguments often influence the policy decisions that political leaders make. If political leaders believe their primary responsibility is national security, then building a safe international system for all countries is of secondary importance. Barry Buzan (1991) concisely describes the security challenge:

> In the case of security, the discussion is about the pursuit of freedom from threat. When this discussion is in the context of the international system, security is about the ability of states and societies to maintain their independent identity and their functional integrity.

Today, many security specialists suggest that the most important contemporary trend is the broad process of **globalization** that is taking place. Globalization challenges what we expect a nation-state to provide its citizens. It might hinder the ability of leaders to protect boundaries, provide order at home, and maintain and promote a productive economic system. We learned in Chapter 1 that the process of globalization challenges a state's legitimacy, efficiency, and identity, which brings new risks and dangers. These include the increase in radical or extremist groups who are willing to use **terrorism** across the world, global climate change, a breakdown of the global monetary system, and the proliferation of weapons of mass destruction. These threats to security, on a global level, are viewed as being largely outside the control of a single state or groups of nation-states. Theorists believe only the development of a global security **community** can deal with such threats adequately.

In the aftermath of 9/11, Jonathan Friedman argued that we are living in a world "where polarization, both vertical and horizontal, both class and ethnic, has become rampant, and where violence has become more globalized and fragmented at the same time, and is no longer a question of wars between states but of sub-state conflicts, globally networked and financed, in which states have become one actor, increasingly privatized, amongst others" (J. Friedman 2003, ix). Many feel that the post–9/11 era is a new and extremely dangerous period in world history. However, whether the world today is so different from the past is a matter of much contemporary discussion. To consider this issue we need to look at the way security has been traditionally conceived.

Globalization A historical process involving a fundamental shift or transformation in the spatial scale of human social organization that links distant communities and expands the reach of power relations across regions and continents.

Terrorism The use of violence by nonstate groups or, in some cases, states to inspire fear by attacking civilians and/or symbolic targets and eliminating opposition groups. This is done for purposes such as drawing widespread attention to a grievance, provoking a severe response, or wearing down an opponent's moral resolve to effect political change.

Community A human association in which members share common symbols and wish to cooperate to realize common objectives.

WHAT'S YOUR WORLDVIEW?

A traditional view of security suggests that states need a strong military to survive. With a more diverse set of security challenges, what resources and expertise do states need?

Mainstream and Critical Approaches to Security

As we discussed in Chapter 2, from the Peace of Westphalia onward, states have been regarded as the only legitimate, and by far the most powerful, actors in the international system. They have been the universal standard of political legitimacy, with no higher authority to regulate their interactions with one another. States have therefore taken the view that there is no alternative but to seek their

On the flight deck of the *Charles de Gaulle* aircraft carrier, a French pilot inspects his military plane before participating in a strike against the Islamic State. In response to the Paris attacks, France has taken on an important role in the U.S.-led coalition against the Islamic State. Is it possible to win a war against an extremist ideology?

own protection in what has been described as a self-help world. For most modern political leaders and academics, realism has been the analytic lens best suited to understanding war and security; other lenses that we discuss in the chapter must all respond to realism.

We also saw in Chapter 3 that many academics have developed theories attempting to explain international politics as something other than a struggle among power-seeking countries. These alternatives to both realism and some strains of liberalism have become vibrant intellectual challenges to those mainstream ideas about the causes of war and peace.

Realist and Neorealist Views on Global Security

The historical debate about how best to achieve national security tends to paint a rather pessimistic picture of the implications of state sovereignty. Realists viewed the international system as a rather brutal arena in which states would seek to achieve their own security at the expense of their neighbors. According to this view, permanent peace was unlikely to be achieved. All that states could do was try to balance the power of other states to prevent any one from achieving overall hegemony.

Structural realism, a permutation of realism, argues that states tend to act aggressively toward one another because:

- The international system is anarchic, which implies that there is no central authority capable of controlling state behavior.
- States claiming sovereignty will inevitably develop offensive military capabilities to defend themselves and extend their power. Hence, they are potentially dangerous to one another.
- Uncertainty, leading to a lack of trust, is inherent in the international system. States can never be sure of the intentions of their neighbors, and therefore, they must always be on their guard.
- States will want to maintain their independence and sovereignty, and as a result, survival will be the most basic driving force influencing their behavior.
- Although states are rational, they will often make miscalculations. In a world of imperfect information, potential antagonists will always have an incentive to misrepresent their own capabilities to keep their opponents guessing. This may lead to mistakes about real state interests.

According to this view, national security (or insecurity) is largely the result of the anarchic structure of the international system. The implication is that international politics in the future is likely to be as violent as international politics in the past. In a 1990 article entitled "Back to the Future," John Mearsheimer argued that the end of the Cold War was likely to usher in a return to the traditional multilateral, balance-of-power politics of the past. Mearsheimer viewed the Cold War as a period of peace and stability brought about by the bipolar structure of power that prevailed. With the collapse of this system, he argued that extreme nationalism and ethnic rivalries would lead to widespread instability and conflict, reflective of the kind of great-power rivalries that had blighted international relations since the seventeenth century.

Indeed, most contemporary neorealists or structural-realist writers see little prospect of a significant improvement in security in the post–Cold War world. The 1991 Gulf War, the violent disintegration of the former Yugoslavia and parts of the former Soviet Union, continuing violence in the Middle East, and the wars in Afghanistan and Iraq after the 2003 invasion all support the notion that we continue to live in a world of mistrust and constant security competition. They suggest there are two main factors that continue to make cooperation difficult: the first is the prospect of cheating; the second is the concern states have regarding relative gains.

Neorealists do not deny that states often cooperate or that in the post–Cold War era there are even greater opportunities than in the past for states to work together. They argue, however, that there are distinct limits to this cooperation because the people who lead states have always been and remain fearful that others will attempt to gain advantages by cheating on any agreements reached. This risk is regarded as particularly important given the nature of modern military technology, which can bring about very rapid shifts in the balance of power between states. "Such a development," Mearsheimer has argued, "could create a window of opportunity for the cheating side to inflict a decisive defeat on the victim state" (1994–1995, 20). States realize that this is the case, and although they join alliances and sign arms control agreements, they remain cautious and aware of the need to provide for their own national security in the last resort.

Cooperation is also inhibited, according to many neorealist writers, because states tend to be concerned with **relative gains** rather than **absolute gains**. Instead of being interested in cooperation because it will benefit both partners, states always need to be aware of how much they are gaining compared with the cooperating state. Because all states will attempt to maximize their gains in a competitive, mistrustful, and uncertain international environment, the thinking goes, cooperation will always be very difficult to achieve and hard to maintain.

Liberal Institutionalist Views on Global Security

One of the main characteristics of the neorealist approach to global security is the belief that international institutions do not play a very important role in the prevention of war. Institutions are seen as the product of state interests and the constraints imposed by the international system. According to this view, interests and constraints shape decisions on whether to cooperate or compete, not the institutions.

Relative gains One of the factors that realists argue constrain the willingness of states to cooperate. States are less concerned about whether everyone benefits (absolute gains) and more concerned about whether someone may benefit more than someone else.

Absolute gains The notion that all states seek to have more power and influence in the system to secure their national interests. Offensive neorealists are also concerned with increasing power relative to other states. One must have enough power to secure interests and more power than any other state in the system—friend or foe.

Political leaders and international relations specialists have challenged such views. British foreign secretary Douglas Hurd, for example, made the case in June 1992 that institutions had played, and continued to play, a crucial role in enhancing security, particularly in Europe. He argued that the West had developed "a set of international institutions which have proved their worth for one set of problems" (Hurd, quoted in Mearsheimer 1994–1995). He argued that the great challenge of the post–Cold War era was to adapt these institutions to deal with the new circumstances that prevailed.

Hurd and other Western leaders believed that a framework of complementary, mutually reinforcing institutions—such as the European Union (EU), **North Atlantic Treaty Organization (NATO)**, the Western European Union (WEU), and the Organization for Security and Co-operation in Europe (OSCE)—could be developed to promote a more durable and stable European security system for the post–Cold War era. Although the past may have been characterized by frequent wars and conflict, they see important changes taking place in international relations that may relax the traditional security competition among states. This approach, known as liberal institutionalism, argues that international institutions are much more important in helping achieve global cooperation and stability than structural realists realize (see Chapter 3). Certainly, the fact that there has not been a war in Western Europe in more than seventy years supports this perspective. Supporters also point to the developments within the European Union and NATO in the post–Cold War era and claim that, by investing major resources, states clearly demonstrate their belief in the importance of institutions. The creation of the Eurozone of shared currency and NATO's deployment of troops outside Europe also provide evidence of this trend.

As such, the liberal-institutionalist approach suggests that international institutions operating on the basis of reciprocity will be a component of any lasting peace. Although international institutions themselves are unlikely to eradicate war from the international system, they can play a part in helping achieve greater cooperation among states.

One question liberal institutionalists might examine is why war is absent in some parts of the contemporary world. The North Atlantic region, for example, has been described as a **security community**, a group of states for whom war has disappeared as a means of resolving disputes with one another, although they may continue to use war against opponents outside the security community. One common characteristic of these states is that they are all democracies and it has been suggested that although democracies will go to war, they are not prepared to fight against another democracy. As we discussed in

North Atlantic Treaty Organization (NATO)
Organization established by treaty in April 1949 including twelve (later sixteen) countries from Western Europe and North America. The most important aspect of the NATO alliance was the U.S. commitment to the defense of Western Europe. Today NATO has twenty-eight member states.

Security community
A regional group of countries that have the same guiding philosophic ideals—usually liberal-democratic principles, norms, values, and traditions—and tend to have the same style of political systems.

Since the end of the Cold War, NATO members have taken on new security tasks. Here, Turkish commandos have captured five pirates operating in the Gulf of Aden near Somalia.

Chapter 3, the **democratic peace thesis** argues that where groups of democracies inhabit a region, war will become extinct in that region, and as democracy spreads throughout the world, war will decline. However, we must keep in mind the danger that wars will occur as democracies attempt to overthrow nondemocratic regimes in attempts to spread democracy. When the Bush administration invaded Iraq in 2003, they argued that a democratic Iraq would become the seed from which democracy and therefore peace would grow in the Middle East. In cases like this, war ends up being fought in the name of peace.

The Constructivist Approach to Global Security

Constructivists often assert that international relations are affected not only by power politics but also by ideas. This assertion places most constructivist thinkers in the liberal tradition. According to this view, the fundamental structures of international politics are **social** rather than strictly **material**. Constructivists therefore argue that changes in the nature of social interaction between states can bring a fundamental shift toward greater international security.

Constructivists think about international politics very differently than neorealists. The latter tend to view structure as made up only of a distribution of material capabilities. Constructivists, on the other hand, view structure as the product of social relationships. Social structures are made possible by shared knowledge, material resources, and practices. According to this perspective, the security dilemma is a social structure in which leaders of states are so distrustful that they make worst-case assumptions about one another's intentions. As a result, they define their interests in "self-help" terms. In contrast, a security community is a social structure composed of shared knowledge in which states trust one another to resolve disputes without war.

The emphasis on the structure of shared knowledge is important in constructivist thinking. Social structures include material things, like tanks and economic resources, but these acquire meaning only through the shared knowledge in which they are embedded. The idea of power politics, or **realpolitik**, has meaning to the extent that states accept the idea as a basic rule of international politics. According to social-constructivist writers, power politics is an idea that does affect the way states behave, but it does not describe all interstate behavior. States are also influenced by other ideas and **norms**, such as the rule of law and the importance of institutional cooperation and restraint.

Although constructivists argue that security dilemmas are not ruled by fate—or any higher autonomous power—they differ over whether they can be escaped. For some, the fact that structures are socially constructed does not necessarily mean that they can be changed. Many constructivists, however, are more optimistic. They point to the changes in ideas represented by perestroika and glasnost, concepts that Soviet Communist Party general secretary Mikhail Gorbachev introduced in the USSR during the second half of the 1980s, which led to a shared knowledge about the end of the Cold War. Once both sides accepted that the Cold War was over, it really was over. According to this view, understanding the crucial

Democratic peace thesis A central plank of liberal-internationalist thought, the democratic peace thesis makes two claims: first, liberal polities exhibit restraint in their relations with other liberal polities (the so-called separate peace), but second, they are imprudent in relations with authoritarian states. The validity of the democratic peace thesis has been fiercely debated in the international relations literature.

Social structure An arrangement based on ideas, norms, values, and shared beliefs. According to constructivists, the social domain does not exist in nature but is constructed through processes of interaction and the sharing of meaning.

Material structure An arrangement based on economic, political, and military resources.

Realpolitik First used to describe the foreign policy of Bismarck in Prussia, it describes the practice of diplomacy based on the assessment of power, territory, and material interests, with little concern for ethical realities.

Norms These specify general standards of behavior and identify the rights and obligations of states. Together, norms and principles define the essential character of a regime, and these cannot be changed without transforming the nature of the regime.

role of social structure is important in developing policies and processes of inter-action that will lead toward cooperation rather than conflict. If there are opportu-nities for promoting social change, most constructivists believe it would be irresponsible not to pursue such policies.

The Feminist Approach to Global Security

Although constructivists and realists disagree about the relationship between ideas and material factors, they tend to agree on the central role of the state in debates about international security. Other theorists, however, believe that the state has been given too much prominence. Keith Krause and Michael C. Williams have defined critical security studies in the following terms: "Contemporary de-bates over the nature of security often float on a sea of unvoiced assumptions and deeper theoretical issues concerning to what and to whom the term *security* refers. . . . What most contributions to the debate thus share are two inter-related concerns: what security is and how we study it" (1997, 34). What they also share is a wish to de-emphasize the role of the state and to reconceptualize security. For critical-security theorists, states should not be the center of analysis because not only are they extremely diverse in character, but also they are often part of the problem of insecurity in the international system. While they can be providers of security, they can also be a source of threat to their own people. Therefore, atten-tion should be focused on the individual rather than the state. Although a number of different approaches make up critical security studies, the feminist approach is one that challenges the traditional emphasis on the central role of the state in stud-ies of international security. Although there are significant differences among fem-inist theorists, all share the view that books and articles on international politics in general, and international security in particular, have been written from a "mascu-line" point of view. In her work, Ann Tickner (1992, 191) argues that women have "seldom been recognized by the security literature" despite the fact that conflicts affect women as much as, if not more than, men. The vast majority of casualties and refugees in war are women and children, and the rape of women is often used as a tool of war (see Chapter 7).

Feminist writers argue that if gender is brought more explicitly into the study of security, not only will new issues and critical perspectives be added to the se-curity agenda, but the result will be a fundamentally different view of the nature of international security. If we look at the language used to describe war, we can see one way security is gendered. As Carol Cohn wrote in her essay "Sex and Death in the Rational World of Defense Intellectuals" (1987), the defense-policy-making world tends to be dominated by men who employ sexual and other euphe-misms to describe their work. These include "servicing the target" instead of "bombing it"; "collateral damage" instead of "dead civilians"; "patting the missile" instead of "getting a tour of a Trident missile–carrying submarine." Cohn and others write that this is the result of war being "man's work."

Contemporary conflicts like those in Bosnia and Sudan pose a critical problem for the international community of whether to intervene in the domestic affairs of sovereign states to safe-guard minority and individual human rights (see Chapter 7). This dilemma reflects the historic transformation of human society that is taking place at the beginning of the twenty-first century. Many global theorists argue that it is now increasingly necessary to think of the security of individuals and of groups within the emergent global society, especially women scholars and practitioners. Although states remain an important factor in the international system, they are being transformed as they struggle to deal with the range of new challenges—including those of security—that face them.

The European Union's Naval Force meets with policymakers in the United Arab Emirates to consider whether militants in Somalia could potentially collaborate with the Islamic State. For the last several years, the European Union has helped to protect vessels from piracy off the coast of Somalia. Notice how the range of security challenges is expanding exponentially. Are state security systems ready for these challenges?

Marxist and Radical Liberal or Utopian Approaches to Security

Marxists believe that capitalism is the source of most of the world's security problems. Workers are exploited, alienated, and estranged from their societies. Thus, workers in poor states are prime targets for radical leaders planning to challenge the rich and the powerful by overthrowing governments that repress the voices of those on the margins. In a global economy, Marxists represent workers around the world and support a global revolution. Globalization has spread capitalist ideas as well as the ideas of those who see capitalism as a source of conflict and inequality. Marxist ideas have inspired many secular radicals who seek to create systems of governance that provide for basic human needs and address the inequalities within most societies. Although there are no states that are openly supporting Marxist revolutions, there are anarchist and Marxist terrorist networks and cells that present a security challenge to all states. For these groups, the source of insecurity is poverty and the denial of access to societal resources.

For radical liberals or utopians, the major security concern may be the **military-industrial complex**, a term coined by U.S. President Dwight D. Eisenhower as he warned the American public of the power and influence of the defense industries and their special relationship with the military. Part of this concern is over a strategic culture that emphasizes national security over human security. Current military budgets distract from efforts aimed at eliminating global poverty and providing for economic well-being and social justice. More than that, current military spending exacerbates the problems of environmental degradation and allows repressive elites

Military-industrial complex
The power and influence of the defense industries and their special relationship with the military. Both have tremendous influence over elected officials.

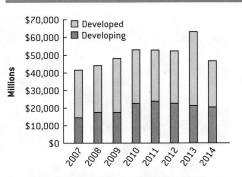

Arms Deliveries Worldwide (in Millions of Dollars).

Which region accounts for the most arms delivery—the North or the South? Based on what you have studied so far in this course, how would you explain the trends you see in this graph?

to deny citizens basic human rights. Thus, for radical liberals, in a worldview that puts national interests over human interests, realist thinking is the source of insecurity.

The Changing Character of War

Postmodernity An international system where domestic and international affairs are intertwined, national borders are permeable, and states have rejected the use of force for resolving conflict. The European Union is an example of the evolution of the state-centric system (Cooper 2003).

Weapons of mass destruction (WMD) A category defined by the United Nations in 1948 to include "atomic explosive weapons, radioactive material weapons, lethal chemical and biological weapons, and any weapons developed in the future which have characteristics comparable in destructive effects to those of the atomic bomb or other weapons mentioned above."

In the contemporary world, powerful pressures are significantly changing national economies and societies. Some of these pressures reflect the impact of globalization; others are the result of the broader effects of **postmodernity**, an international system where domestic and international affairs are intertwined. The cumulative effect has been to change perceptions of external threats. These changed perceptions have in turn influenced beliefs regarding the utility of force as an instrument of policy and the forms and functions of war. In the past two centuries, the modern era of history, some states have used war as a brutal form of politics (typified by the two world wars). In the post–Cold War period, however, the kinds of threats that have driven the accumulation of military power in the developed world have not taken the form of traditional state-to-state military rivalry. Instead, they have been more amorphous and less predictable threats such as terrorism, insurgencies, and internal crises in other countries.

In an era of unprecedented communications technologies, new fields of warfare have emerged. The tangible capacity for war making has also been developing. Military technology with enormous destructive capacity is becoming available to more and more states. This is important, not just because the technology to produce and deliver **weapons of mass destruction (WMD)** is spreading, but also because highly advanced conventional military technology is becoming more widely available. One of the effects of the end of the Cold War was that there was a massive process of disarmament by the former Cold War enemies. This surplus weaponry flooded the global arms market, much of it highly advanced equipment that was sold off comparatively cheaply.

The Nature of War

Wars are fought for reasons. The Western understanding of war, following the ideas of the Prussian military thinker and soldier Carl von Clausewitz, is that it is instrumental, a means to an end. Wars in this perspective are not random violence; they reflect a conscious decision to engage in them for a rational political purpose. Writing in the early 1800s, Clausewitz defined war as an act of violence intended to compel one's opponent to fulfill one's will. Often, people who initiate wars rationalize them by appealing to common belief and value systems. There are

Protesters in central London urge policymakers to take a new approach to national security. "You can't bomb your way to a better world." If countries focused on human security, would we have less violence in the world?

wide varieties of factors that can contribute to the outbreak of war, such as nationalism, class conflict, human nature, and so on. These are the main drivers of change rather than war itself. War is not something that is imposed by an outside force. The willingness to go to war comes from within states and societies.

One of Clausewitz's central arguments is war is a form of social and political behavior. If we operate with a broad and flexible understanding of what constitutes politics, this remains true today. As our understanding of politics, and of the forms it can take, has evolved in the postmodern era, we should expect the same to be true of the character of war because that is itself a form of politics.

The political nature of war has been evolving in recent decades under the impact of globalization, which has increasingly eroded the economic, political, and cultural autonomy of the state. Contemporary warfare takes place in a local context, but it is also played out in wider fields and influenced by nongovernmental organizations, intergovernmental organizations, regional and global media, and users of the Internet. In many ways, contemporary wars are fought partly on television, and the media therefore have a powerful role in providing a framework of understanding for the viewers of the conflict. Reaching beyond the effect of twenty-four-hour-a-day television news channels, Al-Qaeda and ISIS, for instance, use the Internet to disseminate propaganda. The award-winning documentary *Control Room* showed how the 2003 invasion of Iraq became an exercise in the U.S. government trying to restrict the images a globalized audience saw on its televisions. One effect of the constant coverage of international violence by the global media may be to gradually weaken the legal, moral, and political constraints against the use of force by making it appear routine. The advent of such "war fatigue" might make recourse to war appear a normal feature of international relations.

Nevertheless, war, in terms of both preparation and its actual conduct, may be a powerful catalyst for change, but technological or even political modernization does not necessarily imply moral progress. Evolution in war, including its contemporary forms, may involve change that is morally problematic, as is the case with the forces of globalization more generally. War is a profound agent of historical change, but it is not the fundamental driving force of history. For many analysts, war's nature as the use of organized violence in pursuit of political goals always remains the same and is unaltered even by radical changes in political forms, in the motives leading to conflict, or by technological advances (Gray 1999, 169).

For Clausewitz and Gray, there is an important distinction between the *nature* and the *character* of war. The former refers to the constant, universal, and inherent qualities that ultimately define war throughout the ages, such as violence, chance, and uncertainty. The latter relates to the

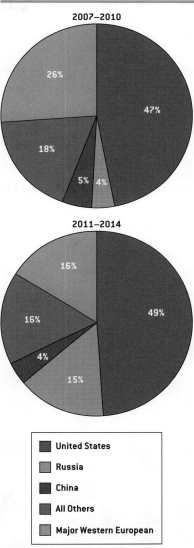

United States

Russia

China

All Others

Major Western European

Arms Transfer Agreements Worldwide.

The conventional arms suppliers here are shown as percentages. Do you notice a shift between the two date ranges compared here? Is it significant? How would you explain the relative stability of conventional arms suppliers worldwide?

impermanent, circumstantial, and adaptive features that war develops and that account for the different periods of warfare throughout history, each displaying attributes determined by sociopolitical and historical preconditions while also influencing those conditions.

A number of questions follow from this survey of war in relation to its contemporary and future forms. Does the current era have a dominant form of war, and if so, what is it? In what ways are the processes associated with globalization changing contemporary warfare? In what ways are the characteristics of postmodernity reflected in contemporary modes of warfare?

The Revolution in Military Affairs

Revolution in military affairs (RMA) The effect generated by the marriage of advanced communications and information processing with state-of-the-art weapons and delivery systems. It is a means of overcoming the uncertainty and confusion that are part of any battle in war.

Although many observers have suggested that the character of war is changing significantly, their reasons for coming to this conclusion are often quite different. One school of thought focuses on the concept of the **revolution in military affairs (RMA)**. This concept became popular after the American victory in the 1991 Gulf War. The manner in which superior technology and doctrine appeared to give the United States an almost effortless victory, if the Iraqi war deaths are ignored, suggested that future conflicts would be decided by the possession of technological advantages such as advanced guided weapons and space satellites. However, the subsequent popularity of the RMA concept has not produced a clear consensus on what exactly the RMA is or what its implications might be. Although analysts agree that RMAs involve a radical change or some form of discontinuity in the history of warfare, there is disagreement regarding how and when these changes or discontinuities take place or what their causes are.

Proponents of RMA argue that recent breakthroughs and likely future advances in military technology mean that military operations will be conducted with such speed, precision, and selective destruction that the whole character of war will change and this will profoundly affect the way military and political affairs are conducted. Most of the RMA literature focuses on the implications of developments in technology. In the conflicts in Kuwait (1991), Serbia (1999), and Iraq (2003), American technology proved vastly superior to that of the opponent. In particular, computing and space technology allowed the U.S. forces to acquire information about the enemy to a degree never before seen in warfare and allowed precision targeting of weapon systems to destroy vital objectives without inflicting unnecessary casualties on civilians (although absolute precision and reliability proved impossible to achieve). Advanced communications allowed generals to exercise detailed and instant control over the developing battle and to respond quickly. Opponents lacking counters to these technologies found themselves helpless in the face of overwhelming American superiority. However, the RMA emphasis

Intelligence satellites, like those aboard this rocket, have been launched by many states to improve their radar and monitoring capabilities. Knowing what the enemy is saying and thinking is an important element of war fighting strategy. Can this intelligence actually prevent future wars?

on military technology and **tactics** risks producing an oversimplified picture of what is an extremely complex phenomenon in which nontechnological factors can play a crucial part in the outcome.

Most of the literature and debate on the RMA is based on a particularly Western concept of fighting in war and tends to take for granted the dominance conferred by technological superiority. The current RMA may be useful only in certain well-defined situations. For example, there is little discussion of what might happen if the United States were to fight a country with similar capabilities or that is able to deploy countermeasures. There has been far less discussion of how a state might use unconventional or asymmetric responses to fight effectively against a more technologically sophisticated opponent. Asymmetry works both ways. **Asymmetric conflicts** since 1990 have been fought by U.S.-led coalitions against Iraq (in 1991 and again in 2003), Yugoslavia, and Afghanistan. Because of the extreme superiority in combat power of the coalition, the battle phases of these asymmetric conflicts have been fairly brief and have produced relatively few combat deaths compared with the Cold War period. However, in the post-conventional insurgency phases in Iraq and Afghanistan, asymmetry has produced guerrilla-style conflict against the technological superiority of the coalition forces.

The conflicts in Iraq and Afghanistan (see the Case Study in this chapter) raised major questions about the pattern of warfare likely after the RMA. United States military supremacy across the combat spectrum does not translate well in wars against networks of radical terrorists. In Afghanistan, the United States has tried a counterinsurgency (COIN) strategy with mixed results. A COIN policy involves fighting the enemy and stabilizing the country by helping develop an effective government. A COIN strategy might include:

1. providing security for the local population and preventing attacks against civilians;
2. protecting infrastructure and providing safe regions for civilians;
3. helping local government provide basic services for citizens; and
4. helping shift loyalties from insurgents to local authorities.

Counterinsurgency is expensive, and it requires patience and a commitment on the part of occupation forces (and the public who pay for it) to stay for a long time.

The Obama administration's drawdown in troop strength and the reluctance of some NATO allies to continue sending troops to combat regions in Afghanistan have forced a shift from a more costly and time-consuming COIN policy to a more direct counterterrorism (CT) policy. Counterterrorism is more about direct military actions. It refers to the identification, tracking, and elimination of terrorist networks. This may be the future of warfare in asymmetrical situations. A CT strategy includes:

1. using technology to hunt and track the enemy;
2. sharing intelligence with other states; and

Tactics The conduct and management of military capabilities in or near the battle area.

Asymmetric conflicts In symmetrical warfare, armies with comparable weapons, tactics, and organizational structures do battle. Wars are fought on near-equal terms. When stakes are high and those actors in conflict are not equal in terms of weapons and technology, the weaker side adopts asymmetrical tactics. These include guerrilla warfare, roadside bombs, attacks on civilians, and other terrorist tactics.

Part of the coalition strategy in Afghanistan involved allies of the United States working with Afghani military forces. Here Canadian troops work with local forces. Canada has recently withdrawn its troops, and as the Western forces leave, the Taliban has returned. Does this suggest that war was won but not the peace?

3. targeting insurgent leadership with unmanned drones and covert operations.

Counterterrorism is an aggressive way to fight wars, but it requires fewer troops than counterinsurgency, and it does not require a long-term commitment to state building.

Postmodern War

Global society is moving from the modern to the postmodern age. This process has been under way for several decades and is the result of a wide range of economic, cultural, social, and political changes that are altering the meaning of the "state" and the "nation." It has been marked by a shift from production to information as a core output of advanced economies. As this happens, it will affect the character of war.

In some parts of the world, the state is deliberately transferring functions, including military functions, to private authorities and businesses. Over the past decade, the "outsourcing" of war has become an increasing trend, as more and more states have contracted out key military services to privatized military firms (PMFs) like Academi (formerly known as Xe Services LLC, or Blackwater). These companies sell a wide range of war-related services to states, overwhelmingly in the logistical and security roles rather than direct combat. The growth of PMFs reflects a broader global trend toward the privatization of public assets. Through the provision of training and equipment, PMFs have influenced the outcomes of several recent wars, including those in Angola, Croatia, Ethiopia, and Sierra Leone. Privatized military firms played a significant role in the 2003 U.S.-led invasion of Iraq. They have also become the targets of criticism and lawsuits for wrongful death, as with the case of the Blackwater guards who in 2007 killed several unarmed Iraqi civilians.

In other areas, political actors have seized previously state-held functions. For example, many of the world's armies are relying more on child soldiers, paramilitary forces, and private armies. At the same time, globalization has weakened the national forms of identity that have dominated international relations in the past two centuries, and it has reinvigorated earlier forms of political identity and organization, such as religious, ethnic, and clan loyalties.

The greatly increased role of the media is another feature of this evolution. As we discussed earlier in the chapter, live broadcasts make media far more important in terms of shaping or even constructing understandings of particular wars by making war more transparent. Journalists have effectively been transformed from observers into active participants, facing most of the same dangers

U.S. Drone Warfare: A Robotic Revolution in Modern Combat

BACKGROUND

In the early years of its wars in Afghanistan and Iraq, the United States sparsely used its newly emerging unmanned aerial vehicle (UAV) drone technology. In 2001, the U.S. Predator UAV fleet numbered only ten and only did reconnaissance. By 2012, however, the United States was using drones not just for reconnaissance, but also for precision attacks on critical enemy targets. In both Iraq and Afghanistan, the U.S. military has used drones as an extension of conventional warfare. The use of drones has been successful in two major ways: first, by identifying and killing enemy combatants, and second, by avoiding deployment of traditional human forces. Drones perform the "Three Ds": dull jobs, dirty jobs, and dangerous jobs. Patrick Lin (2011) cites the emergence of a "fourth D": the capacity to perform with dispassion. Peter Singer (2012), a specialist on twenty-first-century warfare, suggests that the use of drones is "worryingly seductive" because it creates a policy view that war can be less costly in terms of blood and treasure.

The United States uses drone warfare more extensively than any other country, with drone bases in Afghanistan and in several African countries. This photograph records the first drone landing on a nuclear aircraft carrier, the deployment of which makes it possible for the United States to use drones anywhere in the world.

THE CASE

Targeted killing of enemy fighters and their leaders appears to be an official policy of the U.S. government. On September 2, 2012, a U.S.-directed drone strike in Yemen killed thirteen civilians, including three women and three security officials. The strike occurred in a city known as Rada in the Al-Baitha province of Yemen. An estimated 200 suspected Al-Qaeda members resided there at the time of the attack. This was the fourth reported U.S. strike that week, among the hundreds that have taken place in countries including Yemen, Pakistan, and Afghanistan. Since 2004, CIA-directed drone strikes in Pakistan alone have killed more than 2,400 people, possibly as many as 3,997, including somewhere between 423 and 965 civilians, according to the Bureau of Investigative Journalism in London. In 2005, the CIA is said to have used drone strikes in Pakistan three times; in 2010, there were 128 reported strikes. President Bush's administration authorized some 52 strikes between 2001 and 2008, and the Obama administration authorized nearly 300 strikes between 2009 and 2012. As of February 2016, there have been two reported drone strikes in Pakistan, but as many as 61 in Afghanistan. The United States and the United Kingdom are currently using these weapons, and more than fifty nations are expected to have or soon develop similar military technology, including China and Iran, as well as nonstate actors including Hezbollah. In September 2015, it was reported that the CIA and the Joint Special Operations Command collaborated to fly drones over Syria in attempt to strike senior members of the Islamic State.

OUTCOME

Drones are a particularly potent instrument of combat, presenting a new and geographically unbound use of force. Predator drones have a better track record for accuracy than fighter jets. Leaders might believe that drones are morally preferable to other weapons of war because they enable capable, accurate, surgical strikes that limit civilian casualties, and their operators are not put at any risk. In 2009, then U.S. Secretary of Defense Leon Panetta stated that the use of drones was "the only game in town in terms of confronting or trying to disrupt the Al Qaeda leadership." A major concern is that countries that

Continued

CASE STUDY

U.S. Drone Warfare: A Robotic Revolution in Modern Combat *continued*

develop these UAVs might be more inclined to launch attacks. Yet proponents of drone and other robot technology state that the technology protects soldiers and augments their ability to succeed while keeping them safe from the battlefield.

For Discussion

1. Any new weapon technology raises moral questions in light of the rules of war. Any lethal operations inside sovereign countries that are not at war with those

using drones raise several legal and moral questions. Consider the following: the U.S. government has implied that all military-age males in a drone strike area are legitimate targets. Do you agree with that position? Why or why not?

2. Do drones threaten to lower the threshold for lethal violence? Explain your position.

3. Is the decision to use drones ethically permissible? Is it ethically obligatory? Why or why not?

New wars Wars of identity between different ethnic communities or nations, and wars that are caused by the collapse of states or the fragmentation of multiethnic states. Most of these new wars are internal or civil wars.

Failed state A state that fails to provide basic services and provide for their citizens. Such a state cannot protect its boundaries, provide a system of law and order, or maintain a functioning marketplace and means of exchange.

as soldiers and helping shape the course of the war through their reporting. Just as modernity and its wars were based on the mode of production, so postmodernity and its wars reflect the mode of information.

Globalization and New Wars

Mary Kaldor (1999) has suggested that a category of **new wars** has emerged since the mid-1980s. Just as earlier wars were linked to the emergence and creation of states, new wars are related to the disintegration and collapse of states, and much of the pressure on such states has come from the effects of globalization. In the past decade, 95 percent of armed conflicts have taken place within states rather than between them. The new wars occur in situations where the economy of the state is performing extremely poorly, or even collapsing, so that the tax revenues and power of the state decline dramatically, producing an increase in corruption and criminality. As the state loses control, access to weapons and the ability to resort to violence are increasingly privatized. Paramilitary groups proliferate, organized crime grows, and political legitimacy collapses. One of the effects of these developments is that the traditional distinction between the soldier and the civilian becomes blurred, or disappears altogether.

Many features of the new wars are not new, in that they have been common in earlier periods of history—ethnic and religious wars, for example, or conflicts conducted with great brutality. However, it can be argued that the initiators of the new wars have been empowered by the new conditions produced by globalization. These new wars are made possible by the inability of certain governments to successfully exercise many of the functions associated with the traditional Westphalian state. Such conflicts will typically occur in **failed states**,

WHAT'S YOUR WORLDVIEW?

So-called new wars tend to be internal wars between cultural or ethnic groups. Adversaries in these wars seek to eliminate those from different cultural communities. Ethnic cleansing and genocide are the results. Does the international community have a responsibility to prevent these types of war?

countries like Somalia where the government has lost control of significant parts of the national territory and lacks the resources to reimpose control.

For some observers, the economic rationale, rather than politics, is what drives the new wars, so that war has become a continuation of economics by other means. It is the pursuit of personal wealth, rather than political power, that is the motivation of the combatants. In some conflicts, therefore, war has become the end rather than the means.

New Roles for NATO?

We may be on the verge of seeing a new role for NATO as an antiterrorist force and as a protector of civilians in failing or fragile states. Since 2001, NATO has taken two collective actions, one to respond to the terrorist attack on the United States and a second to protect Libyan civilians who were under attack by the Muammar Qaddafi regime. Cynics may argue that this is simply a way for the powerful states to maintain their control, but with the Responsibility to Protect (R2P) agreement (discussed further in Chapter 7), it may mean that we will have more classic humanitarian interventions and more collective military actions.

On September 12, 2001, in an act of solidarity, the NATO allies invoked Article 5 of the Washington Treaty, which states that an attack on one constitutes an attack on all. In December 2014, NATO's International Security Assistance Force ended its combat mission in Afghanistan, and today, the NATO-led Resolute Support Mission is working to prevent Afghanistan from becoming a haven for terrorists. Forty countries have contributed troops to protect civilians and build the capacity of the Afghan government to take responsibility for security and for the other duties of government. The Resolute Support Mission provides training, advice, and assistance in areas such as budgeting, civilian oversight of the Afghan Security Institutions, policy planning, and strategic communications.

Acting with the mandate provided by UN Security Council Resolutions 1970 and 1973, NATO began enforcing a no-fly zone over Libya in March 2011. Later that month, NATO leaders announced that they would implement all aspects of the UN resolution and begin protecting civilians and civilian-populated areas under attack by the forces loyal to the Qaddafi regime. Operation Unified Protector was the first act of humanitarian intervention since the 1999 NATO action to protect Albanian Kosovars from ethnic cleansing. NATO fighter jets supported the rebels and the transitional government with airstrikes, which ended when the dictator Muammar Qaddafi was captured and killed by members of the Libyan National Liberation Army. As of this writing, Libya is still under the transitional government and instability rules.

Nuclear Proliferation and Nonproliferation

Although all wars since 1945 have been fought without the actual use of nuclear weapons, the issue of nuclear proliferation represents one of the more marked illustrations of globalization. Although only five states (China, France, Russia

[Soviet Union], the United Kingdom, and the United States) are acknowledged by the Treaty on the Non-Proliferation of Nuclear Weapons, also known as the Non-Proliferation Treaty (NPT), as possessing nuclear weapons, others have the capability to construct nuclear devices. This was emphasized in May 1998 when India and Pakistan, previously regarded as "threshold" or near-nuclear states, demonstrated their respective capabilities by conducting a series of nuclear tests followed by ballistic missile launches.

The increase in the number of nuclear powers highlights another aspect of nuclear globalization: the potential emergence of a regionally differentiated world. Whereas in some regions nuclear weapons have assumed a lower significance in strategic thinking than they once held, other regions might be moving in the opposite direction. In Latin America, the South Pacific, Southeast Asia, Africa, and Central Asia the trend has been toward developing the region as a Nuclear Weapon Free Zone. In other regions, such as South Asia, the trend appears to be toward a higher profile for nuclear capabilities. What is unclear is the impact nuclearization (meaning nuclear weapons acquisition) will have in regions where states are moving toward denuclearization (meaning a process of removing nuclear weapons).

ENGAGING WITH THE WORLD

Global Security Institute

The Global Security Institute (GSI) offers a series of programs on disarmament as well as an internship program. It is dedicated to strengthening international cooperation and security based on the rule of law, with a particular focus on nuclear arms control, nonproliferation, and disarmament. Visit www.gsinstitute.org.

Proliferation Optimism and Pessimism

One thesis that has sparked diverging responses asserts that the gradual spread of nuclear weapons to additional states should be welcomed rather than feared. The thesis is based on the proposition that, just as **nuclear deterrence**, the idea that states will be deterred from using nuclear weapons because of concerns of retaliation in kind by adversaries, maintained stability during the Cold War, so can it induce stabilizing effects in other conflict situations. This argument is challenged by those who hold that more will be worse, not better, and that measures to stem nuclear proliferation represent the best way forward (Sagan and Waltz 1995, 2003). Two leading thinkers on nuclear matters, Kenneth Waltz and Scott Sagan, present opposing views. Waltz states that a controlled spread of nuclear weapons in countries like Pakistan and India is better than a rapid arms race. He contends that leaders of the new nuclear weapons countries would show the same restraint that the United States and the former Soviet Union demonstrated

Nuclear deterrence Explicit, credible threats to use nuclear weapons in retaliation to deter an adversary from attacking with nuclear weapons.

when they developed their nuclear arsenals. Sagan, on the other hand, asserts that developing countries lack the stable political institutions that the United States and the Soviet Union had during the late 1940s and early 1950s. Their military-run or weak civilian governments, without the positive constraining mechanisms of civilian control, and military biases could serve to encourage nuclear weapons use—especially during a crisis.

The responses to nuclear proliferation encompass unilateral, bilateral, regional, and global measures that collectively have been termed the nuclear nonproliferation regime. Advocates of this regime argue that such measures (including treaties like the NPT, export controls, international safeguards, nuclear-supplier agreements, and other standard-setting arrangements) have constrained nuclear acquisition. Conversely, there have been several criticisms of this regime. Among the criticisms are that it is a product of a bygone first nuclear age (1945–1990) and it is not suited to the demands of the potentially more dangerous second nuclear age (1990–present). It is unable to alleviate the security dilemma that many states confront and, hence, does not address the security motivation driving nuclear weapons acquisition. It is also a discriminatory arrangement because the NPT only requires that the five NWSs pursue nuclear disarmament in good faith (under its Article VI), whereas all other parties—designated as **non–nuclear weapon states (NNWS)**—must forgo the acquisition of nuclear weapons.

Thus, there has always been a tension between two notions of the NPT: as primarily a nonproliferation measure or as a means for achieving nuclear disarmament. This tension was evident during discussion at the NPT Conference in

Non–nuclear weapon states (NNWS) A state that is party to the Treaty on the Nonproliferation of Nuclear Weapons, meaning that it does not possess nuclear weapons.

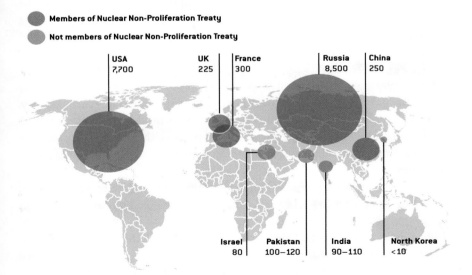

● Members of Nuclear Non-Proliferation Treaty

● Not members of Nuclear Non-Proliferation Treaty

| USA | UK | France | Russia | China |
| 7,700 | 225 | 300 | 8,500 | 250 |

| Israel | Pakistan | India | North Korea |
| 80 | 100–120 | 90–110 | <10 |

Map 6.1 **Global Map of Nuclear Arsenals.**
All numbers are estimates because exact numbers are top secret. Size of circle proportional to number of warheads.

1995, when the treaty was extended indefinitely after an initial twenty-five years in operation (under Article X). It was also evident at the NPT Review Conference in 2000, when the five NWSs reiterated their commitment to the goal of nuclear weapons elimination. India was a leading critic of this position, asserting that states have an inherent right to provide for their defense. During these dialogues, emphasis was placed on the need for all parties to improve transparency in their nuclear operations and for additional measures to enhance verification and compliance.

Nuclear Weapons Effects

The effects of nuclear weapons are considerable. Because of this, the UN Commission for Conventional Armaments in 1948 introduced a new category, weapons of mass destruction or WMD, to distinguish nuclear weapons from conventional forms. More recently, another concept, known as CBRN (referring to chemical, biological, radiological, and nuclear capabilities), has appeared in academic and policy papers. Some analysts have also argued that the term WMD should be unraveled because each of the weapons types has different effects, with nuclear weapons being the true WMD (Panofsky 1998).

Nuclear weapons are always dangerous because they can destroy the world as we know it. When used in conflict, nuclear weapons have indiscriminate effects—civilian deaths and injuries are impossible to avoid. Awareness of the effects stems from the two weapons dropped on Hiroshima and Nagasaki at the end of World War II, the only time nuclear weapons have been used. The weapons that destroyed these Japanese cities were relatively small in comparison to the destructive forces generated by later testing of thermonuclear weapons. The largest weapon of this kind known to have been tested was estimated to be a fifty-megaton device (i.e., the equivalent of 50 million tons of TNT) produced by the Soviet Union in 1961.

In recent years there has been a trend away from nuclear weapons with large explosive potential. Most security experts and world leaders agree that the spread of WMDs and the means to deliver them is the chief threat to global security. Yet, even among these leaders and experts, there is little agreement on how to control this proliferation. The risk is greater because the desire to possess nuclear weapons is spreading among states and among nonstate actors like terrorist groups.

Recently, the United States and other members of the UN Security Council came together to negotiate and reach a deal with Iran that would cease its nuclear weapons program. After twenty months of negotiations between Iran and several world powers including the United States, United Kingdom, France, China, and Russia, along with Germany and the European Union, an agreement was reached that would prevent Iran from developing a nuclear weapon in return for lifting sanctions that have crippled Iran's economy. The negotiation process was difficult and many, including Prime Minister Benjamin Netanyahu of Israel, as well as many Republican leaders in the U.S. Congress, suspect that Iran will ignore the terms of the deal and this arrangement will ultimately allow them to develop a nuclear weapon.

In return for the lifting of sanctions, Iran will shut down some 12,000 nuclear centrifuges and will ship 98 percent of its enriched fuel to outside countries in a fuel swap. They will also destroy their core plutonium reactor and inspectors from the International Atomic Energy Agency will monitor the entire process.

The Current Nuclear Age

In Prague on April 5, 2009, President Obama talked about ridding the world of nuclear weapons:

IAEA Director General Yukiya Amano talks with the head of Iran's Atomic Energy Organization, Ali Akbar Salehi, in an effort to gather information on allegations that Iran had in the past tried to build atomic weapons. Iran is prevented from developing weapons in the new agreement but can develop weapons after 2025. Can world leaders prevent future nuclear proliferation?

The existence of thousands of nuclear weapons is the most dangerous legacy of the Cold War. No nuclear war was fought between the United States and the Soviet Union, but generations lived with the knowledge that their world could be erased in a single flash of light. Cities like Prague that existed for centuries, that embodied the beauty and the talent of so much of humanity, would have ceased to exist.

Today, the Cold War has disappeared but thousands of those weapons have not. In a strange turn of history, the threat of global nuclear war has gone down, but the risk of a nuclear attack has gone up. More nations have acquired these weapons. Testing has continued. Black market trade in nuclear secrets and nuclear materials abound. The technology to build a bomb has spread. Terrorists are determined to buy, build or steal one. Our efforts to contain these dangers are centered on a global non-proliferation regime, but as more people and nations break the rules, we could reach the point where the center cannot hold.

Prior to this speech by Obama, the Global Zero movement was launched in 2008. Led by 200 global leaders and thousands of citizens, the goal of the movement is to work toward the elimination of all nuclear weapons. The leadership of Global Zero announced a two-phase plan aimed at stopping the spread of nuclear weapons, the first being securing all existing weapons, and finally eliminating them. For the first phase of the project, the group asked the United States and Russia to cut their weapons stock down to 1,000 warheads and other nuclear states to freeze their arsenals. While this is one possible scenario for the future, a 2015 article in *The Economist* suggests we have entered a new nuclear age, one that is more dangerous than the Cold War given the existence of rogue regimes and new rivalries among the major nuclear powers.

During the Cold War, most had faith in the idea that neither side would risk mutually assured destruction (MAD) and launch a nuclear weapon. However, this new age is one where states might use nuclear weapons to secure a strategic advantage. In 2015, President Obama budgeted for $350 billion to modernize the U.S. nuclear arsenal. Russia also increased its defense budget, one-third of which is devoted to nuclear weapons. China is also adding to its nuclear stocks and is investing in submarines and mobile missiles. The actions of both India and Pakistan are unknown.

What is the best response to this era of uncertainty and potential global nuclear violence? The Non-Proliferation Treaty (NPT), if enforced, creates a rule-based system that will control the spread of nuclear weapons. The *security dilemma* is mitigated by a vigorous arms control regime supported by the major powers and the international community.

Nuclear Motivations

Given the economic cost of creating a nuclear weapons program, an obvious question is this: Why would a state in the developing world choose to divert scarce resources to a program of questionable value? It is necessary to consider a range of factors that might influence nuclear weapons acquisition. These could include militarism and traditional technological factors that influence the availability of nuclear technology, as well as having a cadre of trained nuclear scientists. Another factor is domestic politics, including imperatives within a political party, or a domestic political situation that might propel a state toward nuclear weapons. Matters of diplomacy also influence the acquisition of nuclear weapons. Through diplomatic bargaining, the acquisition of a nuclear capability can be used to influence or bargain with both perceived allies and enemies. Ultimately, acquiring a nuclear capability deters other states from intervening in one's affairs.

Sagan (2004, 45–46) argues that beyond the *realist/neorealist* argument for building nuclear weapons—states develop these weapons when they face a significant threat—one must consider the influence of domestic interest groups and bureaucratic agencies that benefit from the production of nuclear weapons, missile systems, and other related technologies. In addition, one must consider the value of these weapons in domestic political debates about security and their normative value as symbols of power and modernity. What does it mean to be a major power? Nuclear weapons serve an important symbolic function and help to shape a state's identity (Sagan 2004, 64). In our current international system, the possession of nuclear weapons identifies a country as a major player, and thus some countries want to be seen as a member of this exclusive club.

Nuclear terrorism The use of or threat to use nuclear weapons or nuclear materials to achieve the goals of rogue states or revolutionary or radical organizations.

Studies conducted during the 1970s and 1980s on **nuclear terrorism** indicated that there were risks associated with particular groups acquiring a nuclear device or threatening to attack nuclear installations. One study by the International Task Force on Prevention of Nuclear Terrorism concluded that it was possible for a terrorist group to build a crude nuclear device provided it had sufficient quantities of chemical high explosives and weapons-usable fissile materials. More significant, it was felt that such a group would be more interested in generating social disruption by making a credible nuclear threat rather than actually detonating a nuclear device and causing mass killing and destruction (Leventhal and Alexander 1987). More recent occurrences have served to alter this latter judgment.

Events in the mid-1990s, such as the first bombing of the World Trade Center in New York in 1993 and the attack against the U.S. government building in Oklahoma in April 1995, revealed the extent of damage and loss of life that could be caused. Although both instances involved traditional methods of inflicting damage, the use of nerve agents (chemical weapons) in an underground train network in central Tokyo in March 1995 to cause both death and widespread panic has been viewed as representing a quantum change in methods. These concerns have intensified since the tragic events of September 11, 2001, when the World Trade Center was destroyed by a coordinated attack using civilian aircraft loaded with aviation fuel as the method of destruction. The attacks changed the assumption about terrorist use of CBRN capabilities (Wilkinson 2003).

Nuclear Capabilities and Intentions

The nuclear programs in Iraq, Iran, Pakistan, and North Korea have raised important issues concerning capabilities and intentions. These instances reveal the difficulties in obtaining consensus in international forums on how to respond to **noncompliance** and the problems associated with verifying treaty compliance in situations where special inspection or nuclear development arrangements are agreed. In the case of Iraq, a special inspection arrangement known as a UN Special Committee was established following the 1991 Gulf War to oversee the dismantlement of the WMD program that had come to light as a result of the conflict. By the late 1990s, problems were encountered over access to particular sites, and UN Special Committee inspectors were withdrawn. Disagreements also surfaced among the five permanent members of the UN Security Council concerning how to implement the UN resolutions that had been passed in connection with Iraq since 1991. These had not been resolved at the time of the 2003 intervention in Iraq, and subsequent inspections in that country were unable to find evidence of significant undeclared WMD.

Noncompliance The failure of states or other actors to abide by treaties or rules supported by international regimes.

The complexity associated with compliance is evident in the ongoing case of Iran. The country became the subject of attention from the International Atomic Energy Agency (IAEA) over delays in signing a protocol, added to Iran's safeguards agreement, requiring increased transparency by NNWS. Although Iran later signed the protocol, the discovery by the IAEA of undeclared facilities capable of enriching uranium fueled speculation. In an effort to find a solution, a dialogue between Iran, France, Germany, and the United Kingdom began in October 2003. Although an agreement was reached in November 2004, the situation was not resolved, and by 2006, the UN Security Council passed resolutions, under Chapter VII of the UN Charter, requiring Iran to comply with its international obligations. During the administration of former President of Iran Mahmoud Ahmadinejad, the IAEA had difficulty getting Iran to agree to verification mechanisms, which complicated an already dangerous Middle East security picture. Since the 2015 Iran nuclear deal was reached, which calls for Iran to cease its nuclear weapons program, the international community hopes that a compliant Iran will no longer pose a nuclear threat to regional—and global—politics.

Decisions regarding war and purchasing weapons needed to fight a war are state actions. However, increasingly since the end of the Cold War, states are facing security threats from nonstate actors. During the Cold War, the bipolar regime dominated a range of issues, reducing ethnonationalism or religious fundamentalism to secondary status. As a result of globalization, the declining centrality of the state has created space for groups with subnational or pan-national agendas to act. The subject of the next section—terrorism—is the preferred method of intervention for many of these nonstate groups.

Terrorism and Extremism

Terrorism and globalization share at least one quality—both are complex phenomena open to subjective interpretation. Definitions of terrorism vary widely, but all depart from a common point. Terrorism is characterized, first and foremost, by the use of violence. This tactic of violence takes many forms and often indiscriminately targets noncombatants. The purpose for which violence is used, and its root causes, is where most of the disagreements about terrorism begin.

Historically, the term *terrorism* described state violence against citizens, for example during the French Revolution or the Stalinist era of the Soviet Union. Over the past half-century, however, the definition of terrorism has evolved to mean the use of violence by nonstate groups or networks to achieve political change. Terrorism differs from criminal violence in its degree of political legitimacy. Those sympathetic to terrorist causes suggest that violence, including the death of innocent people, is the only remaining option that can draw attention to the plight of the aggrieved. Such causes have included ideological, ethnic, and religious exclusion or persecution.

Defining terrorism can be difficult because groups often advocate multiple grievances and compete with one another for resources and support. In addition, the relative importance of these grievances within groups can change over time. Those targeted by terrorists are less inclined to see any justification, much less legitimacy, behind attacks that are designed to spread fear by killing and maiming civilians. As a result, the term *terrorist* has a pejorative value that is useful in delegitimizing those who commit such acts.

Audrey Kurth Cronin, an academic authority on terrorism, has outlined different types of terrorist groups and their historical importance in the following way:

> There are four types of terrorist organizations currently operating around the world, categorized mainly by their source of motivation: left-wing terrorists, right-wing terrorists, ethnonationalist/separatist terrorists, and religious or "sacred"

terrorists. All four types have enjoyed periods of relative prominence in the modern era, with left-wing terrorism intertwined with the Communist movement and currently practiced by Maoists in Peru and Nepal, right-wing terrorism employed by Neo-Nazi skinheads in several European countries drawing its inspiration from Fascism, and the bulk of ethnonationalist/separatist terrorism accompanying the wave of decolonization especially in the immediate post–World War II years and in places like Northern Ireland and Spain. Currently, "sacred" terrorism is becoming more significant. Of course, these categories are not perfect, as many groups have a mix of motivating ideologies—some ethnonationalist groups, for example, have religious characteristics or agendas—but usually one ideology or motivation dominates. (Cronin 2002/3, 39)

ISIS soldiers lead Christians along a beach in Libya on the way to be slaughtered by their captors. ISIS has used violence and terror to achieve their goal of creating a new Caliphate and eliminating all nonbelievers.

Even with the use of violence by states, there is disagreement on what constitutes the legitimate application of armed force. For example, during the 1980s Libya sponsored terrorist acts as an indirect method of attacking the United States, France, and the United Kingdom. Those states, in turn, condemned Libyan sponsorship as contravening international norms and responded with the customary methods of global politics: sanctions, international court cases, and occasional uses of force. Disagreement associated with the invasion of Iraq in 2003 relates to interpretations over whether the conditions for "just war" were met prior to commencement of military operations. Some suggest that the conditions were not met and that actions by the coalition should be considered an "act of terrorism" conducted by states. Leaders in the United States and the United Kingdom dismiss the charge on the basis that a greater evil was removed. Violating international norms in the pursuit of terrorists runs the risk of playing into perceptions that the state itself is a terrorist threat.

As with other forms of irregular, or asymmetric, warfare, terrorism is designed to achieve political change for the purpose of obtaining power to right a perceived wrong. However, according to some analysts, terrorism is the weakest form of irregular warfare with which to alter the political landscape. The reason for this weakness is that terrorist groups rarely possess the broader support of the population that characterizes insurgency and revolution, and the methods of terrorists often alienate potential supporters of the cause. Terrorist groups often lack support for their objectives because the changes they seek are based on radical ideas that do not have widespread appeal. To effect change, terrorists must provoke drastic responses that act as a catalyst for change or weaken their opponent's moral resolve.

As with definitions of terrorism, there is general agreement on at least one aspect of globalization. Technologies allow the transfer of goods, services, and

THEORY IN PRACTICE

The Realist-Theory Perspective and the War on Terrorism

THE CHALLENGE

Debates about political theories have had an important role in government debates about how secular Western democracies can best fight terrorism. The realist tradition asserts that countries are the most important, sometimes the only, actors that matter in international politics. Many political scientists in the realist tradition also maintain that questions of morality should not restrain the actions of a country that is under threat of an attack.

OPTIONS

These components of realism can explain why the Bush administration was seemingly surprised by the September 11, 2001, attacks and why the government reacted the way it did to those events. For example, on August 6, 2001, National Security Adviser Condoleezza Rice gave President Bush a briefing that included a memo titled "Bin Laden Determined to Strike in US," which documented plans of the Al-Qaeda organization (*The 9/11 Commission Report*, New York: Norton; p. 261). This was the most recent of a series of warnings about possible terrorist attacks on the United States or on American interests around the world. Realist theory

helps us to understand why the Bush administration did not act aggressively on these reports: The theory asserts that *states* are the primary threat to other *states*. Despite the previous successful Al-Qaeda attacks on the U.S. embassies in Kenya and Tanzania, and the near-sinking of the destroyer USS *Cole*, members of the Bush administration might have believed that a small nonstate group was not able to launch another attack. In addition, the Bush administration was preoccupied with North Korea's nuclear weapons program and an incident in which a Chinese fighter aircraft had damaged a U.S. Navy maritime surveillance aircraft, forcing it to land in China. Logically for President Bush and his advisers, North Korea and China presented a more pressing threat to the United States.

Realist international relations theory also provides an explanation for the Bush administration's actions after September 11, 2001. If, as the memo said, bin Laden was determined to attack the United States, President Bush was equally determined that it would not happen again. Therefore, the United States soon attacked Afghanistan, seeking to depose the Taliban government that had offered

sanctuary to bin Laden and other members of the Al-Qaeda leadership. More telling, however, was the Bush administration's decision to label as "unlawful combatants" anyone whom U.S. military personnel captured and detain them at the U.S. Navy base at Guantánamo, Cuba, or in secret prisons around the world. The increasingly unpopular practice of "extraordinary rendition" was another component of the policy. Extraordinary rendition was the capture and transfer of suspected terrorists to unspecified foreign sites for purposes of detention and often torture. Some nongovernmental human rights organizations called the actions violations of international law, but the Bush administration, echoing a key aspect of the realist perspective, called the decisions morally necessary to protect the United States.

For Discussion

The terrorist challenge facing nation-states raises the enduring question of international relations: when is it appropriate for national leaders to violate international law and moral codes of conduct to protect their citizens? Is torture acceptable if it protects a nation-state?

information almost anywhere quickly and efficiently. In the case of information, the transfer can be secure and is nearly instantaneous. The extent of social, cultural, and political change brought on by globalization, including increasing interconnectedness and homogeneity in the international system, remains the subject of much disagreement and debate. These disagreements, in turn, influence discussion of the extent to which globalization has contributed to the rise of modern terrorism. There is little doubt that the technologies associated with globalization have been used to improve the effectiveness and reach of terrorist groups. For example, social media has played an important role in helping groups like the Islamic State recruit young people to their cause. The relationship between globalization and terrorism is best understood as the next step in the evolution of political violence since terrorism became a transnational phenomenon in the 1960s. To understand the changes perceived in terrorism globally, it is useful to understand the evolution of terrorism from a primarily domestic political event to a global phenomenon.

Terrorism: From Domestic to Global Phenomena

Historically, nonstate terrorist groups have used readily available means to permit small numbers of individuals to spread fear as widely as possible. In the late nineteenth and early twentieth centuries, anarchists relied on railroads for travel and killed with revolvers and dynamite. Yet terrorists and acts of terrorism rarely had an impact beyond national borders, in part because the activists often sought political change within a specific country. Three factors led to the birth of transnational terrorism in 1968: (1) the expansion of commercial air travel, (2) the availability of televised news coverage, and (3) broad political and ideological interests among extremists that converged on a common cause. As a result, terrorism grew from a local to a transnational threat. Air travel gave terrorists unprecedented mobility.

For example, the Japanese Red Army trained in one country and attacked in another, as with the 1972 Lod Airport massacre in Israel. In the United States, some radicals forced airplanes to go to Cuba. Air travel appealed to terrorists because airport security measures, including passport control, were less stringent when terrorists began hijacking airlines, referred to as **skyjackings**. States also acquiesced to terrorist demands, frequently for money, which encouraged further incidents. The success of this tactic spurred other terrorist groups, as well as criminals and political refugees, to follow suit. Incidents of hijacking increased dramatically from five in 1966 to ninety-four in 1969. Shared political ideologies stimulated cooperation and some exchanges between groups as diverse as the Irish Republican Army (IRA) and the Basque separatist organization Euzkadi Ta Askatasuna (ETA). Besides sharing techniques and technical experience, groups demanded the release of imprisoned "fellow revolutionaries" in different countries, giving the impression of a coordinated global terrorist network. The reality

Skyjackings The takeover of a commercial airplane for the purpose of taking hostages and using these hostages to bargain for a particular political or economic goal.

In 1988, terrorists planted a bomb that blew up a Pan American jet over Lockerbie, Scotland. It took twenty-five years to identify the suspects—two Libyans who were supported by the Libyan government—a pariah state at the time seeking to change the distribution of power and influence in North Africa and the Middle East. Are states still involved in terrorist activities aimed at changing the status quo?

Attacks causing one death, cumulative total			
Austria	1	Ireland	2
Belgium	1	Italy	3
Britain	14	Netherlands	3
France	4	Spain	9
Greece	5	Sweden	1

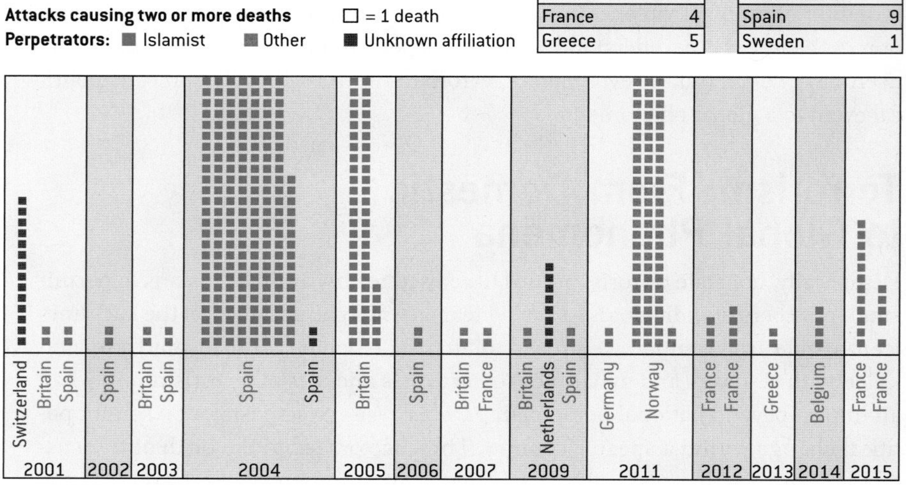

Figure 6.1 Thirteen Years of Terror in Western Europe.

This figure illustrates political violence between September 10, 2001, and January 15, 2015, in Western Europe, as well as who the perpetrators are.

was that groups formed short-term relationships of convenience, based around weapons, capabilities, and money, to advance local political objectives. For example, members of the IRA did not launch attacks in Spain to help the ETA, but they did share resources.

Televised news coverage and the Internet also played a role in expanding the audience, who could witness the theater of terrorism in their own homes. People who had never heard of "the plight of the Palestinians" became more aware of the issue after live coverage of incidents such as the hostage taking conducted by Black September during the 1972 Munich Olympics. Although some considered media coverage "the oxygen that sustains terrorism," terrorists discovered that reporters and audiences lost interest in repeat performances over time. To sustain viewer interest and compete for coverage, terrorist groups undertook increasingly spectacular attacks, such as the seizure of Organization of Petroleum Exporting Countries delegates by "Carlos the Jackal," whose real name was Ilich Ramírez Sánchez, in Austria in December 1975. Terrorism experts speculated that terrorist leaders understood that horrific, mass-casualty attacks might cross a threshold of violence. This might explain why few terrorist groups attempted to acquire or use WMD, including nuclear, chemical, and biological weapons.

The Impact of Globalization on Terrorism

Al-Qaeda Most commonly associated with Osama bin Laden, "The Base" (its meaning in Arabic) is a religious-based group whose fighters swear an oath of fealty to the leadership that succeeded bin Laden.

Al-Qaeda, "The Base" or "The Foundation," received global recognition as a result of its attacks conducted in New York and Washington, D.C., on September 11, 2001. Since then, and even after the death of Osama bin Laden in 2011, experts

TABLE 6.2	Al-Qaeda and Its Extremist Affiliates

Group Name	Description
Al-Qaeda in the Arabian Peninsula (AQAP)	Originally a Saudi-based organization set up by bin Laden after 9/11. In 2009, AQAP joined with a group in Yemen where it focuses its terrorism; AQAP also has a focus on the United States as a target.
Al-Qaeda in the Islamic Maghreb (AQIM)	Founded in 2003 as a successor to the 1990s Algerian jihad, it emerged from the Salafist Group for Preaching and Combat. Their targets are the French and American crusaders. This group has extended its terrorism to Libya, Mali, Mauritania, and Niger.
Al-Shabaab	Founded in 2012 with loyalty toward Al-Qaeda, Al-Shabaab means "young men" in Arabic. These are Somali militants taking advantage of a failed state and attacking the United States and UN peacekeepers. They are best known for their attack on a shopping mall in Kenya.
Boko Haram	This Salafist Islamist sect emerged in Northeast Nigeria in 2003 and clashes with government authorities. In Hausa, their name means "Western education is forbidden." In 2014, this group abducted 276 young school girls.
Jemaah Islamiyah	This militant Islamist group seeks to establish an Islamic state across Southeast Asia. The group has targeted U.S. and Western interests in Indonesia, Singapore, and the Philippines, and has attacked tourist areas in Bali in 2002 and 2005.

Source: Daniel Byman, Al Qaeda, The Islamic State and the Global Jihadist Movement (Oxford 2015).

have debated what Al-Qaeda is, what it represents, and the actual threat it poses (see Table 6.2 for a list of its affiliates and extent of its reach). In early 2006, the Office of the Chairman of the Joint Chiefs of Staff in the Pentagon released the *National Military Strategic Plan for the War on Terrorism*, which sought to characterize the fluid nature of militant Islamic terrorism:

> There is no monolithic enemy network with a single set of goals and objectives. The nature of the threat is more complicated. In the GWOT [global war on terrorism], the primary enemy is a transnational movement of extremist organizations, networks, and individuals—and their state and nonstate supporters—which have in common that they exploit Islam and use terrorism for ideological ends. The Al Qaeda Associated Movement (AQAM), comprised of Al Qaeda and affiliated radical groups, is the most dangerous present manifestation of such extremism. The [Al Qaeda network's] adaptation or evolution resulted in the creation of an extremist "movement," referred to by intelligence analysts as AQAM, extending extremism and terrorist tactics well beyond the original organization. This adaptation has resulted in decentralizing control in the network and franchising its extremist efforts within the movement. (National Military Strategic Plan for the War on Terrorism [Unclassified], 13)

Efforts to explain the vitality of global terrorism in general—and Al-Qaeda in particular—focus on three areas linked to aspects of globalization: culture, economics, and religion.

The Shanghai Cooperation Organization: Fighting Terrorism in the Former Communist Bloc

Although often missing from the headlines of North American media, terrorism is a threat to countries not directly involved in the global war on terrorism. Debates in the United States and Western Europe about the proper methods to stop attacks frequently center on matters of ethics and morality. To put it briefly, what *should* Western-style democracies do to confront terrorist groups, especially those with Islamist links that seek to destroy open societies based on tolerance? *Can* democracy and inclusive institutions survive if Western governments must occasionally bend their own laws to safeguard society?

Such questions of appropriate methods to combat terrorism tend not to restrain the governments of China and the former Soviet republics Russia, Kazakhstan, Kyrgyzstan, Tajikistan, and Uzbekistan, which together created the Shanghai Cooperation Organization (SCO) in June 2001. None of these countries are paragons of democratic virtue. According to the annual survey of the human rights organization Freedom House, Kyrgyzstan ranks the highest of the six SCO countries, and it is only partly free.

Government officials in all of the countries regularly suppress and occasionally murder independent journalists who criticize those who hold political power. Opposition political parties find their offices closed, their assets seized, their telephones tapped, and their members harassed and arrested. Religious minorities are often jailed if they practice their rituals in public. All of this sounds like the description of terror: a state repressing its own subjects or citizens.

Yet from the time of its founding, the SCO called itself an antiterror institution, and its greatest threat is Islamist radical groups. Certainly, given the role that Taliban fighters played in defeating the Soviet invasion of Afghanistan in the 1980s and the Islamic aspect to the Russian war in Chechnya, it made sense that Russia would see an Islamic threat. However, media organizations in the United States miss the effect that separatist groups have in Chinese politics—for example, the Muslim Uighurs who live in the Sinkiang region in the west of the country. According to the CIA's World Factbook, Islam is the primary religious identification for the majority of people in Kyrgyzstan (75%), Tajikistan (90%), and Uzbekistan (88%). Each member state of the SCO must, therefore, take a different approach to its own Muslim problem. The leaders of the most Islamic

states fear that a Taliban style of Sunni Islam might become popular and challenge the legitimacy of the secular governments. Both Russia and China fear that Islamic radicals might push for independence.

Thus, for SCO member states, the greatest threat is not external attack but internal collapse. As a result, terrorism and separatism are linked in the Shanghai Convention on Combating Terrorism, Separatism, and Extremism signed in June 2001. The SCO held its first joint antiterror war games in August 2003 in Kazakhstan. There was perhaps a message in the choice of host country for the exercise. Kazakhstan's population is about 24 percent Russian and has, after China and Russia, the fewest number of people who self-identify as Muslims: about 70 percent. In Kazakhstan, Russians have the most to fear from Islamic radicals, yet at the same time, the exercises might offend the fewest number of Muslims.

Despite the antiterrorist stand of the SCO, some U.S. government officials have been wary of the motives of the group. Some feared that China and Russia might apply pressure to the Central Asian states to have them force the United States to leave the bases it had in Kyrgyzstan in support of its war against the Taliban in Afghanistan. Neo-conservatives in the United States who advocated the spread of democracy also expressed concerns that China and Russia might form an alliance similar to the Holy Alliance that Russia, Prussia, and Austria-Hungary created after the Napoleonic wars. The early-1800s alliance was strongly antidemocratic, repressing political and civil liberties. Some analysts believe that by seeking to slow an inevitable process of liberalism, the Holy Alliance brought about the destruction that it wanted to avoid.

Since its founding, the SCO has expanded its mandate to include joint security and economic development programs. In July 2015, India and Pakistan began the accession process to become SCO members, but at the time of this writing, their membership has not been finalized; a number of other states serve as observer states and dialogue partners. However, the organization's regional influence is limited due to underfunding and the limited power capabilities of members to make collective decisions. More often than not, member states are preoccupied by their own independent agendas, which weaken cohesion and breed mistrust.

GLOBAL PERSPECTIVE *continued*

For Discussion

1. Do you find it strange that authoritarian states want to fight terrorism? Might they respond to terrorism differently?
2. Could this coalition of authoritarian states actually work against the spread of democracy and the ending of global terrorism?
3. All the states in this coalition have significant Muslim populations. Are their concerns about internal order or global terrorism?

Cultural Explanations

Culture is one way to explain why militant Islam's call for armed struggle has been successful in underdeveloped countries. Culture also explains many of the ethnic conflicts, and violence between religious and language groups, across the world. The 1990s were a period of unprecedented ethnic violence and terrorism that included the genocide in Rwanda and the ethnic cleansing in the former Yugoslavia. Many fundamentalist groups believe that violence is the only method to preserve traditions and values against a cultural tsunami of Western products and **materialism**. Once sought after as an entry method to economic prosperity, Western secular, materialist values are increasingly rejected by those seeking to regain or preserve their own unique cultural identity. The phenomenon of rejecting the West is not new; one could argue that it began almost 200 years ago as the strength of the Ottoman Empire waned. Since then, the social changes associated with globalization and the spread of free market capitalism appear to be overwhelming the identity or values of groups who perceive themselves as the losers in the new international system. In an attempt to preserve their threatened identity and values, groups actively distinguish themselves from despised "others." At the local level, this cultural friction could translate into conflicts divided along religious or ethnic lines to safeguard **identity**.

Young British Muslims come together at the Active Change Foundation youth center in Leytonstone to launch a social media campaign, being led by the East London–based charity against ISIS using #notinmyname to register their revulsion and the rejection of terrorist groups that claim their actions are in the name of Islam. President Obama has stated many times that our struggle is against those who inappropriately use a religion to justify their actions.

Economic Explanations

Not everyone agrees that defense of cultural identity is the primary motivation for globalized terrorist violence. Others see economic aspects as the crucial

Materialism In this context, it is the spreading of a global consumer culture and popular-culture artifacts like music, books, and movies. Christopher Lasch called this the "ceaseless translation of luxuries into necessities." These elements are seen as undermining traditional cultural values and norms.

Identity The understanding of the self in relationship to an "other." Identities are social and thus always formed in relationship to others. Constructivists generally hold that identities shape interests; we cannot know what we want unless we know who we are. But because identities are social and produced through interactions, identities can change.

Imperialism The practice of foreign conquest and rule in the context of global relations of hierarchy and subordination. It can lead to the establishment of an empire.

motivating factor in the use of violence to effect political change. Although globalization provides access to a world market for goods and services, the net result has also been perceived as a form of Western economic **imperialism**. The United States and the postindustrial states of Western Europe form the global North or economic core that dominates international economic institutions, sets exchange rates, and determines fiscal policies. The actions and policies can be unfavorable to the underdeveloped countries, or global South, that make up the periphery or gap. Political decisions by the leaders of underdeveloped countries to deregulate or privatize industries to be competitive globally could lead to significant social and economic upheaval. The citizenry might shift loyalties to illegal activities such as terrorism if the state breaks its social contract (Junaid 2005, 143–144).

Wealth is also linked to personal security and violence. With little opportunity to obtain wealth locally, individuals will leave to pursue opportunities in other countries. The result is emigration and the rapid growth of burgeoning urban centers that act as regional hubs for the flow of global resources. Movement, however, is no guarantee that individual aspirations will be realized. In cases where they are not, individuals might turn to violence for reasons that are criminal (e.g., personal gain) or political (e.g., to change the existing political system through insurgency or terrorism). Paradoxically, rising standards of living and greater access to educational opportunities associated with globalization could lead to increased expectations. If those expectations are unmet, individuals may turn to extreme political views and action against "the system" that denies them the opportunity to realize their ambitions.

However, the explanation that recent terrorist violence is a reaction to economic globalization could be flawed for a number of reasons, including the personal wealth and social upbringing of a number of members of global terrorist groups, as well as trends in regional patterns of terrorist recruitment. Many former leaders and members of transnational terrorist groups, including the German Red Army Faction and the Italian Red Brigades, came from respectable middle- and upper-class families. The same holds true for a number of modern-day antiglobalization anarchists. Within militant Islamic groups, most of their leaders and senior operatives attended graduate schools around the globe in fields as diverse as engineering and theology and were neither poor nor downtrodden (Sageman 2004, 73–74).

> ### WHAT'S YOUR WORLDVIEW?
>
> *Poverty might not be a direct cause of terrorist activities, but do you think it contributes to attitudes that make people susceptible to recruitment by radical groups?*

Postmodern or **"new" terrorism** Groups and individuals subscribing to millennial and apocalyptic ideologies and system-level goals. Most value destruction for its own sake, unlike most terrorists in the past, who had specific goals, usually tied to a territory.

Religion and "New" Terrorism

In the decade prior to 9/11, a number of scholars and experts perceived that fundamental changes were taking place in the character of terrorism. The use of violence for political purposes, to change state ideology or the representation of ethnic minority groups, had failed in its purpose and a new trend was emerging. **Postmodern** or **"new" terrorism** was conducted for different reasons altogether and seemed to be driven by the power of ideas of the kind that constructivist international relations theory describes. Motivated by promises of rewards in the afterlife, some terrorists are driven by religious reasons to kill as many of the non-believers and unfaithful as possible (Laqueur 1996, 32–33). Although suicide tactics had been observed in Lebanon as early as 1983, militant Islam had previously been viewed as a state-sponsored, regional phenomenon (Wright 1986, 19–21).

New terrorism is seen as a reaction to the perceived oppression of Muslims worldwide and the spiritual bankruptcy of the West. As globalization spreads and societies become increasingly interconnected, Muslims have a choice: accept Western beliefs to better integrate, or preserve their spiritual purity by rebelling. Believers in the global **jihad** view the rulers of countries such as Pakistan, Saudi Arabia, or Iraq as apostates who have compromised their values in the pursuit and maintenance of secular, state-based power. The only possible response is to fight against such influences through jihad. Jihad is understood by most Islamic scholars and imams to mean the internal struggle for purity spiritually, although it has also been interpreted historically as a method to establish the basis for just war. Extremists who espouse militant Islam understand jihad in a different way. For the jihadi terrorist, there can be no compromise with either infidels or apostates.

Jihad In Arabic, *jihad* means "struggle." Jihad can refer to a purely internal struggle to be a better Muslim or a struggle to make society more closely align with the teachings of the Koran.

The difference in value structures between secular and religious terrorists makes the responses to the latter difficult. Religious terrorists will kill themselves and others because they believe that they will receive rewards in the afterlife. Differences in value structures make the deterrence of religious terrorism difficult, if not impossible, as secular states cannot credibly threaten materially the ideas that terrorists value spiritually. Secular terrorism has had as its goal the pursuit of power to correct flaws within society but retain the overarching system. Religious terrorism, by contrast, does not seek to modify but rather to replace the normative structure of society (Cronin 2002/3, 41).

The use of religion, as a reaction to and an explanation for the phenomenon of global terrorism, contains some of the same incongruities as those focused on cultural and economic aspects. For Western observers, religious reasons appear to explain how individual terrorists are convinced to take their own lives and kill others. Personal motivations can include promises of financial rewards for family members, gaining fame within a community, taking revenge for some grievance, or simply achieving a form of self-actualization. Yet few religious terrorist leaders, planners, and coordinators martyr themselves. Religion provides terrorist groups with a crucial advantage: the mandate and sanction of the divine to commit otherwise illegal or immoral acts. There is a substantial difference between religious motivation as the single driving factor to commit acts of terrorism and the ultimate purpose for which violence is being used.

The Current Challenge: The Islamic State

The Islamic State is part of the Al-Qaeda family. It has about 30,000 well-equipped fighters and they control an area the size of Indiana, including the Iraqi city of Mosul, the country's second largest city. The Islamic State earns about $2 million a day on the black market selling oil but they also sell the spoils of war and sponsor a variety of illegal activities such as smuggling antiquities and human trafficking. Many experts suggest that they are a bigger threat than Al-Qaeda because the Islamic State is attracting recruits from around the world. The Islamic State is an actual governing state providing basic services for all those who are under its control. It is a cruel state for those who do not believe their conservative Sunni Islamic views and Sharia law governs the actions of all citizens.

The goal of the Islamic State is to erase the colonial boundaries imposed by Western powers and create an Islamic empire that stretches from Spain to South and Southeast Asia. Those standing in the way of this new Islamic Caliphate are the nonbelievers and Western liberal ideas that promote democracy and individual freedoms that contradict elements of Islamic thought and Sharia law. The Islamic State follows the seven-stage strategy developed by Al-Qaeda in 2005 in its pursuit of an Islamic Caliphate (Hoffman 2016):

- **Stage I: The Awakening Stage—2000 to 2003**
  Coincides with the September 11, 2001 attacks and the reawakening of the Caliphate by this attack on the West and the United States.
- **Stage II: The Eye-Opening Stage—2003 to 2006**
  With the U.S. invasion of Iraq, the war with the enemy begins and a prolonged war will weaken the United States and the West.
- **Stage III: The Rising Up and Standing on the Feet Stage—2007 to 2010**
  Expanding extremism and terror tactics to new venues across Africa and globally.
- **Stage IV: The Recovery Stage—2010 to 2013**
  Regroup after the death of bin Laden and take advantage of the changes promoted by the Arab Spring to topple apostate regimes like Syria.
- **Stage V: Declaration of the Caliphate Stage—2013 to 2016**
  Islamic State moves ahead of Al-Qaeda by establishing rule over a large area and acting like a state.
- **Stage VI: The Total Confrontation—2016 to 2020**
  The Caliphate is created, and in turn the leaders create an Islamic army to fight the holy war between believers and nonbelievers.
- **Stage VII: The Definitive Stage–2020 to 2022**
  The Caliphate triumphs over the entire world.

Analysts see the Islamic State is at Stage V and is now trying to pull the United States and the West into a major confrontation. Their apocalyptic prophecies suggest this will be the final battle and they will defeat the nonbelievers. All their victories suggest that the prophecies are true and act as great recruiting tools for young Muslims looking to fulfill personal religious goals.

Additionally, another concern for the West is the return of battle-tested Islamic State fighters to their homelands to carry out attacks. Extremists who were trained and then fought for the Islamic State Caliphate in Syria and Iraq carried out the Paris attacks, which resulted in the deaths of more than 100 people, and inspired the attack in San Bernardino, California, which left fourteen people

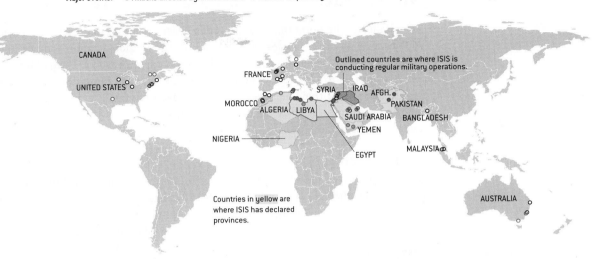

Major events: ● Attacks directed by/linked to ISIS ○ Attacks inspired by ISIS ○ Arrests of suspected ISIS militants or supporters

Outlined countries are where ISIS is conducting regular military operations.

Countries in yellow are where ISIS has declared provinces.

Map 6.2 Where ISIS Has Directed and Inspired Attacks.
Can a nation-state respond to networks like this without global cooperation?

dead. This is what political analyst Bruce Hoffman calls the "boomerang effect" and may be how the Islamic State takes its extremist violence to countries across the world and brings the West into the "total confrontation" (see Map 6.2). The Syrian civil war may ultimately be the conflict that triggers this event (see Table 6.3).

TABLE 6.3 Inter-Actor Relationship Guide to the Syrian War

LEGEND : Allies | It's Complicated | Enemies | Intentionally Blank

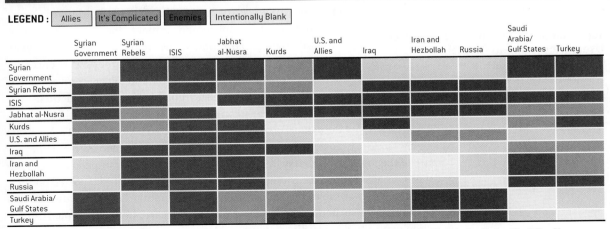

	Syrian Government	Syrian Rebels	ISIS	Jabhat al-Nusra	Kurds	U.S. and Allies	Iraq	Iran and Hezbollah	Russia	Saudi Arabia/ Gulf States	Turkey
Syrian Government											
Syrian Rebels											
ISIS											
Jabhat al-Nusra											
Kurds											
U.S. and Allies											
Iraq											
Iran and Hezbollah											
Russia											
Saudi Arabia/ Gulf States											
Turkey											

Sources: Almukhtar, Sarah, K.K. Rebecca Lai, and Sergio Pecanha. "Untangling the Overlapping Conflicts in the Syrian War." The New York Times 18 Oct. 2015, International sec.: 14. Print.
Kirk, Joshua. "The Middle East Friendship Chart." Slate.com. 17 July 2015. Web. 22 Oct. 2015.

Globalization, Technology, and Terrorism

Few challenge the point that terrorism has become much more pervasive worldwide as a result of the processes and technologies of globalization. The technological advances associated with globalization have improved the capabilities of terrorist groups to plan and conduct operations with far more devastation and coordination than their predecessors could have imagined. In particular, technologies have improved the capability of groups and cells to carry out attacks on a wider and more lethal scale.

Proselytizing

States traditionally have had an advantage in their ability to control information flows and use their resources to win the battle of hearts and minds against terrorist groups. Terrorist leaders understand how the Internet has changed this dynamic: "We [know that we] are in a battle, and that more than half of this battle is taking place in the battlefield of the media. And that we are in a media battle in a race for the hearts and minds of our Umma" (Office of the Director of National Intelligence 2005, 10).

The continued expansion of the number of Internet service providers, especially in states with relaxed or ambivalent content policies or laws, combined with capable and cheap computers, software, peripherals, and wireless technologies, has empowered individuals and groups to post tracts on or send messages throughout the World Wide Web. One form of empowerment is the virtual presence that individuals have. Although prominent jihadi terrorists' physical presence can be removed through imprisonment or death, their virtual presence and influence are immortalized on the World Wide Web.

Another form of empowerment for terrorist groups, brought on by globalization, is the volume, range, and sophistication of propaganda materials. Terrorist groups were once limited to mimeographed manifestos and typed communiqués. Terrorist supporters and sympathizers now build their own websites. An early example was a website sympathetic to the Peruvian Tupac Amaru Revolutionary Movement. This website posted the group's communiqués and videos during the seizure of the Japanese embassy in Lima in 1996. Webmasters sympathetic to terrorist groups also control the content and connotation of the material posted on their websites. The website of the Sri Lankan group Liberation Tigers of Tamil Eelam, for example, posts items that cast the group as an internationally accepted organization committed to conflict resolution. Messages, files, and polemics can be dispatched to almost anywhere on the globe via the Internet or text messaging, almost instantaneously.

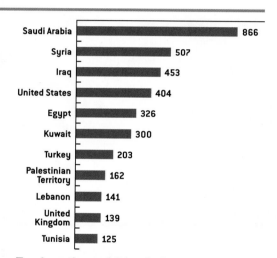

Saudi Arabia	866
Syria	507
Iraq	453
United States	404
Egypt	326
Kuwait	300
Turkey	203
Palestinian Territory	162
Lebanon	141
United Kingdom	139
Tunisia	125

Top Locations of Islamic State Twitter Users (According to Profile).

Terrorist organizations such as ISIS use social media, especially Twitter, to reach supporters. The expansion of social media and the Internet is helping ISIS and other terrorist organizations in reaching foreign supporters.

Terrorist groups in Chechnya and the Middle East have also made increasing use of video cameras to record the preparations for attacks, and their results, including successful roadside bombings and the downing of helicopters. With the right software and a little knowledge, individuals or small groups can download or obtain digital footage and music and produce videos that appeal to specific groups. Video footage is useful in inspiring potential recruits and seeking donations from support elements within the organization. For example, terrorist recruiters distributed videos of sniper and other attacks against coalition forces in Iraq, produced by the Al-Qaeda media-production group As-Sahab. The competition among global news outlets like CNN, MSNBC, and Al Jazeera ensures that the images of successful or dramatic attacks reach the widest audience possible.

> **WHAT'S YOUR WORLDVIEW?**
>
> *Would you be willing to live with fewer personal freedoms if it meant better security? For example, would you accept rules that would allow governments to monitor your communications and your computer activity?*

Security of Terrorist Organizations

Terrorist cells without adequate security precautions are vulnerable to discovery and detection. Translations of captured Al-Qaeda manuals, for example, demonstrate the high value their writers place on security, including surveillance and countersurveillance techniques. The technological enablers of globalization assist terrorist cells and leaders in preserving security in a number of ways, including distributing elements in a coordinated network, remaining mobile, and utilizing clandestine or encrypted communications.

The security of terrorist organizations has historically been preserved by limiting communication and information exchanges between cells. This ensures that if one cell is compromised, its members only know each other's identities and not those of other cells. Thus, the damage done to the organization is minimized. Security is even more important to **clandestine** or **"sleeper" cells** operating on their own without central direction. The use of specific codes and ciphers, known only to a few individuals, is one way of preserving the security of an organization. Although code and ciphers inevitably have been broken and information has been obtained through interrogation, such activities take time. During that time, terrorist groups adjust their location and operating methods in an attempt to stay ahead of counterterrorist forces. Technological advancements, including faster processing speeds and software developments, now mean that those sympathetic to terrorist causes can contribute virtually through servers located hundreds or thousands of miles away.

Clandestine or **"sleeper" cell** Usually, a group of people sent by an intelligence organization or terrorist network that remains dormant in a target country until activated by a message to carry out a mission, which could include prearranged attacks.

Mobility

The reduced size and increased capabilities of personal electronics also give terrorists mobility advantages. Mobility has always been a crucial consideration for terrorists and insurgents alike, given the superior resources that states have been able to bring to bear against them. In open societies that have well-developed infrastructures, terrorists have been able to move rapidly within and between borders, and this complicates efforts to track them because they exploit the very societal values they seek to destroy.

The globalization of commerce has also improved terrorist mobility. The volume of air travel and goods that pass through ports has increased exponentially through globalization. Between states, measures have been taken to ease the flow of goods, services, and ideas, to improve efficiency, and to reduce costs. One example is the European Schengen Agreement, in which border security measures between EU member states have been relaxed to speed deliveries. Market demands for efficiencies of supply, manufacture, delivery, and cost have complicated states' efforts to prevent members of terrorist groups from exploiting gaps in security measures. Additional mobility also allows terrorist groups to transfer expertise, as demonstrated by the arrest of three members of the IRA suspected of training counterparts in the Fuerzas Armadas Revolucionarias de Colombia in Bogotá in August 2001.

Terrorist use of transportation is not necessarily overt, as the volume of goods transported in support of a globalized economy is staggering and difficult to monitor effectively. For example, customs officials cannot inspect all of the vehicles or containers passing through border points or ports. To illustrate the scale of the problem, the United States receives 10 million containers per year, and one port, Los Angeles, processes the equivalent of 12,000 twenty-foot containers daily. Western government officials fear that terrorist groups will use containers as a convenient and cheap means to ship WMD.

Combating Terrorism

States plagued by transnational terrorism responded individually and collectively to combat the phenomenon during the Cold War. These responses ranged in scope and effectiveness and included passing antiterrorism laws, taking preventative security measures at airports, and creating special-operations counterterrorism forces such as the West German Grenzschutzgruppe-9 (GSG-9). Successful rescues in Entebbe (1976), Mogadishu (1977), and Prince's Gate, London (1980), demonstrated that national counterterrorism forces could respond effectively both domestically and abroad. A normative approach to tackling the problem, founded on the principles of international law and collective action, was less successful. Attempts by the United Nations to define and proscribe transnational terrorism bogged down in the General Assembly over semantics (i.e., deciding on the definition of a terrorist), but other cooperative initiatives were successfully implemented. These included the conventions adopted through the International Civil Aviation Organization to improve information sharing and legal cooperation, such as The Hague Convention for the Suppression of Unlawful Seizure of Aircraft (1970). Another collective response to improve information sharing and collaborative action was the creation of the

Public Safety and Terrorism Sub-Directorate within Interpol in 1985. However, most initiatives and responses throughout this decade were unilateral, regional, or ad hoc in nature.

Counterterrorism Activities

Paul Pillar (2001, 29–39), a former high-level CIA official, suggests that counter-terrorist policies must address at least four important issue areas. These include the following:

- Develop a thorough *understanding* of the variety of economic, political, and sociocultural issues and conditions that contribute to decisions by individuals or groups to use terrorist tactics. Know that some people who become terrorists will not give up that role no matter what is done to correct unacceptable conditions.
- Completely assess the *capabilities* of terrorist groups and design programs that reduce their ability to attack.
- Review and understand the *intentions* of terrorists and make certain not to reward any of their activities with concessions.
- Create a *defense* based on counterterrorist measures that would convince terrorists that it is not worth an attack (deterrence).

There are a number of policy instruments available to those trying to prevent further terrorist attacks (Pillar 2001 and Purdy 2004–2005). The first counterterrorist instrument that states might use is *diplomacy*. Leaders might use persuasion and various incentives to encourage foreign governments to suppress certain group activities and to abide by rules and procedures that might prevent terrorist activities. Global policies are welcome, but usually bilateral diplomatic agreements are more effective. It is easier to reward or punish a single state for its compliance or noncompliance with a bilateral or regional agreement than try to monitor the activities of some 200 nation-states.

A second counterterrorism strategy is the *mobilization of NGOs* to promote international law and educate the world about the causes of terrorism, the importance of the rule of law, and the human costs of violence and terrorism.

A third counterterrorist activity is *law enforcement*. Terrorist activities are illegal—violating both national and international law. New laws, special courts, prisons, and new penalties are all part of the war on terrorism. Police forces across the world are now cooperating to identify, arrest, and punish terrorist groups. Stricter law enforcement and increased surveillance, however, have caused some concerns related to the loss of certain civil liberties. The most controversial aspects of the global war on terrorism have been the long-term imprisonment of terrorists, the use of torture and other punitive forms of interrogation, and the illegal transferring of prisoners to nondemocratic states where torture is regularly used.

A fourth counterterrorism strategy involves the use of *financial controls* that track, freeze, and seize financial resources that support terrorist activities. The 1999 International Convention for the Suppression of the Financing of Terrorism criminalizes the collection of funds for any terrorist activity. Unfortunately, because of numerous offshore accounts, Internet banking, and a global banking and financial system that makes it easy to hide and transfer funds, controlling this financial process is extremely difficult and will require both private- and public-sector collaboration.

A fifth counterterrorist strategy is the *use of military force*. The use of military force against states that support terrorism is a just cause and is supported by international law. Problems arise when the enemy is a nonstate actor, a network of terrorist organizations operating in a variety of states. How do you justify retaliating strikes against sovereign states that might not support terrorists within their boundaries?

The strategic use of force might be the only way to respond to groups willing to use force to achieve their goals. If supported by the international community and international law, force can be an effective tool. The multilateral effort to end Taliban rule in Afghanistan, and the continuing NATO operation, provides an example of a just multilateral effort to close terrorist training camps, arrest leaders of Al-Qaeda, and build an effective state that is capable of providing for its citizens.

The final counterterrorist tool is *intelligence and covert action*. This involves both the use of technical intelligence, such as the monitoring of phone calls and e-mails, and human intelligence, and information collected by spies. The

A training exercise for London's emergency services. The exercise was planned in the wake of the *Charlie Hebdo* attacks in Paris in January 2015. The entire world is spending millions of dollars reacting to potential extremist attacks.

collection of information is not easy, because extremists and others willing to use terrorism are difficult to find. Pillar (2001, 110) also points out that analysis is as difficult as collecting information. He suggests that there might just be too much information, and it is difficult to decide what is relevant and what is simply useless chatter.

To deal with transnational terrorism, the global community must address its most problematic modern aspect: the appeal of messages that inspire terrorists to commit horrific acts of violence. Killing or capturing individuals does little to halt the spread of extremist viewpoints that occur under the guise of discussion and education. In the case of Islam, for example, radical mullahs and imams twist the tenets of the religion into a doctrine of action and hatred, where spiritual achievement occurs through destruction rather than personal enlightenment. In other words, suicide attacks offer the promise of private goods (spiritual reward) rather than public goods (positive contributions to the community over a lifetime). Precisely how the processes and technologies of globalization can assist in delegitimizing the pedagogy that incites terrorists will remain one of the most vexing challenges for the global community for years to come.

Conclusion

Questions of war and peace are central to the existence of every country. In this chapter, we have examined the many ways academics analyze security affairs and how these ideas influence the decisions political leaders make on war and weapons procurement, especially nuclear weapons and nuclear proliferation. Terrorism, another salient issue in global security, remains a complex phenomenon in which violence is used to obtain political power to redress grievances that might have become more acute through the process of globalization. The challenge for the global community will be in utilizing its advantages to win the war of ideas that motivates and sustains those responsible for the current wave of terrorist violence.

CONTRIBUTORS TO CHAPTER 6: *John Baylis, Darryl Howlett, James D. Kiras, Steven L. Lamy, and John Masker.*

KEY TERMS

Absolute gains, p. 213
Al-Qaeda, p. 236
Asymmetric conflicts, p. 221

Clandestine or "sleeper" cell, p. 245
Community, p. 211

Democratic peace thesis, p. 215
Failed states, p. 224
Globalization, p. 211

Identity, p. 239
Imperialism, p. 240
Jihad, p. 241
Material structure, p. 215

REVIEW QUESTIONS

1. Why is security a "contested concept"? How do academic disagreements about the term reflect the theory perspectives we studied in Chapter 3?

2. According to realists, why do states find it difficult to cooperate? How do constructivists explain cooperation?

3. Is the tension between national and global security resolvable?

4. Has international security changed since the United States began its global war on terrorism? How?

5. What are the main arguments for and against the proliferation of nuclear weapons? To what extent might these arguments be the result of a person's theory-based worldview?

6. How might nonstate actors represent a new nuclear-proliferation challenge?

7. Why do some authors believe that war between the current great powers is highly unlikely?

8. What is "asymmetric warfare"?

9. When and how did terrorism become a truly global phenomenon?

10. Of all the factors that motivate terrorists, is any one more important than others, and if so, why?

11. What role does technology play in terrorism, and will it change how terrorists operate in the future? If so, how?

12. What is the primary challenge that individual states and the global community as a whole face in confronting terrorism?

13. How can globalization be useful in diminishing the underlying causes of terrorism?

➤ For more information, quizzes, case studies, and other study tools, please visit us at **www.oup.com/us/lamy.**

THINKING ABOUT GLOBAL POLITICS

Perspectives on the Arms Race

OBJECTIVE

The goal of this exercise is difficult to reach: consensus on a national security policy or national strategy for the United States with regard to nuclear weapons. After doing some research online and in your library, you will explore with your classmates the importance of worldviews in determining national interests. Your professor might put you into groups.

PROCEDURE

This is not a debate but a discussion. You should try to consider the assumptions of national security from three significant groups participating in arms debates within the United States. These are the major groups:

- Arms advocates (Realists)
- Arms control advocates (Liberals)
- Disarmament advocates (Select an Alternative Theory; see Chapter 3)
  - Review with your classmates the basic worldview positions and corresponding policy priorities of each group (reread Chapters 2 and 3).

- Divide your class into three groups representing these views.
- Explore these general questions in your discussion:
  a. What does the United States want its nuclear weapons to do?
  b. What should our nuclear strategy be?
  c. How can the United States use nuclear weapons to achieve its foreign policy and national security goals?

FOLLOW-UP

Take the evening to review your readings from the semester so far (both in this textbook and in whatever supplemental readings your professor has assigned). Make a list of statements made in these materials that support your position, which you will use in your next class. During class, your professor might choose to have you (or a group leader) write these statements on the board and ask others in the class to respond to your selections.

7

Human Rights and Human Security

Armenian Americans march in New York City to mark the centennial of the killing of 1.5 million Armenians under the Ottoman Empire in 1915. Only twenty nation-states recognize this as an incident of genocide; the United States is not one of them.

Free expression is the base of human rights, the root of human nature and the mother of truth. To kill free speech is to insult human rights, to stifle human nature and to suppress truth.

—LIU XIABO

Human security naturally connects several kinds of freedom—such as freedom from want and freedom from fear, as well as freedom to take action on one's behalf.

—COMMISSION ON HUMAN SECURITY

The term *genocide* was created after World War II, as leaders of the antifascist coalition struggled to understand the magnitude of human tragedy before them. Immediately after the war, the victorious powers promised "never again" would countries stand by while tyrants massacred their own people or launched wars of aggression.

And yet sadly, since 1945, genocidal violence has occurred in the Congo, Cambodia, East Timor, Rwanda, Bosnia, Kosovo, Chechnya, Somalia, Darfur, and many other places. In this chapter, we will examine the linked concepts of human rights and human security, both of which emerged from the effects of World War II. We will see that there are many reasons for hope that the world community will be able one day to stop human rights abuses and provide security to all people. But because the successful promotion of both human rights and human security depends on the international community, there may be as many reasons to be pessimistic about the prospects for a better world. After all, protecting the rights of individuals can infringe on the prerogatives of governments and thus on the notion of sovereign equality of countries. As we have seen elsewhere in this book, however, globalization is changing many traditions in world affairs.

This tension between the rights of the *individual* and the rights of *society* is a significant barrier to the creation of human security. As we will see in the first section of this chapter, there were intellectual disagreements in the nineteenth and early twentieth centuries about answers to basic questions: What is a human right? What rights should be protected? And by whom? Must these rights be universal?

We are still looking for answers to these questions. How can we discuss such a broad issue as global security on a smaller, human scale? What should it look like and why is it important? What opportunities still exist for political and military leaders to circumvent, undermine, and exploit international laws?

Introduction

As in other areas of the study of global politics, there are disagreements about human rights and human security. Like the debates in other areas, the splits tend to be down the same lines as the international relations theories we discussed in Chapter 3 (see Table 7.1). However, the fundamental question is a simple one. *Do countries have an obligation to improve the living conditions and protect the rights of people who live in other countries?*

Furthermore, if there is such an obligation, what are its legal foundations? And who would define the terms of human rights? Clearly, such rights would rest within a legal system. But whose? And what kind? Some of the contemporary disagreement about the obligation to promote human rights and human security stems from a history of colonialism. For example, the modern concept of individual human rights originally developed in Europe. Yet, as many European countries colonized other regions of the world (and even other parts of Europe), these rights were often not extended to other peoples who were seen as not human. Today, for many people who live in Africa and Asia, these

TABLE 7.1	**Comparing Worldviews on Aspects of Human Rights**			
	Realist	**Liberal**	**Utopian**	**Marxist**
Impact on National Security	• Corporate and governmental leaders want international governments that support them, even if establishing these governments causes violence and repression.	• Citizens should have the right to self-determination and open governments that are responsive to public opinion. • Those holding sovereign power need to act responsibly. • An individual should submit to an established authority unless this authority violates an individual's conscience: disobedience is a lesser evil than the slaughter of the innocent.	• Self-determination increases the likelihood of long-term peace by facilitating the participation of all groups in the determination of their own affairs.	• The biggest security threat is global poverty and a capitalist system that rewards the rich and fails to provide employment and quality of life for those on the margins.

TABLE 7.1 *continued*

	Realist	Liberal	Utopian	Marxist
Economic Consequences	• Government activities should not advocate radical change, even if this change is designed to help abolish poverty for the lower classes.	• Through the reciprocity of mutual needs a great society of states develops, characterized by common norms and customs. These norms and customs are embodied in the law of nations and in natural law and are binding on all nations. States abide by these rules out of long-term, enlightened self-interest.	• Self-determination facilitates a more equitable sharing of the economic resources of the globe. • Collective responsibility and human equality apply both internally within a society and externally between societies.	
Human Rights Implications	• There should be no radical socioeconomic changes aimed at achieving human rights for the dispossessed.	• Humans are endowed equally with the right to do what is necessary for self-preservation, and to be the sole arbiters of what is necessary to expand their own liberty.	• Human rights are profoundly important guidelines for policymaking. • Self-determination is a fundamental human right that contributes to spiritual and psychological well-being and should therefore be universally nurtured.	• A global capitalist class will allow for some human rights but none that would challenge its power and economic interests. The right to quality of life and access to societal resources or an equitable distribution of societal resources is not part of a capitalist system.
Environment	• Corporations focus resources and productive capacity on maximizing profit rather than fulfilling human needs.	• Rights involve protection of quality of life, and that includes clean air and water, and a healthy lifestyle. The rule of law can be used to protect the environment, and actions need to be taken collectively.	• If the rights of other societies are respected, productivity will eventually conform to meeting universal human needs. • Existing productive capacity for unessential goods should be converted into production of food and other essential items, leading to the better disposal of pollutants and conservation of resources.	• The environment is not a resource to be abused and exploited for the good of a few. It must serve the interests of all, and all should have access to environmental resources to create a high quality of life.

human rights may appear to derive from their problematic colonial heritage. Why should it necessarily mean something different to be human in Africa than in Europe?

What Are Human Rights?

Human rights The inalienable rights such as life, liberty, and the pursuit of happiness that one is entitled to because one is human.

The theory of **human rights** developed in Europe during the Middle Ages, and it rested on the idea of **natural law**—that humans have an essential nature. Natural law theorists differed on many issues, but they agreed on the following: (1) there are universal moral standards that support individual rights; (2) there is a general duty to adhere to these standards; and (3) the application of these standards is not limited to any particular legal system, community, state, race, religion, or civilization (Finnis 1980). These central propositions are the origin of modern rhetoric on *universal* human rights.

Natural law The idea that humans have an essential nature, which dictates that certain kinds of human goods are always and everywhere desired; because of this, there are common moral standards that govern all human relations, and these common standards can be discerned by the application of reason to human affairs.

Natural law provided the theory, but in the rougher world of medieval political practice, rights had different connotations. During this time, rights were concessions extracted from a superior, usually by force. The Magna Carta (1215) is a case in point. In it, the barons of England obliged King John to grant to them and their heirs in perpetuity a series of liberties that are, for the most part, very specific and related to particular grievances. The Magna Carta is based on the important principle that the subjects of the king owe him duty only if he meets their claims. Thus, the Magna Carta is a political contract.

Although rights as part of natural law and those established by political contract are not inherently incompatible, these two kinds of rights are based on opposing principles. Whereas rights based on natural law are derived from the notion of human flourishing and are universal, **charter rights** are the result of a political contract and, by definition, are limited to the parties to the contract and thus restricted in time and space.

Charter rights Civil liberties guaranteed in a written document such as a constitution.

The Liberal Account of Rights

The complex language of medieval thinking on rights carried over into the modern period. Political philosophers such as Hugo Grotius, Thomas Hobbes, and John Locke continued to use notions of natural law, albeit in radically different ways from their predecessors. Gradually, a synthesis of the concepts of natural rights and charter rights emerged. Known as the **liberal account of rights**, this position is made up of two basic components:

Liberal account of rights The belief that humans have inherent rights that the state has a responsibility to protect.

1. Human beings possess rights to life, liberty, the secure possession of property, the exercise of freedom of speech, and so on, which are inalienable—cannot be traded away—and unconditional. The only acceptable reason for constraining any one individual is to protect the rights of another.

2. The primary function of government is to protect these rights. Political institutions are to be judged on their performance of this function, and

political obligation rests on their success in this. In short, political life is based on a kind of implicit or explicit contract between people and government.

From a philosophical and conceptual point of view, this position is easy to denigrate as a mishmash of half-digested medieval ideas. It assumes that individuals and their rights predate society—and yet how could they exist without being part of a society? For philosopher Jeremy Bentham, the function of government was to promote the general good (which he called utility), and the idea that individuals might have the right to undermine this seemed to him madness, especially since no one could tell him where these rights came from. Karl Marx, on the other hand, and many subsequent radicals pointed out that the liberal position stresses property rights to the advantage of the rich and powerful. All these points raise compelling questions, but they underestimate the powerful rhetorical appeal of the liberal position. Most people are less likely to be worried about the philosophical inadequacies associated with the liberal position on human rights than they are to be attracted by the obvious benefits of living in a political system based on or influenced by it.

One of the uncertain features of the liberal position is the extent to which the rights it describes are universal. For example, the fundamental document of the French Revolution, the Declaration of the Rights of Man and of the Citizen, is by its very title intended to be of universal scope. However, the universalism of Article 1, "Men are born and remain free and equal in respect of rights," is then followed by Article 3, "The nation is essentially the source of all sovereignty. . . ." When revolutionary and Napoleonic France moved to bring the Rights of Man to the rest of Europe, the end result looked to most

contemporaries remarkably like a French empire. The liberal position, while universal in principle, is particular in application, and it more or less takes state boundaries for granted.

The humanitarianism and international standard setting of the nineteenth and twentieth centuries brought these issues to the foreground. The Congress of Vienna of 1815 saw the great powers accept an obligation to end the slave trade, which was finally abolished by the Brussels Convention of 1890, while slavery itself was formally outlawed by the Slavery Convention of 1926. The Hague Conventions of 1907 and the Geneva Conventions of 1926 were designed to introduce humanitarian considerations into the conduct of war. The International Labor Office, formed in 1901, and its

Anti-drug agents in Panama spray seized drugs with gasoline before they destroy them. Poverty is one of the main causes of violence and repression in the developing world. The drug trade has provided jobs, but it has also created gang violence that has claimed many lives and law enforcement tactics that deny basic human rights.

WHAT'S YOUR WORLDVIEW?

What ideas about human rights come from non-Western societies and religious traditions? Are western ideals and non-Western ideals about human rights in opposition? In what ways, if any, are such rights and practices viewed differently?

successor, the International Labor Organization, attempted to set standards in the workplace via measures such as the Convention Concerning Forced or Compulsory Labor of 1930.

In short, for Western European proponents of the liberal account of rights, human rights were intended to be protections for individuals against oppressive rulers, whether unelected monarchs or the choice of democratic majorities. The English and French colonizers of Asia and Africa took that notion of individual rights with them, and many believed it could take root in other cultures. As we will see, our modern notion of human rights is tied to the colonial experience, and over the centuries, this notion has evolved and been the subject of many disagreements.

Human Rights and State Sovereignty

Humanitarian measures taken together may provide a framework for some kind of global governance, but in many states, it is difficult to override a policy of **nonintervention**—not intervening in the affairs of other states—which is related to the notion of sovereignty. For example, abolishing the slave trade, which involved international transactions, was much easier than abolishing slavery, which concerns what states do to their own people; indeed, pockets of slavery survive to this day in parts of Africa, Asia, and the Middle East.

When it comes to humanitarian impulses, the difficulty in realizing them is that a basic principle of international society is the sovereignty of states, which requires respect toward and noninterference with the institutions of member states. In nineteenth-century England, radical liberals, such as statesmen John Bright and Richard Cobden, were bitterly critical of traditional diplomacy but supported the norm of nonintervention. They argued that their opponents, who claimed moral reasons in support of interventions, were in fact motivated by power politics.

Cobden was a consistent anti-interventionist and anti-imperialist; other liberals were more selective. Prime Minister of Great Britain William Gladstone's 1870s campaign to throw the Ottoman Empire out of Europe was based on the more common view that different standards applied to "civilized" and "uncivilized" peoples. In Gladstone's view, the Ottoman Empire—although a full member of international society since 1856—could not claim the rights of a sovereign state because its institutions did not meet the requisite standards. Indeed, this latter position was briefly established in international law in the notion of **standards of civilization**, a nineteenth-century, European discourse about what made a country civilized or uncivilized. In the twenty-first century, this notion may disturb and unsettle us, yet current conventional thinking on human rights is based on very similar ideas.

The willingness of liberals to extend their thinking on human rights toward direct intervention characterized the second half of the twentieth

Nonintervention The principle that external powers should not intervene in the domestic affairs of sovereign states.

Standards of civilization A nineteenth-century, European discourse about which values and norms made a country civilized or barbaric and uncivilized. The conclusion was that civilized countries should colonize barbaric regions for the latter's benefit.

century. The horrors of World War I stimulated attempts to create a peace system based on a form of international government, and although the League of Nations Covenant of 1919 had no explicit human rights provision, the underlying assumption was that its members would be states governed by the rule of law and respecting individual rights. The UN Charter of 1945, in the wake of World War II, does have some explicit reference to human rights—a tribute to the impact of the horrors of that war and, in particular, the murder of millions of Jews, Roma people, and Slavs in the extermination camps of National Socialist Germany. In this context, the need to assert a universal position was deeply felt, and the scene was set for the burst of international human rights legislation during the postwar era.

International Human Rights Legislation

The post–World War II humanitarian impulse led to a flurry of lawmaking and standard setting, which gave rise to what are known as *generations* of rights. First-generation rights focus on individual rights such as free speech, freedom of religion, and voting rights—rights that protect the individual from the potential abuses of the state. Second-generation rights include social, economic, and cultural rights. This group of rights includes the right to employment, housing, health care, and education. First- and second-generation rights are covered by the Universal Declaration of Human Rights and the European Union's Charter of Fundamental Rights. Third-generation rights are more focused on collective or group rights and have not been adopted by most states. These include the right to natural resources, the right to self-determination, the right to clean air, and the right to communicate. Many of these rights emerge from major global conferences that focus on transboundary issues such as the environment, racism, information and communications, and the rights of minorities and women.

The Universal Declaration of Human Rights

In 1948, the UN General Assembly established a baseline of human rights for its member states to follow. The **Universal Declaration of Human Rights** set out thirty basic political, civil, economic, and social rights that sought to define which specific rights all people share as humans. In the words of the Preamble to the declaration, "the peoples of the United Nations reaffirmed their faith in fundamental human rights, in the dignity and worth of the human person and of the equal rights of men and women. . . ." The enumerated entitlements included freedom from torture, freedom of opinion, equal treatment before the law, freedom of movement within a country, the right to own property, the right to education, and the right to work.

There were two shortcomings in the Universal Declaration. First, it was nonbinding on the member states of the United Nations. Countries' leaders could

Universal Declaration of Human Rights The principal normative document on human rights, adopted by the UN General Assembly in 1948 and accepted as authoritative by most states and other international actors.

Under the 1993 Chemical Weapons Convention there is a worldwide ban on the production, stockpiling, and use of chemical weapons. A country using chemical weapons is breaking international law. Further, any country using chemical weapons is guilty of violating human rights. Pictured above are two Syrian sisters, survivors of a 2014 chemical weapons attack in Moadamiya, Syria, speaking at a news conference in Washington, D.C. That attack killed more than 2,100 Syrian citizens. Syria is in shambles but the leaders of Syria go unpunished for their violation of international law.

pledge to support the goals of the document but then point to a range of political or economic problems that stopped them from full implementation. Article 29 bolstered their rationale for nonintervention: "Everyone has duties to the community in which alone the free and full development of his personality is possible." A second difficulty was the European origins of these rights. As the wave of decolonization swept Asia and Africa, newly independent countries eagerly embraced the tenets of human rights law. Unfortunately, as civil strife threatened to split some of these countries, some leaders blamed it on the pattern of oppression that the colonizers had created, and they used the provisions of Article 29 as the political justification for postcolonial repression.

Despite its shortcomings, the Universal Declaration of Human Rights is, symbolically, a central piece of legislation. This was the first time in history that the international community had attempted to define a comprehensive code for the internal government of its members. During the late 1940s, the West dominated the United Nations, and the contents of the declaration represented this fact, with its emphasis on political freedom. The voting was forty-eight for and none against. Eight states abstained, for interestingly different reasons.

South Africa abstained. The white-dominated regime in South Africa denied political rights to the majority of its people and clearly could not accept that "all are born free and equal in dignity and rights" (Article 1), claiming it violated the protection of the domestic jurisdiction of states guaranteed by Article 2(7) of the UN Charter. This is a clear and uncomplicated case of a first-generation (political) rights issue.

The Soviet Union and five Soviet-bloc countries abstained. Although Stalin's USSR was clearly a tyranny, the Soviet government did not officially object to the political freedoms set forth in the declaration. Instead, the Soviet objection was to the absence of sufficient attention to social and economic rights by comparison to the detailed elaboration of "bourgeois" freedoms and property rights. The Soviets saw the declaration as a Cold War document designed to stigmatize socialist regimes—a not wholly inaccurate description of the motives of its promulgators.

Saudi Arabia abstained. It was one of the few non-Western members of the United Nations in 1948 and just about the only one whose system of government was not, in principle, based on some Western model. Saudi Arabia objected to the declaration on religious grounds, explicitly objecting to Article 18, which specifies the freedom to change and practice the religion of one's choice. These provisions did not merely contravene specific Saudi laws, which, for example, forbade (and still forbid) the practice of the Christian religion in Saudi Arabia, but they also contravened the tenets of Islam, which does not recognize a right of apostasy, or the renunciation of a religious belief. Here, to complete the picture, we have an assertion of third-generation rights and a denial of the universalism of the declaration. These themes emerged at the beginning of the universal human rights regime and would characterize the politics of human rights for the next sixty years.

Nobel Peace Prize winner Malala Yousafzai has become a champion for girls' education rights. Here she speaks with a young Syrian refugee now living in Jordan. Why is educating children, especially girls, seen as such a threat in some countries?

Subsequent UN Legislation

Building on the promise of the Universal Declaration, the United Nations took the lead in creating major legally binding international conventions that define rights of specific groups, including women, children, and migrant workers, and that aim to eliminate torture and racial discrimination. There are ten core human rights instruments, each of which has a committee of experts that monitor the implementation and enforcement of these treaties. Some of the more important conventions or covenants that have attracted attention recently due to global challenges and events include the following:

- International Covenant on Civil and Political Rights (1966): challenged by authoritarian rule in many states including Egypt, China, Russia, Turkey, and Pakistan.
- Convention on the Elimination of All Forms of Discrimination Against Women (1979): challenged by governments in Saudi Arabia, Pakistan, Sudan, Afghanistan, and Iraq. Islamist extremist groups in the Middle East, Africa, and Asia also pose a significant challenge to the convention.
- Convention against Torture and Other Cruel, Inhuman or Degrading Treatment or Punishment (1984): challenged by many authoritarian states and the United States in its war on terrorism. The Bush administration used the law to its advantage and changed the definitions of torture in order to circumvent the prohibitions against torture and cruel and inhumane activities when dealing with suspected terrorists.

WHAT'S YOUR WORLDVIEW?

The Bush administration changed the definition of torture and challenged the four Geneva Conventions for the Protection of Victims of War. What happens when a major power decides to change the laws that govern the treatment of prisoners of war? What does this say about the efficacy of international law?

These conventions and others provide the intellectual and legal basis for the concept of human security, which we examine later in the chapter.

Enforcement of Human Rights Legislation

A significant number of states, global civil society actors, parliamentarians, lawyers, trade unions, and global social movements have embraced the Universal Declaration of Human Rights, and each promotes these rights and uses them as guidelines in its professional and personal activities. The UN Commission on Human Rights has the power to monitor, report, and advise, but the United Nations lacks the resources and authority to enforce these rights. Member states may, however, publicly criticize or shame states guilty of violating the rights of their citizens. Some states, such as the social democratic countries of Europe, have placed conditions on aid and trade agreements, demanding that states follow the rights articulated in all UN legal conventions. With the 2005 Responsibility to Protect (R2P) agreement, states have the obligation to prevent abuse and to protect citizens from governments that abuse the rights of their citizens.

ENGAGING WITH THE WORLD

Human Rights Watch Film Festival

The Human Rights Watch Film Festival is a program of the well-respected organization Human Rights Watch, which is dedicated to defending and protecting human rights. The festival chooses films that expose human rights abuses through storytelling in a way that challenges viewers to empathize with and demand justice for all people. It is held annually in twenty cities across the United States and abroad. Visit https://ff.hrw.org to learn more.

What Is Human Security?

Human security The security of people, including their physical safety, their economic and social well-being, respect for their dignity, and the protection of their human rights.

Like the doctrines of human rights, the concept of **human security** represents a powerful but controversial attempt by sections of the academic and policy community to redefine and broaden the meaning of security. Traditionally, security meant protection of the sovereignty and territorial integrity of states from external military threats. This was the essence of the concept of national security, which dominated security analysis and policymaking during the Cold War period. In the 1970s and 1980s, academic literature on security, responding to the Middle East oil crisis and the growing awareness of worldwide environmental degradation, began to describe security in broader, nonmilitary terms. Yet the state remained the object of security, or the entity to be protected.

The concept of human security challenges the state-centric notion of security by focusing on the individual. Human security is about security for the people rather than for states or governments. Hence, it has generated much debate. Critics wonder whether such an approach would widen the boundaries of security studies too much and whether "securitizing" the individual is the best way to address the challenges facing the international community from the forces of globalization. On the other side, advocates of human security find the concept effectively highlights the dangers to human safety and survival posed by poverty, disease, environmental stress, and human rights abuses as well as armed conflict. These disagreements notwithstanding, the concept of human security captures a growing realization that, in an era of rapid globalization, security must encompass a broader range of concerns and challenges than simply defending the state from external military attack.

Origin of the Concept

The origin of the concept of human security can be traced to the publication of the *Human Development Report* of 1994, issued by the UN Development Programme. The report defined the scope of human security to include seven areas:

- *Economic security*—ensuring basic income for all people, usually from productive and remunerative work or, as the last resort, from some publicly financed safety net.
- *Food security*—ensuring that all people at all times have both physical and economic access to basic food.
- *Health security*—guaranteeing a minimum of protection from diseases and unhealthy lifestyles.
- *Environmental security*—protecting people from the short- and long-term ravages of nature, human threats in nature, and deterioration of the natural environment.
- *Personal security*—protecting people from physical violence, whether from the state or external states, from violent individuals and substate factors, from domestic abuse, or from predatory adults.
- *Community security*—protecting people from the loss of traditional relationships and values and from sectarian and ethnic violence.
- *Political security*—ensuring that people live in a society that honors their basic human rights, and ensuring the freedom of individuals and groups from government attempts to exercise control over ideas and information.

The seven areas appear to describe the basic purpose of every country; and yet, as with other UN programs, the *Human Development Report* has had numerous critics. The primary complaint has been that the report has issued an unfunded mandate: it could be used to admonish countries that did not reach the standards, yet the report provided little or no funding to reach them. As you will see in the next section, this tension between standard setting in human rights and human security and assessing country performance has been a consistent strain since 1945. The leaders of many governments resent what they perceive as interference in the sovereign affairs of their countries.

Human Security and Development

Human development The notion that it is possible to improve the lives of people. Basically, it is about increasing the number of choices people have. These may include living a long and healthy life, access to education, and a better standard of living.

Unlike many other efforts to redefine security, where political scientists played a major role, human security was the handiwork of a group of development economists, such as the late Pakistani economist Mahbub ul Haq, who conceptualized the UN Development Programme's *Human Development Report*. They were increasingly dissatisfied with the orthodox notion of development, which viewed it as a function of economic growth. Instead, they proposed a concept of **human development** that focuses on building human capabilities to confront and overcome poverty, illiteracy, diseases, discrimination, restrictions on political freedom, and the threat of violent conflict: "Individual freedoms and rights matter a great deal, but people are restricted in what they can do with that freedom if they are poor, ill, illiterate, discriminated against, threatened by violent conflict or denied a political voice . . ." (UN Development Programme 2011, 18–19).

Closely related to the attempt to create a broader paradigm for development was the growing concern about the negative impact of defense spending on development, or the "guns versus butter" dilemma. As a global study headed by Inga Thorsson of Sweden concluded, "the arms race and development are in a competitive relationship" (Roche 1986, 8). Drawing on this study, a UN-sponsored International Conference on the Relationship Between Disarmament and Development, in 1986 in Paris, sought "to enlarge world understanding that human security demands more resources for development and fewer for arms."

Human Security and Refugees

One of the most disturbing trends in recent years is the number of refugees fleeing conflicts across the world. The numbers are staggering and their presence has raised some very interesting questions about the responsibility we all have to those in need. According to the International Rescue Committee, there are about 20 million refugees and over 40 million people displaced in their own land. The countries where these refugees have landed do not have the resources to provide adequate housing, food, health care, education, and security for them. What is needed is more humanitarian assistance that addresses poverty in crisis regions as well resources to provide for all who arrive in foreign lands.

In 1950, the United Nations High Commissioner for refugees (UNHCR) was established to help people who were left without homes after World War II. Until recently, half of the refugees of concern to the UNHCR were in Asia and about 28 percent were in African countries. The UNHCR has been successful in its attempt to emphasize three policy strategies: repatriation, or returning people to their homelands; integrating refugees into a place of residence; or resettling the refugees in a country sympathetic to their plight. At this time, the most serious flash point for refugees and human security may be in Syria, where a civil war has been on-going since 2011.

The number of refugees fleeing the Syrian conflict to neighboring countries, such as Lebanon and several European states, has exceeded four million, which confirms that the Syrian crisis is the world's single largest refugee crisis in almost a quarter of a century under the UNHCR's mandate. Not all refugees fleeing to Europe are from Syria, however; Germany expects to take in about 800,000 refugees from Syria, Iraq, Afghanistan, Ukraine, and other conflict-affected regions. Germany has received the most migrants with over 362,000 asylum applications filed as of November 2015. As of January 2016, European Union countries have received over 942,000 claims for asylum from refugees.

Human security includes freedom from fear, freedom from want, and the rule of law. Here, a Syrian refugee boy plays with a tire at Zaatari refugee camp, in Mafraq, Jordan. Human security issues raised by the existence of this refugee tent city have shifted from emergency relief to providing basic human needs for the long term. We may have to rethink the purposes and targets of humanitarian assistance if the refugee crises persist.

Since the war began, over 11 million Syrians have been displaced by the civil war. The United Nations estimates that 6.5 million people are internally displaced, meaning that they have been forced to leave their homes, but that they still reside within the borders of Syria, and over 250,000 have been killed in the conflict. The Syrian civil war and refugee crisis has caused the international community to reassess migration policies and look for solutions that meet the needs of both national and human security. Unfortunately, questions remain regarding how to best respond to the crisis and what roles host countries should play in terms of providing relief and fostering integration.

Common Security

The move toward human security was also advanced by the work of several international commissions. They offered a broader view of security that looked beyond the Cold War emphasis on East-West military competition. Foremost among them was the Palme Commission of 1982, which proposed the doctrine of **common security**, emphasizing noncompetitive, cooperative approaches to achieving human security for all. Its report stressed that "in the Third World countries, as in all our countries, security requires economic progress as well as freedom from military fear" (Palme Commission 1982, xii). In 1987, the report of the World Commission on Environment and Development (also known as the Brundtland Commission) highlighted the linkage between environmental degradation and conflict: "The real sources of insecurity encompass unsustainable development, and its effects can become intertwined with traditional forms of conflict in a manner that can extend and deepen the latter" (Brundtland et al. 1987, 230).

Common security At times called "cooperative security," it stresses noncompetitive approaches and cooperative approaches through which states—both friends and foes—can achieve security. The belief that no one is secure until all people are secure from threats of war.

More recently, Pope Francis has added his voice to the conversation about climate change and human security. In his Papal Encyclical, *Laudato Si, On Care for Our Common Home*, the Pope suggests that the first victims of climate change will be the poor. This is not a new message but it points to the need to address our economic priorities and understand that the changing climate will create a new group of refugees that will be pushed out of their homes by nature or by the rich or powerful seeking a place to survive or resources to consume.

History of Humanitarian Activism and Intervention

As the concepts of human rights and human security have developed, many opinion leaders and politicians in democratic societies have become increasingly aware that the state must take action in the face of challenges to human lives and dignity. In effect, many politicians have come to believe that the state should do more than defend borders and that cooperative and purposeful international action might be necessary to safeguard people.

One reason human security has become a more salient issue in recent decades is that civil wars and intrastate conflicts are more frequent. These have entailed huge losses of life, ethnic cleansing, displacement of people within and across borders, and disease outbreaks. Traditional national security approaches have not been sufficiently sensitive toward conflicts that arise over cultural, ethnic, and religious differences, as happened in Eastern Europe, Africa, and Central Asia in the post–Cold War era (Tow and Trood 2000).

Another reason for greater humanitarian awareness is the spread of democratization (see Map 7.1), which has been accompanied by more emphasis on human rights and **humanitarian intervention**. Proponents of interventions take the position that the international community is justified in intervening in the internal affairs of states accused of gross violation of human rights. This has led to the realization that while the concept of national security has not been rendered irrelevant, it no longer sufficiently accounts for the kinds of danger that threaten societies, states, and the international community.

The notion of human security has also been brought front and center by crises induced by accelerating globalization. For example, the widespread poverty, unemployment, and social dislocation caused by the Asian financial crisis of 1997 underscored people's vulnerability to the effects of economic globalization (Acharya

Humanitarian intervention
The use of military force by external actors to end a threat to people within a sovereign state.

Samantha Power, the U.S. Ambassador to the United Nations, speaks with a wounded woman in the Central African Republic. Sectarian violence has disrupted the peace in this fragile state and created a major human security challenge. The United Nations has warned of a high risk of genocide, and ethnic cleansing targeting the Muslim population is a major concern.

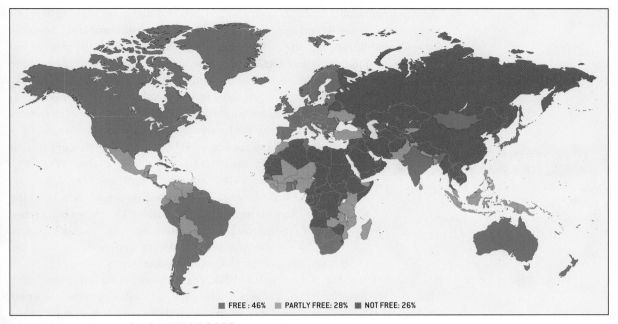

Map 7.1 **Democracy in the World 2015.**

This map from Freedom House represents a specifically American view of democracy. In many countries, democracy is only tenuously established, and human rights abuses continue. Source: Freedom in the World 2015, "Discarding Democracy: A Return to the Iron Fist," Freedom House Report (pp. 14–15), http://www.freedomhouse.org/report/freedom-world/freedom-world-2015.

2004). This vulnerability played a major role in the 2010–2011 **Arab Spring** revolutionary uprisings, which began in Tunisia and spread across Egypt, Libya, Syria, Yemen, Bahrain, Saudi Arabia, and Jordan. At the heart of these protests was a desire for more democratic and transparent political systems and more open and equitable economic systems. Citizens across the Arab world demanded the end of authoritarian rule and sought greater access to resources and wealth that were held by very few in their countries. During the recent global economic recession, however, international aid agencies saw a sharp decline in donations for countries and individuals, thus undermining their ability to meet basic needs.

Arab Spring Protests and revolutionary uprisings that began in Tunisia in 2010 and spread across Egypt, Libya, Syria, Yemen, Bahrain, Saudi Arabia, and Jordan in 2011. At their core was a desire for more democratic and transparent political systems and more open and equitable economic systems.

Intervention and Nonintervention in the 1990s

It has become common to describe the immediate post–Cold War period as something of a golden era for humanitarian activism and intervention. Thomas Weiss (2004, 136) argues that "the notion that human beings matter more than sovereignty radiated brightly, albeit briefly, across the international political horizon of the 1990s." This was symbolized for many by NATO's intervention to halt Serb atrocities in Kosovo in March 1999 and the Australian-led intervention to end mass atrocities in East Timor. But the 1990s also saw the world stand aside during the genocides in Rwanda and Srebrenica. To make sense of these developments, let's focus on international interventions in northern Iraq, Somalia, Rwanda, and Kosovo and divide our discussion into three parts: the place of humanitarian impulses in decisions to intervene; the legality and legitimacy of the interventions; and the effectiveness of these military interventions.

In the cases of northern Iraq in April 1991 and Somalia in December 1992, domestic public opinion played an important role in pressuring policymakers into using force for humanitarian purposes. In the face of a massive refugee crisis caused by Saddam Hussein's oppression of the Kurds in the aftermath of the 1991 Gulf War, U.S., British, French, and Dutch military forces intervened to create protected "safe havens" for the Kurdish people. Similarly, the U.S. military intervention in Somalia in December 1992 was a response to sentiments of compassion on the part of U.S. citizens. This sense of solidarity disappeared, however, once the United States began sustaining casualties.

The fact that the White House pulled the plug on its Somali intervention after the loss of eighteen U.S. Rangers in a firefight in October 1993 indicates how capricious public opinion is. Television pictures of starving and dying Somalis had persuaded the outgoing Bush administration to launch a humanitarian rescue mission, but once the U.S. public saw dead Americans dragged through the streets of Mogadishu, the Clinton administration announced a timetable for withdrawal. What the Somalia case demonstrates is that the "CNN effect" is a double-edged sword: it can pressure governments into humanitarian intervention yet with equal speed produce public disillusionment and calls for withdrawal. These cases also suggest that even if there are no vital national interests at stake, liberal states might launch humanitarian rescue missions if sufficient public pressure is mobilized. Certainly, there is no evidence in either of these cases to support the realist claim that states cloak power-political motives behind the guise of humanitarianism.

By contrast, the French intervention in Rwanda in July 1994 seems to be an example of abuse. France had propped up the one-party Hutu state for twenty years, even providing troops when the Rwandan Patriotic Front (RPF), consisting largely of members of the rival Tutsi population and operating out of neighboring Uganda, threatened to overrun the country in 1990 and 1993. French President François Mitterrand was reportedly anxious to restore waning French influence in Africa and was fearful that an RPF victory in French-speaking Rwanda would bring the country under the influence of Anglophones. France therefore did not intervene until the latter stages of the genocide against the Tutsis, which was ended primarily by the RPF's military victory. Thus, it seems that French behavior accorded with the realist premise that states will risk their soldiers only in defense of the national interest. French leaders may have been partly motivated by humanitarian sentiments, but this seems to be a case of a state abusing the concept of humanitarian intervention because the primary purpose of the intervention was to protect French national interests.

The moral question raised by French intervention is why international society failed to intervene when the genocide began in early April 1994. French intervention may have saved some lives, but it came far too late to halt the genocide. Some 800,000 people were killed in a mere hundred days. The failure of international society to stop the genocide indicates that state leaders remain gripped by the mindset of national interests trumping human interests. There was no intervention for the simple reason that those with the military capability to stop the genocide were unwilling to sacrifice troops and treasure to protect Rwandans. International solidarity in the face of genocide was limited to moral outrage and the provision of humanitarian aid.

If the French intervention in Rwanda can be criticized for being too little too late, NATO's intervention in Kosovo in 1999 was criticized for being too much too soon. At the beginning of the war, NATO said it was intervening to prevent a humanitarian catastrophe. To do this, NATO aircraft were given two objectives: reduce Serbia's military capacity and coerce Slobodan Milošević, President of the Federal Republic of Yugoslavia, into accepting a peace agreement with the Albanian majority population of Kosovo. (Kosovo was an autonomous province within Serbia, which lay within the greater Yugoslavia.) NATO claimed that the resort to force was justifiable for the following reasons. First, it was argued that Serbian actions in Kosovo had created a humanitarian emergency and breached a range of international legal commitments. Second, NATO governments argued that the Serbs were committing crimes against humanity, possibly including genocide. Third, it was contended that the Milošević regime's use of force against the Kosovar Albanians challenged global norms of common humanity.

Closer analysis of the justifications articulated by Western leaders suggests that while humanitarianism may have provided the primary impulse for action, it was by no means the exclusive impulse, and the complexity of the motives of the interveners colored the character of the intervention. Indeed, NATO was propelled into action by a mixture of humanitarian concern and self-interest gathered around three sets of issues. The first might be called the "Srebrenica syndrome"—a fear that, left unchecked, Milošević's henchmen would replicate the carnage of Bosnia. The second is related directly to self-interest and was a concern that protracted conflict in the southern Balkans would create a massive refugee crisis in Europe. Finally, NATO governments were worried that if they failed to contain the crisis, it would spread to several neighboring states, especially Macedonia, Albania, and Bulgaria (Bellamy 2002, 3). This suggests that humanitarian intervention might be prompted by mixed motives. It only becomes a problem if the nonhumanitarian motives undermine the chances of achieving the humanitarian purposes.

CASE STUDY

A Failed Intervention

The Darfur Genocide refers to the current mass slaughter of civilians in Western Sudan, which has claimed the lives of more than 300,000 people and displaced nearly 2.5 million others. The killings began in the early 2000s and continue today. The genocide is being carried out by a group of government-armed and -funded Arab militias known as the Janjaweed, which translates to "devils on horseback." The Janjaweed are destroying Darfurians by burning villages, raping, and torturing civilians.

U.S. Secretary of State Colin Powell declared the ongoing conflict in Darfur genocide on September 4, 2004, and on February 18, 2006, President George W. Bush called for the number of international troops in Darfur to be doubled. On September 17, 2006, British Prime Minister Tony Blair wrote an open letter to the members of the European Union calling for a unified response to the crisis. In supporting the United Nations Security Council Resolution in 2007 to authorize the deployment of up to 26,000 peacekeepers to try to stop the violence in Darfur, British Prime Minister Gordon Brown said in a speech before the UN General Assembly that the Darfur crisis was "the greatest humanitarian disaster the world faces today." The British government also endorsed the International Criminal Court's (ICC) indictment

Women and children living in the ZamZam camp for displaced people in northern Darfur. The Sudanese government is trying to convince the United Nations that things are stable, citizens are protected, and the peacekeeping forces should leave, yet several NGOs claim that atrocities continue and the world must return its attention to this region. Why do you think the world seems to have moved on and forgotten these victims of violence?

against Sudanese President Omar al-Bashir for committing crimes against humanity, war crimes, and genocide and urged the Sudanese government to cooperate with the ICC.

Unfortunately, the world seems to have forgotten about Darfur but the killing and human rights violations have continued. The government of Sudan has been able to contain the flow of information by closing the UN Human Rights Office in the capital of Khartoum and convincing peacekeepers to leave regions they deem stable. Once the peacekeepers leave, the atrocities begin again. In 2014, the Satellite Sentinel Project, an organization dedicated to ending genocide and crimes against humanity, was able to confirm evidence that the Sudanese government had burned and bombed some six villages in Darfur's eastern Jebel Marra region.

The government of Sudan has used aid money from Qatar to build model villages for those displaced by the continuing violence. However, Human Rights Watch recently uncovered an incident of mass rape in one of these model villages. In October 2014 in the village of Tabit, soldiers from the Sudanese army raped over 200 women in a thirty-six-hour period. Human rights courts have ruled that rape by police or soldiers is an act of torture because it is used as an instrument of terror and is a tactic of social control and ethnic domination.

The crimes against humanity continue today with only NGOs demanding action. The international community has imposed some sanctions but enforcement is uneven. The United States and its European allies have no stomach for another intervention after Afghanistan, Iraq, Libya, and Syria. A major constraint is the fact that both China and Russia have worked to block many UN resolutions in attempts to appease the Sudanese government. From its seat on the UN Security Council, China has been Sudan's chief diplomatic ally. China invests heavily in Sudanese oil (Sudan is China's largest overseas oil provider) and China supplies Sudan's military with helicopters, tanks, and fighter planes. For decades, Russia and China have maintained a strong economic and politically strategic partnership and have opposed the presence of UN peacekeeping troops in Sudan. Russia strongly supports Sudan's territorial integrity and opposes the creation of an independent Darfur state. Russia is also Sudan's strongest investment partner and considers Sudan an important global ally in Africa.

CASE STUDY *continued*

For Discussion

1. Genocide continues and states have often not responded despite the fact that many states have signed international agreements requiring a collective response to this criminal behavior. Why do you think states have failed to act collectively to stop genocide and other crimes against humanity?

2. Do some research to find out what kinds of sanctions have been imposed on Sudan by the international community. Why do you think these have failed to stop the genocide? Would different types of sanctions be more effective?

Universalism Challenged

Paradoxically, the success of the global human rights regime caused a growing backlash to the development of international norms of behavior. If taken seriously and at face value, human rights laws after 1945 would create a situation where all states would be obliged to conform to a quite rigid template that dictated most aspects of their political, social, and economic structures and policies. And so, from 1945, opponents of both the human rights and the human security regimes objected that (1) the norms were an unwarranted intrusion in the affairs of sovereign states and (2) these norms also sought to overturn existing assumptions about the role of the state and its jurisdiction.

Conventional defenders of human rights and human security argue that universalism would be a good thing; the spread of best practice in these matters is in the interest of all people. Others disagree. Does post-1945 law constitute best practice? The feminist critique of universal human rights is particularly appropriate here. The universal documents all, in varying degrees, privilege a patriarchal view of the family as the basic unit of society. Even such documents as the Convention on the Elimination of All Forms of Discrimination Against Women (CEDAW) of 1979 do no more than extend to women the standard liberal package of rights, and modern feminists debate whether this constitutes a genuine advance (Peters and Wolper 1995).

More fundamentally, is the very idea of "best practice" sound? We have already met one objection to the idea in the Saudi abstention of 1948. The argument is simple: universalism is destructive not only to undesirable differences between societies but also to desirable and desired differences. The human rights movement stresses the *common* humanity of the peoples of the world, but for many, the qualities that distinguish us from one another are as important as the characteristics that unify us. For example, the Declaration of Principles of Indigenous Rights adopted in Panama in 1984 by a nongovernmental group, the World Council of Indigenous Peoples, lays out positions that are designed to preserve the traditions, customs, institutions, and practices of indigenous peoples (many of which, it need hardly be said, contradict contemporary liberal norms). As with feminist critiques, the argument here is that the present international human rights regime rests too heavily on the experiences of one part of humanity, in this case, Western Europe, Canada, and the United States. Of course, in practice, the cultural critique and the feminist critique may lead in different directions.

This philosophical point took on a political form in the 1990s. In the immediate post–Cold War world, and especially after the election of U.S. President Bill Clinton in 1992, there was some talk of the United States adopting active policies of democracy promotion. A number of East Asian governments and intellectuals asserted in response the notion that there were specifically "Asian values" that required defending from this development. The argument was that human rights boil down to no more than a set of particular social choices that need not be

GLOBAL PERSPECTIVE

Asian Values

That Western states, intergovernmental organizations, and NGOs have sometimes taken it upon themselves to promote human rights has always been resented as hypocritical in the non-Western world, where the imperialist record of the West over the last four centuries has not been forgotten. In the 1990s, this resentment led a number of the leaders of the quasi-authoritarian newly industrializing nations of Southeast Asia to assert the existence of Asian values that could be counterpoised to the (allegedly) Western values associated with the international human rights regime.

Such thinking was partially reflected in the Bangkok Declaration of 1993, made by Asian ministers in the run-up to the Vienna Conference of that year (for texts, see Tang 1994). Western notions of human rights were seen as excessively individualistic, as opposed to Asian societies' stress on the family, and insufficiently supportive of (if not downright hostile to) religion. Further, some regarded the West as morally decadent because of the growth of gay rights and the relative success of the women's movement in combating gender discrimination. Some have argued that such positions are simply intended to legitimate authoritarian rule, although it should be noted that "Asian values" can perform this task only if the argument strikes a chord with ordinary people.

More to the point, are the conservative positions expressed by proponents of Asian values Asian in any genuine sense? Many Western conservatives and fundamentalists share their critique of the West, while progressive Asian human rights activists are critical. Notions such as "the West" or "Asia" are unacceptably essentialist. All cultures and civilizations contain different and often conflicting tendencies; the world of Islam or of "Confucian capitalism" is no more monolithic than is Christianity or Western secularism. The Asian values argument petered out at the end of the 1990s, but the problems it illustrated remain.

Human rights activist Ka Hsaw Wa (left), an ethnic Karen from Myanmar, has led the struggle for minority national rights and environmentalism within that country.

For Discussion

1. Is this really a debate between Asian and Western values, or is it a debate between universal views on rights versus more limited views on rights? Why?

2. Will the world ever come to agreement on a universal view of rights that applies to all? Why or why not?

considered binding by those whose values (and hence, social choices) are differently formed—for example, by Islam or Confucianism rather than by an increasingly secularized Christianity. The wording of the Vienna Declaration on Human Rights of 1993, which refers to the need to bear in mind "the significance of national and regional particularities and various historical, cultural and religious backgrounds" when considering human rights, partially reflects this viewpoint—and has been criticized for this by some human rights activists.

Returning to the history of rights, it is here that the distinction between rights grounded in natural law and rights grounded in a contract becomes crucial. As noted earlier, it is only if rights are grounded in some account of human progress and reason that they may be regarded as genuinely universal in scope. But is this position, as its adherents insist, free of cultural bias, a set of ideas that all rational beings must accept? It seems not, at least insofar as many apparently rational Muslims, Hindus, Buddhists, atheists, utilitarians, and so on clearly do not accept its doctrines. It seems that either the standards derived from natural law (or a similar doctrine) are cast in such general terms that virtually any continuing social system will exemplify them, or if the standards are cast more specifically, they are not in fact universally desired.

Of course, we are under no obligation to accept all critiques of universalism at face value. Human rights may have first emerged in the West, but this does not in itself make rights thinking Western. Perhaps an apparently principled rejection of universalism is, in fact, no more than a rationalization of tyranny. How do we know that the inhabitants of Saudi Arabia, say, prefer not to live in a democratic system with Western liberal rights, as their government asserts? There is an obvious dilemma here: if we insist that we will only accept democratically validated regimes, we will be imposing an alien test of legitimacy on these societies. Yet what other form of validation is available?

In any event, the body of legal acts for the protection of universal human rights applies, does it not, even if rights are essentially convenient fictions? Again, defenders of difference will argue that international law is itself a Western, universalist notion, and they rightly note that the Western record of adherence to universal norms does not justify any claim to moral superiority. They point to the many crimes of the age of imperialism as well as to contemporary issues such as the treatment of asylum seekers and refugees and, of course, the byproducts of the global war on terrorism such as torture and imprisonment without trial.

There is no neutral language for discussing human rights. Whatever way the question is posed reflects a particular viewpoint, and this is no accident. It is built into the nature of the discourse. Is there any way the notion of universal rights can be saved from its critics? Two modern approaches seem fruitful. Even if we find it difficult to specify human *rights*, it may still be possible to talk of human *wrongs*. Similarly, some have argued that it is easier to specify what is *unjust* than what is *just* (see Booth 1999). To use Michael Walzer's terminology (1994), there may be no thick moral code that is universally acceptable, to which all local codes conform, but there may be a thin code that at least can be used to delegitimize some actions. Thus, for example, the Genocide Convention of 1948 seems a plausible example of a piece of international legislation that outlaws an obvious wrong, and while some local variations in the rights associated with gender may be unavoidable, it is still possible to say that practices that severely restrict human capabilities, such as female genital mutilation, are simply wrong. Any code that did not condemn such suffering would be unworthy of respect.

This may not take us as far as some would wish. Essential to this approach is the notion that there are some practices that many would condemn but that must be tolerated, but it may be the most appropriate response to contemporary pluralism. An alternative approach involves recognizing that human rights are based on a particular culture—Richard Rorty (1993) calls this the "human rights culture"—and it requires defending them in these terms rather than by reference to some cross-cultural code. This approach would involve abandoning the idea that human rights exist. Instead, it involves proselytizing on behalf of the sort of culture in which rights are deemed to exist. The essential point is that human life is safer, pleasanter, and more dignified when rights are acknowledged than when they are not.

Humanitarian Dimensions

Both human rights and human security have become part of an international discourse about proper norms of behavior and the best methods to promote these norms. The disagreements that exist today tend to be questions about the responsibilities of governments to live up to these standards. In this section, we discuss some dimensions of this discourse, with particular emphasis on political and economic rights and security, human rights and human security during times of conflict, rights to and security of natural resources, and women's rights.

Political and Economic Rights and Security

"No one shall be subjected to torture or to cruel, inhuman or degrading treatment or punishment" (UN Declaration, Article 5, Covenant on Civil and Political Rights, Article 7, Convention on Torture, etc.). Although this immunity is well established, what does this mean in practice for someone faced with the prospect of such treatment? If the person is fortunate enough to live in a country governed by the rule of law, domestic courts may uphold his or her immunity, and the international side of things will come into play only on the margins. A European who is dissatisfied with treatment at home may be able to take a legal dispute over a particular practice beyond his or her national courts to the European Commission on Human Rights and the European Court of Human Rights. In non-European countries governed by the rule of law, no such direct remedy is available, but the notion of universal rights at least reinforces the rhetorical case for rights that are established elsewhere.

The more interesting case emerges if potential victims do not live in such a law-governed society—that is, if their government and courts are the problem and not the source of a possible solution. What assistance should they expect from the international community? What consequences will flow from their government's failure to live up to its obligations? The problem is that even in cases where violations are quite blatant, it may be difficult to see what other states are able to do, even supposing they are willing to act.

During the Cold War, the West regularly issued verbal condemnations of human rights violations by the Soviet Union and its associates but rarely acted on these condemnations. The power of the Soviet Union made direct intervention imprudent, and even relatively minor sanctions would be adopted only if the general state of East-West relations suggested this would be appropriate. Similar considerations apply today to relations between Western countries and China. Conversely, violations by countries associated with the West are routinely overlooked or, in some cases, even justified; the global war on terrorism provides contemporary examples.

Of the 515 million gamers in China, only 9 million use a PlayStation 4 or Xbox One console. The Chinese government censors Sony and Microsoft's respective content, claiming that it is trying to protect children from the violence and sexual content found in many games. Do you think this is a denial of a core freedom or a suitable way to protect the community?

All told, it seems unlikely that individuals who are ill-treated by nonconstitutional regimes will find any real support from the international community unless their persecutors are weak, of no strategic significance, and commercially unimportant. Even then, it is unlikely that effective action will be taken unless one additional factor is present—namely, the force of public opinion. The growth of humanitarian nongovernmental organizations has produced a context in which the force of public opinion can sometimes make itself felt, not necessarily in the oppressing regime, but in the policy-formation processes of the potential providers of aid. This in turn may goad states into action.

The situation with respect to second-generation rights is more complicated. Consider, for example, "the right of everyone to an adequate standard of living for himself and his family, including adequate food, clothing and housing, and to the continuous improvement of living conditions" (Covenant on Economic, Social and Cultural Rights, Article 11.1) or the "right of everyone to be free from hunger" (Article 11.2). It has been argued that such rights are, or should be, central.

> ### WHAT'S YOUR WORLDVIEW?
>
> *With the rise of new security challenges, one must ask if states are prepared to respond. In this era of globalization, can states deliver on their promise to provide security for their citizens and still maintain certain rights and freedoms?*

The covenant makes the realization of these rights an obligation on its signatories, but this is arguably a different kind of obligation from the obligation to refrain from, for example, "cruel or degrading" punishments. In the latter case, as with other basically political rights, the remedy is clearly in the hands of national governments. The way to end torture is, simply, for states to stop torturing.

The right not to be tortured is associated with a duty not to torture. The right to be free from hunger, on the other hand, is not a matter of a duty on the part of one's own and other states not to pursue policies that lead to starvation. It also involves a duty to act to "ensure an equitable distribution of world food supplies in relation to need" (Covenant on Economic, Social and Cultural Rights, Article 11.2[b]). The distinction here is sometimes seen as that between "negative" and "positive" rights, although this is not entirely satisfactory, because negative (political) rights often require positive action if they are to be protected effectively. In any event, there are problems with the notion of economic rights.

First, it is by no means clear that, even assuming goodwill, these social and economic goals could always be met, and to think in terms of having a right to something that could not be achieved is to misuse language. In such circumstances, a right simply means "a generally desirable state of affairs," and this weakening of the concept may have the effect of undermining more precise claims to rights that actually can be achieved (e.g., the right not to be tortured).

Second, some states may seek to use economic and social rights more directly to undermine political rights. Dictatorial regimes in poor countries quite frequently justify the curtailment of political rights in the name of promoting economic growth or economic equality. In fact, there is no reason to accept the general validity of this argument—Amartya Sen argues cogently that development and freedom go together (Sen 1999)—but it will still be made and not always in bad faith.

Finally, if it is accepted that all states have a positive duty to promote economic well-being and freedom from hunger everywhere, then the consequences go beyond the requirement of the rich to share with the poor. Virtually all national social and economic policies become a matter for international regulation. Rich states would have a duty to make economic and social policy with a view to its consequences on the poor, but so would poor states. The poor's right to assistance creates a duty on the rich to assist, but this in turn creates a right of the rich to insist that the poor have a duty not to worsen their plight—for example, by failing to restrict population growth or by inappropriate economic policies. Aid programs promoted by the Commonwealth and World Bank, and the structural-adjustment programs of the International Monetary Fund, regularly include conditions of this kind. They are, however, widely resented because they contradict another widely supported economic and social right: "All peoples have the right of self-determination. By virtue of that right they freely determine their political status and freely pursue their economic, social and cultural development" (Covenant on Economic, Social and Cultural Rights, Article 1.1). Even when applied in a well-meaning and consistent way, external pressures to change policy are rarely popular, even with those they are intended to benefit.

On the other hand, it is certainly true that people suffering from brutal poverty and severe malnourishment are unlikely to be able to exercise any rights at all unless their condition is attended to. It may be true that the transfers required to raise living standards to an acceptable level across the world are sufficiently modest and that they would not raise the problems we have outlined. Still, most economic and social rights are best seen as collectively agreed-on aspirations rather than as rights as the term has conventionally been used.

Human Rights and Human Security During Conflict

What is the reason for the continued importance of national security over human rights and human security? For developing countries, state sovereignty and territorial integrity take precedence over security of the individual. Many countries in the developing world are artificial nation-states whose boundaries were drawn arbitrarily by the colonial powers in the nineteenth century without regard for the ethnic composition or historical linkages among peoples. State responses to ethnic separatist movements (now conflated with terrorism), which are partly rooted in people's rejection of colonial-imposed boundaries, have been accompanied by the most egregious violations of human security by governments. Moreover, many third world states, as well as China, remain under authoritarian rule. Human security is stymied by the lack of political space for alternatives to state ideologies and by restrictions on civil liberties imposed by authoritarian regimes to ensure their own survival.

In the developed as well as the developing world, one of the most powerful challenges to human rights and human security has come from the war on terrorism led by the United States. The terrorist attacks of 9/11 revived the traditional emphasis of states on national security (Suhrke 2004, 365). Although terrorists target innocent civilians and thus threaten human security, governments have used the war on terrorism to restrict and violate civil liberties. The U.S. decision to put Saddam Hussein on trial in an Iraqi court rather than the International Criminal Court (ICC) illustrated the continued U.S. defiance of a key policy instrument of human security, even though it focused on the more Western-oriented conception of "freedom from fear." The U.S. questioning of the applicability of the Geneva Conventions, and the abandoning of its commitments on the issue of torture in the context of war in Iraq, further undermined the agenda of human security. So did Russia's flouting of a wide range of its international commitments—including the laws of war, Conference on Security and Co-operation in Europe (CSCE) and Organization for Security and Co-operation in Europe (OSCE) commitments, and international and regional conventions on torture—in the context of its war in Chechnya and its current support of insurgents in Ukraine.

A pioneering report released by the Human Security Center, formerly affiliated with the University of British Columbia, in 2005 points to several significant trends in armed conflicts around the world, most notably an overall downward trend (see Figure 7.1). What explains this trend in armed conflicts? The report lists several factors:

- growing democratization (the underlying assumption here being that democracies tend to be better at peaceful resolution of conflicts);
- rising economic interdependence (which increases the costs of conflict);

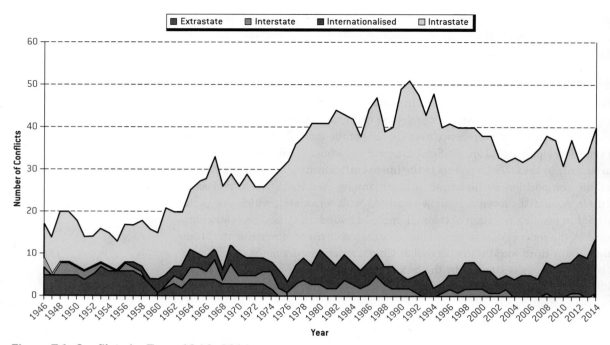

Figure 7.1 **Conflicts by Type, 1946–2014.**

- the declining economic utility of war, owing to the fact that resources can be more easily bought in the international marketplace than acquired through force;
- the growth in the number of international institutions that can mediate in conflicts;
- the impact of international norms against violence such as human sacrifice, witch burning, slavery, dueling, war crimes, and genocide; and
- the end of colonialism and the end of the Cold War.

Another specific reason for the downward trend identified by the report is the dramatic increase in the role of the United Nations in areas such as preventive diplomacy, peacemaking activities, and post-conflict peacebuilding. The willingness of the UN Security Council to use military action to enforce peace agreements, the deterrent effects of war crime trials by the ICC and other tribunals, and the greater resort to reconciliation and addressing the root causes of conflict have all contributed to a general decrease in armed conflicts since the early 1990s.

The optimism created by the report did not last long, however. The 2009/2010 Human Security Report found a 25 percent increase in armed conflicts between 2003 and 2008, a large percentage of which were related to Islamist political violence. While the war on terrorism played an important part in the increasing number and the deadliness of conflicts, viewed from a longer-term perspective, the level of conflict in the Islamic world is lower than two decades earlier. Yet the possibility of increasing violence remains given the failure of the Arab Spring, the rise of ISIS and the ongoing Syrian civil war, and general instability in transitional societies.

Moreover, there are some horrific costs associated with these conflicts. For example, deaths directly or indirectly attributed to the conflict in the Democratic Republic of the Congo since 1998 have surpassed casualties sustained by Britain in World Wars I and II combined. In Iraq, a team of American and Iraqi epidemiologists estimated that Iraq's mortality rate more than doubled following the U.S. invasion, from 5.5 deaths per 1,000 people in the year before the invasion to 13.3 deaths per 1,000 people per year in the postinvasion period. Violence continues even though the war officially ended in December 2011. As of February 2016, preliminary data from the Iraq Body Count Project estimates that more than 150,000 Iraqi civilians have been killed since the U.S. invasion in March 2003 (iraqbodycount.org).

The share of civilian casualties in armed conflict has increased since World War II. Civilians accounted for 10 percent of the victims during World War I and 50 percent of the victims during World War II. In recent wars, civilians constitute between 80 and 85 percent of the victims. Many of these victims are children, women, the sick, and the elderly (*Gendering Human Security* 2001, 18). Additionally, international terrorist incidents and related fatalities have also increased in recent years. According to the National Consortium for the Study of Terrorism and Responses to Terrorism at the University of Maryland, the number of terrorist attacks resulting in the deaths of more than 100 civilians averaged about 4.2 per year between 1978 and 2013. In 2014, that number increased dramatically to 26 per year.

Furthermore, some of the most serious issues of human security in armed conflicts still need to be overcome, such as the recruitment of child soldiers and the use of land mines. Although exact figures are unknown, the United Nations estimates that there are some 300,000 child soldiers involved in more than thirty conflicts in the world today. According to the International Campaign to Ban Landmines, land mines and unexploded ordinances cause about 4,000 casualties each year. Progress has been made but there are still sixty countries around the world contaminated by land mines. Despite the justified optimism generated by the Ottawa Treaty (formally known as the Convention on the Prohibition of the Use, Stockpiling, Production, and Transfer of Anti-Personnel Mines and on their Destruction), there are still thirty-five states that have not signed the treaty and most of them have stockpiles of land mines and reserve the right to use them. Collectively these states have about 50 million mines, and China, Russia, the United States, India, and Pakistan maintain the largest stockpiles.

Finally, the decline in armed conflicts around the world is not necessarily irreversible. Some of the factors contributing to the decline of conflicts, such as democratization and the peace-operations role of the United Nations, can suffer setbacks due to lack of support from major powers and the international community. And there remain serious possible threats to international peace and security that can cause widespread casualties, such as a conflict in the Korean Peninsula and war between China and Taiwan.

It is worth noting that battle deaths themselves are not an adequate indicator of threats to human security posed by armed conflict. Many armed conflicts have indirect consequences on human life and well-being. Wars are a major source of economic disruption, disease, and ecological destruction, which in turn undermine human development and thus create a vicious cycle of conflict and underdevelopment. As the *Human Development Report* (UN Development Programme 2005, 12) put it: "Conflict undermines nutrition and public health, destroys education systems, devastates livelihoods and retards prospects for economic growth." Those who take a broad definition of human security must look at threats to the survival and safety of the individual not only from violent conflict but also from nonviolent factors such as disease, environmental degradation, and natural disasters.

Women, Conflict, and Human Security

The relationship between gender and human security has multiple dimensions. The UN Inter-Agency Committee on Women and Gender Equality notes five aspects: (1) violence against women and girls; (2) gender inequalities in control over resources; (3) gender inequalities in power and decision-making; (4) women's human rights; and (5) women (and men) as actors, not victims (UN Inter-Agency Committee on Women and Gender Equality 1999, 1). Recent conflicts have shown women as victims of rape, torture, and sexual slavery. For example, between 250,000 and 500,000 women were raped during the 1994 genocide in Rwanda. Such atrocities against women are now recognized as a crime against humanity (Rehn and Sirleaf 2002, 9).

War-affected areas often see a sharp increase in domestic violence directed at women and a growth in the number of women trafficked to become forced laborers or sex workers. It has been noted that women become targets of rape and sexual violence because they serve as a social and cultural symbol. Hence, violence against them may be undertaken as a deliberate strategy to undermine the social fabric of an opponent. According to the UNHCR, women and girls comprise approximately half of any refugee or internally displaced population. Another important aspect of the gender dimension of human security is the role of women as actors in conflicts. This involves considering the participation of women in combat. In the Eritrean war of independence, women made up 25 to 30 percent of combatants. A similar proportion of women were fighting with the Tamil Tigers. And although the Islamic State is generally oppressive toward women, approximately 10 percent of its Western recruits are female. Women play an even larger role in support functions, such as logistics, staff, and intelligence services, in a conflict. Securing women's participation in combat may be motivated by a desire, among the parties to a conflict, to increase the legitimacy of their cause. It signifies "a broad social consensus and solidarity, both to their own population and to the outside world" (*Gendering Human Security* 2001, 18).

Gendered Perspective on Human Rights

THE CHALLENGE

Before the emergence of a global feminist movement, it was conventional for human rights treaties to be cast in language that assumes that the rights bearer is a man and the head of a household. Many feminists argue that this convention reflects more than an old-fashioned turn of phrase. The classic political and civil rights (freedom of speech, association, from arbitrary arrest, etc.) assume that the rights bearer will be living, or would wish to live, a life of active citizenship, but until very recently, such a life was denied to nearly all women in nearly all cultures. Instead of this public life, women were limited to the private sphere and subjected to the arbitrary and capricious power of the male head of the household. Only recently in Western liberal democracies have women been able to vote, to stand for office, or to own property in their own name, and issues such as the criminalization of rape in marriage and the effective prevention of domestic violence against women are still controversial. The situation is even worse in some non-Western polities. It may be that a genuinely gender-neutral account of human rights is possible, but some radical feminists argue that an altogether different kind of thinking is required (see Mackinnon 1993).

OPTIONS

Both cultural critics and feminists argue, convincingly, that the model of a rights bearer inherent in the contemporary international human rights regime is based on the experiences of Western men. Agreement collapses, however, when the implications of this common position are explored. Liberal feminists wish to see the rights of men extended to women, whereas radical feminists wish to promote a new model of what it is to be human that privileges neither men nor women. Most cultural critics, on the other hand, wish to preserve inherited status and power differences based on gender.

A global press and the Internet have made local and national decisions the concern of communities across the globe. Indonesian Muslim students protest the French decision to ban Muslim headscarves and other religious clothing in public schools.

APPLICATION

The contradictions here are sharpest when it comes to relations between the world of Islam and the human rights regime, largely because relations between Islam and the West are so fraught on other grounds that all differences are magnified. Radical or traditional Islamists argue for conventional gender roles, support quite severe restrictions on the freedom of women, and promote the compulsory wearing of restrictive clothing such as the niqab or the burqa. Many of these petty restrictions have no basis in the Koran or the sayings of the Prophet Muhammad and can simply be understood as methods of preserving male dominance—although it should be said that they are often accepted by Muslim women as ways of asserting their identity. More serious for the human rights regime are those verses of the Koran that unambiguously deny gender equality. It is often (and truly) said that the Koran's attitude toward the status of women was in advance of much contemporary seventh-century thought—including Christian and Jewish thought of the age. However, it remains the case that, for example, in a Sharia court, the evidence of a woman is worth less than that of a man, and sexual intercourse outside marriage is punishable for a woman even in the case of rape. The other Abrahamic religions continue to preserve misogynist vestiges, but mainstream Christian and Jewish theologians have reinterpreted those aspects of their traditions that radically disadvantage women. Given the importance attached to the literal text of the Koran, this reinterpretation will prove more difficult for Muslims, though many Islamic thinkers discuss women's rights. The role of women under Islam will be a continuing problem for the international human rights regime as it attempts to divest itself of its Western Judeo-Christian heritage and adopt a more inclusive framework. Of course, it will be an even bigger problem for women who live in oppressive Muslim regimes.

For Discussion

1. Should local cultural standards outweigh externally derived norms?
2. The rights of women all over the world, including in many OECD countries, are at risk. To what extent is the focus on women in Islamic societies justified?
3. Are certain human rights not universal?

In recent years, there has been a growing awareness of the need to secure the greater participation of women in international peace operations. The UN Department of Peacekeeping Operations noted in a 2000 report:

> Women's presence [in peacekeeping missions] improves access and support for local women; it makes male peacekeepers more reflective and responsible; and it broadens the repertoire of skills and styles available within the mission, often with the effect of reducing conflict and confrontation. Gender mainstreaming is not just fair, it is beneficial. (Cited in Rehn and Sirleaf 2002, 63.)

In 2000, UN Security Council Resolution 1325 was passed, which mandated a review of the impact of armed conflict on women and the role of women in peace operations and conflict resolution. The review, *Women, Peace and Security*, was released in 2002. In his introduction to the report, then UN Secretary-General Kofi Annan noted that "women still form a minority of those who participate in peace and security negotiations, and receive less attention than men in post-conflict agreements, disarmament and reconstruction" (United Nations 2002, ix). There is still a long way to go before the international community can fully realize the benefits of greater participation by women in UN peace operations and conflict-resolution activities.

Globalization has made it more difficult for leaders of countries to assert that national cultural norms are more important than global standards of behavior. Transnational corporations, the globalized entertainment industry, and the United Nations itself all penetrate national borders and erode traditional values. As we will see in the next section, the international community of countries is actively involved in this process.

The Role of the International Community

Because of the broad and contested nature of the idea of human security, it is difficult to evaluate policies undertaken by the international community that can be specifically regarded as human security measures. But the most important multilateral actions include the creation of the International Criminal Court (ICC), the signing of the Ottawa Treaty, and the 2005 Responsibility to Protect document adopted by the United Nations, which (as discussed in Chapter 5) asserted the moral obligations for states to intervene against human rights violations in other states.

The ICC was established on July 1, 2002, with its headquarters in The Hague, Netherlands, although its proceedings may take place anywhere. It is a permanent institution with "the power to exercise its jurisdiction over persons for the most serious crimes of international concern" (Rome Statute, Article 1). These crimes include genocide, crimes against humanity, war crimes, and the crime of aggression, although the court would not exercise its jurisdiction over the crime of aggression until such time as the state parties agree on a definition of the crime and set out the conditions under which it may be prosecuted. The ICC is a "court of last resort." It is "complementary to national criminal jurisdictions," meaning that it can only exercise its jurisdiction when national courts are unwilling or unable to investigate or prosecute such crimes (Rome Statute, Article 1). The court can only prosecute crimes that were committed on or after July 1, 2002, the date its founding treaty entered into force. Since its establishment, the ICC has opened investigations in several countries, including Uganda, the Democratic Republic of the Congo, Sudan, the Central African Republic, Kenya, Libya, and Mali.

UN High Commissioner for Refugees special envoy, Angelina Jolie, speaks to refugees from the Syrian civil war at a military camp in Jordan. How can special envoys help bring attention to issues of human security?

The Convention on the Prohibition of the Use, Stockpiling, Production, and Transfer of Anti-Personnel Mines and on Their Destruction, signed in Ottawa on December 3–4, 1997, bans the development, production, acquisition, stockpiling, transfer, and use of antipersonnel mines (Ottawa Treaty, Article 1, General Obligations, 1997). It also obliges signatories to destroy existing stockpiles. Among the countries that have yet to sign the treaty are the People's Republic of China, the Russian Federation, and the United States.

The surge in UN peacekeeping and peacebuilding operations has contributed to the decline in conflict and enhanced prospects for human security. There have been seventy-one UN peacekeeping operations since 1948, and there are currently sixteen peacekeeping operations under way. In 2006, a UN Peacebuilding Commission was inaugurated, whose goal is to assist in post-conflict recovery and reconstruction, including institution building and sustainable development, in countries emerging from conflict. The United Nations has also been at center stage in promoting the idea of humanitarian intervention, a central policy element of human security. The concept of humanitarian intervention was endorsed by the report of the UN Secretary-General's High-Level Panel on Threats, Challenges and Change, *A More Secure World* (2004, 66, 106), a subsequent report entitled *In Larger Freedom* (United Nations 2005), and finally, by the UN General Assembly in September 2005.

United Nations specialized agencies play a crucial role in promoting human security. For example, the UN Development Programme and the World Health Organization (WHO) have been at the forefront of fighting poverty and disease, respectively. Other UN agencies, such as the UN High Commissioner for Refugees (UNHCR), UN Children's Fund (UNICEF), and UN Development Fund for Women (UNIFEM), have played a central role in getting particular issues, such as refugees and the rights of children and women, onto the agenda for discussion and in providing a platform for advocacy and action (MacFarlane and Khong 2006).

WHAT'S YOUR WORLDVIEW?

The failure of the international community to respond to crises in Africa and the Middle East raises questions about who will or should act to protect citizens. Do you think the United Nations should have its own independent military force for humanitarian intervention, peacemaking, and even state building? Is this the only way to ensure that something is done about these crimes against humanity?

Nongovernmental organizations (NGOs) contribute to human security in a number of ways: giving information and early warning about conflicts, providing a channel for relief operations (often being the first to do so in areas of conflict or natural disaster), and supporting government- or UN-sponsored peacebuilding and rehabilitation missions. Nongovernmental organizations also play a central role in promoting sustainable development. A leading NGO with a human security mission is the International Committee of the Red Cross (ICRC). Established in Geneva, it has a unique authority based on the international humanitarian law of the Geneva Conventions to protect the lives and dignity of victims of war and internal violence, including the war-wounded, prisoners, refugees, civilians, and other noncombatants, and to provide them with assistance. Other NGOs include Médicins Sans Frontières (Doctors Without Borders; emergency medical assistance), Save the Children (protection of children), and Amnesty International (human rights).

At times, these agencies overlap in the services they provide or the issue for which they advocate. As you will see, this tends to be the case in international relations. However, given the complex nature of international human rights law and the demands of providing for human security, each organization can play a part in helping advance the international agenda.

At the UN Millennium Assembly in 2000, former Canadian Prime Minister Jean Chrétien announced that Canada would sponsor an International Commission on Intervention and State Sovereignty (ICISS). The government invited Gareth Evans, a former Australian foreign minister and current head of the International Crisis Group, and Mohamed Sahnoun, a former Algerian diplomat and an experienced UN adviser, to serve as cochairs. At the behest of Canadian Foreign Minister Lloyd Axworthy, the commission was charged with finding "new ways of reconciling seemingly irreconcilable notions of intervention and state sovereignty" (ICISS 2001, 81). This was a very careful review of the right of humanitarian intervention. The key question the commission explored is whether it is appropriate for states to take coercive military action in another state for the purposes of protecting citizens at risk in that other state.

The *basic principles* (ICISS 2001, xi) of the report fit nicely with many of the universal goals of religious NGOs.

Basic Principles

A. State sovereignty implies responsibility, and the primary responsibility for the protection of its people lies within the state itself.

B. Where a population is suffering serious harm, as a result of internal war, insurgency, repression or state failure, and the state in question is unwilling or unable to halt or avert it, the principle of nonintervention yields to the international Responsibility to Protect. Elements, or specific responsibilities:

1. **The Responsibility to Prevent**: This means addressing the causes of conflict and other crises that put populations at risk.

Syrian government forces began a new offensive south of Aleppo city on October 17, 2015, backed by Russian air strikes. Prior to the withdrawal of its forces beginning in March 2016, the Russian government claimed it was only striking ISIS but its presence added to the number of deaths and Syrian citizens leaving the region.

2. **The Responsibility to React**: Refers to the necessity to respond to situations that put individuals at risk with appropriate measures, which might include various forms of intervention.
3. **The Responsibility to Rebuild**: After a natural disaster or military intervention, the international community must provide assistance for recovery and reconstruction. In addition, the international community should assist with reconciliation efforts aimed at addressing the causes of conflict and violence.
4. **The Responsibility to Protect (R2P)**: Documents and resulting strategies all emphasize the importance of prevention. Clearly stated, that means addressing fundamental *human security* issues: freedom from fear, freedom from want, and the need for the rule of law to provide for a just and peaceful society.

The 2011 situation in Libya presented the most recent test of the R2P principle. In March 2011, the UN Security Council authorized an intervention to protect the citizens of Libya from attacks by pro-Qaddafi forces. World leaders maybe sought to avoid another 1995 Srebrenica massacre, and once again, NATO used its superior air power and surveillance resources to protect citizens, prevent more conflict, and rebuild Libya as a democratic state. The United Nations has not been able to authorize an intervention in Syria to protect the citizens and slow down the flow of refugees because both China and Russia, as permanent members of the UN Security Council, will veto any application of R2P. This may raise questions about the decision-making processes of the United Nations that favors great-power interests over human interests.

Conclusion

For more than sixty years, leaders and citizens of countries have worked to develop the paired concepts of human rights and human security. Although governments around the world—including some in Europe and North America, the intellectual homelands of the concepts—from time to time violate the very freedoms they endorsed when they ratified the various human rights treaties, it is understood that these are transgressions of longstanding norms of behavior. Certainly, more can be done to promote freedom from fear and freedom from want.

Perhaps the greatest challenge today in the issue area of human rights and human security is the need to change the ways government officials and citizens see the role of the state. Does it exist solely to defend the country along the lines suggested in the Westphalian model of an independent and sovereign state? Or do we have an obligation as humans to help other humans in need? Until this is resolved, debates about human rights and human security will continue.

CONTRIBUTORS TO CHAPTER 7: *Amitav Acharya, Alex J. Bellamy, Chris Brown, Nicholas J. Wheeler, Steven L. Lamy, and John Masker.*

KEY TERMS

Arab Spring, p. 267
Charter rights, p. 256
Common security, p. 265
Human development, p. 264

Human rights, p. 256
Human security, p. 262
Humanitarian
  intervention, p. 266

Liberal account of
  rights, p. 256
Natural law, p. 256
Nonintervention, p. 258

Standards of
  civilization, p. 258
Universal Declaration of
  Human Rights, p. 259

REVIEW QUESTIONS

1. What is the relationship between rights and duties?
2. Why is the promotion of human rights so rarely seen as an appropriate foreign policy goal of states?
3. What are the problems involved in assigning rights to peoples as opposed to individuals?
4. In what ways can gender bias be identified in the modern human rights regime?
5. What is the relationship between democracy and human rights? Is it always the case that democracies are more likely to respect human rights than authoritarian regimes?
6. Can the compromising of human rights in the face of the threat of terrorism ever be justified as the lesser of two evils?

7. What is human security? How is it different from the concept of national security?
8. Describe the main difference between the two conceptions of human security: freedom from fear and freedom from want. Are the two understandings irreconcilable?
9. How do you link poverty and health with human security?
10. What are the main areas of progress in the promotion of human security by the international community?
11. What are the obstacles to human security promotion by the international community?
12. Why do we need to give special consideration to the suffering of women in conflict zones?

For more information, quizzes, case studies, and other study tools, please visit us at **www.oup.com/us/lamy.**

THINKING ABOUT GLOBAL POLITICS

What Should Be Done? National Interests versus Human Interests

BACKGROUND

Takastand is a new nation-state that once was part of a large authoritarian empire. It is resource-rich and is located in a strategic region that is important to many of the major powers, including China, India, Russia, and the United States. It is a multiethnic state with five major ethnocultural communities. Although it professes to be a democratic state, one political party controls the government. This political party also represents the dominant ethnic community, and it openly discriminates against the other ethnic communities. The police and the military have led secret raids against ethnic minorities, and international human rights organizations have found mass graves. The Takastand government denies any connections to the human rights abuses and blames international criminal networks or fundamentalist religious groups that are attempting to overthrow the government. The government also believes that stability is more important than rights at this stage of the country's development. Furthermore, the government's claim that it is being attacked by fundamentalist Islamic forces backed by Al-Qaeda has led to significant security assistance from the U.S. government and its NATO partners.

Most of the opposition groups claim that they stand for individual rights and freedoms and democracy, and they all claim that they will implement a true democracy that protects the rights and freedoms of all citizens. They also claim that they will end the country's dependency on the West and that they will challenge the hegemony of the United States and its allies.

Although this is a very poor country, it has significant energy reserves, but most of the profits end up in the hands of the political and military elites. Close to 85 percent of the wealth is controlled by 13 percent of the population. A number of European governments and NGOs have established effective development programs focusing on the United Nations' Sustainable Development Goals. More women and children in rural areas are now receiving health care, food, and education. The government representatives in these regions control the programs and usually demand payments to allow them to continue. Recently, they have arrested NGO workers and local activists who challenged their authority. Four NGO project leaders were arrested, prosecuted before a military court, and sentenced to death.

ASSIGNMENT

This action has prompted an international conference to address the human security problems and the repression in Takastand. The conference is modeled after similar conferences held to decide how to help Rwanda, Iraq, and Afghanistan. Your assignment is to describe how the world should respond. Take a look at other international-assistance conferences and use those models for your work. Is this a military, political, economic, or human rights issue? Then follow these three steps in planning your conference. This can be a group activity.

Step One

What issues should the conference address? Consider economic, political, military, and human rights and security issues.

Step Two

Consider who should be involved. Should this be an action of the United Nations, or should the great powers take care of this crisis? What role should NGOs play in this human security crisis?

Step Three

Answer these questions:

- Is stability in this region more important than human rights? Why or why not?
- Is it more important to provide access to economic opportunities or to provide cultural and political freedoms? Why?
- Should citizens of some countries be forced to give up rights and freedoms so that others may have access to material goods and resources that help them enjoy the good life? Why?

8

Global Trade and Finance

Tattered EU and Greek flags fly from flagpoles at a beach in Anavissos village, southwest of Athens. The Greek economic crisis continued in 2015: tensions between the Greek government and bailout lenders brought the country close to a financial collapse and exit from the Eurozone.

Trade is the oldest and most important economic nexus among nations. Indeed, trade along with war has been central to the evolution of international relations.

—ROBERT GILPIN

Perhaps the removal of trade restrictions throughout the world would do more for the cause of universal peace than can any political union of peoples separated by trade barriers.

—FRANK CHODOROV

The global economy creates great opportunities for citizens around the world but it also increases the linkages among various actors and can increase the chances that vulnerabilities will spread among actors in the global system. The economic crisis in Greece that began in 2009 and came to a head in early 2015 threatened economic stability in all the states that are members of the Eurozone and heightened concerns about the stability of global financial markets. When Greece agreed to its third financial bailout, the crisis eased.

In August 2015, the Chinese market fell 8.5 percent, resulting in market problems in Europe and the United States. Investors feared that China's economy would slow down if not collapse. The Chinese economy recovered, but when an economy of this size begins to slow down, public and private actors feel the effects worldwide. In such a global economy, is there a way to protect national economies? Which economic system is best for meeting a national government's responsibility to provide economic well-being for its citizens?

Nobel Prize–winning economist Joseph Stiglitz stated in 2010 that one of the legacies of the last economic crisis will be a new debate on which kind of economic system "is most likely to deliver the greatest benefit." Communism is out of the debate, but what about Asian capitalism with its emphasis on an economy that enriches the state, or the Nordic social democratic strategy that is creating economic stability and growth in Sweden? Time will tell whether the future of capitalism will include more or less government intervention in the market and whether states will continue to provide their citizens with a wide variety of social services.

After reading and discussing this chapter, you should be able to:

Explain how the global economic and trade system developed since the end of World War II.

Identify the key actors in global economics and trade.

Describe the roles and interactions of these key actors, particularly in managing the forces of globalization.

Explain the nature of the global trading system, the financial and banking system, and the global economy.

Explain the impact of economic globalization on quality of life in both rich and poor states.

Great Depression The global economic collapse that ensued following the U.S. Wall Street stock market crash in October 1929. Economic shock waves rippled around a world already densely interconnected by webs of trade and foreign direct investment.

The economic collapse of 2008–2009 was more than bad personal finances and massive government bailouts for banks and corporations. Indeed, in early 2009, Dennis Blair, the then Director of National Intelligence for the United States, warned members of the Senate that the global economic crisis was the most serious security challenge facing the United States and the world. Blair stated that 25 percent of the countries in the world have experienced low-level instability attributed to unemployment and poor economic conditions. Economic refugees might topple weak governments, and failed states might never get off the bottom. Even wealthy states have been adversely affected by the global economic crisis; after all, working and effective global trade and financial systems are also critical elements of global security.

Introduction

The globalization of world politics involves, among other things, a globalization of economics. As we discussed in previous chapters, politics and economics are inseparable within social relations. Economics does not explain everything, but no account of world politics (and hence, no analysis of globalization as a key issue of contemporary world history) is adequate if it does not explore the economic dimension of global politics and the global marketplace. This global market is built on the assumptions of *economic liberalism*—described by Adam Smith (1723–1790) as a system of natural liberty in which government intervention is minimal and individuals are encouraged to invent, develop businesses, and meet their basic human needs. Liberal economic thinking has emerged as the dominant economic belief system, and since the end of the USSR and its state capitalism, some would argue the only game in town. However, *mercantilist* and *socialist* belief systems still influence economic decision-making in some states. For example, state capitalism best describes the Chinese economy and socialist ideas shape the economies of many Nordic countries.

When the **Great Depression** struck in 1929, international trade measures such as increased tariffs exacerbated the preexisting domestic market distortions. International trade, however, did not lend itself to solutions like the International Monetary Fund and World Bank of the Bretton Woods system. John Maynard Keynes, Harry Dexter White, and the other economists and political leaders who met in New Hampshire in July 1944 planned a third part of the system, the International Trade Organization (ITO). Unfortunately, largely because of opposition in the U.S. Senate, the Havana Charter of the ITO never entered into force. In its place, the GATT secretariat—which was intended to oversee trade on a temporary basis—took on the task of organizing global trade negotiations.

Most of global politics is about peaceful practices and transactions among nation-states. Economic decisions related to trade and economic development make up most of the foreign policy activities of nation-states, regardless of their size and wealth. The current global market was created by political agreements made by national leaders at the regional and global level. Thus, to understand political economy, students of international relations need to focus on the interaction of states and markets. Political economy is the study of how states and other political actors intervene in the economy to serve the interests of their state and nonstate actors, like private corporations that employ their citizens. The extent of political intervention in the market has been a fixture of global politics for centuries but, since the end of World War II, the creation of regimes or governing arrangements to manage the global economy has increased significantly. Some might argue that as the processes of globalization have increased, so have the efforts of states to manage it.

In his book *The Imperious Economy* (1982), David Calleo made the argument that the United States used its power, imagination, and energy to shape the global economy and the institutions of global governance. The United States created a "Western liberal dream" or a "Pax Americana" described as follows:

> *A closely-knit world system of vigorously prosperous democracies, enjoying security from military aggression, permitting the free movement of goods, money, and enterprise among themselves, and promoting the rapid development and integration of those nations whom liberal progress has left behind.*

This U.S.-led liberal order helped finance and provide essential political and military support for the European Common Market and other regional organizations.

With the end of the Cold War, the liberal international economic order (LIEO) faced several challenges. For example, the major global economic institutions created during the Cold War needed to be reformed in order to include the nation-states of the former Soviet bloc and to address the persistent income gap between the more developed North and the developing South. Further, the global economic system had to deal with the emergence of China and other Asian states as economic players. However, the most significant challenge was the rapid pace of economic globalization. The critical question facing policymakers and scholars alike was whether the global political and economic institutions created in the aftermath of World War II could successfully manage economic globalization. Would the United Nations and its agencies like the World Health Organization (WHO) and the UN Development Programme (UNDP) have the financial resources and expertise to address issues of poverty that hinder poor states from participating in the global economy? Would the International Monetary Fund have the resources and political support to prevent financial instability as national economies declined due to job loss? Would the World Trade Organization (WTO) be able to prevent trade disputes as protectionist policies aimed at preventing job loss disrupted trade deals? As we will see in this chapter, much of political economy is all about the creation of regimes aimed at managing globalization and creating peaceful strategies for managing complex interdependence.

Bretton Woods system
A system of economic and financial accords that created the IMF, the World Bank, and GATT/WTO following World War II. It is named after the hamlet in northern New Hampshire where leaders from forty-four countries met in 1944.

World Bank Group (WBG)
A collection of five agencies, the first established in 1945, with head offices in Washington, D.C. The WBG promotes development in medium- and low-income countries with project loans, structural-adjustment programs, and various advisory services.

World Trade Organization (WTO) A permanent institution established in 1995 to replace the provisional GATT. It has greater powers of enforcement and a wider agenda, covering services, intellectual property, and investment issues as well as merchandise trade.

The Emergence of a Global Trade and Monetary System

The post–World War II period was the high point of U.S. political, economic, and military power. The U.S. dollar replaced the British pound sterling as the chief reserve currency and the dollar was considered as good as gold by countries rebuilding after the war or those emerging from a colonial past. An ounce of gold cost $35 and this provided economic stability for all currencies that used the dollar as a reserve currency. However, this monetary aspect of pegging the dollar to gold eventually ended because of U.S. balance-of-payment issues and the decline of the value of the dollar. Most economists agree that letting the value of the dollar float marked the end of the **Bretton Woods system** that was established in 1944 at a resort in rural New Hampshire. There, the United States and its allies created a number of financial institutions aimed at managing the global economy, referred to as the Bretton Woods institutions: the International Monetary Fund (IMF), the **World Bank Group (WBG)**, and the **World Trade Organization (WTO)**. The institutions created at the time (the last listed by its current incarnations) survive to this day and continue to play a major role in shaping the global economy. In the following paragraphs, we will discuss the key actors who have the power to determine access to global economic resources in order to develop a more complete understanding of the economic world.

The International Monetary Fund began when representatives from forty-four nation-states signed articles of agreement in 1944 and began operations in 1947. The goal of this organization was to secure international monetary cooperation, stabilize currency exchange rates, and work to expand international currency liquidity to promote trade and job creation. The IMF uses tools like Special Drawing Rights (SDRs) to transfer funds from the IMF to national banks in order to address balance-of-payments problems.

The International Bank for Reconstruction and Development (IBRD), now known as the World Bank, was originally established to give loans to economically stable countries that could afford to repay them. This strict requirement for loans was first challenged by the **Marshall Plan** and the Dodge Line, which provided grants to European states and Japan for reconstruction. In 1947, the World Bank shifted its goals from reconstruction to development, emphasizing economic liberalization as the ruling narrative for dealing with global economic problems, especially in the developing world, and promoted this strategy through its loans and programs. The World Bank consists of the

How did the Bretton Woods conference of 1944 set up a political and economic system that clearly benefited the United States and its allies?

IBRD and the International Development Association (IDA), which was founded in 1960 to provide "soft" or interest-free loans or credits and grants to the poorest developing countries.

The World Bank Group also includes three additional organizations. The International Finance Corporation (IFC) was established in 1956 to provide funds for private-sector institutions to encourage the development of local investment markets and to stimulate the international flow of capital into developing markets. In order to promote foreign direct investment into developing countries, the Multilateral Investment Guarantee Agency (MIGA) was established in 1988. This agency provides political risk insurance to investors and lending institutions. With any financial transaction, there is a chance that disagreements and disputes will arise and these disputes could potentially prevent the completion of important development activities. The International Centre for Settlement of Investment Disputes provides the essential services for resolving such disputes.

Another important set of actors that play an important role in promoting trade and finance in the global economy are regional development banks. These multilateral financial institutions provide low-interest loans and grants for a variety of programs including infrastructure development, health, education, and environmental and natural resource management. There are four major regional development banks:

- African Development Bank (AfDB)
- Asian Development Bank (ADB)
- European Bank for Reconstruction and Development (EBRD)
- Inter-American Development Bank (IDB)

The United States is a member of each of these banks and is involved in providing financial assistance in the form of soft or hard loans. Soft loans have low interest rates and a long period for repayment; hard loans have higher interest rates and are usually asset-based. The funding for these regional banks comes from financial markets and donor states.

Many scholars and policymakers believe that protectionist trade policies or *beggar thy neighbor* trade policies may have contributed to the start of both world wars. Negotiations to eliminate or reduce tariffs began in the late 1940s and by 1947 the General Agreement on Tariffs and Trade (GATT), a system of treaties among more than 100 nation-states, established rules for the conduct of international trade. The GATT reflected a postwar consensus on free trade that was promoted by and served U.S. national interests. The GATT and the WTO provided a transparent and predictable rule-based trading system, and today the WTO also provides members with a dispute settlement process that serves to resolve conflicts of interest.

In addition to the WTO procedures and rules, states have established both bilateral and multilateral trade agreements. Free trade areas are established to

Marshall Plan Officially known as the European Recovery Program, it was a program of financial and other economic aid for Europe after World War II. Proposed by Secretary of State George Marshall in 1948, it was offered to all European states, including the Soviet Union.

WHAT'S YOUR WORLDVIEW?

How far should governments go to control or manage the world economy? Can the market self-regulate and create opportunities for all citizens across the world?

Poverty According to the United Nations, poverty is a denial of choices and opportunities, a violation of human dignity. It means lack of basic capacity provided by material possessions or money to participate effectively in society.

New International Economic Order (NIEO) A declaration adopted by the UN General Assembly calling for a restructuring of the international order toward greater equity for developing countries, particularly in reference to a wide range of trade, financial, commodity, and debt-related issues.

WHAT'S YOUR WORLDVIEW?

In a global economy run by transnational corporations seeking cheap labor, cheap resources, and minimal rules concerning safety, health, and the environment, should governments seek to protect their citizens and their jobs?

A Chinese investor looks at the Shanghai Composite Index at a stock brokerage house in Fuyang City. Chinese stocks rose in July 2015 after the government unleashed an unprecedented series of support measures to stave off the prospect of a full-blown crash that threatened to destabilize the world's second-biggest economy. Asian capitalism depends upon extensive state interventions to manage the economy.

eliminate tariffs on most trade deals and some agreements also include the reduction of restrictions on investments and services. Critics have suggested that most free trade agreements favor large corporations and encourage companies to move jobs overseas. Although expanded trade produces cheap goods and services, it may also lead to lower domestic wages. Economic globalization is often associated with wage stagnation and growth in inequality within and between states.

It is also worth noting that the global economy is influenced by the actions of multinational or transnational corporations (MNCs or TNCs). Some critics of globalization argue that global corporations, transnational banks, consulting firms, and financial institutions are controlling the world's resources and deciding which countries get rich and which remain poor. Many critics see the globalization process as uneven or even predatory. Investors and transnational corporations are in search of the *lowest common denominator*; namely, cheap labor, fewer rules and regulations, low-cost commodities, and safe and stable areas in which to invest or build their production facilities.

Developing states began criticizing the liberal economic order at the Summit of Non-Aligned Nations in Algiers in 1973. During this time, the Organization of the Petroleum Exporting Countries (OPEC) challenged the global pricing of oil and shifted wealth to oil-producing countries at the expense of large multinational corporations. The success of OPEC inspired other commodity-producing countries to think about establishing cartels to increase the prices of coffee, tin, rubber, and other exports from developing states. At about the same time, economic and political scholars in the developing world were promoting dependency theory as an explanation for the persistence of global **poverty**. This theory suggested that dependence is a situation in which the economy of state A is dependent on the growth in state B. Political elites in both states work to maintain the economic system that benefits them.

In April 1974, the United Nations adopted the Declaration on the Establishment of a **New International Economic Order (NIEO)**. The NIEO demands were aimed at addressing the persistence of poverty and the slow pace of economic development in the global South. The document called for actions such as indexing the prices of commodities by linking them to the costs of manufactured goods, increasing the amount of official development assistance, and lowering tariffs on manufactured goods from developing countries. As the developing world challenged the equity of the

Contending Views of Capitalism

Ever since Deng Xiaoping introduced **free market** reforms in 1978 and opened China to the outside world, China's economy grew at a rate of about 10 percent per year, although in 2015, it slipped to approximately 7 percent. China quickly became the industrial workshop for the world and is currently the world's second-largest economy. The concern among many is whether China will use its economic wealth and influence to extend its power in a nationalistic or mercantilist way. China is a successful state capitalist system, and because of its economic strength, it was able to avoid most of the economic crisis from 2008 to the present. However, in 2015, China devalued its currency, which caused world financial markets to suspect a potential weakening of its economy. There are many in Washington and in European capitals who see China as both an economic and potentially a military or security threat. Many people are asking if the future will be a peaceful one with the great powers, including China and India, working together to find solutions to the global economic crisis, or if instead there will be a new scramble for resources and markets that increases the tensions and conflicts among the major powers. Many free market capitalists have complained about China's monetary policies and its use of subsidies to support certain industries. One reason for the concern is a misunderstanding or lack of knowledge about the differences between the Anglo-American

form of capitalism, known as the *Washington Consensus*, with its emphasis on minimal government and free market solutions, and the Asian form of capitalism, the *Beijing Consensus*, with its emphasis on the economy serving the interests of the state.

Writer and journalist James Fallows provides an excellent description of the purpose of economic life in the Anglo-American and Asian models.* The purpose of economic life in the Anglo-American model is to raise the individual consumer's standard of living,

Female Chinese workers sew clothes to be exported to the United States and Europe at a garment factory in Huaibei City in East China's Anhui province.

whereas the Asian model places priority on increasing national strength by making the state more independent and self-sufficient. In terms of power, the Asian model seeks to concentrate power to serve the common good, and the Anglo-American model seeks to break up any concentrated power. From this perspective, economic development "means that people have more choice" and a greater number of opportunities to pursue personal wealth. In the Asian capitalist system, the primary goal is to

"develop the productive base of the country" by supporting the industries at home and those abroad that are owned by your citizens around the world. This also means using government resources to support efforts at securing both markets and strategic resources essential for economic growth. This state capitalist view suggests that the consumer's welfare and interests are less important than the corporation that is producing goods and services for the welfare of the state. Not surprisingly, then, China is considered an economic superpower by most of the world's leading economists.

The Obama administration has continued to pressure China to address a number of issues, including the value of its currency, its use of subsidies, and its failure to address issues related to the protection of intellectual property rights. In 2015, the Obama administration considered imposing sanctions against China for the purported cybertheft of U.S. trade secrets and allegedly hacking into the Office of Personnel Management and stealing the personal data of nearly 21.5 million people.

The Chinese government generally dismisses international criticism as unwarranted finger pointing. China had a $594.5 billion trade surplus with the world in 2015, and its exports to the United States outpace imports by a four-to-one margin. Evidence is mounting that China is following a two-pronged strategy to maintain its economic growth. First, it uses the WTO to fight protectionism among its trade partners.

Continued

Contending Views of Capitalism *continued*

China has filed more cases with the WTO's trade tribunals in Geneva than any other country. Second, China is holding down the value of its currency, and since 2007, it has also suppressed a series of IMF reports that document the undervaluation of its currency.

Historically, every rising power has used the resources of the state to help key economic players grow. After World War II, Marshall Plan funds combined with other public investments to rebuild European industries and create thriving welfare states. Many nation-states still own or have major control over key industries such as energy, telecommunications, financial services, and manufacturing. So is China the only culprit here, or are we witnessing a shift from Anglo-American liberal capitalism to a

state capitalist system? Will the current economic crisis force many states to take over key economic sectors to provide employment, secure key resources, and protect the interests of their citizens?

*James Fallows, *Looking at the Sun: The Rise of the New East Asian Economic and Political System* (New York: Vintage Books, 1995).

For Discussion

1. A January 2012 issue of *The Economist* included a special section on state capitalism called "The Visible Hand," which argued that the future of capitalism may mean more government control of the economy. What do you think about that idea?

Should government play a more extensive role in our economic lives?

2. The neoliberal institutions that we expect to manage the global economy (e.g., the IMF) push for less government intervention in the economy. Will these institutions need to change their guidelines or should they be replaced with new institutions based on new global realities?

3. Both China and India are members of the G20, and their economic and political power is on the rise. Is this the end of Western hegemony? What might a more pluralistic form of global governance look like?

Free market A market ruled by the forces of supply and demand, where all buying and selling is not constrained by government regulations or interventions.

liberal economic order, it became clear that the world was clearly divided about the efficacy of the system.

Despite such challenges, the core capitalist states did not give up on the developing world. Recall that before the Soviet Union collapsed, this was both an economic and political battle for global influence. The United Nations has provided the foundation for the creation of important organizations aimed at encouraging economic growth in the developing world. Most notable is the UN Development Programme (UNDP), which works in nearly 170 countries and territories helping to eradicate poverty and reduce inequalities and exclusion. Additionally, the UN Conference on Trade and Development (UNCTAD), self-described as the Trade Union of the Poor, is responsible for dealing with development issues, particularly international trade—the main driver of development.

Global Trade and Finance Actors in a Globalizing Economy

Countless discussions of globalization have brought its economic aspects front and center. For example, the late Milton Friedman, a Nobel Prize–winning economist, remarked that it has become possible "to produce a product anywhere, using resources from anywhere, by a company located anywhere, to be sold anywhere" (cited in Naisbitt 1994, 19). Global governance bodies like the Bank for International Settlements (BIS), the Group of Eight (G8), the International Monetary Fund (IMF), the Organisation for Economic Co-operation and Development (OECD), the UN Conference on Trade and Development (UNCTAD), the World Bank Group (WBG), and the World Trade Organization (WTO) have all put economic globalization high on their agendas (see Table 8.1). Usually, these official

TABLE 8.1	Major Public Global Governance Agencies for Trade and Finance
Asian Infrastructure Investment Bank	Established in 2015, this bank is led by the Chinese. There are fifty-seven members and the bank has $100 billion in capital. It is clearly challenging the current "development regime" by focusing on infrastructure and fast approval of applications. This bank will help to extend Chinese political and economic influence.
Bank for International Settlements (BIS)	Established in 1930 with headquarters in Basel. The bank has sixty member shareholding central banks (2015), although many other public financial institutions also use BIS facilities. The bank promotes cooperation among central banks and provides various services for global financial operations.
Group of Eight (G8)	Established in 1975 as the G5 (France, Germany, Japan, the United Kingdom, and the United States); subsequently expanded as the G7 to include Canada and Italy and, since 1998, as the G8 to include the Russian Federation. The G8 conducts semiformal collaboration on world economic problems. Government leaders meet in annual G8 summits, while finance ministers and/or their leading officials periodically hold other consultations.
Group of Twenty (G20)	Established in 1999, this group is made up of finance ministers and central bank governors of nineteen countries and the European Union. Members include Argentina, Australia, Brazil, Canada, China, France, Germany, India, Indonesia, Italy, Japan, Mexico, Russia, Saudi Arabia, South Africa, South Korea, Turkey, the United Kingdom, and the United States. The G20 is an informal forum that was created after the financial crisis in the mid-1990s. The members discuss national policies, plans for international cooperation, and ideas for reforming institutions that manage the global economy.
General Agreement on Tariffs and Trade (GATT)	Established in 1947 with offices in Geneva. Membership had reached 122 states when it was absorbed into the WTO in 1995. The GATT coordinated eight rounds of multilateral negotiations to reduce state restrictions on cross-border merchandise trade.
International Monetary Fund (IMF)	Established in 1945 with headquarters in Washington, D.C. Membership consists of 188 states (2015). The IMF monitors short-term cross-border payments and foreign exchange positions. When a country develops chronic imbalances in its external accounts, the IMF supports corrective policy reforms, often called "structural-adjustment programs." Since 1978, the IMF has undertaken comprehensive surveillance both of the economic performance of individual member states and of the world economy as a whole.

Continued

TABLE 8.1 *continued*	
International Organization of Securities Commissions (IOSCO)	Established in 1983 with headquarters in Montreal; secretariat now in Madrid. Membership consists of 205 official securities regulators (2015) as well as (nonvoting) trade associations and other agencies. The IOSCO aims to promote high standards of regulation in stock and bond markets, to establish effective surveillance of transborder securities transactions, and to foster collaboration between securities markets in the detection and punishment of offenses.
New Development Bank BRICS (NDB BRICS)	Formerly referred to as the BRICS Development Bank, it is a multilateral development bank operated by the BRICS states (Brazil, Russia, India, China, and South Africa) as an alternative to the existing U.S.-dominated World Bank and International Monetary Fund.
Organisation for Economic Co-operation and Development (OECD)	Founded in 1962 with headquarters in Paris. Membership consists of thirty-four states with advanced industrial economies (2015). The OECD provides a forum for multilateral intergovernmental consultations on almost all policy issues except military affairs; measures have especially addressed environmental questions, taxation, and transborder corporations. At regular intervals, the OECD secretariat produces an assessment of the macroeconomic performance of each member, including suggestions for policy changes.
United Nations Conference on Trade and Development (UNCTAD)	Established in 1964 with offices in Geneva. Membership consists of 194 states (2015). The UNCTAD monitors the effects of world trade and investment on economic development, especially in the South.
World Bank Group (WBG)	A collection of five agencies, the first of which was established in 1945, with head offices in Washington, D.C. The WBG promotes development in medium- and low-income countries with project loans, structural-adjustment programs, and various advisory services.
World Trade Organization (WTO)	Established in 1995 with headquarters in Geneva. Membership consists of 162 states (2015). The WTO is a permanent institution to replace the provisional GATT. It has a wider agenda covering services, intellectual property, and investment issues as well as merchandise trade. The WTO also has greater powers of enforcement through its Dispute Settlement Mechanism. The organization's Trade Policy Review Body conducts surveillance of members' commercial measures.

circles have endorsed and encouraged the trend, as have most national governments. Meanwhile, many social movements have focused their critiques of globalization on economic aspects of the process. Their analyses have depicted contemporary globalization of trade and finance as a major cause of higher unemployment, a general decline in working standards, increased inequality, greater poverty for some (see Chapter 9), recurrent financial crises, and large-scale environmental degradation (see Chapter 10).

In their different ways, all of these assessments agree that economic globalization is a key development of contemporary history. True, the scale and impact of the trend are often exaggerated. However, it is just as wrong to argue, as some skeptics have done, that claims about a new globalizing economy rest on nothing but hype and myth. Instead, as in the case of most historical developments, economic globalization involves an intricate interplay of changes and continuities. Certainly, the economic crisis that began in 2008, and continues in parts of Europe and Asia, shows how interconnected and globalized the world's economy has become.

One key reason for disagreements over the extent and significance of economic globalization relates to the contrasting definitions that different analysts have applied to notions of what it means to be global. What, more precisely, is "global" about the global economy? The following paragraphs distinguish three contrasting ways the globalization of trade and finance has been broadly conceived—namely, in terms of (1) the crossing of borders, (2) the opening of borders, and (3) the transcendence of borders. Although the three conceptions overlap to some extent, they involve important differences of emphasis.

Cross-Border Transactions

Skepticism about the significance of contemporary economic globalization has often arisen when analysts have conceived the process in terms of increased cross-border movements of people, goods, money, investments, messages, and ideas. From this perspective, globalization is seen as equivalent to internationalization. No significant distinction is drawn between global companies and international companies, between global trade and international trade, between global money and international money, or between global finance and international finance.

When conceived in this way, economic globalization is nothing particularly new. Commerce between different territorial-political units has transpired for centuries and in some cases even millennia. Trading between Arabia and China via South and Southeast Asia occurred with fair regularity more than 1,000 years ago. Long-distance monies of the premodern Mediterranean world, such as the Byzantine solidus from the fifth century onward and the Muslim dinar from the eighth to the thirteenth centuries, circulated widely. Banks based in Italian city-states maintained (temporary) offices along long-distance trade routes as early as the twelfth century and by the seventeenth century, companies based in Amsterdam, Copenhagen, London, and Paris operated overseas trading posts.

Indeed, on certain measures, cross-border economic activity reached similar levels in the late nineteenth century as it did 100 years later. Relative to world population of the time, the magnitude of permanent migration was in fact considerably greater than today. When measured in relation to world output, cross-border investment in production facilities stood at roughly the same level on the eve of World War I as it did in the early 1990s. International markets in loans and securities also flourished during the heyday of the gold-sterling standard between 1870 and 1914. Under this regime, the British pound, fixed to a certain value in gold, served as a global currency and thereby greatly facilitated cross-border payments. Again citing proportional (rather than aggregate) statistics, several researchers (e.g., Zevin 1992) have argued that these years witnessed larger capital flows between countries than in the late twentieth century.

Mexico's President Enrique Peña Nieto announces that German automaker BMW plans to invest $1 billion to build a new luxury car factory in the northern Mexican state of San Luis Potosí, which will start production in 2019. Globalization of finance, technology, and specialized training allows large corporations to move where costs are low and the chances for higher profits exist.

Interdependence A condition where states (or peoples) are affected by decisions taken by others. Interdependence can be symmetric (i.e., both sets of actors are affected equally), or it can be asymmetric (i.e., the impact varies between actors).

Protectionism Not an economic policy but a variety of political actions taken to protect domestic industries from more efficient foreign producers. Usually, this means the use of tariffs, nontariff barriers, and subsidies to protect domestic interests.

Meanwhile, the volume of international trade grew at some 3.4 percent per annum in the period 1870–1913 until its value was equivalent to 33 percent of world output (Barraclough 1984, 256; Hirst and Thompson 1999, 21). By this particular calculation, cross-border trade was greater at the beginning than at the end of the twentieth century.

For the skeptics, then, the contemporary globalizing economy is nothing new. In their eyes, recent decades have merely experienced a phase of increased cross-border trade and finance. Moreover, they note, just as growth of international **interdependence** in the late nineteenth century was substantially reversed with a forty-year wave of **protectionism** after 1914, so economic globalization of the present day may prove to be temporary. Governments can block cross-border flows if they wish, and national interest may dictate that states once more tighten restrictions on international trade, travel, foreign exchange, and capital movements. According to skeptics, contemporary economic globalization gives little evidence of an impending demise of the state, a weakening of national loyalties, and an end of war. Skeptics point out that most so-called global companies still conduct the majority of their business in their country of origin, retain strong national character and allegiances, and remain heavily dependent on states for the success of their enterprises.

Open-Border Transactions

In contrast to the skeptics, enthusiasts for contemporary globalization of trade and finance generally define these developments as part of the long-term

---

ENGAGING WITH THE WORLD

WTO Secretariat

The WTO Secretariat maintains a limited internship program for postgraduate university students wishing to gain practical experience and deeper knowledge of the multilateral trading system. Intake to the program is on a continuing basis, with no specific recruitment period. Assignments are intended to enhance interns' knowledge and understanding of the WTO and of trade policy more generally. To learn more, visit www.wto.org.

The Trans-Pacific Partnership

Once the Trans-Pacific Partnership (TPP) is ratified, it will be the world's largest trade agreement linking twelve countries that account for 40 percent of the world's gross domestic product. What does this mean for the states involved, and those not involved? Any trade agreement creates sharp divisions between members and nonmembers. Obviously, it becomes more attractive to trade within the community created by the agreement. However, these agreements often create divisions at home as well. Many domestic interests such as labor unions and environmental groups complain about the loss of jobs, lowering of wages, decreases in benefits, and the failure to enact stricter environmental regulations. Within each of the member countries, there will be changes in policies that will shape future debates.

For example, Japanese agricultural workers oppose the TPP because it would eliminate the current tariffs on agricultural imports from other countries that make the prices of Japanese agricultural products much lower. According to Japanese Prime Minister Shinzō Abe, the TPP is critical for both the economy and security of Japan. The government hopes that the TPP will jump-start a moribund economy that has not grown much in the last twenty years. Japan and some of the other Asian member countries, namely Vietnam and Malaysia, are concerned that China's dominance in the region will soon extend to setting the economic rules of engagement in Asia. These states see the TPP as a way of countering Chinese influence in both economic and political sectors. In recent disputes with Japan over the control of the Senkaku Islands and navigation and fishing rights, China cut off Japan's access to rare earth minerals that are essential for the production of many of Japan's high-tech instruments. The TPP will reduce the effectiveness of this form of coercive diplomacy and will reduce the vulnerability of member states.

The United States has been trying to create a free trade pact in this region since the early 1990s. The TPP is a critical element of President Obama's pivot to Asia with the primary goal being the establishment of a set of trading rules that will work in the United States' favor and counter China's effort to create trading rules for the region. U.S. leaders are not opposed to China joining the pact but they expect China to play by the rules that were negotiated by the United States and the other eleven partner countries. Opposition in the United States is mainly from labor unions and some Democratic members of Congress who are concerned about the loss of jobs and the lack of environmental protections in the agreement.

Participants at a 2015 rally held by the Central Union of Agricultural Co-operatives in Japan hold signs to protest the Trans-Pacific Partnership trade agreement. Why do you think domestic workers in Japan and the other eleven states feel that this trade agreement will work against them?

In Australia, industries that rely on exports strongly support the deal because it will create new trading partners and help to grow existing trade deals. Outside the business sector, there are some real concerns about several of the treaty's clauses that suggest that large corporations can prevent governments from passing legislation that protects consumers, workers, and the environment. Labor union representatives have focused on the danger of trading away Australia's sovereign rights, as well as trading away Australian jobs.

All parties to the agreement must figure out ways to manage the processes of globalization to serve their interests and meet their obligations to their citizens. This often requires giving up some sovereignty and opening up their national economies to the forces of globalization that promote competition between economic and political actors.

For Discussion

1. Clearly, domestic interest groups shape global trade policy. Which groups favor more open global treaties and which groups work against them? Why?
2. The TPP is a trading pact but it is also designed to prevent Chinese economic control in the Asia Pacific region. Will great-power rivalry like this extend into other regions?
3. Why is this trade agreement so controversial in the United States?

evolution toward a global society. This conception of globalization entails not an extension of internationalization but the progressive removal of official restrictions on transfers of resources between countries. In the resultant world of open borders, global companies replace international companies, global trade replaces international trade, global money replaces international money, and global finance replaces international finance. This process results in markets that are much larger than regional arrangements like the European Union (EU) and the North American Free Trade Association (NAFTA). From this perspective, globalization is a function of liberalization—that is, the degree to which products, communications, financial instruments, fixed assets, and people can circulate throughout the world economy free from state-imposed controls.

Exemplifying efforts to create a more global economy and promote global economic growth is the Trans-Pacific Partnership (TPP), the largest regional trade agreement in history. The TPP is a multinational trade agreement between several Pacific Rim countries regarding matters such as trade barriers, intellectual property, and standards for labor and environmental law. This partnership will end more than 18,000 tariffs that participating countries have placed on U.S. exports in past years. As of October 2015, the United States, Japan, and ten other Pacific Rim countries have agreed to a web of common rules that will govern trade in the Pacific region. Before the agreement becomes law, the twelve participating countries must ratify it, but there are some concerns that the treaty is bad for domestic workers because it would make imports cheaper, and the natural pace and direction of globalization is to shift production toward areas where labor is cheapest and other costs are very low.

Globalists regard the forty-year interlude of protectionism (c. 1910–1950) as a temporary detour from a longer historical trend toward the construction of a single integrated world economy. In their eyes, the tightening of border controls in the first half of the twentieth century was a major cause of economic depressions, authoritarian regimes, and international conflicts such as the world wars. In contrast, the emergent open world economy will yield prosperity, liberty, democracy, and peace for all humanity. From this perspective, often termed *neoliberalism*, contemporary economic globalization continues the universalizing project of modernity launched several centuries ago.

Recent history has indeed witnessed considerable opening of borders in the world economy. Since 1948, a succession of interstate accords through the General Agreement on Tariffs and Trade (GATT) has brought major reductions in customs duties, quotas, and other measures that previously inhibited cross-border movements of merchandise. Average tariffs on manufactures in countries of the North fell from more than 40 percent in the 1930s to less than 4 percent by 1999. The GATT's successor agency, the World Trade Organization, has greater competences both to enforce existing trade agreements and to pursue new avenues of liberalization—for example, with respect to shipping, telecommunications, and investment flows. Meanwhile, regional frameworks like the European Union and NAFTA have removed (to varying degrees) official restrictions on trade between participating countries. Encouraged by such liberalization, cross-border trade expanded between

1950 and 1994 at an annual rate of just over 6 percent. Total international trade multiplied fourteen-fold in real terms over this period, and expansion of trade in manufactures was even greater, with a twenty-six-fold increase (World Trade Organization 1995).

Borders have also opened considerably to money flows since 1950. In 1959, the gold-dollar standard became fully operational through the IMF. Under this regime, major currencies—especially the U.S. dollar—could circulate worldwide (though not in communist-ruled countries) and be converted to local monies at an official **fixed exchange rate**. The gold-dollar standard thereby broadly re-created the situation that prevailed under the gold-sterling standard in the late nineteenth century. Contrary to many expectations, the U.S. government's termination of dollar-gold convertibility on demand in 1971 did not trigger new restrictions on cross-border payments. Instead, a regime of **floating exchange rates** developed. Moreover, from the mid-1970s onward, most states with developed economies reduced or eliminated restrictions on the import and export of national currencies. In these circumstances, the average volume of daily transactions on the world's wholesale foreign exchange markets burgeoned from $15 billion in 1973 to $1,900 billion in 2004.

Alongside the liberalization of trade and money movements between countries, recent decades have also witnessed the widespread opening of borders to investment flows. These movements involve both direct investments (i.e., fixed assets like research facilities and factories) and portfolio investments (i.e., liquid assets like loans, bonds, and stocks). One result is that the 2008 global economic implosion began with the sale of securities of unwise mortgages made in the United States.

In general, states have welcomed **foreign direct investment (FDI)** into their jurisdictions in contemporary history. Indeed, many governments have actively lured externally based business by lowering corporate tax rates, reducing restrictions on the repatriation of profits, and relaxing labor and environmental standards. Since 1960, there has been a proliferation of what are variously called international, multinational, transnational, or global corporations (hence, the frequently encountered abbreviations MNC and TNC). The number of such companies grew from 3,500 in 1960 to nearly 80,000 in 2006. In 2014, global FDI inflows were $1.23 trillion and were projected to grow to $1.4 trillion by 2015 (UN Conference on Trade and Development World Investment Report 2015, 2

Substantial liberalization has also occurred since the 1970s with respect to cross-border portfolio investments, which contributed to the 2008 economic recession and the continuing global crisis. For example, many states now permit nonresidents to hold bank accounts within their jurisdictions. Other processes of **deregulation** have removed legal restrictions on ownership and trading of stocks and bonds by nonresident investors. Further legislation has reduced controls on participation in a country's financial markets by externally based banks, brokers, and fund managers. As a result of such deregulation (e.g., the repeal of

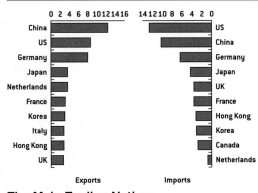

The Main Trading Nations.

These two graphs illustrate the top ten exporting and importing countries in terms of percentage share of world exports and imports. What patterns do you see in these graphs? What do these patterns suggest about global trade?

Fixed exchange rate The price a currency will earn in a hard currency. Here a government is committed to keep it at a specific value.

Floating exchange rate The market decides what the actual value of a currency is compared to other currencies.

Foreign direct investment (FDI) The capital speculation by citizens or organizations of one country into markets or industries in another country.

Deregulation The removal of all regulation so that market forces, not government policy, control economic developments the Glass-Steagall Act in 1999), financial institutions from all over the world have converged on global cities like Hong Kong, New York, Paris, and Tokyo.

In sum, legal obstructions to economic transactions between countries have greatly diminished worldwide in contemporary history. At the same time, cross-border flows of merchandise, services, money, and investments have reached unprecedented levels, at least in aggregate terms. To this extent, enthusiasts for globalization as liberalization can argue against the skeptics that borders have opened more than ever. However, significant official restrictions on cross-border economic activity persist. They include countless trade restrictions and continuing **capital controls** in many countries. While states have overall welcomed FDI, as of yet there is no multilateral regime to liberalize investment flows comparable to the GATT/WTO with respect to trade or the IMF with respect to money. In addition, many governments have loosened visa and travel restrictions in recent times, but **immigration controls** in general are as tight as ever. To this extent, skeptics have grounds to affirm that international borders remain very much in place and can be opened or closed as states choose.

Transborder Transactions

As mentioned earlier, most debates concerning economic globalization have unfolded between skeptics, who regard the current situation as a limited and reversible expansion of cross-border transactions, and globalists, who see an inexorable trend toward an open world economy. However, these two positions do not exhaust the possible interpretations. Indeed, neither of these conventional perspectives requires a distinct concept of globalization. Both views resurrect arguments that were elaborated using other vocabulary long before the word *globalization* entered widespread circulation in the 1990s. In a third conception, human lives are increasingly played out in the world as a single place. In this usage, globalization refers to a transformation of geography that occurs when a host of social conditions becomes less tied to territorial spaces.

Along these lines, in a globalizing economy, patterns of production, exchange, and consumption become increasingly delinked from a geography of territorial distances and territorial borders. *Global* economic activity—for industries and people linked to it—extends across widely dispersed terrestrial locations and moves between locations scattered across the planet, often in effectively no time. Although the patterns of *international* economic interdependence are strongly influenced by territorial distances and national divisions, patterns of *global* trade and finance often have little correspondence to distance and state boundaries. With air travel, satellite links, the Internet, telecommunications, transnational organizations, global consciousness (i.e., a mindset that conceives of the planet as a single place), and more, much contemporary economic activity transcends borders. In this third sense, globalization involves the growth of a **transborder** (as opposed to cross-border or open-border) economy.

This rise of **supraterritoriality** (transcendence of territorial geography) is evidenced by, among other things, more transactions between countries. However,

Capital controls The monetary policy device that a government uses to regulate the flows into and out of a country's capital account (i.e., the flows of investment-oriented money into and out of a country or currency).

Immigration controls A government's control of the number of people who may work, study, or relocate to its country. It may include quotas for certain national groups for immigration.

Transborder Economic, political, social, or cultural activities crossing or extending across a border.

Supraterritoriality Social, economic, cultural, and political connections that transcend territorial geography.

the geographic character of these global movements is different from the territorial framework that has traditionally defined international interdependence. This qualitative shift means that contemporary statistics on international trade, money, and investment can only be crudely compared with figures relating to earlier times. Moreover, economic statistics ignore or do not count activities that are not modern but are nonetheless vital in some societies; for example, a woman gathering firewood to cook the evening meal in a traditional society or a grandparent providing unpaid childcare in present-day New York City. Hence, the issue is not so much the amount of trade between countries but the way much of this commerce shapes transborder production processes and global marketing networks. The problem is not only the quantity of money that moves between countries but also the instantaneity with which most funds are transferred. The question is not simply the number of international securities deals as much as the emergence of stock and bond issues that involve participants from multiple countries at the same time. In short, if one accepts this third conception of globalization, then both the skeptics and the enthusiasts are largely missing the crucial point of historical change.

Global Trade

The distinctiveness of transborder, supraterritorial economic relations will become clearer with the help of illustrations of global trade given in this section. Others regarding global finance are discussed in the next section. In each case, their significance relates mainly to contemporary history (although the phenomena in question made some earlier appearances).

The rules of the global trading system are largely only those the countries themselves put on the firms that operate within their borders. Most of the world's trade takes place within the framework of the World Trade Organization; however, the organization is a multilateral discussion forum, not a global trade system. Member states of the WTO agree, among other things, to lower tariffs and to eliminate nontariff barriers to trade, but its member states must enforce the agreements. The principle that guides the WTO is that multilateral free trade pacts are better than bilateral deals. Another key principle is **most favored nation status**, whereby member states pledge not to discriminate against their trading partners.

Of course, disputes occur in the world's trading system, often to serve a domestic political purpose. For example, the United States and the European Union from time to time have disagreements about bovine growth hormone in beef products grown in the United States, and the United States has had a long-running dispute with China over trade-related aspects of intellectual property rights. To address such disagreements, the WTO has a dispute-resolution panel that keeps the process at the multilateral level so that members will not take unilateral action that could undermine the WTO's goals. Frequently, however, once a country begins the Dispute Settlement Body process, both parties settle the dispute before

Most favored nation status
The status granted to most trading partners that says trade rules with that country will be the same as those given to their most favored trading partner.

Global sourcing Obtaining goods and services across geopolitical boundaries. Usually, the goal is to find the least expensive labor and raw material costs and the lowest taxes and tariffs.

Intrafirm trade The international trade from one branch of a TNC to an affiliate of the same company in a different country.

it reaches the full panel. Because of the risk of retaliation, members prefer to utilize the good offices, reconciliation, and mediation services of the secretary-general, as provided for in Article 5 of the WTO covenant.

Transborder Production

Transborder production arises when a single process is spread across widely dispersed locations both within and between countries. Global coordination links research centers, design units, procurement offices, material-processing installations, fabrication plants, finishing points, assembly lines, quality-control operations, advertising and marketing divisions, data-processing offices, after-sales services, and so on.

Transborder production can be contrasted with territorially centered production. In the latter instance, all stages of a given production process—from initial research to after-sales service—occur within the same local or national unit. In global production, however, the stages are dispersed across different countries. Each of the various links in the transborder chain specializes in one or several functions, thereby creating economies of scale or exploiting cost differentials between locations. Through **global sourcing**, a company draws materials, components, machinery, finance, and services from anywhere in the world. Territorial distance and borders figure only secondarily, if at all, in determining the sites. Indeed, a firm may relocate certain stages of production several times in short succession in search of profit maximization.

Before the 1940s, such global factories were unknown. They did not gain major prominence until the 1960s, and most have spread since the 1970s. Trans-border production has developed primarily in the manufacture of textiles, garments, motor vehicles, leather goods, sports articles, toys, optical products, consumer electronics, semiconductors, airplanes, and construction equipment.

With the growth of global production, a large proportion of purportedly international transfers of goods and services have entailed **intrafirm trade** within transborder companies. When the intermediate inputs and finished goods pass from one country to another, they are officially counted as "international" commerce; yet they primarily involve movements within a global company rather than between national economies. Conventional statistics do not measure intrafirm transfers, but estimates of the share of such exchanges in total cross-border trade have ranged from 25 to more than 40 percent.

Much (though far from all) transborder production has taken advantage of what are variously called special economic zones (SEZs), export processing zones (EPZs), or free production zones (FPZs). Within these enclaves, the ruling national or provincial government exempts assembly plants and other facilities for transborder production from the usual import and export duties. The authorities may also grant other tax reductions, subsidies, and waivers of certain labor and environmental regulations. The first such zone was established in 1954 in Ireland, but

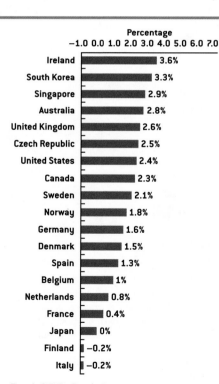

Real GDP Growth.

GDP real growth rate compares GDP growth on an annual basis adjusted for inflation and expressed as a percentage (2014 estimate in percentage).

most were created after 1970, mainly in Asia, the Caribbean, and the *maquiladora* areas along the Mexican frontier with the United States. Several thousand EPZs are now in place across more than 100 countries. One distinguishing trait of these manufacturing centers is their frequent heavy reliance on female labor.

Transborder Products

Much of the output of both transborder and country-based production has acquired a planet-spanning market in the contemporary globalizing economy. Hence, a considerable proportion of international trade now involves the distribution and sale of **global goods**, often under a transworld brand name. Consumers dispersed across many corners of the planet purchase the same articles at the same time. The country location of a potential customer for, say, a Samsung Galaxy smartphone, Beyoncé's latest album, or Kellogg's Corn Flakes is of secondary importance. Design, packaging, and advertising determine the market far more than territorial distances and borders.

Global goods Products that are made for a global market and are available across the world.

Like other aspects of globalization, supraterritorial markets have a longer history than many contemporary observers appreciate. For example, Campbell Soup and Heinz began to become household names in widely dispersed locations across the world in the mid-1880s following the introduction of automatic canning. From the outset, Henry Ford regarded his first automobile, the Model T, as a world car. Coca-Cola was bottled in twenty-seven countries and sold in seventy-eight by 1929 (Pendergrast 1993, 174). Overall, however, the numbers of goods, customers, and countries involved in these earlier global markets were relatively small.

In contrast, global goods pervade the contemporary world economy. They encompass a host of food products (for example, Dunkin' Donuts has over 3,100 stores in 30 countries); bottled beverages (Red Bull energy drink is available in more than 169 countries); printed publications (*The Hunger Games* trilogy was published in 51 languages and sold in 56 markets), and travel services (Airbnb has listings in over 34,000 cities in 190 countries). See Tables 8.2 and 8.3 for more insight into the pervasiveness of global goods. In all these sectors and more, global products inject a touch of the familiar almost anywhere on Earth a person might visit.

Today, many stores carry transborder articles. Moreover, since the 1970s, a number of retail chains have gone global. Examples include Japan-based 7-Eleven, Sweden-based IKEA and H&M, UK-based Body Shop, and U.S.-based Toys"R"Us. Owing largely to the various megabrands and transborder stores,

Skype was created in 2003 by innovators in Sweden, Denmark, and Estonia. In May 2011, Microsoft acquired Skype for $8.5 billion. Microsoft's Skype division headquarters are in Luxembourg, but most of the development team and 44 percent of the division's overall employees are still in Tallinn and Tartu, Estonia. Millions of people use this service and it has transformed both personal and professional communication around the world. Could this sort of service transform the way we understand people and cultures other than our own?

TABLE 8.2	**Your Global Morning as a College Student**

With an 8 A.M. class, you rely on a good working alarm clock to wake up. You also rely on a global production and distribution system.

If you use an old-fashioned alarm clock, rather than your smartphone, your alarm clock is a product of the Sony Corporation, a Japanese-based multinational corporation. The clock was assembled in a Sony plant in Brazil from components produced in Japan, Mexico, and Germany. It was shipped to the United States in a Greek-owned ship manufactured in Sweden, licensed in Liberia, and staffed by a Portuguese crew.

You do not have much to wear to class because you have not had time to do laundry.

You are wearing the international. Your shorts were made in Japan from cotton exported to Japan from the United States. Your socks were made in Vietnam using wool grown in Australia.

You have just enough time to stop at the dining hall for some breakfast.

Your stomach is full of the international. The bacon you ate was brought to you by the UPS Corporation, a multinational shipping company. The pig your bacon came from consumed grain that was grown in Canada. The bread you ate was Wonder Bread, a product of International Telephone and Telegraph, another multinational company. The technology that toasted your bread is a product from another multinational, General Electric. The butter that you put on your toast contains dried milk imported from Germany. Finally, the coffee you drank is a product of the Nestlé Corporation, a Swiss multinational.

You wonder how the Red Sox did last night and whether the U.S. soccer team won its qualifying round for the World Cup, so you take a look at the local newspaper.

Now you are reading the international. Much of the news on the front page that you skimmed is about events outside the United States and the role the United States plays as a global leader. The newspaper received much of its news from the British Broadcasting Corporation, Agence France-Presse, the Associated Press, and Reuters, all transnational information agencies. The major sports story today is about the World Cup and the various international athletes.

TABLE 8.3	**An Example of a Global Product: Your Lenovo ThinkPad**
Memory	Ten manufacturers worldwide, the largest in Korea
Case and keyboard	Made in Thailand
Wireless card	Intel, made in Malaysia
Battery	Made in Asia (various locations in the region possible)
Display screen	Two major screen makers are Samsung and LG Philips in South Korea
Graphics controller chip	ATI, made in Canada, or TMSC, made in Taiwan
Microprocessor	Intel, made in the United States
Hard drive	Made in Thailand
Assembly	Mexico

shopping centers of the twenty-first century are in good part global emporia.

Other supraterritorial markets have developed since the 1990s through **electronic commerce**. Today's global consumer can—equipped with a credit card, telephone, or Internet access—shop across the planet from home. Mail-order outlets and telesales units have undergone exponential growth, while e-commerce on the World Wide Web has expanded hugely.

Through transborder production and transworld products, global trade has become an integral part of everyday life for a notable proportion of the world's firms and consumers. Indeed, these developments could help explain why the recessions of contemporary history have not provoked a wave of protectionism, despite frequently expressed fears of "trade wars." In previous prolonged periods of commercial instability and economic hardship (e.g., during the 1870s–1890s and 1920s–1930s), most states responded by imposing major protectionist restrictions on cross-border trade. Reactions to the recession that began in 2008 have been more complicated (see Milner 1988). Although many territorial interests have pressed for protectionism, global commercial interests have generally resisted it.

Did IBM officials consider U.S. national security interests when they sold their personal computer business to the Chinese corporation Lenovo? Should U.S. leaders be concerned or is this the nature of the global economy?

Electronic commerce The buying and selling of products and services over the telephone or Internet. Amazon and eBay are examples of leaders in this area of commerce.

Global Finance

Finance has attracted some of the greatest attention in contemporary debates on globalization, especially following a string of crises in Latin America (1994–1995), Asia (1997–1998), Russia (1998), Brazil (1999), Argentina (2001–2002), and the 2008 global financial collapse that is still being felt in some areas of the world. The rise of supraterritoriality has affected both the forms money takes and the ways it is deployed in banking, securities, derivatives, and (although not detailed here) insurance markets. As international cross-border activities, such dealings have quite a long history. However, as commerce that unfolds through telephone and computer networks that make the world a single place, global finance has experienced its greatest growth since the 1980s.

> **WHAT'S YOUR WORLDVIEW?**
>
> *With all these transnational institutions and policies, is it possible for any state or even a group of states to manage the global economy? Who should be charged with protecting average people and their savings accounts?*

Global Money

The development of global production and the growth of global markets have each encouraged—and been facilitated by—the spread of global monies. It was noted earlier that the fixed and later floating exchange regimes operated through the IMF have allowed a number of national currencies to enter transworld use. Today, retail outlets in scores of countries deal in multiple currencies on demand.

No national denomination has been more global in this context than the U.S. dollar. About as many dollars circulate outside as inside the United States. Indeed, in certain financial crises, this global money has displaced the locally issued currency in the everyday life of a national economy. Such "dollarization" has occurred in parts of Latin America and Eastern Europe. Since the 1970s, the German mark (now superseded by the euro), Japanese yen, Swiss franc, and other major currencies have also acquired a substantial global character. Hence, huge stocks of notionally "national" money are now used in countless transactions that never touch their home soil.

Foreign exchange dealing has become a thoroughly supraterritorial business and has no central meeting place. Many deals have nothing directly to do with the countries where the currencies involved are initially issued or eventually spent. Trading can also take place without distance. Transactions generally occur over the telephone and are confirmed by telex or e-mail between buyers and sellers regardless of distance. Meanwhile, shifts in exchange rates are communicated instantaneously on video monitors across the main dealing rooms worldwide.

Transborder money also takes other forms besides certain national currencies. Gold has already circulated across the planet for several centuries, although it moves cumbersomely through territorial space rather than instantly through telecommunication lines. A more fully supraterritorial denomination is the **Special Drawing Right (SDR)**, issued through the IMF since 1969. Special Drawing Rights reside only in computer memories and not in wallets for everyday transactions.

Special Drawing Right (SDR) Members of the IMF have the right to borrow this asset from the organization up to the amount that the country has invested in the IMF. The SDR is based on the value of a "basket" of the world's leading currencies: British pound, euro, Japanese yen, and U.S. dollar.

Sabah Al-Khalid Al-Sabah, Kuwait's Deputy Prime Minister and Minister of Foreign Affairs, and Christine Lagarde, the IMF's managing director, meet during the "Islamic Finance: Meeting Global Aspirations" conference in Kuwait City. Lagarde was there to support Islamic finance that has the potential to extend banking services to many who are underserved in the Muslim world.

Other supraterritorial money has entered daily use in plastic form. Bank cards are used to extract local currency from automated teller machines (ATMs) worldwide. Additionally, several types of smart cards (e.g., Mondex, part of the MasterCard network) can simultaneously hold multiple currencies as digital cash on a microchip. Certain credit cards like Visa and MasterCard are accepted at millions of venues the world over to make purchases in whatever local denomination.

Through the spread of transborder currencies, distinctly supraterritorial denominations, digital purses, and global credit and debit cards, contemporary globalization has significantly altered the shape of money. No longer is money restricted to the national, state, or territorial form that prevailed from the nineteenth to the middle of the twentieth century.

Global Banking

Globalization has touched banking mainly in terms of the growth of transborder deposits, the advent of transborder bank lending, the expansion of transborder branch networks, and the emergence of instantaneous transworld interbank fund transfers.

So-called eurocurrency deposits are bank assets denominated in a national money different from the official currency in the country where the funds are held. For instance, euroyen are Japanese yen deposited in, say, Canada. Eurocurrency accounts first appeared in the 1950s but mainly expanded after 1970, especially with the flood of petrodollars (money earned from the sale of oil) that followed major rises of oil prices in 1973–1974 and 1979–1980. Eurocurrencies are supraterritorial; they do not attach neatly to any country's money supply, nor are they systematically regulated by the national central bank that issued them.

Globalization has also entered the lending side of banking. Credit creation from eurocurrency deposits first occurred in 1957, when American dollars were borrowed through the British office of a Soviet bank. However, euroloans mainly proliferated after 1973 following the petrodollar deluge. Today, it is common for a loan to be issued in one country and denominated in the currency of a second country (or perhaps a basket of currencies of several countries) for a borrower in a third country by a bank or syndicate of banks in a fourth or additional countries.

Global banking takes place not only at age-old sites of world finance like London, New York, Tokyo, and Zurich but also through multiple **offshore finance centers**. Much like EPZs in relation to manufacturing, offshore financial arrangements offer investors low levels of taxation and regulation. Although a few offshore finance centers, including Luxembourg and Jersey (a dependency of the United Kingdom that is part of the Channel Islands), predate World War II, most have emerged since 1960 and are now found in over forty jurisdictions. For example, less than thirty years after passing relevant legislation in 1967, the Cayman Islands hosted more than 500 offshore banks with total deposits of $442 billion (S. Roberts 1994; Bank for International Settlements 1996, 7).

Offshore finance centers The extraterritorial banks that investors use for a range of reasons, including the desire to avoid domestic taxes, regulations, and law enforcement agencies.

The supraterritorial character of much contemporary banking also lies in the instantaneity of interbank fund transfers. Electronic messages have largely replaced territorial transfers by check or draft—and cost far less. The largest conduit for such movements is the Society for Worldwide Interbank Financial Telecommunications (SWIFT). Launched in 1977, SWIFT connects more than 10,800 financial institutions in 208 countries. In 2015, over 6.1 billion electronic payments were sent, which equates to approximately 24.22 million messages per day.

Global Securities

Globalization has altered not only banking but also the shape of securities markets. A security is a tradable financial asset, such as stocks or bonds; securities markets, which are part of the greater financial market, are where securities can be bought and sold. Thanks to globalization, some bonds and stocks have become relatively detached from territorial space and many investor portfolios (groupings of financial assets) have acquired a transborder character. Electronic interlinkage of trading sites has created conditions that allow for securities dealing to take place anywhere and at any time. Each of these factors contributed to the 2008 economic collapse; subprime U.S. home mortgages were sold in European markets and traded twenty-four hours a day seven days a week. A subprime mortgage is a loan with a higher interest rate attached intended for individuals with poor credit scores. When the housing market collapsed in the United States and more people failed to pay their mortgages, the mortgage bundles purchased by banks around the world lost their value. The U.S. mortgage crisis certainly contributed to the current global crisis, which is more about sovereign debt and the lack of available credit from banks trying to recover from the previous crisis in 2007–2008.

Contemporary globalization has seen the emergence of several major securities instruments with a transborder character. These bonds and equities can involve issuers, currencies, brokers, and exchanges across multiple countries at the same time. For example, a so-called eurobond is denominated in a currency that is alien to a substantial proportion of the parties involved: the borrower who issues it, the underwriters who distribute it, the investors who hold it, or the exchange(s) that list it. This transborder financial instrument is thereby different from a foreign bond, which is handled in one country for an external borrower. Cross-border bonds of the latter type have existed for several hundred years, but eurobonds first appeared in 1963. In that year, the state highway authority in Italy issued bonds denominated in U.S. dollars through managers in Belgium, Britain, Germany, and the Netherlands, with subsequent quotation on the London Stock Exchange.

On a similar pattern, a euroequity issue involves a transborder syndicate of brokers selling a new share release for simultaneous listing on stock exchanges in several countries. This supraterritorial process contrasts with an international offer, where a company based in one country issues **equity** in a second country. Like foreign bonds, international share quotations have existed almost as long as stock markets themselves. However, the first transborder equity issue occurred in 1984, when 15 percent of a privatization of British Telecommunications was offered on exchanges in Japan, North America, and Switzerland concurrently with the majority share release in the United Kingdom. Transworld placements of new shares have occurred less frequently than eurobond issues. However, it has become quite common for major transborder firms to list their equity on different stock exchanges across several time zones, particularly in Asia, Europe, and North America.

Not only various securities instruments but also many investor portfolios have acquired a transborder character in the context of contemporary financial globalization. For example, an investor in one country may leave assets with a fund manager in a second country who in turn places those sums on markets in a collection of third countries. Thus, even when individual securities have a territorial character, they can be combined in a supraterritorial investment package. Indeed, a number of pension funds, insurance companies, and unit trusts have created explicitly designated "global funds" whose component securities are

Equity A number of equal portions in the nominal capital of a company; the shareholder thereby owns part of the enterprise; also called "stock" or "share."

Southern Debt in Global Finance

The global character of much contemporary finance is well illustrated by the struggles that many middle- and low-income countries have had with large transborder debts. The problems developed in the 1970s, when a surge in oil prices generated huge export earnings of so-called petrodollars, which were largely placed in bank deposits. The banks in turn needed to lend the money, but demand for loans in the OECD countries was low at the time owing to recession. So instead, large bank loans went to countries of the South (in some cases, partly to help pay for the increased cost of oil imports). Often, the lenders were insufficiently careful in extending these credits, and often, the borrowers were reckless in spending the money. Starting with Mexico in August 1982, a string of borrowing governments in the South defaulted on their transborder loans.

The initial response to this situation of unsustainable debts was to implement short-term emergency rescue packages for each country as it ran into crisis. Payments were rescheduled, and additional loans were provided to cover unpaid interest charges. This piecemeal approach only tended to make things worse. From 1987 onward, a series of comprehensive plans for third world debt relief were promoted. During the following decade, unsustainable commercial bank loans were gradually written off or converted into long-term bonds. Many bilateral loans from Northern governments to Southern borrowers were also canceled. However, in the mid-1990s, major problems persisted in regard to debts owed by low-income countries to multilateral lenders such as the IMF and the World Bank.

A much-touted Highly Indebted Poor Countries (HIPC) initiative, launched in 1996 and recast in 1999, brought slow and limited returns. In 2005, the G8 Summit parties agreed to write off the debts of eighteen HIPCs to the multilateral agencies.

Programs of debt relief for low-income countries have received major support from global citizen campaigns. Activists formed the first Debt Crisis Network in the mid-1980s and regional coalitions such as the European Network on Debt and Development emerged in the early 1990s. These efforts coalesced and broadened in the global Jubilee 2000 campaign of the late 1990s, which, among other things, assembled 70,000 people in a "human chain" around the G8 Summit in Birmingham, UK, in 1998. Most commentators agree that these global citizen mobilizations significantly increased, improved, and accelerated programs of debt relief.

For Discussion

1. Why was it considered so important to pay off the debts of developing countries? Would a similar system work to help Greece today?
2. How much do you think colonialism and the Cold War contributed to the debt in developing countries?
3. The Jubilee movement was a transnational social movement that had some success. Why do you think we have not seen a similar movement in support of the Millennium Development Goals and subsequent Sustainable Development Goals?

drawn from multiple corners of the world. Many transborder institutional investors have furthermore registered offshore for tax and other cost advantages. For example, the Africa Emerging Markets Fund has its investments in Africa, its listing in Ireland, and its management office in the United States.

Finally, securities markets have gone global through the growing supraterritorial character of many exchanges since the 1970s. The open-outcry trading floors of old have largely given way to electronic transactions by telephone and computer networks. These telecommunications provide the infrastructure for distanceless deals (called "remote trading") in which brokers, in principle, can be located anywhere on Earth. Most major investment banks (Daiwa Securities, Dresdner Kleinwort, Fidelity, etc.) now coordinate offices across several time zones in round-the-clock, round-the-world trading of bonds and shares. The first

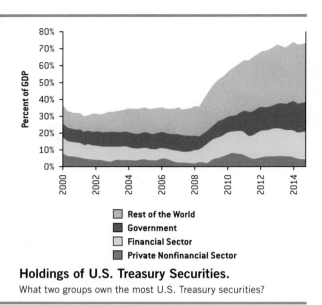

Holdings of U.S. Treasury Securities.

What two groups own the most U.S. Treasury securities?

Futures Derivatives that oblige a buyer and seller to complete a transaction at a predetermined time in the future at a price agreed on today. Futures are also known as "forwards."

Options Derivatives that give parties a right (without obligation) to buy or sell at a specific price for a stipulated period of time up to the contract's expiry date.

computerized order-routing system became operational in 1976, connecting brokers across the United States instantly to the trading floor of the New York Stock Exchange. Since 1996, similar developments have linked brokers anywhere in the European Union directly to its main exchanges. For its part, the wholly computer-based National Association of Securities Dealers Automated Quotations system (NASDAQ) has, since its launch in 1971, had no central meeting place at all. This transborder cyberspatial network has become the world's largest stock market, listing around 3,700 companies with a combined market value of over $9.6 trillion as of 2016.

Global Derivatives

A fourth area of finance suffused with globalization—and a major villain in the drama of the 2008–2009 economic collapse—is the derivatives industry. A derivative product is a contract, the value of which depends on (hence, is "derived" from) the price of some underlying asset (e.g., a raw material or an equity) or a particular reference rate (e.g., an interest level or stock market index). Derivatives connected to tangible assets like raw minerals and land date from the middle of the nineteenth century, and derivatives based on financial indicators have proliferated since their introduction in 1972.

Derivatives contracts take two principal forms. The first type, called **futures** or "forwards," oblige a buyer and seller to complete a transaction at a predetermined time in the future at a price agreed on today. The second main type, called **options**, give parties a right (without obligation) to buy or sell at a specified price for a stipulated period of time up to the contract's expiry date.

Additional technical details and the various rationales relating to derivatives need not detain us here; for our purposes, we will emphasize the magnitude of this financial industry. Public derivatives exchanges have proliferated worldwide since 1982 along with even larger over-the-counter (OTC) markets. The notional value of outstanding OTC financial derivatives contracts alone reached $553 trillion in June 2015 (Bank for International Settlements 2015, 2).

Like banking and securities, much derivatives business has become relatively distanceless and borderless. For example, a number of the contracts relate to supraterritorial indicators, such as the world price of copper or the interest rate on euro–Swiss franc deposits. In addition, much derivatives trading is undertaken through global securities houses and transworld telecommunications links. A number of derivatives instruments are traded simultaneously on several exchanges around the world. For example, contracts related to three-month eurodollar interest rates have been traded concurrently on Euronext.liffe (a pan-European derivatives exchange), the New York Futures Exchange (NYFE), the

Sydney Futures Exchange (SFE), and the Singapore Exchange (SGX). Owing to these tight global interconnections, major losses in the derivatives markets can have immediate worldwide repercussions.

Continuity and Change in Economic Globalization

Having now reviewed the development of a supraterritorial dimension in the contemporary world economy and emphasized its significance, we need to recognize continuities alongside these changes. One can appreciate the importance of globalization without slipping into globalism. In the following sections, we will discuss four factors of continuity: the unevenness of globalization, which we call irregular incidence; the enduring importance of territoriality; the role of the state in an era of globalization; and the persistence of nationalism and cultural diversity.

Irregular Incidence

Globalization has not been experienced everywhere and by everyone to the same extent. In general, transborder trade and finance have developed furthest in East Asia, North America, and Western Europe, in urban areas relative to rural districts, and in wealthier and professional circles. At the same time, few people and places are today completely untouched by economic globalization.

Supraterritorial trade and finance have transpired disproportionately in the North and most especially in its cities. For instance, although McDonald's fast food is available in nearly 36,000 establishments across more than 100 countries, the vast majority of these meals are consumed in a handful of those lands. In contrast to currencies issued in the North, the national denominations of countries in Africa have had scarcely any mutual convertibility. More than three-quarters of foreign direct investment, credit card transactions, stock market capitalization, derivatives trade, and transborder loans flow within the North.

This marginalization of the South is far from complete, however. For instance, certain products originating in the South have figured significantly in global markets (e.g., wines from Chile and South Africa and vacation packages in the Caribbean). Electronic banking has even reached parts of rural China. A number of offshore finance centers and large sums of transborder bank debt are found in the South. Global portfolios have figured strongly in the development of new securities markets in major cities of Africa, Asia, Eastern Europe, and Latin America since the mid-1980s. The Singapore Exchange (SGX) and the São Paulo–based Bolsa de Mercadorias & Futuros (BM&F) have played a part in the burgeoning derivatives markets of recent decades.

Indeed, involvement in global trade and finance is often as much a function of class as of the North-South divide. The vast majority of the world's population—including many in the North—have lacked the means to purchase most global products. Likewise, placing investments in global financial markets depends on wealth, the distribution of which does not always follow a North-South pattern.

For example, elites in the oil-exporting countries of Africa, Latin America, and the Middle East have owned substantial amounts of petrodollars.

Transborder markets and investments can be shown to have contributed significantly to growing wealth gaps within countries as well as between North and South (Scholte 2005, chapter 10). For example, the global mobility of capital, in particular to low-wage production sites and offshore finance centers, has encouraged many countries, including the United States, to reduce upper tax brackets and to downgrade some social welfare provisions. Such steps have contributed to growing inequality across much of the contemporary world. Increasingly, poverty has become connected as much to supraterritorial class, gender, and race structures as to country of domicile.

The Persistence of Territory

The transcendence of territorial space in the contemporary world economy must not be overestimated. Evidence presented earlier in this chapter suggests that distance and borders have lost the determining influence on economic geography that they once had. However, this is not to say that the nation-state has lost all significance in the contemporary organization of production, exchange, and consumption.

On the contrary, after several decades of accelerated globalization, a great deal of commercial activity is still linked to specific countries and has only a secondary supraterritorial dimension. Although transborder manufacturing through global factories has affected a significant proportion of certain industries, many globally distributed products (such as Boeing jets and Ceylon teas) are prepared within a single country.

Many types of money, too, have remained restricted to a national or local domain. Likewise, the great bulk of retail banking has stayed territorial, as clients deal with their local branch offices. In spite of substantial growth since the 1980s, transborder share dealing remains a small fraction of total equity trading. Moreover, a large majority of turnover on most stock exchanges continues to involve shares of firms headquartered in the same country.

Most global commercial activity has not been wholly detached from territorial geography. Local circumstances have strongly influenced corporate decisions regarding the location of transborder production facilities. In the foreign exchange markets, dealers have mainly been clustered in half a dozen cities, even if their transactions are largely cyberspatial and can have immediate consequences anywhere in the world. It remains rare for a transborder company to issue a large proportion of its stock outside its country of origin.

Hence, the importance of globalization is that it has ended the monopoly of territoriality in defining the spatial character of the world economy. The global dimension of contemporary world commerce has grown alongside, and in complex relations with, its territorial aspects. Globalization has been reconfiguring economic, social, and political geography (along with concurrent processes of re-gionalization and localization) but it has by no means eliminated territoriality.

The Survival of the State

Similarly, globalization has repositioned the (territorial) state rather than sig-naled its demise. The expansion of transborder trade and finance has made claims of Westphalian sovereign statehood obsolete, but states themselves remain significant. Through both unilateral decisions and multilaterally coordi-nated policies, states have done much to facilitate economic globalization and influence its course.

As already mentioned, states have encouraged the globalization of com-merce through various policies of liberalization and the creation of special eco-nomic zones and offshore finance centers. At the same time, some governments in the developing world have also slowed globalization within their jurisdiction by retaining certain restrictions on transborder activity. However, most states have eventually responded to strong pressures to liberalize. In any case, gov-ernments have often lacked effective means to fully enforce their territorially bound controls on globally mobile capital. With respect to immigration restric-tions, states have largely sustained their borders against economic globaliza-tion, but even then, substantial traffic in unregistered migrants occurs.

Yet states are by no means powerless in the face of economic globalization. Even the common claim that global finance lies beyond the state requires quali-fication. After all, governments and central banks continue to exert a major influence on money supplies and interest rates, even if they no longer monopo-lize money creation and they lack tight control over the euromarkets. Likewise, particularly through cooperative action, states can significantly shift exchange rates, even if they have lost the capacity to fix the conversion ratios and are sometimes overridden by currency dealers. Governments have also pursued collective regulation of transborder banking to some effect via the Basel Com-mittee on Banking Supervision, set up through the Bank for International Set-tlements in 1974. The survival of offshore finance centers, too, depends to a considerable extent on the goodwill of governments, both the host regime and external authorities. Recent years have seen increased intergovernmental con-sultations, particularly through the OECD, to obtain tighter official oversight of offshore finance. Similarly, national regulators of securities markets have col-laborated since 1984 through the International Organization of Securities Commissions (IOSCO).

In short, there is little sign that global commerce and the state are antitheti-cal, given that the two have shown considerable mutual dependency. States have provided much of the regulatory framework for global trade and finance, albeit sharing these competences with other regulatory agencies. Sadly, despite the po-tential for collective action, none of the measures countries undertook could stop the pace of the economic collapse in late 2008.

The Continuance of Nationalism and Cultural Diversity

Much evidence also confounds the common presumption that economic globalization is effecting cultural homogenization and a rise of cosmopolitan orientations over national **identities**. Identities are social and thus always formed in relationship to others. Constructivists generally hold that identities shape interests; we cannot know what we want unless we know who we are. But because identities are social and produced through interactions, identities can change. The growth of transborder production, the proliferation of global products, the multiplication of supraterritorial monies, and the expansion of transworld financial flows have shown little sign of heralding an end of cultural difference in the world economy.

It is true that global trade and finance are moved by much more than national loyalty. Consumers have repeatedly ignored exhortations to buy American and the like in favor of global products. (This is one reason why U.S. automakers Chrysler and General Motors had to beg for cash bailouts from the federal government in 2008–2009.) Shareholders and managers have rarely put national sentiments ahead of the profit margin. Foreign exchange dealers readily desert their national currency to reap financial gain.

However, in other respects, national identities and solidarities have survived—and sometimes thrived—in the contemporary globalizing economy. Most transborder companies have retained a readily recognized national affiliation. Most firms involved in global trade and finance have kept a mononational board of directors, and the operations of many of these enterprises continue to reflect a national style of business practice connected with the country of origin. Different national conventions have persisted in global finance as well. For instance, since equities have traditionally held a smaller place in German finance, globalization in that country has mainly involved banks and the bond markets. Cultural diversity has also persisted in transborder marketing. Local peculiarities have often affected the way a global product is sold and used in different places. Advertising has often been adjusted to local tastes to be more effective.

Like globalization in general, its economic dimension has not had universal scope. Nor has the rise of global trade and finance marked the end of territorial space, the demise of the state, or full-scale cultural homogenization. However, recognition of these qualifications does not entail a rejection of notions of globalization on the lines of the skeptics noted earlier.

Identity The understanding of the self in relationship to an "other." Identities are social and thus always formed in relationship to others. Constructivists generally hold that identities shape interests; we cannot know what we want unless we know who we are. But because identities are social and produced through interactions, identities can change.

A Greek pensioner looks at customers who use an ATM as she sits outside a bank in Athens. Due to the debt crisis, people were able to withdraw only up to 120 euros (approximately $135) per week from their retirement funds.

Conclusion

Prior to the summer of 2008, the world's economy seemed to be gaining wealth. Aside from the historic high price for petroleum products, most economic sectors showed no sign of distress. Yet the seeds of the economic recession that began in 2008 were already planted. As you read in this chapter, the complex relationship of trade in goods and financial instruments was seemingly doomed to fail. Too much money was invested in arcane instruments like derivatives and mortgages disguised as secure investments. The globalized trade and finance sectors were largely unregulated by host countries. Governments tried financial methods that worked in past recessions and economic crises. Slowly, many of these reforms and interventions—both new and old—have worked to arrest the economic crisis and to help many countries stabilize their banking industries and their financial markets. The U.S. economy is slowly recovering, but partisan political disputes and the rising cost of health care and social security, without an increase in taxes and other revenues, may trigger another economic crisis in the United States that will create economic instability around the world. Europe's debt crisis is far from over and may result in slow growth in the rest of the world. In addition, several emerging economic leaders, such as India, China, and Brazil, are not growing as fast as they were before the crisis. The worst of the financial crisis might be past, but the pain of loss is still being felt in rich and poor states across the world.

CONTRIBUTORS TO CHAPTER 8: *Steven L. Lamy and John Masker.*

KEY TERMS

Bretton Woods system, p. 292

Capital controls, p. 304

Deregulation, p. 303

Electronic commerce, p. 309

Equity, p. 312

Fixed exchange rate, p. 303

Floating exchange rate, p. 303

Foreign direct investment (FDI), p. 303

Free market, p. 295

Futures, p. 314

Global goods, p. 307

Global sourcing, p. 306

Great Depression, p. 290

Identity, p. 318

Immigration controls, p. 304

Interdependence, p. 300

Intrafirm trade, p. 306

Marshall Plan, p. 292

Most favored nation status, p. 305

New International Economic Order (NIEO), p. 294

Offshore finance centers, p. 311

Options, p. 314

Poverty, p. 294

Protectionism, p. 300

Special Drawing Right (SDR), p. 310

Supraterritoriality, p. 304

Transborder, p. 304

World Bank Group (WBG), p. 292

World Trade Organization (WTO), p. 292

REVIEW QUESTIONS

1. In what ways did the Bretton Woods framework for the postwar economy try to avoid the economic problems of the interwar years?

2. What was the breakdown in the Bretton Woods system?

3. What are the three main conceptions of economic globalization?

4. To what extent is economic globalization new to contemporary history?

5. How does transborder production differ from territorial production?

6. What are some of the reasons that the economic crisis has gone global?

7. How has globalization of trade and finance affected state capacities for economic regulation?

8. How have global products altered ideas of cultural diversity?

9. To what extent can it be said that global capital carries no national flag?

10. Assess the relationship between globalization and income inequality.

11. In what ways might global commerce be reshaped to promote greater distributive justice?

> For more information, quizzes, case studies, and other study tools, please visit us at **www.oup.com/us/lamy.**

THINKING ABOUT GLOBAL POLITICS

Globalization: Productive, Predatory, or Inconsequential?

INTRODUCTION

Globalization has become a buzzword that many pundits and scholars use to describe anything and everything happening in the world today. All the authors in this text share several definitions, and these suggest that globalization is more than just an economic process. But what makes this era of globalization different from previous eras? Is it a positive, negative, or marginal process? How do the various processes of globalization shape issues and events in the political, economic, social, and cultural worlds? This exercise will explore some of these questions.

DISCUSSION

1. Find a definition of globalization that makes the most sense to you. What are the different dimensions of globalization? What does *globalization from above and below* mean?

2. Globalization is said to cause *denationalization or delocalization*. What does that mean?

3. Is globalization a recent process? What makes this era different from previous periods of world trade and interdependence? Were the periods of colonialism and imperialism early phases of globalization?

4. What factors push globalization, making it faster, wider, and deeper?

5. Is the process of globalization taking power away from the state, or does it actually enhance the power of some states and weaken others? How?

FOLLOW-UP EXERCISE

What do we expect a state to do? In theory, we expect a state to provide services and resources in three areas:

1. *defining activities*, which include supporting a means of exchange or marketplace, providing a system of law and order, and protecting the boundaries of the state;

2. *accumulation-of-wealth activities*, such as building infrastructure; and

THINKING ABOUT GLOBAL POLITICS | *continued*

3. *redistribution activities*, such as providing health care and education.

Professor Manuel Castells (2005) has written that globalization has led to four crises within states: an *efficiency crisis*, a *legitimacy crisis*, an *identity crisis*, and an *equity crisis*. Is this just an academic claim, or are countries really suffering in these areas? Find at least two countries where one, several, or all of these crises are having a major impact on a state's capacity to provide for its citizens in the three basic areas listed. More precisely, how does globalization influence a state's ability to provide defining activities, accumulation-of-wealth activities, and redistribution activities?

Poverty, Development, and Hunger

The thirty-ninth G8 summit was held in Northern Ireland in June 2013 and a variety of charities in the United Kingdom launched the IF (Enough Food for Everyone) campaign to pressure the G8 countries to increase funding for development and hunger projects. Each of these paper flowers represents the millions of children who die each year from malnutrition. Are you part of an organization that seeks to make such a difference in the world by addressing issues like global poverty?

Wherever there is great property there is great inequality. For one very rich man there must be at least five hundred poor, and the affluence of the few supposes the indigence of the many.

—ADAM SMITH

All societies used to be poor. Most are now lifting out of it; why are others stuck? The answer is traps. Poverty is not intrinsically a trap, otherwise we would all still be poor. Think, for a moment, of development as chutes and ladders. In the modern world of globalization there are some fabulous ladders; most societies are using them. But there are also some chutes, and some societies hit them. The countries at the bottom are an unlucky minority, but they are stuck.

—PAUL COLLIER

As we saw in Chapter 5 and will explore further in this chapter, advocacy campaigns linked to celebrities like Radiohead, U2, and Angelina Jolie have come to play an important part in shaping the range of choices that politicians make about eliminating poverty, building economic development, and ending hunger worldwide.

Since 1945, we have witnessed not only increasing individual and NGO advocacy but also unprecedented official development policies and impressive global economic growth. Yet global polarization is increasing, with the economic gap growing between rich and poor states and people. As we have seen in other issue areas in this book, people who work in the academic discipline of international relations have had different ways of thinking about this gap.

- Traditionally, realists have concentrated on issues relating to war and have seen national security and development economics as separate issue areas.
- Mainstream realist and liberal scholars have largely neglected the challenges that global underdevelopment presents to human security—freedom from fear, freedom from want, and the rule of law.
- Dependency theorists have been interested in persistent and deepening inequality and relations between North and South, but for decades, they received little attention in the discipline.

Washington Consensus The belief of key opinion formers in Washington that global welfare would be maximized by the universal application of neoliberal economic policies that favor a minimalist state and an enhanced role for the market.

Global governance The regulation and coordination of transnational issue areas by nation-states, international and regional organizations, and private agencies through the establishment of international regimes. These regimes may focus on problem-solving or the simple enforcement of rules and regulations.

- During the 1990s, debate flourished, and several subfields developed that touched on matters of poverty, development, and hunger, albeit tangentially (e.g., global environmental politics, gender, international political economy).
- The contributions of a range of theorists and scholars in the 1990s significantly raised the concerns of the majority of humanity and states: postcolonial theorists, Marxist theorists (Hardt and Negri), scholars adopting a human security approach (Nef, Thomas), and the few concerned directly with development (Saurin, Weber).

Now in the twenty-first century, the discipline is better placed to engage with the interrelated issues of poverty, development, and hunger by influencing the diplomatic world, where interest in these issues is growing, spurred on by fears of terrorist threats and recognition of the uneven impact of globalization (Thomas and Wilkin 2004).

Introduction

Despite the trend toward increased activism, poverty, hunger, and disease remain widespread, and women and girls continue to comprise the majority of the world's poorest people. Since the 1980s and 1990s, the worldwide promotion of neoliberal economic policies (the so-called **Washington Consensus**) by **global governance** institutions has been accompanied by increasing inequalities within and among states. During this period, the Second World countries of the former Eastern bloc were incorporated into the third world grouping of states, and millions of people previously cushioned by their governments were thrown into poverty. As a result, the developing world is characterized by rising social inequalities, and, within the third world countries, the adverse impact of globalization has been felt acutely. Countries have been forced to adopt free market policies as a condition of debt rescheduling and in the hope of attracting new investment to spur development. The global picture is very mixed, with other factors such as gender, class, race, and ethnicity contributing to local outcomes (Buvinic 1997, 39).

In 2000, the United Nations recognized the enormity of the current challenges with the acceptance of the Millennium Development Goals (MDGs). These set time-limited, quantifiable targets across eight areas, including poverty, health, gender, education, environment, and development. The first goal was the eradication of extreme poverty and hunger, with the target of halving the proportion of people living on less than $1.25 a day by 2015. The results of the MDG process were mixed, but in general, the process was successful. For example, the number of people in extreme poverty decreased from 1,926 (in millions) in 1990 to 836 (in millions) in 2015. The number of people with access to primary education and clean water has also increased from 1990 to 2015. Thus, these goals provided a useful framework for development. In the final Millennium Development Goals Report 2015, UN Secretary-General Ban Ki-moon suggested that there was still significant work to be done as UN members adopted the Sustainable Development Goals, which build on the success of the MDGs, in September 2015:

> *Yet for all the remarkable gains, I am keenly aware that inequalities persist and that progress has been uneven. The world's poor remain overwhelmingly concentrated in some parts of the world. In 2011, nearly 60 per cent of the world's one billion extremely poor people lived in just five countries. Too many women continue to die during pregnancy or from childbirth-related complications. Progress tends to bypass women and those who are lowest on the economic ladder or are disadvantaged because of their age, disability or ethnicity. Disparities between rural and urban areas remain pronounced.*

The attempts of the majority of governments, international nongovernmental organizations (INGOs), and nongovernmental organizations (NGOs) since 1945 to address global hunger and poverty can be categorized into two very broad types depending on the explanations they provide for the existence of these problems and the respective solutions they prescribe. These can be identified as the dominant mainstream, or orthodox, approach, which provides and values a particular body of developmental knowledge, and a critical alternative approach, which incorporates other more marginalized understandings of the development challenge and process (see Table 9.1). Most of this chapter will be devoted to an examination of the differences between the mainstream/ orthodox approach and the critical alternative approach in view of the three related topics of poverty, development, and hunger, with particular emphasis placed on development. The chapter concludes with an assessment of whether the desperate conditions in which so many of the world's citizens find themselves today are likely to improve.

After reading and discussing this chapter, you will have a better sense of the factors that cause poverty and the status of efforts aimed at addressing global poverty. You will also know about the global institutions that are dedicated to addressing the problems of development.

Agnes Mukamtwari and her son Daniel have been aided by the Millennium Villages project in Rwanda. She has been able to pay her debts and even has health insurance. Global poverty was dramatically reduced in East and Southeast Asia but sub-Saharan Africa lags behind.

TABLE 9.1	Mainstream and Alternative Conceptions of Poverty, Development, and Hunger		
	Poverty	**Development**	**Hunger**
Mainstream approach	Unfulfilled material needs	Linear path—traditional to modern	Not enough food to go around
Critical alternative approach	Unfulfilled material and nonmaterial needs	Diverse paths, locally driven	There is enough food; the problem is distribution and entitlement

ENGAGING WITH THE WORLD

Oxfam Internships in Canada

Are you interested in becoming a volunteer intern at Oxfam? Internship positions at this organization provide a substantive, challenging professional development experience that will expand your understanding of ways to build lasting solutions to global poverty and injustice. Visit www.oxfam.org/en/countries/volunteer-us.

Poverty

Different conceptions of poverty underpin the mainstream and alternative views of development. There is basic agreement on the material aspects of poverty, such as lack of food, clean water, and sanitation, but disagreement on the importance of nonmaterial aspects. Also, key differences emerge in regard to how material needs should be met and, hence, about the goal of development.

Most governments, international organizations (e.g., the IMF and World Bank), and citizens in the West and elsewhere, adhere to the orthodox conception of **poverty**, which refers to a situation where people do not have the money to buy adequate food or satisfy other basic needs and are often classified as un- or underemployed.

Since 1945, this mainstream understanding of poverty based on money has come about as a result of the globalization of Western culture and the attendant expansion of the free market economy. Thus, a community that provides for itself outside monetized cash transactions and wage labor, such as a hunter-gatherer group, is regarded as poor. This meaning of poverty has been almost universalized. Poverty is seen as an economic condition dependent on cash transactions in the marketplace for its eradication. These transactions in turn depend on development defined as economic growth. The same economic yardstick is used to measure all societies and to judge if they merit development assistance.

Poverty has widely been regarded as a characteristic of the third world, and it has a gendered face that realist and liberal perspectives often ignore. By the

Poverty According to the United Nations, poverty is a denial of choices and opportunities, a violation of human dignity. It means lack of basic capacity provided by material possessions or money to participate effectively in society.

mid-1990s, an approach had developed whereby it was seen as incumbent on the developed countries to help the third world eradicate poverty. As studies show that women and children are the most severely impacted by the consequences of poverty, development economists are paying more attention to female poverty and women's roles in economic development. The solution advocated to overcome global poverty is the further integration of the global economy (C. Thomas 2000) and of women into this process (Pearson 2000; H. Weber 2002). Increasingly, however, as globalization has intensified, poverty defined in such economic terms has come to characterize significant sectors of the population in advanced developed countries such as the United States (see Bello 1994).

But for some, poverty cannot be measured in terms of cash. Critical alternative views of poverty place the emphasis not only on money but also on spiritual values, community ties, and the availability of common resources. In traditional subsistence methods, a common strategy for **survival** is provision for oneself and one's family via **community**-regulated access to common water, land, and food. The work of the UN Development Programme (UNDP) since the early 1990s is significant here for distinguishing between income poverty (a material condition) and human poverty (encompassing human dignity, opportunity, and choices).

The issue of poverty and the challenge of poverty alleviation moved up the global political agenda at the close of the twentieth century, as evidenced by the UN's Millennium Development Goals. World Bank figures for the 1990s showed a global improvement in reducing the number of people living on less than $1 a day (its orthodox measurement of extreme poverty, changed later to $1.25). Despite this improvement, the picture was uneven. In sub-Saharan Africa, the situation deteriorated, and elsewhere, such as the Russian Federation, the Commonwealth of Independent States, Latin America and the Caribbean, and some non-oil-producing Middle Eastern states, the picture remained bleak. In 2005, the World Bank stated that almost half the world—more than 3 billion people—lived below the poverty line. On a positive note, though, the world met the Millennium Development Goal target of halving global poverty. The number of people living on less than $1.25 has been reduced from 1.9 billion in 1990 to 836 million in 2015. However, the target of halving the proportion of people suffering from hunger was missed. Another narrow miss was the goal of achieving universal primary education. Enrollment increased from 83 percent in 2000 to 91 percent in 2015.

Survival In this context, it is the survival of the person by the provision of adequate food, clean water, clothing, shelter, medical care, and protection from violence and crime.

Community A human association in which members share common symbols and wish to cooperate to realize common objectives.

> **WHAT'S YOUR WORLDVIEW?**
>
> *The poorest 1.3 billion are living below the $1.25 per day global extreme poverty line and over 800 million are going hungry. With all our technology, 750 million lack access to clean water. We can close these gaps but they persist. What choices could you make that might help address these conditions?*

Development

Having considered the orthodox and critical alternative views of poverty, we now turn to an examination of the important topic of development. This examination will be conducted in three main parts. The first part starts by examining the orthodox view of development and then proceeds to an assessment of its effect on postwar development in the third world. The second part examines the critical alternative view of development and its application to subjects such as empowerment and democracy. In the third part, we consider the ways the orthodox approach to development has responded to some of the criticisms made of it by the critical alternative approach.

When we consider the topic of **development**, it is important to realize that all conceptions of development necessarily reflect a particular set of social and political values. Since World War II, the dominant understanding—favored by the majority of governments and multilateral lending agencies—has been **modernization theory**, a theory that considers development synonymous with economic growth within the context of a free market international economy. Economic growth is identified as necessary for combating poverty, defined as the inability of people to meet their basic material needs through cash transactions. This is reflected in the influential reports of the World Bank, where countries are categorized according to their income. Countries that have lower national incomes per capita are regarded as less developed than those with higher incomes, and they are perceived as being in need of increased integration into the global marketplace.

As the wave of decolonization swept the world in the 1960s and early 1970s, an alternative view of development has emerged from a few governments, UN agencies, grassroots movements, NGOs, and some academics. Their concerns have centered broadly on entitlement and distribution. Poverty is identified as the inability to provide for the material needs of oneself and one's family by subsistence or cash transactions and by the absence of an environment conducive to human well-being broadly conceived in spiritual and community terms. These voices of opposition are growing significantly louder as ideas polarize following the apparent universal triumph of economic liberalism at the end of the Cold War. The language of opposition is changing to incorporate matters of democracy such as political empowerment, participation, meaningful self-determination for the majority, protection of the commons, and an emphasis on growth that benefits the poor. The fundamental differences between the orthodox and the alternative views of development can be seen in Table 9.2 and are supplemented by this chapter's Case Study, which illustrates the impact of ideas about development from the contemporary coffee-producing sector. In the following two sections, we will examine how the orthodox view of development has been applied at a global level and assess what measure of success it has achieved.

Post-1945 International Economic Liberalism and the Orthodox Development Model

During World War II, there was a strong belief among the Allied powers that the protectionist trade policies of the 1930s had contributed significantly to the outbreak of the war. As we learned in Chapter 8, even before World War II had ended, the United States and the United Kingdom drew up plans for the creation of a stable postwar international order. Providing the institutional bases were the United Nations (UN), its affiliates the International Monetary Fund (IMF) and the World Bank Group, plus the General Agreement on Tariffs and Trade (GATT).

Development In the orthodox view, top-down; reliance on "expert knowledge," usually Western and definitely external; large capital investments in large projects; advanced technology; expansion of the private sphere. In the alternative view, bottom-up; participatory; reliance on appropriate (often local) knowledge and technology; small investments in small-scale projects; protection of the commons.

Modernization theory A theory that considers development synonymous with economic growth within the context of a free market international economy.

TABLE 9.2	**Development: A Contested Concept**

The Orthodox View	The Alternative View
Poverty: A situation suffered by people who do not have the *money to buy food* and satisfy other *basic material needs*.	**Poverty:** A situation suffered by people who are not able to meet their *material and nonmaterial needs* through their own effort.
Purpose: Transformation of traditional subsistence economies defined as "backward" into industrial, commodified economies defined as "modern." Production of surplus. Individuals sell their labor for money, rather than producing to meet their family's needs.	**Purpose:** Creation of human well-being through sustainable societies in social, cultural, political, and economic terms.
Core ideas and assumptions: The possibility of unlimited economic growth in a free market system. Economies would reach a "takeoff" point, and thereafter, wealth would trickle down to those at the bottom. Superiority of the Western model and knowledge. Belief that the process would ultimately benefit everyone. Domination, exploitation of nature.	**Core ideas and assumptions:** Sufficiency. The inherent value of nature, cultural diversity, and the community-controlled commons (water, land, air, forest). Human activity in balance with nature. Self-reliance. Democratic inclusion, participation: for example, a voice for marginalized groups such as women and indigenous groups. Local control.
Measurement: Economic growth; gross domestic product (GDP) per capita; industrialization, including of agriculture.	**Measurement:** Fulfillment of basic material and nonmaterial human needs of everyone; condition of the natural environment; political empowerment of marginalized.
Process: Top-down; reliance on "expert knowledge," usually Western and definitely external; large capital investments in large projects; advanced technology; expansion of the private sphere.	**Process:** Bottom-up; participatory; reliance on appropriate (often local) knowledge and technology; small investments in small-scale projects; protection of the commons.

The latter three provided the foundations of a liberal international economic order based on the pursuit of free trade but allowing an appropriate role for state intervention in the market in support of national security and national and global stability (Rapley 1996). This has been called **embedded liberalism**. Because the decision-making procedures of these international economic institutions favored a small group of developed Western states, their relationship with the United Nations, which in the General Assembly has more democratic procedures, has not always been an easy one.

In the early postwar years, reconstruction of previously developed states took priority over assisting developing states. This reconstruction process really took off in the context of the Cold War, with the transfer of huge sums of money from the United States to Europe in the form of bilateral aid from the Marshall Plan of 1947. In the 1950s and 1960s, as decolonization progressed and developing countries gained power in the UN General Assembly, the focus of the World Bank and the UN system generally shifted to the perceived needs of developing countries. The United States was heavily involved as the most important funder of the World Bank and the United Nations and also in a bilateral capacity.

There was a widespread belief in the developed Western countries, among the managers of the major multilateral institutions, and throughout the UN system,

Embedded liberalism A liberal international economic order based on the pursuit of free trade but allowing an appropriate role for state intervention in the market in support of national security and national and global stability.

Ideas and Development in the Contemporary Coffee-Producing Sector

Contemporary debate on the coffee sector provides a graphic example of competing ideas and values concerning development, and it has relevance far beyond coffee. The impact of commodity price volatility and a long-term decline in terms of trade of primary products has profound effects on the livelihoods of millions of rural householders in the poorest countries. In the case of coffee, about 25 million small farmers in more than fifty countries depend directly on coffee production. During the 1980s, export production increased in poor countries, fueled significantly by policy advice from the World Bank and International Monetary Fund (IMF) that hard-currency earnings had to be boosted through increased commodity exports to pay off spiraling third world debt. Oversupply since the early 1980s resulted in a decline of about 70 percent in nominal coffee prices, with prices reaching a thirty-year low in 2001. The impact on livelihoods of smallholder peasant farmers and plantation workers was devastating. At the eleventh World Coffee Conference in Salvador da Bahia in September 2005, twelve groups representing peasant farmers and workers launched an alternative approach to coffee production in the Salvador Declaration:

For a truly sustainable coffee sector, all who take part in coffee production must share its wealth: small-scale producers, permanent and seasonal rural workers, industry and retail workers. Many say that the solutions to the crisis are only associated with methods of production, including increased investment in substitutes for local coffee varieties, use of toxic fertilisers and pesticides, and mechanization—all aimed at greater productivity. This vision . . . allows for the consolidation of production and marketing by a small group of companies that do not practise social responsibility but make decisions that impact millions of people while they reap the lion's share of the benefits of the trade. This vision is not sustainable. . . .

Real sustainability of the coffee sector should not be viewed through an economic lens alone but must include ethical and political perspectives.

From an ethical perspective, the citizenship rights of people who participate in wealth generation must be guaranteed. Those rights are: stability of prices; recognition of efforts to protect the rural landscape and biological diversity by improving cultivation, harvest, and post harvesting practices; and recognition of the basic rights of rural workers, including the fundamental rights of association and collective bargaining, particularly for seasonal rural workers . . .

From a political perspective, . . . governments [must] agree to and implement public policies that guarantee the rights of coffee producers and rural workers. It should be possible to develop a sustainable model based on food security and sovereignty.

In conclusion, we expect the World Coffee Conference to acknowledge . . . the issue of sustainability from the perspective of all actors involved in the coffee chain and sanction space for direct representation by small-scale farmers and rural workers organisations . . . (and) seek to establish the basis for fair trade between nations.

Oxfam 2006, pp. 11–12.

Fair trade NGOs seek to get a fair price for producers of tea, coffee, cocoa, and other food products grown in the developing world. However, companies that sell fair trade–certified food might be doing much better than "fair." In 2014, imports of Fair Trade Certified produce to the United States rose by 26 percent; Whole Foods Market purchases 75 percent of this produce to sell in its stores. Is this a good way to close the poverty gap?

For Discussion

1. Do ethics matter in most economic development stories? Why or why not?
2. Are you willing to pay more for a cup of coffee if you know the coffee farmers were paid a fair wage? Why or why not?
3. How do we all benefit if those producing valuable commodities are paid well and live in stable and free countries?
4. Sustainable development means considering the needs of future generations when we make choices today. Why is it so hard to develop this foresight?

that third world states were economically backward and needed to be "developed." Western-educated elites in those countries believed this process would require intervention in their economies. In the context of independence movements, the development imperative came to be shared by many citizens in the third world. The underlying assumption was that the Western lifestyle and mode of economic organization were superior and should be universally aspired to.

The Cold War provided a context in which there was a competition between the West and the Eastern bloc to win markets in the third world. The United States believed that the path of liberal economic growth would result in development and that development would result in a global capitalist system, which favors the United States. The USSR, by contrast, attempted to sell its centralized economic system as the most rapid means for the newly independent states to achieve industrialization and development. Unfortunately for the Soviet government, because of its own food-supply and consumer-goods production problems, the country's material foreign assistance was usually limited to military equipment.

The majority of third world states were born into and accepted a place within the Western, capitalist orbit, primarily because of preexisting economic ties with their former colonial occupiers, but a few, either by choice or lack of options, ended up in the socialist camp. Yet in the early postwar and postcolonial decades, all newly independent states favored an important role for the state in development.

With the ending of the Cold War and the collapse of the Eastern bloc after 1989, this neoliberal economic and political philosophy came to dominate development thinking across the globe. The championing of unadulterated liberal economic values played an important role in accelerating the globalization process, representing an important ideological shift. The embedded liberalism of the early postwar decades gave way to the neoclassical economic policies that favored a minimalist state and an enhanced role for the market: the Washington Consensus. The belief was that global welfare would be maximized by the **liberalization** of trade, finance, and investment and by the restructuring of national economies to provide an enabling environment for capital. Such policies would also ideally ensure the repayment of debt. The former Eastern bloc countries were now seen to be in transition from centrally planned to market economies, and throughout the third world, the role of government was reduced and the market given the role of major engine of growth and associated development. This approach was presented as common sense, with the attendant idea that "There Is No Alternative," or TINA (C. Thomas 2000). It informed the strategies of the IMF and World Bank, and, importantly, through the Uruguay Round of trade discussions carried out under the auspices of GATT, it shaped the World Trade Organization (WTO).

By the end of the 1990s, the G7 (later the G8, when Russia joined in 1996) and associated international financial institutions were championing a slightly modified version of the neoliberal economic orthodoxy, labeled the **post–Washington Consensus**, which stressed growth benefiting the poor and poverty reduction based on institutional strength, continued domestic policy reform, and growth through trade liberalization. Henceforth, locally owned national poverty-reduction

Liberalization Government policies that reduce the role of the state in the economy, such as the dismantling of trade tariffs and barriers, the deregulation and opening of the financial sector to foreign investors, and the privatization of state enterprises.

Post–Washington Consensus A slightly modified version of the Washington Consensus promoting economic growth through trade liberalization coupled with pro-poor growth and poverty-reduction policies.

Regional diversity Each region of the world has experienced economic development differently based on traditions, culture, historical development, and even geographic location.

strategy (PRS) papers would be the focus for funding (Cammack 2002). These papers quickly became the litmus test for funding from an increasingly integrated lineup of global financial institutions and donors.

The Post-1945 International Economic Order: Results

There has been an explosive widening of the gap between the rich and the poor since 1945 compared with previous history. Nevertheless, there have been major gains for developing countries since 1945 as measured by the orthodox criteria of economic growth, GDP per capita, and industrialization. A striking feature of both is the marked **regional diversity**. The East Asian experience has been generally positive throughout this period, but not so for Africa. China has been strong since the early 1980s, and India has fared better since the late 1980s.

In the 1990s, the picture was far from positive. The UNDP reports "no fewer than 100 countries—all developing or in transition—have experienced serious economic decline over the past three decades. As a result, per capita income in these 100 countries is lower than it was 10, 20, even 30 years ago" (UN Development Programme 1998, 37). Moreover, the 1990s saw twenty-one countries experience decade-long declines in social and economic indicators compared with only four in the 1980s (UN Development Programme 2003). Financial crises spread across the globe and indicated marked reversals in Mexico, the East Asian states, Brazil, and Russia. The African continent looked increasingly excluded from any economic benefits of globalization, and thirty-three countries there ended the 1990s more heavily indebted than they had been two decades earlier (Easterly 2002). By the end of the century, not a single former second or third world country had joined the ranks of the first world in a solid sense. Significant growth occurred in a handful of countries, such as China, India, and Mexico—the new globalizers—but the benefits were not well distributed within those countries. Despite significant improvements in global social indicators like adult literacy, access to safe water, and infant mortality rates, global deprivation continues. This is illustrated vividly in Figure 9.1.

Having outlined the broad development achievements and failures of the postwar international economic order, we will now evaluate these from two different development perspectives: a mainstream orthodox view and a critical alternative view.

Economic Development: Orthodox and Alternative Evaluations

The orthodox liberal assessment of the past sixty years of development suggests states that have integrated most deeply into the global economy through trade liberalization have grown the fastest, and it praises these "new globalizers." It acknowledges that neoliberal economic policy has resulted in greater inequalities

Goals and Targets	Africa		Asia				Oceania	Latin America and the Caribbean	Caucasus and Central Asia
	Northern	Sub-Saharan	Eastern	South-Eastern	Southern	Western			

GOAL 1 | Eradicate extreme poverty and hunger

Reduce extreme poverty by half	low poverty	very high poverty	low poverty	moderate poverty	high poverty	low poverty	—	low poverty	low poverty
Productive and decent employment	large deficit	very large deficit	moderate deficit	large deficit	large deficit	large deficit	very large deficit	moderate deficit	small deficit
Reduce hunger by half	low hunger	high hunger	moderate hunger	moderate hunger	high hunger	moderate hunger	moderate hunger	moderate hunger	moderate hunger

GOAL 2 | Achieve universal primary education

Universal primary schooling	high enrolment	moderate enrolment	high enrolment	high enrolment	high enrolment	high enrolment	high enrolment	high enrolment	high enrolment

GOAL 3 | Promote gender equality and empower women

Equal girls' enrolment in primary school	close to parity	close to parity	parity	parity	parity	close to parity	close to parity	parity	parity
Women's share of paid employment	low share	medium share	high share	medium share	low share	low share	medium share	high share	high share
Women's equal representation in national parliaments	moderate representation	moderate representation	moderate representation	low representation	low representation	low representation	very low representation	moderate representation	low representation

GOAL 4 | Reduce child mortality

Reduce mortality of under-five-year-olds by two thirds	low mortality	high mortality	low mortality	low mortality	moderate mortality	low mortality	moderate mortality	low mortality	low mortality

GOAL 5 | Improve maternal health

Reduce maternal mortality by three quarters	low mortality	high mortality	low mortality	moderate mortality	moderate mortality	low mortality	moderate mortality	low mortality	low mortality
Access to reproductive health	moderate access	low access	high access	moderate access	moderate access	moderate access	low access	high access	moderate access

GOAL 6 | Combat HIV/AIDS, malaria and other diseases

Halt and begin to reverse the spread of HIV/AIDS	low incidence	high incidence	low incidence	low incidence	low incidence	low incidence	low incidence	low incidence	low incidence
Halt and reverse the spread of tuberculosis	low mortality	high mortality	low mortality	moderate mortality	moderate mortality	low mortality	moderate mortality	low mortality	moderate mortality

GOAL 7 | Ensure environmental sustainability

Halve proportion of population without improved drinking water	high coverage	low coverage	high coverage	high coverage	high coverage	high coverage	low coverage	high coverage	moderate coverage
Halve proportion of population without sanitation	moderate coverage	very low coverage	moderate coverage	low coverage	very low coverage	high coverage	very low coverage	moderate coverage	high coverage
Improve the lives of slum-dwellers	low proportion of slum-dwellers	very high proportion of slum-dwellers	moderate proportion of slum-dwellers	moderate proportion of slum-dwellers	moderate proportion of slum-dwellers	moderate proportion of slum-dwellers	moderate proportion of slum-dwellers	moderate proportion of slum-dwellers	—

GOAL 8 | Develop a global partnership for development

Internet users	moderate usage	low usage	high usage	moderate usage	low usage	high usage	low usage	high usage	high usage

The progress chart operates on two levels. The text in each box indicates the present level of development. The colours show progress made towards the target according to the legend below:

■ Target met or excellent progress.
■ Good progress.
□ Fair progress.

■ Poor progress or deterioration.
▨ Missing or insufficient data.

For the regional groupings and country data, see mdgs.un.org. Country experiences in each region may differ significantly from the regional average. Due to new data and revised methodologies, this Progress Chart is not comparable with previous versions.

Sources: United Nations, based on data and estimates provided by: Food and Agriculture Organization of the United Nations; Inter-Parliamentary Union; International Labour Organization; International Telecommunication Union; UNAIDS; UNESCO; UN-Habitat; UNICEF; UN Population Division; World Bank; World Health Organization - based on statistics available as of June 2015.

Compiled by the Statistics Division, Department of Economic and Social Affairs, United Nations.

Figure 9.1 2015 Progress Chart for UN Millennium Development Goals.

within and between states but regards inequality positively as a spur to competition and the entrepreneurial spirit.

It was clear at least from the late 1970s that "trickle-down" (the idea that overall economic growth as measured by increases in the GDP would automatically bring benefits for the poorer classes) had not worked. Despite impressive rates of growth in GDP per capita enjoyed by some developing countries, this success was not reflected in their societies at large, and while a minority became substantially wealthier, the mass of the population saw no significant change. For some bankers in multilateral organizations and conservative politicians in rich countries, the even greater polarization in wealth evident in recent decades is not regarded as a problem as long as the social and political discontent the inequality creates is not so extensive as to potentially derail implementation of the liberalization project itself. This discontent will be alleviated by the development of national poverty-reduction strategies (PRSs), which it is claimed put countries and their peoples in the driver's seat of development policy, thus empowering the local community and ensuring a better distribution of benefits.

Advocates of a critical alternative approach emphasize the pattern of distribution of gains within global society and within individual states rather than growth. They believe that the economic liberalism that underpins the process of globalization has resulted, and continues to result, in growing economic differentiation between and within countries and that this is problematic. Moreover, they note that this trend has been evident during the very period when key global actors have been committed to promoting development worldwide and, indeed, when there were fairly continuous world economic growth rates and positive rates of GDP growth per capita (Brown and Kane 1995; see Table 9.3).

Dependency theorists such as Andre Gunder Frank (1967) regard the increasing gap between rich and poor as inevitable and undesirable. These theorists stressed how the periphery, or third world, was actively underdeveloped by activities that promoted the growth in wealth of the core Western countries and of elites in the periphery.

At the beginning of the twenty-first century, however, exponents of a critical alternative—in contrast to their orthodox colleagues—question the value of national PRSs, arguing that while a new focus on issues such as health and education is important, the more fundamental issue of possible links between Washington Consensus policies and poverty creation is ignored.

The orthodox and alternative evaluations are based on different values, and they are measuring different things. Glyn Roberts's words are pertinent: "GNP growth statistics might mean a good deal to an economist or to a maharajah, but they do not tell us a thing about the quality of life in a Third World fishing village" (1984, 6).

A Critical Alternative View of Development

Since the early 1970s, there have been numerous efforts to stimulate debate about development and to highlight its contested nature. Critical alternative

| TABLE 9.3 | Growth of World Output, 2007–2015 |

Annual percentage change	2007–2010[a]	2011	2012[b]	2013[c]	2014[c]	2015[c]	Change from WESP 2013 forecast[d]	
							2013	2014
World	**1.8**	**2.8**	**2.4**	**2.1**	**3.0**	**3.3**	**−0.3**	**−0.2**
Developed economies	**0.3**	**1.5**	**1.3**	**1.0**	**1.9**	**2.4**	**−0.1**	**−0.1**
United States of America	0.3	1.8	2.8	1.6	2.5	3.2	−0.1	−0.2
Japan	0.0	−0.6	1.9	1.9	1.5	1.2	1.3	0.7
European Union	0.2	1.7	−0.4	−0.1	1.4	1.9	−0.7	−0.3
EU-15	0.1	1.5	−0.5	−0.1	1.4	1.8	−0.6	−0.2
New EU members	2.0	3.0	0.6	0.5	2.1	2.7	−1.5	−0.8
Euro area	0.2	1.6	−0.7	−0.5	1.1	1.6	−0.8	−0.3
Other European countries	1.1	1.6	1.9	1.7	2.6	2.9	0.2	0.7
Other developed countries	1.6	2.4	2.5	2.0	2.6	2.9	0.0	−0.4
Economies in transition	**2.9**	**4.6**	**3.2**	**2.0**	**3.3**	**4.0**	**−1.6**	**−0.9**
South-Eastern Europe	2.6	1.9	−0.9	1.8	2.6	3.1	0.6	0.0
Commonwealth of Independent States and Georgia	2.9	4.8	3.4	2.0	3.4	4.1	−1.8	−1.0
Russian Federation	2.4	4.3	3.4	1.5	2.9	3.6	−2.1	−1.3
Developing economies	**5.9**	**5.9**	**4.7**	**4.6**	**5.1**	**5.3**	**−0.5**	**−0.5**
Africa	4.8	0.8	5.7	4.0	4.7	5.0	−0.8	−0.4
North Africa	4.6	−6.1	7.2	2.3	3.3	4.3	–	–
East Africa	6.5	6.5	6.0	6.0	6.4	6.4	–	–
Central Africa	4.8	3.9	5.8	4.2	4.8	4.1	–	–
West Africa	6.0	6.1	6.7	6.7	6.9	6.8	–	–
Nigeria	6.9	6.8	6.5	6.5	6.9	6.7	−0.3	−0.3
Southern Africa	3.9	4.0	3.5	3.6	4.2	4.4	–	–
South Africa	2.6	3.5	2.5	2.7	3.3	3.7	−0.4	−0.5
East and South Asia	7.6	7.0	5.5	5.6	5.8	6.0	−0.4	−0.5
East Asia	7.7	7.1	5.9	6.0	6.1	6.1	−0.2	−0.4
China	10.8	9.3	7.7	7.7	7.5	7.3	−0.2	−0.5
South Asia	6.9	6.4	4.2	3.9	4.6	5.1	−1.1	−1.1
India	8.1	7.3	5.1	4.8	5.3	5.7	−1.3	−1.2
Western Asia	4.0	6.9	3.9	3.6	4.3	3.9	0.3	0.2
Latin America and the Caribbean	3.4	4.4	3.0	2.6	3.6	4.1	−1.3	−0.8

Continued

TABLE 9.3 *continued*

Annual percentage change	2007–2010[a]	2011	2012[b]	2013[c]	2014[c]	2015[c]	Change from WESP 2013 forecast[d] 2013	Change from WESP 2013 forecast[d] 2014
South America	4.5	4.6	2.5	3.2	3.4	4.1	−0.8	−1.0
Brazil	4.6	2.7	0.9	2.5	3.0	4.2	−1.5	−1.4
Mexico and Central America	1.4	4.1	4.0	1.5	4.0	4.2	−2.4	−0.6
Mexico	1.2	4.0	3.9	1.2	4.0	4.2	−2.6	−0.6
Caribbean	3.5	2.7	2.8	2.4	3.3	3.8	−1.3	−0.5
By Level of Development								
High-income countries	0.6	1.7	1.5	1.2	2.1	2.5	−0.1	−0.1
Upper-middle-income countries	5.9	5.9	5.1	4.6	5.3	5.4	−0.8	−0.5
Lower-middle-income countries	6.1	5.8	4.4	4.7	5.0	5.4	−0.8	−1.0
Low-income countries	6.1	6.2	6.0	5.7	6.1	6.1	−0.2	0.2
Least developed countries	6.9	3.6	4.9	5.4	5.7	5.7	−0.3	0.2
Memorandum items								
World trade[e]	3.0	6.7	2.9	2.3	4.7	5.2	−2.0	−0.2
World output growth with PPP-based weights	3.0	3.7	3.0	2.9	3.6	4.0	−0.4	−0.4

[a]*Average percentage change.*
[b]*Actual or most recent estimates.*
[c]*Forecast, based in part on Project LINK and baseline projections of the UN/DESA World Economic Forecasting Model.*
[d]*See* World Economic Situation and Prospects 2013 *(United Nations publication, Sales No. E.13.II.C.2).*
[e]*Includes goods and services.*
Source: UN/DESA.
Source: United Nations, World Economic Situation and Prospects 2014. *(New York: 2014), 2. http://www.un.org/en/development/desa/policy/wesp/wesp_current/wesp2014.pdf.*

The Terms of Development

THE CHALLENGE

Can any theory of international relations explain the problems of economic underdevelopment? International relations specialists even have trouble deciding what to call the countries of the world once held in European colonial bondage. *Third world* made sense at one time. The term originated with Alfred Sauvy, a French demographer, who in 1952 compared the economic and political conditions of European colonies with those endured by the Third Estate in France prior to the revolution. The typology was a simple one: first world countries had capitalist free market economies, second world countries in the Soviet bloc and China had centrally planned economies, and third world countries lacked industrial bases and provided raw materials for

THEORY IN PRACTICE   *continued*

export. With the end of the Cold War, this tripartite typology made less sense.

OPTIONS

Until 1989, "third world" provided a less demeaning alternative to terms often found in the political science literature on Africa, Asia, Oceania, and Latin America: *underdeveloped* or *less developed country* (LDC), sometimes called *least developed country* (also LDC). A brief look at a map reveals another problem. The *global South* is another term often used to indicate the former European colonies in Africa, Asia, and Latin America; the other side of this dyad is the *global North*, meant to describe the former colonial occupiers. But not all countries in the global South are poor, and not all countries that were once colonial occupiers—Portugal and Spain, for instance—are rich. Instead, there are pockets of wealth and poverty in both the South and the North.

APPLICATION

There is another problem for theorists. What do we mean by the term *development* itself? The term might mean industrial output and its related exchange of goods and services. If that is the case, then the term implies that industrialization is a proper goal. The problem of global climate change suggests that industrialization, as it has been practiced, is not a good thing (see Chapter 10). Moreover, the term, according to some gender theorists, only considers transactions that can be counted or that rely on an amount

calculated in a currency. This method of accounting can overlook transactions that take place in a barter market or economic activities traditionally done by women: raising crops for household consumption, cutting firewood, caring for children. In a capitalist economy, in Western Europe or the United States, such activities could have a dollar amount attached. For example, the U.S. tax code gives a deduction for the cost of childcare.

Residents play table tennis at the Santa Marta slum in Rio de Janeiro, Brazil. Police and government officials are rooting out gangs and bringing services to these favelas to make the city safer for the 2016 Summer Olympics.

The realist perspective looks at the problems of economic and political underdevelopment, using the standard definitions found in scholarly books: countries are poor because they are poor. Since international politics is a constant struggle for power in conditions of anarchy, then some countries must lose in that struggle. This perspective can help explain the series of internal and transborder wars in central Africa since the late 1980s. Short on their own resources, the neighbors of the Congo tried to destabilize that country to gain access to mineral wealth.

Radical perspectives like Marxism once offered hope for a restructured global system. However, whatever comfort the doctrine once promised, the demise of the Soviet Union ended it. What was left was a theory that outlined the causes and results of political and economic exploitation but proposed an apparently bankrupt solution.

For analysts in the liberal tradition, the policy prescription does not offer much hope either. This tradition tends to recommend that the former colonies integrate themselves into the global economy, perhaps by planting a cash crop for export or by utilizing untapped resources. As we have seen in this chapter, however, countries that borrow money from international financial institutions can get caught in a debt trap if the price for the export commodity declines. This can leave the country economically worse off.

Unfortunately, no matter what they are called—the third world, the global South, the LDCs—for many countries, poverty and hunger prevail.

For Discussion

1. Instead of disagreeing about terminology, should leaders work on comprehensive plans to help the poor of the world?
2. Are there alternative views of development that might challenge the orthodox position?
3. What does a state-centric focus (on states as the primary actor in global politics) overlook?

ideas have been put forward that we can synthesize into an alternative approach. These have originated with various NGOs, grassroots development organizations, individuals, UN organizations, and private foundations. The Nobel Prize committee recognized the alternative approach when in 2006 it gave the Peace Prize to Muhammad Yunus and the microcredit loan institution, Grameen Bank, which he founded in Bangladesh. The Grameen Bank provides credit (in the form of small loans) to the poor without requiring collateral. Disparate **social movements** not directly related to the development agenda have contributed to the flourishing of the alternative viewpoints—for example, the women's movement, the peace movement, movements for democracy, and green movements (C. Thomas 2000). In 1975, the Dag Hammarskjöld Foundation published the noteworthy *What Now? Another Development?* which argued that the process of development should be

> **Social movement** A mode of collective action that challenges ways of life, thinking, dominant norms, and moral codes; seeks answers to global problems; and promotes reform or transformation in political and economic institutions.

- need-oriented (material and nonmaterial);
- endogenous (coming from within a society);
- self-reliant (in terms of human, natural, and cultural resources);
- ecologically sound; and
- based on structural transformations (of economy, society, gender, and power relations).

Since then, various NGOs, such as the World Development Movement, have campaigned for a form of development that incorporates aspects of this alternative approach. Grassroots movements have often grown up around specific issues, such as dams (for example, on the Narmada River in India) or access to common resources (the rubber tappers of the Brazilian Amazon; the Chipko movement, which began as a women's movement to secure trees in the Himalayas). Such campaigns received a great impetus in the 1980s with the growth of the green movement worldwide. The two-year preparatory process before the 1992 UN Conference on Environment and Development (UNCED) in Rio de Janeiro, Brazil, gave indigenous groups, women, children, and other previously voiceless groups a chance to express their views. This momentum has continued, and it has become the norm to hold alternative NGO forums parallel to all major UN conferences.

Democracy, Empowerment, and Development

Democracy is at the heart of the alternative conception of development. Grassroots movements play an important role in challenging entrenched structures of power in formal democratic societies. In the face of increasing globalization, with the further erosion of local community control over daily life and the further extension of the power of the market and **transnational corporations**, people are standing up for their rights as they define them. They are making a case for local control and local empowerment as the heart of development. They are protecting what they identify as the immediate source of their survival—water, forest, and land. They are rejecting the dominant agenda of private and public (government-controlled) spheres and setting an alternative

> **Transnational corporation** A company or business that has affiliates in different countries.

one. Examples include the Chiapas uprising in Mexico (which attempted to bring attention to the needs of indigenous people after NAFTA went into effect) and Indian peasant protests against foreign-owned seed factories. Protests at the annual meetings of the WTO and protests of the IMF and World Bank have become routine since the late 1990s and are indicative of an increasingly widespread discontent with the process of globalization and the distribution of its benefits.

Such protests symbolize the struggle for substantive democracy that communities across the world are working for. In this context, development is about facilitating a community's participation and lead role in deciding what sort of development is appropriate for it; it is not about assuming the desirability of the Western model and its associated values. This alternative conception of development therefore values diversity above universality and is based on a different conception of rights.

These antiglobalization demonstrators dressed as clowns pass by a burning police car in Frankfurt, Germany. Blockupy European anticapitalist activists tried to blockade the new headquarters of the European Central Bank to protest against government austerity and capitalism. Poverty and economic hardships are global conditions—no region of the world is immune to poverty.

For some commentators, national PRSs offer the opportunity—albeit as yet unrealized—for greater community participation in development policy making in the South. If all parties operate in the spirit that was intended, the PRS process could enhance representation and voice for states and peoples in the South, and it offers the best hope available for expanding national ownership of economic policy.

Now that we have looked at the critical alternative view of development, we will look at the way the orthodox view has attempted to respond to the criticisms of the alternative view.

The Orthodoxy Incorporates Criticisms

In the mainstream debate, the focus has shifted from growth to sustainable development. The concept was championed in the late 1980s by the influential Brundtland Commission (officially entitled the World Commission on Environment and Development; see Brundtland et al. 1987) and supported in the 1990s by a series of UN global conferences. Central to the concept of **sustainable development** is the idea that the pursuit of development by the present generation should not be at the expense of future generations. Similarly, when faced with critical NGO voices, the World Bank in 1994 came up with its Operational Policy 4.20 on gender. The latter aimed to "reduce gender disparities and enhance women particularly in the economic development of their countries by integrating gender considerations in its country assistance programs" (www.worldbank.org).

Most recently, incorporating the language of poverty reduction into World Bank and IMF policies includes words like "growth with equity" and "pro-poor

Sustainable development
Development that meets the needs of the present without compromising the ability of future generations to meet their own needs.

growth," which some would argue are nothing more than buzzwords because they underlie macroeconomic policy that remains unchanged. An examination of the contribution of the development orthodoxy to increasing global inequality is not on the agenda. The gendered outcomes of macroeconomic policies are largely ignored.

Despite promises of new funding at the UN Monterrey Conference on Financing for Development in 2002, new transfers of finance from developed to developing countries have been slow in coming; meanwhile, most expected new promises to be made by the G8 during their summit in 2009. In addition to new finance, that summit saw commitments to write off $40 billion of debt owed by the heavily indebted poor countries (HIPCs). However, the commitment was not

TABLE 9.4	Sustainable Development Goals
Goal	**Description**
Goal 1	End poverty in all its forms everywhere.
Goal 2	End hunger, achieve food security and improved nutrition and promote sustainable agriculture.
Goal 3	Ensure healthy lives and promote well-being for all at all ages.
Goal 4	Ensure inclusive and quality education for all and promote lifelong learning.
Goal 5	Achieve gender equality and empower all women and girls.
Goal 6	Ensure access to water and sanitation for all.
Goal 7	Ensure access to affordable, reliable, sustainable and modern energy for all.
Goal 8	Promote inclusive and sustainable economic growth, employment and decent work for all.
Goal 9	Build resilient infrastructure, promote sustainable industrialization and foster innovation.
Goal 10	Reduce inequality within and among countries.
Goal 11	Make cities inclusive, safe, resilient and sustainable.
Goal 12	Ensure sustainable consumption and production patterns.
Goal 13	Take urgent action to combat climate change and its impacts.
Goal 14	Conserve and sustainably use the oceans, seas and marine resources.
Goal 15	Sustainably manage forests, combat desertification, halt and reverse land degradation, halt biodiversity loss.
Goal 16	Promote just, peaceful and inclusive societies.
Goal 17	Revitalize the global partnership for sustainable development.

Source: United Nations Development Programme 2016.

Life in Zimbabwe: Poverty, Hunger, Development, and Politics

BACKGROUND

It is possible the average person in Zimbabwe was not aware of the global economic downturn of 2009. If people in the southern African country did know about the collapse of banks and, according to the IMF, the loss of perhaps 51 million jobs worldwide, this knowledge would not have changed their lives very much. With a 2008 per capita GDP of $200, things could not have gotten much worse.

THE CASE

The previous year had seen an array of problems that few developing countries had seen recently. First, a series of bad harvests had pushed more people than usual to rely on food aid provided mainly by foreign aid agencies, such as the UN's World Food Programme, and some EU countries. In power since 1980, President Robert Mugabe's government had banned aid from Britain because the former colonial power had sought to have Zimbabwe suspended from the Commonwealth, an organization of now-independent former British colonies. Critics of Mugabe's government blame the famine not just on low rainfall but, even more, on the badly planned land reform effort that took land away from the most prosperous farmers and gave it to landless Zimbabweans. Although the Mugabe government called the reform program "Zimbabwe for Zimbabweans," not only people of European descent lost land but also people who were not members of President Mugabe's ethnic group. Resistance to land reform led to riots, as government paramilitary units

In Zimbabwe, a corrupt and inept government tried to reduce prices on basic commodities and left markets with nothing.

forced people from their farms and into illegal squatter camps.

The famine exacerbated preexisting economic problems. Zimbabwe had little to offer for export earnings beyond the agricultural sector, which provided more than 400,000 jobs. When the land reform began, unemployment increased, as did the inflation rate, because the government printed more money to cover its operating expenses. The U.S. CIA *World Factbook* estimates that prior to the currency reform of January 2009, Zimbabwe's annual inflation rate was 11.2 million percent. With the formation of a new government in 2009, the Zimbabwean economy has been on the rebound. GDP grew by more than 5 percent in 2009 and 2011. International and regional banks have released favorable investment reports. However, the amount of resources for public services is very low. This internal economic debacle coincided with the rapid price rise for a barrel of oil. Like many other developing countries, Zimbabwe does not have domestic sources of petroleum products and must import what it needs. In 2016, Robert Mugabe is in charge for his thirty-sixth year, and economic experts suggest that his policies will be as destructive as ever. Those with resources are likely to leave or be looking for an exit.

Many analysts of African affairs say that bad harvests, bad weather, and high oil prices are not to blame for Zimbabwe's troubles. Rather, they assert, President Mugabe himself is to blame for the current situation. Left alone by Great Britain and other countries, the president established his personalist regime that favored his family and other members of his ethnic group and intimidated other ethnic groups in Zimbabwean society. If a person wanted to advance in the country, the person had to be a member of Mugabe's political party, Zimbabwe African National Union–Popular Front (ZANU–PF). Like other parties in the country but unlike political parties in most liberal democracies, it is linked to an ethnic group, but membership in the party was not guaranteed. Parliamentary elections in March 2008 sparked another crisis. When the Movement for Democratic Change (MDC) won more seats than ZANU–PF and Mugabe came in second to MDC's leader Morgan Tsvangirai in the presidential election, people knew that trouble was ahead. Mugabe's supporters violently harassed MDC members, an action that caused

Continued

Life in Zimbabwe: Poverty, Hunger, Development, and Politics *continued*

Tsvangirai to withdraw from the race. (The current government of national unity is a coalition of ZANU–PF and the MDC, and it was formed in February 2009.)

OUTCOME

Given this string of unfortunate internal events, an average Zimbabwean can be forgiven if the failure of banks in Iceland, New York, and London is not a cause for great alarm. If workers at Macy's, Home Depot, or Merrill Lynch lose their jobs, this is not news for a resident of Harare. The subprime mortgage crisis in the United States must sound otherworldly to a person who lives in a galvanized metal shack in a shantytown on the outskirts of Bulawayo.

For Discussion

1. In times of global economic stress, should states with developed economies increase their assistance to states like Zimbabwe?
2. To what extent are Zimbabwe's problems the result of European colonization?
3. Do states have an obligation to help other states even if authoritarian leaders lead those states?

implemented with immediate effect and did not cover all needy countries. The North-South agenda has changed little in the years since the Rio Summit, when sustainable development hit the headlines.

In September 2015, the assembled members of the United Nations adopted a new sustainable development agenda that continues the efforts around the Millennium Development Goals. These seventeen Sustainable Development Goals (see Table 9.4) are to be realized by 2030 and will require global cooperation across public, private, and civil society organizations. Agenda 2030 repeats the call for the eradication of poverty but also includes climate change mitigation as an element of sustainable development.

It is important to note that some parts of the UN family have been genuinely responsive to criticisms of mainstream development. The UN Development Programme is noteworthy for its advocacy of the measurement of development based on life expectancy, adult literacy, and average local purchasing power—the Human Development Index (HDI). The HDI results in a very different assessment of countries' achievements than does the traditional measurement of development based on per capita GDP (A. Thomas et al. 1994, 22). For example, China, Sri Lanka, Poland, and Cuba fare much better under HDI assessments than they do under more orthodox assessments, whereas Saudi Arabia and Kuwait fare much worse.

An Appraisal of the Responses of the Orthodox Approach to Its Critics

In 2000, a series of official + 5 miniconferences were held, such as Rio + 5, Copenhagen + 5, and Beijing + 5, to assess progress in specific areas since the major UN conferences five years earlier. The assessments suggested that the international community had fallen short in its efforts to operationalize conference action plans and to mainstream these concerns in global politics.

Voices of criticism are growing in number and range. Even among supporters of the mainstream approach, voices of disquiet are heard, as increasingly the maldistribution of the benefits of economic liberalism are seen as a threat to local, national, regional, and even global order. Moreover, some regard the social protest that accompanies economic globalization as a potential obstacle to the neoliberal project. Thus, supporters of globalization are keen to temper its most unpopular effects by modification of neoliberal policies. Small but nevertheless important changes are taking place. For example, the World Bank has guidelines on the treatment of indigenous peoples, resettlement, the environmental impact of its projects, gender, and disclosure of information. It is implementing social safety nets when pursuing structural-adjustment policies, and it is promoting microcredit as a way to empower women. With the IMF, it developed an HIPC initiative to reduce the debt burden of the poorest states. What is important, however, is whether these guidelines and concerns really inform policy and whether these new policies and facilities result in practical outcomes that have an impact on the fundamental causes of poverty.

The bank has admitted that such changes have been incorporated largely due to the efforts of NGOs, which have monitored its work closely and undertaken vigorous international campaigns to change its general operational processes and the way it funds projects. These campaigns continue. The Bretton Woods Campaign, Fifty Years Is Enough, Jubilee 2000, and, most recently, the Make Poverty History campaign have been particularly significant in calling for open, transparent, and accountable decision-making by global economic institutions, for local involvement in project planning and implementation, and for debt write-off. The U2 Singer Bono and his One Campaign have been very active in advocating for change and supporting all efforts to end poverty. In addition to the NGO pressure for change, pressure is building within the institutional champions of the neoliberal development orthodoxy.

There is a tremendously long way to go in terms of gaining credence for the core values of the alternative model of development in the corridors of power nationally and internationally. Nevertheless, the alternative view has had some noteworthy successes in modifying orthodox development. These may be significant for those whose destinies have until now been largely determined by the attempted universal application of a selective set of local, essentially Western, values.

Hunger

In addressing the topic of global hunger, it is necessary to examine a paradox. Although "the production of food to meet the needs of a burgeoning population has been one of the outstanding global achievements of the post-war period" (International Commission on Peace and Food 1994, 104, 106), in 2015 nearly

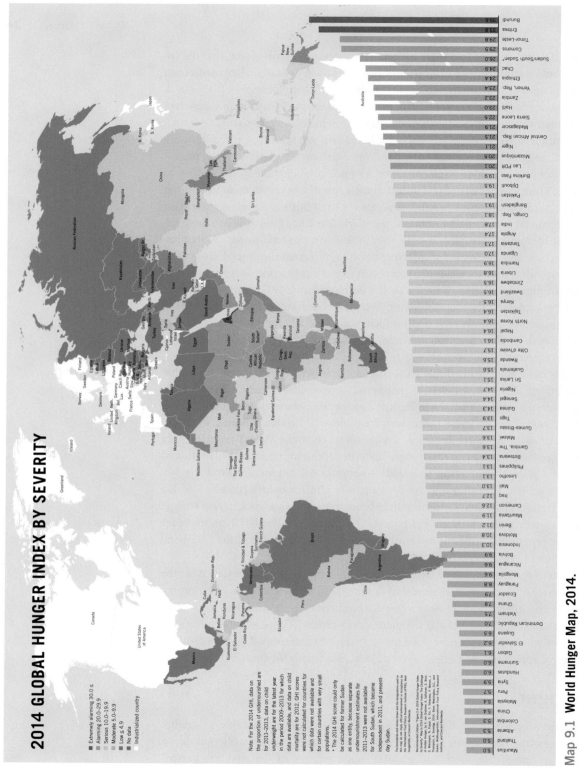

Map 9.1 World Hunger Map, 2014.

What patterns of hunger do you see around the world? What responsibilities might industrial nation-states have toward helping less developed nation-states?

795 million people around the world did not have enough food (World Food Programme). Poor nutrition is the cause of death for nearly 3.1 million children each
year. The current depth of hunger across different world regions is shown in
Map 9.1. Famines may be exceptional phenomena, but why is hunger an ongoing problem?

The Orthodox, Nature-Focused Explanation of Hunger

The orthodox explanation of hunger, first espoused by Thomas Robert Malthus in
his *Essay on the Principle of Population* in 1798, focuses on the relationship between
human population growth and the food supply. It asserts that population growth
naturally outstrips the growth in food production so that a decrease in the per capita
availability of food is inevitable. Eventually, a point is reached at which starvation,
or some other disaster, drastically reduces the human population to a level that can
be sustained by the available food supply. This approach places great stress on
human overpopulation as the cause of the problem and seeks ways to reduce the
fertility of the human race or, rather, that part of the human race which seems to
reproduce faster than the rest—the poor of the third world. Supporters of this approach, such as Paul Ehrlich and Dennis and Donella Meadows (1972), argue that
there are natural limits to population growth—principally that of the carrying capacity of the land—and that when these limits are exceeded, disaster is inevitable.

The available data on the growth of the global human population indicate
that it has quintupled since the early 1800s and is expected to grow from 7.4 billion in 2016 to 10 billion in 2050. More than 50 percent of this increase is expected to occur in seven countries: Bangladesh, Brazil, China, India, Indonesia,

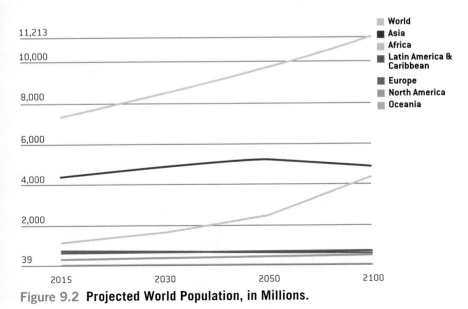

Figure 9.2 **Projected World Population, in Millions.**

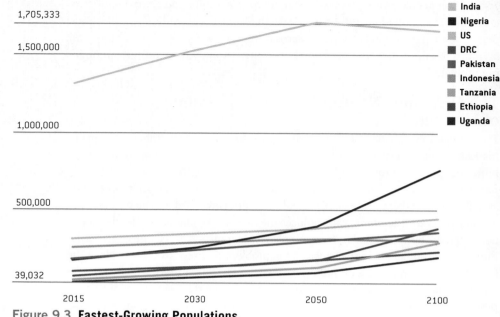

Figure 9.3 **Fastest-Growing Populations.**

TABLE 9.5 World Population, 2015 and 2050 (Projected)

Most Populous Countries, 2015			Most Populous Countries, 2050		
Rank	Country	Population (millions)	Rank	Country	Population (millions)
1	China	1,372	1	India	1,660
2	India	1,314	2	China	1,366
3	United States	321	3	United States	398
4	Indonesia	256	4	Nigeria	397
5	Brazil	205	5	Indonesia	366
6	Pakistan	199	6	Pakistan	344
7	Nigeria	182	7	Brazil	226
8	Bangladesh	160	8	Bangladesh	202
9	Russia	144	9	Democratic Republic of the Congo	194
10	Mexico	127	10	Ethiopia	165

Source: Population Reference Bureau.

Nigeria, and Pakistan. Figure 9.2 illustrates the projected world population growth to 2100 and shows that the rate of world population growth is set to increase. Table 9.5 lists the most populous countries—almost all of which are located in the third world. Figures like these have convinced many adherents of the orthodox approach to hunger that it is essential for third world countries to adhere to strict family-planning policies that one way or another limit their population growth rates. Indeed, in the case of the World Bank, most women-related efforts until very recently were in the area of family planning.

The Entitlement, Society-Focused Explanation of Hunger

Critics of the orthodox approach to hunger and its associated implications argue that it is too simplistic in its analysis and ignores the vital factor of food distribution. It fails to account for the paradox that despite the enormous increase in food production per capita that has occurred over the postwar period (largely due to the development of high-yielding seeds and industrial agricultural techniques), little impact has been made to reduce the huge numbers of people in the world who experience chronic hunger. For example, the UN Food and Agriculture Organization (FAO) estimates that although there is enough grain alone to provide everyone in the world with 3,600 calories a day (i.e., 1,200 more than the United Nations' recommended minimum daily intake), there are still nearly 795 million hungry people.

Furthermore, critics note that the third world, where the majority of malnourished people are found, produces much of the world's food, whereas those who consume most of it are in the Western world. Meat consumption tends to rise with household wealth, and a third of the world's grain is used to fatten animals. A worrying recent trend is the use of corn grown in the United States to produce green fuel, thus reducing what is available to feed the hungry people overseas. Such evidence leads opponents of the orthodox approach to argue that we need to look much more closely at the social, political, and economic factors that determine how food is distributed and why access to food is achieved by some and denied to others.

A convincing alternative to the orthodox explanation of hunger was set forward in Amartya Sen's pioneering book, *Poverty and Famines: An Essay on Entitlement and Deprivation* (1981). From the results of his empirical research work on the causes of famines, Sen concluded that hunger is due to people not having enough to

> ### WHAT'S YOUR WORLDVIEW?
>
> *The One Campaign and NGOs like Oxfam have worked hard to end global poverty and hunger, so why do poverty and hunger persist? What appear to be the root causes? The best solutions?*

In parts of the developing world such as Kenya, enough food is available. However, the increased global demand for biofuels has started to push farmers to grow crops like corn that they can sell in that emerging market for a higher price.

eat rather than there not being enough to eat. He discovered that famines have frequently occurred when there has been no significant reduction in the level of per capita food availability and, furthermore, that some famines have occurred during years of peak food availability. For example, the Bangladesh famine of 1974 occurred in a year of peak food availability, yet because floods wiped out the normal employment opportunities of rural laborers, the latter were left with no money to purchase the food that was readily available, and many of them starved.

Therefore, what determines whether people starve or eat is not so much the amount of food available to them but whether or not they can establish an entitlement to that food. If there is plenty of food available in the stores, but a family does not have the money to purchase that food and does not have the means of growing their own food, then they are likely to starve. With the globalization of the market and the associated curtailing of subsistence agriculture, the predominant method of establishing an entitlement to food has become the exercise of purchasing power, and consequently, those without purchasing power will go hungry amid a world of plenty (Sen 1981, 1983).

Sen's focus on entitlement enables him to identify two groups who are particularly at risk of losing their access to food: landless rural laborers, such as in South Asia and Latin America, and pastoralists, such as in sub-Saharan Africa. The landless rural laborers are especially at risk because no arrangements are in place to protect their access to food. In the traditional peasant economy, there is some **security** of land ownership, and therefore, rural laborers have the possibility of growing their own food. However, this possibility is lost in the early stages of the transition to capitalist agriculture, when the laborers are obliged to sell their land and join the wage-based economy. Unlike in the developed countries of the West, no social security arrangements are in place to ensure that their access to

Security The measures taken by states to ensure the safety of their citizens, the protection of their way of life, and the survival of their nation-state. Security can also mean the ownership of property that gives an individual the ability to secure the enjoyment or enforcement of a right or a basic human need.

A young boy walks across a flooded street in a temporary housing area in Kabul, Afghanistan. His country is one of the most impoverished nations in Asia. With 36 percent of its population living below the poverty line, Afghanistan is second only to Bangladesh as Asia's poorest country. Many Afghans live under the poverty line in a country devastated by years of fighting that continues daily.

food is maintained. In this context, it is important to note that the IMF/World Bank austerity policies of the 1980s ensured that any welfare arrangements previously enjoyed by vulnerable groups in developing countries were largely removed; therefore, these policies directly contributed to a higher risk of hunger in the third world.

Building on the work of Sen, researcher Susan George in *The Hunger Machine* (Bennett and George 1987, 1–10) details how different groups of people experience unequal levels of access to food. She identifies six factors that are important in determining who goes hungry:

1. The North-South divide between developed and developing countries
2. National policies on how wealth is shared
3. The rural-urban bias
4. Social class
5. Gender
6. Age

One could add to the list two other very important, and often neglected, factors: race and disability. Consequently, a person is more likely to experience hunger if he or she is disabled rather than able-bodied, black rather than white, a child rather than an adult, poor rather than wealthy, a rural dweller rather than a town dweller, and an inhabitant of a developing country rather than an inhabitant of a developed country.

Globalization and Hunger

It is possible to explain the contemporary occurrence of hunger by reference to the process of globalization. Globalization means that events occurring in one part of the globe can affect, and can be affected by, events occurring in other, distant parts of the globe. Often, as individuals, we remain unaware of our role in this process and its ramifications. When we drink a cup of tea or coffee or eat imported fruit and vegetables, in the developed countries, we tend not to reflect on the changes experienced at the site of production of these cash crops in the developing world. However, it is possible to look at the effect of the establishment of a global system of food production as opposed to a local, national, or regional system. This has been done by David Goodman and Michael Redclift in their book *Refashioning Nature: Food, Ecology, and Culture* (1991), and the closing part of this discussion on hunger is based largely on their findings.

Since 1945, a global food regime has been established, and now in the twenty-first century, we are witnessing an increasingly global organization of food provision and of access to food with transnational corporations playing the major role. Local subsistence producers, who traditionally have produced to meet the needs of their family and community, may now be involved in cash-crop production for a distant market. Alternatively, they may have left the land and become

Much of the agricultural production involves small farmers without modern technology. An unidentified woman filters millet in Malankaka near Maradi in the African country of Mali. Would more technology help produce more food? What other factors prevent the production of food in a country like this?

involved in the process of industrialization. The most important actor in the development and expansion of this global food regime has been the United States, which, at the end of World War II, was producing large food surpluses. These surpluses became cheap food exports and initially were welcomed by the war-ravaged countries of Europe. Many developing countries also welcomed them because the then-prevalent model of development depended on the creation of a pool of cheap wage labor to serve the industrialization process. Hence, to encourage people off the land and away from subsistence production, the incentive to produce for oneself and one's family had to be removed. Cheap imported food provided this incentive, while the resulting low prices paid for domestic subsistence crops made them unattractive to grow; indeed, for those who continued to produce for the local market, such as in Sudan, the consequence has been the production of food at a loss (Bennett and George 1987, 78). Not surprisingly, the production of subsistence crops for local consumption drastically declined in the postwar period in the developing world.

The postwar, U.S.-dominated, global food regime has therefore had a number of unforeseen consequences. First, the domestic production of food staples in developing countries was disrupted. Second, consumer preferences in the importing countries changed in line with the cheap imports, and export markets for American-produced food were created. This created a dependency on food aid (Goodman and Redclift 1991, 123). Third, there has been a stress on cash-crop production. The result has been the drive toward export-oriented, large-scale, intensively mechanized agriculture in the South. Technical progress resulted in the green revolution, with massively increased yields produced from high-yield seeds and industrialized agricultural practices. In some respects, this has been an important achievement. However, the cost has been millions of peasants thrown off the land because their labor was no longer required; the greater concentration of land was in a smaller number of hands; and there was environmental damage from pesticides, fertilizers, and inappropriate irrigation techniques.

Since the early 1980s, the reform of national economies via structural-adjustment policies has further undermined the national organization of agriculture and given a further boost to the activities of agribusiness. The aggressive pursuit of unilateralist trade policies by the United States, such as the invocation of free trade to legitimize opening the Korean agricultural market, has added to this. Global trade liberalization, especially the Uruguay Round's Agreement on Agriculture (the original text of which was drafted by the multinational Cargill's vice president Dan Amstutz; Oxfam 2003, 23), is further eroding local food security and throwing peasant producers and their families off the land. This has fueled resentment in the South about the global rules governing agriculture. In India, disputes over intellectual property rights regarding high-yielding crop seeds have resulted in violent protest by peasant farmers at foreign-owned seed factories. In the North, NGOs have campaigned against the double standards operated by their governments in expecting Southern countries to liberalize their food markets while the Northern countries continue to heavily subsidize and protect their own.

Conclusion

In this chapter, we have seen how poverty, development, and hunger are more than merely domestic political issues. Academic theories of international relations tended to ignore these problems until the mid-1980s, when the third world debt crisis threatened to undermine key parts of the global financial system. Political leaders in the rich countries of the North—and in many cases, the South—acted the way realism predicted: to protect the interests of their own states.

CONTRIBUTORS TO CHAPTER 9: *Caroline Thomas, Steven L. Lamy, and John Masker.*

KEY TERMS

Community, p. 327
Development, p. 328
Embedded
   liberalism, p. 329
Global governance, p. 324
Liberalization, p. 331

Modernization
   theory, p. 328
Post–Washington
   Consensus, p. 331
Poverty, p. 326
Regional diversity, p. 332

Security, p. 348
Social movement, p. 338
Survival, p. 327
Sustainable
   development, p. 339

Transnational
   corporation, p. 338
Washington
   Consensus, p. 324

REVIEW QUESTIONS

1. What does poverty mean?
2. Explain the orthodox approach to development and outline the criteria by which it measures development.
3. Assess the critical alternative model of development.
4. How effectively has the orthodox model of development neutralized the critical alternative view?
5. Compare and contrast the orthodox and alternative explanations of hunger.
6. What are the pros and cons of the global food regime established since World War II?

7. Account for the growing gap between rich and poor states and people after fifty years of official development policies.
8. Use a gendered lens to explore the nature of poverty.
9. Is the recent World Bank focus on poverty reduction evidence of a change of direction by the bank?
10. Which development pathway—the traditional or the alternative—do you regard as more likely to contribute to global peace in the twenty-first century?
11. Are national poverty-reduction strategies contributing to national ownership of development policies in the third world?

For more information, quizzes, case studies, and other study tools, please visit us at **www.oup.com/us/lamy.**

Development Assistance as Foreign Policy Statecraft

EXPECTATIONS

You will be asked to evaluate contending arguments for aid (official development assistance, or ODA) and then make a case supporting ODA and a case against ODA for developing states.

PROCEDURE

Step One

Participants will be divided into three groups and asked to evaluate proposals requesting development assistance with a specific worldview in mind. The groups and their designated worldview are:

1. Western Security Organization: realists who have a competitive view of international relations.
2. European Social Democrats: liberal internationalists favoring multilateral cooperation.
3. World Federalists: modern-day utopians or radical liberals who seek to create a world government based on human-centric values and world law.

Step Two

Your task is to make recommendations on how much and what kind of aid or development assistance should be allocated. You may recommend the following:

A. Project Aid: funds for specific activities such as the construction of roads and irrigation systems.
B. Program Aid: funds that are loaned to correct problems in a country's capital flow. The funds are used to correct balance-of-payment problems or to enable the country to increase its supply of capital either in the form of savings or foreign currency.
C. Technical Assistance: this includes experts and advisers, training or educational programs, and the supply of equipment for projects.
D. Food Aid: food, medicine, and equipment sent to countries to feed the starving or increase the available stocks of food.
E. Specific Aid: to deal with emergency situations (e.g., drought relief, natural disasters).

F. Military Assistance: to maintain order and make certain the country is stable and the government is not at risk because of extreme poverty or radical movements.

Step Three

You must decide on ODA allocations for the following countries:

Country 1 has requested $100 million in aid from the developed donor countries. The country is governed by a weak democratic system. A Marxist party is strong but holds few government positions. The party currently in power was always pro–United States and now is an active participant in U.S.-led multilateral activities. The economy depends heavily on the export of one crop and one mineral. There is little industry. The aid money will be used to improve and extend the road system, improve the dock and port facilities in the country's only port city, and fund agricultural extension projects.

Country 2 has requested $50 million in aid. The country is governed by a socialist party and has strong ties with Europe's more social democratic states. The president of the country often participates in meetings of heads of state of nonaligned nations, and the country's leaders are very active in multilateral organizations. This country has a diversified economy that exports agricultural products, some minerals, and light manufactured goods. The requested aid will be used to improve the national university, send students abroad for advanced college degrees in business management and science, import farm machinery, and purchase high-tech equipment to develop manufacturing in computers and technology related to the environment.

Country 3 has requested $150 million in aid. The country is totally dependent on outside support. It has suffered from a severe drought, and three tribal groups continue to challenge the military government. The country's only resources are uranium and an abundance of cheap labor. Most aid has ended up in the hands of the elites and has not been used to improve the quality of life of most of the population. Recently, the leaders have begun to discuss a possible alliance with Syria and Iran. The aid will be used to develop a comprehensive education system, develop facilities in rural areas, and build a national highway and rail system.

Based on the assumptions of your group's worldview:

1. Rank the three countries in terms of aid priority.
2. Select an appropriate program (e.g., military assistance and drought relief for Country X).
3. Be prepared to defend your choices. Each group will have an opportunity to decide on its priorities and then present them. Each group should also be

prepared to critically review the allocations made by the other groups.

Step Four

As you debate your group's position on these requests, consider the following questions. You may want to ask the other groups to justify their positions by responding to these questions. As you finish the exercise, these three questions may provide a useful debriefing or evaluation of your debate:

1. What is the strongest argument for giving or not giving some form of aid to each country?
2. What assumptions about each country and the international system defined your allocation priorities?
3. Discuss the relative strengths and weaknesses of bilateral and multilateral aid programs. Would you agree with the statement that suggests the complexity of world development problems requires multilateral responses?

10

Environmental Issues

The Black Marble, or the Earth, our very fragile home at night. This is an image of Asia and Australia with some of the brighter lights revealing wildfires in Western Australia. Lights in uninhabited areas include images of fishing boats, gas flaring, lightning, oil drilling, and mining operations.

The "control of nature" is a phrase conceived in arrogance, born of the Neanderthal age of biology and philosophy, when it was supposed that nature exists for the convenience of man.

—RACHEL CARSON

The climate is a common good, belonging to all and meant for all. At the global level, it is a complex system linked to many of the essential conditions for human life.

—POPE FRANCIS

In 2011, *Newsweek* magazine stated that "weather panic" is the new normal. As global temperatures rise, climate scientists predict side effects such as droughts, flooding, and ferocious storms. Many scientists, citizens, and business and government leaders have identified climate change as the greatest challenge to economic and political stability across the world. There is minimal scientific disagreement but plenty of political debate regarding the direct link, but CO_2 emissions are rising by record amounts and that is seen as the source of climate change. Without a doubt, the world's environmental problems have only gotten worse since 1987, when the Brundtland Commission released its UN-sponsored report on the global environment, *Our Common Future*. The report provided the foundation for the 1992 Earth Summit and introduced concepts like sustainable development and foresight capacity that urged leaders and citizens alike to consider the well-being of future generations and the earth when making economic and political decisions.

Despite leadership from former politicians such as Nobel Prize–winner Al Gore, and strong grassroots efforts in some industrial countries to "Reduce, Reuse, and Recycle"—to "Think Globally, Act Locally"—why are other international leaders and many other citizens unwilling to change their lifestyles to respond to urgent challenges like climate change, air and water pollution, and resource scarcity? Why is it so hard to reach agreement when scientific reports clearly confirm the severity of environmental degradation across the globe? Why are some leaders of political and economic organizations rejecting climate science? Although there are no easy answers to these global problems, such questions can at least be understood more

355

After reading and discussing this chapter, you should be able to:

Define key terms of environmental politics and associated scientific information.

Explain connections between globalization and environmental issues.

Describe the features of environmental protection regimes for climate change, global commons, transboundary pollution, and biodiversity.

Describe the problems associated with regime formation in environmental affairs.

Explain the term *free rider* as it applies to environmental issues.

Describe the role of the United Nations in the creation of environmental rules and norms.

Explain the connections among economic development, war, and environmental degradations.

Ecological footprint A measure that demonstrates the load placed on Earth's carrying capacity by individuals or nations. It does this by estimating the area of productive land and water system required to sustain a population at its specified standard of living.

Ecologies The communities of plants and animals that supply raw materials for all living things.

clearly with a careful examination of the facts, along with some perspective afforded us by considering the history and theory of international cooperation involving environmental issues.

Introduction

Although humankind as a whole now appears to be living well above Earth's carrying capacity, the **ecological footprints** of individual states vary to an extraordinary extent. See Map 10.1, which illustrates the size of countries in proportion to their carbon emissions. If everyone were to enjoy the current lifestyle of the developed countries, more than three additional planets would be required.

This situation is rendered all the more unsustainable by the process of globalization, even though the precise relationship between environmental degradation and the overuse of resources, on the one hand, and globalization, on the other, is complex and sometimes contradictory. Globalization has stimulated the relocation of industry to the global South, caused urbanization as people move away from rural areas, and contributed to ever-rising levels of consumption, along with associated emissions of effluents and waste gases. While often generating greater income for poorer countries exporting basic goods to developed-country markets, ever-freer trade can also have adverse environmental consequences by disrupting local **ecologies** (communities of plants and animals), cultural habits, and livelihoods.

However, some analysts believe there is little evidence that globalization has stimulated a "race to the bottom" in environmental standards, and some even argue that growing levels of affluence have brought about local environmental improvements, just as birth rates tend to fall as populations become wealthier. Economists claim that globalization's opening up of markets can increase efficiency and reduce pollution provided that the environmental and social damage associated with production of a good is properly factored into its market price. Similarly, as we will see in this chapter, globalization has promoted the sharing of knowledge and the influential presence of nongovernmental organizations (NGOs) in global environmental politics. Whatever the ecological balance sheet of globalization, the resources on which human beings depend for survival, such as fresh water, a clean atmosphere, and a stable climate, are now under serious threat.

Global problems may need global solutions and pose a fundamental requirement for **global environmental governance**. Yet the history of environmental cooperation demonstrates that local or regional action remains a vital aspect of responses to many problems. One of the defining characteristics of environmental politics is the awareness of such interconnections and of the need to "Think Globally—Act Locally." Nongovernmental organizations have been very active in this respect, as we saw in Chapter 5.

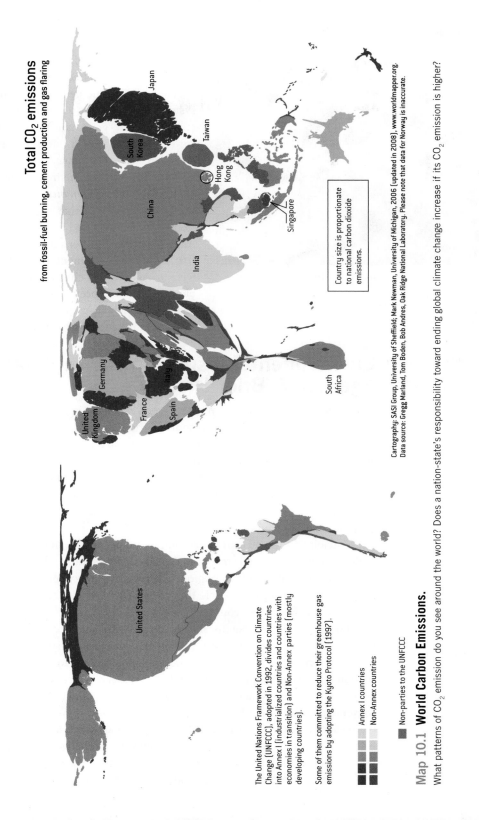

Total CO$_2$ emissions
from fossil-fuel burning, cement production and gas flaring

Japan

South Korea

Taiwan

Hong Kong

China

Singapore

India

Germany

Italy

France

Spain

United Kingdom

South Africa

United States

Country size is proportionate to national carbon dioxide emissions.

The United Nations Framework Convention on Climate Change (UNFCCC), adopted in 1992, divides countries into Annex I (industrialized countries and countries with economies in transition) and Non-Annex parties (mostly developing countries).

Some of them committed to reduce their greenhouse gas emissions by adopting the Kyoto Protocol (1997).

Annex I countries
Non-Annex countries

Non-parties to the UNFCCC

Cartography: SASI Group, University of Sheffield; Mark Newman, University of Michigan, 2006 (updated in 2008), www.worldmapper.org. Data source: Gregg Marland, Tom Boden, Bob Andres, Oak Ridge National Laboratory. Please note that data for Norway is inaccurate.

Map 10.1 **World Carbon Emissions.**

What patterns of CO$_2$ emission do you see around the world? Does a nation-state's responsibility toward ending global climate change increase if its CO$_2$ emission is higher?

357

One of the last frontiers is the Arctic, and demonstrations against drilling are likely to increase. In 2015, Greenpeace led a campaign in London against the Shell Oil Company. Shell recently announced that they are pulling out of drilling efforts in the Alaskan Arctic region.

Despite the global dimensions of environmental change, an effective response still must depend on a fragmented international political system of more than 190 sovereign states. Global environmental governance consequently involves bringing to bear interstate relations, international law, and transnational organizations in addressing shared environmental problems. Using the term *governance*—as distinct from *government*—implies that regulation and control need to be exercised in the absence of a central government, delivering the kinds of service that a world government would provide if it were to exist. In this chapter, we will briefly explore essential concepts employed in regime analysis, which is commonly applied in the study of international governance.

Global environmental governance The performance of global environmental regulative functions, often in the absence of a central government authority. It usually refers to the structure of international agreements and organizations but can also involve governance by the private sector or NGOs.

Environmental Issues on the International Agenda: A Brief History

Before the era of globalization, there were two traditional environmental concerns: conservation of natural resources and damage caused by pollution. No forms of pollution respect international boundaries, and action to mitigate or avert environmental harm sometimes had to involve more than one state. Early international agreements were designed to conserve specific resources, such as fisheries (1867 convention between France and Great Britain) or fur seals (1891, 1892, 1911 conventions between Great Britain, the United States, and Russia). In 1935, the Trail Smelter case demonstrated that reducing transboundary pollution required joint effort and could be accomplished peacefully. In this landmark case, pollutants from a mineral smelter in Canada drifted south and contaminated portions of the U.S. state of Washington. The resulting treaty between the two countries asserted the legal principle that countries are liable for damage that their citizens cause in another country.

There were also numerous, mostly unsuccessful, attempts to regulate exploitation of maritime resources lying beyond national jurisdiction, including several multilateral fisheries commissions. The development of the 1946 International Convention for the Regulation of Whaling (and its International Whaling Commission [IWC]) marked a move away from the goal of the late-nineteenth-century fur seal conventions, which entailed conserving an industry by regulating catches, toward the preservation of the great whales by declaring an international moratorium on whaling. This shift still generates bitter confrontation between NGOs, most IWC members, and the small number of nations—Japan, Norway, and Iceland—that wish to resume commercial whaling and kill what they call "research whales."

After World War II, global economic recovery resulted in damaging pollution to the atmosphere, watercourses, and the sea, notably the Mediterranean, leading to international agreements in the 1950s and 1960s regarding matters such as discharges from oil tankers. These efforts, though, were not the stuff of great power politics. Such "apolitical" matters were the domain of new UN **specialized agencies**, like the Food and Agriculture Organization (FAO), but were hardly central to diplomacy at the UN General Assembly in New York.

However, the salience of environmental issues grew in the 1960s, and in 1968, the UN General Assembly accepted a Swedish proposal for what became the 1972 UN Conference on the Human Environment "to focus governments' attention and public opinion on the importance and urgency of the question." The conference led to the creation of the UN Environment Programme. Yet it was already clear that for the countries of the South, which constituted the majority in the UN General Assembly, environmental questions could not be separated from their demands for development, aid, and the restructuring of international economic relations. This political context surrounded the

Specialized agencies International institutions that have a special relationship with the central system of the United Nations but are constitutionally independent, having their own assessed budgets, executive heads and committees, and assemblies of the representatives of all state members.

TABLE 10.1	**Recent Global Environmental Actions**
1987	Release of the Brundtland Commission report, *Our Common Future*
	Montreal Protocol on Substances that Deplete the Ozone Layer
1988	Establishment of the Intergovernmental Panel on Climate Change (IPCC)
1989	Basel Convention on the Control of Transboundary Movements of Hazardous Wastes and Their Disposal
1992	UN Conference on Environment and Development (UNCED) results in the Rio Declaration on Environment and Development and Agenda 21
	UN Framework Convention on Climate Change (UNFCCC)
	Convention on Biological Diversity
	Commission on Sustainable Development
1997	Kyoto Protocol
2002	World Summit on Sustainable Development
2008	First Commitment Period of Kyoto begins
2009	Copenhagen Accord
2010	Cancun Agreements
2012	Rio+20 UN Conference on Sustainable Development
2015	UN Conference on Climate Change

Sustainable development
Development that meets the needs of the present without compromising the ability of future generations to meet their own needs.

emergence of the concept of **sustainable development** (development that meets the needs of the present without compromising future ability to meet needs). Before the Brundtland Commission formulated this concept in 1987, however, the environment was pushed to the periphery of the international agenda by the global economic downturn of the 1970s and then the onset of the second Cold War, or the end of détente.

Environmental degradation continued nonetheless. Awareness of new forms of transnational pollution, such as sulfur dioxide ("acid") rain, joined existing concerns over point-source pollution (when the pollutant comes from a definite source), followed by a dawning scientific realization that some environmental problems—the thinning of the stratospheric ozone layer and the possibility of climate change—were truly global in scale. The attendant popular concern over such issues and the relaxation of East-West tension created the opportunity for a second great UN conference where the connection between environment and development was explicitly drawn. Although this conference was subject to many subsequent interpretations, its political essence was an accommodation of the environmental concerns of developed states and the development demands of the South.

The 1992 UN Conference on Environment and Development (UNCED), or Earth Summit, raised the profile of the environment as an international issue while concluding international conventions on climate change and the preservation of biodiversity. The event's underlying politics were evidenced in its title: it was a conference on "environment and development," where the most serious arguments concerned aid pledges to finance environmental improvements. The United Nations created a process to review the implementation of the Earth Summit agreements, including meetings of the new Commission on Sustainable Development (CSD) and convening a special session of the UN General Assembly in 1997.

On the tenth anniversary of the UNCED in 2002, the World Summit on Sustainable Development (WSSD) was held in Johannesburg, South Africa. The change of wording indicated how conceptions of environment and development had shifted since the 1970s. Now discussion was embedded in recognition of the importance of globalization and of the dire state of the African continent. Poverty eradication was clearly emphasized along with practical progress in providing clean water, sanitation, and agricultural improvements. One controversial element, however, was what role private–public sector partnerships would play in such provision.

These UN conferences marked the stages by which the environment entered the international political mainstream, but they also reflected underlying changes in the scope and perception of environmental problems. As scientific understanding expanded, it became common, by the 1980s, to speak in terms of global environmental change. This was represented most graphically by the discovery of the ozone hole and the creeping realization that human activities might be dangerously altering the global climate.

Alongside environmental degradation and advances in scientific knowledge, the international politics of the environment has responded to the issue-attention cycle in developed countries, peaking at certain moments and then declining. The causes are complex, and during the 1960s, they reflected the countercultural and radical movements of the time along with wider public reactions to a series of trends and events. The most influential of these was the publication of Rachel Carson's book *Silent Spring* (1962), which powerfully conjoined the conservationist and antipollution agendas by bringing to light the damage inflicted on bird life by industrial pesticides like DDT. Well-publicized environmental disasters, such as the 1959 mercury poisoning at Minamata in Japan and the 1967 wreck of the *Torrey Canyon* oil tanker close to beaches in southwestern England, fed public concern. The failure of established political parties to respond effectively to these issues encouraged the birth of several new high-profile NGOs—Friends of the Earth, Greenpeace, and the World Wildlife Fund for Nature—alongside more established pressure groups such as the U.S. Sierra Club and the British Royal Society for the Protection of Birds. The interest in international environmental action, and most of the NGOs exerting pressure to this end, was an almost exclusively developed-world phenomenon.

In recent years, public alarm over the impact of climate change has propelled environmental issues up the political agenda again. Environmental activists and the public demand international action and governance, but what exactly does this mean?

In seeking natural explanations for the occurrence of natural catastrophes, geologists and other scientists look to the history of Earth, which they divide into two periods. The Holocene period, or the recent 10,000 years of Earth, is considered a period of weather and temperature stability. This is when humans began building civilizations. In the current geologic era, the Anthropocene, the world has been remade by human behavior. The biggest change is the emission of CO_2, which traps heat near the planet and creates more energy in the atmosphere. Climate scientists predict that rising temperatures will have serious side effects, such as deeper droughts, more floods, more moisture in the air, and potentially more serious storms like hurricanes and tornadoes. These conditions are what some now call a period of *weather panic* or global *weather weirding*. According to climate scientists, 2015 was the hottest year globally in recorded history. The more heat, the more problems we can expect with the weather.

UN Secretary-General Ban Ki-moon, President Ollanta Humala of Peru, and President François Hollande of France discuss the costs of climate change. The wealthy countries of the world must decide how they will help developing states with their economies as they cut back on emissions.

We typically think of developing countries when thinking of deforestation, but this is Romania. Poverty forces people to cut down trees in a natural haven in Romania where bears and wolves still reside. The entire area has been threatened by legal and illegal logging.

Kyoto Protocol A global environmental treaty passed in 1997 that set binding targets for thirty-seven industrialized countries and the European community for reducing greenhouse-gas emissions.

Oxfam reported that the number of natural disasters increased from 133 a year in the 1980s to more than 350 a year now. Skeptics argue that there have always been periods of weird weather and extreme events, but scientists argue that these events are becoming severer and more frequent. The scientific community has asked world political leaders to make hard choices and support action in response.

Although in 2009 the UN Framework Convention on Climate Change Conference of Parties failed to replace or extend the **Kyoto Protocol** in 2009, which set targets for reducing environmentally harmful gas emissions, it did result in the Copenhagen Accord. The Accord included a list of national pledges on greenhouse gas reductions (and a pledge for China and India to make improvements in energy efficiency rather than reductions). It was also acknowledged that there was a need to keep temperature rises below 2 degrees centigrade, a need to set up a climate fund to assist developing countries, and a need to work on halting deforestation. These arrangements did not amount to a renewal of the Kyoto Protocol or a new comprehensive climate agreement, but the governments did commit themselves to producing such an agreement by 2015.

The Paris Climate Summit 2015

In late 2015, world leaders gathered in Paris for the UN Conference on Climate Change. At the forefront of the discussions was the topic of greenhouse gas emissions from human activities and that increasingly high levels are driving climate change. Climate change has the greatest impact on the poor and most vulnerable people. Equity plays a central role in the entire climate regime and the climate policies discussed in Paris focused on strategies geared toward poverty alleviation and sustainable development. This latest gathering demonstrated that climate change is truly a global challenge that requires collaboration and coordination at the international level. In order to be effective, the agreement reached in Paris must do the following:

1. Enable states to move forward on their national strategies for carbon emissions reduction, knowing that other states have supported the agreement and will be enacting their own plans.
2. Create a framework for a low carbon economy.
3. Provide financial and scientific support for developing states to pursue low carbon economic activities and adapt to the effects of climate change.
4. Ensure that there is an effective 'global inventory' to assess progress toward climate safety.

TABLE 10.2	Climate Change Facts from the Intergovernmental Panel on Climate Change (IPCC) and the United Nations
Fact One	Average global temperature rose .85 degrees Celsius from 1880 to 2012. How might this relate to food security? For each 1 degree of temperature increase, grain yields decline 5 percent. A warmer climate means less food production.
Fact Two	The warming of oceans, the melting of snow and ice has resulted in the rising of sea levels. A recent study measuring the melting of the Greenland ice sheet will drive up sea levels in coming decades. If the full ice sheet melts, seas will rise about twenty feet.
Fact Three	Global emissions of carbon dioxide have increased by almost 50 percent since 1990. Emissions grew more quickly between the years 2000 and 2010 than in each of the three previous decades.
Fact Four	There are some technological strategies as well as changes in personal behavior that will work to slow the increase in global mean temperature to 2 degrees Celsius above pre-industrial levels.
Fact Five	Responding to climate change involves a two-part strategy: 1) *Mitigation* defined as reducing emissions and stabilizing heat-trapping greenhouse gases; 2) *Adaptation* defined as reducing the vulnerability of individuals to the harmful effects of climate change.

Sources: https://www.ipcc.ch/pdf/assessment-report/ar5/syr/AR5_SYR_FINAL_SPM.pdf, accessed May 5, 2016.

The Environment and International Relations Theory

Academics who study the international relations of the environment try to understand the circumstances under which potentially effective international cooperation can occur. Most scholars have used the concept of regime as the basis for their understanding. Note, for instance, how the defining characteristics of regimes—principles, norms, rules, and decision-making procedures—can be applied to the environmental cases mentioned in this chapter. Those who try to explain the record of environmental regimes tend to adopt a liberal-institutionalist stance, stressing as a key motivating factor the joint gains arising from cooperative solutions to the problem of providing public goods such as a clean atmosphere (see Chapter 3). One significant addition to the regime literature made by scholars of environmental politics points out the importance of scientific knowledge and the roles of NGOs in this area. Whereas orthodox regime approaches assume that behavior is based on the pursuit of power or interest, analysts of international environmental cooperation have noted the independent role played by changes in knowledge (particularly, scientific understanding). This cognitive approach appears in studies of the ways that transnationally organized groups of scientists and policymakers—often referred to as *epistemic communities*—have influenced the development of environmental regimes.

Liberal-institutionalist analysis of regime creation may still be the predominant approach to global environmental change, but it is not the only one. It makes the important assumption that the problem to solve is how to obtain global

State system The regular patterns of interaction between states but without implying any shared values between them. This is distinguished from the view of a "society" of states.

governance in a fragmented system of sovereign states. Marxist writers would reject this formulation (see Chapter 3). For them, the **state system** is part of the problem rather than the solution, and the proper object of study is the way global capitalism produces relationships that are profoundly damaging to the environment. The global spread of neoliberal policies accelerates those features of globalization—consumerism, the relocation of production to the South, and the thoughtless squandering of resources—driving the global ecological crisis (see Chapter 8). Proponents of this view also highlight the incapacity of the state to do anything other than assist such processes. It follows that the international cooperation efforts described here at worst legitimize this state of affairs and at best provide some marginal improvements to the devastation wrought by global capitalism. For example, proponents would point to how free market concepts are now routinely embedded in discussions of sustainable development and how the WTO rules tend to subordinate attempts to provide environmental regulation of genetically modified organisms (GMOs). This argument is part of a broader debate among political theorists concerning whether the state can ever be "greened." The opposing view suggests that when coping with a threat as large and immediate as climate change, state and international cooperation remain the only plausible mechanisms for providing the necessary global governance, and we simply need to do the best we can with existing state and international organizational structures.

Desertification The extreme deterioration of land in arid and dry subhumid areas due to loss of vegetation and soil moisture; it results chiefly from human activities and is influenced by climatic variations. This condition is principally caused by overgrazing, overdrafting of groundwater, and diversion of water from rivers for human consumption and industrial use; all of these processes are fundamentally driven by overpopulation.

With the end of the Cold War, some realist international relations specialists began to apply their ideas about anarchy and war to the study of environmental politics. As a result, they contended that conflict, not cooperation, shaped the issue, and they sought proof of this hypothesis. Largely ignoring examples of cooperation, like the Antarctic Treaty system (see Table 10.3), they argued that environmental change contributes to the incidence of both internal conflict and interstate war, even though the causal connections are complex and involve many factors. It is already evident that **desertification** (the extreme deterioration of land due to loss of vegetation and soil moisture) and the degradation of other vital resources are intimately connected with cycles of poverty, destitution, and war in Africa. But these factors can also be attributed to the effects of European

TABLE 10.3	The Antarctic Treaty Regime
1959	Antarctic Treaty
1972	Convention for the Conservation of Antarctic Seals
1980	Convention on the Conservation of Antarctic Marine Living Resources (CCAMLR)
1988	Convention on the Regulation of Antarctic Mineral Resource Activities (CRAMRA)
1991	Protocol on Environmental Protection to the Antarctic Treaty (Madrid Protocol)

colonization of the continent. However, if we consider such predicted consequences of climate change as mass migrations of populations across international boundaries and acute scarcity of water and other resources, the outlines of potential future conflicts come into sharper focus.

Thus, the more immediate *and* persistent consequence of warfare may be the destruction of **ecosystems** (systems of organisms sharing a habitat) that such conflict causes. For example, during World War I, artillery shelling devastated farmland along the trench lines in northern France and Belgium, creating eerie moonscapes for years after the war. Similarly, in Vietnam, the detrimental environmental effects of U.S. weapons, including the use of the herbicide Agent Orange (a form of the carcinogenic compound dioxin) and the carpet-bombing of wide swaths of jungle and rice paddies, remain visible today. More recently, tank-training exercises in the Mojave Desert of California have increased erosion of the fragile landscape. During both Gulf Wars, fires set at oil wells sent carcinogenic materials aloft to be carried downwind, where people who breathed the air became sick. In addition, the depleted-uranium antitank bullets fired during those wars put radioactive material into the air and soil. Even the less obvious effects of warfare can have unforeseen, negative impacts. A recent lawsuit filed in the U.S. federal courts has charged that U.S. Navy sonar-training exercises can hurt the hearing of migrating whales, causing them to become disoriented.

Recent research suggests that climate change and environmental degradation might be the source of major violence against specific ethnic communities. The violence in Rwanda between Hutus and Tutsis may have been a fight over productive farmland and the killing of African tribesmen in Darfur by Northern Arabs may have been about access to water and other resources. Therefore, existing ethnic tensions may be accentuated by weather events and climate change.

Left out of most discussions about international relations theory and the environment is the **ecotopian** perspective. The **deep ecology** movement, or the **ecocentric** view, represents a radical or transformational perspective. Deep ecologists are purists rejecting the idea of inherent human superiority and giving equal moral weight to all elements of nature. Many of the utopians who seek system transformation have called for an alliance between red (socialist) and green (environmentalist) organizations to address the two overarching political issues of our time: human inequality and environmental destruction.

Deep ecologists lack faith in capitalist systems that are technologically dependent, prone to move toward large centralized corporate control, and protected by undemocratic, elitist political institutions. Strongly opposed to materialism and consumerism, they argue that our throw-away, shop-till-you-drop consumer culture should be replaced by an emphasis on meeting basic human needs. Otherwise, they fear, the environment will be devastated. Ecological and natural laws should help shape morality in human affairs, and the costs of environmental degradation must be considered when policy choices

Ecosystem A system of interdependent living organisms that share the same habitat, functioning together with all of the physical factors of the environment.

Ecotopian Someone who believes in protecting and preserving the environment and promotes progressive political goals that promote environmental sustainability, social justice, and economic well-being.

Deep ecology Often identified with the Norwegian philosopher Arne Naess, the core belief is that the living environment has a right to live and flourish. The "deep" refers to the need to think deeply about the impact of human life on the environment.

Ecocentric Having a nature- or ecology-centered rather than a human-centered set of values.

The "Doomsday" Seed Vault

BACKGROUND

One day in February 2008, like a scene out of a post-apocalyptic science fiction movie, more than 200 invited guests hunkered inside puffy parkas at the official opening of the Svalbard Global Seed Vault. Unfortunately dubbed in news media the "Doomsday Vault," the facility is located on an island over 600 miles north of Norway and not far from the North Pole. There, at the end of a 400-foot tunnel carved into a mountain and isolated from the outside by a series of air locks, governments store as many as 2 billion seeds representing almost 4.5 million species of food plants. It is intended to be the storehouse of last resort for the world's plants.

THE CASE

The seed vault is the idea of an NGO based in Rome, Italy, called the Global Crop Diversity Trust. An affiliate of the Food and Agriculture Organization, the trust administers the facility, which cost more than $9 million. The vault is one response to fears about the long-term effects global warming might have on biodiversity and crop output. It is a repository for samples of food seeds in the event that a temperature increase causes plant extinctions. The location of the tunnel is one sign that the host Norwegian government, which covered the entire cost of construction, and Global Crop Diversity Trust, believe the threat of global warming is very real. It is far above the current high tide mark and well above where mean high tide will be if the Arctic, Antarctic, and Greenland ice sheets all melt.

Billing itself as "A Foundation for Food Security," the Global Crop Diversity Trust gives grants in support of food-plant research and to maintain gene banks in accordance with the goals of the 1983 International Treaty on Plant Genetic Resources for Food and Agriculture and the 1993 Biodiversity Convention. In addition, the trust seeks to maintain vital food products eaten in the developing world such as bananas, sorghum, barley, cassava, lentils, and several varieties of beans.

There seems to be little not to like about the Svalbard Global Seed Vault, aside from the eminent threat of highly negative effects of global warming. However, the Global Crop Diversity Trust website (www.croptrust.org) FAQ section provides some hints about one possible controversy. The site carefully asserts that national governments will deposit seeds and that each government will retain ownership of its seeds. A look at the donors section of the website suggests an explanation for this statement of seed ownership. There among the list of donors, such as EU governments, USAID, the Rockefeller Foundation, and the Bill and Melinda Gates Foundation, are the names of two giants of the agribusiness chemical industry: DuPont and Syngenta AG. Prior to changing its name to Syngenta AG in 2001, the chemical firm was known by several names, including Ciba. Ciba invented both DDT and 2, 4-D. DDT was the villain in Rachel Carson's *Silent Spring*; 2, 4-D is better known as a component of Agent Orange, an herbicide that U.S. forces sprayed in uncounted millions of gallons on Vietnam during the 1960s and early 1970s.

OUTCOME

As we have seen so far in this book, perspective matters when seeking to understand international politics. Some environmental activists resent the fact that agribusiness seems to be trying to exploit global warming by supporting the Global Crop Diversity Trust, especially because the chemical industry bears some of the guilt for causing the greenhouse-gas problem in the first place. However, as Syngenta AG's website indicates, the company is trying to do its best to save biodiversity. Which side is correct? The answer may be buried under a mountain in the permafrost zone at the end of a tunnel 600 miles from the North Pole.

The entrance to the Svalbard Global Seed Vault is located near Longyearbyen on Spitsbergen, Norway.

For Discussion

1. If the goal of the Global Seed Vault is good, does it matter who the donors are?
2. Should the concept of national sovereignty extend to control of the world's seeds?
3. Our reliance on technology and plants resistant to all sorts of natural enemies has increased our vulnerability. Does it make sense for us to return to more natural or organic ways of agriculture?

Regime Theory and the Montreal Protocol

THE CHALLENGE

Academic advocates of international regime theory discussed in this chapter contend that four factors—context, knowledge, interest, and power—can explain why and when countries decide to create a formal commitment in a given issue area. The same four factors also help explain what kinds of restraints countries permit on their behaviors. The evolution of international cooperation to protect the ozone layer provides an excellent case to test this hypothesis. In brief, if there are significant disagreements about the scientific evidence and one or more countries want to limit cooperation, then it is unlikely that other countries will be able to establish an effective international regime.

OPTIONS

The consequences of the thinning of the stratospheric ozone layer include excessive exposure to UVB radiation, resulting in increased rates of skin cancer for human beings and damage to immune systems. Stratospheric ozone depletion arose from a previously unsuspected source—artificial chemicals containing fluorine, chlorine, and bromine that were involved in chemical reaction with ozone molecules at high altitudes. Most significant were the CFCs (chlorofluorocarbons), developed in the 1920s as "safe" inert industrial gases, and which had been blithely produced and used over the next fifty years for a variety of purposes from refrigeration, to air conditioning, and as propellants for hair spray. Despite growing scientific knowledge, there was no universal agreement on the dangers posed by these chemicals, and production and use continued— except, significantly, where the U.S. Congress decided to ban some nonessential uses. This meant that the U.S. chemical industry found itself under a costly obligation to find alternatives. Until a U.S.-based chemical company developed an alternative to the harmful CFC compound, U.S. diplomats blocked serious discussions at the international level. As evidence on the problem began to mount, UNEP acted to convene an international conference in Vienna. It produced a relatively weak "framework convention"—the 1985 Vienna Convention for the Protection of the Ozone Layer—agreeing that international action might be required and that the parties should continue to communicate and to develop and exchange scientific findings. These findings proved to be very persuasive, particularly with the added public impetus provided by the dramatic discovery of the Antarctic ozone hole.

APPLICATION

Within two years, the Montreal Protocol was negotiated. Some analysts point to a change in U.S. negotiating stance as the reason for the rapid passage of the protocol. Why did this change occur? An American chemical giant found a replacement compound for the ozone-depleting CFCs, seemingly confirming part of the regime-creation hypothesis. In the Montreal Protocol, parties agreed to a regime under which the production and trading of CFCs and other ozone-depleting substances would be progressively phased out. The developed countries achieved this for CFCs by 1996, and Meetings of the Parties have continued to work on the elimination of other substances since that time. There was some initial resistance from European chemical producers, but the U.S. side had a real incentive to ensure international agreement because otherwise its chemical industry would remain at a commercial disadvantage. The other problem faced by the negotiators involved the developing countries, which themselves were manufacturing CFC products. As the Indian delegate stated, it was the developed countries' mess and their responsibility to clear it up! Why should developing countries be forced to change over to higher-cost CFC alternatives? There were two responses. The first was an article in the protocol giving the developing countries a period of grace. The second was a fund, set up in 1990, to finance the provision of alternative non-CFC technologies for the developing world.

Illegal production and smuggling of CFCs were evident in the 1990s. This tested the monitoring and compliance systems of the protocol (which included a possible use of trade sanctions against offenders). Nonetheless, the regime has generally proved to be effective and has continually widened its scope of activities to deal with further classes of ozone-depleting chemicals. The damage to the ozone layer will not be repaired until the latter part of the twenty-first century, given the long atmospheric lifetimes of the chemicals involved. However, human behavior has been significantly altered to the extent that the scientific subsidiary body of the Montreal Protocol has been able to report a measurable reduction in the atmospheric concentration of CFCs. Therefore, it seems that the context, knowledge, interest, and power hypothesis is correct.

For Discussion

1. How might the alternative theories we have studied explain the case of CFCs and regime creation?
2. Can you think of examples in which a leader in one environmental issue is a laggard on another?
3. Given the apparent pace of climate change in the polar regions, is the regime-creation process too slow to solve Earth's problems?

WHAT'S YOUR WORLDVIEW?

How do theoretical approaches like constructivism, radical-liberal, ecotopian, and some feminist theories of international relations help us understand environmental problems in ways that traditional theories like realism and liberalism do not?

are made. Following their recommendations would certainly require a significant transformation in our political and economic thinking and in our policy priorities.

Clearly, the environmental degradation caused by wars and the instruments of war is impossible to dismiss yet even more difficult to address; by its very nature, warfare is a breakdown of international cooperation. However, when states are not at war and cooperation *is* a viable option, what does it look like and how does it function? Now that we have explored some of the theories surrounding international environmental cooperation, in the next section we will further discuss global mechanisms—or how states and transnational actors attempt to solve environmental issues through formal agreements and cooperative actions.

The Functions of International Environmental Cooperation

Because environmental issues, such as pollution control, often involve more than one country—or region, or hemisphere—states must establish international governance regimes to regulate these transboundary environmental problems and sustain the global commons. Yet these regimes encompass more than formal agreements between states, although such agreements are very important. Moreover, there are other functions and consequences of international cooperation beyond regime formation, which we will learn about in the following sections.

Transboundary Trade and Pollution Control

When animals, fish, water, or pollution cross national frontiers, the need for international cooperation arises. The regulation of transboundary environmental problems is a long-established function of international cooperation reflected in hundreds of multilateral, regional, and bilateral agreements providing for joint efforts to manage resources and control pollution.

An important example is the 1979 Convention on Long-Range Trans-boundary Air Pollution (LRTAP) and its various protocols. They responded to the growing problem of acidification and acid rain by providing mechanisms to study atmospheric pollution problems in Europe and North America and securing commitments by the states involved to control and reduce their emissions. Another set of multilateral environmental agreements (MEAs) regulates the transboundary movement of hazardous wastes and chemicals in the interest of protecting human health and the environment. These agreements require that when hazardous chemicals and pesticides are traded, the government from whose territory the exports originate shall obtain the "prior informed consent" of the importing country (see Table 10.4).

Controlling, taxing, and even promoting trade have always been some of the more important functions of the state, and trade restrictions can also be used as

TABLE 10.4	Some Environmental Treaties with Weight in International Environmental Law
	Atmospheric Pollution
1985	Convention on Long-Range Transboundary Air Pollution
1988	Protocol Concerning the Control of Emissions of Nitrogen Oxides
1988	Protocol on the Reduction of Sulfur Emissions or Their Transboundary Fluxes
	Stratospheric Ozone Layer
1985	Vienna Convention for the Protection of the Ozone Layer
1987	Montreal Protocol on Substances That Deplete the Ozone Layer
	Hazardous Wastes
1989	Basel Convention on the Control of Transboundary Movements of Hazardous Wastes and Their Disposal
1991	Bamako Convention on the Ban of the Import into Africa and the Control of Transboundary Movement and Management Within Africa of Hazardous Wastes
	Marine Pollution
1969	International Convention on Civil Liability for Oil Pollution Damage
1971	Brussels Convention Relating to Civil Liability in the Field of Maritime Carriage of Nuclear Material
1973–1978	International Convention for the Prevention of Pollution from Ships (MARPOL)
1992	London Convention on the Prevention of Marine Pollution by Dumping Wastes and Other Matter
	Wildlife
1971	Ramsar Convention on Wetlands of International Importance Especially as Waterfowl Habitat
1973	International Convention for the Regulation of Whaling
1973	Convention on International Trade in Endangered Species (CITES)
1979	Bonn Convention on the Conservation of Migratory Species of Wild Animals

an instrument for nature conservation. The 1973 Convention on International Trade in Endangered Species (CITES) does this by attempting to monitor, control, or prohibit international trade in species (or products derived from them) whose continued survival might be put at risk by the effects of such trade. Species at risk are "listed" in three appendixes to the convention. Some 600 animal and 300 plant species currently receive the highest level of protection (a trade ban) through listing in Appendix I. However, decisions on the "up-listing" and "down-listing"

African penguins at Boulders Beach, South Africa. This species is classified as endangered because it is undergoing a very rapid population decline, probably as a result of commercial fisheries and shifts in prey populations. We can save these penguins and other endangered species if we consider their lives when we make choices that are sustainable and consider ecological factors.

of species are sometimes controversial, as in the case of the African elephant or the northern spotted owl, bald eagle, and gray wolf in the United States.

The use of trade penalties and restrictions by MEAs has been a thorny issue whenever the objective of environmental protection has come into conflict with the rules of the GATT/WTO trade regime (see Chapters 5 and 8). Such a problem arose when the international community attempted to address the controversial question of new biotechnology and genetically modified organisms (GMOs). The claims of (primarily American) biotechnology corporations, which had made huge investments in developing GMO seed, pharmaceuticals, and food products, that these innovations had positive environmental and development potential (through reducing pesticide use and increasing crop yields) were met with much resistance. European publics, supermarkets, and some developing countries were very wary of GMO technologies on safety and other grounds, which led to pressure for controls on their transboundary movement and to the negotiation of the Biosafety Protocol to the Convention on Biological Diversity (CBD) in 1992. Signed in 2000, the resulting Cartagena Protocol established an advanced informed agreement procedure between governments to be applied when GMOs are transferred across frontiers for ultimate release into the environment. The criteria to guide decisions on blocking imports reflected a precautionary approach rather than insistence on conclusive scientific evidence of harmfulness. Much of the argument in negotiating the Cartagena Protocol concerned the relationship of these new environmental rules to the

ENGAGING WITH THE WORLD

Worldwide Opportunities on Organic Farms (WWOOF)

WWOOF is an organization that links people who want to volunteer on organic farms with farmers who are looking for volunteer help. Volunteers are paired with a farm anywhere within participating countries. In return for volunteer help, WWOOF hosts offer food, accommodations, and opportunities to learn about organic lifestyles. For more information, check out www.wwoof.net.

requirements of the trade regime and arose from the concern of the United States, and other potential GMO exporters, that the protocol would permit a disguised form of trade protectionism. Whether the WTO trade rules should take precedence over the emerging biosafety rules was debated at length, until the parties agreed to avoid the issue by providing that the two sets of rules should be mutually supportive.

Norm Creation

The development of international environmental law and associated norms of acceptable behavior has been both rapid and innovative over the last thirty years. Some of the norms mentioned earlier are in the form of technical policy concepts that have been widely disseminated and adopted as a result of international discussion. The precautionary principle has gained increasing, but not uncritical, currency (see Table 10.5 for other international environmental laws that affect norm creation). Originally coined by German policymakers, the precautionary principle states that where there is a likelihood of environmental damage, banning an activity should not require full and definitive scientific proof. As we saw in the earlier example of GMOs, the latter has tended to be the requirement in trade law. The norm of "prior informed consent" has also been promoted alongside that of "the polluter pays." In the longer term, one of the key effects of the climate-change regime (dealt with in detail later) may be the dissemination of new approaches to pollution control, such as emissions trading and joint implementation.

The UN Earth Summits were important in establishing environmental norms. The 1972 Stockholm Conference produced its Principle 21, which combines sovereignty over the use of national resources with state responsibility for ensuring that activities within their jurisdiction do not cause external pollution. This should not be confused with Agenda 21, issued by the 1992 Earth Summit.

TABLE 10.5	Principles of International Environmental Law That Affect Norm Creation

State Responsibility to Protect Environment

Preventive Action

Good Neighborliness

Sustainable Development

Precautionary Principle

Polluter Pays

Common, Differentiated Responsibility

A river of trash flows through Port-au-Price, Haiti. Our global consumer society may make any chance to deal with environmental degradation and control of such hazardous waste difficult.

Agenda 21 was a complex, voluntary action plan for sustainable development put forth by the United Nations. Agenda 21 was frequently derided, not least because of its nonbinding character, but this internationally agreed compendium of environmental "best practice" subsequently had a wide impact and remains a point of reference. For example, many local authorities have produced their own Agenda 21s. Under the Aarhus Convention (1998), North American and European governments agreed to guarantee to their publics a number of environmental rights, including the right to obtain environmental information held by governments, to participate in policy decisions, and to have access to judicial processes.

Aid and Capacity Building

Technology transfer The process of sharing skills, knowledge, technologies, methods of manufacturing, and facilities among governments and private actors (e.g., corporations) to ensure that scientific and technological developments are accessible to a wider range of users for application in new products, processes, materials, or services.

Capacity building The provision of funds and technical training to allow developing countries to participate in global environmental governance.

Although not a specific norm of the type dealt with earlier, sustainable development provides a normative framework built on an underlying deal between developed and developing worlds. Frequent North-South arguments about the levels of aid and **technology transfer** that would allow developing countries to achieve sustainable development have ended in disappointment and unfulfilled pledges. In 1991, the UN Environment Programme, UN Development Programme, and the World Bank created the Global Environmental Facility (GEF) as an international mechanism specifically for funding environmental projects in developing countries. Since its founding, the GEF has provided $14.5 billion in grants and organized $74.5 billion in additional financing for nearly 4,000 projects. Most environmental conventions now aim at **capacity building** through arrangements for the transfer of funds, technology, and expertise because most of their member states lack the resources to participate fully in international agreements. The stratospheric-ozone and climate-change regimes aim to build capacity and could not exist in their current form without providing for this function.

Scientific Understanding

International environmental cooperation relies on shared scientific understanding, as evidenced by the form of some important contemporary environmental regimes. An initial framework convention will signal concern and establish mechanisms for developing and sharing new scientific data, thereby providing the basis for taking action in a control protocol. Generating and sharing scientific information have long been functions of international cooperation in public bodies such as the World Meteorological Organization (WMO) and myriad academic organizations such as the International Council for the Exploration of the Seas (ICES) and the International Union for the Conservation of Nature (IUCN).

Disseminating scientific information on an international basis makes sense, but it needs funding from governments because, except in areas like pharmaceutical research, the private sector has no incentive to do the work. International environmental regimes usually have standing scientific committees and subsidiary bodies to support their work. Perhaps the greatest international effort to generate new and authoritative scientific knowledge has been in the area of **climate change** through the Intergovernmental Panel on Climate Change (IPCC).

Climate change A change in the statistical distribution of weather over periods that range from decades to millions of years. It can be a change in the average weather or a change in the distribution of weather events.

Set up in 1988 under the auspices of the WMO and UN Environmental Programme, the IPCC brings together the majority of the world's climate-change scientists in three working groups: on climate science, impacts, and economic and social dimensions. They have produced assessment reports in 1990, 1995, 2001, 2007, and 2014, which are regarded as the authoritative scientific statements on climate change. The reports are drafted carefully and cautiously with the involvement of government representatives and represent a consensus view.

The Fourth Assessment Report, published in February 2007, concluded that "warming of the climate system is unequivocal, as is now evident from observations of increases in global average air and ocean temperatures, widespread melting of snow and ice and rising global sea level" (IPCC 2007, 4). Most of the temperature increase "is *very likely* due to the observed increase in anthropogenic greenhouse gas concentrations" (IPCC 2007, 8; original italics). The use of words is significant here, for the IPCC defines *very likely* as more than 90 percent certain. This represents a change from the previous report, which had only estimated that human activity was *likely*, or more than 66 percent certain, to be responsible for temperature increases.

In 2008, the IPCC agreed to prepare the most recent available IPCC report, published in 2014 (AR5), which stated, "Each of the last three decades has been successively warmer at the Earth's surface than any preceding decade since 1850" (IPCC 2014, 9). The report also concluded that it is "very likely that the Arctic sea ice cover will continue to shrink and thin and that Northern Hemisphere spring snow cover will decrease during the 21st century as global mean surface temperature rises," which means that the global glacier volume will continue to decrease (IPCC 2014, 13).

Like many recent scientific reports on climate change, the AR5 report also points out that "Human influence on the climate system is clear. This is evident from the increasing greenhouse gas concentrations in the atmosphere, positive radiative forcing, observed warming, and understanding of the climate system" (IPCC 2014, 19).

Governing the Commons

The **global commons** are usually understood as areas and resources not under sovereign jurisdiction—that is, not owned by anybody. The high seas and the deep ocean floor come within this category (beyond the two hundred nautical mile exclusive economic zone that states could claim under the 1992 UN

WHAT'S YOUR WORLDVIEW?

The scientific community has presented very convincing data that climate change is real and the burning of fossil fuels has contributed to the resulting global warming and significant weather events. Why do you think so many people refuse to accept these findings?

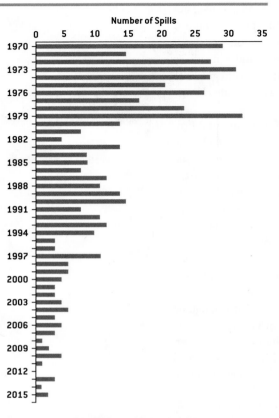

Number of Oil Spills, 1970–2015.

Since 1970, the number of incidents involving large oil spills from tankers has been declining

Convention on the Law of the Sea), as does Antarctica (based on the 1959 Antarctic Treaty). Outer space is another highly important commons area, with use vital to modern telecommunications, broadcasting, navigation, and surveillance. Finally, there is the global atmosphere.

The global commons have an environmental dimension not only as resources but also as a kind of garbage dump for waste products from cities and industry. The fish and whale stocks of the high seas have been relentlessly overexploited to the point where some species have been wiped out and long-term protein sources for human beings are imperiled. The ocean environment has been polluted by land-based effluent and oil and other discharges from ships. It has been a struggle to maintain the unique wilderness of the Antarctic in the face of increasing pressure from human beings, and even outer space now faces an environmental problem in the form of increasing orbital debris left by decades of satellite launches. Similarly, the global atmosphere has been degraded in a number of highly threatening ways, through damage to the stratospheric ozone layer and, most important, by the enhanced **greenhouse effect** now firmly associated with changes to Earth's climate. This is often characterized as a "tragedy of the commons." Where there is unrestricted access to a resource owned by no one, there will be an incentive for individuals to grab as much as they can, and if the resource is finite, there will come a time when it is ruined by overexploitation as the short-term interests of individual users overwhelm the longer-run collective interest in sustaining the resource.

Global commons The areas and resources not under national sovereignty that belong to no single country and are the responsibility of the entire world. The oceans beyond the 200-mile limit, outer space, and Antarctica are global commons areas.

Greenhouse effect The trapping of the sun's warmth in Earth's lower atmosphere due to gases that act like the glass of a greenhouse.

Environmental Regimes

Within the jurisdiction of governments, it may be possible to solve the problem of the "tragedy of the commons" by turning the global commons into private property or nationalizing them, but such a solution is, by definition, unavailable. Therefore, the function of international cooperation in this context is to provide a substitute for world government to ensure that global commons are not misused and subject to tragic collapse. Regimes have been created that have enjoyed varying degrees of effectiveness. Many of the functions that have been discussed can be found in these global commons regimes, but their central contribution is a framework of rules to ensure mutual agreement between users about acceptable standards of behavior and levels of exploitation consistent with sustaining commons ecology.

Enforcement poses difficult challenges due to the incentives for users to "free ride" by taking more than a fair share or refusing to be bound by the collective arrangements. Free riding can potentially destroy regimes because other parties will then see no reason to restrain themselves either. In local commons regimes, inquisitive neighbors might deter rule breaking, and a similar role at the international level can be performed by NGOs. However, it is very difficult to enforce compliance by sovereign states; this is a fundamental difficulty for international law and hardly unique to environmental regimes. Mechanisms have been developed to cope with the problem, but how effective they, and the environmental regimes to which they apply, can be is hard to judge; this involves determining the extent to which governments are in legal and technical compliance with their international obligations. Moreover, it also involves estimating the extent to which state behavior has been changed as a result of the international regime concerned. Naturally, the ultimate and most demanding test of the effectiveness of global commons regimes is whether or not the resources or ecologies concerned are sustained or even improved.

> ### WHAT'S YOUR WORLDVIEW?
>
> *International relations describes a world of nation-states with sovereignty over issues within their borders. How would you convince these states to give up or share sovereignty to address common problems like air or water pollution or climate change?*

Some of the first and least-successful global commons regimes were the various fisheries commissions for the Atlantic and elsewhere, which sought agreement on limiting catches to preserve stocks. Pollution from ships has been controlled by MARPOL (the 1973 international marine environmental convention—short for "marine pollution"), and there is a patchwork of other treaties to manage such issues as the dumping of radioactive waste at sea. For the Antarctic, a remarkably well-developed set of rules designed to preserve the ecological integrity of this last great wilderness has been devised within the framework of the 1959 Antarctic Treaty. The Antarctic regime is a rather exclusive club: the treaty's "Consultative Parties" include the states that had originally claimed sovereignty over parts of the area, and new members of the club must demonstrate their involvement in scientific research on the frozen continent. There is a comprehensive agreement on conserving the marine ecosystem around the continent, and in the late 1980s, preparations for regulated mineral mining were defeated by a new 1988 Protocol on Environmental Protection, which included a fifty-year mining ban. The success of a restricted group of countries, with only a minimal level of formal organization, in governing this crucial laboratory for understanding global environmental change, demonstrates what can be achieved by international action.

Antarctic science was crucial to the discovery of a problem that resulted in what is perhaps the best example of effective international action to govern the commons. In 1985, a British

A Chinese technician from an environmental protection bureau wears a facemask as he takes a water sample from a river where large quantities of dead fish were found near the site of massive blasts in Binhai New Area in Tianjin, China, in August 2015. Often rapid economic development outpaces rules related to safety, health, and environmental protection.

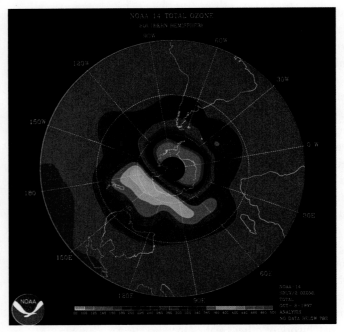

International agreements have reduced the amount of ozone-depleting gases that industries release, but the gases remain a cause of atmospheric damage, as this NASA satellite image shows.

A scavenger in Lagos, Nigeria, sorts out iron and plastic to sell while a bulldozer clears the garbage and birds surrounding it in the Olususun dumpsite, the city's largest dump. Nigeria's most populous city is turning these problems into an advantage by starting a program to convert waste into methane gas to generate electricity.

Antarctic Survey balloon provided definitive evidence of serious thinning of the stratospheric ozone layer (see this chapter's Theory in Practice box for more information). A diminishing ozone layer is a global problem par excellence because the ozone layer protects Earth and its inhabitants from the damaging effects of the sun's ultraviolet radiation. The problem's causes were isolated, international support was mobilized, and a set of rules and procedures were developed that proved to be effective, at least in reducing the concentration of the offending chemicals in the atmosphere, if not yet fully restoring the stratospheric ozone layer.

Climate Change

Unlike the ozone-layer problem, which was clearly the result of damage caused when people used chlorofluorocarbons (CFCs), climate change and the enhanced greenhouse effect had long been debated among scientists. Only in the late 1980s did sufficient international scientific and political consensus emerge to stimulate action—a clear case of the development and influence of an epistemic community. There were still serious disagreements, however, over the likelihood that human-induced changes in mean temperatures were altering the global climate system.

Naturally occurring greenhouse gases in the atmosphere insulate Earth's surface by trapping solar radiation. Before the Industrial Revolution, carbon dioxide concentrations in the atmosphere were around 280 parts per million. They have since grown exponentially. In 2007, they were measured at 379 ppm; in 2015, they surpassed 400 ppm. This rising concentration is due to burning fossil fuels and reductions in some of the "sinks" for carbon dioxide (anything that absorbs more carbon dioxide that it releases), notably forests. Methane emissions have also risen with the growth of agriculture (Intergovernmental Panel on Climate Change 2007, 11).

The best predictions of the IPCC are that if nothing is done to curb intensive fossil fuel emissions there will be a likely rise in mean temperatures on the order of 4.3–11.5 degrees Fahrenheit (2.4–6.4 degrees Celsius) by 2099. The exact consequences of this are difficult to predict based on current climate modeling, but sea level rises and turbulent weather are generally expected. While at Copenhagen the 2 degree target had been agreed, by 2015 there was international agreement in Paris that to avoid dangerous climate change temperature increases should be held '. . . well below 20 degrees C and' to pursue efforts to limit increases to 1.5 degrees C." In the first decade of the twenty-first century, unusual weather patterns, storm events, and the melting of polar ice sheets added a dimension of public concern to the fears expressed by the scientific community.

As a common problem, climate change is on a quite different scale from anything that the international system has previously encountered. Climate change is not a normal international environmental problem; it threatens huge changes in living conditions and challenges existing patterns of energy use and security. There is almost no dimension of international relations that climate change does not actually or potentially affect, and it has already become the subject of "high politics," discussed at G8 summits and in high-level meetings between political leaders.

One way of examining the dimensions of the problem and the steps taken at the international level to respond to the threat of climate change is to make a comparison to the stratospheric-ozone problem discussed in the previous section. There are, of course, some similarities. Chlorofluorocarbons are in themselves greenhouse gases, and the international legal texts on climate change make it clear that controlling them is the responsibility of the Montreal Protocol. The experience with stratospheric ozone and other recent conventions has clearly influenced efforts to build a climate-change regime. At the very start of climate discussions, the same approach was adopted: a framework convention followed by protocols.

The UN Framework Convention on Climate Change (UNFCCC) was signed at the 1992 Earth Summit in Rio de Janeiro, Brazil. It envisaged the reduction of greenhouse-gas emissions and their removal by carbon sequestration, a process through which carbon-based gases are injected into the ground or into peat bogs. The signatories hoped that including a commitment from the developed nations to cut their emissions back to 1990 levels by 2000 would be a start. In a U.S. election year, this proved to be impossible, and the parties to the convention had to be content with a nonbinding declaration that an attempt would be made. There was a binding commitment, however, for parties to draw up national inventories of emissions sources and sinks. As this included the developing nations, many of whom were ill-equipped to fulfill this obligation, there was also funding for capacity building. Most important, the convention locked the signatories into holding a continuing series of annual Conferences of Parties (CoPs) to consider possible actions

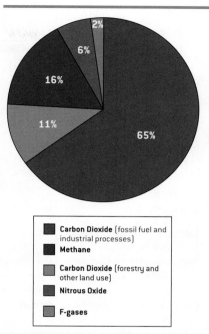

Legend:
- Carbon Dioxide (fossil fuel and industrial processes)
- Methane
- Carbon Dioxide (forestry and other land use)
- Nitrous Oxide
- F-gases

Global Greenhouse Gas Emissions by Type of Gas.

The key greenhouse gases in the atmosphere are carbon dioxide, methane, nitrous oxide, and fluorinated gases (F-gases). Do some research to determine what sort of human activities are responsible for emitting these types of gases.

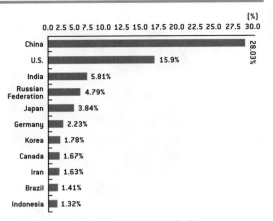

Largest Producers of CO$_2$ Emissions Worldwide, 2015.

Since the Industrial Revolution, carbon dioxide concentrations have grown exponentially. If nothing is done to curb intensive fossil fuel emissions, what will happen to the average global temperature? What effects might that have?

WHAT'S YOUR WORLDVIEW?

The United Nations' Sustainable Development Goals, adopted in September 2015, are aimed at ending poverty, fighting inequality and injustice, and managing climate change by 2030. What factors work against success here? What factors suggest the global community might succeed?

Emissions trading A system which provides that the rights to emit carbon can be bought and sold.

Joint Implementation A system that allows a developed country to receive credits against its own emissions-reduction target by financing projects in another developed country, the argument being that money is best spent where it can achieve the greatest reduction in world emissions of greenhouse gases.

and review the adequacy of existing commitments, supported by regular meetings of the subsidiary scientific and implementation bodies. By 1997, the parties agreed on a "control" measure—the Kyoto Protocol, which set targets for emissions reductions by developed countries.

The problem faced by the framers of the Kyoto Protocol was vastly more complex and demanding than that which their counterparts at Montreal had confronted so successfully in 1987. Instead of controlling a single set of industrial gases for which substitutes were available, reducing greenhouse-gas emissions would involve major changes in energy production, transportation, and agriculture—the fundamentals of life in modern societies. Reducing greenhouse-gas emissions challenges the whole idea of sustainable development. Doing so would involve real sacrifices in living standards and create tough political choices for governments, although there are potential economic benefits from cutting emissions through the development of alternative-energy technologies.

The Kyoto Protocol to the Climate Convention entered into force in 2005. It committed developed countries to make an average 5.2 percent cut in their greenhouse-gas emissions from a 1990 baseline. Within this range, different national targets were negotiated: 8 percent for the European Union, 6 percent for Japan, and 7 percent for the United States. Unfortunately, the United States, representing one of the worst greenhouse-gas-offending countries by several indicators, eventually refused to participate because its economic competitors, China and India, were not required to make similar cuts. These targets were to be achieved by the first commitment period: 2008–2012. In order to achieve these targets, three mechanisms were agreed on:

First, there was **emissions trading**, which provided that rights to emit carbon could be bought and sold. The European Union established its own emissions trading system and carbon markets began to grow up elsewhere. The second and third offset mechanisms, **Joint Implementation** and the **Clean Development Mechanism** (CDM), allowed countries to meet their own national targets by investing in carbon reduction projects elsewhere in the world. There has been extensive use of the CDM, especially in China.

Even with what appeared to be a flexible framework and some useful reduction mechanisms built into the Kyoto Protocol, there was much disagreement and international posturing. One reason for dissent was that, despite an unprecedented international scientific effort in support of the IPCC to establish the causes and consequences of warming, there was not the kind of scientific consensus that had promoted agreement on CFCs—at least not in 1997. At the time, there was disagreement over the significance of human activities and over projections of future change (which has since narrowed dramatically). There were those who had an economic interest in denying or misrepresenting the science, including fossil fuel interests and oil producing countries, such as Saudi Arabia. At the other end of the spectrum, the Alliance of Small Island States, some of whose members' territory would disappear under projected sea level rises, were desperately concerned that such projections be taken seriously.

Even though the effects of climate change are not fully understood, there is enough evidence for some nations to calculate that there might be benefits to them from climatic alterations. Regions of Russia, for example, might become more temperate with rises in mean temperature and thus more suitable for agricultural production (although one could argue equally well the extremely damaging effects of melting permafrost in Siberia). In North America, variations in rainfall patterns have already begun to disrupt agriculture that relies on irrigation. Snowfall patterns in the major mountain ranges are changing, and some species of frogs and insects—especially honeybees necessary for crop pollination—are slowly disappearing. One generalization that can be made with certainty is that the developing nations, with limited infrastructure and major populations located at sea level, are most vulnerable. In recognition of this and on the understanding that a certain level of warming is now inevitable, international attention has begun to shift toward the problem of adaptation to the effects of climate change as well as mitigation of its causes.

At the heart of the international politics of climate change as a global environmental problem is the structural divide between North and South (see Chapters 8 and 9). One of the most significant principles set out in the UN Framework Convention on Climate Change was that of common but differentiated responsibilities. That is to say, although climate change was the common concern of all, it had been produced as a consequence of the development of the old industrialized nations, and it was their responsibility to take the lead in cutting emissions.

The Kyoto Protocol, in its first phase, accomplished relatively little and much more greenhouse gas reduction occurred under the Montreal protocol in the same period, for chlorofluorocarbons are also powerful greenhouse gases. Given the fact that by 2005 developing countries were responsible for the majority of current emissions, and that in 2007 China overtook the United States as the primary

Clean Development Mechanism A system that allows a developed country to receive credits against its own emissions-reduction target by financing projects in a developing country, the argument being that money is best spent where it can achieve the greatest reduction in world emissions of greenhouse gases.

What is happening to the bees? Bee experts say conditions that create a honeybee die-off include mild winters and unseasonably warm early spring weather, which creates conditions for an explosion in the mite populations that kill off many colonies.

Common but Differentiated Responsibilities?

A key principle of the climate-change regime, written into the 1992 UNFCCC, was the notion of "common but differentiated responsibilities." This, in effect, meant that although all nations had to accept responsibility for the world's changing climate, it was developed nations that were immediately responsible because they had benefited from the industrialization generally regarded as the source of the excess carbon dioxide emissions (see Map 10.1).

Consider the relationship between national carbon dioxide emissions and share of global population. The United States emits around 15 to 16 percent of the global total but has only 4.5 percent of the global population. China is the world's biggest emitter of carbon dioxide, producing approximately 28 percent of the global total and has nearly 20 percent of the world's population. On the other hand, the thirty-five least developed nations emit less than 1 percent and account for more than 10 percent of the world's population.

Accordingly, the developed countries were listed in Annex I of the convention, and it was agreed that they, rather than developing countries, would have to lead the way in making emissions reductions.

This approach was followed in the Kyoto Protocol, where only developed-country parties are committed to make reductions. Even before the protocol was agreed, the U.S. Senate passed the Byrd-Hagel Resolution making it clear that it would not ratify any agreement where developing nations, who were now economic competitors of the United States, did not also need to make emissions reductions.

However, in 2004, the International Energy Agency published projections that underlined how globalization was radically changing the pattern of energy-related carbon dioxide emissions; it estimated that emissions would rise by 62 percent by 2030 but, most significantly, that at some point in the 2020s, developing-world emissions would overtake those of the developed OECD countries.

It therefore became clear that to have any chance of success, the future climate-change regime would have to include emissions reductions by countries such as China and India but that they in turn would not even consider reductions if the United States remained outside the Kyoto system.

The fundamental question is thus: *On what basis should countries be asked to reduce their emissions*?

The most radical and equitable answer might be to give each individual a fixed carbon allowance, probably allowing rich people to maintain something of their lifestyle by buying the allowances of the poor. A more likely alternative is to find ways of creating and then raising a global carbon price so that alternatives to fossil fuel become economically attractive. Which approach would you support? Why? What alternatives can you imagine?

For Discussion

1. Why is climate change such a politically charged issue?
2. Developing states want a chance to develop like the rich countries of the global North. What is the argument against their development? Should they care about the environment?
3. Economic interests and environmental concerns are often in conflict. As states develop, do they have a responsibility to prevent further environmental degradation?

Sources: "Global CO2 emissions are set to stall in 2015," The Econo-mist, December 8, 2015, http://www.economist.com/blogs/graphicde-tail/2015/12/climate-change.

"The largest producers of CO2 emissions worldwide in 2015, based on their share of global CO2 emissions," Statista, accessed February 2, 2016, http://www.statista.com/statistics/271748/the-largest-emitters-of-co2-in-the-world/.

emitter, it became increasingly clear that an effective climate agreement would have to include all the Parties to the Convention. This continues to be very difficult to achieve because of the legitimate claims to development and climate justice made by Southern countries and, of course, because many of the emissions from a country like China have been displaced by the globalization of production from Europe and America. It is also true that developed countries, suffering from the world economic crisis of 2008, were not prepared to take risks with their economies. In 2007, it was agreed that there would be two negotiation tracks, one on the future of Kyoto and the other on the future of the Convention. The United States was prepared to participate in the latter because it avoided Kyoto "targets and timetables."

In 2009, the UNFCCC met in Copenhagen, but failed to produce a new legally binding and comprehensive agreement on climate change. Instead, the United States and the BASIC countries (a coalition of large emerging economies including Brazil, South Africa, India, and China) struck a deal known as the Copenhagen Accord. Unlike Kyoto, this agreement provided for countries to offer their "contributions" to emissions reductions that they regarded as appropriate. All countries would participate, breaking down the strict divide between developed and developing countries, but the principle of common but differentiated responsibilities would remain. How strictly contributions will be assessed and how far they will be legally binding remains to be seen.

The contributions offered under the Copenhagen Accord were not sufficient to put the world on a pathway that would avoid breaching the 2 degree Celsius threshold. the UN Conference on Climate Change in Paris in 2015, where representatives from 196 governments set a goal of limiting warming by 1.5 degrees Celsius above pre-industrial levels. The Paris talks were an opportunity to lock in climate action commitments at the national level. The European Union pledged to cut its emissions by 40 percent, while the United States stated

Former U.S. Vice President and Nobel Peace Prize laureate Al Gore warned that the world must act quickly to slow the melting of the world's polar ice packs and glaciers before they reach a critical rate due to global warming.

that it would cut its emissions by 26 to 28 percent by 2025. China agreed to cut its emissions as well.

While the goal of 1.5 degrees Celsius is better than the goal of 2 degrees Celsius that was set in Copenhagen, it is a meaningless one if states do not take essential measures. How can they be encouraged to do so? One important way is to make sure that there is 'transparent' reporting of national actions so that it will be clear whether governments are living up to their promises. Who will make certain countries meet their goals? The following is a list of outcomes from the Paris talks:

- *Pledges to curb emissions*: Before the conference began, some 180 countries had submitted plans or *intended nationally defined contributions* (INDCs) to cut their emissions. Nationally determined contributions are part of the agreement but are not legally binding. The aspects of the Agreement that are binding cover procedures for reporting, transparency and analysis. INDCs are part of the agreement but they are not legally binding. It must be noted that existing INDCs are not sufficient to prevent global temperatures from rising beyond 2 degrees Celsius.
- *Long-term global goal for net zero emissions*: Participants promised to reduce global emissions as soon as possible. The goal is to reach net zero emissions between 2050 and 2100. The UN climate science panel has stated that net zero emissions must happen by 2070 to avoid major environmental problems.
- *Take stock every five years*: The agreement includes a review mechanism aimed at checking on the national pledges every five years. In some cases, they will ask countries to ramp up their pledges to keep under 2 degrees Celsius. The first review will be in 2023.
- *Loss and damage*: This is a mechanism for providing funds for countries that face major losses from extreme weather events. To get this accepted, the United States was protected from financial claims from vulnerable countries.
- *Money*: Funds need to be provided to developing countries so that they can adapt to climate change and find alternatives to fossil fuels. Developed states will provide $100 billion a year beyond 2020. The agreement states that by 2025 the amount of the fund will be reassessed and will likely increase.

Parties to the Paris conference will achieve a great deal if they work in a multilateral fashion towards goals related to climate change, economic development, and other social and political issues. Cooperation is critical for success, as is sacrifice and setting aside national interests for the good of global and common interests.

Conclusion

In this chapter, we have seen that cooperation to protect the global environment, though sometimes difficult to achieve, is possible. The determinants of

THINKING ABOUT GLOBAL POLITICS *continued*

	Future One	Future Two	Future Three	Future Four
Society	As well as being individuals, most people live in social groups. People need support from one another to grow and be happy.	People benefit most when there is equal opportunity for all people to seek their own best interest. Government must not tell them what to do or what not to do.	People must cooperate, not compete. They must blend their own self-interest into that of the greater good.	Well-informed individuals can exercise freedom of choice to satisfy their own interest. This will contribute to creative problem-solving and increased well-being for all.
Environment	The world around us is to be used. New inventions will make some resources (e.g., the sun and wind) useful before or after others (coal and gas) are used up.	The land and sea around us are full of riches. They should be used to the fullest in making us happy and prosperous.	It is important to preserve the balance between ourselves and the land and sea around us. They belong both to us and to those who come after us.	By inventing new ways of using our resources, we can prosper without harming our natural riches.
Government	Central government should be strong and guarantee a job for all with equal pay for equal work. It must also allow people to develop private businesses.	Central government should play a very limited role in our lives. Its main jobs are to keep peace at home and protect us from attack.	Attention should be turned away from central government and toward local community government. Local government aids social and natural harmony.	Central government should give some support to its citizens. It should provide education and information and protect our natural resources.
Economics	Maximum effort will be made to cut our dependency on foreign resources. The government will pay for basic human services such as health care and education.	Large-scale industry can best use the natural resources of our land and oceans. They are most fit to lead development and make the most money in a world eager to buy our goods.	Local economies promote doing more with less in the design of all systems and question the ever-growing demand for consumer goods. Industries favor reuse or recycling of materials.	New industries with advanced equipment and the invention of new technologies should be encouraged. All new industries must be responsible for using our resources with care.

GLOSSARY

Absolute gains The notion that all states seek to have more power and influence in the system to secure their national interests. Offensive neorealists are also concerned with increasing power relative to other states. One must have enough power to secure interests and more power than any other state in the system—friend or foe.

Adaptation strategies Changes in foreign policy behavior in reaction to changes in the international system or international events and adjusting national goals to conform to the effects of events external to that state.

Acquiescent strategy A foreign policy strategy in which a state defers to the interests of a major power.

African Union (AU) Created in 2002 and consisting of fifty-four member states, this union was formed as a successor to the Organization of African Unity. It maintains fourteen goals primarily centered on African unity and security, human rights, peace security and stability, economy, sustainable development, and equality.

Al-Qaeda Most commonly associated with Osama bin Laden, "The Base" (its meaning in Arabic) is a religious-based group whose fighters swear an oath of fealty to the leadership that succeeded bin Laden.

Anarchic system A realist description of the international system that suggests there is no common power or central governing structure.

Anarchy A system operating in the absence of any central government. It does not imply chaos but, in realist theory, the absence of political authority.

Appeasement A policy of making concessions to a territorially acquisitive state in the hope that settlement of more modest claims will assuage that state's expansionist appetites.

Arab Spring Protests and revolutionary uprisings that began in Tunisia in 2010 and spread across Egypt, Libya, Syria, Yemen, Bahrain, Saudi Arabia, and Jordan in 2011. At their core was a desire for more democratic and transparent political systems and more open and equitable economic systems.

Armistice A ceasefire agreement between enemies in wartime. In the case of World War I, the armistice began at 11 A.M. on November 11, 1918.

Arms embargo Similar to economic sanctions, an arms embargo stops the flow of arms from one country to another.

Arms race A central concept in realist thought. As states build up their military to address real or perceived threats to their national security, they may create insecurity in other states. These states in turn develop their military capacities and thus begin an arms race. This never-ending pursuit of security creates the condition we know as a security dilemma.

Association of Southeast Asian Nations (ASEAN) A geopolitical and economic organization of several countries located in Southeast Asia. Initially formed as a display of solidarity against communism, it has since redefined its aims and broadened to include the acceleration of economic growth and the promotion of regional peace.

Asymmetric conflicts In symmetrical warfare, armies with comparable weapons, tactics, and organizational structures do battle. Wars are fought on near-equal terms. When stakes are high and those actors in conflict are not equal in terms of weapons and technology, the weaker side adopts asymmetrical tactics. These include guerrilla warfare, roadside bombs, attacks on civilians, and other terrorist tactics.

Balance of power In the international system, a state of affairs in which there is parity and stability among competing forces, and no one state is sufficiently strong to dominate all the others.

Bipolar An international political order in which two states dominate all others. It is often used to describe the nature of the international system when the two superpowers, the Soviet Union and the United States, were dominant powers during the Cold War.

Blitzkrieg The German term for "lightning war." This was an offensive strategy that used the combination of mechanized forces—especially tanks—and aircraft as mobile artillery to exploit breaches in an enemy's front line.

Bretton Woods system A system of economic and financial accords that created the IMF, the World Bank, and GATT/WTO following World War II. It is named after the hamlet in northern New Hampshire where leaders from forty-four countries met in 1944.

Capacity building The provision of funds and technical training to allow developing countries to participate in global environmental governance.

Capital controls The monetary policy device that a government uses to regulate the flows into and out of a country's capital account (i.e., the flows of investment-oriented money into and out of a country or currency).

Capitalism A system of production in which human labor and its products are commodities that are bought and sold in the marketplace.

Charter rights Civil liberties guaranteed in a written document such as a constitution.

Civic nationalism The idea that an association of people can identify themselves as belonging to the nation and have equal and shared political rights and allegiance to similar political procedures.

civil society The totality of all individuals and groups in a society who are not acting as participants in any government institutions or acting in the interests of commercial companies.

Clandestine or **"sleeper" cell** Usually, a group of people sent by an intelligence organization or terrorist network that remains dormant in a target country until activated by a message to carry out a mission, which could include prearranged attacks.

Class A social group that in Marxism is identified by its relationship with the means of production and the distribution of societal resources. Thus, we have the bourgeoisie, or the owners or upper classes, and the proletariat, or the workers.

Classical realism The belief that it is fundamentally the nature of people and the state to act in a way that places interests over ideologies. The drive for power and the will to dominate are held to be fundamental aspects of human nature.

Clean Development Mechanism A system that allows a developed country to receive credits against its own emissions-reduction target by financing projects in a developing country, the argument being that money is best spent where it can achieve the greatest reduction in world emissions of greenhouse gases.

Climate change A change in the statistical distribution of weather over periods that range from decades to millions of years. It can be a change in the average weather or a change in the distribution of weather events.

Coercive diplomacy The use of diplomatic and military methods that force a state to concede to another state. These methods may include the threat of force and the mobilization of the military to gradually "turn the screw" but exclude the actual use of force. The implication is that war is the next step if diplomacy fails.

Cold War The period from 1946 to 1991 defined by ideological conflict and rivalry between the United States and the Soviet Union. This was a global struggle for the hearts and minds of citizens around the world that was characterized by political conflict, military competition, proxy wars, and economic competition.

Collective security An arrangement where "each state in the system accepts that the security of one is the concern of all, and agrees to join in a collective response to aggression" (Roberts and Kingsbury 1993, 30).

Common security At times called "cooperative security," it stresses noncompetitive approaches and cooperative approaches through which states—both friends and foes—can achieve security. The belief that no one is secure until all people are secure from threats of war.

Community A human association in which members share common symbols and wish to cooperate to realize common objectives.

Comparative advantage A theory developed by David Ricardo stating that two countries will both gain from trade if, in the absence of trade, they have different relative costs for producing the same goods. Even if one country is more efficient in the production of all goods than the other (absolute advantage), both countries will still gain by trading with each other as long as they have different relative efficiencies.

Concert of Europe An informal institution created in 1815 by the five great powers of Europe (Austria, Britain, France, Prussia, and Russia), whereby they agreed on controlling revolutionary forces, managing the balance of power, and accepting interventions to keep current leaders in power. This system kept the peace in Europe from 1815 until World War I.

Congress of Vienna A meeting of major European leaders (1814–1815) that redrew the political map of Europe after the Napoleonic Wars. The congress was an attempt to restore a conservative political order in the continent.

Constructivism An approach to international politics that concerns itself with the centrality of ideas and human consciousness. As constructivists have examined global politics, they have been broadly interested in how the structure constructs the actors' identities and interests, how their interactions are organized and constrained by that structure, and how their very interaction serves to either reproduce or transform that structure.

Containment An American political strategy for resisting perceived Soviet expansion.

Cosmopolitan culture A pattern of relations within which people share the same goals and aspirations, generally to improve that culture for all members.

Cosmopolitan democracy A condition in which international organizations, transnational corporations, and global markets are accountable to the peoples of the world.

Critical theory Theories that are critical of the status quo and reject the idea that things can be fixed under the present system. These theories challenge core assumptions of the dominant paradigm and argue for transformation and not just reform.

Deep ecology Often identified with the Norwegian philosopher Arne Naess, the core belief is that the living environment has a right to live and flourish. The "deep" refers to the need to think deeply about the impact of human life on the environment.

Defensive realism A structural theory of realism that views states as security maximizers—more concerned with absolute power as opposed to relative power. According to this view, it is unwise for states to try to maximize their share of power and seek hegemony.

Democratic deficit Leaders have created many policymaking institutions at the global, regional, and national levels with policymaking power led by individuals who are appointed and not elected. Thus, policy decisions are not subject to review by citizens.

Democratic peace thesis A central plank of liberal-internationalist thought, the democratic peace thesis makes two claims: first, liberal polities exhibit restraint in their relations with other liberal polities (the so-called separate peace), but second, they are imprudent in relations with authoritarian states. The validity of the democratic peace thesis has been fiercely debated in the international relations literature.

Deregulation The removal of all regulation so that market forces, not government policy, control economic developments.

Desertification The extreme deterioration of land in arid and dry subhumid areas due to loss of vegetation and soil moisture; it results chiefly from human activities and is influenced by climatic variations. This condition is principally caused by overgrazing, overdrafting of groundwater, and diversion of water from rivers for human consumption and industrial use; all of these processes are fundamentally driven by overpopulation.

Détente The relaxation of tension between East and West; Soviet-American détente lasted from the late 1960s to the late 1970s and was characterized by negotiations and nuclear arms control agreements.

Development In the orthodox view, top-down; reliance on "expert knowledge," usually Western and definitely external; large capital investments in large projects; advanced technology; expansion of the private sphere. In the alternative view, bottom-up; participatory; reliance on appropriate (often local) knowledge and technology; small investments in small-scale projects; protection of the commons.

Diplomacy The process by which international actors communicate as they seek to resolve conflicts without going to war and find solutions to complex global problems.

Doctrine A stated principle of government policy, mainly in foreign or military affairs, or the set of beliefs held and taught by an individual or political group.

Ecocentric Having a nature- or ecology-centered rather than a human-centered set of values.

Ecological footprint A measure that demonstrates the load placed on Earth's carrying capacity by individuals or nations. It does this by estimating the area of productive land and water system required to sustain a population at its specified standard of living.

Ecologies The communities of plants and animals that supply raw materials for all living things.

Economic base For Marxists, the substructure of the society is the relationship between owners and workers. Capitalists own the means of production and control technology and resources. The workers are employed by the capitalists, and they are alienated, exploited, and estranged from their work and their society.

Economic sanctions A tool of statecraft that seeks to get a state to behave by coercion of a monetary kind—for example, freezing banking assets, cutting aid programs, or banning trade.

Ecosystem A system of interdependent living organisms that share the same habitat, functioning together with all of the physical factors of the environment.

Ecotopian Someone who believes in protecting and preserving the environment and promotes progressive political goals that promote environmental sustainability, social justice, and economic well-being.

Electronic commerce The buying and selling of products and services over the telephone or Internet. Amazon and eBay are examples of leaders in this area of commerce.

Embedded liberalism A liberal international economic order based on the pursuit of free trade but allowing an appropriate role for state intervention in the market in support of national security and national and global stability.

Emissions trading A system which provides that the rights to emit carbon can be bought and sold.

Empire A distinct type of political entity, which may or may not be a state, possessing both a home territory and foreign territories. This may include conquered nations and colonies.

Enlightenment A movement associated with rationalist thinkers of the eighteenth century. Key ideas (which some would argue remain mottoes for our age) include secularism, progress, reason, science, knowledge, and freedom. The motto of the Enlightenment is *"Sapere aude!"* (Have courage to know!) (Kant 1991, 54).

Equity A number of equal portions in the nominal capital of a company; the shareholder thereby owns part of the enterprise; also called "stock" or "share."

Ethic of responsibility For realists, it represents the limits of ethics in international politics; it involves the weighing up of consequences and the realization that positive outcomes may result from amoral actions.

Ethics Ethical studies in international relations and foreign policy include the identification, illumination, and application of relevant moral norms to the conduct of foreign policy and assessing the moral architecture of the international system.

Ethnonationalism A strain of nationalism marked by the desire of an ethnic community to have absolute authority over its own political, economic, and social affairs. Loyalty and identity shift from the state to an ethnic community that seeks to create its own state.

European Union (EU) The union formally created in 1992 following the signing of the Maastricht Treaty. The origins of the European Union can be traced back to 1951 and the creation of the European Coal and Steel Community, followed in 1957 with a broader customs union (the Treaty of Rome, 1958). Originally a grouping of six countries in 1957, "Europe" grew by adding new members in 1973, 1981, and 1986. Since the fall of the planned economies in Eastern Europe in 1989, Europe has grown and now includes twenty-eight member states.

Export-led growth An outward-oriented economy that is based on exploiting its own comparative advantages, such as cheap labor or resources, to capture a share of the world market in a given industry.

Failed or **collapsed state** A state that fails to provide basic services and provide for their citizens. Such a state cannot protect its boundaries, provide a system of law and order, or maintain a functioning marketplace and means of exchange.

Feminism A political project to understand so as to end women's inequality and oppression. Feminist theories tend to be critical of the biases of the discipline. Many feminists focus their research on the areas where women are excluded from the analysis of major international issues and concerns.

Fixed exchange rate The price a currency will earn in a hard currency. Here a government is committed to keep it at a specific value.

Floating exchange rate The market decides what the actual value of a currency is compared to other currencies.

Foreign direct investment (FDI) The capital speculation by citizens or organizations of one country into markets or industries in another country.

Foreign policy The articulation of national interests and the means chosen to secure those interests, both material and ideational, in the international arena.

Foreign policy style Often shaped by a state's political culture, history, and traditions, this describes how a country deals with other states and how it approaches any decision-making situation. For example, does it act unilaterally or multilaterally? Does it seek consensus on an agreement or does it go with majority rule?

Foreign policy tradition A tradition that includes national beliefs about how the world works and a list of national interests and priorities based on these beliefs. It also refers to past actions or significant historical events that act as analogs and give guidance to leaders about what strategy would best secure their national interests.

Fourteen Points President Woodrow Wilson's vision of international society, first articulated in January 1918, included the principle of self-determination, the conduct of diplomacy on an open (not secret) basis, and the establishment of an association of nation-states to provide guarantees of independence and territorial integrity (League of Nations).

Fragile state A state that has not yet failed but whose leaders lack the will or capacity to perform core state functions.

Free market A market ruled by the forces of supply and demand, where all buying and selling is not constrained by government regulations or interventions.

Free trade An essential element of capitalism that argues for no barriers or minimal barriers to the exchange of goods, services, and investments among states.

Functionalism An idea formulated by early proponents of European integration that suggests cooperation should begin with efforts aimed at resolving specific regional or transnational problems. It is assumed that resolution of these problems will lead to cooperation, or spillover, in other policy areas.

Futures Derivatives that oblige a buyer and seller to complete a transaction at a predetermined time in the future at a price agreed on today. Futures are also known as "forwards."

Genocide The deliberate and systematic extermination of an ethnic, national, tribal, or religious group.

Glasnost A policy of greater openness pursued by Soviet leader Mikhail Gorbachev from 1985, involving more toleration of internal dissent and criticism.

Global capital markets Banks, investment companies, insurance companies, trusts, hedge funds, and stock exchanges that transfer funds to industries and other commercial enterprises globally.

Global commons The areas and resources not under national sovereignty that belong to no single country and are the responsibility of the entire world. The oceans beyond the 200-mile limit, outer space, and Antarctica are global commons areas.

Global environmental governance The performance of global environmental regulative functions, often in the absence of a central government authority. It usually refers to the structure of international agreements and organizations but can also involve governance by the private sector or NGOs.

Global goods Products that are made for a global market and are available across the world.

Global governance The regulation and coordination of transnational issue areas by nation-states, international and regional organizations, and private agencies through the establishment of international regimes. These regimes may focus on problem-solving or the simple enforcement of rules and regulations.

Global politics The politics of global social relations in which the pursuit of power, interests, order, and justice transcends regions and continents.

Global polity The collective structures and processes by which "interests are articulated and aggregated, decisions are made, values allocated and policies conducted through international or transnational political processes" (Ougaard 2004, 5).

Global sourcing Obtaining goods and services across geopolitical boundaries. Usually, the goal is to find the least expensive labor and raw material costs and the lowest taxes and tariffs.

Globalization A historical process involving a fundamental shift or transformation in the spatial scale of human social organization that links distant communities and expands the reach of power relations across regions and continents.

Government The people and agencies that have the power and legitimate authority to determine who gets what, when, where, and how within a given territory.

Great Depression The global economic collapse that ensued following the U.S. Wall Street stock market crash in October 1929. Economic shock waves rippled around a world already densely interconnected by webs of trade and foreign direct investment.

Great power A state that has the political, economic, and military resources to shape the world beyond its borders. In most cases, such a state has the will and capacity to define the rules of the international system.

Greenhouse effect The trapping of the sun's warmth in Earth's lower atmosphere due to gases that act like the glass of a greenhouse.

Gross domestic product (GDP) The sum of all economic activity that takes place within a country.

Grotian A liberal tradition in international relations theory named for Hugo Grotius that emphasizes the rule of law and multilateral cooperation. Grotians believe the international system is not anarchic, but interdependent: a society of states is created in part by international law, treaties, alliances, and diplomacy, which states are bound by and ought to uphold.

Group of Twenty (G20) An assembly of governments and leaders from twenty of the world's largest economies: Argentina, Australia, Brazil, Canada, China, France, Germany, India, Indonesia, Italy, Japan, Mexico, Republic of Korea, Russian Federation, Saudi Arabia, South Africa, Turkey, United Kingdom, United States, and the European Union.

Hard power The material threats and inducements leaders employ to achieve the goals of their state.

Hegemony A system regulated by a dominant leader, or political (and/or economic) domination of a region. It also means power and control exercised by a leading state over other states.

Holocaust The attempts by the Nazis to murder the Jewish population of Europe. Some 6 million Jewish people were killed in concentration camps, along with a further million that included Soviet prisoners, Roma, Poles, communists, homosexuals, and the physically or mentally disabled.

Human development The notion that it is possible to improve the lives of people. Basically, it is about increasing the number of choices people have. These may include living a long and healthy life, access to education, and a better standard of living.

Human rights The inalienable rights such as life, liberty, and the pursuit of happiness that one is entitled to because one is human.

Human security The security of people, including their physical safety, their economic and social well-being, respect for their dignity, and the protection of their human rights.

Humanitarian intervention The use of military force by external actors to end a threat to people within a sovereign state.

Hyperpower The situation of the United States after the Cold War ended. With the Soviet Union's military might greatly diminished and China having primarily only regional power-projecting capability, the United States was unchallenged in the world.

Idealism Referred to by realists as *utopianism* since it underestimates the logic of power politics and the constraints this imposes on political action. Idealism as a substantive theory of international relations is generally associated with the claim that it is possible to create a world of peace based on the rule of law.

Ideational/ideal interest The psychological, moral, and ethical goals of a state as it sets foreign and domestic policy.

Identity The understanding of the self in relationship to an "other." Identities are social and thus always formed in relationship to others. Constructivists generally hold that identities shape interests; we cannot know what we want unless we know who we are. But because identities are social and produced through interactions, identities can change.

Immigration controls A government's control of the number of people who may work, study, or relocate to its country. It may include quotas for certain national groups for immigration.

Imperialism The practice of foreign conquest and rule in the context of global relations of hierarchy and subordination. It can lead to the establishment of an empire.

Integration A process of ever-closer union between states in a regional or international context. The process often begins with cooperation to solve technical problems.

Intercontinental ballistic missiles (ICBMs) Weapons system the United States and Soviet Union developed to threaten each other with destruction. The thirty- to forty-minute flight times of the missiles created a situation that is sometimes called "mutually assured destruction" (MAD) or "the balance of terror."

Interdependence A condition where states (or peoples) are affected by decisions taken by others. Interdependence can be symmetric (i.e., both sets of actors are affected equally), or it can be asymmetric (i.e., the impact varies between actors).

International Court of Justice (ICJ) The main judicial organ of the United Nations consisting of fifteen judges elected jointly by the General Assembly and Security Council. The ICJ handles disputes between states, not individuals and states, and although a state does not have to participate in a case, if it elects to do so it must obey the decision.

International Criminal Court (ICC) The first permanent, treaty-based, international criminal court, established to help end impunity for the perpetrators of the most serious crimes of concern to the international community. The ICC is governed by the Rome Statute and an independent international organization.

International institutions Complexes of norms, rules, and practices that prescribe behavioral roles, constrain activity, and shape expectations.

International law The formal rules of conduct that states acknowledge or contract between themselves.

International nongovernmental organization (INGO) A formal nongovernmental organization with members from at least three countries.

International organization Any institution with formal procedures and formal membership from three or more countries. The minimum number of countries is set at three, rather than two, because multilateral relationships have significantly greater complexity than bilateral relationships.

International relations The study of the interactions of states (countries) and other actors in the international system.

Interparadigm debate The debate between the main theoretical approaches in the field of global politics.

Intervention The direct involvement within a state by an outside actor to achieve an outcome preferred by the intervening agency without the consent of the host state.

Intrafirm trade The international trade from one branch of a TNC to an affiliate of the same company in a different country.

Intransigent foreign policy A foreign policy that challenges the rules established by the great powers or rule-making states.

Jihad In Arabic, *jihad* means "struggle." Jihad can refer to a purely internal struggle to be a better Muslim or a struggle to make society more closely align with the teachings of the Koran.

Joint Implementation A system that allows a developed country to receive credits against its own emissions-reduction target by financing projects in another developed country, the argument being that money is best spent where it can achieve the greatest reduction in world emissions of greenhouse gases.

Kantian A revolutionary tradition in international relations theory named for Immanuel Kant that emphasizes human interests over state interests.

Kyoto Protocol A global environmental treaty passed in 1997 that set binding targets for thirty-seven industrialized countries and the European community for reducing greenhouse-gas emissions.

League of Nations The first permanent collective international security organization aimed at preventing future wars and resolving global problems. The League failed due to the unwillingness of the United States to join and the inability of its members to commit to a real international community.

Legitimacy An authority that is respected and recognized by those it rules and by other rulers or leaders of other states. The source of legitimacy can be laws or a constitution and the support of the society.

Levels of analysis Analysts of global politics may examine factors at various levels—such as individual, domestic, systemic, and global—to explain actions and events. Each level provides possible explanations on a different scale.

Liberal account of rights The belief that humans have inherent rights that the state has a responsibility to protect.

Liberal democracy A state with democratic or representative government and a capitalist economy that promotes multilateralism and free trade. Domestic interests, values, and institutions shape foreign policy. Liberal democracies champion freedom of the individual, constitutional civil and political rights, and laissez-faire economic arrangements.

Liberal feminism A position that advocates equal rights for women but also supports a more progressive policy agenda, including social justice, peace, economic well-being, and ecological balance.

Liberal internationalism A perspective that seeks to transform international relations to emphasize peace, individual freedom, and prosperity and to replicate domestic models of liberal democracy at the international level.

Liberalism A theoretical approach that argues for human rights, parliamentary democracy, and free trade—while also maintaining that all such goals must begin *within a state*.

Liberalism of privilege The perspective that developed democratic states have a responsibility to spread liberal values for the benefit of all peoples of the earth.

Liberalization Government policies that reduce the role of the state in the economy, such as the dismantling of trade tariffs and barriers, the deregulation and opening of the financial sector to foreign investors, and the privatization of state enterprises.

Machiavellian A tradition in international relations theory named for Niccolò Machiavelli that characterizes the international system as anarchic; states are constantly in conflict and pursue their own interests as they see fit.

Market democracies See *liberal democracies*.

Marshall Plan Officially known as the European Recovery Program, it was a program of financial and other economic aid for Europe after World War II. Proposed by Secretary of State George Marshall in 1948, it was offered to all European states, including the Soviet Union.

Marxism A theory critical of the status quo, or dominant capitalist paradigm. It is a critique of the capitalist political economy from the view of the revolutionary proletariat, or workers. Marxists' ideal is a stateless and classless society.

Material Things we can see, measure, consume, and use, such as military forces, oil, and currency.

Materialism In this context, it is the spreading of a global consumer culture and popular-culture artifacts like music, books, and movies. Christopher Lasch called this the "ceaseless translation of luxuries into necessities." These elements are seen as undermining traditional cultural values and norms.

Middle powers These states, because of their position and past roles in international affairs, have very distinctive interests in world order. Middle powers are activists in international and regional forums, and they are confirmed multilateralists in most issue areas.

Military-industrial complex The power and influence of the defense industries and their special relationship with the military. Both have tremendous influence over elected officials.

Modern state A political unit within which citizens identify with the state and see the state as legitimate. This state has a monopoly over the use of force and is able to provide citizens with key services.

Modernization theory A theory that considers development synonymous with economic growth within the context of a free market international economy.

Most favored nation status The status granted to most trading partners that says trade rules with that country will be the same as those given to their most favored trading partner.

Multilateral diplomacy Cooperation among three or more states based on, or with a view to formulating, reciprocally binding rules of conduct.

Multilateralism The process by which states work together to solve a common problem.

Multinational corporation or **enterprise (MNC/MNE)** A business or firm with administration, production, distribution, and marketing located in countries around the world. Such a business moves money, goods, services, and technology around the world depending on where the firm can make the most profit.

Munich Agreement of 1938 An agreement negotiated after a conference held in Munich between Germany and the United Kingdom and other major powers of Europe along with Czechoslovakia. It permitted Nazi Germany's annexation of Czechoslovakia's Sudetenland, an area along the Czech border that was inhabited primarily by ethnic Germans.

Nation A community of people who share a common sense of identity, which may be derived from language, culture, or ethnicity; this community may be a minority within a single country or live in more than one country.

Nation-state A political community in which the state claims legitimacy on the grounds that it represents all citizens, including those who may identify as a separate community or nation.

National interest The material and ideational goals of a nation-state.

National security A fundamental value in the foreign policy of states secured by a variety of tools of statecraft, including military actions, diplomacy, economic resources, and international agreements and alliances. It also depends on a stable and productive domestic society.

National self-determination The right or desire of distinct national groups to become states and to rule themselves.

nationalism The idea that the world is divided into nations that provide the overriding focus of political identity and loyalty, which in turn should be the basis for defining the population of states. Nationalism also can refer to this idea in the form of a strong sense of identity (*sentiment*) or organizations and movements seeking to realize this idea (*politics*).

Natural law The idea that humans have an essential nature, which dictates that certain kinds of human goods are always and everywhere desired; because of this, there are common moral standards that govern all human relations, and these common standards can be discerned by the application of reason to human affairs.

Neoclassical realism A version of realism that combines both structural factors such as the distribution of power and unit-level factors such as the interests of states.

Neoliberalism Theory shaped by the ideas of commercial, republican, sociological, and institutional liberalism. Neoliberals see the international system as anarchic but believe relations can be managed by the establishment of international regimes and institutions. Neoliberals think actors with common interests will try to maximize absolute gains.

New International Economic Order (NIEO) A declaration adopted by the UN General Assembly calling for a restructuring of the international order toward greater equity for developing countries, particularly in reference to a wide range of trade, financial, commodity, and debt-related issues.

New wars Wars of identity between different ethnic communities or nations, and wars that are caused by the collapse of states or the fragmentation of multiethnic states. Most of these new wars are internal or civil wars.

Niche diplomacy Every state has its national interests and its areas of comparative advantage over other international actors. This is its area of expertise and where it has the greatest interest. Hence, this is where the state concentrates its foreign policy resources.

Noncompliance The failure of states or other actors to abide by treaties or rules supported by international regimes.

Nongovernmental organization (NGO) An organization, usually a grassroots one, with policy goals but not governmental in makeup. An NGO is any group of people relating to each other regularly in some formal manner and engaging in collective action, provided the activities are noncommercial and nonviolent and are not on behalf of a government.

Nonintervention The principle that external powers should not intervene in the domestic affairs of sovereign states.

Non–nuclear weapon states (NNWS) A state that is party to the Treaty on the Nonproliferation of Nuclear Weapons, meaning that it does not possess nuclear weapons.

Nonpolar An international system in which power is not concentrated in a few states but is diffused among a variety of state and nonstate actors.

Nonpolar world A world in which there are many power centers, and many of them are not nation-states. Power is diffused and in many hands in many policy areas.

Nonstate actor Any participant in global politics that is neither acting in the name of government nor created and served by government. Nongovernmental organizations, terrorist networks, global crime syndicates, and multinational corporations are examples.

Normative orientation In foreign policy, promoting certain norms and values and being prescriptive in one's foreign policy goals.

Normative theory The systematic analyses of the ethical, moral, and political principles that either govern or ought to govern the organization or conduct of global politics. The belief that theories should be concerned with what ought to be rather than merely diagnosing what is.

Norms These specify general standards of behavior and identify the rights and obligations of states. Together, norms and principles define the essential character of a regime, and these cannot be changed without transforming the nature of the regime.

North Atlantic Treaty Organization (NATO) Organization established by treaty in April 1949 including twelve (later sixteen) countries from Western Europe and North America. The most important aspect of the NATO alliance was the U.S. commitment to the defense of Western Europe. Today NATO has twenty-eight member states.

Nuclear deterrence Explicit, credible threats to use nuclear weapons in retaliation to deter an adversary from attacking with nuclear weapons.

Nuclear terrorism The use of or threat to use nuclear weapons or nuclear materials to achieve the goals of rogue states or revolutionary or radical organizations.

Offensive realism A structural theory of realism that views states as power maximizers.

Offshore finance centers The extraterritorial banks that investors use for a range of reasons, including the desire to avoid domestic taxes, regulations, and law enforcement agencies.

Oligarchs A term from ancient Greece to describe members of a small group that controls a state.

Options Derivatives that give parties a right (without obligation) to buy or sell at a specific price for a stipulated period of time up to the contract's expiry date.

Organization of African Unity (OAU) A regional organization founded in 1963 as a way to foster solidarity among African countries, promote African independence, and throw off the vestiges of colonial rule. The Organization of African Unity had a policy of noninterference in member states, and it had no means for intervening in conflicts; as a result, this organization could be only a passive bystander in many violent conflicts.

Organization of American States (OAS) A regional international organization composed of thirty-five member states. It is the world's oldest regional organization, founded in 1890 as the International Union of American Republics and changing its name to Organization of American States in 1948. The goals of this organization are to create "an order of peace and justice, to promote their solidarity, to strengthen their collaboration, and to defend their sovereignty, their territorial integrity, and their independence."

Ostpolitik The West German government's "Eastern Policy" of the mid-to-late 1960s, designed to develop relations between West Germany and members of the Warsaw Pact.

Paradigm A model or example. In the case of international relations theory, the term is a rough synonym for "academic perspective." A paradigm provides the basis for a theory, describing what is real and significant in a given area so that we can select appropriate research questions.

Paradox A seemingly absurd or self-contradictory statement that, when investigated or explained, may prove to be well founded or true.

Peace enforcement Designed to bring hostile parties to agreement and may occur without the consent of the parties.

Peace of Utrecht (1713) The agreement that ended the War of the Spanish Succession and helped to consolidate the link between sovereign authority and territorial boundaries in Europe. This treaty refined the territorial scope of sovereign rights of states.

Peace of Westphalia (1648) Ended the Thirty Years' War and was crucial in delimiting the political rights and authority of European monarchs.

Peacekeeping The interposition of third-party military personnel to keep warring parties apart.

Peacemaking Active diplomatic efforts to seek a resolution to an international dispute that has already escalated.

Perestroika Gorbachev's policy of restructuring, pursued in tandem with glasnost and intended to modernize the Soviet political and economic system.

Pluralism A political theory holding that political power and influence in society do not belong just to the citizens nor only to elite groups in various sectors of society but are distributed among a wide number of groups in the society. It can also mean a recognition of ethnic, racial, and cultural diversity.

Post-conflict peace building Activities launched after a conflict has ended that seek to end the condition that caused the conflict.

Postmodern or **"new" terrorism** Groups and individuals subscribing to millennial and apocalyptic ideologies and system-level goals. Most value destruction for its own sake, unlike most terrorists in the past, who had specific goals, usually tied to a territory.

Postmodern state A political unit within which citizens are less nationalistic and more cosmopolitan in their outlook on both domestic and foreign policy.

Postmodernity An international system where domestic and international affairs are intertwined, national borders are permeable, and states have rejected the use of force for resolving conflict. The European Union is an example of the evolution of the state-centric system (Cooper 2003).

Post–Washington Consensus A slightly modified version of the Washington Consensus promoting economic growth through trade liberalization coupled with pro-poor growth and poverty-reduction policies.

Poverty According to the United Nations, poverty is a denial of choices and opportunities, a violation of human dignity. It means lack of basic capacity provided by material possessions or money to participate effectively in society.

Power This is a contested concept. Many political scientists believe that power is the capacity to do things and, in social and political situations, to affect others to get the outcome one wants. Sources of power include material or tangible resources and control over meaning or ideas.

Premodern state A state within which the primary identity of citizens or subjects is to national, religious, or ethnic communities.

Prescription Recommendations for state survival in the international system based on international relations traditions.

Preservative strategy A foreign policy aimed at preserving power and status in the international system.

Preventive diplomacy Measures that states take to keep a disagreement from escalating.

Problem-solving theory Realism and liberalism are problem-solving theories that address issues and questions within the dominant paradigm or the present system. How can we fix capitalism? How can we make a society more democratic? These are problem-solving questions that assume nothing is wrong with the core elements of the system.

Promotive foreign policy A foreign policy that promotes the values and interests of a state and seeks to create an international system based on these values.

Protectionism Not an economic policy but a variety of political actions taken to protect domestic industries from more efficient foreign producers. Usually, this means the use of tariffs, nontariff barriers, and subsidies to protect domestic interests.

Protectionist An economic policy of restraining trade between states through methods such as tariffs on imported goods, restrictive quotas, and a variety of other government regulations designed to allow "fair competition" among imports and goods and services produced domestically.

Protestant Reformation A social and political movement begun in 1517 in reaction to the widespread perception that the Catholic Church had become corrupt and had lost its moral compass.

Public diplomacy The use of media, the Internet, and other cultural outlets to communicate the message of a state.

Radical liberalism The utopian side of liberalism best exemplified by the academic community called the World Order Models Project (WOMP). These scholars advocate a world in which states promote values like social justice, economic well-being, peace, and ecological balance. The scholars see the liberal order as predatory and clearly in need of transformation.

Rapprochement The reestablishment of more friendly relations between the People's Republic of China and the United States in the early 1970s.

Realism A theoretical approach that analyzes all international relations as the relation of states engaged in the pursuit of power. Realists see the international system as anarchic, or without a common power, and they believe conflict is endemic in the international system.

Realpolitik First used to describe the foreign policy of Bismarck in Prussia, it describes the practice of diplomacy based on the assessment of power, territory, and material interests, with little concern for ethical realities.

Reciprocity A form of statecraft that employs a retaliatory strategy, cooperating only if others do likewise.

Regime A set of implicit or explicit principles, norms, rules, and decision-making procedures around which actors' expectations converge in a given area of international relations. Often simply defined as a governing arrangement in a regional or global policy area.

Regional diversity Each region of the world has experienced economic development differently based on traditions, culture, historical development, and even geographic location.

Relative gains One of the factors that realists argue constrain the willingness of states to cooperate. States are less concerned about whether everyone benefits (absolute gains) and more concerned about whether someone may benefit more than someone else.

Responsibility to Protect Resolution supported by the United Nations in 2005 to determine the international community's responsibility in preventing mass atrocities, reacting to crises, protecting citizens, rebuilding, and preventing future problems.

Revolution in military affairs (RMA) The effect generated by the marriage of advanced communications and information processing with state-of-the-art weapons and delivery systems. It is a means of overcoming the uncertainty and confusion that are part of any battle in war.

Risk culture A pattern of relations within which people share the same perils.

Security The measures taken by states to ensure the safety of their citizens, the protection of their way of life, and the survival of their nation-state. Security can also mean the ownership of property that gives an individual the ability to secure the enjoyment or enforcement of a right or a basic human need.

Security community A regional group of countries that have the same guiding philosophic ideals—usually liberal-democratic principles, norms, values, and traditions—and tend to have the same style of political systems.

Security dilemma In an anarchic international system, one with no common central power, when one state seeks to improve its security it creates insecurity in other states.

Self-help In realist theory, in an anarchical environment, states cannot assume other states will come to their defense even if they are allies. Each state must take care of itself.

Skyjackings The takeover of a commercial airplane for the purpose of taking hostages and using these hostages to bargain for a particular political or economic goal.

Social movement A mode of collective action that challenges ways of life, thinking, dominant norms, and moral codes; seeks answers to global problems; and promotes reform or transformation in political and economic institutions.

Social structure An arrangement based on ideas, norms, values, and shared beliefs. According to constructivists, the social domain does not exist in nature but is constructed through processes of interaction and the sharing of meaning.

Society of states An association of sovereign states based on their common interests, values, and norms.

Soft power The influence and authority deriving from the attraction that a country's political, social, and economic ideas, beliefs, and practices have for people living in other countries.

Sovereign equality The idea that all countries have the same rights, including the right of noninterference in their internal affairs.

Sovereignty The condition of a state having control and authority over its own territory and being free from any higher legal authority. It is related to, but distinct from, the condition of a government being free from any external political constraints.

Special Drawing Right (SDR) Members of the IMF have the right to borrow this asset from the organization up to the amount that the country has invested in the IMF. The SDR is based on the value of a "basket" of the world's leading currencies: British pound, euro, Japanese yen, and U.S. dollar.

Specialized agencies International institutions that have a special relationship with the central system of the United Nations but are constitutionally independent, having their own assessed budgets, executive heads and committees, and assemblies of the representatives of all state members.

Standard operating procedures (SOPs) The prepared-response patterns that organizations create to react to general categories of events, crises, and actions.

State A legal territorial entity composed of a stable population and a government; it possesses a monopoly over the legitimate use of force; its sovereignty is recognized by other states in the international system.

State sovereignty The concept that all countries are equal under international law and that they are protected from outside interference; this is the basis on which the United Nations and other international and regional organizations operate.

State system The regular patterns of interaction between states but without implying any shared values between them. This is distinguished from the view of a "society" of states.

Statecraft The methods and tools that national leaders use to achieve the national interests of a state.

Strategic Arms Reductions Treaty (START) Negotiations between the United States and Soviet Union over limiting nuclear arsenals began in 1982 and progressed at a very slow pace over eight years. The eventual treaty in 1991 broke new ground because it called for a reduction of nuclear arms rather than just a limit on the growth of these weapons.

Strategic Defense Initiative (SDI) A controversial strategic policy advocated by the Reagan administration and nuclear physicists such as Edward Teller, who helped create the hydrogen bomb. The plan, which is often derisively nicknamed "Star Wars," called for a defensive missile shield that would make Soviet offensive missiles ineffective by destroying them in flight.

Structural realism (neorealism) A theory of realism that maintains the international system and the condition of anarchy or no common power push states and individuals to act in a way that places interests over ideologies. This condition creates a self-help system. The international system is seen as a structure acting on the state with individuals below the level of the state acting as agency on the state as a whole.

Summit diplomacy A direct meeting between heads of government (of the superpowers in particular) to resolve major problems. The summit became a regular mode of contact during the Cold War.

Superpower A state with a dominant position in the international system. It has the will and the means to influence the actions of other states in favor of its own interests, and it projects its power on a global scale to secure its national interests.

Superstructure The government or political structure that is controlled by those who own the means of production.

Supranational global organization An authoritative international organization that operates above the nation-state.

Supraterratoriality Social, economic, cultural, and political connections that transcend territorial geography.

Survival In this context, it is the survival of the person by the provision of adequate food, clean water, clothing, shelter, medical care, and protection from violence and crime.

Sustainable development Development that meets the needs of the present without compromising the ability of future generations to meet their own needs.

Tactics The conduct and management of military capabilities in or near the battle area.

Technology transfer The process of sharing skills, knowledge, technologies, methods of manufacturing, and facilities among governments and private actors (e.g., corporations) to ensure that scientific and technological developments are accessible to a wider range of users for application in new products, processes, materials, or services.

Terrorism The use of violence by nonstate groups or, in some cases, states to inspire fear by attacking civilians and/or symbolic targets and eliminating opposition groups. This is done for purposes such as drawing widespread attention to a grievance, provoking a severe response, or wearing down an opponent's moral resolve to effect political change.

Theocracy A state based on religion.

Theory A proposed explanation of an event or behavior of an actor in the real world. Definitions range from "an unproven assumption" to "a working hypothesis that proposes an explanation for an action or behavior." In international relations, we have intuitive theories, empirical theories, and normative theories.

Thirty Years' War (1618–1648) The last of the great wars in Europe fought nominally for religion.

Trade liberalization The removal or reduction of barriers to free trade such as tariffs or quotas on the trading of specific goods.

Tradition In international relations, a way of thinking that describes the nature of international politics. Such traditions include Machiavellian, Grotian, and Kantian.

Transborder Economic, political, social, or cultural activities crossing or extending across a border.

Transnational actor Any nongovernmental actor, such as a multinational corporation or a global religious humanitarian organization, that has dealings with any actor from another country or with an international organization.

Transnational advocacy network (TAN) A network of activists—often, a coalition of NGOs—distinguishable largely by the centrality of principled ideas or values in motivating its formation.

Transnational corporation A company or business that has affiliates in different countries.

Transnational nonstate actor Any nonstate or nongovernmental actor from one country that has relations with any actor from another country or with an international organization.

Treaty of Versailles, 1919 Formally ended World War I (1914–1918).

Trench warfare Warfare in which armies dug elaborate defensive fortifications in the ground, as both sides did in World War I. Because of the power of weapons like machine guns and rapid-fire cannons, trenches often gave the advantage in battle to the defenders.

Truman Doctrine A statement made by U.S. President Harry Truman in March 1947 that it "must be the policy of the United States to support free people who are resisting attempted subjugation by armed minorities or by outside pressures."

United Nations Founded in 1945 following World War II, it is an international organization composed of 193 member states dedicated to addressing issues related to peace and security, development, human rights, humanitarian affairs, and international law.

United Nations Charter (1945) The legal regime that created the United Nations. The charter defines the structure of the United Nations, the powers of its constitutive agencies, and the rights and obligations of sovereign states party to the charter.

United Nations Economic and Social Council (ECOSOC) This council is intended to coordinate the economic and social work of the United Nations and the UN family organizations. The ECOSOC has a direct link to civil society through communications with nongovernmental organizations (NGOs).

United Nations General Assembly Often referred to as a "parliament of nations," it is composed of all member states, which meet to consider the world's most pressing problems. Each state has one vote, and a two-thirds majority in the General Assembly is required for decisions on key issues. Decisions reached by the General Assembly only have the status of recommendations and are not binding.

United Nations Secretariat The Secretariat carries out the administrative work of the United Nations as directed by the General Assembly, Security Council, and other organs. The Secretariat is led by the secretary-general, who provides overall administrative guidance.

United Nations Security Council The council made up of five permanent member states (sometimes called the P-5)—namely, Great Britain, China, France, Russia, and the United States—and ten nonpermanent members. The P-5 all have a veto power over all Security Council decisions.

United Nations Trusteeship Council Upon creation of the United Nations, this council was established to provide international supervision for eleven trust territories administered by seven member states in an effort to prepare them for self-government or independence. By 1994, all trust territories had attained self-government or independence, and the council now meets on an ad hoc basis.

Universal Declaration of Human Rights The principal normative document on human rights, adopted by the UN General Assembly in 1948 and accepted as authoritative by most states and other international actors.

Venture philanthropy The practice of supporting philanthropists or social entrepreneurs by providing them with networking and leveraging opportunities.

Veto power The right of the five permanent members of the Security Council (United States, Russia, China, France, and Great Britain) to forbid any action by the United Nations.

Warsaw Pact An agreement of mutual defense and military aid signed in May 1955 in response to West Germany's rearmament and entry into NATO. It comprised the USSR and seven communist states (though Albania withdrew support in 1961). The pact was officially dissolved in July 1991.

Washington Consensus The belief of key opinion formers in Washington that global welfare would be maximized by the universal application of neo-liberal economic policies that favor a minimalist state and an enhanced role for the market.

Weapons of mass destruction (WMD) A category defined by the United Nations in 1948 to include "atomic explosive weapons, radioactive material weapons, lethal chemical and biological weapons, and any weapons developed in the future which have characteristics comparable in destructive effects to those of the atomic bomb or other weapons mentioned above."

Widening school of international security Sometimes called the Copenhagen school, these are authors who extend the definition of security to include economic, political, societal, and environmental policy areas.

World Bank Group (WBG) A collection of five agencies, the first established in 1945, with head offices in Washington, D.C. The WBG promotes development in medium- and low-income countries with project loans, structural-adjustment programs, and various advisory services.

World Trade Organization (WTO) A permanent institution established in 1995 to replace the provisional GATT. It has greater powers of enforcement and a wider agenda, covering services, intellectual property, and investment issues as well as merchandise trade.

Acharya, A. (2004), "A Holistic Paradigm," *Security Dialogue* 35: 355–356.

Acharya, A. (2007), *Promoting Human Security: Ethical, Normative and Educational Frameworks in South East Asia* (Paris: United Nations Scientific, Cultural and Educational Organization).

Addams, J. (1922), *Peace and Bread in Time of War*. With introduction by Katherine Joslin. Urbana: University of Illinois Press, 2002. Reprint.

Adler, E. (1992), "The Emergence of Cooperation: National Epistemic Communities and the International Evolution of the Idea of Nuclear Arms Control," *International Organization* 46: 101–145.

Allison, G. (1971), *Essence of Decision; Explaining the Cuban Missile Crisis* (Boston: Little, Brown).

Allison, G. (2000), "The Impact of Globalization on National and International Security." In J. S. Nye and J. D. Donahue (eds.), *Governance in a Globalizing World*, 72–85 (Washington, D.C.: Brookings Institution).

Andrew, H. (2002), "Norms and Ethics in International Relations." In W. Carlnaes, T. Risse, and B. Simmons (eds.), *Handbook of International Relations* (Thousand Oaks, Calif.: Sage).

Anheier, H., Glasius, M., and Kaldor, M. (eds.) (2004), *Global Civil Society Yearbook 2004* (London: Sage).

Armstrong, D. (1993), *Revolution and World Order: The Revolutionary State in International Society* (Oxford: Clarendon Press).

Aron, R. (1966), *The Century of Total War* (Garden City, N.Y.: Doubleday).

Axworthy, L. (2003), *Navigating a New World* (Toronto: Alfred A. Knopf Canada).

Bacevich, A. (2008), "Introduction." In R. Niebuhr, *The Irony of American History* (Chicago: University of Chicago Press).

Bakker, E. (2006), *Jihadi Terrorists in Europe, Their Characteristics and the Circumstances in Which They Joined the Jihad: An Exploratory Study* (Clingendael: Netherlands Institute of International Relations).

Bank for International Settlements (1996), *International Banking and Financial Market Developments* (Basel: Bank for International Settlements).

Bank for International Settlements (2006), Semiannual OTC Derivatives Statistics at End-June 2006. www.bis.org/ statistics (accessed June 25, 2007).

Bank for International Settlements (2015), Statistical Release: OTC Derivatives Statistics at End-June 2015. http://www.bis.org/publ/otc_hy1511.pdf (accessed February 12, 2016).

Barnett, M. (2011), "Social Constructivism." In J. Baylis, S. Smith, and P. Owens, *The Globalization of World Politics* (Oxford: Oxford University Press).

Barraclough, G. (ed.) (1984), *The Times Atlas of World History* (London: Times Books).

BBC News (2016), "Migrant Crisis: Migration to Europe Explained in Seven Charts." *BBC News*, March 4, http:// www.bbc.com/news/world-europe-34131911 (accessed March 8, 2016).

Beitz, C. (1979), *Political Theory and International Relations* (Princeton, N.J.: Princeton University Press).

Bellamy, A. J. (2002), *Kosovo and International Society* (Basingstoke: Palgrave).

Bello, W. (1994), *Dark Victory: The United States, Structural Adjustment, and Global Poverty* (London: Pluto Press).

Bennett, J., and George, S. (1987), *The Hunger Machine* (Cambridge: Polity Press).

Bethell, L. (1970), *The Abolition of the Brazilian Slave Trade: Britain, Brazil, and the Slave Trade Question 1807–1869* (Cambridge: Cambridge University Press).

Bloom, M. (2005), *Dying to Win: The Allure of Suicide Terror* (New York: Columbia University Press).

Bloomberg News (2016), "China Trade Surplus Swells as Exports Rise in Boost for Yuan." *Bloomberg News*, January 12, http://www.bloomberg.com/news/ articles/2016-01-13/china-s-exports-unexpectedly- rebound-as-yuan-weakness-kicks-in (accessed February 12, 2016).

Booth, K. (1999), "Three Tyrannies." In T. Dunne and N. J. Wheeler (eds.), *Human Rights in Global Politics* (Cambridge: Cambridge University Press).

Booth, K. (ed.) (2004), *Critical Security Studies in World Politics* (Boulder, Colo.: Lynne Rienner).

Booth, K., and Dunne, T. (1999), "Learning Beyond Frontiers." In T. Dunne and N. J. Wheeler (eds.), *Human Rights in Global Politics*, 303–328 (Cambridge: Cambridge University Press).

Braun, L. (1987), *Selected Writings on Feminism and Socialism* (Bloomington: Indiana University Press).

Breman, J. G. (2001), "The Ears of the Hippopotamus: Manifestations, Determinants, and Estimates of the Malaria Burden." *American Journal of Tropical Medicine and Hygiene* 64(1/2): 1–11. http://www.ajtmh.org/cgi/reprint/64/1_suppl/1-c (accessed June 25, 2007).

Brewer, A. (1990), *Marxist Theories of Imperialism: A Critical Survey*, 2nd ed. (London: Routledge).

Brittan, A. (1989), *Masculinity and Power* (Oxford: Basil Blackwell).

Brocklehurst, H. (2007), "Children and War." In A. Collins (ed.), *Contemporary Security Studies*, 367–382 (Oxford: Oxford University Press).

Brodie, B. (ed.) (1946), *The Absolute Weapon: Atomic Power and World Order* (New York: Harcourt Brace).

Brown, D. (2006), "Study Claims Iraq's 'Excess' Death Toll Has Reached 655,000." *Washington Post*, October 11, A12.

Brown, L. R., and Kane, H. (1995), *Full House: Reassessing the Earth's Population Carrying Capacity* (London: Earthscan).

Brundtland, G. H., et al. (1987), *Our Common Future: Report of the World Commission on Environment and Development* (The Brundtland Report) (Oxford: Oxford University Press).

Bull, H. (1977), *The Anarchical Society: A Study of Order in World Politics* (London: Macmillan).

Bureau of Investigative Journalism, The (2016), *Get the Data: Drone Wars* (London: The Bureau of Investigative Journalism). https://www.thebureauinvestigates.com/category/projects/drones/drones-graphs (accessed February 24, 2016).

Buvinic, M. (1997), "Women in Poverty: A New Global Underclass." *Foreign Policy*: 38–53.

Buzan, B. (1991), *People, State & Fear: An Agenda for International Security Studies in the Post–Cold War Era*, 2nd ed. (Hertfordshire: Harvester Wheatsheaf). First published in 1983.

Calleo, D. (1982), *The Imperious Economy* (Cambridge: Harvard University Press).

Cammack, P. (2002), "The Mother of All Governments: The World Bank's Matrix for Global Governance." In R. Wilkinson and S. Hughes (eds.), *Global Governance: Critical Perspectives* (London: Routledge).

Carver, T. (1996), *Gender Is Not a Synonym for Women* (Boulder, Colo.: Lynne Rienner).

Castells, M. (2005), "Global Governance and Global Politics," *Political Science and Politics* 38(1): 9–16.

Centers for Disease Control (2005), Fact Sheet: Tuberculosis in the United States, March 17. http://www.cdc.gov/tb/pubs/TBfactsheets.htm (accessed June 25, 2007).

Chalk, P. (1996), *West European Terrorism and Counter-Terrorism: The Evolving Dynamic* (New York: St. Martin's Press).

Ching, F. (1999), "Social Impact of the Regional Financial Crisis." In Linda Y. C. Lim, F. Ching, and Bernardo M. Villegas (eds.), *The Asian Economic Crisis: Policy Choices, Social Consequences and the Philippine Case* (New York: Asia Society). http://www.asiasociety.org/publications/update_crisis_ching.html (accessed June 25, 2007).

Christensen, T., Jørgensen, K. E., and Wiener, A. (eds.) (2001), *The Social Construction of Europe* (London: Sage).

Clark, I. (1980), *Reform and Resistance in the International Order* (Cambridge: Cambridge University Press).

Clark, I. (1989), *The Hierarchy of States: Reform and Resistance in the International Order* (Cambridge: Cambridge University Press).

Coglianese, C. (2000), "Globalization and the Design of International Institutions." In J. S. Nye and J. D. Donahue (eds.), *Governance in a Globalizing World*, 297–318 (Washington, D.C.: Brookings Institution Press).

Cohn, C. (1987), "Sex and Death in the Rational World of Defense Intellectuals," *Signs* 12(4): 687–718.

Connell, R. W. (1995), *Masculinities* (London: Routledge).

Cooper, A., Higgott, R., and Nossal, K. R. (1993), *Relocating Middle Powers* (Vancouver: University of British Columbia Press).

Cooper, R. (2000), *The Breaking of Nations: Order and Chaos in the 21st Century* (New York: Atlantic Monthly Press).

Council on Foreign Relations (2016), *Global Conflict Tracker* (New York: Council on Foreign Relations). http://www.cfr.org/global/global-conflict-tracker/p32137#!/conflict/civil-war-in-syria (accessed February 8, 2016).

Cox, R. (1981), "Social Forces, States and World Orders: Beyond International Relations Theory," *Millennium Journal of International Studies* 10(2): 126–155.

Cox, R. (1989), "Middlepowermanship, Japan, and the Future World Order," *International Journal* 44(4): 823–862.

Crenshaw, M. (ed.) (1983), *Terrorism, Legitimacy, and Power* (Middletown, Conn.: Wesleyan University Press).

Cronin, A. K. (2002–2003), "Behind the Curve: Globalization and International Terrorism," *International Security* 27(3): 30–58.

Davis, Z. S., and Frankel, B. (eds.) (1993), *The Proliferation Puzzle: Why Nuclear Weapons Spread and What Results* (London: Frank Cass).

Department for International Development (2005), *Fighting Poverty to Build a Safer World* (London: HMSO). http://www.dfid.gov.uk/pubs/files/securityforall.pdf (accessed June 25, 2007).

Department for International Development (2006), *Eliminating World Poverty: Making Governance Work for the Poor*, Cm 6876 (London: HMSO). http://www.dfid.gov.uk/pubs/files/whitepaper2006/wp2006section3.pdf, (accessed June 25, 2007).

Doyle, M. W. (1986), "Liberalism and World Politics," *American Political Science Review* 80(4): 1151–1169.

Doyle, M. W. (1995a), "Liberalism and World Politics Revisited." In C. W. Kegley (ed.) *Controversies in International Relations Theory: Realism and the Neoliberal Challenge*, 83–105 (New York: St. Martin's Press).

Doyle, M. W. (1995b), "On Democratic Peace" *International Security*, 19(4): 164–184.

Doyle, M. W. (1997), *Ways of War and Peace: Realism, Liberalism, and Socialism* (New York: W. W. Norton).

Easterly, W. (2002), "How Did Heavily Indebted Poor Countries Become Heavily Indebted? Reviewing Two Decades of Debt Relief," *World Development* 30(10): 1677–1696.

The Economist. (2015), "From Cold War to Hot War," *The Economist*: 19–22.

Ekins, P. (1992), *A New World Order: Grassroots Movements for Global Change* (London: Routledge).

Elshtain, J. B. (1987), *Women and War* (New York: Basic Books).

Elshtain, J. B., and Tobias, S. (eds.) (1990), *Women, Militarism, and War: Essays in History, Politics, and Social Theory* (Totowa, N.J.: Rowman & Littlefield).

Enloe, C. (1989), *Bananas, Beaches and Bases: Making Feminist Sense of International Politics* (London: Pandora Books).

Enloe, C. (1993), *The Morning After: Sexual Politics at the End of the Cold War* (Berkeley: University of California Press).

Enloe, C. (2000), *Maneuvers: The International Politics of Militarizing Women's Lives* (Berkeley: University of California Press).

Environmental Degradation and Conflict in Darfur: A Workshop Organized by the University of Peace of the United Nations and the Peace Research Institute, University of Khartoum, Khartoum, December 15–16, 2004.

Falk, R. (1995a), "Liberalism at the Global Level: The Last of the Independent Commissions," *Millennium Special Issue: The Globalization of Liberalism?* 24(3): 563–576.

Falk, R. (1995b), *On Humane Governance: Toward a New Global Politics* (Cambridge: Polity Press).

Fanon, F. (1990), *The Wretched of the Earth* (Harmondsworth: Penguin).

Fausto-Sterling, A. (1992), *Myths of Gender: Biological Theories About Women and Men* (New York: Basic Books).

Fausto-Sterling, A. (2000), *Sexing the Body: Gender Politics and the Construction of Sexuality* (New York: Basic Books).

Finnemore, M. (1996a), "Norms, Culture, and World Politics: Insights from Sociology's Institutionalism," *International Organization* 50(2): 325–347.

Finnemore, M. (1996b), *National Interests in International Society* (Ithaca, N.Y.: Cornell University Press).

Finnemore, M., and Sikkink, K. (October 1998), "International Norm Dynamics and Political Change," *International Organization* 52: 887–918.

Finnis, J. (1980), *Natural Law and Natural Rights* (Oxford: Clarendon Press).

Forsythe, D. P. (1988), "The United Nations and Human Rights." In L. S. Finkelstein (ed.), *Politics in the United Nations System* (Durham, N.C., and London: Duke University Press).

Fox-Keller, E. (1985), *Reflections on Gender and Science* (New Haven, Conn.: Yale University Press).

Frank, A. G. (1967), *Capitalism and Underdevelopment in Latin America* (New York: Monthly Review Press).

Friedman, J. (ed.) (2003), *Globalization, the State and Violence* (Oxford: AltaMira Press).

Friedman, T. (2005), *The World Is Flat: A Brief History of the 21st Century* (New York: Farrar, Straus, Giroux).

Fukuyama, F. (1989), "The End of History," *The National Interest* 16 (Summer): 3–18.

Gaddis, J. L. (2004), *Surprise, Security and the American Experience* (Cambridge, Mass.: Harvard University Press).

Gardner, G. T. (1994), *Nuclear Nonproliferation: A Primer* (London and Boulder, Colo.: Lynne Rienner).

Gendering Human Security: From Marginalisation to the Integration of Women in Peace-Building (Oslo: Norwegian Institute of International Affairs and Fafo Forum on Gender Relations in Post-Conflict Transitions, 2001). http://www.fafo.no/pub/rapp/352/352.pdf (accessed June 25, 2007).

George, A. (1991), *Forceful Persuasion* (Washington, D.C.: USIP).

Giddens, A. (2000), *Runaway World: How Globalization is Shaping Our Lives* (London: Routledge).

Gioseffi, D. (ed.) (2003), *Women on War: An International Anthology of Women's Writings from Antiquity to the Present*, 2nd ed. (New York: Feminist Press at the City University of New York).

Glendon, M. A. (2002), *A World Made New: Eleanor Roosevelt and the Universal Declaration of Human Rights* (New York: Random House).

Goel, V., and Wingfield, N. (2015), "Mark Zuckerberg Vows to Donate 99% of His Facebook Shares for Charity," *The New York Times*, December 1, http://www.nytimes.com/2015/12/02/technology/mark-zuckerberg-facebook-charity.html?_r=1 (accessed February 26, 2016).

Goldstein, J., and Keohane, R. (eds.) (1993), *Ideas and Foreign Policy: Beliefs, Institutions, and Political Change* (Ithaca, N.Y.: Cornell University Press).

Gong, G. W. (1984), *The Standard of "Civilization" in International Society* (Oxford: Clarendon Press).

Goodman, D., and Redclift, M. (1991), *Refashioning Nature: Food, Ecology, and Culture* (London: Routledge).

Gottlieb, R. S. (ed.) (1989), *An Anthology of Western Marxism: From Lukacs and Gramsci to Socialist-Feminism* (Oxford: Oxford University Press).

Gowa, J. (1983), *Closing the Cold Window: Domestic Politics and the End of Bretton Woods* (Ithaca, N.Y.: Cornell University Press).

Grace, C. S. (1994), *Nuclear Weapons: Principles, Effects and Survivability* (London: Brassey's).

Gray, C. S. (1996), "The Second Nuclear Age: Insecurity, Proliferation, and the Control of Arms." In W. Murray (ed.), *The Brassey's Mershon American Defense Annual, 1995–1996: The United States and The Emerging Strategic Environment*, 135–154 (Washington, D.C.: Brassey's).

Gray, C. S. (1999), "Clausewitz Rules, OK? The Future Is the Past—with GPS," *Review of International Studies* 25: 161–182.

Green, D. (1995), *Silent Revolution: The Rise of Market Economics in Latin America* (London: Latin America Bureau).

Greenwood, B. M., Bojang, K., Whitty, C. J., and Targett, G. A. (2005), "Malaria," *The Lancet* 365(9469): 1487–1498.

Gunaratna, R. (2002), *Inside Al Qaeda: Global Network of Terror* (New York: Columbia University Press).

Haass, R. (2008), "The Age of Nonpolarity," *Foreign Affairs* 87(3): 44–56.

Haraway, D. (1989), *Primate Visions: Gender, Race, and Nature in the World of Modern Science* (New York: Routledge).

Haraway, D. (1991), *Symians, Cyborgs, and Women: The Re-Invention of Nature* (New York: Routledge).

Harrington, M. (1989), *Socialism Past and Future* (New York: Arcade Publishing).

Hartsock, N. (1998), *The Feminist Standpoint Revisited and Other Essays* (Boulder, Colo.: Westview Press).

Hebron, L., and Stack, J. F. (2011), *Globalization* (Boston: Longman).

Held, D. (1993), "Democracy: From City-States to a Cosmopolitan Order? In D. Held (ed.), *Prospects for Democracy: North, South, East, West*, 13–52 (Cambridge: Polity Press).

Held, D. (1995), *Democracy and the Global Order: From the Modern State to Cosmopolitan Governance* (Cambridge: Polity Press).

Held, D., and McGrew, A. (2002), *Globalization/Anti-Globalization* (Cambridge: Polity Press; 2nd ed., 2007).

Henderson, J., Jackson, K., and Kennaway, R. (eds.) (1980), *Beyond New Zealand: The Foreign Policy of a Small State* (Auckland, N.Z.: Methuen).

Hennessy, R., and Ingraham, C. (eds.) (1997), *Materialist Feminism: A Reader in Class, Difference, and Women's Lives* (London: Routledge).

Hettne, B. (1999), "Globalization and the New Regionalism: The Second Great Transformation." In B. Hettne, A. Intoai, and O. Sunkel (eds.), *Globalism and the New Regionalism* (Basingstoke: Macmillan).

Higgins, R. (1994), *Problems and Process: International Law and How We Use It* (Oxford: Oxford University Press).

Hill, C. (2003), *The Changing Politics of Foreign Policy* (Houndmills, Basingstoke: Palgrave Macmillan).

Hirst, P., and Thompson, G. (1999), *Globalization in Question: The International Economy and the Possibilities of Governance* (Cambridge: Polity Press).

Hoffman, B. (2016), "ISIS Is Here: Return of the Jihadi," *The National Interest* (January–February 2016 Digital Edition).

Hoffman, S. (1981), *Duties Beyond Borders: On the Limits and Possibilities of Ethical International Politics* (Syracuse, N.Y.: Syracuse University Press).

Holbraad, C. (1984), *Middle Powers in International Politics* (London: Macmillan).

Holsti, K. (1991), *Peace and War: Armed Conflicts and International Order 1648–1989* (Cambridge: Cambridge University Press).

Homer-Dixon, T. (1991), "On the Threshold: Environmental Changes as Causes of Acute Conflict," *International Security* 16: 76–116.

Homer-Dixon, T. (1994), "Environmental Scarcities and Violent Conflict: Evidence from Cases," *International Security* 19(1): 5–40.

Huckerby, J. (2015), "When Women Become Terrorists." *The New York Times*, January 21, http://www.nytimes.com/2015/01/22/opinion/when-women-become-terrorists.html (accessed February 8, 2016).

Hudson, J. (2014), "Congress Approves Arming of Syrian Rebels." *Foreign Policy*. http://foreignpolicy.com/2014/09/18/congress-approves-arming-of-syrian-rebels/ (accessed February 17, 2016).

Hudson, V. (2007), *Foreign Policy Analysis. Classic and Contemporary Theory* (Lanham, Md.: Rowman and Littlefield).

Human Rights Watch. *World Report 2015: China: Events of 2014* (New York: Human Rights Watch.)

Human Security Report Project. *Human Security Report 2012: Sexual Violence, Education, and War: Beyond the Mainstream Narrative* (Vancouver: Human Security Press, 2012).

Humphreys, M., and Varshney, A. (2004), "Violent Conflict and the Millennium Development Goals: Diagnosis and Recommendations," CGSD Working Paper No. 19 (New York: Center on Globalization and Sustainable

Development, The Earth Institute at Columbia University). http://www.earthinstitute.columbia.edu/cgsd/documents/humphreys_conflict_and_MDG.pdf (accessed June 25, 2007).

Huntington, S. (1993), "The Clash of Civilizations," *Foreign Affairs* 72(3): 22–169.

Huntington, S. (1996), *The Clash of Civilizations and the Remaking of the World Order* (New York: Simon & Schuster).

Hurrell, A., and Woods, N. (1995), "Globalization and Inequality," *Millennium*, 24(3): 447–70.

Hymans, J. E. (2006). *The Psychology of Nuclear Proliferation* (Cambridge: Cambridge University Press).

Ikenberry, G. J. (1999), "Liberal Hegemony and the Future of American Post-War Order." In T. V. Paul and J. A. Hall (eds.), *International Order and the Future of World Politics*, 123–145 (Cambridge: Cambridge University Press).

Ingebritsen, C., Neumann, I., Gstohl, S., and Beyer, J. (2006), *Small States in International Relations* (Seattle: University of Washington Press).

Intergovernmental Panel on Climate Change (IPCC) (2007), *Climate Change 2007: The Physical Science BASIS*, Contribution of Working Group 1 to the Fourth Assessment Report of the Intergovernmental Panel on Climate Change. www.ipcc.ch.

International Commission on Intervention and Sovereignty (2001), *The Responsibility to Protect* (Ottawa, Canada: International Development Research Centre).

International Commission on Peace and Food (ICPF) (1994), *Uncommon Opportunities: An Agenda for Peace and Equitable Development* (London: Zed).

Jolly, R., and Ray, D. B. (2006), *National Human Development Reports and the Human Security Framework: A Review of Analysis and Experience* (Brighton: Institute of Development Studies).

Junaid, S. (2005), *Terrorism and Global Power Systems* (Oxford: Oxford University Press).

Kant, I. (1991), *Political Writings*, H. Reiss (ed.) (Cambridge: Cambridge University Press).

Karp, A. (1995), *Ballistic Missile Proliferation: The Politics and Technics* (Oxford: Oxford University Press for Stockholm International Peace Research Institute).

Keck, M., and Sikkink, K. (1998), *Activists Beyond Borders: Transnational Advocacy Networks in International Politics* (Ithaca, N.Y.: Cornell University Press).

Keohane, R. (1984), *After Hegemony: Cooperation and Discord in the World Political Economy* (Princeton, N.J.: Princeton University Press).

Keohane, R. (ed.) (1989a), *International Institutions and State Power: Essays in International Relations Theory* (Boulder, Colo.: Westview Press).

Keohane, R. (1989b), "Theory of World Politics: Structural Realism and Beyond." In R. Keohane (ed.), *International Institutions and State Power: Essays in International Relations Theory* (Boulder, Colo.: Westview Press).

Keohane, R. (2002a), "The Globalization of Informal Violence, Theories of World Politics, and the 'Liberalism of Fear.'" In R. Keohane (ed.), *Power and Governance in a Partially Globalized World*, 272–287 (London: Routledge).

Keohane, R. (2002b), "The Public Delegitimation of Terrorism and Coalitional Politics." In K. Booth and T. Dunne (eds.), *Worlds in Collision: Terror and the Future of Global Order*, 141–151 (London: Palgrave Macmillan).

Keohane, R., and Nye, J. (eds.) (1972), *Transnational Relations and World Politics* (Cambridge, Mass.: Harvard University Press).

Kinsella, H. M. (2003), "For a Careful Reading: The Conservativism of Gender Constructivism," *International Studies Review* 5: 294–297.

Kinsella, H. M. (2005a), "Discourses of Difference: Civilians, Combatants, and Compliance with the Laws of War," *Review of International Studies* (Special Issue): 163–185.

Kinsella, H. M. (2005b), "Securing the Civilian: Sex and Gender and Laws of War." In M. Barnett and R. Duvall (eds.), *Power in Global Governance*, 249–272 (Cambridge: Cambridge University Press).

Kinsella, H. M. (2006), "Gendering Grotius: Sex and Sex Difference in the Laws of War," *Political Theory* 34(2): 161–191.

Kirkpatrick, J. (1979), "Dictatorships and Double Standards," *Commentary* 68(5): 34–45.

Kissinger, H. A. (1977), *American Foreign Policy*, 3rd ed. (New York: W. W. Norton).

Knutsen, T. (1997), *A History of International Relations* (Manchester: Manchester University Press).

Koehler, S. (February 7, 2007), "Professor Explains Continuous Threat from Land Mines," *Ozarks Local News*. http://www.banminesusa.org (accessed June 25, 2007).

Krause, K., and Williams, M. C. (eds.) (1997), *Critical Security Studies: Concepts and Cases* (London: UCL Press).

Laqueur, W. (1996), "Post-Modern Terrorism," *Foreign Affairs* 75(5): 24–37.

Lavoy, P. (1995), "The Strategic Consequences of Nuclear Proliferation: A Review Essay," *Security Studies* 4(4): 695–753.

Leventhal, P., and Alexander, Y. (eds.) (1987), *Preventing Nuclear Terrorism* (Lexington, Mass., and Toronto: Lexington Books).

Lind, W. S., and colleagues (October 1989), "The Changing Face of War: Into the Fourth Generation," *Marine Corps Gazette*: 22–26.

Little, R. (1996), "The Growing Relevance of Pluralism?" In S. Smith, K. Booth, and M. Zalewski (eds.), *International Theory: Positivism and Beyond*, 66–86 (Cambridge: Cambridge University Press).

Longino, H. E. (1990), *Science as Social Knowledge: Values and Objectivity in Scientific Inquiry* (Princeton, N.J.: Princeton University Press).

Luard, E. (ed.) (1992), *Basic Texts in International Relations* (London: Macmillan).

MacFarlane, N., and Khong, Y. F. (2006), *Human Security and the UN: A Critical History* (Bloomington: Indiana University Press).

Mackinnon, C. (1993), "Crimes of War, Crimes of Peace." In S. Shute and S. Hurley (eds.), *On Human Rights* (New York: Basic Books).

Marx, K. (1888), "Theses on Feuerbach." In *Selected Works*, K. Marx and F. Engels, 28–30 (London: Lawrence and Wishart, 1968).

Marx, K. (1992), *Capital*, student ed. C. J. Arthur (ed.) (London: Lawrence & Wishart). First published 1867.

Marx, K., and Engels, F. (1848), *The Communist Manifesto*, intr. by E. Hobsbawm (London: Verso, 1998).

Mathews, J. (1997), "Power Shift," *Foreign Affairs* 76(1): 50–66.

Mead, W. R. (2001), *Special Providence: American Foreign Policy and How It Changed the World* (New York: Knopf).

Meadows, D. H., Meadows, D. L., and Randers, J. (1972), *The Limits to Growth* (London: Earth Island).

Mearsheimer, J. (1994–1995), "The False Promise of International Institutions," *International Security* 19(3): 5–49.

Mearsheimer, J. (2001), *The Tragedy of Great Power Politics* (New York: W. W. Norton).

Metz, S. (2004), *Armed Conflict in the 21st Century: The Information Revolution and Post Modern Warfare* (Honolulu, Hawaii: University Press of the Pacific).

Meyer, S. M. (1984), *The Dynamics of Nuclear Proliferation* (Chicago: University of Chicago Press).

Milner, H. V. (1988), *Resisting Protectionism: Global Industries and the Politics of International Trade* (Princeton, N.J.: Princeton University Press).

Mingst, K. (2004), *Essentials of International Relations* (New York: W. W. Norton).

Mitrany, D. (1943), *A Working Peace System* (London: RIIA).

Morgenthau, H. J. ([1948], 1955, 1962, 1978), *Politics Among Nations: The Struggle for Power and Peace*, 2nd ed. (New York: Alfred A. Knopf).

Morgenthau, H. J. (1952), *American Foreign Policy: A Critical Examination* (also published as *In Defence of the National Interest*) (London: Methuen).

Morgenthau, H. J. (1960), *Politics Among Nations* (New York: Alfred A. Knopf).

Morgenthau, H. J. (1985), *Politics Among Nations*, 6th ed. (New York: McGraw-Hill).

Mousseau, F., and Mittal, A. (October 26, 2006), Free Market Famine: Foreign Policy in Focus Commentary. www.fpif.org/pdf/gac/0610famine.pdf (accessed June 25, 2007).

Muldoon, J. (2004), *The Architecture of Global Governance: An Introduction to the Study of International Organizations* (Boulder, Colo.: Westview Press).

Naisbitt, J. (1994), *Global Paradox: The Bigger the World-Economy, the More Powerful Its Smallest Players* (London: Brealey).

Nardelli, A. (2015), "Germany Receives Nearly Half of All Syrian Asylum Spplicants." *The Guardian*, November 5, http://www.theguardian.com/world/2015/nov/05/asylum-applications-to-germany-see-160-rise (accessed February 8, 2016).

Nardin, T. (1983), *Law, Morality and the Relations of States* (Princeton, N.J.: Princeton University Press).

National Consortium for the Study of Terrorism and Responses to Terrorism (2015), *Mass-Fatality, Coordinated Attacks Worldwide, and Terrorism in France.* http://www.start.umd.edu/pubs/START_ParisMassCasualtyCoordinatedAttack_Nov2015.pdf (accessed February 8, 2016).

National Counter Terrorism Center (2005), NCTC Fact Sheet and Observations Related to 2005 Terrorist Incidents. www.NCTC.gov (accessed June 25, 2007).

National Security Strategy (2001, 2002). *National Security Strategy of the United States of America* (Washington, D.C.: U.S. Government Printing Office).

Norchi, C. (2004), "Human Rights: A Global Common Interest." In Jean Krasno, ed., *The United Nations: Confronting the Challenges of a Global Society* (Boulder, Colo.: Lynne Rienner Publishers).

Nussbaum, M. (1996), *For Love of Country: Debating the Limits of Patriotism* (Boston: Beacon Press).

Nye, J. S. (2004), *Soft Power* (New York: Public Affairs).

O'Brien, R. (1992), *Global Financial Integration: The End of Geography* (London: Pinter).

Office of the Director of National Intelligence (2005), Letter from Al-Zawahiri to Al-Zarqawi, October 11.

Ogilvie-White, T. (1996), "Is There a Theory of Nuclear Proliferation?" *The Nonproliferation Review* 4(1): 43–60.

Ogilvie-White, T., and Simpson, J. (2003), "The NPT and Its Prepcom Session: A Regime in Need of Intensive Care," *The Nonproliferation Review* 10(1): 40–58.

Olson, J. S. (ed.) (1988), *Dictionary of the Vietnam War* (New York: Greenwood Press).

Onwudiwe, I. D. (2001), *The Globalization of Terror* (Burlington, Vt.: Ashgate).

Ougaard, M. (2004), *Political Globalization—State, Power, and Social Forces* (London: Palgrave).

Owens, P. (2007), *Between War and Politics: International Relations and the Thought of Hannah Arendt* (Oxford: Oxford University Press).

Oxfam (2003). "Boxing Match in Agricultural Trade," Briefing Paper No. 32. www.oxfam.org (accessed June 25, 2007).

Oxfam (2006), Grounds for Change: Creating a Voice for Small Farmers and Farm Workers with Next International Coffee Agreement. http://www.oxfam.org/en/policy/briefingnotes/bn0604_coffee_groundsforchange (accessed June 25, 2007).

Palme Commission (1982), *Common Security: A Programme for Disarmament. The Report of the Palme Commission* (London: Pan Books).

Panofsky, W. K. H. (1998), "Dismantling the Concept of 'Weapons of Mass Destruction,' " *Arms Control Today* 28(3): 3–8.

Pape, R. (2006), *Dying to Win: The Strategic Logic of Suicide Terrorism* (New York: Random House).

Pastor, R. (1999), *A Century's Journey: How the Great Powers Shape the World* (New York: Basic Books).

Pearson, R. (2000), "Rethinking Gender Matters in Development." In T. Allen and A. Thomas (eds.), *Poverty and Development into the Twenty-First Century*, 383–402 (Oxford: Oxford University Press).

Pendergrast, M. (1993), *For God, Country, and Coca-Cola: The Unauthorized History of the Great American Soft Drink and the Company That Makes It* (London: Weidenfeld & Nicolson).

Peters, J. S., and Wolper, A. (eds.) (1995), *Women's Rights, Human Rights: International Feminist Perspectives* (New York: Routledge).

Petzold-Bradley, E., Carius, A., and Vincze, A. (eds.) (2001), *Responding to Environmental Conflicts: Implications for Theory and Practice* (Dordrecht, the Netherlands: Kluwer Academic).

Pogge, T. (2002), *World Poverty and Human Rights: Cosmopolitan Responsibilities and Reforms* (Cambridge: Polity Press).

Power and Interest News Report (2006), "Asia's Coming Water Wars," August 22. http://www.pinr.com (accessed June 25, 2007).

Price, R. (1998), "Reversing the Gun Sights: Transnational Civil Society Targets Land Mines," *International Organization* 52(3): 613–644.

Price, R., and Tannenwald, N. (1996), "Norms and Deterrence: The Nuclear and Chemical Weapons Taboos." In P. J. Katzenstein (ed.), *The Culture of National Security: Norms and Identity in World Politics*, 114–152 (New York: Columbia University Press).

Pugh, M. (2001), "Peacekeeping and Humanitarian Intervention." In B. White, R. Little, and M. Smith (eds.), *Issues in World Politics*, 2nd ed. (London: Palgrave).

Rabasa, A., Chalk, P., et al. (2006), *Beyond al-Qaeda: Part 2, The Outer Rings of the Terrorist Universe* (Santa Monica, Calif.: RAND).

Rapley, J. (1996) *Understanding Development* (Boulder, Colo.: Lynne Rienner).

Rehn, E., and Sirleaf, E. J. (2002), Women, War, Peace: The Independent Experts' Assessment on the Impact of Armed Conflict on Women and Women's Role in Peace-Building. http://www.unifem.org/resources/item_detail.php?ProductID=17 (accessed June 25, 2007).

Reus-Smit, C. (1999), *The Moral Purpose of the State* (Princeton, N.J.: Princeton University Press).

Reus-Smit, C. (2001), "The Strange Death of Liberal International Theory," *European Journal of International Law* 12(3): 573–593.

Rhodes, E. (2003), "The Imperial Logic of Bush's Liberal Agenda," *Survival* 45: 131–154.

Rice, S. (2006), "The Threat of Global Poverty," *The National Interest* 83: 76–82.

Richardson, J. L. (1997), "Contending Liberalisms: Past and Present," *European Journal of International Relations* 3(1): 5–33.

Rischard, J. F. (2002), *High Noon: Twenty Global Problems, Twenty Years to Solve Them* (New York: Basic Books).

Roberts, A. (1996), "The United Nations: Variants of Collective Security." In N. Woods (ed.), *Explaining International Relations Since 1945*, 309–336 (Oxford: Oxford University Press).

Roberts, A., and Kingsbury, B. (1993), "Introduction: The UN's Roles in International Society Since 1945." In A. Roberts and B. Kingsbury (eds.), *United Nations, Divided World* (Oxford: Clarendon Press).

Roberts, G. (1984), *Questioning Development* (London: Returned Volunteer Action).

Roberts, S. (1994), "Fictitious Capital, Fictitious Spaces: The Geography of Offshore Financial Flows." In S. Corbridge et al. (eds.), *Money, Power and Space* (Oxford: Blackwell).

Roche, D. (1986), "Balance Out of Kilter in Arms/Society Needs," *Financial Post*, January 18, 8.

Rodrik, D. (1999), *The New Global Economy and Developing Countries: Making Openness Work* (Washington, D.C.: Overseas Development Council, 148).

Rorty, R. (1993), "Sentimentality and Human Rights." In S. Shute and S. Hurley (eds.), *On Human Rights* (New York: Basic Books).

Rosamond, B. (2000), *Theories of European Integration* (Basingstoke: Macmillan).

Rose, G. (1998), "Neoclassical Realism and Theories of Foreign Policy," *World Politics* 51(1): 144–172.

Rosenau, J. (1981), *The Study of Political Adaptation* (London: Pinter Publishers).

Sagan, S. D., and Waltz, K. N. (1995), *The Spread of Nuclear Weapons: A Debate* (New York and London: W. W. Norton; 2nd ed., 2003).

Sageman, M. (2004), *Understanding Terror Networks* (Philadelphia: University of Pennsylvania Press).

Sargent, L. (ed.) (1981), *Women and Revolution: A Discussion of the Unhappy Marriage of Marxism and Feminism* (Boston: South End).

Scholte, J. A. (2005), *Globalization: A Critical Introduction* (Basingstoke: Macmillan; 2nd ed., 2005).

Schwarz, A. (1999), *A Nation in Waiting: Indonesia's Search for Stability* (Sydney: Allen & Unwin).

Schweller, R. L. (1996), "Neo-Realism's Status-Quo Bias: What Security Dilemma?" *Security Studies* 5: 90–121.

Schweller, R. L. (1998), *Deadly Imbalances: Tripolarity and Hitler's Strategy of World Conquest* (New York: Columbia University Press).

Seidler, V. (1989), *Rediscovering Masculinity: Reason, Language, and Sexuality* (London: Routledge).

Sen, A. (1981), *Poverty and Famines* (Oxford: Clarendon Press).

Sen, A. (1983), "The Food Problem: Theory and Policy." In A. Gauhar (ed.), *South-South Strategy* (London: Zed).

Sen, A. (1999), *Development as Freedom* (Oxford: Oxford University Press).

Shue, H. (1996), *Basic Rights*, 2nd ed. (Princeton, N.J.: Princeton University Press).

Simon Fraser University, Human Security Research Group (2011), "Human Security Report 2009–2010," Retrieved from: http://www.hsrgroup.org/human-security-reports/20092010/text.aspx

Smith, K. E., and Light, M. (eds.) (2001), *Ethics and Foreign Policy* (Cambridge: Cambridge University Press).

Smith, M. J. (1986), *Realist Thought from Weber to Kissinger* (Baton Rouge: Louisiana State University Press).

Smith, M. J. (2002), "On Thin Ice: First Steps for the Ballistic Missile Code of Conduct," *Arms Control Today* 32(6): 9–13.

Smith, S. (1999), "The Increasing Insecurity of Security Studies: Conceptualising Security in the Last Twenty Years," *Contemporary Security Policy* 20(3): 72–101.

Spivak, G. C. (1988), "Can the Subaltern Speak?" In C. Nelson and L. Grossberg (eds.), *Marxism and the Interpretation of Culture* (Basingstoke: Macmillan).

Steans, J. (1998), *Gender and International Relations: An Introduction* (Cambridge: Polity Press).

Suganami, H. (1989), *The Domestic Analogy and World Order Proposals* (Cambridge: Cambridge University Press).

Suhrke, A. (2004), "A Stalled Initiative," *Security Dialogue* 35(3): 365.

Tang, J. H. (ed.) (1994), *Human Rights and International Relations in the Asia-Pacific Region* (London: Pinter).

Tasch, B. (2015), "The 23 Poorest Countries in the World," *Business Insider*, July 13, http://www.businessinsider.com/the-23-poorest-countries-in-the-world-2015-7 (accessed February 26, 2016).

Thomas, A., et al. (1994), *Third World Atlas*, 2nd ed. (Milton Keynes: Open University Press).

Thomas, C. (2000), *Global Governance, Development, and Human Security* (London: Pluto).

Thomas, C., and Wilkin, P. (2004), "Still Waiting After All These Years: The Third World on the Periphery of International Relations," *British Journal of Politics and International Relations* 6: 223–240.

Thucydides ([1954], 1972), *The Peloponnesian War*, R. Warner (trans.) (London: Penguin).

Tickner, J. A. (1992), *Gender in International Relations: Feminist Perspectives on Achieving Global Security* (New York: Columbia University Press).

Tow, W. T., and Trood, R. (2000), "Linkages Between Traditional Security and Human Security." In W. T. Tow, R. Thakur, and In-Taek Hyun (eds.), *Asia's Emerging Regional Order* (New York: United Nations University Press).

UN Conference on Trade and Development, Division on Transnational Corporations and Investment (1996), *Transnational Corporations and World Development* (London: International Thomson Business Press).

UN Conference on Trade and Development (2006a), *Trade and Development Report* (Geneva: United Nations Conference on Trade and Development).

UN Conference on Trade and Development (2006b), *World Investment Report 2006* (Geneva: United Nations Conference on Trade and Development).

UN Conference on Trade and Development (2015), *World Investment Report 2015: Reforming International Investment Governance* (Geneva: United Nations Conference on Trade and Development).

UN Development Programme (1994), *United Nations Human Development Report* (New York: Oxford University Press).

UN Development Programme (1997), *United Nations Human Development Report 1997* (New York: United Nations Development Programme).

UN Development Programme (1998), *United Nations Human Development Report 1998* (Oxford: Oxford University Press).

UN Development Programme (2003), *United Nations Human Development Report* (New York: United Nations Development Programme).

UN Development Programme (2005), *Human Development Report 2005: International Cooperation at a Crossroads* (New York: United Nations Development Programme).

UN Development Programme (2015), *Human Development Report 2015: Work for Human Development* (New York: United Nations Development Programme).

United Nations (2002), *Women, Peace, and Security: Study Submitted by the Secretary-General Pursuant to Security Council Resolution 1325 (2000)* (New York: United Nations). http://www.un.org/womenwatch/feature/wps (accessed June 25, 2007).

United Nations (2004), *A More Secure World.* UN Secretary-General's High-Level Panel on Threats, Challenges, and Change. http://www.un.org/secureworld

United Nations (March 2005), *In Larger Freedom: Towards Development, Security and Human Rights for All: Report of the Secretary-General.*

United Nations Framework Convention on Climate Change (2015), *Paris Agreement* (Paris: Conference of the Parties, Twenty-first session).

United Nations High Commissioner for Refugees (2015), 2015 UNHCR country operations profile—Sudan (New York: United Nations). http://www.unhcr.org/pages/49e483b76.html (accessed February 8, 2016).

United Nations Inter-Agency Committee on Women and Gender Equality (December 7–8, 1999), *Final Communiqué, Women's Empowerment in the Context of Human Security* (Bangkok, Thailand: ESCAP). http://www.un.org/womenwatch/ianwge/collaboration/finalcomm1999.htm (accessed June 25, 2007).

United Nations Peacekeeping (2016), *Peacekeeping Fact Sheet* (New York: United Nations). http://www.un.org/en/peacekeeping/resources/statistics/factsheet.shtml (accessed February 26, 2016).

University of British Columbia, Human Security Center (2005), *Human Security Report 2005: War and Peace in the 21st Century* (New York: Oxford University Press).

University of British Columbia, Human Security Center (2006), *The Human Security Brief 2006.* http://www.humansecuritybrief.info (accessed June 25, 2007).

Uppsala Conflict Data Program (UCDP), *Uppsala University, Uppsala, Sweden/Human Security Report Project, School for International Studies,* Simon Fraser University, Vancouver, Canada.

U.S. Department of State (March 31, 2003), *Country Reports on Human Rights Practices, Burma.* http://www.state.gov/g/drl/rls/hrrpt/2002/18237.htm (accessed June 25, 2007).

Vincent, R. J. (1974), *Nonintervention and International Order* (Princeton, N.J.: Princeton University Press).

von Grebmer, K., et al. (2013). "2013 Global Hunger Index— The Challenge of Hunger: Building Resilience to Achieve Food and Nutrition Security. 'Global Hunger Index Scores by Severity' map" (Bonn, Germany: Welthungerhilfe; Washington, D.C.: International Food Policy Research Institute; Dublin, Ireland: Concern Worldwide).

Wallerstein, I. (1979), *The Capitalist World-Economy* (Cambridge: Cambridge University Press).

Walt, S. (2002), "The Enduring Relevance of the Realist Tradition." In I. Katznelson and H. V. Milner (eds.), *Political Science: The State of the Discipline* (New York: W. W. Norton).

Waltz, K. (1959), *Man, the State and War* (New York: Columbia University Press).

Waltz, K. (1979), *Theory of International Politics* (Reading, Mass.: Addison-Wesley).

Waltz, K. (1989), "The Origins of War in Neorealist Theory." In R. I. Rotberg and T. K. Rabb (eds.), *The Origin and Prevention of Major Wars,* 39–52 (Cambridge: Cambridge University Press).

Walzer, M. (1977), *Just and Unjust Wars: A Moral Argument with Historical Illustration* (Harmondsworth: Penguin and New York: Basic Books).

Walzer, M. (1994), *Thick and Thin: Moral Argument at Home and Abroad* (Notre Dame, Ind.: University of Notre Dame Press).

Walzer, M. (1995), "The Politics of Rescue," *Dissent* (Winter): 35–40.

Weaver, O., Buzan, B., Kelstrup, M., and Lemaitre, P. (1993), *Identity, Migration and the New Security Agenda in Europe* (London: Pinter).

Weber, H. (2002), "Global Governance and Poverty Reduction." In S. Hughes and R. Wilkinson (eds.), *Global Governance: Critical Perspectives* (London: Palgrave).

Weber, M. (1949), *The Methodology of the Social Sciences,* E. Shils and H. Finch (eds.) (New York: Free Press).

Weiss, T. G. (2004), "The Sunset of Humanitarian Intervention? The Responsibility to Protect in a Unipolar Era," *Security Dialogue* 35(2): 135–153.

Wendt, A. (1992), "Anarchy Is What States Make of It: The Social Construction of Power Politics," *International Organisation* 46(2): 391–425.

Wendt, A. (1995), "Constructing International Politics," *International Security* 20(1).

Wendt, A. (1999), *Social Theory of International Politics* (Cambridge: Cambridge University Press).

Wessel, I., and Wimhofer, G. (eds.) (2001), *Violence in Indonesia* (Hamburg: Abera-Verlag).

Weston, B. H., Falk, R., and D'Amato, A. (1990), *Basic Documents in International Law*, 2nd ed. (St. Paul, Minn.: West Publishing).

Wheeler, N. J., and Booth, K. (1992), "The Security Dilemma." In J. Baylis and N. J. Rengger (eds.), *Dilemmas of World Politics: International Issues in a Changing World* (Oxford: Oxford University Press).

Wiener, A., and Diez, T. (eds.) (2004), *European Integration Theory* (Oxford: Oxford University Press).

Wilkinson, P. (2003), "Implications of the Attacks of 9/11 for the Future of Terrorism." In M. Buckley and R. Fawn (eds.), *Global Responses to Terrorism* (London: Routledge).

Wood, B. (1998), *The Middle Powers and the General Interest* (Ottawa: North-South Institute).

World Food Programme (2016), Hunger Statistics (Rome: World Food Programme). https://www.wfp.org/hunger/stats (accessed January 28, 2016).

World Health Organization (n.d.), Roll Back Malaria: The Economic Costs of Malaria (Geneva: WHO). http://www.rbm.who.int/cmc_upload/0/000/015/363/RBMInfosheet_10.htm (accessed June 25, 2007).

World Health Organization (February 2006), Avian Influenza ("Bird Flu")—Fact Sheet. www.who.int/mediacentre/factsheets/avian_influenza/en (accessed June 25, 2007).

World Trade Organization (1995), *International Trade: Trends and Statistics* (Geneva: WTO).

World Trade Organization (2013), *9th WTO Ministerial Conference, Bali, 2013, Briefing Note: Regional Trade Agreements* (Geneva: WTO).

Wright, R. (1986), *Sacred Rage: The Wrath of Militant Islam* (New York: Simon & Schuster).

Yale University Cambodian Genocide Program. http://www.yale.edu/cgp

Zakaria, F. (1998), *From Wealth to Power: The Unusual Origins of America's World Role* (Princeton, N.J.: Princeton University Press).

Zalewski, M. (1993), "Feminist Standpoint Theory Meets International Relations Theory: A Feminist Version of David and Goliath," *Fletcher Forum of World Affairs* 17(2).

Zalewski, M., and Parpart, J. (eds.) (1998), *The "Man" Question in International Relations* (Boulder, Colo.: Westview Press).

Zengerle, P., and Lawder, D. (2014), "U.S. Congress Approves Arming Syrian Rebels, Funding Government," *Reuters*. http://www.reuters.com/article/us-iraq-crisis-congress-vote-idUSKBN0HD2P820140919 (accessed February 17, 2016).

Zevin, R. (1992), "Are World Financial Markets More Open? If So, Why and with What Effects?" In T. Banuri and J. B. Schor (eds.), *Financial Openness and National Autonomy: Opportunities and Constraints* (Oxford: Clarendon Press).

PHOTO CREDITS

Chapter 1

p. 2: Kyodo via AP Images; p. 6: AP Photo/Charles Dharapak; p. 8: AP Photo/Geert Vanden Wijngaert, FILE; p. 10: Jack Dempsey/AP Images for IKEA; p. 11: Dennis Van Tine/STAR MAX/IPx 5/20/15; p. 13: AP Photo/Denis Farrell; p. 15: Kyodo via AP Images; p. 17: Doreen Fiedler/picture-alliance/dpa/AP Images; p. 21: AP Photo/Musadeq Sadeq; p. 25 (top): AP Photo/Bernat Armangue; p. 25 (bottom): AP Photo/Alexander Zemlianichenko

Chapter 2

p. 28: AP Photo/Karl-Heinz Kreifelts; p. 33: North Wind Picture Archives via AP Images; p. 36: AP Photo; p. 37: Getty Images; p. 38: AP Photo; p. 41: Time & Life Pictures/Getty Images; p. 44: AP Photo; p. 47: AP Photo; p. 53: AP Photo/Hani Mohammed; p. 56: Robert Geiss/picture-alliance/dpa/AP Images; p. 58: AP Photo/Evan Vucci; p. 61: AP Photo/Saurabh Das; p. 64: AP Photo/Jens Meyer; p. 65: Stefan Rousseau/PA Wire

Chapter 3

p. 70: AP Photo/Andrew Harnik; p. 73: AP Photo/Evgeniy Maloletka; p. 77: AP Photo; p. 82: AP Photo/Eraldo Peres; p. 88: AP Photo/Martin Meissner; p. 89: Time & Life Pictures/Getty Images; p. 92: AP Photo/Virginia Mayo; p. 94: Carlos Barria/Pool Photo via AP; p. 95: AP Photo/Ben Curtis; p. 100: AP Photo/Herbert Knosowski; p. 106: AP Photo/Bilal Hussein; p. 109: AP Photo/Miguel Medina, Pool

Chapter 4

p. 114: (Pool photo)(Kyodo via AP Images); p. 119: AP Photo/Yves Logghe; p. 121: Paul Chiasson/The Canadian Press via AP; p. 122: AP Photo/Farah Abdi Warsameh; p. 136: Agencia EL UNIVERSAL/RML (GDA via AP Images); p. 140: AP Photo/Keystone, Jean-Christophe Bott, File; p. 142: AP Photo/Najim Rahim; p. 143: AP Photo/Bikas Das; p. 145: AP Photo/Peter Dejong; p. 147: Lynsey Addario; p. 150: AP Photo/Adel Hana; p. 152: The United States Navy

Chapter 5

p. 156: AP Photo/Aimen Zine, File; p. 160: Kyodo via AP Images; p. 162: AP Photo/Abd Raouf; p. 165: AP Photo; p. 172: Photo by Dasril Roszandi/NurPhoto (Sipa via AP Images); p. 181: AP Photo/Hassene Dridi; p. 184: AP Photo; p. 186: AP Photo/Nader Daoud; p. 189: Alex Masi/Corbis/AP Images; p. 190: Per-Anders Pettersson/Getty Images; p. 191: AP Photo/Aijaz Rahi; p. 193: AP Photo/Eduardo Verdugo; p. 196: AP Photo/Sayyid Azim; p. 200: AP Photo/Lennart Preiss; p. 201: Photo by Oscar Gonzalez/NurPhoto (Sipa via AP Images)

Chapter 6

p. 206: AP Photo/Manu Brabo, File; p. 209: AP Photo/Lefteris Pitarakis, File; p. 212: AP Photo/Hasan Jamali; p. 214: AP Photo/Turkish Military HQ; p. 217: AP Photo/Kamran Jebreili; p. 218: AP Photo/Lefteris Pitarakis; p. 220: AP Photo/Kyodo News; p. 222: AP Photo/David Guttenfelder; p. 223: AP Photo/Steve Helber; p. 229: AP Photo/Vahid Salemi; p. 233: AP Photo, File; p. 235: AP Photo/Martin Cleaver, File; p. 239: Press Association via AP Images; p. 248: AP Photo/Matt Dunham

Chapter 7

p. 252: AP Photo/Mark Lennihan; p. 257: AP Photo/Arnulfo Franco; p. 260: AP Photo/Susan Walsh, File; p. 261: AP Photo/Muhammed Muheisen; p. 265: AP Photo/Raad Adayleh; p. 266: AP Photo/Jerome Delay; p. 270: AP Photo/UNAMID, Albert Gonzalez Farran, File; p. 272: AP Photo/Bullit Marquez; p. 275: AP Photo/Jae C. Hong; p. 281: AP Photo/Desi Sari; p. 283: Associated Press via AP Photo; p. 285: AP Photo/Vladimir Isachenkov

Chapter 8

p. 288: AP Photo/Yorgos Karahalis; p. 292: AP Photo/Abe Fox; p. 294: Imaginechina via AP Images; p. 295: Imaginechina via AP Images; p. 300: AP Photo/Moises Castillo; p. 301: Kyodo via AP Images; p. 307: Imaginechina via AP Images; p. 309: Imaginechina via AP Images; p. 310: AP Photo; p. 318: AP Photo/Thanassis Stavrakis

Chapter 9

p. 322: Rex Features via AP Images; p. 325: Jesko Johannsen/picture-alliance/dpa/AP Images; p. 330: Media for Medical/UIG via Getty Images; p. 337: AP Photo/Felipe Dana; p. 339: AP Photo/Michael Probst, File; p. 341: AP Photo; p. 347: AP Photo/Gregory Bull; p. 348: AP Photo/Rahmat Gul; p. 350: AP Photo/George Osodi

Chapter 10

p. 354: NASA EO/Rex Features via AP Images; p. 358: Rex Features via AP Images; p. 361: AP Photo/Jason DeCrow; p. 362: Kathrin Lauer/picture-alliance/dpa/AP Images; p. 366: Jens Büttner/picture-alliance/dpa/AP Images; p. 370: Rex Features via AP Images; p. 372: AP Photo/Ricardo Arduengo; p. 375: Imaginechina via AP Images; p. 376 (top): AP Photo/NOAA; p. 376 (bottom): AP Photo/Sunday Alamba; p. 379: AP Photo/Wichita Falls Times Record News, Torin Halsey; p. 381: AP Photo/Rune Stoltz Bertinussen/Scanpix Norway

FIGURE CREDITS

Chapter 2
p. 49: © Natural Resources Defense Council; p. 62: *Vital Signs 2006-2007*, The Worldwatch Institute

Chapter 4
p. 139: Source: Stockholm International Peace Research Institute (SIPRI); p. 141: CIA World Factbook

Chapter 5
p. 166: © United Nations; p. 191: Union of International Associations; p. 168: "The United Nations System" © United Nations Department of Public Information, 2007; p. 199: *2012 Global Go To Think Tanks Report and Policy Advice. FINAL UNITED NATIONS UNIVERSITY EDITION, JANUARY 28, 2013. Think Tanks and Civil Societies Program* © *2012, University of Pennsylvania, International Relations Program*

Chapter 6
p. 217: Source: Conventional Arms Transfers to Developing Nations, 2007–2014, page 19; p. 219: Source: Conventional Arms Transfers to Developing Nations, 2007–2014, page 20; p. 244: Source: The Brookings Project on U.S. Relations with the Islamic World Analysis Paper. No. 20, March 2015. "The ISIS Twitter Census: Defining and describing the population of ISIS supporters on Twitter." By J.M. Berger and Jonathon Morgan. Page 12.

Chapter 7
p. 278: Source: © UCDP 2015

Chapter 8
p. 303: Source: Australian Trade Commission and the World Trade Organization, 2015; p. 306: Source: Central Intelligence Agency, The World Factbook; p. 314: Source: Federal Reserve Bank of St. Louis

Chapter 9
p. 333: United Nations, based on data and estimates provided by: Food and Agriculture Organization of the United Nations; Inter-Parliamentary Union; International Labour Organization; International Telecommunication Union; UNAIDS; UNESCO; UN-Habitat; UNICEF; UN Population Division; World Bank; World Health Organization—based on statistics available as of June 2013. Compiled by Statistics Division, Department of Economic and Social Affairs, United Nations; p. 345: Source: United Nations; p. 346: Source: United Nations

Chapter 10
p. 374: The International Tanker Owners Pollution Federation Limited; p. 377: Source: IPCC (2014); Exit EPA Disclaimer based on global emissions from 2010. Details about the sources included in these estimates can be found in the Contribution of Working Group III to the Fifth Assessment Report of the Intergovernmental Panel on Climate Change; p. 378: © Statista 2016

MAP CREDITS

Frontmatter
xxx–xxxvii: Cartography © Philip's; xxx: Cartography © Philip's; xxxi: Cartography © Philip's; xxxii: Cartography © Philip's; xxxiii: Cartography © Philip's; xxxiv: Cartography © Philip's; xxxv: Cartography © Philip's; xxxvi: Cartography © Philip's; xxxvii: Cartography © Philip's

Chapter 2
p. 35: Cartography © Philip's; p. 39: Cartography © Philip's; p. 40: Cartography © Philip's

Chapter 6
p. 227: Federation of American Scientists; Nuclear Threat Initiative; p. 243: New York Times/Sources: Institute for the Study of War, Soufan Group, State Department, Justice Department. http://www.nytimes.com/interactive/2015/06/17/world/middleeast/map-isis-attacks-around-the-world.html?_r=2

Chapter 7
p. 267: Freedom in the World 2013: Democratic Breakthroughs in the Balance. Selected Data from Freedom House's Annual Survey of Political Rights and Civil Liberties. Freedom House: http://www.freedomhouse.org/sites/default/files/FIW%202013%20Booklet.pdf

Chapter 9
p. 344: von Grember et al. (2013). Reprinted with permission from the International Food Policy Research Institute

Chapter 10
p. 357: Cartography: SASI Group, University of Sheffield; Mark Newman, University of Michigan, 2006 (updated 2008), www.worldmapper.org/Data source: Gregg Marland, Tom Boden, Bob Andres, Oak Ridge National Laboratory. Please note that data for Norway is inaccurate.